The
C++
Programming
Language

Second Edition

Bjarne Stroustrup

AT&T Bell Laboratories
Murray Hill, New Jersey

ADDISON-WESLEY PUBLISHING COMPANY

Reading, Massachusetts · Menlo Park, California · New York
Don Mills, Ontario · Wokingham, England · Amsterdam · Bonn
Sydney · Singapore · Tokyo · Madrid · San Juan · Milan · Paris

Library of Congress Cataloging-in-Publication Data

Stroustrup, Bjarne.
    The C++ programming language / Bjarne Stroustrup. -- 2nd ed.
       p.   cm.
    Includes bibliographical references and index.
    ISBN 0-201-53992-6
    1. C++ (Computer program language)   I. Title.   II. Title: C plus
plus programming language.
QA76.73.C15S79   1991
005. 13' 3--dc20   91-27307
                                                CIP

AT&T

Reprinted with corrections September, 1991

This book was typeset in Times and Courier by the author, using a Linotronic 200P phototype-setter and a DEC VAX 8550 running the 10th edition of the UNIX operating system.

1 2 3 4 5 6 7 8 9 10-HA-9594939291

Preface

The road goes ever on and on.
– Bilbo Baggins

As promised in the first edition of this book, C++ has been evolving to meet the needs of its users. This evolution has been guided by the experience of users of widely varying backgrounds working in a great range of application areas. The C++ user-community has grown a hundredfold during the six years since the first edition of this book; many lessons have been learned, and many techniques have been discovered and/or validated by experience. Some of these experiences are reflected here.

The primary aim of the language extensions made in the last six years has been to enhance C++ as a language for data abstraction and object-oriented programming in general and to enhance it as a tool for writing high-quality libraries of user-defined types in particular. A "high-quality library," is a library that provides a concept to a user in the form of one or more classes that are convenient, safe, and efficient to use. In this context, *safe* means that a class provides a specific type-safe interface between the users of the library and its providers; *efficient* means that use of the class does not impose significant overheads in run-time or space on the user compared with hand-written C code.

This book presents the complete C++ language. Chapters 1 through 10 give a tutorial introduction; Chapters 11 through 13 provide a discussion of design and software development issues; and, finally, the complete C++ reference manual is included. Naturally, the features added and resolutions made since the original edition are integral parts of the presentation. They include refined overloading resolution, memory management facilities, and access control mechanisms, type-safe linkage, `const` and `static` member functions, abstract classes, multiple inheritance, templates, and exception handling.

C++ is a general-purpose programming language; its core application domain is systems programming in the broadest sense. In addition, C++ is successfully used in many application areas that are not covered by this label. Implementations of C++ exist from some of the most modest microcomputers to the largest supercomputers and for almost all operating systems. Consequently, this book describes the C++ language itself without trying to explain a particular implementation, programming environment, or library.

This book presents many examples of classes that, though useful, should be classified as "toys." This style of exposition allows general principles and useful techniques to stand out more clearly than they would in a fully elaborated program, where they would be buried in details. Most of the useful classes presented here, such as linked lists, arrays, character strings, matrices, graphics classes, associative arrays, etc., are available in "bulletproof" and/or "goldplated" versions from a wide variety of commercial and non-commercial sources. Many of these "industrial strength" classes and libraries are actually direct and indirect descendants of the toy versions found here.

This edition provides a greater emphasis on tutorial aspects than did the first edition of this book. However, the presentation is still aimed squarely at experienced programmers and endeavors not to insult their intelligence or experience. The discussion of design issues has been greatly expanded to reflect the demand for information beyond the description of language features and their immediate use. Technical detail and precision have also been increased. The reference manual, in particular, represents many years of work in this direction. The intent has been to provide a book with a depth sufficient to make more than one reading rewarding to most programmers. In other words, this book presents the C++ language, its fundamental principles, and the key techniques needed to apply it. Enjoy!

Acknowledgments

In addition to the people mentioned in the acknowledgements section in the preface to the first edition, I would like to thank Al Aho, Steve Buroff, Jim Coplien, Ted Goldstein, Tony Hansen, Peter Juhl, Brian Kernighan, Andrew Koenig, Bill Leggett, Lorraine Mingacci, Warren Montgomery, Mike Mowbray, Rob Murray, Jonathan Shopiro, Mike Vilot, and Peter Weinberger for commenting on draft chapters of this second edition. Many people influenced the development of C++ from 1985 to 1991. I can mention only a few: Andrew Koenig, Brian Kernighan, Doug McIlroy, and Jonathan Shopiro. Also thanks to the many participants of the "external reviews" of the reference manual drafts and to the people who suffered through the first year of X3J16.

Murray Hill, New Jersey   *Bjarne Stroustrup*

Preface to the first Edition

Language shapes the way we think,
and determines what we can think about.
– B.L.Whorf

C++ is a general purpose programming language designed to make programming more enjoyable for the serious programmer. Except for minor details, C++ is a superset of the C programming language. In addition to the facilities provided by C, C++ provides flexible and efficient facilities for defining new types. A programmer can partition an application into manageable pieces by defining new types that closely match the concepts of the application. This technique for program construction is often called *data abstraction*. Objects of some user-defined types contain type information. Such objects can be used conveniently and safely in contexts in which their type cannot be determined at compile time. Programs using objects of such types are often called *object based*. When used well, these techniques result in shorter, easier to understand, and easier to maintain programs.

The key concept in C++ is *class*. A class is a user-defined type. Classes provide data hiding, guaranteed initialization of data, implicit type conversion for user-defined types, dynamic typing, user-controlled memory management, and mechanisms for overloading operators. C++ provides much better facilities for type checking and for expressing modularity than C does. It also contains improvements that are not directly related to classes, including symbolic constants, inline substitution of functions, default function arguments, overloaded function names, free store management operators, and a reference type. C++ retains C's ability to deal efficiently with the fundamental objects of the hardware (bits, bytes, words, addresses, etc.). This allows the user-defined types to be implemented with a pleasing degree of efficiency.

C++ and its standard libraries are designed for portability. The current implementation will run on most systems that support C. C libraries can be used from a C++

program, and most tools that support programming in C can be used with C++.

This book is primarily intended to help serious programmers learn the language and use it for nontrivial projects. It provides a complete description of C++, many complete examples, and many more program fragments.

Acknowledgments

C++ could never have matured without the constant use, suggestions, and constructive criticism of many friends and colleagues. In particular, Tom Cargill, Jim Coplien, Stu Feldman, Sandy Fraser, Steve Johnson, Brian Kernighan, Bart Locanthi, Doug McIlroy, Dennis Ritchie, Larry Rosler, Jerry Schwarz, and Jon Shopiro provided important ideas for development of the language. Dave Presotto wrote the current implementation of the stream I/O library.

In addition, hundreds of people contributed to the development of C++ and its compiler by sending me suggestions for improvements, descriptions of problems they had encountered, and compiler errors. I can mention only a few: Gary Bishop, Andrew Hume, Tom Karzes, Victor Milenkovic, Rob Murray, Leonie Rose, Brian Schmult, and Gary Walker.

Many people have also helped with the production of this book, in particular, Jon Bentley, Laura Eaves, Brian Kernighan, Ted Kowalski, Steve Mahaney, Jon Shopiro, and the participants in the C++ course held at Bell Labs, Columbus, Ohio, June 26-27, 1985.

Murray Hill, New Jersey   *Bjarne Stroustrup*

Contents

0

Notes to the Reader

"The time has come," the Walrus said,
"to talk of many things."
– L.Carroll

This chapter consists of an overview of this book, a list of references, and some ancillary notes on C++. The notes concern the history of C++, ideas that influenced the design of C++, and thoughts about programming in C++. This chapter is not an introduction: the notes are not a prerequisite for understanding the following chapters, and some notes assume knowledge of C++.

The Structure of This Book
This book has three parts: Chapters 1 through 10 provide a tutorial introduction to C++. Chapters 11 through 13 present a discussion of design and software development issues arising in connection with the use of C++. Finally, the complete C++ reference manual is included. Complete information about language features can be found only in the reference manual. However, the tutorial chapters provide examples, opinions, recommendations, warnings, and exercises that have no place in a manual.

The emphasis of this book is on program organization rather than on the writing of algorithms. Consequently, where there was a choice, a trivial algorithm was chosen over a clever and harder-to-understand algorithm. For example, a bubble sort is used where a quicksort would be more appropriate for real code. Often, re-implementation with a more suitable algorithm is left as an exercise.

Chapter 1 is a quick tour of the major concepts and features of the C++ programming language. Its purpose is to give a high-level acquaintance with C++. Detailed explanations of language features and techniques are postponed to later chapters. The discussion focuses on the language features supporting data abstraction and object-oriented programming, but also briefly introduces the key features used for procedural programming.

Chapters 2, 3, and 4 describe features of C++ that are not involved in defining new types: the fundamental types, expressions, and control structures for C++ programs. In other words, they describe the subset of C++ that is essentially C. They go into considerably greater detail than Chapter 1.

Chapters 5 through 8 describe C++'s facilities for defining new types, features that do not have counterparts in C. Chapter 5 presents the basic class concept, showing how user-defined types (classes) can be defined and how objects of such types can be initialized, accessed, and finally cleaned up. Chapter 6 explains how to define unary and binary operators for a user-defined type, how to specify conversions between user-defined types, and how to specify creation, deletion, and copying of a value of a user-defined type. Chapter 7 describes the concept of a derived class, which enables a programmer to build more complex classes from simpler ones and to handle objects in an efficient and type-safe manner in contexts in which their type cannot be known at compile time. Chapter 8 presents templates, that is, C++'s facilities for defining families of types and functions. It demonstrates their use in the definition of container classes such as lists and associative arrays.

Chapter 9 presents exception handling and discusses ideas for error handling and strategies for fault tolerance. Chapter 10 presents the `ostream` and `istream` classes provided for input and output in the *standard library*.

Chapters 11 through 13 discuss issues that arise when C++ is used in the design and implementation of large software systems. Chapter 11 concentrates on design and management issues, Chapter 12 discusses the relation between the C++ programming language and design issues; and Chapter 13 presents library design techniques.

Finally, the C++ reference manual is included.

References to parts of this book are of the form §2.3.4 (Chapter 2, sub-section 3.4). Chapter r is the reference manual; for example, §r.8.5.5.

Implementation Notes

Several independently developed and distributed implementations of C++ exist. A wealth of tools, libraries, and software development environments are also available. A mass of text books, manuals, journals, newsletters, electronic bulletin boards, mailing lists, conferences, and courses is available to inform you about the latest developments in C++, its use, details, tools, libraries, implementations, etc. If you plan to use C++ seriously, I strongly suggest that you gain access to at least two such sources – each source has a bias, so use at least two.

The major program fragments in this book were taken directly from source files that were compiled on a DEC VAX11/8550 running the 10th Edition UNIX[25] system. The compiler used is a direct descendant of the original C++ compiler developed by the author. The language used here is "pure C++;" that is, no implementation-dependent extensions are used. Therefore, the examples ought to run on any C++ implementation. However, the template and exception handling facilities are at the time of writing recent additions to C++, so your compiler may not yet support them.

Exercises
Exercises can be found at the end of chapters. The exercises are mainly of the write-a-program variety. Always write enough code for a solution to be compiled and run with at least a few test cases. The exercises vary considerably in difficulty, so they are marked with an estimate of their difficulty. The scale is exponential so that if a (∗1) exercise takes you five minutes, a (∗2) might take an hour, and a (∗3) might take a day. The time needed to write and test a program depends more on the reader's experience than on the exercise itself. A (∗1) exercise might take a day if the reader first has to get acquainted with a new computer system to run it. On the other hand, a (∗5) exercise might be done in an hour by someone who happens to have the right collection of programs handy.

Any book on programming in C can be used as a source of extra exercises for Chapters 2 through 4. Aho et al.[1] present many common data structures and algorithms in terms of abstract data types. It can therefore be used as a source of exercises for Chapters 5 through 8. However, the language used in that book lacks both member functions and derived classes. Consequently, the user-defined types can often be expressed more elegantly in C++.

Design Notes
Simplicity was an important design criterion for C++; where there was a choice between simplifying the manual and other documentation or simplifying the compiler, the former was chosen. Great importance was also attached to retaining compatibility with C; this precluded cleaning up C syntax.

C++ has no high-level data types and no high-level primitive operations. For example, there is no matrix type with an inversion operator or a string type with a concatenation operator. If a user wants such a type, it can be defined in the language itself. In fact, defining a new general-purpose or application-specific type is the most fundamental programming activity in C++. A well designed user-defined type differs from a built-in type only in the way it is defined and not in the way it is used.

Features that would incur run-time or memory overheads even when not used were avoided. For example, ideas that would make it necessary to store "housekeeping information" in every object were rejected; if a user declares a structure consisting of two 16-bit quantities, that structure will fit into a 32-bit register.

C++ was designed to be used in a traditional compilation and run-time environment, the C programming environment on the UNIX system. There are, however, good reasons for using C++ in an environment with significantly more support available. Facilities such as dynamic loading, incremental compilation, and a database of type definitions can be put to good use without affecting the language.

C++ types and data-hiding features rely on compile-time analysis of programs to prevent accidental corruption of data. They do not provide secrecy or protection against someone deliberately breaking the rules. They can, however, be used freely without incurring run-time or space overheads. The idea is that to be useful, a language feature must not only be elegant, it must also be affordable in the context of a real program.

Historical Note

Clearly C++ owes most to C[8]. C is retained as a subset, and so is C's emphasis on facilities that are low-level enough to cope with the most demanding systems programming tasks. C in turn owes much to its predecessor BCPL[13]; in fact, BCPL's // comment convention has been (re)introduced in C++. If you know BCPL you will notice that C++ still lacks a VALOF block. The other main source of inspiration was Simula67[2,3]; the class concept (with derived classes and virtual functions) was borrowed from it. The Simula67 inspect statement was deliberately not introduced into C++. The reason for that is to encourage modularity through the use of virtual functions. C++'s facility for overloading operators and the freedom to place a declaration wherever a statement can occur resembles Algol68[24].

Since the original edition of this book, the language has been extensively reviewed and refined. The major areas for revision were overloading resolution, linking, and memory management facilities. In addition, several minor changes were made to increase C compatibility. Several generalizations and a few major extensions were added: these include multiple inheritance, static member functions, const member functions, protected members, templates, and exception handling. The overall theme of these extensions and revisions was to make C++ a better language for writing and using libraries. These changes are described in references 10, 18, 20, 21, and 23.

The template facility was partly designed to formalize macro usage, partly inspired by the Ada generics (both their strengths and their weaknesses), and partly inspired by Clu's parameterized modules. Similarly, the C++ exception handling mechanism was partly inspired partly by Ada, by Clu[11], and partly by ML[26]. Other developments in the 1985 to 1991 time span – such as multiple inheritance, static member functions, and pure virtual functions – are generalizations driven by experience with the use of C++ rather than ideas imported from other languages.

Earlier versions of the language, collectively known as "C with Classes"[16], have been in use since 1980. The language was originally invented because the author wanted to write some event-driven simulations for which Simula67 would have been ideal, except for efficiency considerations. "C with Classes" was used for major simulation projects in which the facilities for writing programs that use (only) minimal time and space were severely tested. "C with Classes" lacked operator overloading, references, virtual functions, and many details. C++ was first installed outside the author's research group in July, 1983; quite a few current C++ features had not yet been invented, however.

The name C++ (pronounced C plus plus) was coined by Rick Mascitti in the summer of 1983. The name signifies the evolutionary nature of the changes from C. "++" is the C increment operator. The slightly shorter name C+ is a syntax error; it has also been used as the name of an unrelated language. Connoisseurs of C semantics find C++ inferior to ++C. The language is not called D, because it is an extension of C and does not attempt to remedy problems by removing features. For yet another interpretation of the name C++, see the appendix of Orwell[12].

C++ was designed primarily so that the author and his friends would not have to program in assembler, C, or various modern high-level languages. Its main purpose is to make writing good programs easier and more pleasant for the individual programmer. Until recently, there never was a C++ paper design; design, documentation, and implementation went on simultaneously. There never was a "C++ project" either, or a "C++ design committee." Throughout, C++ evolved, to cope with problems encountered by users, and through discussions between the author and his friends and colleagues.

Lately, the explosive growth of C++ use has caused some changes. Sometime during 1987, it became clear that formal standardization of C++ was inevitable and that we needed to start preparing the ground immediately for a standardization effort[22]. The result was a conscious effort to maintain contact between C++ compiler implementers and major users through paper and electronic mail and through face-to-face meetings at C++ conferences and elsewhere.

AT&T Bell Laboratories made a major contribution to this by allowing me to share drafts of revised versions of the C++ reference manual with such implementers and users. Because many of these people work for companies that could be seen as competing with AT&T, the significance of this contribution should not be underestimated. A less enlightened company could have caused major problems of language fragmentation simply by doing nothing. As it happened, about a hundred individuals from a couple of dozen organizations read and commented on what became the current reference manual and the base document for the ANSI C++ standardization effort. Their names can be found in *The Annotated C++ Reference Manual*[4]. The reference manual proper is part of this book. Finally, the X3J16 committee of ANSI was convened in December of 1989 at the initiative of Hewlett-Packard. It is expected that the ANSI (American national) standardization of C++ will be part of the ISO (international) standardization effort for C++.

C++ evolved hand-in-hand with some of the key classes presented in this book. For example, I designed the `complex`, `vector`, and `stack` classes together with the operator overloading mechanisms. The string and list classes was developed by Jonathan Shopiro and me as part of the same effort. Jonathan's string and list classes were the first such classes to see extensive use as part of a library. The `task` library described in reference 19 and in exercise 13 in §6.8 was part of the first C with classes program ever written. I wrote it and its associated classes to support Simula-style simulations. The task library has been revised and reimplemented, notably by Jonathan Shopiro, and is still in extensive use. The stream library as described in the first edition of this book was designed and implemented by me. Jerry Schwarz transformed it into the iostreams library (§10) using (among other ideas) Andrew Koenig's manipulator technique (§10.4.2). The `Map` class (§8.8) was designed by Andrew Koenig. Similarly, Andrew wrote the `Pool` class (§13.10) to make a library version of the class-specific memory management technique (§5.5.6) I had devised. The development of the template facility was influenced by the `Vector`, `Map`, `Slist`, and `sort` templates presented in Chapter 8.

C and C++

C was chosen as the base language for C++ because (1) it is versatile, terse, and relatively low-level; (2) it is adequate for most system programming tasks; (3) it runs everywhere and on everything; and (4) it fits into the UNIX programming environment. C has its problems, but a language designed from scratch would have some too, and we know C's problems. Most importantly, working with C enabled ''C with Classes'' to be a useful (if awkward) tool within months of the first thought of adding Simula-like classes to C.

As C++ became more widely used, and as the facilities it provided over and above those of C became more significant, the question of whether to retain compatibility was raised again and again. Clearly some problems could be avoided if some of the C heritage was rejected (see, for example, Sethi[15]). This was not done because (1) there are millions of lines of C code that might benefit from C++, provided that a complete rewrite from C to C++ were unnecessary; (2) there are millions of lines of library functions and utility software code written in C that could be used from/on C++ programs provided C++ were link compatible with and syntactically very similar to C; (3) there are hundreds of thousands of programmers who know C and therefore need only learn to use the new features of C++ and not relearn the basics; and (4) because C++ and C will be used on the same systems by the same people for years, the differences should be either very large or very small to minimize mistakes and confusion. The definition of C++ has been revised to ensure that a construct that is both legal C and legal C++ actually has the same meaning in both languages.

The C language has itself evolved, partly under the influence of the development of C++ (see Rosler[14]). The ANSI C standard[27] contains a function declaration syntax borrowed from ''C with Classes.'' Borrowing works both ways; for example, the `void*` pointer type was invented for ANSI C and first implemented in C++. As promised in the first edition of this book, the definition of C++ has been reviewed to remove gratuitous incompatibilities; C++ is now more compatible with C than it originally was; see §r.18. The ideal is for C++ to be as close to ANSI C as possible – but no closer[9]. One hundred percent compatibility is not and never was a goal because that would compromise the type safety and smooth integration of user-defined and built-in types that are among the essential aims of C++.

Knowing C is not a prerequisite for learning C++. Programming in C encourages many techniques and tricks rendered unnecessary by C++ language features. For example, explicit type conversion, ''casting,'' is less frequently needed in C++ than it is in C (see also the ''Note to C programmers'' below). However, *good* C programs tend to be C++ programs. For example, note that every program in Kernighan and Ritchie: The C Programming Language (2nd Edition)[8] is a C++ program. Experience with any statically typed language will be a help with learning C++.

Efficiency and Structure

C++ was developed from the C programming language and, with few exceptions, retains C as a subset. The base language, the C subset of C++, is designed so that there is a very close correspondence between its types, operators, and statements and the objects computers deal with directly: numbers, characters, and addresses. Except for the new, delete, and throw operators and the try block, individual C++ expressions and statements need no hidden run-time support or subroutines.

C++ can use the same function call and return sequences as C – or even more efficient ones. When even such relatively efficient mechanisms are too expensive, a C++ function can be substituted inline, thus enjoying the notational convenience of functions without run-time overhead.

One of the original aims for C was to replace assembly coding for the most demanding systems programming tasks. When C++ was designed, care was taken not to compromise the gains in this area. The difference between C and C++ is primarily in the degree of emphasis on types and structure. C is expressive and permissive. C++ is even more expressive, but to gain that increase in expressiveness, the programmer must pay more attention to the types of objects. Knowing the types of objects, the compiler can deal correctly with expressions when the programmer would otherwise have had to specify operations in painful detail. Knowing the types of objects also enables the compiler to detect errors that would otherwise have persisted until testing. Note that using the type system to get function argument checking, to protect data from accidental corruption, to provide new types, to provide new operators, etc., does not in itself increase run-time or space overheads.

The emphasis on structure in the design of C++ reflects the increase in the scale of programs written since C was designed. You can make a small program (less than 1000 lines) work through brute force even when breaking every rule of good style. For a larger program, this is simply not so for an individual. If the structure of a 10,000 line program is bad, you will find that new errors are introduced as fast as old ones are removed. C++ was designed to enable larger programs to be structured in a rational way so that it would not be unreasonable for a single person to cope with 25,000 lines of code. C++ has by now been shown to over-fulfill that goal.

Much larger programs exist, but the ones that work generally turn out to consist of many nearly independent parts, each one well below the limits previously mentioned. Naturally, the difficulty of writing and maintaining a program depends on the complexity of the application and not simply on the number of lines of program text, so the exact numbers used to express the preceding ideas should not be taken too literally.

However, not every piece of code can be well structured, hardware independent, easy to read, etc. C++ possesses features that are intended for manipulating hardware facilities in a direct and efficient way without regard for safety or ease of comprehension. It also possesses facilities for hiding such code behind elegant and safe interfaces.

Naturally, the use of C++ for larger programs leads to the use of C++ by groups of programmers. C++'s emphasis on modularity, strongly typed interfaces, and flexibility pays off here. C++ has as good a balance of facilities for writing *large* programs as any language. However, as programs get larger, the problems associated with their development and maintenance shift from being language problems to more global problems of tools and management. Chapters 11 and 12 explore some of these issues.

This book emphasizes techniques for providing general-purpose facilities, generally useful types, libraries, etc. These techniques will serve programmers of small programs as well as programmers of large ones. Furthermore, because all non-trivial programs consist of many semi-independent parts, the techniques for writing such parts serve programmers of both systems and applications.

One might suspect that specifying a program using a more detailed type structure would lead to a larger program source text. With C++ this is not so; a C++ program declaring functions argument types, using classes, etc., is typically a bit shorter than the equivalent C program not using these facilities. Also, where libraries are used a C++ program will *appear* much shorter than its C equivalent, assuming, of course, that a functioning C equivalent could actually have been built.

Philosophical Note

A programming language serves two related purposes: it provides a vehicle for the programmer to specify actions to be executed, and it provides a set of concepts for the programmer to use when thinking about what can be done. The first aspect ideally requires a language that is "close to the machine," so that all important aspects of a machine are handled simply and efficiently in a way that is reasonably obvious to the programmer. The C language was primarily designed with this in mind. The second aspect ideally requires a language that is "close to the problem to be solved" so that the concepts of a solution can be expressed directly and concisely. The facilities added to C to create C++ were primarily designed with this in mind.

The connection between the language in which we think/program and the problems and solutions we can imagine is very close. For this reason, restricting language features with the intent of eliminating programmer errors is at best dangerous. As with natural languages, there are great benefits from being at least bilingual. The language provides a programmer with a set of conceptual tools; if these are inadequate for a task, they will simply be ignored. For example, seriously restricting the concept of a pointer simply forces the programmer to use a vector plus integer arithmetic to implement structures, pointers, etc. Good design and the absence of errors cannot be guaranteed merely by the presence or the absence of specific language features.

The type system should be especially helpful for non-trivial tasks. The C++ class concept has, in fact, proven itself to be a powerful conceptual tool.

Thinking about Programming in C++

Ideally, one approaches the task of designing a program in three stages: first gain a clear understanding of the problem, then identify the key concepts involved in a solution, and finally express that solution in a program. However, the details of the problem and the concepts of the solution often become clearly understood only through the effort to express them in the program – this is where the choice of programming language matters.

In most applications there are concepts that are not easily represented in a program as one of the fundamental types or as a function without associated static data. Given such a concept, declare a class to represent it in the program. A class is a type; that is, it specifies how objects of its class behave: how they are created, how they can be manipulated, and how they are destroyed. A class also specifies how objects are represented, but at the early stages of the design of a program, that is not (and should not be) the major concern. The key to writing a good program is to design classes so that each cleanly represents a single concept. Often this means that the programmer must focus on the questions: How are objects of this class created? Can objects of this class be copied and/or destroyed? What operations can be done on such objects? If there are no good answers to such questions, the concept probably wasn't "clean" in the first place, and it might be a good idea to think a bit more about the problem and the proposed solution instead of immediately starting to "code around" the problems.

The concepts that are easiest to deal with are the ones that have a traditional mathematical formalism: numbers of all sorts, sets, geometric shapes, etc. There really ought to be standard libraries of classes representing such concepts, but this is not the case at the time of writing. There is a bewildering wealth of such libraries but as yet no formal or de facto standard. C++ is still young, and its libraries have not yet matured to the same degree as the language itself.

A concept does not exist in a vacuum; there are always clusters of related concepts. Organizing the relationship between classes in a program – that is, determining the exact relationship between the different concepts involved in a solution – is often harder than laying out the individual classes in the first place. The result had better not be a muddle in which every class (concept) depends on every other. Consider two classes, A and B: Relationships such as "A calls functions from B," "A creates Bs," and "A has a B member" seldom cause major problems. Relationships such as "A uses data from B" can typically be eliminated.

One of the most powerful intellectual tools for managing complexity is hierarchical ordering, that is, organizing related concepts into a tree structure with the most general concept at the root. In C++, derived classes represent such structures. A program can often be organized as a set of trees or directed acyclic graphs of classes. That is, the programmer specifies a number of base classes, each with its own set of derived classes. Virtual functions (§6.2.5) can often be used to define a set of operations for the most general version of a concept (a base class). When necessary, the interpretation of these operations can be refined for particular special cases (derived classes).

Naturally, this organization has its limits. Sometimes even a directed acyclic graph seems insufficient for organizing the concepts of a program; some concepts seem to be inherently mutually dependent. If a set of mutually dependent classes is so small that it is easy to understand, the cyclic dependencies need not be a problem. The idea of `friend` classes (§5.4.1) can be used to represent sets of mutually dependent classes in C++.

If you can organize the concepts of a program only into a general graph (and not a tree or a directed acyclic graph), and if you cannot localize the mutual dependencies, then you are most likely in a predicament that no programming language can help you out of. Unless you can conceive of some easily stated relationships between the basic concepts, the program is likely to become unmanageable.

Another form of commonality can be expressed through templates. A class template specifies a family of classes. For example, a list template specifies "list of T" where "T" can be any type. Thus a template is a mechanism for specifying how one type is generated given another type as an argument. The most common templates are container classes such as lists, arrays, and associative arrays.

Remember that much programming can be simply and clearly done using only primitive types, data structures, plain functions, and a few classes from a standard library. The whole apparatus involved in defining new types should not be used except when there is a real need.

The question "How does one write good programs in C++?" is very similar to the question "How does one write good English prose?" There are two kinds of answers: "Know what you want to say," and "Practice. Imitate good writing." Both kinds of advice appear to be as appropriate for C++ as they are for English – and as hard to follow.

Rules of Thumb

Here is a set of "rules" you might consider while learning C++. As you get more proficient you can evolve them into something suitable for your kind of applications and your style of programming. They are deliberately very simple, so they lack detail. Don't take them too literally. To write a good program takes intelligence, taste, and patience. You are not going to get it right the first time; experiment!

[1] When you program, you create a concrete representation of the ideas in your solution to some problem. Let the structure of the program reflect those ideas as directly as possible:

    [a] If you can think of "it" as a separate idea, make it a class.

    [b] If you can think of "it" as a separate entity, make it an object of some class.

    [c] If two classes have something significant in common, make that commonality a base class.

    [d] If a class is a container of objects, make it a template.

[2] When you define a class that does not implement a mathematical entity like a matrix or a complex number, or a low-level type such as a linked list:

    [a] Don't use global data.

    [b] Don't use global (nonmember) functions.

    [c] Don't use public data members.

    [d] Don't use friends, except to avoid [a], [b], or [c].

    [e] Don't access data members of another object directly.

    [f] Don't put a "type field" in a class; use virtual functions.

    [g] Don't use inline functions, except as a significant optimization.

Note to C Programmers

The better one knows C, the harder it seems to avoid writing C++ in C style, thereby losing some of the potential benefits of C++. So please take a look at the "Differences from C" section of the reference manual (§r.18). Here are a few pointers to the areas in which C++ has better ways of doing something than C has. Macros are almost never necessary in C++; use const (§2.5) or enum (§2.5.1) to define manifest constants, inline (§4.6.2) to avoid function-calling overhead, and templates (§8) to specify families of functions and types. Don't declare a variable before you need it so that you can initialize it immediately – a declaration can occur anywhere a statement can. Don't use malloc() – the new operator (§3.2.6) does the same job better. Unions are needed less often than in C because derived classes often provide an alternative; try doing without them and when you do need a union keep it out of major interfaces – try anonymous unions (§2.6.2). Try to avoid void*, pointer arithmetic, C arrays, and casts except deep within the implementation of some function or class. Note that to obey C linkage conventions, a C++ function must be declared extern "C" (§4.4).

Most importantly, try thinking of a program as a set of interacting concepts represented as classes and objects, instead of the program as a bunch of data structures with functions twiddling their bits.

References

There are few direct references in the text, but here is a short list of books and papers that are mentioned directly or indirectly.

[1]   A.V. Aho, J.E. Hopcroft, and J.D. Ullman: *Data Structures and Algorithms*. Addison-Wesley, Reading, Massachusetts. 1983.

[2]   O-J. Dahl, B. Myrhaug, and K. Nygaard: *SIMULA Common Base Language*. Norwegian Computing Center S-22. Oslo, Norway. 1970.

[3]   O-J. Dahl and C.A.R. Hoare: *Hierarchical Program Construction* in *Structured Programming*. Academic Press, New York. 1972. pp. 174-220.

[4]   Margaret A. Ellis and Bjarne Stroustrup: *The Annotated C++ Reference Manual*. Addison-Wesley. Reading, Massachusetts. 1990.

[5]   A. Goldberg and D. Robson: *SMALLTALK-80 – The Language and Its Implementation*. Addison-Wesley, Reading, Massachusetts. 1983.

[6]   R.E. Griswold et.al.: *The Snobol4 Programming Language*. Prentice-Hall, Englewood Cliffs, New Jersey. 1970.

[7]   R.E. Griswold and M.T. Griswold: *The ICON Programming Language*. Prentice-Hall, Englewood Cliffs, New Jersey. 1983.

[8]   Brian W. Kernighan and Dennis M. Ritchie: *The C Programming Language*. Prentice-Hall, Englewood Cliffs, New Jersey. 1978. Second edition 1988.

[9]   Andrew Koenig and Bjarne Stroustrup: *C++: As close to C as possible – but no closer*. The C++ Report. Vol.1 No.7. July 1989.

[10] Andrew Koenig and Bjarne Stroustrup: *Exception Handling for C++ (revised)*. Proc USENIX C++ Conference, April 1990. Also, Journal of Object Oriented Programming, Vol.3 No.2. July/Aug 1990. pp. 16-33.

[11] Barbara Liskov et al.: *CLU Reference Manual*. MIT/LCS/TR-225.

[12] George Orwell: *1984*. Secker and Warburg, London. 1949.

[13] Martin Richards and Colin Whitby-Strevens: *BCPL - The Language and Its Compiler*. Cambridge University Press. 1980.

[14] L. Rosler: *The Evolution of C - Past and Future*. AT&T Bell Laboratories Technical Journal. Vol.63 No.8 Part 2. October 1984. pp. 1685-1700.

[15] Ravi Sethi: *Uniform Syntax for Type Expressions and Declarations*. Software Practice & Experience, Vol.11. 1981. pp. 623-628.

[16] Bjarne Stroustrup: *Adding Classes to C: An Exercise in Language Evolution*. Software Practice & Experience, Vol.13. 1983. pp. 139-61.

[17] Bjarne Stroustrup: *The C++ Programming Language*. Addison-Wesley. 1986.

[18] Bjarne Stroustrup: *Multiple Inheritance for C++*. Proc. EUUG Spring Conference, May 1987. Also, USENIX Computer Systems, Vol 2 No 4, Fall 1989.

[19] Bjarne Stroustrup and Jonathan Shopiro: *A Set of C classes for Co-Routine Style Programming*. Proc. USENIX C++ conference, Santa Fe. November 1987. pp. 417-439.

[20] Bjarne Stroustrup: *Type-safe Linkage for C++*. USENIX Computer Systems, Vol.1 No.4. Fall 1988.

[21] Bjarne Stroustrup: *Parameterized Types for C++*. Proc. USENIX C++ Conference, Denver. October 1988. pp. 1-18. Also, USENIX Computer Systems, Vol.2 No.1. Winter 1989.

[22] Bjarne Stroustrup: *Standardizing C++*. The C++ Report. Vol.1 No.1. January 1989.

[23] Bjarne Stroustrup: *The Evolution of C++: 1985-1989*. USENIX Computer Systems, Vol.2 No.3. Summer 1989.

[24] P.M. Woodward and S.G. Bond: *Algol 68-R Users Guide*. Her Majesty's Stationery Office, London. 1974.

[25] *UNIX Time-Sharing System: Programmer's Manual. Research Version, Tenth Edition*. AT&T Bell Laboratories, Murray Hill, New Jersey. February 1985.

[26] Aake Wilkstroem: *Functional Programming Using ML*. Prentice-Hall, Englewood Cliffs, New Jersey. 1987.

[27] X3 Secretariat: *Standard - The C Language*. X3J11/90-013. Computer and Business Equipment Manufactures Association, 311 First Street, NW, Suite 500, Washington, DC 20001, USA.

References to books relating to design and larger software development issues can be found at the end of Chapter 11.

1

A Tour of C++

The first thing we do, let's
kill all the language lawyers.
– Henry VI, part II

This chapter is a quick tour of the major concepts and features of the C++ programming language. Its purpose is to give a fairly high-level acquaintance with C++. Detailed explanations of language features and techniques are postponed to later chapters. The discussion focuses on the language features supporting data abstraction and object-oriented programming, but it also briefly introduces the key features used for procedural programming.

1.1 Introduction

The C++ programming language is designed to
- be a better C
- support data abstraction
- support object-oriented programming

This chapter explains what this means without going into the finer details of the language definition:

§1.2 informally distinguishes "procedural programming," "modular programming," "data abstraction" and "object-oriented programming" from each other and presents the mechanisms that are essential for supporting these styles of programming. The styles of programming typically used in C are discussed under the headings "procedural programming" and "modular programming." C++ is "a better C" because C++ provides better support for these styles of programming than C does. C++ does so without loss of generality or efficiency compared with C while remaining almost completely a superset of C. The discussion of data abstraction and object-oriented programming equates "support for data abstraction" with the ability to define and use new types and equates "support for object-oriented programming" with the ability to express type hierarchies.

§1.3 presents the basic facilities for procedural and modular programming provided by C++. In particular, it introduces functions, pointers, iteration, input/output, and the notion of programs composed out of separately compiled modules. Chapters 2, 3, and 4 cover these facilities in detail.

§1.4 presents features needed to make data abstraction effective. In particular, it introduces classes, the simplest access control mechanism, constructors and destructors, operator overloading, user-defined type conversions, exception handling, and templates. Chapters 5, 7, 8, and 9 cover these facilities in detail.

§1.5 discusses facilities needed to support object-oriented programming. In particular, derived classes and virtual functions are introduced and some implementation issues are presented. Chapter 6 covers these facilities in detail.

§1.6 discusses some limits to perfection imposed on general-purpose programming languages in general, and C++ in particular, by efficiency demands, competing demands from diverse application areas, education, and the need to function in traditional compile and run-time environments.

Should you find any part of this chapter incomprehensible, you are strongly encouraged to read the corresponding chapters and then return to this overview with a more detailed understanding of the basic language features. The purpose of this chapter is to give you a general overview of C++, *not* to provide you with the information necessary to start programming in it.

1.2 Programming Paradigms

Object-oriented programming is a technique for programming – a paradigm for writing "good" programs for a set of problems. If the term "object-oriented programming language" means anything, it must mean a programming language that provides mechanisms that support the object-oriented style of programming well.

There is an important distinction here. A language is said to *support* a style of programming if it provides facilities that makes it convenient (reasonably easy, safe, and efficient) to use that style. A language does not support a technique if it takes exceptional effort or skill to write such programs; it merely *enables* the technique to be used. For example, you can write structured programs in Fortran and object-oriented programs in C, but it is unnecessarily hard to do so because these languages do not directly support those techniques.

Support for a paradigm comes not only in the obvious form of language facilities that allow direct use of the paradigm, but also in the more subtle form of compile-time and/or run-time checks against unintentional deviation from the paradigm. Type checking is the most obvious example of this; ambiguity detection and run-time checks can be used to extend linguistic support for paradigms. Extra-linguistic facilities such as standard libraries and programming environments can also provide significant support for paradigms.

One language is not necessarily better than another because it possesses a feature the other does not. There are many examples to the contrary. The important issue is not so much what features a language possesses, but that the features it does possess are sufficient to support the desired programming styles in the desired application areas:

[1] All features must be cleanly and elegantly integrated into the language.

[2] It must be possible to use features in combination to achieve solutions that would otherwise have required extra, separate features.

[3] There should be as few spurious and ''special-purpose'' features as possible.

[4] A feature should be such that its implementation does not impose significant overheads on programs that do not require it.

[5] A user need only know about the subset of the language explicitly used to write a program.

The first principle is an appeal to aesthetics and logic, the next two are expressions of the ideal of minimalism, and the last two principles can be summarized as ''what you don't know won't hurt you.''

C++ was designed to support data abstraction and object-oriented programming in addition to traditional C programming techniques under these constraints. It was *not* meant to force any particular programming style upon all users.

Let's now consider some programming styles and the key language mechanisms necessary for supporting them. The presentation of language features is not intended to be exhaustive.

1.2.1 Procedural Programming

The original (and probably still the most commonly used) programming paradigm is:

> *Decide which procedures you want;*
> *use the best algorithms you can find.*

The focus is on the processing, the algorithm needed to perform the desired computation. Languages support this paradigm by providing facilities for passing arguments to functions and returning values from functions. The literature related to this way of thinking is filled with discussion of ways of passing arguments, ways of distinguishing different kinds of arguments, different kinds of functions (procedures, routines, macros, ...), etc. Fortran is the original procedural language; Algol60, Algol68, Pascal, and C are later inventions in the same tradition.

A typical example of ''good style'' is a square root function. Given an argument, it produces a result. To do this, it performs a well understood mathematical computation:

```
double sqrt(double arg)
{
    // the code for calculating a square root
}

void some_function()
{
    double root2 = sqrt(2);
    // ...
}
```

The double slash, //, begins a comment that extends to the end of the line.

From the point of view of program organization, functions are used to create order in a maze of algorithms.

1.2.2 Modular Programming

Over the years, the emphasis in the design of programs has shifted away from the design of procedures and toward the organization of data. Among other things, this reflects an increase in program size. A set of related procedures with the data they manipulate is often called a *module*. The programming paradigm becomes:

> *Decide which modules you want;*
> *partition the program so that data is hidden in modules.*

This paradigm is also known as the ''data-hiding principle.'' Where there is no grouping of procedures with related data, the procedural programming style suffices. Also, the techniques for designing ''good procedures'' are now applied for each procedure in a module. The most common example of a module is the definition of a stack module. The main problems that have to be solved are:

[1] Provide a user interface for the stack (for example, functions push() and pop()).

[2] Ensure that the representation of the stack (for example, an array of elements) can be accessed only through this user interface.

[3] Ensure that the stack is initialized before its first use.

Modula-2 directly supports this notion; C merely enables its use. Here is a plausible external interface for a C-style stack module:

```
    // declaration of the interface for
    //  module stack of characters:

void push(char);
char pop();
const int stack_size = 100;
```

Assuming that this interface is found in a file called stack.h, an implementation can be defined like this:

```
#include "stack.h"          // use the stack interface

static char v[stack_size];  // ``static'' means local to
                            // this file/module

static char* p = v;         // the stack is initially empty


void push(char c)
{
    // check for overflow and push
}


char pop()
{
    // check for underflow and pop
}
```

It would be quite feasible to change the representation of this stack to a linked list. A user does not have access to the representation anyway (because v and p were declared static, that is, local to the file/module in which they were declared). Such a stack can be used like this:

```
#include "stack.h"          // use the stack interface

void some_function()
{
    push('c');
    char c = pop();
    if (c != 'c') error("impossible");
}
```

Because data is only one of the things one might want to "hide," the notion of data hiding is trivially extended to the notion of "information hiding;" that is, the names of variables, constants, functions, and types can also be made local to a module. Although C++ wasn't specifically designed to support modular programming, its class concept does provide support for the concept of a module (§5.4.3 and §5.4.4). In addition, C++ of course supports C's notion of modules implemented using the units of separate compilation as demonstrated above.

1.2.3 Data Abstraction

Programming with modules leads to the centralization of all data of a type under the control of a type manager module. If one wanted two stacks, one would define a stack manager module with an interface like this:

```
class stack_id { /* ... */ };   // stack_id is a type
                                // no details about stacks
                                // are known here

stack_id create_stack(int size); // make a stack and
                                 // return its identifier

void push(stack_id, char);
char pop(stack_id);

destroy_stack(stack_id);              // discard stack
```

This is certainly a great improvement over the traditional unstructured mess, but "types" implemented this way are clearly different from built-in types. Each type-manager module must define a separate mechanism for creating "variables" of its type, there is no established norm for assigning object identifiers, a "variable" of such a type has no name known to the compiler or programming environment, nor do such "variables" obey the usual scope rules or argument passing rules.

A type created through a module mechanism is in most important aspects different from a built-in type and enjoys support inferior to the support provided for built-in types. The problem is that users program in terms of little "object descriptors" (the stack_ids in the example above) rather than in terms of the objects themselves. This implies that a compiler cannot catch "silly little mistakes." For example:

```
void f()
{
    stack_id s1;
    stack_id s2;

    s1 = create_stack(200);
    // Oops: forgot to create s2

    push(s1,'a');
    char c1 = pop(s1);  // pretty ugly

    destroy_stack(s2);
    // Oops: forgot to destroy s1

    s1 = s2;   // this assignment has pointer semantics
               // also: s2 is used after destruction
}
```

In other words, the module concept that supports the data hiding paradigm enables this style of programming, but does not support it.

Languages such as Ada, Clu, and C++ attack this problem by allowing a user to define types that behave in (nearly) the same way as built-in types. Such a type is often called an *abstract data type*. I prefer the term *user-defined type*. A more reasonable definition of *abstract data type* would require a mathematical "abstract" specification. What is referred to as types here would, given such a specification, be concrete specifications of such truly abstract entities. A way of defining "more abstract" types is shown in §4.6. The programming paradigm becomes:

> *Decide which types you want;*
> *provide a full set of operations for each type.*

Where there is no need for more than one object of a type, the data hiding programming style using modules suffices.

Arithmetic types such as rational and complex numbers are common examples of user-defined types:

```
class complex {
    double re, im;
public:
    complex(double r, double i) { re=r; im=i; }
    complex(double r)   // float->complex conversion
        { re=r; im=0; }

    friend complex operator+(complex, complex);
    friend complex operator-(complex, complex); // binary
    friend complex operator-(complex);          // unary
    friend complex operator*(complex, complex);
    friend complex operator/(complex, complex);
    // ...
};
```

The declaration of class (that is, user-defined type) `complex` specifies the representation of a complex number and the set of operations on a complex number. The representation is *private*; that is, `re` and `im` are accessible only to the functions specified in the declaration of class `complex`. Such functions can be defined like this:

```
complex operator+(complex a1, complex a2)
{
    return complex(a1.re+a2.re,a1.im+a2.im);
}
```

and used like this:

```
void f()
{
    complex a = 2.3;
    complex b = 1/a;
    complex c = a+b*complex(1,2.3);
    // ...
    c = -(a/b)+2;
}
```

Most, but not all, modules are better expressed as user defined types.

1.2.4 Problems with Data Abstraction

An abstract data type defines a sort of black box. Once it has been defined, it does not really interact with the rest of the program. There is no way of adapting it to new uses except by modifying its definition. This can lead to severe inflexibility. Consider defining a type shape for use in a graphics system. Assume for the moment that the system has to support circles, triangles, and squares. Assume also that you have:

```
class point{ /* ... */ };
class color{ /* ... */ };
```

You might define a shape like this:

```
enum kind { circle, triangle, square };

class shape {
    point center;
    color col;
    kind k;
    // representation of shape
public:
    point where()         { return center; }
    void move(point to) { center = to; draw(); }
    void draw();
    void rotate(int);
    // more operations
};
```

The "type field" k is necessary to allow operations such as draw() and rotate() to determine what kind of shape they are dealing with (in a Pascal-like language, one might use a variant record with tag k). The function draw() might be defined:

```
void shape::draw()
{
    switch (k) {
    case circle:
        // draw a circle
        break;
    case triangle:
        // draw a triangle
        break;
    case square:
        // draw a square
        break;
    }
}
```

This is a mess. Functions such as draw() must "know about" all the kinds of shapes there are. Therefore the code for any such function grows each time a new shape is added to the system. If you define a new shape, every operation on a shape must be examined and (possibly) modified. You are not able to add a new shape to a system unless you have access to the source code for every operation. Because adding a new shape involves "touching" the code of every important operation on shapes, it requires great skill and potentially introduces bugs into the code handling other (older) shapes. The choice of representation of particular shapes can get severely cramped by the requirement that (at least some of) their representation must fit into the typically fixed sized framework presented by the definition of the general type shape.

1.2.5 Object-Oriented Programming

The problem is that there is no distinction between the general properties of any shape (a shape has a color, it can be drawn, etc.) and the properties of a specific shape (a circle is a shape that has a radius, is drawn by a circle-drawing function, etc.). Expressing this distinction and taking advantage of it defines object-oriented programming. A language with constructs that allow this distinction to be expressed and used supports object-oriented programming. Other languages don't.

The inheritance mechanism (borrowed for C++ from Simula) provides a solution. First, specify a class that defines the general properties of all shapes:

```
class shape {
    point center;
    color col;
    // ...
public:
    point where() { return center; }
    void move(point to) { center = to; draw(); }
    virtual void draw();
    virtual void rotate(int);
    // ...
};
```

The functions for which the calling interface can be defined, but where the implementation cannot be defined except for a specific shape, have been marked "virtual" (the Simula and C++ term for "may be redefined later in a class derived from this one"). Given this definition, we can write general functions manipulating shapes:

```
void rotate_all(shape v[], int size, int angle)
    // rotate all members of array "v" of size "size"
    // "angle" degrees
{
    int i = 0;
    while (i<size) {
        v[i].rotate(angle);
        i = i+1;
    }
}
```

To define a particular shape, we must say that it is a shape and specify its particular properties (including the virtual functions):

```
class circle : public shape {
    int radius;
public:
    void draw() { /* ... */ };
    void rotate(int) {}    // yes, the null function
};
```

In C++, class `circle` is said to be *derived* from class `shape`, and class `shape` is said to be a *base* of class `circle`. An alternative terminology calls `circle` and `shape` subclass and superclass, respectively.

The programming paradigm is:

> *Decide which classes you want;*
> *provide a full set of operations for each class;*
> *make commonality explicit by using inheritance.*

Where there is no such commonality, data abstraction suffices. The amount of commonality between types that can be exploited by using inheritance and virtual functions is the litmus test of the applicability of object-oriented programming to an application area. In some areas, such as interactive graphics, there is clearly enormous scope for object-oriented programming. In other areas, such as classical arithmetic types and computations based on them, there appears to be hardly any scope for more than data abstraction, and the facilities needed for the support of object-oriented programming seem unnecessary.

Finding commonality among types in a system is not a trivial process. The amount of commonality to be exploited is affected by the way the system is designed. When a system is designed, commonality must be actively sought, both by designing classes specifically as building blocks for other types, and by examining classes to see if they exhibit similarities that can be exploited in a common base class.

For attempts to explain what object-oriented programming is without recourse to specific programming language constructs, see references 2 and 6 in Chapter 11.

Having examined the minimum support needed for procedural programming, data hiding, data abstraction, and object-oriented programming, we will go into some detail describing features that – although not essential – can make data abstraction and object-oriented programming more effective.

1.3 "A Better C"

The minimal support for procedural programming consists of functions, arithmetic, selection statements, and looping constructs. In addition, there must be a way of performing input and output operations. C++ inherits these basic language mechanisms from C (including pointers) and I/O is provided through a library. A fairly crude module concept is implemented through the mechanisms for separate compilation.

1.3.1 Program and Output

The minimal C++ program is

```
main() { }
```

It defines a function called `main`, which takes no arguments and does nothing. Curly braces, { and }, are used to express grouping in C++; here, they indicate the start and end of the (empty) body of the function `main`. Every C++ program must have a function named `main()`, and the program starts by executing that function.

Typically, a program produces some output. Here is a program that writes out *Hello, World!*

```
#include <iostream.h>

int main()
{
    cout << "Hello, World!\n";
}
```

The line `#include <iostream.h>` instructs the compiler to *include* the declarations of the standard stream input and output facilities as found in `iostream.h`. Without these declarations, the expression

```
cout << "Hello, World!\n"
```

would make no sense. The operator `<<` (''put to'') writes its second argument onto its first. In this case, the string `"Hello, World!\n"` is written onto the standard output stream `cout`. A string is a sequence of characters surrounded by double quotes. In a string the backslash character \ followed by another character denotes a single special character; in this case, `\n` is the newline character, so that the characters written are `Hello, World!` followed by a newline.

The `int` value returned by `main()`, if any, is the program's return value to ''the system.'' If none is returned, ''the system'' will receive a random value.

The input/output facilities provided by the stream library will be more closely examined in Chapter 10.

1.3.2 Variables and Arithmetic

Every name and every expression has a type that determines the operations that may be performed on it. For example, the declaration

```
int inch;
```

specifies that `inch` is of type `int`; that is, `inch` is an integer variable.

A declaration is a statement that introduces a name into the program. A declaration specifies a type for that name. A type defines the proper use of a name or an expression.

The fundamental types, corresponding most directly to hardware facilities, are:

```
char
short
int
long
```

representing integers, and

```
float
double
long double
```

representing floating-point numbers. A variable of type `char` is of the natural size to hold a character on a given machine (typically a byte), and a variable `int` is of the natural size for integer arithmetic on a given machine (typically a word).

The arithmetic operators can be used for any combination of these types:

```
+       (plus, both unary and binary)
-       (minus, both unary and binary)
*       (multiply)
/       (divide)
%       (remainder)
```

So can the comparison operators:

```
==      (equal)
!=      (not equal)
<       (less than)
>       (greater than)
<=      (less than or equal)
>=      (greater than or equal)
```

In assignments and in arithmetic operations, C++ performs all meaningful conversions between the basic types so that they can be mixed freely:

```
double d;
int i;
short s;
// ...
d = d+i;
i = s*i;
```

Here = is the assignment operator.

1.3.3 Pointers and Arrays

An array can be declared like this:

```
char v[10];   // array of 10 characters
```

Similarly, a pointer can be declared like this:

```
char* p;      // pointer to character
```

In declarations, [] means "array of" and * means "pointer to." All arrays have zero as their lower bound, so v has 10 elements, v[0]..v[9]. A pointer variable can hold the address of an object of the appropriate type:

```
p = &v[3];   // p points to v's fourth element
```

Unary & is the address-of operator.

1.3.4 Tests and Loops

C++ provides a conventional set of statements for expressing selection and looping. Here we will give examples of if-statements, switch-statements, and while-statements.

The following example performs both inch-to-centimeter and centimeter-to-inch conversion; you are supposed to indicate the unit of the input by appending i for inches or c for centimeters:

```
#include <iostream.h>

int main()
{
    const float fac = 2.54;
    float x, in, cm;
    char ch = 0;

    cout << "enter length: ";

    cin >> x;    // read floating point number
    cin >> ch;   // read suffix

    if (ch == 'i') {        // inch
        in = x;
        cm = x*fac;
    }
    else if (ch == 'c') { // cm
        in = x/fac;
        cm = x;
    }
    else
        in = cm = 0;

    cout << in << " in = " << cm << " cm\n";
}
```

The operator >> ("get from") is used as an input operator; cin is the standard input stream. The type of the right-hand operand of >> determines what input is accepted and is the target of the input operation.

A switch statement tests a value against a set of constants. The tests in the preceding example could be written like this:

```
switch (ch) {
case 'i':
     in = x;
     cm = x*fac;
     break;
case 'c':
     in = x/fac;
     cm = x;
     break;
default:
     in = cm = 0;
     break;
}
```

The break statements are used to exit the switch statement. The case constants
must be distinct, and if the value tested does not match any of them, the default is
chosen. The programmer need not provide a default.

Consider copying 10 elements from one array to another:

```
int v1[10];
int v2[10];
// ...
for (int i=0; i<10; i++)  v1[i]=v2[i];
```

This can be read as "starting with i being zero, while i is less than 10, copy the ith
element and increment i." When applied to an integer variable, the increment operator ++ simply adds 1.

1.3.5 Functions

A function is a named part of a program that can be invoked from other parts of the
program as often as needed. Consider a program writing powers of 2:

```
extern float pow(float, int); // pow() defined elsewhere

int main()
{
     for (int i=0; i<10; i++) cout << pow(2,i) << '\n';
}
```

The first line is a function declaration that specifies pow to be a function taking a
float and an int argument and returning a float. A function declaration is used
to enable calls to a function defined elsewhere.

In a call each function argument is checked against its expected type exactly as if a
variable of the declared type were being initialized. This ensures proper type checking and type conversion. For example, a call pow(12.3, "abcd") causes the compiler to complain because "abcd" is a string and not an int. For the call
pow(2,i), the compiler converts the integer constant 2 to a float, as expected by
the function. Pow might be defined like this:

```
float pow(float x, int n)
{
    if (n < 0) error("sorry, negative exponent to pow()");

    switch (n) {
    case 0:     return 1;
    case 1:     return x;
    default:    return x*pow(x,n-1);
    }
}
```

The first part of a function definition specifies the name of the function, the type of the value it returns (if any), and the types and names of its arguments (if any). A value is returned from a function using a `return` statement.

Different functions typically have different names, but for functions performing similar tasks on different types of objects it is sometimes better to let these functions have the same name. When their argument types are different, the compiler can distinguish them anyway and choose the right function to call. For example, one could have one power function for integers and another for floating-point variables:

```
int pow(int, int);
double pow(double, double);
//...
x = pow(2,10);          // call pow(int, int)
y = pow(2.0,10.0);      // call pow(double, double)
```

Such multiple use of a name is called *function-name overloading*, or simply *overloading*; overloading is discussed in Chapter 7.

Arguments to a function can be passed either "by value" or "by reference." For example, consider writing a function that swaps the values of two integer variables. When using the default pass-by-value we must use pointers:

```
void swap(int* p, int* q)
{
    int t = *p;
    *p = *q;
    *q = t;
}
```

The unary * operator is the dereference operator that returns the value of the object pointed to by a pointer. This function can be called like this

```
void f(int i, int j)
{
    swap(&i,&j);
}
```

Using pass-by-reference we can dispense with explicit pointer manipulation:

```
void swap(int& r1, int& r2)
{
      int t = r1;
      r1 = r2;
      r2 = t;
}


void g(int i, int j)
{
      swap(i,j);
}
```

For any type T, T& means "reference to T." A reference is a synonym for the variable it is initialized to. Note that because of overloading, these two swap functions
could co-exist in a program.

1.3.6 Modules

A C++ program almost always consists of several separately compiled "modules."
Each "module" – commonly referred to as a *source file* and occasionally as a
translation unit – contains a sequence of declarations of types, functions, variables,
and constants. An extern declaration allows a function or an object defined in one
source file to be referred to from another source file. For example:

```
extern "C" double sqrt(double);
extern ostream cout;
```

The most common way of ensuring consistency between source files is to place such
declarations in separate files, called *header files*, and then to *include* those header files
in all files needing the declarations. For example, the declaration of sqrt is stored in
the header file for the standard mathematical functions math.h, so if you want to
take the square root of 4, you can write:

```
#include <math.h>
//...
x = sqrt(4);
```

Because a typical header file is included in many source files, it does not contain declarations that should not be replicated. For example, function bodies are provided
only for inline functions and initializers only for constants (§4.3). Except for those
cases, a header file is a repository for type information; it provides an interface
between separately compiled parts of a program.

In an include directive, a file name enclosed in angle brackets, such as
<math.h>, refers to the file of that name in a *standard include directory* (often
/usr/include/CC); files elsewhere are referred to by names enclosed in double
quotes. For example:

```
#include "math1.h"
#include "/usr/bs/math2.h"
```

would include `math1.h` from the user's current directory and `math2.h` from the directory `/usr/bs`.

Here is a small, complete example in which a string is defined in one file and printed out in another. The file `header.h` defines the types needed:

```
// header.h

extern char* prog_name;
extern void f();
```

The file `main.c` is the main program:

```
// main.c

#include "header.h"
char* prog_name = "silly, but complete";
int main()
{
    f();
}
```

and the file `f.c` prints the string:

```
// f.c

#include <iostream.h>
#include "header.h"
void f()
{
    cout << prog_name << '\n';
}
```

Implementations vary in the suffixes used to distinguish files containing C++ programs, in the way C++ compilers are invoked, and in the arguments needed to specify a compilation. However, on my machine you can compile and run this program like this:

```
$ CC main.c f.c -o silly
$ silly
silly, but complete
$
```

In addition to this notion of a module as the unit of compilation, C++ classes provide a way of expressing modularity (§5.4).

1.4 Support for Data Abstraction

The basic support for programming with data abstraction consists of facilities for
defining a set of operations (functions and operators) for a type and for restricting the
access to objects of the type to that set of operations. Once that is done, however, the
programmer soon finds that language refinements are needed for convenient definition and use of the new types. Operator overloading is a good example of this.

1.4.1 Initialization and Cleanup

When the representation of a type is hidden, some mechanism must be provided for a
user to initialize variables of that type. A simple solution is to require a user to call
some function to initialize a variable before using it. For example:

```
class vector {
    // ...
public:
    void init(int size);    // call init() before
                            // the first use of a vector
    // ...
};


void f()
{
    vector v;
    // don't use v here
    v.init(10);
    // use v here
}
```

This is error prone and inelegant. A better solution is to allow the designer of a type
to provide a distinguished function to do the initialization. Given such a function,
allocation and initialization of a variable becomes a single operation (often called
instantiation or construction) instead of two separate operations. Such an initialization function is called a constructor. A constructor is identified by having the same
name as its class. Where construction of objects of a type is nontrivial, one often
needs a complementary operation to clean up objects after their last use. In C++, such
a cleanup function is called a destructor. A destructor is identified by having the same
name as its class prefixed by ˜ (the C++ complement operator). Consider:

```
class vector {
    int  sz;                         // number of elements
    int* v;                          // pointer to integers
public:
    vector(int);                     // constructor
    ˜vector();                       // destructor
    int& operator[](int index);      // subscript operator
};
```

The `vector` constructor can be defined to check for errors and allocate space:

```
vector::vector(int s)
{
    if (s<=0) error("bad vector size");
    sz = s;
    v = new int[s]; // allocate an array of s integers
}
```

The `vector` destructor frees the storage used:

```
vector::~vector()
{
    delete[] v;      // deallocate the array
                     // pointed to by v
}
```

C++ does not require the implementation to reclaim storage allocated by `new` when it becomes unreferenced (''automatic garbage collection''). This is compensated for, however, by enabling a type to maintain its own storage management without requiring intervention by a user. This is a common use for the constructor/destructor mechanism, but many uses of this mechanism are unrelated to storage management; see, for example §9.4.

1.4.2 Assignment and Initialization

Controlling construction and destruction of objects is sufficient for many types, but not for all. It can also be necessary to control all copy operations. Consider class `vector`:

```
void f()
{
    vector v1(100);
    vector v2 = v1; // make a new vector v2 initialized to v1
    v1 = v2;        // assign v2 to v1
    // ...
}
```

It must be possible to define the meaning of the initialization of `v2` and the assignment to `v1`. For example:

```
class vector {
    int* v;
    int  sz;
public:
    // ...
    void operator=(const vector&);   // assignment
    vector(const vector&);           // initialization
};
```

specifies that user-defined operations should be used to interpret `vector` assignment and initialization. Assignment might be defined like this:

```
void vector::operator=(const vector& a)
    // check size and copy elements
{
    if (sz != a.sz) error("bad vector size for =");
    for (int i = 0; i<sz; i++) v[i] = a.v[i];
}
```

Because the assignment operation relies on the "old value" of the vector being assigned to, the initialization operation *must* be different. For example:

```
vector::vector(const vector& a)
    // initialize a vector from another vector
{
    sz = a.sz;                        // same size
    v = new int[sz];                  // allocate element array
    for (int i = 0; i<sz; i++)        // copy elements
        v[i] = a.v[i];
}
```

In C++, a constructor of the form T(const T&) – a *copy constructor* for type T – defines all initialization of objects of type T with another object of type T. In addition to explicit initialization, constructors of the form T(const T&) are used to handle arguments passed "by value" and function return values.

1.4.3 Templates

Why would you want to define a vector of integers anyway? A user typically needs a vector of elements of some type unknown to the writer of the Vector type. Consequently the vector type ought to be expressed in such a way that it takes the element type as an argument:

```
template<class T> class Vector {       // Vector of Ts
    T* v;
    int sz;
public:
    Vector(int s)
    {
        if (s <= 0) error("bad Vector size");
        v = new T[sz = s];   // allocate an array of s Ts
    }
    T& operator[](int i);
    int size() { return sz; }
    // ...
};
```

This defines a *template*. A template is a specification of how to make a family of related classes. In this case, the Vector template specifies how vector classes can be made for individual element types. The template<class T> prefix to the otherwise perfectly ordinary class declaration specifies that a template that requires a type argument (used as the element type) is being declared.

Vectors of specific types can now be defined and used:

```
void f()
{
    Vector<int> v1(100);        // Vector of 100 integers
    Vector<complex> v2(200);    // Vector of 200 complex numbers

    v2[i] = complex(v1[x],v1[y]);
    // ...
}
```

This notion of templates provides what is sometimes called parameterized types or generics. It resembles features from Clu and Ada. Users of a template need not incur any run-time overheads compared with a class where all types involved are specified directly.

1.4.4 Exception Handling

As programs grow, and especially when libraries are used extensively, standards for handling errors (or, more generally, "exceptional circumstances") become important. Ada, Algol68, and Clu each support a standard way of handling exceptions.

Consider again the `vector` example. What *ought* to be done when an out-of-range index value is passed to the subscript operator? The writer of the vector class doesn't know what the user would like done in this case, and the user cannot detect the problem (if the user could, the range error wouldn't happen in the first place). The solution is for the implementer of the vector to detect the range error and then tell the (unknown) user. The user can then take appropriate action. For example:

```
class vector {
    // define a type to be used for exceptions:
    class range { };

    // ...
}
```

Instead of calling an error function, `vector::operator[]()` can invoke the exception handling code, that is "throw the exception:"

```
int& vector::operator[](int i)
{
    if (i<0 || sz<=i) throw range();
    return v[i];
}
```

This will cause the call stack to be unwound until a handler for an exception of `vector`'s Range type (`vector::range`) is found; this handler will then be executed.

An exception handler may be defined for a specific block:

```
void f(int i)
{
    try {                       // exceptions here are handled by
                                // the handler defined below
        vector v(i);
        // ...
        v[i+1] = 7;     // causes range exception
        //...
        g();            // might cause a range exception
                        // using some vector
    }
    catch (vector::range) {
        error("f(): vector range error");
        return;
    }
}
```

Use of the exception handling mechanisms can make error handling more regular and readable. See Chapter 9 for further discussion and details.

1.4.5 Type Conversions

User-defined conversions, such as the one from floating point numbers to complex numbers implied by the constructor complex(double), have proven unexpectedly useful in C++. Such conversions can be applied explicitly or the programmer can rely on the compiler to add them implicitly where necessary and unambiguous:

```
complex a = complex(1);
complex b = 1;              // implicit: 1 -> complex(1)
a = b+complex(2);
a = b+2;                    // implicit: 2 -> complex(2)
```

Type conversions were introduced into C++ because mixed-mode arithmetic is the norm in languages for numerical work and because most user-defined types used for ''calculation'' (for example, matrices, character strings, and machine addresses) have natural mappings to and/or from other types.

Type conversions have also proven useful from the point of view of program organization:

```
complex a = 2;
complex b = a+2;   // means: operator+(a,complex(2))
b = 2+a;           // means: operator+(complex(2),a)
```

Only one function is needed to interpret ''+'' operations, and the two operands are handled identically by the type system. Furthermore, class complex is written without any need to modify the concept of integers to enable the smooth and natural integration of the two concepts.

1.4.6 Multiple Implementations

The basic mechanism for supporting object-oriented programming, derived classes, and virtual functions can be used to support data abstraction by allowing several different implementations for a given type. Consider again the stack example:

```
template<class T>
    class stack {
    public:
        virtual void push(T) = 0; // pure virtual function
        virtual T pop() = 0;       // pure virtual function
    };
```

The =0 notation specifies that no definition is required for the virtual function and that the class is abstract; that is, the class can be used only as a base class. This allows stacks to be used, but not created:

```
class cat { /* ... */ };

stack<cat> s; // error: stack is abstract


void some_function(stack<cat>& s, cat kitty) // ok
{
    s.push(kitty);
    cat c2 = s.pop();
    // ...
}
```

Because no representation is specified in the stack interface, its users are totally insulated from implementation details.

We can now provide several distinct implementations of stacks. For example, we can provide a stack implemented with an array:

```
template<class T>
    class astack : public stack<T> {
        // actual representation of a stack object
        // in this case an array
        // ...
    public:
        astack(int size);
        ~astack();

        void push(T);
        T pop();
    };
```

Elsewhere we can provide a stack implemented using a linked list:

```
template<class T>
    class lstack : public stack<T> {
        // ...
    };
```

We can now create and use stacks:

```
void g()
{
    lstack<cat> s1(100);
    astack<cat> s2(100);

    cat Ginger;
    cat Snowball;

    some_function(s1,Ginger);
    some_function(s2,Snowball);
}
```

Only the creator of stacks, g(), needs to worry about different kinds of stacks; the user some_function() is totally insulated from such details. The price of this flexibility is that all operations on such types must be virtual functions.

1.5 Support for Object-Oriented Programming

The basic support a programmer needs to write object-oriented programs consists of a class mechanism with inheritance and a mechanism that allows calls of member functions to depend on the actual type of an object (in cases where the actual type is unknown at compile time). The design of the member function calling mechanism is critical. In addition, facilities supporting data abstraction techniques (as described above) are important because the arguments for data abstraction and for its refinements to support elegant use of types are equally valid where support for object-oriented programming is available. The success of both techniques hinges on the design of types and on the ease, flexibility, and efficiency of such types. Object-oriented programming allows user-defined types to be far more flexible and general than the ones designed using only data abstraction techniques.

1.5.1 Calling Mechanisms

The key language facility supporting object-oriented programming is the mechanism by which a member function is invoked for a given object for which the exact type isn't known at compile time. For example, given a pointer p, how is a call p->rotate(45) handled? Because C++ relies heavily on static type checking, this expression will make sense only provided the function rotate() has been declared. Further, the notation p->rotate indicates that p must be a pointer to an object of some class and rotate must be a member of that class. The purpose of this checking – as for all static type checking – is to ensure that the program is as consistent in its use of types as can be determined before executing it, in other words, to ensure that large classes of errors are absent in running programs.

Consequently, a class declaration such as the one found in §1.2.5

```
class shape {
     // ...
public:
     // ...
     virtual void rotate(int);
     // ...
};
```

must be available, and p must have been declared

```
T* p;
```

where T is shape or the name of a class derived from shape. We see that the class of the object pointed to by p indeed has a function rotate() and that function accepts an argument of type int. This means that p->rotate(45) is a correct expression.

Because shape::rotate() was declared to be a virtual function, a virtual function call must be used. The call mechanism must look into the object and find some information placed there by the compiler to determine which function rotate is to be called. Once that function is found, say circle::rotate, it can be called using the mechanism described above. A common implementation technique is for the compiler to convert the name rotate into an index into a table of pointers to functions. A shape object will look something like this:

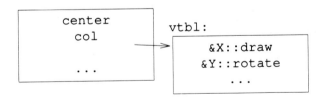

The functions in the virtual function table, the vtbl, allows the object to be used correctly even when the size of the object and the layout of the data in the . . . parts of the object and the vtbl are unknown to the caller. The names of the classes providing the functions that will be called are indicated by X and Y; for a circle object both X and Y are circle. This virtual call mechanism can be made essentially as efficient as the "normal function call" mechanism.

1.5.2 Type Checking

The need to type check virtual function calls can be constraining for library designers. For example, it could be nice to provide a class ''stack of anything'' for general use. C++ doesn't allow this, but the combinations of templates and inheritance can approach the flexibility, ease of design, and ease of use of libraries in languages that rely on dynamic (run-time) type checking, such as Smalltalk, where a ''stack of anything'' can be expressed. As an example, consider a stack template:

```
template<class T> class stack {
    T* p;
    int sz;
public:
    stack(int);
    ~stack();

    void push(T);
    T& pop();
};
```

This stack can then be used as a stack of pointers to `planes` without relaxation of static type checking:

```
stack<plane*> cs(200);

void f()
{
    cs.push(new Saab900);  // Compile-time error:
                           // car* passed, plane* expected

    cs.push(new Saab37B);  // fine: a Saab 37B is a plane

    cs.pop()->takeoff();

    cs.pop()->takeoff();
}
```

Without static type checking the error would not have been detected until run time:

```
// Example assuming dynamic type checking instead of
// static checking. Not C++.

Stack s; // Stack can hold pointers to objects of any type

void f()
{
    s.push(new Saab900);
    s.push(new Saab37B);
```

```
    s.pop()->takeoff();    // fine: a Saab 37B is a plane

    s.pop()->takeoff();    // run-time error:
                           // car cannot take off

}
```

The mechanism for determining whether an operation can be performed on an object at run time is typically expensive as compared to a C++ virtual function call.

The use of static type checking and virtual function calls leads to a somewhat different style of programming than does dynamic type checking. For example, a C++ class specifies a fixed interface to a set of objects (of any derived class), whereas a Smalltalk class specifies an initial set of operations for objects (of any subclass). In other words, a Smalltalk class is a minimal specification, and the user is free to try operations not specified; whereas a C++ class is an exact specification, and the user is guaranteed that only operations specified in the class declaration will be accepted by the compiler.

1.5.3 Multiple Inheritance

When a class A is a base of class B, a B inherits the attributes of an A; that is, a B is an A in addition to whatever else it might be. Given this explanation it seems obvious that it might be useful to have a class B inherit from two base classes A1 and A2. This is called multiple inheritance.

A standard example of the use of multiple inheritance would be to provide two library classes displayed and task for representing objects under the control of a display manager and co-routines under the control of a scheduler, respectively. A programmer could then create classes such as

```
    class my_displayed_task : public displayed, public task {
        // my stuff
    };

    class my_task : public task {   // not a displayed
        // my stuff
    };

    class my_displayed : public displayed {   // not a task
        // my stuff
    };
```

Using just single inheritance only two of these three choices would be open to the programmer. This leads to either code replication or loss of flexibility – and typically both. In C++, this example can be handled as shown above with no significant overheads (in time or space) as compared to single inheritance and without sacrificing static type checking.

Ambiguities are handled at compile time:

```
class task {
public:
    void trace();
    // ...
};


class displayed {
public:
    void trace();
    // ...
};


class my_displayed_task : public displayed, public task {
    // no trace() defined here
};


void g(my_displayed_task* p)
{
    p->trace();   // error: ambiguous
}
```

In this, C++ differs from the object-oriented Lisp dialects that support multiple inheritance. In these Lisp dialects ambiguities are resolved by considering the order of declarations significant, by considering objects of the same name in different base classes identical, or by combining methods of the same name in base classes into a more complex method of the highest class. In C++, one would typically resolve the ambiguity by adding a function:

```
class my_displayed_task : public displayed, public task {
    // ...
public:
    void trace()
    {
        // my own stuff
        displayed::trace();   // call display's trace()
        task::trace();        // call task's trace()
    }
    // ...
};


void g(my_displayed_task* p)
{
    p->trace();   // now fine
}
```

1.5.4 Encapsulation

Consider a class member (either a data member or a function member) that needs to be protected from "unauthorized access." What choices can be reasonable for defining the set of functions that may access that member? The "obvious" answer for a language supporting object-oriented programming is "all operations defined for this object," that is, all member functions. For example:

```
class window {
    // ...
protected:
    Rectangle inside;
    // ...
};

class dumb_terminal : public window {
    // ...
public:
    void prompt();
    // ...
};
```

Here, the base class `window` has specified the `Rectangle` called `inside` to be `protected` so that member functions of derived classes, such as `dumb_terminal::prompt()`, can read it to figure out what part of the window they may manipulate. Other functions cannot access `window::inside`.

This approach combines a large degree of protection from accident (because you do not easily define a new derived class "by accident") with the flexibility needed for "tool building" using class hierarchies (because you can "grant yourself access" to protected members by deriving a class).

A nonobvious implication of this is that there cannot be a complete and final list of all functions that may access the protected member because one can always add another by deriving a new class from the protected member's class and define a member function of that derived class. For the data abstraction style of programming this is often not good enough. The "obvious" choice for a language oriented toward data abstraction is to require the programmer to list the functions that need access in the class declaration. This is C++'s notion of `private`. This notion was used in the `complex` and `shape` examples above.

Encapsulation issues increase dramatically in importance with the size of the program and with the number and geographical dispersion of its users. See §6.6 for more detailed discussions of language support for encapsulation.

1.6   Limits to Perfection

C++ is designed to be "a better C," to support data abstraction, and to support object-oriented programming. It does so under the constraints of being useful for the most demanding systems programming tasks.

A major design problem with a language defined to exploit the techniques of data hiding, data abstraction, and object-oriented programming is that to claim to be a general purpose programming language it must
- Run on traditional machines.
- Coexist with traditional operating systems and languages.
- Compete with traditional programming languages in terms of run-time efficiency.
- Cope with every major application area.

This implies that facilities must be available for effective numerical work (floating-point arithmetic without overheads that would make Fortran appear attractive), and that facilities must be available for access to memory in a way that allows device drivers to be written. It must also be possible to write calls that conform to the often rather strange standards required for traditional operating system interfaces. In addition, it should be possible to call functions written in other languages from a language supporting object-oriented programming and for functions written in the language supporting object-oriented programming to be called from a program written in another language.

Another implication is that a programming language cannot completely rely on mechanisms that cannot be efficiently implemented on a traditional architecture and still expect to be used as a general-purpose language.

The alternative to having "low-level" features in a language is to handle major application areas using separate "low-level" languages (such as C or assembler) for many tasks. C++ is designed to ensure that anything that can be done in C can be done in C++ with no added run-time overhead. In general, C++ is designed with the notion that no overhead is introduced without an explicit request from the programmer.

C++ is designed to rely on compiler technology for consistency of programs and for run-time compactness and efficiency. Strong type checking and encapsulation are seen as the primary means of controlling the complexity of programs. This is particularly important for larger programs that are developed by many people and where the user is not the original programmer or even a programmer at all. Because essentially no programs are written without reliance on libraries written by others, this means essentially all programs.

C++ is designed to support the notion of a program as a model of some aspects of reality and a class as the concrete representation of a concept from the application (§12.2). This makes classes ubiquitous in C++ programs and places stringent demands on the flexibility of the class concept, the compactness of class objects, and the efficiency of their use. Were classes inconvenient or expensive to use, they would be left unused and programs would degenerate into "better C" style programs. The users would thus lose the primary benefits C++ was designed to provide.

Declarations and Constants

*Perfection is achieved
only on the point of collapse.*
– C.N.Parkinson

This chapter presents the fundamental types (char, int, float, etc.)
and the fundamental ways of deriving new types (functions, arrays, pointers, etc.) from them. A name is introduced into a program by a declaration
specifying its type and perhaps an initial value; the concepts of declaration,
definition, scope of names, lifetime of objects, and type are presented. The
notations for literal constants in C++ are described, and so are the methods
for defining symbolic constants. The examples simply demonstrate language features. A more extensive and realistic example is used to present
C++ expressions and statements in the next chapter. The mechanisms for
specifying user-defined types with associated operations are not mentioned
here; they can be found in Chapters 5 and 7.

2.1 Declarations

Before a name (identifier) can be used in a C++ program it must be declared; that is,
its type must be specified to inform the compiler what kind of entity the name refers
to. Here are some examples illustrating the diversity of declarations:

```
char ch;
int count = 1;
char* name = "Njal";
struct complex { float re, im; };
```

```
complex cvar;
extern complex sqrt(complex);
extern int error_number;
typedef complex point;
float real(complex* p) { return p->re; };
const double pi = 3.1415926535897932385;
struct user;
template<class T> abs(T a) { return a<0 ? -a : a; }
enum beer { Carlsberg, Tuborg, Thor };
```

As can be seen from these examples, a declaration can do more than simply associate a type with a name. Most of these *declarations* are also *definitions*; that is, they also define an entity for the name to refer to. For ch, count, name, and cvar, that entity is an appropriate amount of memory to be used as a variable – that memory will be allocated. For real, it is the specified function. For the constant pi, it is the value 3.1415926535897932385. For complex, that entity is a new type. For point, it is the type complex, so that point becomes a synonym for complex. Only the declarations

```
extern complex sqrt(complex);
extern int error_number;
struct user;
```

are not also definitions. That is, the entity they refer to must be defined elsewhere. The code (body) for the function sqrt must be specified by some other declaration, the memory for the int variable error_number must be allocated by some other declaration of error_number, and some other declaration of the type user must define what that type looks like. There must always be exactly one definition for each name in a C++ program, but there can be many declarations, and all declarations must agree on the type of the entity referred to, so this fragment has two errors:

```
int count;
int count;                      // error: redefinition

extern int error_number;
extern short error_number;      // error: type mismatch
```

and this has none (for the use of extern see §4.2):

```
extern int error_number;
extern int error_number;
```

Some definitions specify a "value" for the entities they define:

```
struct complex { float re, im; };
typedef complex point;
float real(complex* p) { return p->re };
const double pi = 3.1415926535897932385;
```

For types, functions, and constants the "value" is permanent; for nonconstant data types the initial value may be changed later:

```
int count = 1;
char* name = "Bjarne";
// ...
count = 2;
name = "Marian";
```

Of the definitions only

```
char ch;
```

does not specify a value. Any declaration that specifies a value is a definition.

2.1.1 Scope

A declaration introduces a name into a scope; that is, a name can be used only in a specific part of the program text. For a name declared in a function (often called a local name), that scope extends from the point of declaration to the end of the block in which its declaration occurs; for a name not in a function or in a class (often called a global name), the scope extends from the point of declaration to the end of the file in which its declaration occurs. A declaration of a name in a block can hide a declaration in an enclosing block or a global name; that is, a name can be redefined to refer to a different entity within a block. After exit from the block, the name resumes its previous meaning. For example:

```
int x;                 // global x

void f()
{
     int x;            // local x hides global x
     x = 1;            // assign to local x
     {
          int x;       // hides first local x
          x = 2;       // assign to second local x
     }
     x = 3;            // assign to first local x
}

int* p = &x;           // take address of global x
```

Hiding names is unavoidable when writing large programs. However, a human reader can easily fail to notice that a name has been hidden; and some errors caused by this are very difficult to find, mainly because they are rare. Consequently, name hiding should be minimized. Using names such as i and x for global variables or for local variables in a large function is asking for trouble.

It is possible to use a hidden global name by using the scope resolution operator ::. For example:

```
int x;

void f2()
{
    int x = 1;          // hide global x
    ::x = 2;            // assign to global x
}
```

There is no way to use a hidden local name.

The scope of a name starts at its point of declaration (after the complete declarator and before the initializer; see §r.3.2); this means that a name can even be used to specify its own initial value. For example:

```
int x;

void f3()
{
    int x = x;          // perverse
}
```

This is not illegal, just silly, and the compiler will warn that x has been "used before set" if you try it. It is, however, possible to use a single name to refer to two different objects in a block without using the : : operator. For example:

```
int x = 11;

void f4()                 // perverse:
{
    int y = x;          // global x
    int x = 22;
    y = x;              // local x
}
```

The variable y is initialized to the value of the global x, 11, and then assigned the value of the local variable x, 22.

Function argument names are considered declared in the outermost block of a function, so

```
void f5(int x)
{
    int x;              // error
}
```

is an error, because x is defined twice in the same scope. Having this an error catches a not uncommon, subtle mistake.

2.1.2 Objects and Lvalues

One can allocate and use "variables" that do not have names, and it is possible to assign to strange looking expressions (for example *p[a+10]=7). Consequently, there is a need for a name for "something in memory." Here is the appropriate quote from the C++ reference manual: "An *object* is a region of storage; an *lvalue* is an expression referring to an object or function" (§r.3.7). The word *lvalue* was originally coined to mean "something that can be on the left-hand side of an assignment." However, not every lvalue may be used on the left-hand side of an assignment; one can have an lvalue referring to a constant (see §2.5). An lvalue that has not been declared const is often called a modifiable lvalue.

2.1.3 Lifetime

Unless the programmer specifies otherwise, an object is created when its definition is encountered and destroyed when its name goes out of scope. Objects with global names are created and initialized once (only) and "live" until the the program terminates. Local objects defined by a declaration with the keyword static also "live" until the end of the program. They are initialized the first time the thread of control passes through their declaration. For example†:

```
int a = 1;

void f()
{
    int b = 1;              // initialized at each call of f()
    static int c = a;   // initialized once only
    cout << " a = " << a++
         << " b = " << b++
         << " c = " << c++ << '\n';
}

int main()
{
    while (a < 4) f();
}
```

produces this output:

```
a = 1 b = 1 c = 1
a = 2 b = 1 c = 2
a = 3 b = 1 c = 3
```

The ++ operator increments: a++ means add 1 to a.

A global or local static variable that is not explicitly initialized is implicitly initialized to zero (§2.4.5).

Using the new and delete operators, the programmer can also create objects whose lifetime's are controlled directly; see §3.2.6.

---

† The #include <iostream.h> directive has been left out of the examples in this chapter to save space. It is necessary to complete examples producing output.

2.2 Names

A name (identifier) consists of a sequence of letters and digits. The first character must be a letter. The underscore character _ is considered a letter. C++ imposes no limit on the number of characters in a name, but some parts of an implementation are not under control of the compiler writer (in particular, the loader), and they, unfortunately, sometimes do. Some run-time environments also make it necessary to extend or restrict the set of characters accepted in an identifier; extensions (for example, allowing the character $ in a name) yield nonportable programs. A C++ keyword (see §r.2.4) cannot be used as a name. Examples of names are:

```
hello      this_is_a_most_unusually_long_name
DEFINED    foO     bAr     u_name      HorseSense
var0       var1    CLASS   _class      ____
```

Examples of character sequences that cannot be used as identifiers are:

```
012        a fool     $sys      class     3var
pay.due    foo~bar    .name     if
```

Uppercase and lowercase letters are distinct, so Count and count are different names; but it is unwise to choose names that differ only slightly from each other. Names starting with underscore are reserved for special facilities in the implementation and the run-time environment, so it is unwise to use such names in application programs.

When reading a program, the compiler always looks for the longest string of characters that could make up a name, so var10 is a single name, not the name var followed by the number 10; and elseif is a single name, not the keyword else followed by the keyword if.

2.3 Types

Every name (identifier) in a C++ program has a type associated with it. This type determines what operations can be applied to the name (that is, to the entity referred to by the name) and how such operations are interpreted. For example:

```
int error_number;
float real(complex* p);
```

Because error_number is declared to be an int, it can be assigned to, used in arithmetic expressions, etc. The function real, on the other hand, can be called with the address of a complex as its argument. It is possible to take the address of either one. Some names, like int and complex, are names of types. A type name is typically used to specify the type of another name in a declaration. The only other operations on a type name are sizeof (for determining the amount of memory required to hold an object of the type) and new (for free-store allocation of objects of the type). For example:

```
int main()
{
    int* p = new int;
    cout << "sizeof(int) = " << sizeof(int) << '\n';
}
```

A type name can also be use to specify explicit conversion from one type to another (§3.2.5). For example:

```
float f;
char* p;
// ...
long ll = long(p);    // convert p to a long
int i = int(f);       // convert f to an int
```

2.3.1 Fundamental Types

C++ has a set of fundamental types corresponding to the most common fundamental storage units of a computer and the most common fundamental ways of using them:

```
char
short int
int
long int
```

to represent integers of different sizes,

```
float
double
long double
```

to represent floating point numbers,

```
unsigned char
unsigned short int
unsigned int
unsigned long int
```

to represent unsigned integers, logical values, bit arrays, etc.,

```
signed char
signed short int
signed int
signed long int
```

to represent explicitly signed types.

Since `int`s are signed by default the `signed int` types are simply synonyms for their plain `int` counterparts; only `signed char` is of interest: `unsigned char`, `signed char`, and (plain) `char` are three distinct types; see also §r.3.6.1.

For a more compact notation, `int` can be dropped from multiword combinations without changing the meaning; thus `long` means `long int` and `unsigned` means

unsigned int. In general, when a type is missing in a declaration, int is
assumed. For example:

```
const a = 1;  // sloppy
static x;     // sloppy
```

each define an object of type int. Leaving type specification out of a declaration and
relying on the default int is generally considered bad taste and can lead to undesirable subtleties; see §r.7.1.

The integer type char is the most suitable for holding and manipulating characters on a given computer; it is typically an 8-bit byte. Sizes of C++ objects are
expressed in terms of multiples of the size of a char, so by definition
sizeof(char) ≡ 1. Depending on the hardware, a char is a signed or an
unsigned integer. The type unsigned char is of course always unsigned, and
using it yields more portable programs, but there can be a significant performance
penalty for using it instead of using plain char. Similarly, the type signed char
is always signed.

The reason for providing more than one integer type, more than one unsigned
type, and more than one floating point type is to allow the programmer to take advantage of hardware characteristics. On many machines there are significant differences
in memory requirements, memory access times, and computation speed between the
different varieties of fundamental types. Knowing a machine, it is usually easy to
choose, for example, the appropriate integer type for a particular variable. Writing
truly portable low-level code is harder. This is what is guaranteed about sizes of fundamental types:

$$1 \equiv sizeof(char) \leq sizeof(short) \leq sizeof(int) \leq sizeof(long)$$

$$sizeof(float) \leq sizeof(double) \leq sizeof(long\ double)$$

$$sizeof(I) \equiv sizeof(signed\ I) \equiv sizeof(unsigned\ I)$$

where I can be char, short, int, or long. In addition, it is guaranteed that a
char has at least 8 bits, a short at least 16 bits, and a long at least 32 bits. A
char can hold a character of the machine's character set. This means that it is usually safe to assume that a char can hold integers in the range 0..127. Assuming
more is hazardous.

The unsigned integer types are ideal for uses that treat storage as a bit array.
Using an unsigned instead of an int to gain one more bit to represent positive
integers is almost never a good idea. Attempts to ensure that some values are positive
by declaring variables unsigned will typically be defeated by the implicit conversion rules. For example:

```
unsigned surprise = -1;
```

is legal (but a compiler can warn about it).

2.3.2 Implicit Type Conversion

The fundamental types can be mixed freely in assignments and expressions. Wherever possible, values are converted so as not to lose information. The exact rules can be found in §r.4 and §r.5.4.

There are cases in which information may get lost or even distorted. Assignment of a value of one type to a variable of another type with fewer bits in its representation is necessarily a potential source of trouble. For example, assume that the following is executed on a machine with two's complement representation of integers and 8-bit characters:

```
int i1 = 256+255;
char ch = i1;        // ch == 255
int i2 = ch;         // i2 == ?
```

One bit (the most significant!) is lost in the assignment `ch=i1`, and `ch` will hold the bit pattern ''all ones'' (that is, 8 ones) when assigned to `i2`! But what could be the value of `i2`? On a DEC VAX, where a `char` is signed, the answer is −1; on a Motorola 68K, where a `char` is unsigned, the answer is 255. C++ does not have a run-time mechanism for detecting this kind of problem, and compile-time detection is too difficult in general, so the programmer must be careful.

2.3.3 Derived Types

From the fundamental types (and from user-defined types), other types can be derived by using the declaration operators

```
*       pointer
&       reference
[]      array
()      function
```

and the structure definition mechanism. For example:

```
int* a;
float v[10];
char* p[20];      // array of 20 character pointers
void f(int);
struct str { short length; char* p; };
```

The rules for composing types using these operators are explained in detail in §r.8. The basic idea is that the declaration of a derived type mirrors its use. For example:

```
int v[10];        // declare an array
i = v[3];         // use an element of the array

int* p;           // declare a pointer
i = *p;           // use the object pointed to
```

All problems in understanding the notation for derived types stem from the fact that `*` and `&` are prefix operators and `[]` and `()` are postfix, so that parentheses must be used to express types in which the operator precedences are awkward. For example, because [ ] has higher precedence than *:

```
int* v[10];      // array of pointers
int (*p)[10];    // pointer to array
```

Most people simply remember how the most common types look.

It is possible to declare several names in a single declaration; instead of a single name, the declaration simply contains a list of comma-separated names. For example, one can declare two integers like this:

```
int x, y;        // int x; int y;
```

When declaring derived types one should note that operators apply to individual names only (and not to any other names in the same declaration). For example:

```
int* p, y;       // int* p;  int y;  NOT int* y;
int x, *p;       // int x;   int* p;
int v[10], *p;   // int v[10];  int* p;
```

The author's opinion is that such constructs make a program less readable and should be avoided.

2.3.4 Void

The type void behaves syntactically as a fundamental type. It can, however, be used only as part of a derived type; there are no objects of type void. It is used to specify that a function does not return a value or as the base type for pointers to objects of unknown type.

```
void f();        // f does not return a value
void* pv;        // pointer to object of unknown type
```

A pointer of any type can be assigned to a variable of type void*. At first this may not seem very useful, because a void* cannot be dereferenced, but this restriction is exactly what makes the void* type useful. Its primary use is for passing pointers to functions that are not allowed to make assumptions about the type of the object, and for returning untyped objects from functions. To use such an object, explicit type conversion must be used. Such functions typically exist at the very lowest level of the system, where real hardware resources are manipulated. For example:

```
void* malloc(unsigned size);
void free(void*);

void f()      // C style allocation
{
    int* pi = (int*)malloc(10*sizeof(int));
    char* pc = (char*)malloc(10);
    // ...
    free(pi);
    free(pc);
}
```

The notation (*type*) *expression* specifies a conversion of the *expression* to the *type*. Thus the void* returned by the first call to malloc() is converted to an int* before assignment to pi. This particular example demonstrates an archaic style; see §3.2.6 for a better way of handling free store allocations.

2.3.5 Pointers

For most types T, T* is the type pointer to T. That is, a variable of type T* can hold the address of an object of type T. Pointers to arrays and pointers to functions unfortunately need a more complicated notation:

```
int* pi;
char** cpp;            // pointer to pointer to char
int (*vp)[10];         // pointer to array of 10 ints
int (*fp)(char, char*);  // pointer to function
                       // taking (char, char*) arguments
                       // and returning an int
```

The fundamental operation on a pointer is *dereferencing*, that is, referring to the object pointed to by the pointer. This operation is also called *indirection*. The dereferencing operator is (prefix) unary *. For example:

```
char c1 = 'a';
char* p = &c1;     // p holds the address of c1
char c2 = *p;      // c2 = 'a'
```

The variable pointed to by p is c1, and the value stored in c1 is 'a', so the value of *p assigned to c2 is 'a'.

It is possible to perform some arithmetic operations on pointers. Here, for example, is a function that counts the number of characters in a zero-terminated string of characters (not counting the terminating 0):

```
int strlen(char* p)
{
    int i = 0;
    while (*p++) i++;
    return i;
}
```

Another way of finding the length is first to find the end of the string and then to subtract the address of the beginning of the string from the address of the end:

```
int strlen(const char* p)
{
    char* q = p;
    while (*q++) ;
    return q-p-1;
}
```

Pointers to functions can be extremely useful; they are discussed in §4.6.9.

2.3.6 Arrays

For a type T, T[size] is the type "array of size elements of type T." The elements are indexed from 0 to size−1. For example:

```
float v[3];      // an array of 3 floats: v[0], v[1], v[2]
int a[2][5];     // two arrays of five ints
char* vpc[32];   // array of 32 character pointers
```

A loop for writing out the integer values of the lowercase letters could be written like this:

```
extern "C" int strlen(const char*); // from <string.h>

char alpha[] = "abcdefghijklmnopqrstuvwxyz";

main()
{
    int sz = strlen(alpha);

    for (int i=0; i<sz; i++) {
        char ch = alpha[i];
        cout << '\'' << ch << '\''
             << " = " << int(ch)
             << " = 0" << oct(ch)
             << " = 0x" << hex(ch) << '\n';
    }
}
```

The function oct() produces an octal representation of its integer argument, and hex() produces a hexadecimal representation of its integer argument; oct() and hex() are declared in <iostream.h>. The function strlen() from

`<string.h>` was used to count characters in `alpha`; alternatively, the size of `alpha` could have been used (§2.4.4). When using the ASCII character set, the output will look like this:

```
'a' = 97 = 0141 = 0x61
'b' = 98 = 0142 = 0x62
'c' = 99 = 0143 = 0x63
...
```

Note that it is not necessary to specify the size of the array `alpha`; the compiler counts the number of characters in the character string specified as the initializer. Using a string as the initializer for an array of characters is a convenient, but unfortunately also a unique, use of strings. There is no similar assignment of a string to an array. For example,

```
char v[9];
v = "a string";            // error
```

is an error because assignment is not defined for arrays. A more advanced notion of a string can be implemented using classes; see §7.10.

Obviously, strings are appropriate only for initializing arrays of characters; for other types, a more elaborate notation must be used. This notation can also be used for character arrays. For example:

```
int   v1[] = { 1, 2, 3, 4 };
int   v2[] = { 'a', 'b', 'c', 'd' };

char v3[] = { 1, 2, 3, 4 };
char v4[] = { 'a', 'b', 'c', 'd' };
```

Note that `v3` and `v4` are arrays of four (not five) characters; `v4` is not terminated by a zero, as convention and most library routines require. Such a `char` array is a programming error waiting to happen.

Multidimensional arrays are represented as arrays of arrays, and using comma notation as used for array bounds in some other languages gives compile-time errors because comma `(,)` is a sequencing operator (see §3.2.2). For example, try this:

```
int bad[5,2];              // error
```

and this:

```
int v[5][2];
int bad = v[4,1];          // error
int good = v[4][1];        // correct
```

A declaration

```
char v[2][5];
```

declares an array with two elements, each of which is an array of type `char[5]`. In the following example, the first of those arrays is initialized with the first five letters and the second to the first five digits.

```
char v[2][5] = {
    { 'a', 'b', 'c', 'd', 'e' },
    { '0', '1', '2', '3', '4' }
};

main() {
    for (int i = 0; i<2; i++) {
        for (int j = 0; j<5; j++)
            cout << "v[" << i << "][" << j
                 << "]=" << v[i][j] << "   ";
        cout << '\n';
    }
}
```

It will produce:

```
v[0][0]=a  v[0][1]=b  v[0][2]=c  v[0][3]=d  v[0][4]=e
v[1][0]=0  v[1][1]=1  v[1][2]=2  v[1][3]=3  v[1][4]=4
```

2.3.7 Pointers and Arrays

In C++, pointers and arrays are very closely related. The name of an array can also be used as a pointer to its first element, so the alphabet example could be written like this:

```
int main()
{
    char alpha[] = "abcdefghijklmnopqrstuvwxyz";
    char* p = alpha;
    char ch;

    while (ch = *p++)
        cout << ch << " = " << int(ch)
             << " = 0" << oct(ch) << '\n';
}
```

The declaration of p could also be written

```
char* p = &alpha[0];
```

This equivalence is extensively used in function calls, in which an array argument is always passed as a pointer to the first element of the array; thus, in this example,

```
void f()
{
    extern "C" int strlen(const char*); // from <string.h>
    char v[] = "Annemarie";
    char* p = v;
    strlen(p);
    strlen(v);
}
```

the same value is passed to `strlen` in both calls. The snag is that it is impossible to avoid this; that is, there is no way of declaring a function so that the array v is copied when the function is called (§4.6.5).

The result of applying the arithmetic operators +, −, ++, or −− to pointers depends on the type of the object pointed to. When an arithmetic operator is applied to a pointer p of type T*, p is assumed to point to an element of an array of objects of type T; p+1 means the next element of that array and p−1 the previous element. This implies that the value of p+1 will be `sizeof(T)` bytes larger than the value of p. For example, executing

```
main()
{
    char cv[10];
    int iv[10];

    char* pc = cv;
    int* pi = iv;

    cout << "char* " << long(pc+1)-long(pc) << '\n';
    cout << "int*  " << long(pi+1)-long(pi) << '\n';
}
```

produced

```
char* 1
int*  4
```

because characters occupy one byte each and integers occupy four bytes each on my machine. The pointer values were converted to the type `long` before the subtraction using explicit type conversion (§3.2.5). They were converted to `long`, and not to the "obvious" type `int`, because in some implementations of C++ a pointer will not fit into an `int` (that is, `sizeof(int)<sizeof(char*)`).

Subtraction of pointers is defined only when both pointers point to elements of the same array (although the language has no way of ensuring that is the case). When subtracting one pointer from another, the result is the number of array elements between the two pointers (an integer). One can add an integer to a pointer or subtract an integer from a pointer; in both cases, the result is a pointer value. If that value does not point to an element of the same array as the original pointer or one beyond, the result of using that value is undefined. For example:

```
void f()
{
    int v1[10];
    int v2[10];

    int i = &v1[5]-&v1[3];    // 2
        i = &v1[5]-&v2[3];    // result undefined

    int* p = v2+2;            // p == &v2[2]
        p = v2-2;             // *p undefined
}
```

Complicated pointer arithmetic is usually unnecessary and often best avoided.

Note that most C++ implementations offer no range checking for arrays and that arrays are not self-describing because the number of elements of an array is not guaranteed to be stored with the array. This array concept is inherently low level. A more advanced notion of arrays can be provided through the use of classes; see §1.4.3.

2.3.8 Structures

A array is an aggregate of elements of the same type; a `struct` is an aggregate of elements of (nearly) arbitrary types. For example:

```
struct address {
    char* name;         // "Jim Dandy"
    long  number;       // 61
    char* street;       // "South St"
    char* town;         // "New Providence"
    char  state[2];     // 'N' 'J'
    int   zip;          // 7974
};
```

defines a new type called `address` consisting of the items you need to send mail to someone (`address` is not general enough to handle all mailing addresses, but sufficient as an example). Note the semicolon at the end; this is one of the very few places in C++ where it is necessary to have a semicolon after a curly brace, so people are prone to forget it.

Variables of the type `address` can be declared exactly as other variables, and the individual members can be accessed using the . (dot) operator. For example:

```
address jd;
jd.name = "Jim Dandy";
jd.number = 61;
```

The notation used for initializing arrays can also be used for variables of structure types. For example:

```
address jd = {
    "Jim Dandy",
    61, "South St",
    "New Providence", {'N','J'}, 7974
};
```

Using a constructor (§5.2.4) is usually better, however. Note that `jd.state` could not be initialized by the string `"NJ"`. Strings are terminated by the character `'\0'` so `"NJ"` has three characters, that is, one more than will fit into `jd.state`.

Structure objects are often accessed through pointers using the `->` operator. For example:

```
void print_addr(address* p)
{
    cout << p->name << '\n'
         << p->number << ' ' << p->street << '\n'
         << p->town << '\n'
         << p->state[0] << p->state[1]
         << ' ' << p->zip << '\n';
}
```

Objects of structure types can be assigned, passed as function arguments, and returned as the result from a function. For example:

```
address current;

address set_current(address next)
{
    address prev = current;
    current = next;
    return prev;
}
```

Other plausible operations, such as comparison (`==` and `!=`), are not defined. However, the user can define such operators; see Chapter 7.

The size of an object of a structure type is not necessarily the sum of the sizes of its members. The reason is that many machines require objects of certain types to be allocated only on some architecture-dependent boundaries (a typical example is that an integer must be allocated on a word boundary) or handle such objects much more efficiently if they are. This leads to "holes" in the structures. For example, (on my machine) `sizeof(address)` is `24`, and not `22` as one might have expected.

Note that the name of a type becomes available for use immediately after it has been encountered, and not just after the complete declaration has been seen. For example:

```
struct link {
    link* previous;
    link* successor;
};
```

It is not possible to declare new objects of a structure type until the complete declaration has been seen, so

```
struct no_good {
    no_good member;
};
```

is an error (the compiler is not able to determine the size of no_good). To allow two (or more) structure types to refer to each other, it is possible to declare a name to be the name of a structure type. For example:

```
struct list;    // to be defined later

struct link {
    link* pre;
    link* suc;
    list* member_of;
};

struct list {
    link* head;
};
```

Without the first declaration of list, the declaration of link would have caused a syntax error.

It is possible to use the name of a structure type before the type is defined as long as the use does not require the size of the structure to be known. For example:

```
class S;   // 'S' is the name of some type

extern S a;

S f();

void g(S);
```

However, these declarations cannot be used unless the type S is defined:

```
void h()
{
    S a;     // error S not declared
    f();     // error S not declared
    g(a);    // error S not declared
}
```

2.3.9 Type Equivalency

Two structure types are different even when they have the same members. For example:

```
struct s1 { int a; };
struct s2 { int a; };
```

are two different types, so

```
s1 x;
s2 y = x;      // error: type mismatch
```

Structure types are also different from fundamental types, so

```
s1 x;
int i = x;      // error: type mismatch
```

There is, however, a mechanism for declaring a new name for a type without introducing a new type. A declaration prefixed by the keyword `typedef` declares not a new variable of the given type, but a new name for the type. For example:

```
typedef char* Pchar;
Pchar p1, p2;
char* p3 = p1;
```

This can be a convenient shorthand.

2.3.10 References

A *reference* is an alternative name for an object. The main use of references is in specifying arguments and return values for functions in general, and for overloaded operators (§7) in particular. The notation X& means *reference to* X. For example:

```
int i = 1;
int& r = i;     // r and i now refer to the same int
int x = r;      // x = 1
r = 2;          // i = 2;
```

A reference must be initialized (there must be something for it to be a name for). Note that initialization of a reference is something quite different from assignment to it. Despite appearances, no operator operates on a reference. For example,

```
int ii = 0;
int& rr = ii;
rr++;           // ii is incremented to 1
```

is legal, but `rr++` does not increment the reference `rr`; rather, `++` is applied to an `int` that happens to be `ii`. Consequently, the value of a reference cannot be changed after initialization; it always refers to the object it was initialized to denote. To get a pointer to the object denoted by a reference `rr`, one can write `&rr`.

The obvious implementation of a reference is as a (constant) pointer that is dereferenced each time it is used. This makes initialization of a reference trivial when the initializer is an lvalue (an object you can take the address of; see §r.3.7). The initializer for a ''plain'' T must be an lvalue. However, the initializer for a const T& need not be an lvalue or even of type T. In such cases:

[1] first, type conversion is applied if necessary (see §.8.4.3);

[2] then, the resulting value is placed in a temporary variable; and

[3] finally, the address of this is used as the value of the initializer.

Consider

```
double& dr = 1;         // error: lvalue needed
const double& cdr = 1;  // ok
```

The interpretation of this is:

```
double* cdrp;    // reference represented as a pointer
double temp;
temp = double(1);
cdrp = &temp;
```

The reason that references to variables and references to constants are distinguished here is that the introduction of a temporary in the case of the variable is highly error-prone; an assignment to the variable would become an assignment to the – soon to disappear – temporary. No such problem exists for references to constants, and references to constants are often important as function arguments; see §4.6.3.

A reference can be used to implement a function that is supposed to change the value of its argument. For example:

```
void incr(int& aa) { aa++; }

void f()
{
    int x = 1;
    incr(x);                         // x = 2
}
```

The semantics of argument passing are defined to be those of initialization, so when called, incr's argument aa became another name for x. However, to keep a program readable it is in most cases best to avoid functions that modify their arguments. It is often preferable to return a value from the function explicitly or to require a pointer argument:

```
int next(int p) { return p+1; }
void inc(int* p) { (*p)++; }

void g()
{
    int x = 1;
    x = next(x);                     // x = 2
    inc(&x);                         // x = 3
}
```

References can also be used to define functions that can be used on both the left-hand and right-hand sides of an assignment. Again, many of the most interesting uses of this are found in the design of nontrivial user-defined types. As an example, let us define a simple associative array. First we define struct `pair` like this:

```
struct pair {
    char* name;
    int val;
};
```

The basic idea is that a string has an integer value associated with it. It is easy to define a function, `find()`, that maintains a data structure consisting of one `pair` for each different string that has been presented to it. To shorten the presentation, a very simple (and inefficient) implementation is used:

```
const int large = 1024;
static pair vec[large+1];

pair* find(const char* p)
/*
    maintain a set of "pair"s:
    search for p, return its "pair" if found
    otherwise return an unused "pair"
*/

{
    for (int i=0; vec[i].name; i++)
        if (strcmp(p,vec[i].name)==0) return &vec[i];

    if (i == large) return &vec[large-1];

    return &vec[i];
}
```

This function can be used by the function `value()` that implements an array of integers indexed by character strings (rather than the other way around):

```
int& value(const char* p)
{
    pair* res = find(p);
    if (res->name == 0) { // hitherto unseen: initialize
        res->name = new char[strlen(p)+1];
        strcpy(res->name,p);
        res->val = 0;       // initial value: 0
    }
    return res->val;
}
```

For a given argument string, `value()` finds the corresponding integer object (*not* the value of the corresponding integer); it then returns a reference to it. This could be used like this:

```
const int MAX = 256; // larger than the largest word

int main()
// count the number of occurrences of each word on input
{
    char buf[MAX];

    while (cin>>buf) value(buf)++;

    for (int i=0; vec[i].name; i++)
        cout << vec[i].name << ": " << vec[i].val << '\n';
}
```

Each time around, the `while`-loop reads one word from the standard input string `cin` into `buf` (see Chapter 8) and then updates the counter associated with it by `find()`. Finally, the resulting table of different words in the input, each with its number of occurrences, is printed. For example, given the input

```
aa bb bb aa aa bb aa aa
```

this program will produce:

```
aa: 5
bb: 3
```

It is easy to refine this into a proper associative array type by using a template class with the selection operator `[]` overloaded (§8.8).

2.4 Literals

C++ provides a notation for values of the fundamental types: character constants, integer constants, and floating-point constants. In addition, zero (0) can be used as a constant of any pointer type, and character strings are constants of type `char[]`. It is also possible to specify symbolic constants. A symbolic constant is a name whose value cannot be changed in its scope. In C++, there are three kinds of symbolic constants: (1) any value of any type can be given a name and used as a constant by adding the keyword `const` to its definition; (2) a set of integer constants can be defined as an enumeration; and (3) any array or function name is a constant.

2.4.1 Integer Constants

Integer constants come in four guises: decimal, octal, hexadecimal, and character constants. Decimal constants are the most commonly used and look as you would expect them to:

```
0    1234    976    12345678901234567890
```

The type of a decimal constant is `int` provided it fits into an `int`; otherwise, it is `long`. The compiler ought to warn about constants that are too long to represent.

A constant starting with zero followed by x (0x) is a hexadecimal (base 16) number, and a constant starting with zero followed by a digit is an octal (base 8) number. Examples of octal constants:

        0   02   077   0123

their decimal equivalents are: 0, 2, 63, and 83. These constants look like this in hexadecimal notation:

        0x0   0x2   0x3f   0x53

The letters a, b, c, d, e, and f, or their uppercase equivalents, are used to represent 10, 11, 12, 13, 14, and 15, respectively. Octal and hexadecimal notations are most useful for expressing bit patterns; using these notations to express genuine numbers can lead to surprises. For example, on a machine on which an int is represented as a two's complement 16-bit integer, 0xffff is the negative decimal number −1; had more bits been used to represent an integer, it would have been 65535.

The suffix U can be used to write explicitly unsigned constants. Similarly, the suffix L can be used to write explicitly long constants. For example,

```
void f(int);
void f(unsigned int);
void f(long int);

void g()
{
    f(3);     // call f(int)
    f(3U);    // call f(unsigned int)
    f(3L);    // call f(long int)
}
```

2.4.2 Floating-Point Constants

A floating-point constant is of type double. Again, a compiler ought to warn about floating-point constants that are too large to be represented. Here are some floating-point constants:

        1.23   .23   0.23   1.   1.0   1.2e10   1.23e−15

Note that a space cannot occur in the middle of a floating point constant. For example, 65.43   e−21 is not a floating-point constant but four separate lexical tokens

        65.43   e   −   21

and will cause a syntax error.

If you want a floating-point constant of type float, you can define one like this using the suffix f:

        3.14159265f   2.0f   2.997925f

2.4.3 Character Constants

A character constant is a character enclosed in single quotes, for example ′a′ and ′0′. Such character constants are really symbolic constants for the integer value of the characters in the character set of the machine on which the C++ program is to run (which is not necessarily the same character set as is used on the computer on which the program is compiled). So, if you are running on a machine using the ASCII character set, the value of ′0′ is 48; but if your machine uses EBCDIC, it is 240. Using character constants rather than decimal notation makes programs more portable. A few characters also have standard names that use the backslash \ as an escape character:

newline	NL (LF)	\n
horizontal tab	HT	\t
vertical tab	VT	\v
backspace	BS	\b
carriage return	CR	\r
form feed	FF	\f
alert	BEL	\a
backslash	\	\\
question mark	?	\?
single quote	′	\′
double quote	″	\"
integer 0	NUL	\0
octal number	*ooo*	*ooo*
hex number	*hhh*	\x*hhh*

These are single characters despite their appearance. The type of a character constant is char. It is also possible to represent a character as a one-, two-, or three-digit octal number (\ followed by octal digits), or as a hexadecimal number (\x followed by hexadecimal digits). There is no limit to the number of hexadecimal digits in the sequence. A sequence of octal or hexadecimal digits is terminated by the first character that is not an octal digit or a hexadecimal digit, respectively. For example:

```
′\6′        ′\x6′        6        ASCII ack
′\60′       ′\x30′       48       ASCII ′0′
′\137′      ′\x05f′      95       ASCII ′_′
```

This makes it possible to represent every character in the machine's character set and, in particular, to embed such characters in character strings (see the next section). Using any numeric notation for characters makes a program nonportable across machines with different character sets.

2.4.4 String Literals

A string literal is a character sequence enclosed in double quotes:

```
"this is a string"
```

Every string literal contains one more character than it appears to have; they are all terminated by the null character ' \0', with the value 0. For example:

```
sizeof("asdf")==5;
```

The type of a string is "array of the appropriate number of characters," so "asdf" is of type char[5]. The empty string is written "" (and has the type char[1]). Note that for every string s, strlen(s)==sizeof(s)-1 because strlen() does not count the terminating 0.

The backslash convention for representing nongraphic characters can also be used within a string. This makes it possible to represent the double quote " and the escape character backslash \ within a string. The most common such character by far is the newline character, ' \n'. For example:

```
cout<<"beep at end of message\007\n";
```

where 7 is the value of the ASCII character BEL (also known – portably – as \a).

It is not possible to have a "real" newline in a string:

```
"this is not a string
but a syntax error"
```

Long strings can be broken by whitespace to make the program text neater. For example:

```
char alpha[] = "abcdefghijklmnopqrstuvwxyz"
               "ABCDEFGHIJKLMNOPQRSTUVWXYZ";
```

Such adjacent strings will be concatenated, so alpha could equivalently have been initialized by the single string:

```
"abcdefghijklmnopqrstuvwxyzABCDEFGHIJKLMNOPQRSTUVWXYZ";
```

It is possible to have the null character in a string, but most programs will not suspect that there are characters after it. For example, the string "asdf\000hjkl" will be treated as "asdf" by standard functions such as strcpy() and strlen().

When embedding a numeric constant in a string using the octal notation, it is wise always to use three digits for the number. The notation is hard enough to read without having to worry about whether the character after a constant is a digit or not. For hexadecimal constants, use two digits. Consider these examples:

```
char v1[] = "a\x0fah\0129";    // 'a' '\xfa' 'h' '\12' '9'
char v2[] = "a\xfah\129";      // 'a' '\xfa' 'h' '\12' '9'
char v3[] = "a\xfad\127";      // 'a' '\xfad' '\127'
```

2.4.5 Zero

Zero (0) is an `int`. Because of standard conversions (§r.4), 0 can be used as a constant of any integer, floating point, or pointer type. No object is allocated with the address 0. The type of zero will be determined by context. It will typically (but not necessarily) be represented by the bit pattern *all-zeros* of the appropriate size.

2.5 Named Constants

The keyword `const` can be added to the declaration of an object to make that object a constant rather than a variable. For example:

```
const int model = 90;
const int v[] = { 1, 2, 3, 4 };
```

Because it cannot be assigned to, a constant must be initialized. Declaring something `const` ensures that its value will not change within its scope:

```
model = 200;           // error
model++;               // error
```

Note that `const` modifies a type; that is, it restricts the ways in which an object can be used, rather than specifying how the constant is to be allocated. It is, for example, perfectly reasonable, and sometimes useful, to declare a function that returns a `const`:

```
const char* peek(int i) // return pointer to constant
{
     return hidden[i];
}
```

A function such as this could be used to allow someone to read a string that should not be overwritten (by that someone).

However, a compiler can take advantage of an object being a constant in several ways (depending on how smart it is, of course). The most obvious is that typically no store needs to be allocated for a constant because the compiler knows its value. Furthermore, the initializer for a constant is often (but not always) a constant expression; if so, it can be evaluated at compile time. However, it is typically necessary to allocate store for an array of constants because the compiler cannot in general figure out which elements of the array are referred to in expressions. On many machines, however, efficiency improvements can be achieved even in this case by placing arrays of constants in read-only storage.

When using a pointer, two objects are involved; the pointer itself and the object pointed to. "Prefixing" a declaration of a pointer with `const` makes the object, but not the pointer, a constant. For example:

```
const char* pc = "asdf";          // pointer to constant
pc[3] = 'a';                      // error
pc = "ghjk";                      // ok
```

To declare a pointer itself, rather than the object pointed to, to be a constant, the operator *const is used. For example:

```
char *const cp = "asdf";          // constant pointer
cp[3] = 'a';                      // ok
cp = "ghjk";                      // error
```

To make both objects constant both must be declared const. For example:

```
const char *const cpc = "asdf"; // const pointer to const
cpc[3] = 'a';                     // error
cpc = "ghjk";                     // error
```

An object that is a constant when accessed through one pointer may be variable when accessed in other ways. This is particularly useful for function arguments. By declaring a pointer argument const, the function is prohibited from modifying the object pointed to. For example:

```
char* strcpy(char* p, const char* q); // cannot modify *q
```

One may assign the address of a variable to a pointer to constant because no harm can come from that. However, the address of a constant cannot be assigned to an unrestricted pointer because this would allow the object's value to be changed. For example:

```
int a = 1;
const int c = 2;
const int* p1 = &c;    // ok
const int* p2 = &a;    // ok
int* p3 = &c;          // error
*p3 = 7;               // change the value of c
```

2.5.1 Enumerations

An alternative method for naming integer constants is often more convenient than const. For example:

```
enum { ASM, AUTO, BREAK };
```

defines three integer constants, called enumerators, and assigns values to them. Because enumerator values are by default assigned increasing from 0, this is equivalent to writing

```
const ASM = 0;
const AUTO = 1;
const BREAK = 2;
```

An enumeration can be named. For example:

```
enum keyword { ASM, AUTO, BREAK };
```

The name of the enumeration becomes a distinct type. An enumeration can be implicitly converted to an `int` by a standard conversion. The opposite conversion (from `int` to enumeration) must be explicit. For example:

```
void f()
{
    keyword k = ASM;
    int i = ASM;
    k = i;   // error
    k = keyword(i);
    i = k;
    k = 4;   // error
}
```

The last assignment shows why there is no implicit conversion from an `int` to an enumeration; most `int` values do not have a representation in a particular enumeration.

Declaring a variable `keyword` instead of plain `int` can give both the user and the compiler a hint as to the intended use. For example:

```
keyword key;

switch (key) {
case ASM:
    // do something
    break;
case BREAK:
    // do something
    break;
}
```

allows the compiler to issue a warning because only two out of three `keyword` values are handled.

Values can also be explicitly given to enumerators. For example:

```
enum int16 {
    sign=0100000,
    most_significant=040000,
    least_significant=1
};
```

Such values need not be distinct, increasing, or positive.

2.6 Saving Space

When programming nontrivial applications, there invariably comes a time when one wants more memory space than is available or affordable. There are two ways of squeezing more space out of what is available:

[1]   putting more than one small object into a byte; and

[2]   using the same space to hold different objects at different times.

The former can be achieved by using *fields*, the latter by using *unions*. These constructs are described in the following sections. Because their typical use is purely to optimize a program, and they are more often than not nonportable, the programmer should think twice before using them. Often a better approach is to change the way data is managed, for example, to rely more on dynamically allocated store (§3.2.6) and less on pre-allocated static storage.

2.6.1 Fields

It seems extravagant to use a char to represent a binary variable – for example, an on/off switch – but a char is the smallest object that can be independently allocated in C++. It is possible, however, to bundle several such tiny variables together as *fields* in a struct. A member is defined to be a field by specifying the number of bits it is to occupy after its name. Unnamed fields are allowed; they do not affect the meaning of the named fields but can be used to make the layout better in some machine-dependent way:

```
struct sreg {
    unsigned int enable : 1;
    unsigned int page : 3;
    unsigned int : 1;                // unused
    unsigned int mode : 2;
    unsigned int : 4;                // unused
    unsigned int access : 1;
    unsigned int length : 1;
    unsigned int non_resident : 1;
};
```

This happens to be the layout of a DEC PDP11/45 status register 0 (assuming that fields are allocated left-to-right in a word). This example also illustrates the other main use of fields: to name parts of an externally imposed layout. A field must be of integral type (§r.3.6.1 and §r.9.6) and is used like other integral types, except that it is not possible to take the address of a field. In an operating system kernel or in a debugger, the type sreg could be used like this:

```
sreg* sr0 = (sreg*)0777572;
//...
if (sr0->access) {                // access violation
    // clean up the mess
    sr0->access = 0;
}
```

However, using fields to pack several variables into a single byte does not necessarily save space. It saves data space, but the size of the code needed to manipulate these variables increases on most machines. Programs have been known to shrink significantly when binary variables were converted from bit fields to characters! Furthermore, it is typically much faster to access a `char` or an `int` than to access a field. Fields are simply a convenient shorthand for using logical operators (§3.2.4) to extract information from and insert information into part of a word.

2.6.2 Unions

Consider designing a symbol table in which an entry holds a name and a value, and the value is either a string or an integer:

```
struct entry {
    char* name;
    char  type;
    char* string_value;    // used if type=='s'
    int   int_value;       // used if type=='i'
};

void print_entry(entry* p)
{
    switch (p->type) {
    case 's':
        cout << p->string_value;
        break;
    case 'i':
        cout << p->int_value;
        break;
    default:
        cerr << "type corrupted\n";
        break;
    }
}
```

Because `string_value` and `int_value` can never be used at the same time, space is clearly lost. It can be easily recovered by specifying that both should be members of a `union`, like this:

```
struct entry {
    char* name;
    char  type;
    union {
        char* string_value;    // used if type=='s'
        int   int_value;       // used if type=='i'
    };
};
```

This leaves all code using an `entry` unchanged, but ensures that when an `entry` is allocated, `string_value` and `int_value` have the same address. This implies that all the members of a union together take up only as much space as the largest member.

Using a union so that a value is always read using the member it was written with is a pure optimization. However, in large programs, it is not easy to ensure that a union is used in this way only, and subtle errors can be introduced through misuse. It is possible to encapsulate a union so that the correspondence between a type field and the types of the union members can be guaranteed to be correct (§5.4.6).

Unions are sometimes used for "type conversion" (this is done mainly by programmers trained in languages without type conversion facilities, where cheating is necessary). For example, on a VAX this "converts" an int to an int* simply by assuming bitwise equivalence:

```
struct fudge {
    union {
        int  i;
        int* p;
    };
};

fudge a;
a.i = 4095;
int* p = a.p;    // bad usage
```

However, this is not really a conversion at all; on some machines an int and an int* do not occupy the same amount of space, and on others no integer can have an odd address. Such use of a union is not portable, and there is an explicit and portable way of specifying type conversion (§3.2.5).

Unions are occasionally used deliberately to avoid type conversion. One might, for example, use a fudge to find the representation of the pointer 0:

```
fudge.p = 0;
int i = fudge.i;    // i need not be 0
```

It is also possible to give a union a name, that is, to make it a type in its own right. For example, fudge could be declared like this:

```
union fudge {
    int  i;
    int* p;
};
```

and (mis)used exactly as before. Named unions do, however, also have legitimate uses; see §5.4.6.

2.7 Exercises

1. (∗1) Get the "Hello, world" program (§1.3.1) to run.
2. (∗1) For each of the declarations in §2.1, do the following: If the declaration is not a definition, write a definition for it. If the declaration is a definition, write a declaration for it that is not also a definition.
3. (∗1) Write declarations for the following: A pointer to a character; an array of 10

integers; a reference to an array of 10 integers; a pointer to an array of character strings; a pointer to a pointer to a character; a constant integer; a pointer to a constant integer; and a constant pointer to an integer. Initialize each one.

4. (*1.5) Write a program that prints the sizes of the fundamental and pointer types. Use the `sizeof` operator.

5. (*1.5) Write a program that prints out the letters `'a'..'z'` and the digits `'0'..'9'` and their integer values. Do the same for other printable characters. Do the same, but use hexadecimal notation.

6. (*1) Print out the bit pattern used to represent the pointer 0 on your system. Hint: see §2.6.2.

7. (*1.5) Write a function that prints the exponent and mantissa of a `double` argument.

8. (*2) What, on your system, are the largest and the smallest values of the following types: `char`, `short`, `int`, `long`, `float`, `double`, `long double`, `unsigned`, `char*`, `int*`, and `void*`? Are there further restrictions on the values? For example, may an `int*` have an odd value? What is the alignment of objects of those types? For example, may an `int` have an odd address?

9. (*1) What is the longest local name you can use in a C++ program on your system? What is the longest external name you can use in a C++ program on your system? Are there any restrictions on the characters you can use in a name?

10. (*1) Write a function that swaps (exchanges the values of) two integers. Use `int*` as the argument type. Write another swap function using `int&` as the argument type.

11. (*1) What is the size of the array `str` in the following example:

```
char str[] = "a short string";
```

What is the length of the string `"a short string"`?

12. (*1.5) Define a table of the names of months of the year and the number of days in each month. Write out that table. Do this twice: once using an array for the names and an array for the number of days, and once using an array of structures, each structure holding the name of a month and the number of days in it.

13. (*1) Use `typedef` to define the types unsigned char, constant unsigned char, pointer to integer, pointer to pointer to char, pointer to arrays of characters, array of 7 integer pointers, pointer to an array of 7 integer pointers, and array of 8 arrays of 7 integer pointers.

14. (*1) Define functions f(char) , g(char&), and h(const char&), and call them with the arguments `'a'`, 49, 3300, c, uc, and sc where c is a `char`, uc is an `unsigned char`, and sc is a `signed char`. Which calls are legal? Which calls cause the compiler to introduce a temporary variable.

3

Expressions and Statements

On the other hand,
we cannot ignore efficiency.
– Jon Bentley

C++ has a small, but flexible, set of statement types for controlling the flow
of control through a program and a rich set of operators for manipulating
data. A single complete example introduces the most commonly used
facilities. After that, expressions are summarized, and explicit type conversion and the use of free store are presented in some detail. Then statements
are summarized, and, finally, indentation style and comments are discussed.

3.1 A Desk Calculator

Statements and expressions are introduced by presenting a desk calculator program
that provides the four standard arithmetic operations as infix operators on floating-
point numbers. The user can also define variables. For example, given the input

```
r=2.5
area=pi*r*r
```

(pi is predefined) the calculator program will write:

```
2.5
19.635
```

where 2.5 is the result of the first line of input and 19.635 is the result of the second.

The calculator consists of four main parts: a parser, an input function, a symbol table, and a driver. Actually, it is a miniature compiler with the parser doing the syntactic analysis, the input function handling input and lexical analysis, the symbol table holding permanent information, and the driver handling initialization, output, and errors. One could add many features to this calculator to make it more useful, but the code is long enough as it is (200 lines), and most features would just add code without providing additional insight into the use of C++.

3.1.1 The Parser

Here is a grammar for the language accepted by the calculator:

```
program:
    END                         // END is end-of-input
    expr_list END

expr_list:
    expression PRINT            // PRINT is '\n' or ';'
    expression PRINT expr_list

expression:
    expression + term
    expression - term
    term

term:
    term / primary
    term * primary
    primary

primary:
    NUMBER                      // C++ floating point
    NAME                        // C++ name except '_'
    NAME = expression
    - primary
    ( expression )
```

In other words, a program is a sequence of lines; each line consists of one or more expressions separated by semicolons. The basic units of an expression are numbers, names, and the operators *, /, +, - (both unary and binary), and =. Names need not be declared before use.

The style of syntax analysis used is usually called *recursive descent*; it is a popular and straightforward top-down technique. In a language such as C++, in which function calls are relatively cheap, it is also efficient. For each production in the grammar, there is a function that calls other functions. Terminal symbols (for example, END, NUMBER, +, and -) are recognized by the lexical analyzer, get_token(); and non-terminal symbols are recognized by the syntax analyzer functions, expr(), term(), and prim(). As soon as both operands of a (sub)expression are known, it is evaluated; in a real compiler, code is generated at this point.

The parser uses a function get_token() to get input. The value of the most recent call of get_token() can be found in the global variable curr_tok. The value of curr_tok is of the enumeration token_value:

```
enum token_value {
      NAME,         NUMBER,       END,
      PLUS='+',     MINUS='-',    MUL='*',        DIV='/',
      PRINT=';',    ASSIGN='=',   LP='(',         RP=')'
};
```

```
token_value curr_tok;
```

Each parser function assumes that get_token() has been called so that curr_tok holds the next token to be analyzed. This allows the parser to look one token ahead and obliges every parser function always to read one token more than is used by the production it was called to handle. Each parser function evaluates ''its'' expression and returns the value. The function expr() handles addition and subtraction; it consists of a single loop that looks for terms to add or subtract:

```
double expr()                         // add and subtract
{
    double left = term();

    for(;;)                           // ``forever''
          switch (curr_tok) {
          case PLUS:
                get_token();          // eat '+'
                left += term();
                break;
          case MINUS:
                get_token();          // eat '-'
                left -= term();
                break;
          default:
                return left;
          }
}
```

This function really does not do much itself. In a manner typical of higher-level functions in a large program, it calls other functions to do the work. Note that an expression such as 2−3+4 is evaluated as (2−3)+4, as specified in the grammar.

The curious notation for(;;) is the standard way to specify an infinite loop; you could pronounce it "forever." It is a degenerate form of a for statement; while(1) is an alternative. The switch statement is executed repeatedly until no + or − is found, and then the return statement in the default case is executed.

The operators += and −= are used to handle the addition and subtraction; left=left+term() and left=left−term() could have been used without changing the meaning of the program. However, left+=term() and left−=term() not only are shorter but also express the intended operation directly. For a binary operator @, an expression x@=y means x=x@y, except that x is evaluated once only; this applies to the binary operators

$$+ \quad - \quad * \quad / \quad \% \quad \& \quad | \quad \char`\^ \quad << \quad >>$$

so that the following assignment operators are possible

$$= \quad += \quad -= \quad *= \quad /= \quad \%= \quad \&= \quad |= \quad \char`\^= \quad <<= \quad >>=$$

Each is a separate lexical token, so a + = 1; is a syntax error because of the space between the + and the =. (% is the modulo, or remainder, operator; &, |, and ˆ are the bitwise logical operators AND, OR, and exclusive OR; << and >> are the left shift and right shift operators.) The functions term() and get_token() must be declared before expr().

Chapter 4 discusses how to organize a program as a set of files. With one exception, the declarations for this desk calculator example can be ordered so that everything is declared exactly once and before it is used. The exception is expr(), which calls term(), which calls prim(), which in turn calls expr(). This loop must be broken somehow; a declaration

```
double expr();   // cannot do without
```

before the definition of prim() will do nicely.

Function term() handles multiplication and division in the same way expr() handled addition and subtraction:

```
double term()                        // multiply and divide
{
    double left = prim();

    for (;;)
        switch (curr_tok) {
        case MUL:
            get_token();             // eat '*'
            left *= prim();
            break;
        case DIV:
            get_token();             // eat '/'
            double d = prim();
            if (d == 0) return error("divide by 0");
            left /= d;
            break;
        default:
            return left;
        }
}
```

Testing to ensure that one does not divide by zero is necessary because the result of dividing by zero is undefined and usually disastrous. The function error() is described later. The variable d is introduced into the program where it is needed, and is initialized immediately. In many languages, a declaration can occur only at the head of a block. This restriction can lead to nasty contortions of programming style and/or to unnecessary errors. Most often, an uninitialized local variable is an indication of bad style; the exceptions are variables that are to be initialized by input operations and variables of array or structure type that cannot be conveniently initialized by single assignments. Note that = is the assignment operator, and == is a comparison operator.

The function `prim` handling a *primary* is of much the same kind as `expr` and `term()`, except that because we are getting lower in the call hierarchy a bit of real work is being done and no loop is necessary:

```cpp
double number_value;
char name_string[256];

double prim()              // handle primaries
{
    switch (curr_tok) {
    case NUMBER:           // floating point constant
        get_token();
        return number_value;
    case NAME:
        if (get_token() == ASSIGN) {
            name* n = insert(name_string);
            get_token();
            n->value = expr();
            return n->value;
        }
        return look(name_string)->value;
    case MINUS:            // unary minus
        get_token();
        return -prim();
    case LP:
        get_token();
        double e = expr();
        if (curr_tok != RP) return error(") expected");
        get_token();
        return e;
    case END:
        return 1;
    default:
        return error("primary expected");
    }
}
```

When a NUMBER (that is, a floating point constant) is seen, its value is returned. The input routine `get_token()` places the value in the global variable `number_value`. Use of a global variable in a program often indicates that the structure is not quite clean – that some sort of optimization has been applied. So it is here; ideally, a lexical token typically consists of two parts: a value specifying the kind of token (a `token_value` in this program) and (when needed) the value of the token. Here, there is only a single, simple variable, `curr_tok`, so that the global variable `number_value` is needed to hold the value of the last NUMBER read. This works only because the calculator always uses one number in the computation before reading another from input. Eliminating this spurious global variable is left as an exercise (§3.5 [15]).

In the same way that the value of the last NUMBER is kept in `number_value`, the character string representation of the last NAME seen is kept in `name_string`. Before doing anything to a name, the calculator must first look ahead to see if it is being assigned to or simply used. In both cases the symbol table must be consulted. The table itself is presented in §3.1.3; here it must be observed that it contains entries of the form:

```
struct name {
    char* string;
    name* next;
    double value;
};
```

where `next` is used only by the functions maintaining the table:

```
name* look(const char*);
name* insert(const char*);
```

Both return a pointer to a `name` corresponding to the character string argument; `look()` complains if the name has not been defined. This means that in the calculator a name can be used without previous declaration, but its first use should be as the left hand of an assignment.

3.1.2 The Input Function

Reading input is often the messiest part of a program. The reason is that if a program must communicate with a person, it must cope with that person's whims, conventions, and seemingly random errors. Trying to force the person to behave in a manner more suitable for the machine is often (rightly) considered offensive. The task of a low-level input routine is to read characters one by one and compose higher-level tokens from them. These tokens are then the units of input for higher-level routines. Here, low-level input is done by `get_token()`. Hopefully, writing a low-level input routine is not an everyday task; in a good system, there will be standard functions for this.

The rules for input to the calculator were deliberately chosen to be somewhat awkward for the stream functions to handle; slight modifications in the token definitions would have made `get_token()` deceptively simple.

The first problem is that the newline character `'\n'` is significant to the calculator, but the stream input functions consider it a *whitespace* character. That is, to those functions, `'\n'` is significant only as a token terminator. To cope with this, whitespace (space, tabs, etc.) must be examined. A do statement is used; it is equivalent to a `while` statement except that the controlled statement is always executed at least once:

```
char ch;

do {           // skip whitespace except '\n'
    if (!cin.get(ch)) return curr_tok = END;
} while (ch!='\n' && isspace(ch));
```

The call `cin.get(ch)` reads a single character from the standard input stream into
`ch`. The test `if (!cin.get(ch))` fails if no character can be read from `cin`; in
this case `END` is returned to terminate the calculator session. The operator `!` (NOT) is
used because `get()` returns a nonzero value in case of success.

The (inline) function `isspace()` from `<ctype.h>` provides the standard test
for whitespace (§10.3.1); `isspace(c)` returns a nonzero value if `c` is a whitespace
character and zero otherwise. The test is implemented as a table lookup, so using
`isspace()` is much faster than testing for the individual whitespace characters; the
same applies to the functions `isalpha()`, `isdigit()`, and `isalnum()` used in
`get_token()`.

After whitespace has been skipped, the next character is used to determine what
kind of lexical token is coming. Let us look at some of the cases separately before
presenting the complete function. The expression terminators `'\n'` and `';'` are
handled like this:

```
switch (ch) {
case ';':
case '\n':
    cin >> ws;  // skip whitespace
    return curr_tok=PRINT;
```

Skipping whitespace (again) is not necessary, but doing it avoids repeated calls of
`get_token()`. The variable `ws` is a standard whitespace object declared in
`<iostream.h>`; its only use is to discard whitespace. An error in the input or the
end of input will not be detected until the next call of `get_token()`. Note the way
several case labels can be used for a single sequence of statements handling those
cases. The token `PRINT` is returned and put into `curr_tok` in both cases.

Numbers are handled like this:

```
case '0': case '1': case '2': case '3': case '4':
case '5': case '6': case '7': case '8': case '9':
case '.':
    cin.putback(ch);
    cin >> number_value;
    return curr_tok=NUMBER;
```

Stacking case labels horizontally rather than vertically is generally not a good idea
because it is harder to read, but having one line for each digit is tedious. Because
operator `>>` is already defined for reading floating point constants into a `double`, the
code is trivial: First the initial character (a digit or a dot) is put back into `cin`, and
then the constant can be read into `number_value`.

A name, that is a NAME token, is defined as a letter possibly followed by some letters or digits:

```
if (isalpha(ch)) {
    char* p = name_string;
    *p++ = ch;
    while (cin.get(ch) && isalnum(ch)) *p++ = ch;
    cin.putback(ch);
    *p = 0;
    return curr_tok=NAME;
}
```

This builds a zero-terminated string in name_string. The functions isalpha()
and isalnum() are provided in <ctype.h>; isalnum(c) is nonzero if c is a
letter or a digit and zero otherwise.

Here, finally, is the complete input function:

```
token_value get_token()
{
    char ch;

    do {            // skip whitespace except '\n'
        if (!cin.get(ch)) return curr_tok = END;
    } while (ch!='\n' && isspace(ch));

    switch (ch) {
    case ';':
    case '\n':
        cin >> ws;        // skip whitespace
        return curr_tok=PRINT;
    case '*':
    case '/':
    case '+':
    case '-':
    case '(':
    case ')':
    case '=':
        return curr_tok=token_value(ch);
    case '0': case '1': case '2': case '3': case '4':
    case '5': case '6': case '7': case '8': case '9':
    case '.':
        cin.putback(ch);
        cin >> number_value;
        return curr_tok=NUMBER;
```

```
    default:                           // NAME, NAME=, or error
        if (isalpha(ch)) {
            char* p = name_string;
            *p++ = ch;
            while (cin.get(ch) && isalnum(ch)) *p++ = ch;
            cin.putback(ch);
            *p = 0;
            return curr_tok=NAME;
        }
        error("bad token");
        return curr_tok=PRINT;
    }
}
```

The conversion of an operator to its token value is trivial because the `token_value` of an operator was defined as the integer value of the operator.

3.1.3 The Symbol Table

The symbol table is searched by a single function:

```
name* look(char* p, int ins =0);
```

Its second argument indicates whether the character string is supposed to have been previously inserted. The initializer =0 specifies a default argument to be used when `look` is called with only one argument. This gives the notational convenience of having `look("sqrt2")` mean `look("sqrt2",0)`, that is, lookup, not insertion. To get the same notational convenience for insertions, a second function is defined:

```
inline name* insert(const char* s) { return look(s,1); }
```

As mentioned previously, table entries are of this type:

```
struct name {
    char* string;
    name* next;
    double value;
};
```

The member `next` is used to link names together in the table.

The table itself is simply an array of pointers to objects of type `name`:

```
const TBLSZ = 23;
name* table[TBLSZ];
```

Because all static objects are by default initialized to zero, this trivial declaration of `table` also ensures proper initialization.

To find an entry for a name in the table, `look()` uses a simple hash code (names with the same hash code are linked together):

```
int ii = 0;                                    // hash
const char* pp = p;
while (*pp) ii = ii<<1 ^ *pp++;
if (ii < 0) ii = -ii;
ii %= TBLSZ;
```

That is, each character in the input string p is "added" to ii (the "sum" of the previous characters) by an exclusive or. A bit in x^y is set if and only if the corresponding bits in the operands x and y are different. Before xor'ing in a character, ii is shifted one bit to the left to avoid using only one byte of it. This can also be expressed like this:

```
ii <<= 1;
ii ^= *pp++;
```

Using ^ is marginally better than using +. The shift is essential for getting a reasonable hash code in both cases. The statements

```
if (ii < 0) ii = -ii;
ii %= TBLSZ;
```

ensure that ii is in the range 0..TBLSZ−1 at the end; % is the modulo (also called remainder) operator.

Here is the complete function:

```
#include <string.h>

name* look(const char* p, int ins =0)
{
    int ii = 0;                                // hash
    const char* pp = p;
    while (*pp) ii = ii<<1 ^ *pp++;
    if (ii < 0) ii = -ii;
    ii %= TBLSZ;

    for (name* n=table[ii]; n; n=n->next)      // search
        if (strcmp(p,n->string) == 0) return n;

    if (ins == 0) error("name not found");

    name* nn = new name;                       // insert
    nn->string = new char[strlen(p)+1];
    strcpy(nn->string,p);
    nn->value = 1;
    nn->next = table[ii];
    table[ii] = nn;
    return nn;
}
```

After the hash code ii has been calculated, the name is found by a simple search through the next fields. Each name is checked using the standard string compare function strcmp(). If the string is found, its name is returned; otherwise, a new name is added.

Adding a name involves creating a new name object on the free store using the new operator (see §3.2.6), initializing it, and adding it to the list of names. The latter is done by putting the new name at the head of the list because this can be done without even testing whether or not there is a list. The character string for the name must also be stored away in free store. The function strlen() is used to find how much store is needed, new is used to allocate it, and strcpy() is used to copy the string to that store. All the string functions are declared in <string.h>:

```
extern int strlen(const char*);
extern int strcmp(const char*, const char*);
extern char* strcpy(char*, const char*);
```

The value returned by strcmp() is 0 if the strings are identical sequences of characters, a negative integer if the first string comes lexicographically before the second, and a positive integer otherwise.

3.1.4 Error Handling

Because the program is so simple, error handling is not a major concern. The error function simply counts the errors, writes out an error message, and returns:

```
int no_of_errors;

double error(const char* s)
{
    cerr << "error: " << s << '\n';
    no_of_errors++;
    return 1;
}
```

The stream cerr is an unbuffered output stream usually used to report errors.

The reason for returning a value is that errors typically occur in the middle of the evaluation of an expression, so that one should either abort that evaluation entirely or else return a value that is unlikely to cause subsequent errors. The latter is adequate for this simple calculator. Had get_token() kept track of the line numbers, error() could have informed the user approximately where the error occurred. This would have been useful when the calculator was used noninteractively.

Often, a program must be terminated after an error has occurred because no sensible way of continuing has been devised. This can be done by calling exit(), which first cleans up things like output streams (§10.5.1) and then terminates the program with its argument as the return value. A more drastic way of terminating a program is a call of abort() that terminates immediately, or immediately after storing information for a debugger (a *core dump*) somewhere; please consult your manual for details.

More stylized error-handling mechanisms can be implemented using exceptions (see §9), but what we have here is quite suitable for a 200 line toy calculator.

3.1.5 The Driver

With all the pieces of the program in place, we need only a driver to initialize and start things. In this simple example, `main()` can do that:

```
int main()
{
    // insert pre-defined names:
    insert("pi")->value = 3.1415926535897932385;
    insert("e")->value  = 2.7182818284590452354;

    while (cin) {
        get_token();
        if (curr_tok == END) break;
        if (curr_tok == PRINT) continue;
        cout << expr() << '\n';
    }

    return no_of_errors;
}
```

Conventionally, `main()` returns zero if the program terminates normally and nonzero otherwise, so returning the number of errors accomplishes this nicely. As it happens, the only initialization needed is to insert the predefined names into the symbol table.

The primary task of the main loop is to read expressions and write out the answer. This is achieved by the line:

```
cout << expr() << '\n';
```

Testing `cin` each time around the loop ensures that the program terminates if something goes wrong with the input stream, and testing for `END` ensures that the loop is correctly exited when `get_token()` encounters end-of-file. A `break` statement exits its nearest enclosing `switch` statement or loop (that is, a `for` statement, `while` statement, or do statement). Testing for `PRINT` (that is, for `'\n'` and `';'`) relieves `expr()` of the responsibility for handling empty expressions. A `continue` statement is equivalent to going to the very end of a loop, so that in this case

```
while (cin) {
    // ...
    if (curr_tok == PRINT) continue;
    cout << expr() << '\n';
}
```

is equivalent to

```
while  (cin) {
    // ...
    if (curr_tok == PRINT) goto end_of_loop;
    cout << expr() << '\n';
end_of_loop: ;
}
```

Loops are described in greater detail in §r.6.

3.1.6 Command Line Arguments

After the program was written and tested, I found it a bother to first start the program, then type the expressions, and finally quit. My most common use was to evaluate a single expression. Were it possible to present that expression as a command line argument, a few keystrokes could be avoided.

As mentioned previously, a program starts by calling main(). When this is done, main() is given two arguments specifying the number of arguments, usually called argc, and an array of arguments, usually called argv. The arguments are character strings, so the type of argv is char*[argc+1]. The name of the program (as it occurs on the command line) is passed as argv[0], so argc is always at least 1. The list of arguments is zero-terminated, that is argv[argc]==0. For example, for the command

```
dc 150/1.1934
```

the arguments have these values:

```
argc        2
argv[0]     "dc"
argv[1]     "150/1.1934"
argv[2]     0
```

It is not difficult to get hold of a command line argument; the problem is how to use it without reprogramming. In this case, it turns out to be trivial because an input stream can be bound to a character string instead of to a file (§10.5.2). For example, cin can be made to read characters from a string rather than from the standard input:

```
int main(int argc, char* argv[])
{
    switch (argc) {
    case 1:                 // read from standard input
        break;
    case 2:                 // read argument string
        cin = *new istrstream(argv[1],strlen(argv[1]));
        break;
    default:
        error("too many arguments");
        return 1;
    }

    // as before
}
```

An `istrstream` is an `istream` that reads from its character string argument. To use an `istrstream` one must include `<strstream.h>` rather than plain `<iostream.h>`. Apart from this, the program is unchanged except for adding the arguments to `main()` and using them in the switch statement. It would be easy to modify `main()` to accept several command line arguments, but this does not appear to be necessary, especially as several expressions can be passed as a single argument:

```
dc "rate=1.1934;150/rate;19.75/rate;217/rate"
```

Quotes are necessary here because *;* is the UNIX system command separator. Other systems will have different conventions for command line arguments.

3.2 Operator Summary

The C++ operators are systematically and completely described in §r.5; please read that section. Here, however, is a summary and some examples. Each operator is followed by one or more names commonly used for it and an example of its use. In these examples a *class_name* is the name of a class, a *member* is a member name, an *object* is an expression yielding a class object, a *pointer* is an expression yielding a pointer, an *expr* is an expression, and an *lvalue* is an expression denoting a nonconstant object. A *type* can be a fully general type name (with *, (), etc.) only when it appears in parentheses; elsewhere there are restrictions.

Unary operators and assignment operators are right associative; all others are left associative. That is, a=b=c, means a=(b=c), a+b+c means (a+b)+c, and *p++ means *(p++), *not* (*p)++.

Operator Summary		
: :	scope resolution	*class_name* : : *member*
: :	global	: : *name*
.	member selection	*object* . *member*
->	member selection	*pointer* -> *member*
[]	subscripting	*pointer* [*expr*]
()	function call	*expr* (*expr_list*)
()	value construction	*type* (*expr_list*)
sizeof	size of object	sizeof *expr*
sizeof	size of type	sizeof (*type*)
++	post increment	*lvalue* ++
++	pre increment	++ *lvalue*
--	post decrement	*lvalue* --
--	pre decrement	-- *lvalue*
~	complement	~ *expr*
!	not	! *expr*
-	unary minus	- *expr*
+	unary plus	+ *expr*
&	address of	& *lvalue*
*	dereference	* *expr*
new	create (allocate)	new *type*
delete	destroy (de-allocate)	delete *pointer*
delete[]	destroy array	delete[] *pointer*
()	cast (type conversion)	(*type*) *expr*
.*	member section	*object* . *pointer-to-member*
->*	member section	*pointer* -> *pointer-to-member*
*	multiply	*expr* * *expr*
/	divide	*expr* / *expr*
%	modulo (remainder)	*expr* % *expr*
+	add (plus)	*expr* + *expr*
-	subtract (minus)	*expr* - *expr*

Each box holds operators with the same precedence. An operator has higher precedence than operators in lower boxes. For example: a+b*c means a+(b*c) because * has higher precedence than +, and a+b-c means (a+b)-c because + and - have the same precedence (and because + is left associative).

Operator Summary (continued)		
<<	shift left	*expr << expr*
>>	shift right	*expr >> expr*
<	less than	*expr < expr*
<=	less than or equal	*expr <= expr*
>	greater than	*expr > expr*
>=	greater than or equal	*expr >= expr*
==	equal	*expr == expr*
!=	not equal	*expr != expr*
&	bitwise AND	*expr & expr*
^	bitwise exclusive OR	*expr ^ expr*
|	bitwise inclusive OR	*expr | expr*
&&	logical AND	*expr && expr*
||	logical inclusive OR	*expr || expr*
? :	conditional expression	*expr ? expr : expr*
=	simple assignment	*lvalue = expr*
*=	multiply and assign	*lvalue *= expr*
/=	divide and assign	*lvalue /= expr*
%=	modulo and assign	*lvalue %= expr*
+=	add and assign	*lvalue += expr*
-=	subtract and assign	*lvalue -= expr*
<<=	shift left and assign	*lvalue <<= expr*
>>=	shift right and assign	*lvalue >>= expr*
&=	AND and assign	*lvalue &= expr*
|=	inclusive OR and assign	*lvalue |= expr*
^=	exclusive OR and assign	*lvalue ^= expr*
,	comma (sequencing)	*expr , expr*

3.2.1 Parentheses

Parentheses are overused in the C++ syntax; they have a confusing number of uses. They are used around arguments in function calls, around the type in a type conversion (casts), in type names to denote functions, and also to resolve precedence conflicts. Fortunately, the latter is not necessary very often because precedence levels and associativity rules are defined to make expressions "work as expected" (that is, to reflect the most common usage). For example:

```
if (i<=0 || max<i) // ...
```

means "if i is less than or equal to 0 or if max is less than i." That is,

```
if ( (i<=0) || (max<i) ) // ...
```

and not the legal but nonsensical

```
if (i <= (0||max) < i) // ...
```

However, parentheses should be used whenever a programmer is in doubt about those rules, and some programmers prefer the slightly longer and less elegant

```
if ( (i<=0) || (max<i) ) // ...
```

Use of parentheses becomes more common as the subexpressions become more complicated, but complicated subexpressions are a source of errors. Therefore, if you start feeling the need for parentheses, you might consider breaking up the expression by using an extra variable. There are also cases when the operator precedence does not result in the "obvious" interpretation. For example:

```
if (i&mask == 0)   // oops! == expression as operand for &
        // ...
```

does not apply a mask to i and then test if the result is zero. Because == has higher precedence than &, the expression is interpreted as i&(mask==0). Fortunately, it is easy enough for a compiler to warn about most such mistakes. In this case parentheses are important:

```
if ((i&mask) == 0) // ...
```

It might also be worth noting that the following does not work the way a naive user might expect:

```
if (0 <= a <= 99) // ...
```

It is legal, but it is interpreted as (0<=a)<=99, where the result of the first comparison is either 0 or 1, but not a (except when a is 1). To test whether a is in the range 0..99 one might use:

```
if (0<=a && a<=99) // ...
```

A common mistake for novices is to use = (assignment) instead of == (equals) in a condition:

```
if (a = 7)   // oops! constant assignment in condition
        // ...
```

This is natural because = means "equals" in many languages. Again, it is easy for a compiler to warn about most such mistakes.

3.2.2 Evaluation Order

The order of evaluation of subexpressions within an expression is undefined. For example:

```
int i = 1;
v[i] = i++;
```

may be evaluated as either v[1]=1 or v[2]=1. Better code can be generated in the absence of restrictions on expression evaluation order. Compilers can warn about

such ambiguities. Unfortunately, most do not.
  The operators

&& ||

guarantee that their left-hand operand is evaluated before their right-hand operand.
For example, b=(a=2,a+1) assigns 3 to b. An example of the use of || was pre-
sented in §3.2.1, and an example of the use of && can be found in §3.3.1. Note that
the sequencing operator , (comma) is logically different from the comma used to separate arguments in a function call. Consider:

```
f1(v[i],i++);               // two arguments.
f2( (v[i],i++) );           // one argument.
```

The call of f1 has two arguments, v[i] and i++, and the order of evaluation of the
argument expressions is undefined. Order dependence of argument expressions is
very poor style and nonportable. The call of f2 has one argument, the comma
expression (v[i],i++), which is equivalent to i++.

  Parentheses can be used to force evaluation order. For example, a*(b/c) may
be evaluated as (a*b)/c only if the user cannot tell the difference. In particular, for
many floating point computations a*(b/c) and (a*b)/c are significantly different.

3.2.3 Increment and Decrement

The ++ operator is used to express incrementing directly, rather than expressing it
indirectly using a combination of an addition and an assignment. By definition,
++*lvalue* means *lvalue*+=1, which again means *lvalue*=*lvalue*+1 provided *lvalue* has
no side effects. The expression denoting the object to be incremented is evaluated
once (only). Decrementing is similarly expressed by the -- operator. The operators
++ and -- can be used as both prefix and postfix operators. The value of ++x is the
new (that is, incremented) value of x. For example, y=++x is equivalent to
y=(x+=1). The value of x++, however, is the old value of x. For example, y=x++
is equivalent to y=(t=x,x+=1,t), where t is a variable of the same type as x.

  Remember that incrementing and decrementing of pointers, like addition and subtraction of pointers, operate in terms of elements of the array pointed into by the
pointer; p++ makes p point to the next element. For a pointer p of type T*, the following holds by definition:

```
long(p+1)  ==  long(p)+sizeof(T);
```

  The increment operators are particularly useful for incrementing and decrementing
variables in loops. For example, one can copy a zero terminated string like this:

```
inline void cpy(char* p, const char* q)
{
     while (*p++ = *q++) ;
}
```

C++ (like C) is both loved and hated for enabling such terse expression-oriented coding. Because

```
while (*p++ = *q++) ;
```

is more than a little obscure to non-C programmers and because the style of coding is not uncommon in C and C++, it is worth examining closer.

Consider first a more traditional way of copying an array of characters:

```
int length = strlen(q);
for (int i = 0; i<=length; i++) p[i] = q[i];
```

This is wasteful because a string is terminated by a zero and the only way to find its length is to read it from the start looking for the zero character; thus we are reading the string twice: once to find its length and once to copy it. So we try this instead:

```
for (int i = 0; q[i]!=0 ; i++) p[i] = q[i];
p[i] = 0; // terminating zero
```

The variable i used for indexing can be eliminated because p and q are pointers:

```
while (*q != 0) {
        *p = *q;
        p++;      // point to next character
        q++;      // point to next character
}
*p = 0; // terminating zero
```

Because the post increment operation allows us first to use the value and then increment it, this can be written like this:

```
while (*q != 0) {
        *p++ = *q++;
}
*p = 0; // terminating zero
```

Note that the value of *p++ = *q++ is *q. We can therefore re-write the example like this:

```
while ((*p++ = *q++) != 0) { }
```

In this case we don't notice that *q is zero until we already have copied it into *p, so we had to eliminate the final assignment of the terminating zero. Finally, we can reduce the example further by observing that we don't need the empty block and that the "!= 0" is redundant because the result of a condition expression is always compared to zero anyway. Thus we get the version we set out to discover:

```
while (*p++ = *q++) ;
```

Is this version less readable than the versions above? Not to an experienced C or C++ programmer. Is this version more efficient in time or space than the versions above? Except for the first version that called strlen(), not really. Which version is the most efficient will vary from machine architecture to machine architecture and from compiler to compiler. The most efficient copy algorithm for your particular machine ought to be found in the standard string copy function:

```
int strcpy(char*, const char*);
```

from `<string.h>`.

3.2.4 Bitwise Logical Operators

The bitwise logical operators

      & | ^   ~   >>   <<

are applied to integers – that is, objects of type `char`, `short`, `int`, `long`, and their `unsigned` counterparts – and the results produced are integers too.

    A typical use of bitwise logical operators is to implement the notion of a small set (a bit vector). In this case, each bit of an unsigned integer represents one member of the set, and the number of bits limits the number of members. The binary operator `&` is interpreted as intersection, `|` as union, and `^` as difference. An enumeration can be used to name the members of such a set. Here is a small example borrowed from an implementation of `<iostream.h>`:

```
class ios {
public:
    enum io_state {
        goodbit=0, eofbit=1, failbit=2, badbit=4
    };
    // ...
};
```

The state of a stream can be reset like this:

```
cout.state = ios::goodbit;
```

The `ios::` prefix is necessary because the `io_state` definition is nested in class `ios` to avoid having names such as `goodbit` interfere with names a user might define.

    One can test whether a stream has been corrupted or an operation has failed like this:

```
if (cout.state&(ios::badbit|ios::failbit))   // stream no good
```

The extra parentheses are necessary because `&` has higher precedence than `|`.

    A function that reaches the end of input can report it like this:

```
cin.state |= ios::eofbit;
```

The `|=` operator is used because the stream might have been corrupted already (that is, `state==ios::badbit`) so that

```
cin.state = ios::eofbit;
```

would have cleared that condition. One could find the way the states of two streams differ like this:

```
ios::io_state diff = cin.state^cout.state;
```

For the type `io_state`, such a difference is not very useful, but for other similar types it is most useful. For example, consider comparing a bit vector that represents the set of interrupts being handled with another that represents the set of interrupts waiting to be handled.

Note that using fields (§r.9.6) is really a convenient shorthand for shifting and masking to extract bit fields from a word. This can, of course, also be done using the bitwise logical operators. For example, one could extract the middle 16 bits of a 32-bit `int` like this:

```
unsigned short middle(int a) { return (a>>8)&0xffff; }
```

Do not confuse the bitwise logical operators with the logical operators:

```
&&        ||        !
```

The latter return either a `0` or a `1`, and they are primarily useful for writing the test in an `if`, `while`, or `for` statement (§3.3.1). For example, `!0` (not zero) is the value `1`, whereas `~0` (complement of zero) is the bit pattern all-ones, which in two's complement representation is the value `−1`.

3.2.5 Type Conversion

Occasionally it is necessary to convert a value of some type explicitly to a value of another. An explicit type conversion produces a value of one type given a value of another. For example:

```
float r = float(1);
```

converts the integer value `1` to the floating point value `1.0f` before the assignment. The result of a type conversion is not an lvalue, so it may not be assigned to (unless the type is a reference type).

There are two notations for explicit type conversion: the traditional C *cast* notation `(double)a` and the functional notation `double(a)`. The functional notation cannot be used for types that do not have a simple name. For example, to convert a value to a pointer type one must either use the cast notation

```
char* p = (char*)0777;
```

or define a new type name:

```
typedef char* Pchar;
char* p = Pchar(0777);
```

In my opinion the functional notation is preferable for nontrivial examples. Consider these two equivalent examples:

```
Pname n2 = Pbase(n1->tp)->b_name;     // functional notation
Pname n3 = ((Pbase)n2->tp)->b_name; // cast notation
```

Since the $->$ operator has higher precedence than a cast has, the latter expression is interpreted as

```
((Pbase)(n2->tp))->b_name
```

By using explicit type conversion on pointer types, it is possible to pretend that an object has any type at all. For example,

```
any_type* p = (any_type*)&some_object;
```

will allow `some_object` to be manipulated as an `any_type` through p. However, if `some_object` is not in fact an `any_type`, strange and undesirable things may happen.

When a type conversion is not necessary it should be avoided. Programs that use explicit type conversions are harder to understand than programs that do not. Programs that use explicit type conversions are, however, easier to understand than programs that avoid conversions by refraining from using types to represent higher-level concepts (for example, a program that operates on a device register by shifting and masking on integers rather than defining the appropriate `struct` and operating on that; see §2.6.1). Furthermore, the correctness of an explicit type conversion depends critically on the programmer's understanding of the ways objects of different types are handled in the language and often also on details of the implementation. For example:

```
int i = 1;
char* pc = "asdf";
int* pi = &i;

i = (int)pc;
pc = (char*)i;   // Beware: pc might change value.
                 // On some machines, sizeof(int)
                 // is less than sizeof(char*)
pi = (int*)pc;
pc = (char*)pi; // Beware: pc might change value.
                 // On some machines a char* is
                 // represented differently from an int*
```

On many machines, no harm will be done, but on others the results are disastrous. At best, such code is nonportable. It is usually safe to assume that pointers to different structures have the same representation. Furthermore, any pointer can be assigned (without explicit type conversion) to a `void*`, and a `void*` can be explicitly converted back to a pointer of any type.

In C++, explicit type conversion is unnecessary in most cases when C needs it. In many programs, explicit type conversion can be completely avoided, and in other programs its use can be localized to a few routines.

3.2.6 Free Store

A named object is either static or automatic (see §2.1.3). A static object is allocated when the program is started and exists throughout the execution of the program. An automatic object is allocated each time execution reaches its definition and exists only until the block that contains it is left. It is often useful, however, to create a new object that exists until it is no longer needed. In particular, it is often useful to create an object that can be used after returning from the function in which it is created. The operator new creates such objects, and the operator delete can be used to destroy them later. Objects allocated by new are said to be *on the free store*. Such objects are typically tree nodes or linked list elements that are part of a larger data structure whose size cannot be known at compile time. Consider how one could write a compiler in the style used for the desk calculator. The syntax analysis functions might build a tree representation of the expressions for use by the code generator. For example:

```
struct enode {
    token_value oper;
    enode* left;
    enode* right;
};



enode* expr()
{
    enode* left = term();

    for (;;)
        switch(curr_tok) {
        case PLUS:
        case MINUS:
            get_token();
            enode* n = new enode;
            n->oper = curr_tok;
            n->left = left;
            n->right = term();
            left = n;
            break;
        default:
            return left;
        }
}
```

A code generator might use the resulting tree like this:

```
void generate(enode* n)
{
    switch (n->oper) {
    case PLUS:
        // do something appropriate
        delete n;
    }
}
```

An object created by new exists until it is explicitly destroyed by delete; then the space it occupied can be reused by new. There is typically no "garbage collector" that looks out for unreferenced objects and makes them available to new for reuse. The delete operator may be applied only to a pointer returned by new or to zero. Applying delete to zero has no effect.

Arrays of objects can also be created using new. For example:

```
char* save_string(const char* p)
{
    char* s = new char[strlen(p)+1];
    strcpy(s,p);
    return s;
}
```

Note that to de-allocate space allocated by new, delete must be able to determine the size of the object allocated. For example:

```
int main(int argc, char* argv[])
{
    if (argc < 2) exit(1);
    char* p = save_string(arg[1]);
    delete[] p;
}
```

This implies that an object allocated using the standard implementation of new will occupy slightly more space than a static object (typically one word more). The "plain" operator delete is used to delete individual objects; delete[] is used to delete arrays.

The free store operators are implemented by the functions (§r.5.3.3–4):

```
void* operator new(size_t);
void operator delete(void*);
```

where size_t is an unsigned integral type defined in <stddef.h>.

The standard implementation of operator new() does not initialize the memory returned.

What happens when new can find no store to allocate? Because even virtual memory is finite, this is bound to happen sometime; a request such as

```
char* p = new char[100000000];
```

will typically cause some kind of trouble. When new fails, it calls a function

specified by a call to the `set_new_handler()` function declared in `<new.h>`.
For example:

```
#include <iostream.h>
#include <new.h>
#include <stdlib.h>

void out_of_store()
{
    cerr << "operator new failed: out of store\n";
    exit(1);
}

int main()
{
    set_new_handler(&out_of_store);
    char* p = new char[100000000];
    cout << "done, p = " << long(p) << '\n';
}
```

will typically never get to write `done`, but will instead produce

```
operator new failed: out of store
```

A `new_handler` might do something more clever than simply terminating the
program. If you know how `new` and `delete` work – for example, because you provided your own `operator new()` and `operator delete()` – the handler might
attempt to find some memory for `new` to return. In other words, a user might provide
a garbage collector, thus rendering use of `delete` optional. Doing this is most definitely not the task for a beginner, though.

For historical reasons, `new` simply returns the pointer 0 if it cannot find enough
store and no `new_handler` has been specified. For example:

```
#include <iostream.h>

int main()
{
    char* p = new char[100000000];
    cout << "done, p = " << long(p) << '\n';
}
```

will produce

```
done, p = 0
```

You have been warned! Note that by providing a `new_handler`, one takes care of
the check for memory exhaustion for every use of `new` in the program (except when a
user has provided separate routines for handling allocation of objects of specific user-
defined types; see §5.5.6).

3.3 Statement Summary

C++ statements are systematically and completely described in §r.6; please read that section. Here, however, is a summary and some examples.

Statement Syntax

statement:
    declaration
    { *statement-list$_{opt}$* }
    expression$_{opt}$;

    `if` (*expression*) *statement*
    `if` (*expression*) *statement* `else` *statement*
    `switch` (*expression*) *statement*

    `while` (*expression*) *statement*
    `do` *statement* `while` (*expression*) ;
    `for` (*for-init-statement* *expression$_{opt}$* ; *expression$_{opt}$*) *statement*

    `case` *constant-expression* : *statement*
    `default` : *statement*
    `break` ;
    `continue` ;

    `return` *expression$_{opt}$* ;

    `goto` *identifier* ;
    identifier : *statement*

statement-list:
    statement
    statement-list statement

for-init-statement:
    declaration
    expression$_{opt}$;

    Note that a declaration is a statement and that there is no assignment statement or procedure call statement; assignment and function call are handled as expressions.

3.3.1 Selection Statements

A value can be tested by either an `if` statement or a `switch` statement:

```
if ( expression ) statement
if ( expression ) statement else statement
switch ( expression ) statement
```

There is no separate boolean type in C++. The comparison operators

```
==        !=        <        <=        >        >=
```

return the integer 1 if the comparison is true and 0 otherwise. It is not uncommon to see TRUE defined as 1 and FALSE defined as 0.

In an if statement, the first (or only) statement is executed if the expression is nonzero, and the second statement (if it is specified) is executed otherwise. This implies that any integer or pointer expression can be used as a condition. In particular, if a is an integer

```
if (a) // ...
```

is equivalent to

```
if (a != 0) // ...
```

The logical operators

```
&&        ||        !
```

are most commonly used in conditions. The operators && and || will not evaluate their second argument unless it is necessary. For example:

```
if (p && 1<p->count) // ...
```

first tests that p is nonzero, and only if it is, tests 1<p->count.

Some simple if statements can conveniently be replaced by *arithmetic if* expressions. For example:

```
if (a <= b)
    max = b;
else
    max = a;
```

is better expressed like this:

```
max = (a<=b) ? b : a;
```

The parentheses around the condition in a conditional expression are not necessary, but I find the code easier to read when they are used.

Some simple switch statements can alternatively be written as a set of if statements. For example:

```
switch (val) {
case 1:
    f();
    break;
case 2;
    g();
    break;
default:
    h();
    break;
}
```

could alternatively be expressed as

```
if (val == 1)
    f();
else if (val == 2)
    g();
else
    h();
```

The meaning is the same, but the first (`switch`) version is preferred because the nature of the operation (testing a value against a set of constants) is explicit in that case. This makes the `switch` statement easier to read for nontrivial examples.

Beware that a case of a switch must be terminated somehow unless you want to carry on executing the next case. For example:

```
switch (val) {                        // beware
case 1:
    cout << "case 1\n";
case 2:
    cout << "case 2\n";
default:
    cout << "default: case not found\n";
}
```

with `val==1` prints

```
case 1
case 2
default: case not found
```

to the great surprise of the uninitiated. It is a good idea to comment the (rare) cases where a fall-through is intentional so that an uncommented fall-through can be assumed to be an error. A `break` is the most common way of terminating a case, but a `return` is often useful, and even a `goto` can sometimes be used. For example:

```
switch (val) {                       // beware
case 0:
    cout << "case 0\n";
case1:
case 1:
    cout << "case 1\n";
    return;
case 2:
    cout << "case 2\n";
    goto case1;
default:
    cout << "default: case not found\n";
    return;
}
```

Called with `val==2`, this produces

```
case 2
case 1
```

Note that a *case label* is not a suitable label for use in a `goto` statement:

```
goto case 2;     // syntax error
```

3.3.2 Goto

C++ possesses the infamous `goto`:

> `goto` *identifier* `;`
> *identifier* `:` *statement*

It has few uses in general high-level programming, but it can be very useful when a C++ program is generated by a program rather than written directly by a person; for example, gotos can be used in a parser generated from a grammar by a parser genera-tor. The `goto` can also be important in the rare cases when optimal efficiency is essential, for example, in the inner loop of some real-time application.

One of the few sensible uses of `goto` in ordinary code is to break out from a nested loop or switch (a `break` breaks out of only the innermost enclosing loop or switch). For example:

```
void f()
{
    int i;
    int j;
```

```
        for (i = 0;  i<n;  i++)
            for (j = 0;  j<m;  j++)
                if (nm[i][j] == a) goto found;
        // not found
        // ...

    found:
        // nm[i][j] == a
    }
```

There is also a `continue` statement that, in effect, goes to the end of a loop statement, as explained in §3.1.5.

3.4 Comments and Indentation

Judicious use of comments and consistent use of indentation can make the task of reading and understanding a program much more pleasant. Several different consistent styles of indentation are used. I see no fundamental reason to prefer one over another (though, like most others, I have my preferences). The same applies to styles of comments.

Comments can be misused in ways that seriously affect the readability of a program. The compiler does not understand the contents of a comment, so it has no way of ensuring that a comment

[1]   is meaningful,

[2]   describes the program, and

[3]   is up to date.

Most programs contain comments that are incomprehensible, ambiguous, and just plain wrong. Bad comments can be worse than no comments.

If something can be stated *in the language itself*, it should be, and not just mentioned in a comment. This remark is aimed at comments such as

```
// variable "v" must be initialized.

// variable "v" must be used only by function "f()".

// call function "init()" before calling
// any other function in this file.

// call function "cleanup()" at the end of your program.

// don't use function "weird()".

// function "f()" takes two arguments.
```

Such comments can often be rendered unnecessary by proper use of C++. For example, one might utilize the linkage rules (§4.2) and the visibility, initialization, and cleanup rules for classes (see §5.5) to make the preceding examples redundant.

Once something has been stated clearly in the language, it should not be mentioned a second time in a comment. For example:

```
a = b+c;          // a becomes b+c
count++;          // increment the counter
```

Such comments are worse than simply redundant: They increase the amount of text the reader has to look at, they often obscure the structure of the program, and they may be wrong. Note, however, that such comments are used extensively for teaching purposes in programming language text books such as this. This is one of the many ways a program in a textbook differs from a real program.

The author's preference is for

[1]   a comment for each source file stating what the declarations in it have in common, references to manuals, general hints for maintenance, etc.;

[2]   a comment for each class or template;

[3]   a comment for each nontrivial function stating its purpose, the algorithm used (unless it is obvious), and maybe something about the assumptions it makes about its environment;

[4]   a comment for each global variable;

[5]   a few comments in places where the code is nonobvious and/or nonportable; and

[6]   very little else.

For example:

```
//   tbl.c: Implementation of the symbol table.

/*
    Gaussian elimination with partial pivoting.
    See Ralston: "A first course ..." pg 411.
*/

//   swap() assumes the stack layout of an AT&T 3B20.

/**********************************

    Copyright (c) 1991 AT&T, Inc.
    All rights reserved

**********************************/
```

A well-chosen and well-written set of comments is an essential part of a good program. Writing good comments can be as difficult as writing the program itself. It is an art well worth cultivating.

Note also that if // comments are used exclusively in a function, then any part of that function can be commented out using /* */ style comments, and vice versa.

3.5 Exercises

1. (*1) Rewrite the following `for` statement as an equivalent `while` statement:

```
for (i=0; i<max_length; i++)
    if (input_line[i] == '?') quest_count++;
```

   Rewrite it to use a pointer as the controlled variable, that is, so that the the test is of the form `*p=='?'`.

2. (*1) Fully parenthesize the following expressions:

```
a = b + c * d << 2 & 8
a & 077 != 3
a == b || a == c && c < 5
c = x != 0
0 <= i < 7
f(1,2)+3
a = - 1 + + b -- - 5
a = b == c ++
a = b = c = 0
a[4][2] *= * b ? c : * d * 2
a-b,c=d
```

3. (*2) Find 5 different C++ constructs for which the meaning is undefined.
4. (*2) Find 10 different examples of nonportable C++ code.
5. (*1) What happens if you divide by zero on your system? What happens in case of overflow and underflow?
6. (*1) Fully parenthesize the following expressions:

```
*p++
*--p
++a--
(int*)p->m
*p.m
*a[i]
```

7. (*2) Write functions: `strlen()` that returns the length of a string, `strcpy()` that copies a string into another, and `strcmp()` that compares two strings. Consider what the argument types and return types ought to be, then compare with the standard versions as declared in `<string.h>` and specified in your manual.

8. (*1) See how your compiler reacts to these errors:

```
void f(int a, int b)
{
    if (a = 3) // ...
    if (a&077 == 0) // ...
    a := b+1;
}
```

   Devise more simple errors and see how the compiler reacts.

9. (*2) Write a function `cat()` that takes two string arguments and returns a string

that is the concatenation of the arguments. Use `new` to find store for the result. Write a function `rev ()` that takes a string argument and reverses the characters in it. That is, after `rev (p)` the last character of `p` will be the first, etc.

10. (*2) What does the following example do?

```
void send(register* to, register* from, register count)
// Duff's device. Helpful comment deliberately deleted.
{
    register n=(count+7)/8;
    switch (count%8) {
        case 0: do {    *to++ = *from++;
        case 7:         *to++ = *from++;
        case 6:         *to++ = *from++;
        case 5:         *to++ = *from++;
        case 4:         *to++ = *from++;
        case 3:         *to++ = *from++;
        case 2:         *to++ = *from++;
        case 1:         *to++ = *from++;
                } while (--n>0);
    }
}
```

Why would anyone write something like that?

11. (*2) Write a function `atoi ()` that takes a string containing digits and returns the corresponding `int`. For example, `atoi ("123")` is 123. Modify `atoi ()` to handle C++ octal and hexadecimal notation in addition to plain decimal numbers. Modify `atoi ()` to handle the C++ character constant notation. Write a function `itoa ()` that creates a string representation of an integer argument.

12. (*2) Re-write `get_token ()` (§3.1.2) to read a line at a time into a buffer and then compose tokens by reading the characters in the buffer.

13. (*2) Add functions such as `sqrt ()`, `log ()`, and `sin ()` to the desk calculator from §3.1. Hint: Predefine the names and call the functions through an array of pointers to functions. Don't forget to check the arguments in a function call.

14. (*3) Allow a user to define functions in the desk calculator. Hint: Define a function as a sequence of operations just as a user would have typed them. Such a sequence can be stored either as a character string or as a list of tokens. Then read and execute those operations when the function is called. If you want a user-defined function to take arguments, you will have to invent a notation for that.

15. (*1.5) Convert the desk calculator to use a `symbol` structure instead of using the static variables `name_string` and `number_value`:

```
struct symbol {
    token_value tok;
    union {
        double number_value;
        char*   name_string;
    };
};
```

16. (*2.5) Write a program that strips comments out of a C++ program. That is, read from cin and remove both `//` comments and `/* */` comments and write the result to cout. Do not worry about making the layout of the output look nice (that would be another, and much harder, exercise). Do not worry about incorrect programs. Beware of `//`, `/*`, and `*/` in comments, strings, and character constants.

17. (*2) Look at some programs to get an idea of the variety of indentation and commenting styles actually used.

4

Functions and Files

To iterate is human,
to recurse divine.
– L. Peter Deutsch

All nontrivial programs are made up of several separately compiled units (conventionally, called files). This chapter describes how separately compiled functions can call each other, how separately compiled functions can share data, and how types used in different files in a program can be kept consistent. Functions are discussed in some detail; this includes argument passing, function name overloading, default arguments, pointers to functions, and, of course, declaration and definition of functions. Finally, macros are presented.

4.1 Introduction

A *file* has just one role in the C++ language, that of providing *file scope* (§r.3.2), that is, the scope for global `static` and `inline` functions and global `static` and `const` ''variables.'' A file is also the traditional unit of storage (in a file system) and the unit of compilation. Systems that do not store, compile, and present C++ programs to the programmer as sets of files do exist. However, the discussion here will concentrate on systems with the traditional use of files.

Having a complete program in one file is usually impossible because the code for the standard libraries and operating system is elsewhere. Furthermore, having all of the user's own code in a single file is typically both impractical and inconvenient. The way a program is organized into files can help the reader understand the overall structure of a program and enable the compiler to enforce that structure. Where the unit of compilation is a file, all of a file must be recompiled whenever a change (however small) has been made to it. For even a moderately sized program, the amount of time spent recompiling can be significantly reduced by partitioning the program into files of suitable size.

Consider the calculator example. It was presented as a single source file. If you typed it in, you undoubtedly had some minor trouble getting the declarations in the right order, and at least one "spurious" declaration had to be used to allow the compiler to handle the mutually recursive functions `expr()`, `term()`, and `prim()`. The text stated that the program had four parts (a lexical analyzer, a parser, a symbol table, and a driver), but this was in no way reflected in the code itself. Actually, the calculator was not written like that. That is simply not the way to do it; even if all considerations of programming methodology, maintenance, and compilation efficiency were disregarded for this "throw away" program, the author would still construct it from several files simply to make the task of programming more pleasant.

To enable separate compilation, the programmer must supply declarations providing the type information needed to analyze a file in isolation from the rest of the program. A program consisting of many separately compiled parts must be consistent in its use of names and types in exactly the same way as must a program consisting of a single source file. To ensure that, the declarations presented in separate compilations must be consistent. Your system will have tools to help ensure this. In particular, the linker can detect many inconsistencies. The linker is the program that binds together the separately compiled parts. A linker is sometimes (confusingly) called a loader.

4.2 Linkage

Unless otherwise stated, a name that is not local to a function or a class must refer to the same type, value, function, or object in every separately compiled part of a program. That is, there can only be one nonlocal type, value, function, or object in a program with that name. For example, consider two files:

```
// file1.c:
    int a = 1;
    int f() { /* do something */ }

// file2.c:
    extern int a;
    int f();
    void g() { a = f(); }
```

The a and `f()` used by `g()` in `file2.c` are the ones defined in `file1.c`. The keyword `extern` indicates that the declaration of a in `file2.c` is (just) a declaration and not a definition. Had a been initialized, `extern` would simply be ignored because a declaration with an initializer is always a definition. An object must be defined exactly once in a program. It may be declared many times, but the types must agree exactly. For example:

```
// file1.c:
    int a = 1;
    int b = 1;
    extern int c;

// file2.c:
    int a;
    extern double b;
    extern int c;
```

There are three errors here: a is defined twice (``int a;'' is a definition meaning
``int a=0;''), b is declared twice with different types, and c is declared twice but
not defined. These kinds of errors (linkage errors) cannot be detected by a compiler
that looks at only one file at a time. Most, however, are detectable by the linker.

The following program is not C++ (even though it is C):

```
// file1.c:
    int a;
    int f() { return a; }

// file2.c:
    int a;
    int g() { return f(); }
```

First, the call of f() in file2.c is an error because f() has not been declared.
Second, the program will not link because a is defined twice.

A name can be made local to a file by declaring it static. For example:

```
// file1.c:
    static int a = 6;
    static int f() { /* ... */ }

// file2.c:
    static int a = 7;
    static int f() { /* ... */ }
```

Because each a and f is declared static, the resulting program is correct. Each file
has its own a and its own f().

When variables and functions are explicitly declared static, a program fragment is easier to understand (you don't have to look elsewhere). Using static for
functions may also have a beneficial effect on the amount of function call overhead by
giving an optimizing compiler an easier job. An object or a function with a name that
is local to a file is said to have *internal linkage*. Conversely, an object or a function
with a name that is not local to a file is said to have *external linkage*.

Names of types – that is, names of classes and enumerations – are usually said to
have no linkage. Names of global classes and enumerations must be unique in a program and must refer to unique definitions, though. So even though the two class definitions are identical this is an error:

```
// file1.c:
    struct S { int a; char b; };
    extern void f(S*);
```

```
// file2.c:
    struct S { int a; char b; };
    void f(S* p) { /* ... */}
```

Beware that checking against such duplicate class declarations is beyond the ability of
most C++ compilation systems and that undetected inconsistent class declarations can
be a source of subtle errors.

Global `inline` functions have internal linkage, and so by default have `const`s.
Synonyms for types – that is, `typedef` names – are local to their file, so the declarations in these two files do not interfere with each other:

```
// file1.c:
    typedef int T;
    const int a = 7;
    inline T f(int i) { return i+a;   }
```

```
// file2.c:
    typedef void T;
    const int a = 8;
    inline T f(double d) { cout<<d;  }
```

A const can be given external linkage by an explicit declaration:

```
// file3.c:
    extern const int a;
    const int a = 77;
```

```
// file4.c:
    extern const int a;
    void g() { cout<<a;  }
```

Here `g()` will print 77.

4.3 Header Files

The types in all declarations of the same object or function must be consistent. Consequently, the source code submitted to the compiler and later linked together must be
consistent. One imperfect but simple method of achieving consistency for declarations in different files is to include *header files* containing interface information in
source files containing executable code and/or data definitions.

The `#include` mechanism is a text manipulation facility for gathering source
program fragments together into a single unit (file) for compilation. The directive

```
#include "to_be_included"
```

replaces the line in which the #include appears with the contents of the file to_be_included. The content should be C++ source text because the compiler will proceed to read it. Often, the inclusion is handled by a separate program, called the C++ preprocessor, invoked implicitly to transform the source file presented by the programmer into a file without include directives before compilation proper is started. Alternatively, the compiler front-end handles these directives as they appear in the source text. On the author's system, if the programmer wants to see the effect of the include directives, the command

```
CC -E file.c
```

can be used to preprocess file.c in the same way as CC would before starting the compiler proper.

To include files from the standard include directory, the angle brackets < and > are used instead of quotes. For example:

```
#include <stream.h>    // from standard include directory
#define "myheader.h"   // from current directory
```

Using <> has the advantage that the names of the standard include directories are not built into the program (often /usr/include/CC is searched first followed by /usr/include). A space is, unfortunately, significant in an include directive:

```
#include < stream.h >   // will not find <stream.h>
```

It may seem extravagant to recompile a file each time it is included somewhere, but the files included typically contain only declarations and not code needing extensive analysis by the compiler. Further, a system can use some form of precompiling of header files provided it is smart enough to do so without changing the semantics of programs.

A header file may contain:

Type definitions	`struct point { int x, y; };`
Templates	`template<class T>`
	`    class V { /* ... */ }`
Function declarations	`extern int strlen(const char*);`
Inline function definitions	`inline char get() { return *p++; }`
Data declarations	`extern int a;`
Constant definitions	`const float pi = 3.141593;`
Enumerations	`enum bool { false, true };`
Name declarations	`class Matrix;`
Include directives	`#include <signal.h>`
Macro definitions	`#define Case break;case`
Comments	`/* check for end of file */`

This rule of thumb for what should be placed in a header file is not a language requirement, but simply a suggestion of a reasonable way of using the `#include` mechanism. Conversely, a header file should never contain:

Ordinary function definitions	`char get() { return *p++; }`
Data definitions	`int a;`
Constant aggregate definitions	`const tbl[] = { /* ... */ };`

Header files are conventionally suffixed by `.h` and files containing function or data definitions by `.c`. They are therefore often referred to as ''.h files'' and ''.c files,'' respectively. Other conventions, such as `.C`, `.cxx`, `.cpp`, and `.cc`, are also found. The manual for your compiler will be quite specific about this issue. Macros are described in §4.7. Note that macros are far less useful in C++ than they are in C because C++ has language constructs such as `const` for defining constants, `inline` for eliminating function call overhead, and `template` for generating families of types and families of functions (§8).

The reason for recommending that the definition of simple constants, but not the definition of constant aggregates, can be placed in header files, is pragmatic. Most compilers are simply not smart enough to ensure that no redundant copies of constant aggregates are generated. Furthermore, the simple cases are far more common and therefore more important for generating good code.

4.3.1 Single Header File

The simplest solution to the problem of partitioning a program into several files is to put the functions and data definitions in a suitable number of source files and to declare the types needed for them to communicate in a single header file that all the other files include. For the calculator program, one could use four `.c` files: `lex.c`, `syn.c`, `table.c`, and `main.c`, and a header file `dc.h` containing declarations of every name used in more than one `.c` file:

```
// dc.h: common declarations for the calculator

#include <iostream.h>

enum token_value {
      NAME,         NUMBER,         END,
      PLUS='+',     MINUS='-',      MUL='*',        DIV='/',
      PRINT=';',    ASSIGN='=',     LP='(',         RP=')'
};


extern int no_of_errors;
extern double error(const char* s);
extern token_value get_token();
extern token_value curr_tok;
extern double number_value;
extern char name_string[256];
```

```
extern double expr();
extern double term();
extern double prim();

struct name {
    char* string;
    name* next;
    double value;
};

extern name* look(const char* p, int ins = 0);
inline name* insert(const char* s) { return look(s,1); }
```

Leaving out the actual code, `lex.c` will look something like this:

```
// lex.c: input and lexical analysis

#include "dc.h"
#include <ctype.h>

token_value curr_tok;
double number_value;
char name_string[256];

token_value get_token() { /* ... */ }
```

Note that using header files in this manner ensures that every declaration of a user-defined object in a header file will at some point be included in the file in which it is defined. For example, when compiling `lex.c` the compiler will be presented with:

```
extern token_value get_token();
// ...
token_value get_token() { /* ... */ }
```

This ensures that the compiler will detect any inconsistencies in the types specified for a name. For example, had `get_token()` been declared to return a `token_value`, but defined to return an `int`, the compilation of `lex.c` would have failed with a type-mismatch error.

File `syn.c` will look like this:

```
// syn.c: syntax analysis and evaluation

#include "dc.h"

double prim() { /* ... */ }
double term() { /* ... */ }
double expr() { /* ... */ }
```

File `table.c` will look like this:

```
// table.c: symbol table and lookup

#include "dc.h"

extern char* strcmp(const char*, const char*);
extern char* strcpy(char*, const char*);
extern int strlen(const char*);

const int TBLSZ = 23;
name* table[TBLSZ];

name* look(char* p, int ins) { /* ... */ }
```

Note that `table.c` itself declares the standard string manipulation functions, so there are no consistency checks on those declarations. It is nearly always better to include a header file than to declare a name `extern` in a `.c` file. This may involve including "too much," but that usually does not seriously affect the time needed for the compilation and will save time for the programmer. As an example of this, note how `strlen()` is redeclared again in `main.c` (below). This is a waste of keystrokes and a potential cause of trouble because the compiler cannot check the consistency of those two declarations (the linker can, though). Naturally, this problem could have been avoided had every `extern` declaration been placed in `dc.h`, as was intended. This "sloppiness" was left in the program because it is very common in C programs, is very tempting to the programmer, and more often than not leads to errors and programs that are hard to maintain. You have been warned!

Finally, file `main.c` will look like this:

```
// main.c: initialization, main loop, and error handling

#include "dc.h"

int no_of_errors;

double error(char* s) { /* ... */ }

extern int strlen(const char*);

int main(int argc, char* argv[]) { /* ... */ }
```

There is an important case where header files becomes a serious nuisance. A set of header files and a library can be used to extend the language with a set of general and application-specific types (see Chapters 5-9). In such cases, it is not unusual to read thousands of lines of header files at the start of every compilation. The contents of library headers are usually "frozen" and change infrequently. A technique for starting the compiler *primed* with the contents of library headers can be most useful; in a sense one is creating a special-purpose language with its own compiler. No standard procedure for creating such a primed compiler has been established.

4.3.2 Multiple Header Files

The single-header style of program partitioning is most useful when the program is small and its parts are not intended to be used separately. Then, it is acceptable that it is not possible to determine which declarations are placed in the header file for what reason. Comments can be a help. An alternative is to let each part of a program have its own header file defining the facilities it provides. Each .c file then has a corresponding .h file specifying what it provides. Each .c file includes its own .h file and maybe also some other .h files specifying what it needs.

Considering this organization for the calculator, we note that error() is used by just about every function in the program, and itself uses only <iostream.h>. This is typical for error functions and implies that error() should be separate from main():

```
// error.h: error handling

extern int no_of_errors;

extern double error(const char* s);
```

```
// error.c

#include <iostream.h>
#include "error.h"

int no_of_errors;

double error(const char* s) { /* ... */ }
```

In this style of use of header files, a .h file and its associated .c file can be seen as a module in which the .h file specifies an interface and the .c file specifies an implementation.

The symbol table is independent of the rest of the calculator except for the use of the error function. This can now be made explicit:

```
// table.h: symbol table declarations

struct name {
    char* string;
    name* next;
    double value;
};

extern name* look(const char* p, int ins = 0);
inline name* insert(const char* s) { return look(s,1); }
```

```
// table.c: symbol table definitions

#include "error.h"
#include <string.h>
#include "table.h"

const int TBLSZ = 23;
name* table[TBLSZ];

name* look(const char* p, int ins) { /* ... */ }
```

Note that the declarations of string manipulating functions are now included from
`<string.h>`. This removes yet another potential source of errors.

```
// lex.h: input and lexical analysis declarations

enum token_value {
    NAME,         NUMBER,        END,
    PLUS='+',     MINUS='-',     MUL='*',      DIV='/',
    PRINT=';',    ASSIGN='=',    LP='(',       RP=')'
};

extern token_value curr_tok;
extern double number_value;
extern char name_string[256];

extern token_value get_token();
```

This interface to the lexical analyzer is quite messy. The lack of a proper token type
shows itself in the need to present a user of `get_token()` with the actual lexical
buffers `number_value` and `name_string`.

```
// lex.c: input and lexical analysis definitions

#include <iostream.h>
#include <ctype.h>
#include "error.h"
#include "lex.h"

token_value curr_tok;
double number_value;
char name_string[256];

token_value get_token() { /* ... */ }
```

The interface to the syntax analyzer is particularly clean:

```
// syn.h: declarations for syntax analysis and evaluation

extern double expr();
extern double term();
extern double prim();

// syn.c: definitions for syntax analysis and evaluation

#include "error.h"
#include "lex.h"
#include "syn.h"

double prim() { /* ... */ }
double term() { /* ... */ }
double expr() { /* ... */ }
```

The main program is, as usual, trivial:

```
// main.c: the main program

#include <iostream.h>
#include "error.h"
#include "lex.h"
#include "syn.h"
#include "table.h"
#include <string.h>

int main(int argc, char* argv[]) { /* ... */ }
```

The number of header files to use for a program is a function of many factors. Many of these factors have more to do with the way files are handled on your system than with C++. For example, if your editor does not have facilities for looking at several files at the same time, using many header files becomes less attractive. Similarly, if opening and reading 10 files of 50 lines each is noticeably more time consuming than reading a single file of 500 lines, you might think twice before using the multiple header file style for a small project. A word of caution: A set of 10 header files plus the standard header files is usually manageable. However, if you partition the declarations of a large program into the logically minimal-sized header files (putting each structure declaration in its own file, etc.), you can easily get an unmanageable mess of hundreds of files.

4.4 Linkage to Non-C++ Code

It is typical for a C++ program to contain parts written in other languages. Similarly, it is common for C++ code fragments to be used as parts of programs mainly written in some other language. The cooperation between program fragments written in different languages or in the same language compiled with compilers that use different linkage conventions can be difficult. For example, languages and different implementations of the same language may differ in their use of registers to hold arguments, the layout of arguments put on a stack, the layout of built-in types such as strings and integers, the function names passed by the compiler to the linker, and the amount of type checking required from the linker. To help, one can specify a linkage convention to be used in an `extern` declaration. For example, this declares `strcpy` and specifies that it should be linked according to the C linkage conventions:

```
extern "C" char* strcpy(char*, const char*);
```

The effect of this declaration differs from the effect of the ''plain'' declaration

```
extern char* strcpy(char*, const char*);
```

only in the linkage convention used for calling `strcpy()`. The semantics of the call, and in particular the checking of the arguments, are identical in both cases. The `extern "C"` directive is particularly useful because of the close relationship between C and C++ and between C and C++ implementations. Note that the C in `extern "C"` names a linkage convention and not a language; often `extern "C"` is used to link to Fortran and assembler routines that happen to conform to some of the same conventions as a C implementation.

Adding "C" to a lot of `extern` declarations can be a nuisance. Consequently, there is a mechanism to add "C" to a group of declarations. For example:

```
extern "C" {
    char* strcpy(char*, const char*);
    int strcmp(const char*, const char*);
    int strlen(const char*);
    // ...
}
```

This construct can be used to enclose a complete C header file to make a header suitable for C++ use. For example:

```
extern "C" {
#include <string.h>
}
```

This technique is commonly used to produce a C++ standard header from a C standard header. Alternatively, conditional compilation can be used to create a common C and C++ header:

```
#ifdef __cplusplus
extern "C" {
#endif

    char* strcpy(char*, const char*);
    int strcmp(const char*, const char*);
    int strlen(const char*);
    // ...

#ifdef __cplusplus
}
#endif
```

The predefined macro name __cplusplus is used to ensure that the C++ constructs are edited out when the file is used as a C header.

Because only linkage conventions are affected by an extern "C" directive, any declaration can appear within a linkage block:

```
extern "C" {
    // any declaration here

    // for example:

    static int st;
    int glob;
}
```

In particular, the scope and storage class of variables are not affected, so st still has internal linkage and glob is still a global variable.

Note that an extern "C" directive specifies the linkage convention (only) and does not affect the semantics of calls to the function. In particular, a function declared extern "C" still obeys the C++ type checking and argument conversion rules and not the weaker C rules. For example:

```
extern "C" int f();

int g()
{
    return f(1); // error: no argument expected
}
```

4.5 How to Make a Library

Phrases such as "put in a library" and "found in some library" are used often (in this book and elsewhere), but what does that mean for a C++ program? Unfortunately, the answer depends on the system used; but this section explains how to make and use a library on a 10th edition UNIX system. Other systems provide similar facilities.

A library is basically a set of .o files obtained by compiling a corresponding set of .c files. There typically are one or more .h files containing the declarations necessary to use those .o files. As an example, consider having to provide (in a convenient way) a set of mathematical functions for some unspecified set of users. The header file could look like this:

```
extern "C" {  // standard math library is often a C program

     double sqrt(double);  // subset of <math.h>
     double sin(double);
     double cos(double);
     double exp(double);
     double log(double);
     // ...
}
```

and the definitions of these functions would be stored in files sqrt.c, sin.c, cos.c, exp.c, and log.c, respectively.

A library called math.a can be made like this

```
$ CC -c sqrt.c sin.c cos.c expr.c log.c
$ ar cr math.a sqrt.o sin.o cos.o expr.o log.o
$ ranlib math.a
```

where $ is the system prompt.

The source files are first compiled giving the equivalent object files. The ar command is then used to make an archive called math.a. Finally, that archive is indexed for faster access. If your system does not have a ranlib command, you probably do not need it; please look in your manual under ar for details. The library can be used like this:

```
$ CC myprog.c math.a
```

Now, what advantage is there in using math.a instead of simply using the .o files directly? For example:

```
$ CC myprog.c sqrt.o sin.o cos.o expr.o log.o
```

For most programs, finding the right set of .o files is distinctly nontrivial. In the example above, they were all included, but if functions in myprog.c call only the functions sqrt() and cos() then it appears that:

```
$ CC myprog.c sqrt.o cos.o
```

would be sufficient. It is not because cos.c uses sin.c.

The linker that the CC command calls to handle a .a file (in this case, math.a) knows how to extract only the necessary .o files from the set that was used to create the .a file. In other words, using a library, one can include many definitions with a single name (including definitions of functions and variables used by internal functions and never seen by the user), yet at the same time ensure that only the minimal number of definitions is included in the resulting program.

4.6 Functions

The typical way of getting something done in a C++ program is to call a function to
do it. Defining a function is the way to specify how an operation is to be done. A
function cannot be called unless it is declared.

4.6.1 Function Declarations

A function declaration gives the name of the function, the type of the value returned
(if any) by the function, and the number and types of the arguments that must be supplied in a call of the function. For example,

```
extern double sqrt(double);
extern elem* next_elem();
extern char* strcpy(char* to, const char* from);
extern void exit(int);
```

The semantics of argument passing are identical to the semantics of initialization.
Argument types are checked and implicit argument type conversion takes place when
necessary. For example, given the preceding declarations,

```
double sr2 = sqrt(2);
```

will correctly call the function `sqrt()` with the floating point value `2.0`. The value
of this checking and type conversion is enormous.

A function declaration may contain argument names. This can be a help to the
reader, but the compiler simply ignores such names.

4.6.2 Function Definitions

Every function that is called in a program must be defined somewhere (once only). A
function definition is a function declaration in which the body of the function is presented. For example:

```
extern void swap(int*, int*);   // a declaration

void swap(int* p, int* q)       // a definition
{
    int t = *p;
    *p = *q;
    *q = t;
}
```

It is not uncommon to have function definitions with unused arguments:

```
void search(table* t, const char* key, const char*)
{
    // no use of the third argument

    // ...
}
```

As shown, the fact that an argument is unused can be indicated by not naming it. Such functions typically arise from simplification of code and from planning ahead for extensions. In both cases, leaving the argument in place, though unused, ensures that other functions calling the function are not affected by the change.

As mentioned, a function can be defined to be `inline`. For example:

```
inline fac(int i) { return i<2 ? 1 : n*fac(n-1); }
```

The `inline` specifier is a hint to the compiler that it should attempt to generate code for a call of `fac()` inline rather than laying down the code for the function once and then calling through the usual function call mechanism (§r.7.1.2). A clever compiler could generate the constant `720` for a call `fac(6)`. The possibility of mutually recursive inline functions, inline functions that recurse or not dependent on input, etc., makes it impossible to guarantee that every call of an `inline` function is actually inlined. The degree of cleverness of a compiler cannot be legislated, so another compiler might generate `6*5*4*3*2*1`, another `6*fac(5)`, and yet another an unoptimized call `fac(6)`.

To make inlining possible in the absence of unusually clever compilation and linking facilities the definition, and not just the declaration, of an inline function must be in scope for inlining to take place. An `inline` specifier does not affect the meaning of a call of the function.

4.6.3 Argument Passing

When a function is called, store is set aside for its formal arguments and each formal argument is initialized by its corresponding actual argument. The semantics of argument passing are identical to the semantics of initialization. In particular, the type of an actual argument is checked against the type of the corresponding formal argument, and all standard and user-defined type conversions are performed. There are special rules for passing arrays (§4.6.5), a facility for passing unchecked arguments (§4.6.8), and a facility for specifying default arguments (§4.6.7). Consider:

```
void f(int val, int& ref)
{
    val++;
    ref++;
}
```

When `f()` is called, `val++` increments a local copy of the first actual argument whereas `ref++` increments the second actual argument. For example,

```
void g()
{
    int i = 1;
    int j = 1;
    f(i,j);
}
```

will increment j but not i. The first argument, i, is passed *by value*, the second
argument, j, is passed *by reference*. As mentioned in §2.3.10, functions that modify
call-by-reference arguments can make programs hard to read and should generally be
avoided (but see §10.2.2). It can, however, be noticeably more efficient to pass a
large object by reference than to pass it by value. In that case, the argument might be
declared const to indicate that the reference is used for efficiency reasons only and
not to enable the called function to change the value of the object:

```
void f(const large& arg)
{
    // the value of "arg" cannot be changed
    // without explicit use of type conversion
}
```

The absence of const in the declaration of a reference argument is taken as a statement of intent to modify the variable:

```
void g(large& arg);    // assume that g() modifies arg
```

So use const where ever possible.

Similarly, declaring a pointer argument const tells readers that the value of an
object pointed to by that argument is not changed by the function. For example:

```
extern int strlen(const char*);    // from <string.h>
extern char* strcpy(char* to, const char* from);
extern int strcmp(const char*, const char*);
```

The importance of this practice increases with the size of a program.

Note that the semantics of argument passing are different from the semantics of
assignment. This is important for const arguments, reference arguments, and arguments of some user-defined types (§1.4.2).

A literal, a constant, and an argument that requires conversion can be passed as a
const& argument, but not as a non-const argument. Allowing conversions for
const T& arguments ensures that such an argument can be given exactly the same
set of values as a T argument by passing the value in a temporary if necessary.

```
float fsqrt(const float&); // fortran-style sqrt

void g(double d)
{
    float r;

    r = fsqrt(2.0f);    // pass ref to temp == 2.0f
    r = fsqrt(r);       // pass ref to r
    r = fsqrt(d);       // pass ref to temp == float(d)
}
```

Disallowing conversions for non-const reference arguments avoids the possibility of silly mistakes arising from the introduction of those temporaries.

```
void update(float& i);

void g(double d)
{
    float r;

    update(2.0f);    // error: const argument
    update(r);       // pass ref to r
    update(d);       // error: type conversion required
}
```

4.6.4 Value Return

A value must be returned from a function that is not declared void. For example:

```
int f() { }     // error
void g() { }    // ok
```

A return value is specified by a return statement. For example:

```
int fac(int n) { return (n>1) ? n*fac(n-1) : 1; }
```

There can be more than one return statement in a function:

```
int fac(int n)
{
    if (n > 1)
        return n*fac(n-1);
    else
        return 1;
}
```

Like the semantics of argument passing, the semantics of function value return are identical to the semantics of initialization. A return statement is considered to initialize a variable of the returned type. The type of a return expression is checked against the type of the returned type, and all standard and user-defined type conversions are performed. For example:

```
double f()
{
    // ...
    return 1;    // implicitly converted to double(1)
}
```

Each time a function is called a new copy of its arguments and automatic variables is created. The store is reused after the function returns, so it is unwise to return a pointer to a local variable. The contents of the location pointed to will change unpredictably:

```
int* f()
{
    int local = 1;
    // ...
    return &local;      // error
}
```

This error is less common than the equivalent error using references:

```
int& f()
{
    int local = 1;
    // ...
    return local;       // error
}
```

Fortunately, the compiler warns about return of references to local variables. Here is another example:

```
int& f() { return 1; }   // error
```

4.6.5 Array Arguments

If an array is used as a function argument, a pointer to its first element is passed. For example:

```
int strlen(const char*);

void f()
{
    char v[] = "an array";
    strlen(v);
    strlen("Nicholas");
};
```

That is, an argument of type T[] will be converted to a T* when passed as an argument. This implies that an assignment to an element of an array argument changes the value of an element of the argument array. In other words, arrays differ from other types in that an array is not (and cannot be) passed by value.

The size of an array is not available to the called function. This can be a nuisance, but there are several ways of circumventing this problem. Strings are zero-terminated, so their size can be computed easily. For other arrays a second argument specifying the size can be passed, or a type containing a pointer and a length indicator can be defined and passed instead of a plain array (see also §1.2.5). For example:

```
void compute1(int* vec_ptr, int vec_size); // one way

struct vec {                                 // another way
    int* ptr;
    int size;
};

void compute2(vec v);
```

Multidimensional arrays are trickier, but often arrays of pointers can be used instead, and they need no special treatment. For example:

```
char* day[] = {
    "mon", "tue", "wed", "thu", "fri", "sat", "sun"
};
```

However, consider defining a function to manipulate a two-dimensional matrix. If the dimensions are known at compile time, there is no problem:

```
void print_m34(int m[3][4])
{
    for (int i = 0; i<3; i++) {
        for (int j = 0; j<4; j++)
            cout << ' ' << m[i][j];
        cout << '\n';
    }
}
```

The matrix is, of course, still passed as a pointer, and the dimensions in the declaration are simply a notational convenience.

The first dimension of an array is irrelevant to the problem of finding the location of an element (§r.8.2.4). It can therefore be passed as an argument:

```
void print_mi4(int m[][4], int dim1)
{
    for (int i = 0; i<dim1; i++) {
        for (int j = 0; j<4; j++)
            cout << ' ' << m[i][j];
        cout << '\n';
    }
}
```

The difficult case is when both dimensions need to be passed. The "obvious solution" simply does not work:

```
void print_mij(int m[][], int dim1, int dim2)  // error
{
    for (int i = 0; i<dim1; i++) {
        for (int j = 0; j<dim2; j++)
            cout << ' ' << m[i][j];      // surprise!
        cout << '\n';
    }
}
```

First, the argument declaration `m[][]` is illegal because the second dimension of a multidimensional array must be known to find the location of an element. Second, the expression `m[i][j]` is (correctly) interpreted as `*(*(m+i)+j)`, but that is unlikely to be what the programmer intended. A correct solution is:

```
void print_mij(int** m, int dim1, int dim2)
{
    for (int i = 0; i<dim1; i++) {
        for (int j = 0; j<dim2; j++)
            cout << ' ' << ((int*)m)[i*dim2+j]; // obscure
        cout << '\n';
    }
}
```

The expression used for accessing the members is equivalent to the one the compiler generates when it knows the last dimension. An extra variable could be introduced to make the code slightly less obscure:

```
int* v = (int*)m;
// ...
v[i*dim2+j]
```

Preferably, this kind of messy code is hidden. Providing a multi-dimensional array type with a proper subscripting operator saves most users from having to worry about the layout of the data in the array; see Exercise 18 in §7.13.

4.6.6 Overloaded Function Names

Most often, it is a good idea to give different functions different names, but when some functions perform the same task on objects of different types, it can be more convenient to give them the same name. Using the same name for different operations on different types is called *overloading*. The technique is already used for the basic operations in C++: There is only one name for addition, +, and yet it can be used to add values of integer, floating-point, and pointer types. This idea is easily extended to handle operations defined by the programmer, that is, functions. For example:

```
void print(int);         // print an int
void print(const char*); // print a character string
```

As far as the compiler is concerned, the only thing functions of the same name have in common is that name. Presumably, the functions are in some sense similar, but the language does not constrain or aid the programmer. Thus overloaded function names are primarily a notational convenience. This convenience is significant for functions with conventional names such as `sqrt`, `print`, and `open`. When a name is semantically significant, as with operators such as +, *, and << (§7.2), and in the case of constructors (§5.2.4 and §7.3.1), this convenience becomes essential. When a function `f` is called, the compiler must figure out which of the functions with the name `f` is to be invoked. This is done by comparing the types of the actual arguments with the types of the formal arguments of all functions called `f`. The idea is to invoke the function that is the best match on the arguments and give a compile time error if no function is the best match. For example:

```
void print (double);
void print (long);

void f ()
{
    print (1L);    // print (long)
    print (1.0);   // print (double)
    print (1);     // error, ambiguous:
                   // print (long (1)) or print (double (1))?
}
```

The detailed argument matching rules are explained in §r.13.2. Here, a simplified version suffices. These rules are applied in order:
[1] Exact match; that is, match using no or only unavoidable conversions (for example, array name to pointer, function name to pointer to function, and T to const T).
[2] Match using integral promotions (as defined in §r.4.1, that is, char to int, short to int, and their unsigned counterparts) and float to double.
[3] Match using standard conversions (as defined in §r.4, for example, int to double, derived* to base*, unsigned int to int).
[4] Match using user-defined conversions (§r.12.3).
[5] Match using the ellipsis ... in a function declaration.
If two matches are found at the highest level where a match is found, the call is rejected as ambiguous. The resolution rules are this elaborate primarily to take account of the elaborate C and C++ rules for numeric types. For example, using all the declarations of `print ()` above we can write:

```
void print (int);
void print (const char*);
void print (double);
void print (long);
void print (char);
```

```
void h(char c, int i, short s, float f)
{
    print(c);     // exact match: invoke print(char)
    print(i);     // exact match: invoke print(int)
    print(s);     // integral promotion: invoke print(int)
    print(f);     // integral promotion: invoke print(double)

    print('a');   // exact match: invoke print(char)
    print(49);    // exact match: invoke print(int)
    print(0);     // exact match: invoke print(int)
    print("a");   // exact match: invoke print(const char*)
}
```

The call print(0) invokes print(int) because 0 is an int. The call print('a') invokes print(char) because 'a' is a char (§r.2.5.2).

Note that the overloading resolution is independent of the order of declaration of the functions considered and that the return types of the functions are not considered.

Given these rules, one can ensure that the simplest algorithm (function) will be used when the efficiency or precision of computations differs significantly for the types involved. For example:

```
int pow(int, int);
double pow(double, double);       // from <math.h>
complex pow(double, complex);     // from <complex.h>
complex pow(complex, int);
complex pow(complex, double);
complex pow(complex, complex);


void k(complex z)
{
    int i = pow(2,2);         // invoke pow(int,int)
    double d = pow(2.0,2);    // invoke pow(double,double
    complex z2 = pow(2,z);    // invoke pow(double,complex)
    complex z3 = pow(z,2);    // invoke pow(complex,int)
    complex z4 = pow(z,z);    // invoke pow(complex,complex)
}
```

4.6.7 Default Arguments

A function often needs more arguments in the general case than are needed in the simplest, and often most frequent, case. This is particularly common for functions that construct objects (for example, constructors; see §5.2.4). Such functions often provide several options for flexibility. Consider a function for printing an integer. Giving the user an option of what base to print it in seems reasonable, but in most programs integers will be printed as decimal integer values.

```
void print (int value, int base =10);

void f ()
{
    print (31);
    print (31,10);
    print (31,16);
    print (31,2);
}
```

might produce this output:

```
31  31  1f  11111
```

The effect of a default argument can alternatively be achieved by overloading:

```
void print (int value, int base);
inline void print (int value) { print (value,10); }
```

However, in this case it is not so obvious to the reader that the intent is to have a single print function plus a shorthand.

A default argument is type checked at the time of the function declaration and evaluated at the time of the call. It is possible to provide default arguments for trailing arguments only, so

```
int f (int, int =0, char* =0);     // ok
int g (int =0, int =0, char*);     // error
int h (int =0, int, char* =0);     // error
```

Note that the space between the * and the = is significant in this context (*= is an assignment operator):

```
int nasty (char*=0);               // syntax error
```

4.6.8 Unspecified Number of Arguments

For some functions, it is not possible to specify the number and type of all arguments expected in a call. Such a function is declared by terminating the list of argument declarations with the ellipsis (. . .), which means ''and maybe some more arguments.'' For example:

```
int printf (const char* ...);
```

This specifies that a call of printf must have at least one argument, a char*, but may or may not have others. For example:

```
printf ("Hello, world\n");
printf ("My name is %s %s\n", first_name, second_name);
printf ("%d + %d = %d\n",2,3,5);
```

Such a function must rely on information not available to the compiler when interpreting its argument list. In the case of printf(), the first argument is a format string containing special character sequences that allow `printf()` to handle other arguments correctly; `%s` means "expect a `char*` argument" and `%d` means "expect an `int` argument;" see also §10.6. However, the compiler does not know that, so it cannot ensure that the expected arguments are really there, or that an argument is of the proper type. For example:

```
printf("My name is %s %s\n",2);
```

will compile and (at best) cause some strange looking output (try it!).

Clearly, if an argument has not been declared, the compiler does not have the information needed to perform the standard type checking and type conversion for it. In this case, a `char` or a `short` is passed as an `int`, and a `float` is passed as a `double`. This is not necessarily what the user expects.

A well-designed program needs at most a few functions for which the argument types are not completely specified. Overloaded functions and functions using default arguments can be used to take care of type checking in most cases when one would otherwise consider leaving argument types unspecified. Only when both the number of arguments *and* the type of arguments vary is the ellipsis necessary. The most common use of the ellipsis is to specify an interface to C library functions that were defined when the alternatives were not available:

```
extern "C" int fprintf(FILE*, const char* ...);
extern "C" int execl(const char* ...);
```

A standard set of macros available for accessing the unspecified arguments in such functions can be found in `<stdarg.h>`. Consider writing an error function that takes one integer argument indicating the severity of the error followed by an arbitrary number of strings. The idea is to compose the error message by passing each word as a separate string argument:

```
extern void error(int ...);
extern char* itoa(int);

main(int argc, char* argv[])
{
    switch (argc) {
    case 1:
        error(0,argv[0],(char*)0);
        break;
    case 2:
        error(0,argv[0],argv[1],(char*)0);
        break;
    default:
        error(1,argv[0],
                "with",itoa(argc-1),"arguments",(char*)0);
    }
    // ...
}
```

The function itoa() returns the character string representing its integer argument. The error function could be defined like this:

```
#include <stdarg.h>

void error(int severity ...)
/*
    "severity" followed by a zero-terminated list of char*s
*/
{
    va_list ap;
    va_start(ap,severity);          // arg startup

    for (;;) {
        char* p = va_arg(ap,char*);
        if (p == 0) break;
        cerr << p << ' ';
    }

    va_end(ap);                     // arg cleanup

    cerr << '\n';
    if (severity) exit(severity);
}
```

First a va_list is defined and initialized by a call of va_start(). The macro va_start takes the name of the va_list and the name of the last formal argument as arguments. The macro va_arg() is used to pick the unnamed arguments in order. In each call the programmer must supply a type; va_arg() assumes that an actual argument of that type has been passed, but it typically has no way of ensuring that. Before returning from a function in which va_start() has been used, va_end() must be called. The reason is that va_start() may modify the stack in such a way that a return cannot successfully be done; va_end() undoes any such modifications.

The casts of the 0 to (char*)0 are necessary because sizeof(int) need not be the same as sizeof(char*). This illustrates the subtleties that face the programmer once type checking has been suppressed using the ellipsis.

4.6.9 Pointer to Function

There are only two things one can do to a function: call it and take its address. The pointer obtained by taking the address of a function can then be used to call the function. For example:

```
void error(char* p) { /* ... */ }

void (*efct)(char*);                // pointer to function

void f()
{
    efct = &error;                  // efct points to error
    (*efct)("error");               // call error through efct
}
```

To call a function through a pointer – for example, efct, – one must first dereference the pointer, *efct. Because the function call operator () has higher precedence than the dereference operator * has, one cannot just write *efct("error");
that means *(efct("error")), which is a type error. The same applies to the
declaration syntax. One can, however, write plain efct("error"), and the compiler will discover that efct is a pointer and call the function pointed to correctly.

Note that pointers to functions have argument types declared just like the functions themselves. In pointer assignments, the complete function type must match
exactly. For example:

```
void (*pf)(char*);        // pointer to void(char*)
void f1(char*);           // void(char*);
int  f2(char*);           // int(char*);
void f3(int*);            // void(int*);

void f()
{
    pf = &f1;             // ok
    pf = &f2;             // error: bad return type
    pf = &f3;             // error: bad argument type

    (*pf)("asdf");        // ok
    (*pf)(1);             // error: bad argument type

    int i = (*pf)("qwer"); // error: void assigned to int
}
```

The rules for argument passing are the same for calls directly to a function and for
calls to a function through a pointer.

It is often convenient to define a name for a pointer-to-function type to avoid
using the somewhat nonobvious syntax all the time. For example:

```
typedef int (*SIG_TYP)(int);        // from <signal.h>
typedef void (*SIG_ARG_TYP)(int);
SIG_TYP signal(int, SIG_ARG_TYP);
```

An array of pointers to functions is often useful. For example, the menu system
for my mouse-based editor is implemented using arrays of pointers to functions to
represent operations. The system cannot be described in detail here, but this is the

general idea:

```
typedef void (*PF)();

PF edit_ops[] = { // edit operations
    &cut, &paste, &snarf, &search
};

PF file_ops[] = { // file management
    &open, &reshape, &close, &write
};
```

Then define and initialize the pointers that define actions selected from a menu associated with the mouse buttons:

```
PF* button2 = edit_ops;
PF* button3 = file_ops;
```

In a complete implementation, more information is needed to define each menu item. For example, a string specifying the text to be displayed must be stored somewhere. As the system is used, the meaning of mouse buttons changes frequently with the context. Such changes are performed (partly) by changing the value of the button pointers. When a user selects a menu item, such as item 3 for button 2, the associated operation is executed:

```
(*button2[3])();
```

One way to gain appreciation of the expressive power of pointers to functions is to try to write such code without them. A menu can be modified at runtime by inserting new functions into the operator table. It is also easy to construct new menus at runtime.

Pointers to functions can be used to provide polymorphic routines, that is, routines that can be applied to objects of many different types:

```
typedef int (*CFT)(void*,void*);

void sort(void* base, unsigned n, unsigned int sz, CFT cmp)
/*
    Sort the "n" elements of vector "base"
    into increasing order
    using the comparison function pointed to by "cmp".
    The elements are of size "sz".

    Very inefficient algorithm: bubble sort
*/
{
```

```
    for (int i=0; i<n-1; i++)
        for (int j=n-1; i<j; j--) {
            char* pj = (char*)base+j*sz;    // b[j]
            char* pj1 = pj-sz;              // b[j-1]
            if ((*cmp)(pj,pj1) < 0) {
                // swap b[j] and b[j-1]:
                for (int k=0; k<sz; k++) {
                    char temp = pj[k];
                    pj[k] = pj1[k];
                    pj1[k] = temp;
                }
            }
        }
}
```

The `sort()` routine does not know the type of the objects it sorts, only the number
of elements (the array size), the size of each element, and the function to call to perform a comparison. The type of `sort()` was chosen to be the same as the type of
the standard C library sort routine, `qsort()`. Real programs use `qsort()`. Such a
sort function could be used to sort a table such as this:

```
struct user {
    char* name;
    char* id;
    int dept;
};

typedef user* Puser;

user heads[] = {
    "Ritchie D.M",      "dmr",    11271,
    "Sethi R.",         "ravi",   11272,
    "Szymanski T.G.",   "tgs",    11273,
    "Schryer N.L.",     "nls",    11274,
    "Schryer N.L.",     "nls",    11275,
    "Kernighan B.W.",   "bwk",    11276
};

void print_id(Puser v, int n)
{
    for (int i=0; i<n; i++)
        cout << v[i].name << '\t'
             << v[i].id << '\t'
             << v[i].dept << '\n';
}
```

To be able to sort, one must first define appropriate comparison functions. A
comparison function must return a negative value if its first argument is less than the
second, zero if they are equal, and a positive number otherwise:

```
int cmp1(const void* p, const void* q)   // Compare name strings
{
    return strcmp(Puser(p)->name, Puser(q)->name);
}


int cmp2(const void* p, const void* q)   // Compare dept numbers
{
    return Puser(p)->dept - Puser(q)->dept;
}
```

This program sorts and prints:

```
int main()
{
    sort(heads,6,sizeof(user),cmp1);
    print_id(heads,6);      // in alphabetical order
    cout << "\n";
    sort(heads,6,sizeof(user),cmp2);
    print_id(heads,6);      // in department number order
}
```

It is possible to take the address of an `inline` function, and also to take the address of an overloaded function (§r.13.3).

Note that the implicit conversion of a pointer to something to a `void*` does not take place for argument types of a pointer to function used as an argument. This means that

```
int cmp3(const mytype*,const mytype*);
```

is not a suitable argument for `sort()`. The reason is that accepting `cmp3` as an argument to `sort()` would violate the guarantee that `cmp3` will be called with arguments of type `mytype*`. If you want to violate that guarantee you'll have to use explicit type conversion.

4.7 Macros

Macros are defined in §r.16. They are very important in C but have far fewer uses in C++. The first rule is: Don't use them if you don't have to. It has been observed that almost every macro demonstrates a flaw in the programming language, in the program, or in the programmer. Because they rearrange the program text before the compiler proper sees it, macros are also a major problem for many programming tools, so when you use macros you should expect inferior service from tools such as debuggers, cross reference tools, and profilers. If you must use macros, please read the reference manual for your own implementation of the C++ preprocessor very carefully first, and try not to be too clever.

A simple macro is defined like this:

```
#define name rest of line
```

When name is encountered as a token, it is replaced by `rest of line`. For example,

```
named = name
```

will be expanded into

```
named = rest of line
```

A macro can also be defined to take arguments. For example:

```
#define mac(a,b) argument1: a argument2: b
```

When `mac` is used, two argument strings must be presented. They will replace a and b when `mac()` is expanded. For example,

```
expanded = mac(foo bar, yuk yuk)
```

will be expanded into

```
expanded = argument1: foo bar argument2: yuk yuk
```

Macro names cannot be overloaded, and recursive calls give the macro processor a problem it cannot handle well:

```
// error:
#define print(a,b) cout<<(a)<<(b)
#define print(a,b,c)  cout<<(a)<<(b)<<(c)

//trouble:
#define fac(n) (n>1)?n*fac(n-1):1
```

Macros manipulate strings and know little about C++ syntax and nothing about C++ types or scope rules. Only the expanded form of a macro is seen by the compiler, so an error in a macro will be reported when the macro is expanded, not when it is defined. This leads to very obscure error messages.

Here are some plausible macros:

```
#define Case break;case
#define forever for(;;)
```

Here are some completely unnecessary macros:

```
#define PI 3.141593
#define BEGIN {
#define END }
```

Here are some examples of dangerous macros:

```
#define SQUARE(a) a*a
#define INCR_xx (xx)++
#define DISP = 4
```

To see why they are dangerous, try expanding this:

```
int xx = 0;                    // global counter

void f() {
    int xx = 0;                // local variable
    xx = SQUARE(xx+2);         // xx = xx+2*xx+2;
    INCR_xx;                   // increments local xx
    if (a-DISP==b) {           // a-= 4==b
        // ...
    }
}
```

If you must use a macro, use the scope resolution operator : : when referring to global names (§2.1.1), and enclose occurrences of a macro argument name in parentheses whenever possible. For example:

```
#define MIN(a,b)  (((a)<(b))?(a):(b))
```

If you must write macros complicated enough to require comments, it is wise to use /* */ comments because C preprocessors that do not know about // comments are sometimes used for C++. For example:

```
#define m2(a) something(a)        /* thoughtful comment */
```

Using macros, you can design your own private language; it will most likely be incomprehensible to others. Furthermore, the C preprocessor is a very simple macro processor. When you try to do something nontrivial, you are likely to find it either impossible or unnecessarily hard to do. The const, inline, and template mechanisms are intended as alternatives to many traditional uses of preprocessor constructs. For example:

```
const int answer = 42;
template<class T>
    inline T min(T a, T b) { return (a<b)?a:b; }
```

4.8 Exercises

1. (*1) Write declarations for the following: a function taking arguments of type pointer to character and reference to integer and returning no value; a pointer to such a function; a function taking such a pointer as an argument; and a function returning such a pointer. Write the definition of a function that takes such a pointer as argument and returns its argument as the return value. Hint: Use typedef.

2. (*1) What does the following mean? What would it be good for?

```
typedef int (rifii&) (int, int);
```

3. (*1.5) Write a program like "Hello, world" that takes a name as a command line

argument and writes ''Hello, *name*''. Modify this program to take any number of names as arguments and say hello to each.

4. (∗1.5) Write a program that reads an arbitrary number of files whose names are given as command line arguments and writes them one after another on cout. Because this program concatenates its arguments to produce its output, you might call it cat.

5. (∗2) Convert a small C program to C++. Modify the header files to declare all functions called and to declare the type of every argument. Where possible, replace #defines with enum, const, or inline. Remove extern declarations from .c files and convert to C++ function definition syntax. Replace calls of malloc() and free() with new and delete. Remove unnecessary casts.

6. (∗2) Implement sort() (§4.6.9) using a more efficient sorting algorithm.

7. (∗2) Look at the definition of struct tnode in §r.9.3. Write a function for entering new words into a tree of tnodes. Write a function to write out a tree of tnodes. Write a function to write out a tree of tnodes with the words in alphabetical order. Modify tnode so that it stores (only) a pointer to an arbitrarily long word stored on free store using new. Modify the functions to use the new definition of tnode.

8. (∗1) Implement the itoa() function used in §4.6.8.

9. (∗2) Know your standard header files. List the files in /usr/include and /usr/include/CC (or wherever the standard header files are kept on your system). Read any that look interesting.

10. (∗2) Write a function to invert a two dimensional array.

11. (∗2) Write an encryption program that reads from cin and writes the encoded characters to cout. You might use this simple encryption scheme: The encrypted form of a character c is c^key[i], where key is a string passed as a command line argument. The program uses the characters in key in a cyclic manner until all the input has been read. Re-encrypting encoded text with the same key produces the original text. If no key (or a null string) is passed, then no encryption is done.

12. (∗3) Write a program to help decipher messages encrypted with the method described above without knowing the key. Hint: See David Kahn: *The Codebreakers*, Macmillan, 1967, New York, pp. 207-213.

13. (∗3) Write an error function that takes a printf-style format string containing %s, %c, and %d directives and an arbitrary number of arguments. Don't use printf(). Look at §10.6 if you don't know the meaning of %s etc. Use <stdarg.h>.

14. (∗1) How would you choose names for pointer to function types defined using typedef?

15. (∗2) Look at some programs to get an idea of the diversity of styles of names actually used. How are uppercase letters used? How is the underscore used? When are short names such as i and x used?

16. (∗1) What is wrong with these macro definitions?

```
#define PI = 3.141593;
#define MAX(a,b)  a>b?a:b
#define fac(a)  (a)*fac((a)-1)
```

17. (*3) Write a macro processor that defines and expands simple macros (like the C preprocessor does). Read from cin and write to cout. At first, don't try to handle macros with arguments. Hint: The desk calculator (§3.1) contains a symbol table and a lexical analyzer that you could modify.

18. (*2) Write a program that calculates the square root of two by calling the standard C library function sqrt(). Do not include the C++ <math.h>. Do exercise again, but call a Fortran square root function.

19. (*2) Implement print() from §4.6.7.

5

Classes

Those types are not "abstract";
they are as real as int *and* float.
– Doug McIlroy

This chapter describes C++'s facilities for defining new types for which access to data is restricted to a specific set of access functions. The ways in which a data structure can be protected, initialized, accessed, and finally cleaned up are explained. Examples include simple classes for symbol table management, stack manipulation, set manipulation, and implementation of a discriminating (that is, "safe") union. The following three chapters will complete the description of C++'s facilities for creating new types and provide more interesting examples.

5.1 Introduction and Overview

The aim of the C++ class concept, as described in this and the following three chapters, is to provide the programmer with a tool for creating new types that can be used as conveniently as the built-in types. Ideally, a user-defined type should not differ from built-in types in the way it is used, only in the way it is created.

A type is the concrete representation of an idea or concept. For example, the C++ type float with its operations +, −, *, etc., provides a restricted, but concrete, version of the mathematical concept of a real number. The reason for designing a new type is to provide a concrete and specific definition of a concept that has no direct and obvious counterpart among the built-in types. For example, one might provide a type trunk_module in a program dealing with telephony, an explosion type for a videogame, or a type list_of_paragraphs for a text processing program. A program that provides types that closely match the concepts of the application is typically easier to understand and easier to modify than a program that does not. A well-chosen set of user-defined types makes a program more concise; it also enables the compiler to detect illegal uses of objects that otherwise would not be detected until the program is tested.

The fundamental idea in defining a new type is to separate the incidental details of the implementation (for example, the layout of the data used to store an object of the type) from the properties essential to the correct use of it (for example, the complete list of functions that can access the data). Such a separation can be expressed by channeling all use of the data structure and internal housekeeping routines through a specific interface.

This chapter consists of four parts:

§5.2 *Classes and Members.* This section introduces the basic notion of a user-defined type called a `class`. Access to objects of a class can be restricted to a set of functions declared as part of the class; such functions are called member functions and friends. Objects of a class are created and initialized by member functions specifically declared for that purpose; such functions are called constructors. A member function can be specifically declared to ''clean up'' objects of a class when they are destroyed; such a function is called a destructor.

§5.3 *Interfaces and Implementations.* This section presents two examples of how a class can be designed, implemented, and used.

§5.4 *Minor Class Features.* This section presents many additional details about classes. It shows how access to private parts of a class can be granted to a function that is not a member of that class (a `friend`). The notions of static class members and pointers to members are presented. This section also shows how to define a discriminating union.

§5.5 *Construction and Destruction.* An object can be created as an automatic, a static, or as an object on the free store. An object can also be a member of some aggregate (an array or class type), which in turn can be allocated in one of those three ways. The use of constructors and destructors is explained in some detail, and the use of user-defined free store allocators and deallocators is described.

5.2 Classes and Members

A `class` is a user-defined type. This section introduces the basic facilities for defining a class, creating objects of a class, manipulating such objects, and finally cleaning up such objects after use.

5.2.1 Member Functions

Consider implementing the concept of a date using a `struct` to define the representation of a `date` and a set of functions for manipulating variables of this type:

```
struct date { int month, day, year; };
date today;
void set_date(date*, int, int, int);
void next_date(date*);
void print_date(const date*);
// ...
```

There are no explicit connections between the functions and the data type. Such a connection can be established by declaring the functions as members:

```
struct date {
    int month, day, year;

    void set(int, int, int);
    void get(int*, int*, int*);
    void next();
    void print();
};
```

Functions declared in this way are called member functions and can be invoked only for a specific variable of the appropriate type using the standard syntax for structure member access. For example:

```
date today;
date my_birthday;

void f()
{
    my_birthday.set(30,12,1950);
    today.set(18,1,1991);

    my_birthday.print();
    today.next();
}
```

Because different structures can have member functions with the same name, one must specify the structure name when defining a member function:

```
void date::next()
{
    if ( ++day > 28 ) {
        // do the hard part
    }
}
```

In a member function, member names can be used without explicit reference to an object. In that case, the name refers to that member of the object for which the function was invoked.

5.2.2 Classes

The declaration of date in the previous subsection provides a set of functions for manipulating a date, but it does not specify that those functions should be the only ones to access objects of type date. This restriction can be expressed by using a class instead of a struct:

```
class date {
    int month, day, year;
public:
    void set(int, int, int);
    void get(int*, int*, int*);
    void next();
    void print();
};
```

The public label separates the class body into two parts. The names in the first, *private*, part can be used only by member functions. The second, *public*, part constitutes the interface to objects of the class. A struct is simply a class where members are public by default; member functions can be defined and used exactly as before. For example:

```
void date::print()       // print using US notation
{
    cout << month << '/' << day << '/' << year ;
}
```

However, nonmember functions are barred from using the private members of class date. For example:

```
void backdate()
{
    today.day--;           // error
}
```

There are several benefits to be obtained from restricting access to a data structure to an explicitly declared list of functions. Any error causing a date to take on an illegal value (for example, December 36, 1985) must be caused by code in a member function, so the first stage of debugging, localization, is completed before the program is even run. This is a special case of the general observation that any change to the behavior of the type date can and must be effected by changes to its members. Another advantage is that a potential user of such a type need only examine the definition of the member functions to learn to use it.

The protection of private data relies on restriction of the use of the class member names. It can therefore be circumvented by address manipulation and explicit type conversion, but this, of course, is cheating.

5.2.3 Self-reference

In a member function, one can refer directly to members of the object for which the member function is invoked. For example:

```
class X {
    int m;
public:
    int readm() { return m; }
};


void f(X aa,X bb)
{
    int a = aa.readm();
    int b = bb.readm();
    // ...
}
```

In the first call of the member `readm()`, m refers to `aa.m`, and in the second it refers to `bb.m`.

A pointer to the object for which a member function is invoked constitutes a hidden argument to the function. The implicit argument can be explicitly referred to as `this`. In every function of a class X, the pointer `this` is implicitly declared as

```
X *const this;
```

and initialized to point to the object for which the member function is invoked. Because `this` is declared `*const`, a constant pointer, it cannot be changed. However, the object pointed to can. Because `this` is a keyword, it cannot be explicitly declared. Class X could equivalently be declared like this:

```
class X {
    int m;
public:
    int readm() { return this->m; }
};
```

Using `this` when referring to members is unnecessary; the major use of `this` is for writing member functions that manipulate pointers directly. A typical example of this is a function that inserts a link on a doubly linked list:

```
class dlink {
    dlink* pre; // previous
    dlink* suc; // next
public:
    void append(dlink*);
    // ...
};
```

```
void dlink::append(dlink* p)
{
    p->suc = suc;        // that is, p->suc = this->suc
    p->pre = this;       // explicit use of "this"
    suc->pre = p;        // that is, this->suc->pre = p
    suc = p;             // that is, this->suc = p
}

dlink* list_head;

void f(dlink* a, dlink* b)
{
    // ...
    list_head->append(a);
    list_head->append(b);
}
```

Links of this general nature are the basis for the list classes described in Chapter 8. To append a link to a list, the objects pointed to by `this`, `pre`, and `suc` must be updated. They are all of type `dlink`, so the member function `dlink::append()` can access them. The unit of protection in C++ is a `class`, not an individual object of a class.

A member function can be declared to be able to read but not write the object for which it is called. The promise not to modify the object for which it is called, `*this`, is indicated by a `const` suffix to the argument list. For example:

```
class X {
    int m;
public:
    readme() const { return m; }
    writeme(int i) { m = i; }
};
```

A `const` member function can be called for a `const` object; an ordinary member function cannot:

```
void f(X& mutable, const X& constant)
{
    mutable.readme();        // ok
    mutable.writeme(7);      // ok
    constant.readme();       // ok
    constant.writeme(7);     // error
}
```

In the example above, a clever compiler could notice that `X::writeme()` tried to modify a `const` object. However, it is not easy for a compiler to detect such things; and because of separate compilation, it is not in general possible for a compiler to ensure "constness" without the help of `const` declarations. For example, `readme()` and `writeme()` might have been defined in some other file:

```
class X {
    int m;
public:
    readme() const;
    writeme(int i);
};
```

This makes declaring `readme() const` essential.

The type of `this` in a `const` member function of class X is `const X *const`. This means that you cannot change the value of an object through `this` without an explicit cast:

```
class X {
    int m;
public:
    // ...
    void implicit_cheat() const { m++; } // error
    void explicit_cheat() const { ((X*)this)->m++; } // ok
};
```

The reason one is allowed to "cast away `const`" is that there are two related yet different concepts of constness. The one, which we could call *physical* constness, is simply "stored in read-only memory." The other, which we could call *logical* constness, is "an object appears constant to its users." An operation on a logically const object may actually change some part of the object's state as long as it does so without spoiling the illusion of constness. Caching values, maintaining statistics, and updating use counts in `const` member functions are examples of logical constness.

Logical constness can usually be achieved either by casting away `const`:

```
class calculator1 {
    int cache_val;
    int cache_arg;
    // ...
public:
    int compute(int i) const;
    // ...
};

int calculator1::compute(int i) const
{
    if (i == cache_arg) return cache_val;
    // do it the hard way
    ((calculator1*)this)->cache_arg = i;
    ((calculator1*)this)->cache_val = val;
    return val;
}
```

or by holding a pointer to non-`const` data:

```
struct cache {
    int val;
    int arg;
};

class calculator2 {
    cache* p;
    // ...
public:
    int compute(int i) const;
    // ...
};

int calculator2::compute(int i) const
{
    if (i == p->arg) return p->val;
    // do it the hard way
    p->arg = i;
    p->val = val;
    return val;
}
```

Note that const must be present in both the declaration and the definition of a const member function. Note also that physical constness may be enforced by placement of an object in read-only memory only for classes without constructors (§r.7.1.6).

5.2.4 Initialization

The use of functions such as set_date() to provide initialization for class objects is inelegant and error prone. Because it is nowhere stated that an object must be initialized, a programmer can forget to do so, or (often with equally disastrous results) do so twice. A better approach is to allow the programmer to declare a function with the explicit purpose of initializing objects. Because such a function constructs values of a given type, it is called a constructor. A constructor is recognized by having the same name as the class itself. For example:

```
class date {
    // ...
    date(int, int, int);
};
```

When a class has a constructor, all objects of that class will be initialized. If the constructor requires arguments, they must be supplied:

```
date today = date(23,6,1983);
date xmas(25,12,0);        // abbreviated form
date my_birthday;          // illegal, initializer missing
```

It is often nice to provide several ways of initializing a class object. This can be done by providing several constructors. For example:

```
class date {
    int month, day, year;
public:
    // ...
    date(int, int, int);  // day month year
    date(int, int);       // day month, today's year
    date(int);            // day, today's month and year
    date();               // default date: today
    date(const char*);    // date in string representation
};
```

Constructors obey the same rules for argument types as do other functions (§4.6.6). As long as the constructors differ sufficiently in their argument types the compiler can select the correct one for each use:

```
date today(4);
date july4("July 4, 1983");
date guy("5 Nov");
date now;                  // default initialized
```

The proliferation of constructors in the date example is typical. When designing a class there is always the temptation to add features just because somebody might want them. Deciding on what features are really needed and including only those takes more thought, but typically leads to smaller and more comprehensible programs. One way of reducing the number of related functions is to use default arguments. In the date, each argument can be given a default value interpreted as ''pick the default: today.''

```
class date {
    int month, day, year;
public:
    // ...
    date(int d =0, int m =0, int y =0);
    // ...
};

date::date(int d, int m, int y)
{
    day = d ? d : today.day;
    month = m ? m : today.month;
    year = y ? y : today.year;
    // check that the date is valid
    // ...
}
```

When using an argument value to indicate ''pick the default,'' the value chosen must be outside the set of possible values for the argument. For day and month this is clearly so, but for `year`, zero may not be an obvious choice. Fortunately there is no year zero on the European calendar; 1AD (`year==1`) comes immediately after 1BC (`year==-1`), but this would probably be too subtle for a real program.

An object of a class with no constructors can be initialized by assigning another object of that class to it. This can also be done where constructors have been declared. For example:

```
date d = today; // initialization by assignment
```

In essence, there is a default constructor defined as memberwise copy of objects of the same class. If that default is not wanted for a class `X`, it can be redefined by defining a copy constructor, `X::X(const X&)`. This will be discussed further in §7.6.

5.2.5 Cleanup

More often than not, a user-defined type has a constructor to ensure proper initialization. Many types also need the inverse operation, a *destructor*, to ensure proper cleanup of objects of the type. The name of the destructor for class `X` is `~X()` (''the complement of the constructor''). In particular, many classes use some memory from the free store (see §3.2.6) that is allocated by a constructor and de-allocated by a destructor. For example, here is a conventional stack type that has been completely stripped of error handling to make it shorter:

```
class char_stack {
    int size;
    char* top;
    char* s;
public:
    char_stack(int sz) { top=s=new char[size=sz]; }
    ~char_stack()      { delete[] s; }   // destructor
    void push(char c)  { *top++ = c; }
    char pop()         { return *--top; }
};
```

When a `char_stack` goes out of scope, the destructor will be called:

```
void f()
{
    char_stack s1(100);
    char_stack s2(200);
    s1.push('a');
    s2.push(s1.pop());
    char ch = s2.pop();
    cout << ch << '\n';
}
```

When `f()` is called, the `char_stack` constructor will be called for `s1` to allocate an array of 100 characters and for `s2` to allocate an array of 200 characters; at the return from `f()`, these two arrays will be freed again.

5.2.6 Inline

When programming using classes, it is common to use many small functions. In essence, a function is provided where a traditionally structured program would simply have some typical way of using a data structure; what was a convention becomes a standard recognized by the compiler. This can lead to horrible inefficiencies because the cost of calling a function (though not at all high compared with other languages) is still much higher than the couple of memory references needed for the body of a trivial function.

The `inline` function facility was designed to handle this problem. A member function defined (not just declared) in the class declaration is taken to be inline. This means, for example, that the code generated for the functions using `char_stacks` presented previously does not contain any function calls except the ones used to implement the output operations! In other words, there is no minimum run-time cost to take into account when designing a class; even the tiniest operation can be provided efficiently. This observation invalidates the most commonly stated reason for using public data members.

A member function can also be declared `inline` outside the class declaration. For example:

```
class char_stack {
    int size;
    char* top;
    char* s;
public:
    char pop();
    // ...
};

inline char char_stack::pop()
{
    return *--top;
}
```

Note that it is not allowed to supply different implementations of inline member functions in different source files (§r.7.1.2). Doing that would compromise the notion that a class is a (single) type.

5.3 Interfaces and Implementations

What makes a good class? Something that has a small and well-defined set of operations. Something that can be seen as a "black box" manipulated exclusively through that set of operations. Something whose actual representation could conceivably be modified without affecting the way that set of operations is used. Something one might want more than one of.

Containers of all sorts provide obvious examples: tables, sets, lists, vectors, dictionaries, etc. Such a class will have an insert operation; typically it will also have operations for checking whether a specific member has been inserted; maybe it will have operations for sorting the members; maybe it will have operations for examining all members in some order; and finally, it may also have an operation for removing a member. Container classes typically have constructors and destructors.

5.3.1 Alternative Implementations

As long as the declaration of the public part of a class and the declaration of the member functions remain unchanged, the implementation of a class can be changed without affecting its users. Consider a symbol table like the one used for the desk calculator example in Chapter 3. It is a table of names:

```
struct name {
    char* string;
    name* next;
    double value;
};
```

Here is a version of a class `table`:

```
// file table.h:

class table {
    name* tbl;
public:
    table()   { tbl = 0; }

    name* look(char*, int = 0);
    name* insert(char* s) { return look(s,1); }
};
```

This table differs from the table defined in Chapter 3 in that it is a proper type. One can declare more than one `table`; one can have a pointer to a `table`, etc. For example:

```
#include "table.h"

table globals;
table keywords;
table* locals;

main()
{
    locals = new table;
    // ...
}
```

Here is an implementation of `table::look()` using a linear search through the linked list of names in the table:

```
#include <string.h>

name* table::look(char* p, int ins)
{
    for (name* n = tbl; n; n=n->next)
        if (strcmp(p,n->string) == 0) return n;

    if (ins == 0) error("name not found");

    name* nn = new name;
    nn->string = new char[strlen(p)+1];
    strcpy(nn->string,p);
    nn->value = 1;
    nn->next = tbl;
    tbl = nn;
    return nn;
}
```

Now consider improving class `table` to use hashed lookup as used in the desk calculator example. Doing so is made more difficult by the constraint that code written using the version of class `table` just defined should still be valid without modification:

```
class table {
    name** tbl;
    int size;
public:
    table(int sz = 15);
    ~table();

    name* look(char*, int =0);
    name* insert(char* s) { return look(s,1); }
};
```

The data structure and the constructor were changed to reflect the need for a specific size of a table when hashing is used. Providing the constructor with a default argument ensures that old code that did not specify a table size is still correct. Default arguments are useful in situations when one must change a class without affecting old code. The constructor and destructor now handle the creation and deletion of hash tables:

```
table::table(int sz)
{
    if (sz < 0) error("negative table size");
    tbl = new name*[size = sz];
    for (int i = 0; i<sz; i++) tbl[i] = 0;
}
```

```
table::~table()
{
    for (int i = 0; i<size; i++) {
        name* nx;
        for (name* n = tbl[i]; n; n=nx) {
            nx = n->next;
            delete n->string;
            delete n;
        }
    }
    delete tbl;
}
```

A simpler and cleaner version of `table::~table()` can be obtained by declaring a destructor for class name. The lookup function is almost identical to the one used in the desk calculator example (§3.1.3):

```
name* table::look(const char* p, int ins)
{
    int ii = 0;
    char* pp = p;
    while (*pp) ii = ii<<1 ^ *pp++;
    if (ii < 0) ii = -ii;
    ii %= size;

    for (name* n=tbl[ii]; n; n=n->next)
        if (strcmp(p,n->string) == 0) return n;

    if (ins == 0) error("name not found");

    name* nn = new name;
    nn->string = new char[strlen(p)+1];
    strcpy(nn->string,p);
    nn->value = 1;
    nn->next = tbl[ii];
    tbl[ii] = nn;
    return nn;
}
```

Clearly, the member functions of a class must be recompiled whenever a change is made to the class declaration. Ideally, such a change would not affect users of the class at all. Unfortunately, this is not so. To allocate a variable of a class type, the compiler needs to know the size of an object of the class. If the size of such objects is changed, files that contain uses of the class must be recompiled. Software that determines the (minimal) amount of information that needs recompiling after a change to a class declaration can be (and has been) written but is not yet in widespread use.

Why, you may ask, was C++ designed in such a way that recompilation of users of a class is necessary after a change to the private part? And why indeed need the private part be present in the class declaration at all? In other words, since users of a class are not allowed to access the private members, why must their declarations be present in the header files the user is supposed to read? The answer is run-time *efficiency*. On many systems, both the compilation process and the sequence of operations implementing a function call are simpler when the size of automatic objects (objects on the stack) is known at compile time.

This problem could be avoided by representing every class object as a pointer to the ''real'' object. Because all such pointers would have the same size, and the allocation of the ''real'' objects could be defined in a file where the private part is available, this would solve the problem. However, this solution imposes a per-object space overhead, an extra memory reference when accessing class members, and worse, involves at least one invocation of the free store allocation and de-allocation routines for each call of a function with an automatic class object. It would also make the implementation of inline member functions that access private data infeasible. Furthermore, such a change would make it impossible to link C++ and C program fragments together (because a C compiler would treat a `struct` in a different way from the way a C++ compiler would). This was deemed unsuitable for C++.

On the other hand, C++ does provide the mechanisms needed to implement abstract types with a looser coupling between the user interface and the implementation. Chapter 6 explains derived classes and abstract base classes and §13.3 explains how to use those mechanisms to implement abstract types. The idea is to provide the most efficient and concrete user-defined types as the default and also the key mechanisms to allow the user to specify more flexible yet (locally) less efficient alternatives.

5.3.2 A Complete Class

Programming without data hiding (using structures) requires less forethought than programming with it (using classes). One can define a structure without too much thought about how it is supposed to be used; but when defining a class, one tends to focus on providing a complete set of operations for the new type; this is an important shift in emphasis. The time spent designing a new type is typically recovered many times over in the development and testing of a program.

Here is an example of a complete type, `intset`, providing the concept ''set of integers:''

```
class intset {
    int cursize, maxsize;
    int *x;
public:
    intset(int m, int n);      // at most m ints in 1..n
    ~intset();
```

```
        int member(int t) const;  // is "t" a member?
        void insert(int t);       // add "t" to set

        void start(int& i) const  { i = 0; }
        int ok(int& i) const      { return i<cursize; }
        int next(int& i) const    { return x[i++]; }
};
```

To test this class we can create and then print a set of random integers. Such a set might constitute a drawing of a lottery. This simple set could also be used to check a sequence of integers for duplicates, but for most applications the set type would have to be a bit more elaborate. As always, errors are possible:

```
#include <iostream.h>

void error(const char *s)
{
    cerr << "set: " << s << '\n';
    exit(1);
}
```

Class intset is used by a main() expecting two integer arguments. The first argument specifies the number of random numbers to be generated. The second argument specifies the range the random integers will be expected in:

```
int main(int argc, char *argv[])
{
    if (argc != 3) error("two arguments expected");
    int count = 0;
    int m = atoi(argv[1]);        // number of set members
    int n = atoi(argv[2]);        // in the range 1..n
    intset s(m,n);

    while (count<m) {
        int t = randint(n);
        if (s.member(t)==0) {
            s.insert(t);
            count++;
        }
    }

    print_in_order(&s);
}
```

The reason that the argument count, argc, has to be 3 for a program requiring two arguments is that the name of the program is always passed as argv[0]. The function

```
    extern "C" int atoi(const char*);
```

is a standard library function for converting the string representation of an integer into

its internal (binary) form. As ever, if you don't like to see the explicit extern "C"
specification you should #include the proper header instead of writing out individual declarations of standard library functions. The random numbers are generated
using the standard function rand ():

```
extern "C" int rand();   // Not too random: beware


int randint(int u)       // in the range 1..u
{
    int r = rand();
    if (r < 0) r = -r;
    return 1 + r%u ;
}
```

The implementation details of a class should be of little interest to a user, but here are
the member functions anyway. The constructor allocates an integer array of the specified maximum set size and the destructor de-allocates it:

```
intset::intset(int m, int n)        // at most m ints in 1..n
{
    if (m<1 || n<m) error("illegal intset size");
    cursize = 0;
    maxsize = m;
    x = new int[maxsize];
}


intset::~intset()
{
    delete x;
}
```

Integers are inserted so that they are kept in increasing order in the set:

```
void intset::insert(int t)
{
    if (++cursize > maxsize) error("too many elements");
    int i = cursize-1;
    x[i] = t;

    while (i>0 && x[i-1]>x[i]) {
        int t = x[i];                    // swap x[i] and [i-1]
        x[i] = x[i-1];
        x[i-1] = t;
        i--;
    }
}
```

A simple binary search is used to find a member:

```
int intset::member(int t) const    //  binary search
{
    int l = 0;
    int u = cursize-1;

    while (l <= u) {
        int m = (l+u)/2;
        if (t < x[m])
            u = m-1;
        else if (t > x[m])
            l = m+1;
        else
            return 1;    // found
    }
    return 0;                        // not found
}
```

Finally, because the representation of an intset is hidden from a user, we must provide a set of operations that allow a user to iterate through the set in some order. A set is not intrinsically ordered, so we cannot simply provide a way of accessing the array (tomorrow, I might reimplement intset as a linked list).

Three functions are provided: start() for initializing an iteration, ok() for checking if there is a next member, and next() for getting the next member:

```
class intset {
    // ...
    void start(int& i) const    { i = 0; }
    int ok(int& i) const        { return i<cursize; }
    int next(int& i) const      { return x[i++]; }
};
```

To allow these three operations to cooperate and to remember how far the iteration has progressed, the user must supply an integer argument. Because the elements are kept in a sorted list, their implementation is trivial. Now the print_in_order function can be defined:

```
void print_in_order(intset* set)
{
    int var;
    set->start(var);
    while (set->ok(var)) cout <<  set->next(var) << '\n';
}
```

An alternative way of providing an iterator is presented in §7.8.

5.4 Minor Class Features

This section describes some more features relating to classes. It presents a way of
granting a nonmember function access to private members (§5.4.1). It describes how
member name conflicts can be resolved (§5.4.2), how class declarations can be nested
(§5.4.3), and how undesirable nesting can be avoided. It introduces the notion of
static members that can be used to represent operations and data that belong to the
class itself rather than to individual objects of the class (§5.4.4). Pointers to members
are introduced (§5.4.5). Finally there is an example showing how one can design a
discriminating (safe) union (§5.4.6).

5.4.1 Friends

Assume that you have defined two classes, vector and matrix. Each hides its
representation and provides a complete set of operations for manipulating objects of
its type. Now define a function multiplying a matrix by a vector. For simplicity,
assume that a vector has four elements, indexed 0..3, and that a matrix has four vectors, indexed 0..3. Assume also that elements of a vector are accessed through a
function elem() and that matrix has a similar function. One approach is to define
a global function multiply() like this:

```
vector multiply(const matrix& m, const vector& v);
{
    vector r;
    for (int i = 0; i<3; i++) { // r[i] = m[i] * v;
        r.elem(i) = 0;
        for (int j = 0; j<3; j++)
            r.elem(i) += m.elem(i,j) * v.elem(j);
    }
    return r;
}
```

This is in some way the "natural" way of doing it, but it may be very inefficient.
Each time multiply() is called, elem() is called 4*(1+4*3) times. If elem()
does proper range checking, this spurious range checking will dominate the run time
of the function and make the function unsuitable for many users. If, on the other
hand, elem() is a special unchecked access function, then we have complicated the
interface to vectors and matrices with a special access function added simply to cir-
cumvent checking.

  If we could make multiply() a member of both class vector and class
matrix, we could dispense with range checking when accessing a matrix element
and still avoid introducing a special elem() function. However, a function cannot
be a member of two classes. What is needed is a language construct that grants a
function access to the private part of a class without requiring membership. A nonmember function that is allowed access to the private part of a class is called a
friend of the class. A function is made a friend of a class by a friend declaration
in that class. For example:

```
class matrix;

class vector {
    float v[4];
    // ...
    friend vector multiply(const matrix&, const vector&);
};


class matrix {
    vector v[4];
    // ...
    friend vector multiply(const matrix&, const vector&);
};
```

There is nothing special about a friend function apart from its right to access the
private part of a class. In particular, a friend function does not have a this
pointer (unless it is a member function in its own right). A friend declaration is a
real declaration. It introduces the name of the function into the scope enclosing the
class in which it was declared a friend and is checked against other declarations of
that name in that scope. A friend declaration can be placed in either the private or
the public part of a class declaration; it does not matter where.

The multiply function can now be written using the elements of the vectors and
the matrix directly:

```
vector multiply(const matrix& m, const vector& v)
{
    vector r;
    for (int i = 0; i<3; i++) { // r[i] = m[i] * v;
        r.v[i] = 0;
        for (int j = 0; j<3; j++)
            r.v[i] += m.v[i][j] * v.v[j];
    }
    return r;
}
```

Note that, like a member function, a friend function is explicitly declared in the
declaration of the class it is a friend of and is thus as much a part of the interface of
that class as a member function is.

A member function of one class can be the friend of another. For example:

```
class x {
    // ...
    void f();
};
```

```
class y {
    // ...
    friend void x::f();
};
```

It is not unusual for all functions of one class to be friends of another. There is even a shorthand for this:

```
class x {
    friend class y;
    // ...
};
```

This friend declaration makes all of **y**'s member functions friends of **x**.

5.4.2 Member Name Qualification

Occasionally, it is useful to distinguish explicitly between class member names and other names. The scope resolution operator : : can be used:

```
class X {
    int m;
public:
    int readm() const { return m; }
    void setm(int m)   { X::m = m; }
};
```

In X::setm() the argument name m hides the member m, so that the member could be referred to using only its qualified name, X::m. The left-hand operand of : : must be the name of a class.

A name prefixed by (just) : : must be a global name. This is particularly useful to enable popular names such as read, put, and open to be used for member function names without losing the ability to refer to the nonmember version. For example:

```
class my_file {
    // ...
public:
    int open(const char*, const char*);
};
```

```
int my_file::open(const char* name, const char* spec)
{
    // ...
    if (::open(name,flag)) { // use the UNIX(2) open()
        // ...
    }
    // ...
}
```

5.4.3 Nested Classes

Class declarations can be nested. For example:

```
class set {
    struct setmem {
        int mem;
        setmem* next;
        setmem(int m, setmem* n) { mem=m; next=n; }
    };
    setmem* first;
public:
    set() { first=0; }
    insert(int m) { first = new setmem(m,first); }
    // ...
};
```

A nested class is hidden in the scope of its lexically enclosing class:

```
setmem m1(1,0); // error setmem not in global scope
```

Unless the nested class is very simple, nested declarations can be messy, so nontrivial classes are often better declared separately:

```
class setmem {
friend class set;          // access by members of set only
    int mem;
    setmem* next;
    setmem(int m, setmem* n) { mem=m; next=n; }

    // many other useful members
};

class set {
    setmem* first;
public:
    set() { first=0; }
    insert(int m) { first = new setmem(m,first); }
    // ...
};
```

Nesting has the advantage of minimizing the number of global names but the disadvantage of hindering unanticipated uses of nested types; see §12.3.

The name of a member class (a nested class) can be accessed from outside its enclosing class just like the name of any other member. For example:

```
class X {
        struct M1 { int m; };
public:
        struct M2 { int m; };

        M1 f(M2);
};

void f()
{
        M1 a;       // error: name 'M1' not in scope
        M2 b;       // error: name 'M1' not in scope
        X::M1 c;    // error: X::M1 private
        X::M2 d;    // ok
}
```

Note that access control applies to names of nested classes.

In member definitions, the scope of the class starts at the X:: qualifier and extends to the end of the declaration. For example:

```
M1 X::f(M2 a)           // error: name 'M1' not in scope
     { /* ... */ }

X::M1 X::f(M2 a)        // ok
     { /* ... */ }

X::M1 X::f(X::M2 a)     // ok, but third X:: is redundant
     { /* ... */ }
```

5.4.4 Static Members

A class is a type, not a data object, and each object of the class has its own copy of the data members of the class. However, some types are most elegantly implemented if all objects of that type share some data. Preferably, such shared data is declared as part of the class. For example, to manage tasks in an operating system or a simulation, a list of all tasks is often useful:

```
class task {
        // ...
        static task* chain;
        // ...
};
```

Declaring the member chain as static ensures that there will be only one copy of it, not one copy per task object. It is still in the scope of class task, however, and can be accessed from "the outside" only if it is declared public. In that case, its name must be qualified by its class name:

```
if (task::chain == 0) // do something
```

In a member function, it can be referred to as plain `task_chain`. The use of `static` class members can considerably reduce the need for global variables.

Declaring a member `static` restricts its scope and makes it independent of the individual objects of the class. This is as useful for function members as for data members:

```
class task {
    // ...
    static task* task_chain;
    static void schedule(int);
    // ...
};
```

A `static` member declaration is only a declaration and the object or function it declares must have a unique definition somewhere in the program. For example:

```
task* task::task_chain = 0;
void task::schedule(int p) { /* ... */ }
```

Naturally, even private members can be defined in this way.

Note that the word `static` is neither necessary nor allowed in the definition of a static class member. Had it been, there would have been a clash between the meaning of `static` as applied to class members and `static` as applied to global objects and functions.

The word `static` is one of the most overused words in C and C++. For `static` data members it has both of the common meanings: `static` as in "statically allocated" as opposed to on the stack or on the free store *and* `static` as in "with restricted visibility" as opposed to with external linkage. For member functions, `static` has only the second meaning.

5.4.5 Pointers to Members

It is possible to take the address of a member of a class. Taking the address of a member function is often useful because the techniques and reasons for using pointers to functions presented in §4.6.9 apply equally to member functions. A *pointer to member* can be obtained by applying the address-of operator `&` to a fully qualified class member name, for example `&class_name::member_name`. A variable of type "pointer to member of class X" can be obtained using a declarator of the form `X::*`. Consider:

```
#include <iostream.h>

struct cl
{
    char* val;
    void  print(int x) { cout << val << x << '\n'; };
    cl(char* v) { val = v; }
};
```

A pointer to member can be declared and used like this:

```
typedef void (cl::*PMFI)(int);

int main()
{
    cl z1("z1 ");
    cl z2("z2 ");
    cl* p = &z2;
    PMFI pf = &cl::print;
    z1.print(1);
    (z1.*pf)(2);
    z2.print(3);
    (p->*pf)(4);
}
```

The use of `typedef` to compensate for the lack of readability of the C declarator syntax is typical. The `.*` and `->*` operators are used to bind a pointer to object to a particular object, thus yielding a function that can be used in a call. The precedence of `()` is higher than that of `.*` and `->*`, so the parentheses are necessary.

In many cases, virtual functions (see §6.2.5) can be used where one would otherwise use pointers to functions.

5.4.6 Structures and Unions

By definition, a `struct` is a class where members are by default public; that is,

```
struct s { ...
```

is simply a shorthand for

```
class s { public: ...
```

A named union is defined as a `struct` where every member has the same address (see §r.9.5). If one knows that only one member of a structure will have a useful value at any one time, a union can save space. For example, one could define a union for holding lexical tokens in a C compiler:

```
union tok_val {
    char* p;                    // string
    char v[8];                  // identifier (max 8 char)
    long i;                     // integer values
    double d;                   // floating-point values
};
```

The problem is that the compiler cannot in general know which member is in use at
any one time, so proper type checking is not possible. For example:

```
void strange(int i)
{
    tok_val x;
    if (i)
        x.p = "2";
    else
        x.d = 2;
    sqrt(x.d);                  // error if i != 0
}
```

Furthermore, a union defined like this cannot be initialized in the way one might consider natural. For example:

```
tok_val val1 = 12;      // error: int assigned to tok_val
tok_val val2 = "12";    // error: char* assigned to tok_val
```

is illegal. Constructors can be used to handle this:

```
union tok_val {
    char* p;        // string
    char v[8];      // identifier (max 8 char)
    long i;         // integer values
    double d;       // floating point values

    tok_val(const char*); // must decide between p and v
    tok_val(int ii)     { i = ii; }
    tok_val(double dd)  { d = dd; }
};
```

This handles cases when the member types can be resolved by the rules for function
name overloading (see §4.6.6 and §7.3). For example:

```
void f()
{
    tok_val a = 10;     // a.i = 10
    tok_val b = 10.0;   // b.d = 10.0
}
```

When this is not possible (for types such as char* and char[8], int and char,
etc.), the proper member can be found only by examining the initializer at run time or
by providing an extra argument. For example:

```
tok_val::tok_val(const char* pp)
{
    if (strlen(pp) <= 8)
        strncpy(v,pp,8);      // short string
    else
        p = pp;               // long string
}
```

Such cases are, in general, better avoided.

The standard function `strncpy()` is used to to copy short strings; `strncpy()` resembles `strcpy()` but takes a third argument indicating the number of characters to be copied.

Using constructors does not prevent accidental misuse of a `tok_val` by assigning a value of one type and then retrieving it as another type. This problem can be solved by embedding the union in a class that keeps track of which type of value is stored:

```
class tok_val {
public:
    enum Tag { I, D, S, N };

private:
    union {
        const char* p;
        char v[8];
        long i;
        double d;
    };

    Tag tag;

    void check(Tag t) { if (tag!=t) error(); }
public:
    Tag get_tag() { return tag; }

    tok_val(const char* pp);
    tok_val(long ii)    { i=ii; tag=I; }
    tok_val(double dd)  { d=dd; tag=D; }

    long& ival()              { check(I); return i; }
    double& fval()            { check(D); return d; }
    const char*& sval() { check(S); return p; }
    char* id()                { check(N); return v; }
};
```

```
tok_val::tok_val(const char* pp)
{
    if (strlen(pp) <= 8) {          // short string
        tag = N;
        strncpy(v,pp,8);            // copy 8 characters
    }
    else {                          // long string
        tag = S;
        p = pp;                     // just store the pointer
    }
}
```

The tok_val class can be used like this:

```
void f()
{
    tok_val t1("short");            // assign to v
    tok_val t2("long string");      // assign to p
    char s[8];
    strncpy(s,t1.id(),8);           // ok
    strncpy(s,t2.id(),8);           // check() will fail
}
```

Making the Tag type and the get_tag() function public ensures that the tok_val type can be used as an argument type. Such types provide a type-safe alternative to some functions declared using the ellipsis. For example, here is a declaration of an error function that can be called with one, two, or three arguments of types char*, int, or double:

```
extern tok_val no_arg;

void error(
    const char* format,
    tok_val a1 = no_arg,
    tok_val a2 = no_arg,
    tok_val a3 = no_arg);
```

5.5 Construction and Destruction

When a class has a constructor, a constructor is called whenever an object of that class is created. When a class has a destructor, the destructor is called whenever an object of that class is destroyed. Objects can be created as

[1] an automatic object, which is created each time its declaration is encountered in the execution of the program and destroyed each time the block in which it occurs is left;

[2] a static object, which is created once at the start of the program and destroyed once at the termination of the program;

[3] a free store object, which is created using the `new` operator and destroyed using the `delete` operator; and

[4] a member object, which is created as a member of another class or as an array element.

An object can also be constructed by explicit use of a constructor in an expression (see §7.3) or as a temporary (§r12.2). In both cases it is an automatic object. In the following subsections it is assumed that objects are of a class with a constructor and a destructor. The class `table` from §5.3.1 is used as an example.

5.5.1 Local Variables

The constructor for a local variable is executed each time the thread of control passes through the declaration of the local variable. The destructor for a local variable is executed each time the local variable's block is exited. Destructors for local variables are executed in reverse order of their construction. For example:

```
void f(int i)
{
        table aa;
        table bb;
        if (i>0) {
                table cc;
                // ...
        }
        // ...
}
```

Here, `aa` and `bb` are constructed (in that order) each time `f()` is called, and `bb` and `aa` are destructed (in that order) each time we return from `f()`. If `i>0` for a call, `cc` will be constructed after and destroyed before `bb`.

Because `aa` and `bb` are objects of a class `table`, `aa=bb` by default means a memberwise copy of `bb` into `aa` (see §2.3.8). Having assignment interpreted this way can cause a surprising (and usually undesired) effect when used on objects of a class for which a destructor has been defined. For example:

```
void h()
{
    table t1(100);
    table t2 = t1;   // trouble
    table t3(200);

    t3 = t2;          // trouble
}
```

Here the `table` constructor is called twice: for `t1` and `t3`. It is not called for `t2` because that variable was initialized by assignment. However, the `table` destructor is called three times: for `t1`, `t2`, and `t3`! Furthermore, the default interpretation of assignment is memberwise copy, so `t1`, `t2`, and `t3` will at the end of `h()` each

contain a pointer to the array of names allocated on the free store when `t1` was created. No pointer to the array of names allocated when `t3` was created will remain.
Such anomalies can be avoided: see §1.4.2 and §7.6.

5.5.2 Static Store

Consider this:

```
table tbl(100);

void f(int i)
{
    static table tbl2(i);
}

int main()
{
    f(200);
    // ...
}
```

Here, the constructor `table::table()` as defined in §5.3.1 will be called twice:
once for `tbl` and once for `tbl2`. The destructor `table::~table()` will also be
called twice: to destroy `tbl` and `tbl2` after exit from `main()`. Constructors for
global static objects in a file are executed in the order in which the declarations occur;
destructors are called in the reverse order. The constructor for a local static object is
called the first time the thread of control passes through the object's definition.

Traditionally, the execution of `main()` has been seen as the execution of the program. This was never so – not even in C – but only by allocating a static object of a
class with a constructor and/or a destructor does the programmer have an obvious and
simple way of specifying code to be executed before and/or after the call of `main()`.

Calling constructors and destructors for static objects serves an extremely important function in C++. It is the way to ensure proper initialization and cleanup of data
structures in libraries. Consider `<iostream.h>`. Where did `cin`, `cout`, and
`cerr` come from? Where did they get initialized? And, most importantly, because
the output streams keep internal buffers of characters, how do these buffers get
flushed? The simple and obvious answer is that the work is done by the appropriate
constructors and destructors before and after the execution of `main()`; see §10.5.1.
There are alternatives to using constructors and destructors for initializing and cleaning up library facilities, but they are all either specialized, ugly, or both.

If a program is terminated using the function `exit()`, the destructors for constructed static objects are called; but if the program is terminated using `abort()`,
they are not. Note that this implies that `exit()` does not terminate a program immediately. Calling `exit()` in a destructor may cause an infinite recursion. If one
wants to ensure that both automatic and static objects are destroyed, exceptions must
be used (§9).

Sometimes when you design a library, it is necessary, or simply convenient, to invent a type with a constructor and a destructor with the sole purpose of initialization and cleanup. Such a type would be used once only: to allocate a static object so that the constructor and the destructor are called.

5.5.3 Free Store

Consider this:

```
main()
{
    table* p = new table(100);
    table* q = new table(200);
    delete p;
    delete p; // probably causes run-time error
}
```

The constructor `table::table()` will be called twice, and so will the destructor `table::~table()`. It is worth noting that C++ offers no guarantee that a destructor is ever called for an object created using `new`. The preceding program never deleted q, but it deleted p twice! Depending on the type of p and q, the programmer may or may not consider this an error. Not deleting an object is typically not an error, only a waste of space. Deleting p twice is a serious error. The result of applying `delete` to the same pointer twice is an infinite loop in my free store management routine, but the behavior is not specified by the language definition and depends on the implementation.

The user can define a new implementation of the `new` and `delete` operators (see §3.2.6 and §6.7). It is also possible to specify the way a constructor or destructor interacts with the `new` and `delete` operators (see §5.5.6 and §6.7.2). Arrays on the free store are discussed in §5.5.5.

5.5.4 Class Objects as Members

Consider

```
class classdef {
    table members;
    int no_of_members;
    // ...
    classdef(int size);
    ~classdef();
};
```

The intention is clearly that a `classdef` should contain a table of members of size `size`, and the problem is to get the constructor `table::table()` called with the argument `size`. It can be done like this:

```
classdef::classdef(int size)
    : members(size)
{
    no_of_members = size;
    // ...
}
```

The arguments for a member constructor (here `table::table()`) are placed in the definition (not in a declaration) of the constructor of the class containing it (here `classdef::classdef()`). The member constructor is then called before the body of the constructor specifying its argument list.

If there are more members needing argument lists for constructors, they can be specified similarly. For example:

```
class classdef {
    table members;
    table friends;
    int no_of_members;
    // ...
    classdef(int size);
    ~classdef();
};
```

The argument lists for the members are separated by commas (not by colons), and the initializer lists for members can be presented in any order:

```
classdef::classdef(int size)
    : friends(size), members(size), no_of_members(size)
{
    // ...
}
```

The constructors are called in the order they are specified in the class declaration.

This style of declaration is essential for types where initialization differs from assignment – that is, for member objects of classes with constructors, for `const` members, and for reference members. However, as shown for `no_of_members` above, it can be used for members of any type.

If a constructor for a member needs no arguments, then no argument list needs to be specified. For example, because `table::table` was defined with a default argument 15, the following is correct:

```
classdef::classdef(int size)
    : members(size), no_of_members(size)
{
    // ...
}
```

and the size of the `friends` table will be 15.

When a class object containing class objects (for example, a `classdef`) is destroyed, the body of that object's own destructor is executed first and then the members' destructors are executed in reverse order of declaration.

Consider the traditional alternative to having class objects as members: to have pointer members and initialize them in a constructor:

```
class classdef {
    table* members;
    table* friends;
    int no_of_members;
    // ...
    classdef(int size);
    ~classdef();
};

classdef::classdef(int size)
{
    members = new table(size);
    friends = new table;          // default table size
    no_of_members = size;
    // ...
}
```

Because the tables were created using `new`, they must be destroyed using `delete`:

```
classdef::~classdef()
{
    // ...
    delete members;
    delete friends;
}
```

Separately created objects like this can be useful, but note that `members` and `friends` point to separate objects that require an allocation and a de-allocation operation each. Furthermore, a pointer plus an object on the free store takes up more space than a member object does.

5.5.5 Arrays of Class Objects

To declare an array of objects of a class with a constructor, that class must have a default constructor, that is, a constructor that can be called with an empty argument list. For example,

```
table tbl[10];
```

will create an array of 10 tables, each initialized by a call to `table::table(15)`, because that is the meaning of `table::table()` given the default argument 15.

There is no way for specifying arguments for a constructor in an array declaration. If it is absolutely necessary to initialize members of an array with different values, games can be played with global or static member variables.

The destructor must be called for each element of an array when that array is

destroyed. This is done implicitly for arrays that are not allocated using new. However, this cannot be done implicitly for arrays on the free store because the compiler
cannot distinguish the pointer to a single object from a pointer to the first element of
an array of objects. For example:

```
void f()
{
    table* t1 = new table;
    table* t2 = new table[10];
    delete t1;   // one table
    delete t2;   // trouble: 10 tables
}
```

In this case the programmer must specify that t2 points to an array:

```
void g(int sz)
{
    table* t1 = new table;
    table* t2 = new table[sz];
    delete t1;
    delete[] t2;
}
```

The allocator holds the number of elements in each array allocated. Requiring the
use of delete[] relieves the allocator of the obligation of having to keep an element count for every object. That obligation would have caused significant time,
space, and C compatibility overheads on C++ implementations.

5.5.6 Small Objects

When using many small objects allocated on the free store, you might find your program consuming considerable time allocating and de-allocating such objects. One
solution is to provide a better general purpose allocator, and another is for the
designer of a class to take over free store management for objects of that particular
class by defining appropriate allocation and deallocation functions.
    Consider class name used in the table examples. It could be defined like this:

```
struct name {
    char* string;
    name* next;
    double value;

    name(char*, double, name*);
    ˜name();
```

```
    void* operator new(size_t);
    void operator delete(void*, size_t);
private:
    enum { NALL = 128 };
    static name* nfree;
};
```

The functions `name::operator new()` and `name::operator delete()`
will be (implicitly) used in preference to the global `operator new()` and
`operator delete()`. The programmer can then take advantage of the fact that
allocating and de-allocating objects of a known type can be handled more efficiently
(in time and space) than with a general implementation of `operator new()` and
`operator delete()`. The idea is to preallocate "chunks" of name objects and
link them together to reduce allocation and de-allocation to simple linked list operations. The variable `nfree` is the head of a list of unused names.

```
void* name::operator new(size_t)
{
    register name* p = nfree;                    // first allocate

    if (p)
        nfree = p->next;
    else {                                        // allocate & link
        name* q = (name*)new char[ NALL*sizeof(name) ];
        for (p=nfree=&q[NALL-1]; q<p; p--) p->next = p-1;
        (p+1)->next = 0;
    }

    return p;
}
```

The allocator used by the `new` operator stores the size of an object with the object in
order for the `delete` operator to function correctly. This space overhead is easily
avoided by using a type-specific allocator. For example, `name::operator`
`new()` uses 16 bytes to store a name on my machine, whereas the standard global
`operator new()` needs 20.

Note that within `name::operator new()` space could not simply be allocated
like this:

```
name* q = new name[NALL];
```

because this would cause infinite recursion when new called `name::name()`.

De-allocation is typically trivial:

```
void name::operator delete(void* p, size_t)
{
    ((name*)p)->next = nfree;
    nfree = (name*) p;
}
```

Casting of the `void*` argument to `name::operator delete()` is necessary because the deallocation function is called after destruction of the object so that we no longer have a proper object of type `name` available, only a `sizeof(name)` sized chunk of memory. The `size_t` arguments to `name::operator delete()` and `name::operator new()` are not used here; they will be explained in §6.7. Note that `name::operator new()` and `name::operator delete()` is used only for objects of type `name` and not for arrays of names.

5.6 Exercises

1. (*1) Modify the desk calculator from Chapter 3 to use class `table`.
2. (*1) Design `tnode` (§r.9.3) as a class with constructors, destructors, etc. Define a tree of `tnode`s as a class with constructors, destructors, etc.
3. (*1) Modify class `intset` (§5.3.2) into a set of strings.
4. (*1) Modify class `intset` into a set of nodes where `node` is a structure you define.
5. (*3) Define a class for analyzing, storing, evaluating, and printing simple arithmetic expressions consisting of integer constants and the operators +, −, *, and /. The public interface should look like this:

   ```
   class expr {
       // ...
   public:
       expr(char*);
       int eval();
       void print();
   };
   ```

   The string argument for the constructor `expr::expr()` is the expression. The function `expr::eval()` returns the value of the expression, and `expr::print()` prints a representation of the expression on `cout`. A program might look like this:

   ```
   expr x("123/4+123*4-3");
   cout << "x = " << x.eval() << "\n";
   x.print();
   ```

   Define class `expr` twice: once using a linked list of nodes as the representation, and once using a character string as the representation. Experiment with different ways of printing the expression: fully parenthesized, postfix notation, assembly code, etc.

6. (∗1) Define a class `char_queue` so that the public interface does not depend on the representation. Implement `char_queue` (1) as a linked list and (2) as a vector. Do not worry about concurrency.
7. (∗2) Define a class `histogram` that keeps count of numbers in some intervals specified as arguments to `histogram`'s constructor. Provide functions to print out the histogram. Handle out of range values. Hint: `<task.h>`.
8. (∗2) Define some classes for providing random numbers of certain distributions. Each class has a constructor specifying parameters for the distribution and a function `draw` that returns the "next" value. Hint: `<task.h>`. See also class `intset`.
9. (∗2) Re-write the `date` example (§5.2.2 and §5.2.4), the `char_stack` example (§5.2.5), and the `intset` example (§5.3.2) without using member functions (not even constructors and destructors). Use `class` and `friend` only. Test each of the new versions. Compare them with the versions using member functions.
10. (∗3) Design a symbol table class and a symbol table entry class for some language. Have a look at a compiler for that language to see what the symbol table really looks like.
11. (∗2) Modify the expression class from Exercise 5 to handle variables and the assignment operator =. Use the symbol table class from Exercise 10.
12. (∗1) Given the program:

```
#include <iostream.h>

main()
{
    cout << "Hello, world\n";
}
```

modify it to produce the output

```
Initialize
Hello, world
Clean up
```

Do not change `main()` in any way.

6

Derived Classes

Do not multiply objects without necessity.
– W.Occam

This chapter describes the C++ concept of derived classes. Derived classes provide a simple, flexible, and efficient mechanism for defining a class by adding facilities to an existing class without reprogramming or recompilation. Using derived classes, one can provide a common interface for several different classes so that objects of those classes can be manipulated identically by other parts of a program. The concept of a virtual function is provided to allow objects to be used appropriately in contexts in which their type cannot be known at compile time. Fundamentally, derived classes exist to make it easier for a programmer to express commonality among classes.

6.1 Introduction and Overview

A concept does not exist in isolation; it co-exists with related concepts and derives much of its power from relationships with related concepts. Since we use classes to represent concepts the issue becomes how to represent relationships between concepts. The notion of a derived class and its associated language mechanisms is provided to express hierarchical relationships, that is, to express commonality between classes. For example, the concepts of a circle and a triangle are related in that they are both shapes; that is, they have the concept of a shape in common. To represent a circle and a triangle in a program without losing the notion of a shape we must explicitly define class `circle` and class `triangle` to have class `shape` in common. This chapter is an exploration of the implications of this simple idea, which is the basis for what is commonly called object-oriented programming.

This chapter consists of six parts:

§6.2 introduces the notions of derived classes, class hierarchies, and virtual functions through a series of small examples.

§6.3 presents the notions of pure virtual functions and abstract classes and presents simple examples of their use.

§6.4 demonstrates the use of derived classes in a complete example.

§6.5 introduces the notion of multiple inheritance – that is, the ability of a class to have more than one direct base class – and presents the mechanisms and techniques for handling the name resolution problems that may occur when multiple inheritance is used.

§6.6 discusses access control mechanisms.

§6.7 presents some techniques for managing free store where derived classes are used.

More examples of these language features and their use can be found in the following chapters.

6.2 Derived Classes

Consider building a program dealing with people employed by a firm. Such a program might have a data structure like this:

```
struct employee {
    char*       name;
    short       age;
    short       department;
    int         salary;
    employee* next;
    // ...
};
```

The next field would be a link in a list of similar employees. Now let us try to define a manager:

```
struct manager {
    employee  emp;      // manager's employee record
    employee* group;    // people managed
    short     level;
    // ...
};
```

A manager is also an employee; the employee data is stored in the emp member of a manager object. This may be obvious to a human reader, but there is nothing that distinguishes the emp member to the compiler. A pointer to a manager (manager*) is not a pointer to an employee (employee*), so one cannot simply use the one where the other is required. In particular, one cannot put a manager onto a list of employees without writing special code. One could either use explicit type conversion on a manager* or put the address of the emp member onto a list of employees, but both are inelegant and can be quite obscure. The correct approach is to state that a manager *is* an employee with a few pieces of information added:

```
struct manager : employee {
    employee* group;
    short      level;
    // ...
};
```

The `manager` is *derived* from `employee`, and conversely, `employee` is a *base class* for `manager`. The class `manager` has the members of class `employee` (name, age, etc.) in addition to the member `group`.

Derivation is often represented graphically by a pointer from the derived class to its base class:

A derived class is often said to inherit from its base, so the relationship is also called *inheritance*. A base class is sometimes called a `superclass` and a derived class a `subclass`. This terminology, however, is confusing to people who observe that an object of a derived class has an object of its base class as a subobject and also that a derived class is larger than its base class in the sense that it holds more data and provides more functions.

With this definition of `employee` and `manager`, we can now create a list of employees, some of whom are managers. For example:

```
void f()
{
    manager m1, m2;
    employee e1, e2;
    employee* elist;
    elist = &m1;        // put m1 on elist
    m1.next = &e1;      // put e1 on elist
    e1.next = &m2;      // put m2 on elist
    m2.next = &e2;      // put e2 on elist
    e2.next = 0;        // terminate elist
}
```

Because a manager is an employee, a `manager*` can be used as a `employee*`. However, an employee is not necessarily a manager, so an `employee*` cannot be used as a `manager*`.

In general, if a class `derived` has a public base class `base`, then a pointer to `derived` can be assigned to a variable of type pointer to `base` without use of explicit type conversion. The opposite conversion, for pointer to `base` to pointer to `derived`, must be explicit. For example:

```
void g()
{
    manager mm;
    employee* pe = &mm;  // ok:
                         // every manager is an employee

    employee ee;
    manager* pm = &ee;   // error:
                         // not every employeee is a manager

    pm->level = 2;       // would be a disaster because ee
                         // doesn't have space allocated
                         // for a 'level'

    pm = (manager*) pe;  // ok: because pe does in fact point
                         // to the manager mm

    pm->level = 2;       // fine: pm points to the manager mm
                         // that has space allocated for
                         // a 'level'
}
```

In other words, an object of a derived class can be treated as an object of its base class when manipulated through pointers. The opposite is not true. Note that the typical C++ implementation has no run-time checks to ensure that type conversions such as the one used to assign pe to pm do in fact leave the result pointing to an object of the expected type (see §13.5).

6.2.1 Member Functions

Simple data structures, such as `employee` and `manager`, are really not that interesting and often not particularly useful, so consider adding functions to them. For example:

```
class employee {
    char* name;
    // ...
public:
    employee* next; // public to allow list manipulation
    void print() const;
    // ...
};
```

```
class manager : public employee {
    // ...
public:
    void print() const;
    // ...
};
```

Some questions must be answered. How can a member function of the derived class manager use members of its base class employee? What members of the base class employee can the member functions of the derived class manager use? What members of the base class employee can a nonmember function use on an object of type manager? In what way can the programmer affect the answer to those questions to suit the application?

Consider:

```
void manager::print() const
{
    cout << " name is " << name << '\n';
    // ...
}
```

A member of a derived class can use a public name of its base class in the same way as other members, that is, without specifying an object. The object pointed to by this is assumed, so name (correctly) refers to this->name. However, the function manager::print() will not compile; a member of a derived class has no special permission to access private members of its base class, so name is not accessible to it.

This comes as a surprise to many, but consider the alternative: that a member function of a derived class could access the private members of its base class. The concept of a private member would be rendered meaningless by a facility that allowed a programmer to gain access to the private part of a class simply by deriving a new class from it. Furthermore, one could no longer find all uses of a private name by looking at the functions declared as members and friends of that class. One would have to examine every source file of the complete program for derived classes, then examine every function of those classes, then find every class derived from these classes, etc. This is at best tedious, and often impractical. Where it is acceptable protected, rather than private, members can be used; see §6.6.1.

Typically, the cleanest solution is for the derived class to use only the public members of its base class. For example:

```
void manager::print() const
{
    employee::print();   // print employee information

    // print manager information
}
```

Note that :: must be used because print() has been redefined in manager. Such reuse of names is typical. The unwary might write this:

```
void manager::print() const
{
    print();    // print employee information

    // print manager information
}
```

and find the program in an unexpected sequence of recursive calls when `manager::print()` is called.

6.2.2 Constructors and Destructors

Some derived classes need constructors. If the base class has a constructor, then that constructor must be called; and if that constructor needs arguments, then such arguments must be provided. For example:

```
class employee {
    // ...
public:
    // ...
    employee(char* n, int d);
};

class manager : public employee {
    // ...
public:
    // ...
    manager(char* n, int l, int d);
};
```

Arguments for the base class's constructor are specified in the definition of a derived class's constructor. In this respect, the base class acts exactly like a member of the derived class. For example:

```
manager::manager(char* n, int l, int d)
    : employee(n,d), level(l), group(0)
{
}
```

The base class constructor `employee::employee()` might look like this:

```
employee::employee(char* n, int d)
    : name(n), department(d)
{
    next = list;
    list = this;
}
```

where `list` is a static member of `employee`.

Class objects are constructed from the bottom up: first the base, then the members, and then the derived class itself. They are destroyed in the opposite order: first the derived class itself, then the members, and then the base. Members and bases are constructed in order of declaration in the class and destroyed in the reverse order.

6.2.3 Class Hierarchies

A derived class can itself be a base class. For example:

```
class employee { /* ... */ };
class manager : public employee { /* ... */ };
class director : public manager { /* ... */ };
```

Such a set of related classes is traditionally called a class hierarchy. Such a hierarchy is most often a tree but can also be a more general graph structure. For example:

```
class temporary { /* ... */ };
class secretary : public employee { /* ... */ };

class tsec
    : public temporary, public secretary { /* ... */ };

class consultant
    : public temporary, public manager { /* ... */ };
```

Thus, as will be explained in detail in §6.5.3, C++ can express a directed acyclic graph of classes. Graphically, the hierarchy defined above can be represented like this:

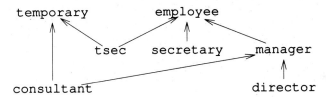

6.2.4 Type Fields

To use derived classes as more than a convenient shorthand in declarations, the following problem must be solved: Given a pointer of type `base*`, to which derived type does the object pointed to really belong? There are three fundamental solutions to the problem:

    [1]   Ensure that only objects of a single type are ever pointed to (§6.4.2);
    [2]   Place a type field in the base class for the functions to inspect; and
    [3]   Use virtual functions (§6.2.5).

    Pointers to base classes are commonly used in the design of *container classes* such as set, vector, and list. In this case, solution 1 yields homogeneous lists, that is, lists of objects of the same type. Solutions 2 and 3 can be used to build heterogeneous lists, that is, lists of (pointers to) objects of several different types. Solution 3 is a special type-secure variation of solution 2. Combinations of solutions 1 and 3 are particularly interesting and powerful; they are described in Chapter 8.

Let us first examine the simple type-field solution, that is, solution 2. The manager/employee example could be redefined like this:

```
struct employee {
        enum empl_type { M, E };
        empl_type type;
        employee* next;
        char*     name;
        short     department;
        // ...
};

struct manager : employee {
        employee* group;
        short     level;
        // ...
};
```

Given this, we can now write a function that prints information about each employee:

```
void print_employee(const employee* e)
{
        switch (e->type) {
        case E:
            cout << e->name << '\t' << e->department << '\n';
            // ...
            break;
        case M:
            cout << e->name << '\t' << e->department << '\n';
            // ...
            manager* p = (manager*)e;
            cout << " level " << p->level << '\n';
            // ...
            break;
        }
}
```

and use it to print a list of employees like this:

```
void f(const employee* elist)
{
        for (; elist; elist=elist->next) print_employee(elist);
}
```

This works fine, especially in a small program written by a single person, but it has the fundamental weakness that it depends on the programmer manipulating types in a way that cannot be checked by the compiler. This typically leads to two kinds of errors in larger programs. The first is failure to test the type field. The second is failure to place all possible cases in a switch such as the one above. Both failures are reasonably easy to avoid when a program is first written, and both are very hard to avoid when modifying a nontrivial program, especially a large program written by someone else. These problems are often made harder to avoid because functions such as `print()` are organized to take advantage of the commonality of the classes involved. For example:

```
void print_employee(const employee* e)
{
    cout << e->name << '\t' << e->department << '\n';
    // ...
    if (e->type == M) {
        manager* p = (manager*)e;
        cout << " level " << p->level << '\n';
        // ...
    }
}
```

Finding all such `if` statements buried in a large function that handles many derived classes can be difficult, and even when they have been found it can be hard to understand what is going on. Furthermore, any addition of a new kind of `employee` involves a change to all the key functions in the system – the ones containing the tests on the type field. This implies the need to access critical source code and the resulting necessary overhead of testing the affected code.

In other words, the type field is an error-prone technique that leads to maintenance problems. The problems increase in severity with the size of a program because the use of a type field causes a violation of the ideals of modularity and data hiding. Each function using a type field must know about the representation and other details of the implementation of every class derived from the one containing the type field.

6.2.5 Virtual Functions

Virtual functions overcome the problems with the type-field solution by allowing the programmer to declare functions in a base class that can be redefined in each derived class. The compiler and loader will guarantee the correct correspondence between objects and functions applied to them. For example:

```
class employee {
    char*    name;
    short    department;
    // ...
    employee* next;
    static employee* list;
public:
    employee(char* n, int d);
    // ...
    static void print_list();
    virtual void print() const;
};
```

The keyword `virtual` indicates that the function `print()` can have different versions for different derived classes and that it is the task of the compiler to find the appropriate one for each call of print (). The type of the function is declared in the base class and cannot be redeclared in a derived class. A virtual function *must* be defined for the class in which it is first declared (unless it is declared to be a pure virtual function; see §6.3). For example:

```
void employee::print() const
{
    cout << name << '\t' << department << '\n';
    // ...
}
```

The virtual function can therefore be used even if no class is derived from its class, and a derived class that does not need a special version of a virtual function need not provide one. When deriving a class, one simply provides an appropriate function if it is needed. For example:

```
class manager : public employee {
    employee* group;
    short      level;
    // ...
public:
    manager(char* n, int l, int d);
    // ...
    void print() const;
};
```

The function print_employee() is now unnecessary because the print() member functions have taken its place. The list of employees was built by the employee constructor (§6.2.2) and can be printed like this:

```
void employee::print_list()
{
    for (employee* p = list; p; p=p->next) p->print();
}
```

Each employee will be written out according to its type. For example:

```
int main()
{
    employee e("J.Brown",1234);
    manager m("J.Smith",2,1234);
    employee::print_list();
}
```

produced:

```
J.Smith 1234
        level 2
J.Brown 1234
```

Note that this will work even if `employee::print_list()` was written and compiled before the specific derived class `manager` was even conceived of! Clearly implementing this involves storing some kind of type information in each object of class `employee`. In a typical implementation, the space taken is just enough to hold a pointer. This space is taken only in objects of a class with virtual functions, not in every class object, or even in every object of a derived class. You pay this overhead only for classes for which you declare virtual functions and had you chosen to use the alternative type field solution a comparable amount of space would have been needed for the type field.

Calling a function using the scope resolution operator `::` as is done in `manager::print()` ensures that the virtual mechanism is not used. Otherwise `manager::print()` would suffer an infinite recursion. The use of a qualified name has another desirable effect: If a `virtual` function is also `inline` (as is not uncommon), then inline substitution can be used where `::` is used in a call. This provides the programmer with an efficient way to handle some important special cases in which one virtual function calls another for the same object. The `manager::print()` function is an example of this. Because the type of the object is determined in the call of `manager::print()`, it need not be dynamically determined again for the resulting call of `employee::print()`.

6.3 Abstract Classes

Many classes resemble class `employee` in that there is a sensible implementation of the virtual functions it defined. However, not all classes follow that pattern. Some classes, such as class `shape`, represent abstract concepts for which objects cannot exist. A `shape` makes sense only as the base of some class derived from it. This can be seen from the fact that it is not possible to provide sensible definitions for its virtual functions:

```
class shape {
    // ...
public:
    virtual void rotate(int) { error("shape::rotate"); }
    virtual void draw() { error("shape::draw"); }
    // ...
};
```

Trying to make a shape of this unspecified kind is silly but legal:

```
shape s;  // silly: ''shapeless shape''
```

It is silly because every operation on s will result in an error.

A better alternative is to declare the virtual functions of class shape *pure virtual functions*. A virtual function is "made pure" by an initializer =0:

```
class shape {
    // ...
public:
    virtual void rotate(int) = 0;  // pure virtual function
    virtual void draw() = 0;       // pure virtual function
    // ...
};
```

A class with one or more pure virtual functions is an *abstract class*, and no objects of that abstract class can be created:

```
shape s;  // error: variable of abstract class shape
```

An abstract class can be used only as a base for another class. For example:

```
class circle : public shape {
    int radius;
public:
    void rotate(int) { }  // ok: overrides shape::rotate
    void draw();          // ok: overrides shape::draw

    circle(point p, int r);
};
```

A pure virtual function that is not defined in a derived class remains a pure virtual function, so that the derived class is also an abstract class. This allows us to build implementations in stages:

```
class X {
public:
    virtual void f() = 0;
    virtual void g() = 0;
};

X b;  // error: declaration of object of abstract class X

class Y : public X {
    void f();  // overrides X::f
};

Y b;  // error: declaration of object of abstract class Y

class Z : public Y {
    void g();  // overrides X::g
};

Z c;  // fine
```

An important use of abstract classes is to provide an interface without exposing any implementation details. For example, an operating system might hide the details of its device drivers behind an abstract class:

```
class character_device {
public:
    virtual int open() = 0;
    virtual int close(const char*) = 0;
    virtual int read(const char*, int) = 0;
    virtual int write(const char*, int) = 0;
    virtual int ioctl(int ...) = 0;
    // ...
};
```

and specify the actual device drivers as classes derived from `character_device`.

With the introduction of abstract classes we have the basic facilities for writing a complete program.

6.4 A Complete Program

Consider writing a program for drawing geometric shapes on a screen. It will naturally consist of three parts:

[1] a screen manager: Low-level routines and data structures defining the screen; it knows about points and straight lines only;

[2] a shape library: A set of definitions of general shapes such as rectangle and circle and standard routines for manipulating them; and

[3] an application program: A set of application-specific definitions and code using them.

Typically, the three parts are written by different people in different organizations and at different times. The parts are also typically written in the order they are presented, with the added complication that the designers of a lower level have no precise idea of what their code will eventually be used for. The following example reflects this. To get the example short enough to present, the shape library provides only a few simple services and the application program is trivial. An extremely simple concept of a screen is used so that the reader can try the program even if no graphics facility is available. It should be easy to replace the screen part of the program with something appropriate without changing the code of the shape library or the application program.

6.4.1 The Screen Manager

The intention was to write the screen manager in C (not C++) to emphasize the separation between the levels of the implementation. This turned out to be tedious, so a compromise was made: The style of usage is C (no member functions, virtual functions, user-defined operators, etc.), but constructors are used, function arguments are properly declared and checked, etc. In retrospect, the screen manager looks very much like a C program that has been modified to take advantage of C++ features without being totally rewritten.

The screen is represented as a two-dimensional array of characters, manipulated by functions `put_point()` and `put_line()` using the structure `point` when referring to the screen:

```
// file screen.h.

const int XMAX=40;
const int YMAX=24;

struct point {
    int x,y;
    point() {}
    point(int a, int b) { x=a; y=b; }
};

extern void put_point(int a, int b);
inline void put_point(point p) { put_point(p.x,p.y); }

extern void put_line(int, int, int, int);
inline void put_line(point a, point b)
    { put_line(a.x,a.y,b.x,b.y); }

extern void screen_init();
extern void screen_destroy();
extern void screen_refresh();
extern void screen_clear();

#include <iostream.h>
```

Before the first use of a put function, the screen must be initialized by
`screen_init()`, and changes to the screen data structure are reflected on the
screen only after a call of `screen_refresh()`. The reader will find that
"refresh" is done simply by printing a new copy of the screen array below the previous version. Here are the functions and data definitions for the screen:

```
#include "screen.h"
#include <stream.h>

enum color { black='*', white=' ' };

char screen[XMAX][YMAX];

void screen_init()
{
    for (int y=0; y<YMAX; y++)
        for (int x=0; x<XMAX; x++)
            screen[x][y] = white;
}
```

The function

```
void screen_destroy() { }
```

is provided simply as a place holder. Such a cleanup function is typically needed for a real system.

Points are written only if they are on the screen:

```
inline int on_screen(int a, int b)   // clipping
{
        return 0<=a && a<XMAX && 0<=b && b<YMAX;
}

void put_point(int a, int b)
{
        if (on_screen(a,b)) screen[a][b] = black;
}
```

The function put_line() is used to draw lines:

```
void put_line(int x0, int y0, int x1, int y1)
/*
        Plot the line (x0,y0) to (x1,y1).
        The line being plotted is b(x-x0) + a(y-y0) = 0.
        Minimize abs(eps) where eps = 2*(b(x-x0) + a(y-y0).
        See Newman and Sproull:
        ''Principles of Interactive Computer Graphics''
        McGraw-Hill, New York, 1979. pp. 33-44.
*/
{
        register int dx = 1;
        int a = x1 - x0;
        if (a < 0) dx = -1, a = -a;

        register int dy = 1;
        int b = y1 - y0;
        if (b < 0) dy = -1, b = -b;

        int two_a = 2*a;
        int two_b = 2*b;
        int xcrit = -b + two_a;
        register int eps = 0;

        for (;;) {
                put_point(x0,y0);
                if (x0==x1 && y0==y1) break;
                if (eps <= xcrit) x0 += dx, eps += two_b;
                if (eps>=a || a<=b) y0 += dy, eps -= two_a;
        }
}
```

Functions are provided to clear the screen and to refresh it:

```
void screen_clear() { screen_init(); }

void screen_refresh()
{
    for (int y=YMAX-1; 0<=y; y--) {      // top to bottom
        for (int x=0; x<XMAX; x++)       // left to right
            cout << screen[x][y];
        cout << '\n';
    }
}
```

You can now imagine that these definitions are available only as compiler output in a
library you cannot modify.

6.4.2 The Shape Library

We must define the general concept of a shape. This must be done in such a way that
it can be shared (as a base class `shape`) by all particular shapes (for example, circles
and squares), and in such a way that any shape can be manipulated exclusively
through the interface provided by class `shape`:

```
struct shape {
    static shape* list;
    shape* next;

    shape() { next = list; list = this; }

    virtual point north() const = 0;
    virtual point south() const = 0;
    virtual point east() const = 0;
    virtual point west() const = 0;
    virtual point neast() const = 0;
    virtual point seast() const = 0;
    virtual point nwest() const = 0;
    virtual point swest() const = 0;

    virtual void draw() = 0;
    virtual void move(int, int) = 0;
};
```

The idea is that shapes are positioned by `move()` and placed on the screen by
`draw()`. Shapes can be positioned relative to each other using the concept of
contact points, named after points on the compass. Each particular shape defines the
meaning of those points for itself, and each defines how it is drawn. The constructor
`shape::shape()` appends the shape to a list of shapes `shape::list`. This list
is maintained using the `next` member in each `shape` object. Because it does not
make sense to create a plain `shape` object, class `shape` is made an abstract class.
    A line can be constructed from either two points or a point and an integer. The
latter constructs a horizontal with the length specified by the integer. The sign of the

integer indicates whether the point is the left or the right endpoint:

```
class line : public shape {
/*
    line from "w" to "e"
    north() is defined as ``above the center
    as far north as the northernmost point''
*/
    point w,e;
public:
    point north() const
        { return point((w.x+e.x)/2,e.y<w.y?w.y:e.y); }
    point south() const
        { return point((w.x+e.x)/2,e.y<w.y?e.y:w.y); }
    point east() const;
    point west() const;
    point neast() const;
    point seast() const;
    point nwest() const;
    point swest() const;

    void move(int a, int b)
        { w.x += a; w.y += b; e.x += a; e.y += b; }
    void draw() { put_line(w,e); }

    line(point a, point b) { w = a; e = b; }
    line(point a, int l) { w = point(a.x+l-1,a.y); e = a; }
};
```

A rectangle is defined similarly:

```
class rectangle : public shape {
/*
    nw ---- n ---- ne
    |              |
    w      c       e
    |              |
    sw ---- s ---- se
*/
    point sw,ne;
public:
    point north() const { return point((sw.x+ne.x)/2,ne.y); }
    point south() const { return point((sw.x+ne.x)/2,sw.y); }
    point east() const;
    point west() const;
    point neast() const { return ne; }
    point seast() const;
    point nwest() const;
    point swest() const { return sw; }
```

```
    void move(int a, int b)
        { sw.x+=a; sw.y+=b; ne.x+=a; ne.y+=b; }
    void draw();

    rectangle(point, point);
};
```

A rectangle is constructed from two points. The code is complicated by the need
to figure out the relative position of those points:

```
rectangle::rectangle(point a, point b)
{
    if (a.x <= b.x) {
        if (a.y <= b.y) {
            sw = a;
            ne = b;
        }
        else {
            sw = point(a.x,b.y);
            ne = point(b.x,a.y);
        }
    }
    else {
        if (a.y <= b.y) {
            sw = point(b.x,a.y);
            ne = point(a.x,b.y);
        }
        else {
            sw = b;
            ne = a;
        }
    }
}
```

To draw a rectangle, its four sides are drawn:

```
void rectangle::draw()
{
    point nw(sw.x,ne.y);
    point se(ne.x,sw.y);
    put_line(nw,ne);
    put_line(ne,se);
    put_line(se,sw);
    put_line(sw,nw);
}
```

In addition to the shape definitions, a library of shapes contains functions for manipulating them. For example:

```
void shape_refresh();              // draw all shapes
void stack(shape* p, const shape* q); // put p on top of q
```

The refresh function is needed to cope with our naive screen. It simply re-draws all shapes. Note that it has no idea what kind of shapes it is drawing:

```
void shape_refresh()
{
    screen_clear();
    for (shape* p = shape::list; p; p=p->next) p->draw();
    screen_refresh();
}
```

Finally, here is a genuine utility function; it stacks one shape on top of another by specifying that the one's south() should be just above the other's north():

```
void stack(shape* p, const shape* q) // put p on top of q
{
    point n = q->north();
    point s = p->south();
    p->move(n.x-s.x,n.y-s.y+1);
}
```

Now imagine that this library is considered proprietary by some company selling software, and that they will sell you only the header file containing the shape definitions and the compiled version of the function definitions. It is still possible for you to define new shapes and take advantage of the utility functions for your own shapes.

6.4.3 The Application Program

The application program is extremely simple. A new shape myshape (looking a little bit like a face when printed) is defined; then a main program is written that draws such a face wearing a hat. Here first is the declaration of myshape:

```
#include "shape.h"

class myshape : public rectangle {
    line* l_eye;
    line* r_eye;
    line* mouth;
public:
    myshape(point, point);
    void draw();
    void move(int, int);
};
```

The eyes and the mouth are separate and independent objects created by myshape's constructor:

```
myshape::myshape(point a, point b)  : rectangle(a,b)
{
    int ll = neast().x-swest().x+1;
    int hh = neast().y-swest().y+1;
    l_eye = new line(
        point(swest().x+2,swest().y+hh*3/4),2);
    r_eye = new line(
        point(swest().x+ll-4,swest().y+hh*3/4),2);
    mouth = new line(
        point(swest().x+2,swest().y+hh/4),ll-4);
}
```

The eye and mouth objects are refreshed separately by the shape_refresh()
function and could in principle be manipulated independently from the my_shape
object to which they belong. That is one way of defining features for a hierarchically
constructed object such as myshape. Another way is illustrated by the nose. There
is no nose defined; it is simply added to the picture by the draw() function:

```
void myshape::draw()
{
    rectangle::draw();
    int a = (swest().x+neast().x)/2;
    int b = (swest().y+neast().y)/2;
    put_point(point(a,b));
}
```

A myshape is moved by moving the base rectangle and the secondary objects
l_eye, r_eye, and mouth:

```
void myshape::move(int a,  int b)
{
    rectangle::move(a,b);
    l_eye->move(a,b);
    r_eye->move(a,b);
    mouth->move(a,b);
}
```

Finally we can construct a few shapes and move them around a bit:

```
int main()
{
    screen_init();
    shape* p1 = new rectangle(point(0,0),point(10,10));
    shape* p2 = new line(point(0,15),17);
    shape* p3 = new myshape(point(15,10),point(27,18));
    shape_refresh();
    p3->move(-10,-10);
    stack(p2,p3);
    stack(p1,p2);
    shape_refresh();
    screen_destroy();
    return 0;
}
```

Note again how functions such as shape_refresh() and stack() manipulate objects of types that were defined long after these functions were written (and possibly compiled).

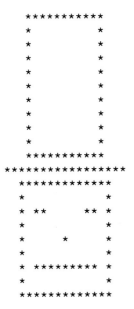

To simplify the discussion, the issues of deletion and copying of shapes were ignored.

6.5 Multiple Inheritance

As shown in §1.5.3 and §6.2.3, a class can have more than one direct base class, that is, more than one class specified after the : in the class declaration. Consider a simulation where concurrent activities are represented by a standard library class task and data gathering and display is achieved through a library class `displayed`. We can then define a class of simulated entities, class `satellite`, as:

```
class satellite : public task, public displayed {
    // ...
};
```

This is usually called multiple inheritance. In contrast, having just one direct base class is called single inheritance.

In addition to whatever operations are defined specifically for a `satellite`, the union of operations on `task`s and `displayed`s can be applied. For example:

```
void f(satellite& s)
{
    s.draw();        // displayed::draw()
    s.delay(10);     // task::delay()
    s.xmit();        // satellite::xmit()
}
```

Similarly, a `satellite` can be passed to functions that expect a `task` or a `displayed`. For example:

```
void highlight(displayed*);
void suspend(task*);

void g(satellite* p)
{
    highlight(p);    // highlight((displayed*)p)
    suspend(p);      // suspend((task*)p);
}
```

The implementation of this clearly involves some (simple) compiler trickery to ensure that the functions expecting a `task` see a different part of a `satellite` than the functions expecting a `displayed`.

Naturally, virtual functions work as usual. For example:

```
class task {
    // ...
    virtual pending() = 0;
}
```

```
class displayed {
    // ...
    virtual void draw() = 0;
};
```

```
class satellite : public task, public displayed {
    // ...
    void pending();
    void draw();
};
```

ensures that `satellite::draw()` and `satellite::pending()` will be called for a `satellite` treated as a `displayed` and `task`, respectively.

Note that with single inheritance (only) the programmer's choices for implementing the classes `displayed`, `task`, and `satellite` would be limited. A `satellite` could be a `task` or a `displayed`, but not both unless `task` was derived from `displayed` or visa versa. Either alternative involves a loss of flexibility.

6.5.1 Multiple Occurrences of a Base

With the ability of specifying more than one base class comes the possibility of having a class as a base twice. For example, had `task` and `displayed` each been derived from a `link` class, a `satellite` would have two links:

```
class task : public link {
    // the link is used to maintain a list
    // of all tasks (the scheduler list)

    // ...
};
```

```
class displayed : public link {
    // the link is used to maintain a list
    // of all displayed objects (the display list)

    // ...
};
```

This causes no problems. Two separate `link` objects are used to represent the links, and the two lists do not interfere with each other. Naturally, one cannot refer to members of the `link` class without risking an ambiguity, but that is handled as shown in the following section. A `satellite` object could be drawn like this:

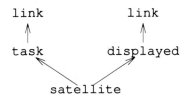

Examples where the common base class shouldn't be represented by two separate objects can also be represented; see §6.5.3.

6.5.2 Ambiguity Resolution

Naturally, two base classes may have member functions with the same name. For example:

```
class task {
    // ...
    virtual debug_info* get_debug();
};

class displayed {
    // ...
    virtual debug_info* get_debug();
};
```

When using a satellite these functions must be disambiguated:

```
void f(satellite* sp)
{
    debug_info* dip = sp->get_debug(); // error: ambiguous
    dip = sp->task::get_debug();        // ok
    dip = sp->displayed::get_debug();   // ok
}
```

However, explicit disambiguation is messy, so it is most often best to resolve such problems by defining a new function in the derived class:

```
class satellite : public task, public displayed {
{
    // ...

    debug_info* get_debug()
    {
        debug_info* dip1 = task::get_debug();
        debug_info* dip2 = displayed::get_debug();
        return dip1->merge(dip2);
    }
}
```

This localizes the information about the base classes of satellite. Because satellite::get_debug() overrides the get_debug() functions from both its base classes this ensures that satellite::get_debug() is called wherever get_debug() is called for a satellite object.

The compiler detects name clashes resulting from using a name defined in more than one base class. This implies that unless there actually is an ambiguous use the programmer need not do anything to resolve it. Most uses of base classes do not imply name clashes, and most names from base classes that might clash don't because they are not used directly on objects of the derived class.

The related problem of two classes providing functions with dissimilar semantics but the same name, such as a draw() function for both a bank account class and a display class, is discussed in §13.8.

Naming the base class when explicitly referring to a base class member is redundant in cases where there is no ambiguity. In particular, where multiple inheritance is not used it would be sufficient to use some notation meaning ''in base classes somewhere.'' This would save the programmer from having to remember the name of a derived class's immediate base class and from (rare) errors arising from reorganization of a class hierarchy. For example, this code from §6.2.5

```
void manager::print()
{
    employee::print();
    // ...
}
```

assumes that `employee` is the direct base class of `manager`. The code would still work as intended if `employee` was an indirect base of `manager` and the direct class didn't define `print()`. However, someone might have rearranged things like this:

```
class employee {
    // ...
    virtual void print();
};


class foreman : public employee {
    // ...
    void print();
};


class manager : public foreman {
    // ...
    void print();
};
```

Now `foreman::print()` isn't called, although it was almost certainly meant to be. A simple trick eliminates this problem:

```
class foreman : public employee {
    typedef employee inherited;
    // ...
    void print();
};


class manager : public foreman {
    typedef foreman inherited;
    // ...
    void print();
};
```

```
void manager::print()
{
    inherited::print();
    // ...
}
```

The scope rules, especially the rules for nested types, ensure that the resulting multi-tude of `inherited` types do not interfere with each other. It seems to be a matter of taste whether this use of `inherited` makes code more or less readable.

6.5.3 Virtual Base Classes

The sections above have emphasized the role of multiple inheritance in merging exist-ing classes to allow smooth integration of separately developed software. This is by far the most common use of multiple inheritance and, fortunately (but not acciden-tally), also the simplest and safest to use.

   Some uses of multiple inheritance involve a closer connection between the classes used as ''sibling'' base classes. Such siblings tend to be designed together. In many cases that does not involve a style of programming significantly different from what was shown above; one simply leaves a bit of extra work to be done in a derived class. Such extra work often takes the form of overriding one or more virtual functions; see §13.2 and §8.7. However, sometimes sibling classes need to share information. Because C++ is a strongly typed language, such sharing must be achieved by explicit declaration of what is to be shared. One mechanism for specifying such sharing is a virtual base class.

   A virtual base class can be used to represent a ''main class'' that can be cus-tomized in several ways:

```
class window {
    // basic stuff
    virtual void draw();
};
```

For simplicity we will consider only one detail of class `window`, the `draw()` func-tion. Various more elaborate `windows` can be specified. Each will define its (more elaborate) version of the draw function. For example:

```
class window_w_border : public virtual window {
    // border stuff
    void draw();
};
```

```
class window_w_menu : public virtual window {
    // menu stuff
    void draw();
};
```

We would now like to define a `window` with border and menu:

```
class window_w_border_and_menu
    : public virtual window,
    public window_w_border,
    public window_w_menu {
    // window_w_border_and_menu stuff
    void draw();
};
```

Each such derived class adds some feature to a window. To use a combination of added features, we must ensure that the same object of class `window` is used to represent all the occurrences of the `window` base class in these derived classes. That is exactly what is achieved by specifying the `windows` as `virtual` classes.

An object of class `window_w_border_and_menu` could be drawn like this:

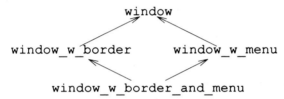

Compare with the drawing of the `satellite` object in §6.5 to see the difference between ordinary and virtual inheritance. In an inheritance graph every base class of a given name that is specified to be virtual will be represented by a single object of that class. On the other hand, each base class not specified `virtual` will have its own object representing it.

Next we have to program the various `draw()` functions. This is not hard, but there is a snag for the unwary. Let us first proceed in the too simple way that leads to the problem:

```
void window_w_border::draw()
{
    window::draw();
    // draw the border
};
```

```
void window_w_menu::draw()
{
    window::draw()
    // draw the menu
};
```

So far so good. This is simple, follows the pattern for such functions used with single inheritance (§6.2.1), and works perfectly. However, the next level of composition reveals the snag:

```
void window_w_border_and_menu::draw() // trouble!
{
    window_w_border::draw();
    window_w_menu::draw();

    // do whatever is specific to
    // window_w_border_and_menu
};
```

At first glance this looks plausible. As ever, we do the operations necessary for the
base classes and then the work needed specifically for the derived class. However,
this causes window::draw() to be called twice! With most graphics systems this
leads not only to a waste of time but also to a corrupted screen. Typically, the second
write erases the first one.

To avoid this effect we have to back off a bit and separate the work done by the
base class from the work done from the base class. This is done by giving each class
both a _draw() function that does just what is specific for the class and a draw()
that does that plus the specific work for each base class. For class window the
change is simply in the introduction of a redundant function:

```
class window {
    // basic stuff
    void _draw();
    virtual void draw() { _draw(); }
};
```

The derived classes will follow this pattern:

```
class window_w_border : public virtual window {
    // border stuff
    void _draw();
    void draw();
};
```

```
void window_w_border::draw()
{
    window::_draw();
    _draw();   // draw the border
};
```

Only for further derived classes does the difference become significant in that it
solves the problem of the double call of window::draw() by calling
window::_draw() exactly once:

```
class window_w_border_and_menu
    : public virtual window,
    public window_w_border,
    public window_w_menu {

    void _draw();
    void draw();
};


void window_w_border_and_menu::draw()
{
    window::_draw();
    window_w_border::_draw();
    window_w_menu::_draw();

    _draw();   // whatever is specific to
               // window_w_border_and_menu
};
```

Having both a `window::draw()` and a `window::_draw()` is not really necessary, but having them both saves a lot of small typos.

In this example `window` acts as the repository of information shared between `window_w_border`, `window_w_menu`, etc., and defines the interface through which they communicate. Note that when single inheritance is used, sharing within a tree is achieved by pushing the shared information toward the root of the tree until it becomes visible to all interested node classes. This can easily have the unfortunate effect of causing the root class or classes near to it to act as a "global" name space for all classes in a tree, and ending up containing a multitude of unrelated items.

It is important that each of these classes can override functions defined in the common `virtual` base; that way each sibling can modify the way others operate. Suppose a `window` has a general `get_input()`:

```
class window {
    // basic stuff
    virtual void draw();
    virtual void get_input();
};
```

One derived class can now implement an operation using `get_input()` without worrying about who supplies it:

```
class window_w_banner : public virtual window {
    // banner stuff
    void draw();
    void update_banner_text();
};
```

```
void window_w_banner::update_banner_text()
{
    // ...
    get_input();
    // change banner_text
}
```

Another derived class can supply get_input() without worrying about who uses
it:

```
class window_w_menu : public virtual window {
    // menu stuff
    void draw();
    void get_input();   // override window::get_input
};
```

This will all come together in a further derived class:

```
class window_w_banner_and_menu
    : public virtual window,
    public window_w_banner,
    public window_w_menu
{
    void draw();
};
```

Ambiguity control is used to ensure that sibling classes do not supply the same function:

```
class window_w_input : public virtual window {
    // ...
    void draw();
    void get_input();   // overrides window::get_input
};
```

```
class window_w_input_and_menu
    : public virtual window,
    public window_w_input,
    public window_w_menu
{                          // error: both window_w_input
                           // and window_w_menu
                           // override window::get_input

    void draw();
};
```

This is detected by the compiler and can be resolved in the usual way by supplying
class window_w_input_and_menu with a function that overrides the ''offend-
ing'' function and resolves the issue somehow:

```
class window_w_input_and_menu
    : public virtual window,
    public window_w_input,
    public window_w_menu
{
    void draw();
    void get_input();
};
```

Here `window_w_input_and_menu::get_input()` will override all the other `get_input()` operations. The details of this resolution mechanism can be found in §r.10.1.1.

6.6 Access Control

A member of a class can be `private`, `protected`, or `public`:

If it is `private`, its name can be used only by member functions and friends of the class in which it is declared.

If it is `protected`, its name can be used only by member functions and friends of the class in which it is declared and by member functions and friends of classes derived from this class (see §5.4.1).

If it is `public`, its name can be used by any function.

This reflects the view that there are three kinds of functions accessing a class: functions implementing the class (its friends and members), functions implementing a derived class (the derived class's friends and members), and other functions.

The access control is applied uniformly to names. What a name refers to does not affect the control of its use. This means that one can have private member functions, constants, etc., as well as private data members. For example:

```
class X {
private:
    enum { A, B };
    void f(int);
    int a;
};
```

```
void X::f(int i)
{
    if (i<A) f(i+B);
    a++;
};
```

```
void g(X& x)
{
    int i = X::A;  // error: X::A is private
    x.f(2);        // error: X::f is private
    x.a++;         // error: X::a is private
};
```

6.6.1 Protected Members

As an example of `protected` members, consider the `window` example from the previous section. There the `_draw()` functions were intended for use by derived classes (only) because they were incomplete in the service they provided and therefore not safe or convenient enough for general use. They were designed as building blocks for further refinement. The `draw()` operations, on the other hand, were designed for general use. This could be expressed by separating the interface of the `window` classes into two, the `protected` interface and the `public` interface:

```
class window {
public:
    virtual void draw();
    // ...
protected:
    void _draw();
    // other tool-building stuff
private:
    // representation, etc.
};
```

This convention can then be followed by derived classes such as `window_w_border` and `window_w_menu`.

The use of the _ prefix for the protected functions that are ''part of the implementation'' follows the convention that names starting with _ should be avoided in code visible to the general user. It is still best to avoid names starting with double underscores, though, even for member names.

Here is a less realistic, but more detailed, example:

```
class X {
// private by default:
    int priv;
protected:
    int prot;
public:
    int publ;
    void m();
};
```

The member `X::m()` has unrestricted access:

```
void X::m()
{
    priv = 1;      // ok
    prot = 2;      // ok
    publ = 3;      // ok
}
```

A member of a derived class has access to public and protected members:

```
class Y : public X {
    void mderived();
};

Y::mderived()
{
    priv = 1;  // error: priv is private
    prot = 2;  // ok: prot is protected and mderived()
               // is a member of the derived class Y
    publ = 3;  // ok: publ is public
}
```

A global function can access only the public members:

```
void f(Y* p)
{
    p->priv = 1;  // error: priv is private
    p->prot = 2;  // error: prot is protected and f()
                  // is not a friend or a member of X or Y
    p->publ = 3;  // ok: publ is public
}
```

6.6.2 Access to Base Classes

Like a member, a base class can be declared `private`, `protected`, or `public`. Consider:

```
class X {
public:
    int a;
    // ...
};

class Y1 : public X {  };
class Y2 : protected X { };
class Y3 : private X { };
```

Because X is a public base of Y1, any function can (implicitly) convert a Y1* to an X* where needed just as it can access the public members of class X. For example:

```
void f(Y1* py1, Y2* py2, Y3* py3)
{
    X* px = py1;    // ok: X is a public base class of Y1
    py1->a = 7;     // ok
    px = py2;       // error: X is a protected base of Y2
    py1->a = 7;     // error
    px = py3;       // error: X is a private base of Y3
    py3->a = 7;     // error
}
```

Consider:

```
class Y2 : protected X {  };
class Z2 : public Y2 { void f(); };
```

Because X is a protected base of Y2, only members and friends of Y2 and members and friends of Y2's derived classes (for example Z2) can (implicitly) convert a Y2* to an X* where needed, just as they can access the public and protected members of class X. For example:

```
void Z2::f(Y1* py1, Y2* py2, Y3* py3)
{
    X* px = py1;    // ok: X is a public base class of Y1
    py1->a = 7;     // ok
    px = py2;       // ok: X is a protected base of Y2
                    // and Z2 is derived from Y2
    py1->a = 7;     // ok
    px = py3;       // error: X is a private base of Y3
    py3->a = 7;     // error
}
```

Consider finally:

```
class Y3 : private X { void f(); };
```

Because X is a private base of Y3, only members and friends of Y3 can (implicitly) convert a Y3* to an X where needed, just as they can access the public and protected members of class X. For example:

```
void Y3::f(Y1* py1, Y2* py2, Y3* py3)
{
    X* px = py1;    // ok: X is a public base class of Y1
    py1->a = 7;     // ok
    px = py2;       // error: X is a protected base of Y2
    py1->a = 7;     // error
    px = py3;       // ok: X is a private base of Y3
                    // and Y3::f is a member of Y3
    py3->a = 7;     // ok
}
```

6.7 Free Store

It is possible to take over memory management for a class by defining `operator new()` and `operator delete()`. This is still possible and often even more useful for a class that is the base for many derived classes. For example, we might like to have the `employee` class (from §6.2.5) provide a specialized allocator and deallocator for itself and all its derived classes:

```
class employee {
    // ...
public:
    // ...
    void* operator new(size_t);
    void operator delete(void*, size_t);
};


void* employee::operator new(size_t s)
{
    // allocate 's' bytes of memory
    // and return a pointer to it
}


void employee::operator delete(void* p, size_t s)
{
    // assume 'p' points to 's' bytes of memory
    // allocated by employee::operator new()
    // and free that memory for reuse
}
```

The use of the hitherto mysterious `size_t` argument now becomes obvious. It is the size of the object actually deleted. Deleting a "plain" `employee` gives an argument value of `sizeof(employee)`; deleting a `manager` gives an argument value of `sizeof(manager)`. This allows a class-specific allocator to avoid storing size information with each allocation. Naturally, a class specific allocator can store such information (like a general purpose allocator must) and ignore the `size_t` argument to `operator delete()`, but that makes it harder to improve significantly on the speed and memory consumption of a general purpose allocator.

How does a compiler know how to supply the right size to `operator delete()`? As long as the type specified in the `delete` operation matches the actual type of the object, this is easy; but consider:

```
class manager : public employee {
    int level;
    // ...
}
```

```
void f()
{
    employee* p = new manager;   // trouble
    delete p;
}
```

The compiler will not get the size right in this case; as in the case with deleting an array, the user must help. This is done by adding a virtual destructor to the base class, `employee`:

```
class employee {
    // ...
public:
    // ...
    void* operator new(size_t);
    void operator delete(void*, size_t);
    virtual ~employee();
};
```

Even an empty destructor will do:

```
employee::~employee() { }
```

This will cause the deallocation to be done from within the destructor (which knows the size) and will further cause every class derived from `employee` to be supplied with a destructor (thus getting the size right) if the user doesn't supply a destructor directly. The example

```
void f()
{
    employee* p = new manager;   // now fine
    delete p;
}
```

now works correctly. Allocation is done by a (compiler generated) call

```
employee::operator new(sizeof(manager))
```

and deallocation by a (compiler generated) call

```
employee::operator delete(p,sizeof(manager))
```

In other words, if you want to supply an allocator/deallocator pair that works correctly for derived classes, you must either supply a virtual destructor in the base class or refrain from using the `size_t` argument in the deallocator. Naturally, the language could have been designed to save you from such concerns. However, that can be done only by also ''saving'' you from the benefits of the optimizations possible in the less safe system.

In general, it is wise to supply a virtual destructor in all classes that act as a base class in the sense that objects of derived classes are manipulated (and possibly deleted) through a pointer to the base. This is almost always the case for classes with even a single virtual function. For example:

```
class X {
    // ...
public:
    // ...
    virtual void f(); // X has a virtual function
                      // so supply virtual destructor:
    virtual ~X();
};
```

6.7.1 Virtual Constructors

After hearing about virtual destructors, the obvious question is ''Can constructors be virtual?'' The short answer is ''no;'' a slightly longer one is ''no, but you can easily get the effect you are looking for.''

A constructor cannot be virtual because it needs the information about the exact type of the object it is creating to construct it correctly. Furthermore, a constructor is not quite an ordinary function. It may interact with memory management routines in ways ordinary member functions don't, and it differs from ordinary member functions in that it is not called for an existing object. Consequently, you cannot have a pointer to a constructor.

Both of these restrictions can be circumvented by defining a function that calls a constructor and returns a constructed object. This is fortunate, because it is not uncommon to need to create a new object without knowing the exact type of the object. For example, inside a compiler one occasionally needs to make a copy of a tree representing an expression. There can be many kinds of expression nodes, but we only want to write the tree cloning operations once. Consequently, we want the expression nodes to have a virtual clone operation.

The most common such ''virtual constructors'' are the default constructor (taking no argument) and the copy constructor (taking an argument of the resulting type). For example:

```
class expr {
    // ...
public:
    // ...
    expr(); // default constructor
    virtual expr* new_expr() { return new expr(); }
};
```

The virtual `new_expr()` function simply returns a default initialized `expr` allocated on the free store. A derived class can override `new_expr()` to return an object of its own type:

```
class conditional : public expr {
    // ...
public:
    // ...
    conditional(); // default constructor
    expr* new_expr() { return new conditional(); }
};
```

This means that given an object of class expr a user can create a new object of "just the same type." For example:

```
void user(expr* p1, expr* p2)
{
    expr* p3 = p1->new_expr();
    expr* p4 = p2->new_expr();
    // ...
}
```

The pointers assigned to p3 and p4 are of the appropriate, but unknown, types.

A virtual copy constructor, often called a clone operation, can be defined using the same technique, but requires more care to deal with the subtleties of copying semantics. For example:

```
class expr {
    // ...
    expr* left;
    expr* right;
public:
    // ...
        // copy 's' into 'this':
    inline void copy(expr* s);

        // create a copy of this object:
    virtual expr* clone(int deep = 0);
};
```

The deep argument caters to the distinction between copying only the object itself (shallow copy) and copying the complete subtree rooted in the object (deep copy). The default, 0, means shallow copy.

The clone() function can be used like this:

```
void fct(expr* root)
{
    expr* c1 = root->clone(1); // deep copy
    expr* c2 = root->clone();  // shallow copy
    // ...
}
```

Being virtual, clone() will clone objects of every class derived from expr.

The actual copy operation can be defined like this:

```
void expr::copy(expression* s, int deep)
{
    if (deep == 0) {   // just copy the members:
        *this = *s;
    }
    else { // chase pointers:
        left = s->clone(1);
        right = s->clone(1);
        // ...
    }
}
```

The `expr::clone()` operation will be called for `expr`s (and not for classes derived from `expr`) only so it can simply allocate and return an `expr` that is a copy of itself:

```
expr* expr::clone(int deep)
{
    expr* r = new expr();   // make a default expression
    r->copy(this,deep);     // copy `*this' into `*r'
    return r;
}
```

This `clone()` operation can be used for classes derived from `expr` without adding data members (often the most common case). For example:

```
class arithmetic : public expr {
    // ...

    // no new data members: can use default clone
};
```

On the other hand, where data members are added, a specific `clone()` operation is needed. For example:

```
class conditional : public expression {
    expr* cond;
public:
    inline void copy(cond* s, int deep = 0);
    expr* clone(int deep = 0);
    // ...
};
```

The `copy()` and `clone()` operations are defined in close parallel to their `expression` counterparts:

```
expr* conditional::clone(int deep)
{
    conditional* r = new conditional();
    r->copy(this,deep);
    return r;
}

void conditional::copy(expr* s, int deep)
{
    if (deep == 0) {
        *this = *s;
    }
    else {
        expr::copy(s,1); // copy the expr part
        cond = s->cond->clone(1);
    }
}
```

This last function definition shows the value of separating the actual copy operation, `expr::copy()`, from the complete clone (that is, create new object and copy) oper-ation `expr::clone()`. The simple copy operation is useful in defining more com-plex copy and clone operations. The distinction between `copy()` and `clone()` parallels the distinction between an assignment operator and a copy constructor (§1.4.2) and also the distinction between the `_draw()` and the `draw()` functions §6.5.3. Note that `copy()` is not a `virtual` function; it need not be because its caller, `clone()`, is. Simple copy operations are also obvious candidates for inlining.

6.7.2 Placement

Operator `new` creates its object on the free store by default. What if we wanted the object allocated "elsewhere?" This can be achieved by overloading the allocation operator. Consider a simple class:

```
class X {
    // ...
public:
    X(int);
    // ...
};
```

We can place objects anywhere by providing an allocator function with "extra" argu-ments:

```
// explicit placement operator:

void* operator new(size_t, void* p) { return p; }
```

and then supplying the extra arguments to the `new` operator like this:

```
char buffer[sizeof(X)];

void f(int i);
{
    X* p = new(buffer) X(i); // place X in buffer
    // ...
}
```

The operator new() used by the new operator is chosen by the usual argument matching rules (§r.13.2); every operator new() has a size_t as its first argument. That size is implicitly supplied by the new operator.

The "placement" operator new() defined above is the simplest such allocator. Another example is an allocator that allocates memory from a specific arena:

```
class Arena {
    // ...
    virtual void* alloc(size_t) =0;
    virtual void free(void*) =0;
};

void* operator new(size_t sz, Arena* a)
{
    return a.alloc(sz);
}
```

Now objects of arbitrary types can be allocated from different Arenas as needed. For example:

```
extern Arena* Persistent;
extern Arena* Shared;

void g(int i);
{
    X* p = new(Persistent) X(i); // X in persistent storage
    X* q = new(Shared) X(i);     // X in shared memory
    // ...
}
```

Placing an object in an area that is not (directly) controlled by the standard free store manager implies that some care is required when destroying the object. The basic mechanism for that is an explicit call of a destructor:

```
void h(X* p)
{
    p->~X(); // call destructor
    Persistent->free(p); // free memory
}
```

Note that explicit calls of destructors, like the use of special-purpose *global* allocators, should be avoided wherever possible. Occasionally they are essential, though, but a novice ought to think thrice before calling a destructor explicitly and should also ask a more experienced colleague first.

6.8 Exercises

1. (∗1) Define

```
class base {
public:
    virtual void iam() { cout << "base\n"; }
};
```

Derive two classes from `base`, and for each define `iam()` to write out the name of the class. Create objects of these classes and call `iam()` for them. Assign the address of objects of the derived classes to `base*` pointers and call `iam()` through those pointers.

2. (∗2) Implement the screen primitives (§6.4.1) in a way that is reasonable for your system.

3. (∗2) Define a class `triangle` and a class `circle`.

4. (∗2) Define a function that draws a line connecting two shapes by finding the two closest "contact points" and connecting them.

5. (∗2) Modify the shape example so that `line` is derived from `rectangle`, or vice versa.

6. (∗2) Consider:

```
class char_vec {
    int sz;
    char element[1];
public:
    static new_char_vec(int s);
    char& operator[](int i) { return element[i]; }
    // ...
}
```

Define `new_char_vec()` to allocate contiguous memory for a `char_vec` object so that the elements can be indexed through `element` as shown. Under what circumstances does this trick cause serious problems?

7. (∗1) Draw data structures that could be used to support the `shape` example from §6.4 and explain how a virtual call might be performed.

8. (∗1.5) Draw data structures that could be used to support the `satellite` example from §6.5 and explain how a virtual call might be performed.

9. (∗2) Draw data structures that could be used to support the `window` example from §6.5.3 and explain how a virtual call might be performed.

10. (∗2) Define a graphical object class with a plausible set of operations to serve as a common base class for a library of graphical objects; look at some graphics library to see what operations were supplied there. Define a database object class with a plausible set of operations to serve as a common base class for objects stored as

sequences of fields in a database; look at some database library to see what operations were supplied there. Define a graphical database object with and without the use of multiple inheritance and discuss the relative merits of the two solutions.

11. (∗2) Write a version of the clone() operation from §6.7.1 that can place its cloned object in an Arena (see §6.7.2) passed as an argument. Implement a simple Arena as a class derived from Arena.

12. (∗2) Given classes Circle, Square, and Triangle derived from a class Shape, define a function intersect() that takes two Shape* arguments and calls suitable functions to determine if the two shapes overlap. It will be necessary to add suitable (virtual) functions to the classes to achieve this. Don't bother to write the functions that does the check for overlap; just make sure the right functions are called.

13. (∗5) Design and implement a library for writing event-driven simulations. Hint: <task.h>. However, that is an old program, and you can do better. There should be a class task. An object of class task should be able to save its state and to have that state restored (you might define task::save() and task::restore()) so that it can operate as a coroutine. Specific tasks can be defined as objects of classes derived from class task. The program to be executed by a task might be specified as a virtual function. It should be possible to pass arguments to a new task as arguments to its constructor(s). There should be a scheduler implementing a concept of virtual time. Provide a function task::delay(long) that "consumes" virtual time. Whether the scheduler is part of class task or separate will be one of the major design decisions. The tasks will need to communicate. Design a class queue for that. Devise a way for a task to wait for input from several queues. Handle run-time errors in a uniform way. How would you debug programs written using such a library?

7

Operator Overloading

*When **I** use a word it means just what*
I choose it to mean – neither more nor less.
– Humpty Dumpty

This chapter describes the mechanism for operator overloading provided in C++. A programmer can define a meaning for operators when applied to objects of a specific class; in addition to arithmetic, logical, and relational operators, call ( ), subscripting [ ], and dereferencing -> can be defined, and both assignment and initialization can be redefined. Explicit and implicit type conversion between user-defined and basic types can be defined. It is shown how to define a class for which an object cannot be copied or destroyed except by specific user-defined functions.

7.1 Introduction

Programs often manipulate objects that are concrete representations of abstract concepts. For example, the C++ data type int, together with the operators +, −, *, /, etc., provides a (restricted) implementation of the mathematical concept of integers. Such concepts typically include a set of operators representing basic operations on objects in a terse, convenient, and conventional way. Unfortunately, only few concepts can be directly supported by a programming language. For example, the notions of complex arithmetic, matrix algebra, logic signals, and strings receive no direct support in C++. Classes provide a facility for specifying a representation of nonprimitive objects in C++ together with a set of operations that can be performed on such objects. Defining operators to operate on class objects sometimes allows a programmer to provide a more conventional and convenient notation for manipulating class objects than could be achieved using only the basic functional notation. For example,

```
class complex {
    double   re, im;
public:
    complex(double r, double i) { re=r; im=i; }
    friend complex operator+(complex, complex);
    friend complex operator*(complex, complex);
};
```

defines a simple implementation of the concept of complex numbers, where a number
is represented by a pair of double precision floating-point numbers manipulated
(exclusively) by the operators + and *. The programmer provides a meaning for +
and * by defining functions named operator+ and operator*. For example,
given b and c of type complex, b+c means (by definition) operator+(b,c).
One can now approximate the conventional interpretation of complex expressions:

```
void f()
{
    complex a = complex(1,3.1);
    complex b = complex(1.2,2);
    complex c = b;

    a = b+c;
    b = b+c*a;
    c = a*b+complex(1,2);
}
```

The usual precedence rules hold; so the second statement means b=b+(c*a), not
b=(b+c)*a.

7.2 Operator Functions

Functions defining meanings for the following operators can be declared:

+	–	*	/	%	^	&	|	~	!
=	<	>	+=	-=	*=	/=	%=	^=	&=
|=	<<	>>	>>=	<<=	==	!=	<=	>=	&&
||	++	--	->*	,	->	[]	()	new	delete

The last five are dereferencing (§7.9), subscript (§7.7), function call (§7.8), free store
allocation, and free store de-allocation (§3.2.6). It is not possible to change the precedence of these operators, nor can the expression syntax be changed. For example, it is
not possible to define a unary % or a binary !. It is not possible to define new operator tokens, but you can use the function call notation when this set of operators is not
adequate. For example, use pow(), not **. These restrictions may seem Draconian,
but more flexible rules can easily lead to ambiguities. For example, defining an operator ** to mean exponentiation may seem an obvious and easy task at first glance, but
think again. Should ** bind to the left (as in Fortran) or to the right (as in Algol)?
Should the expression a**p be interpreted a*(*p) or (a)**(p)?

The name of an operator function is the keyword `operator` followed by the operator itself, for example `operator<<`. An operator function is declared and can be called like any other function; a use of the operator is only a shorthand for an explicit call of the operator function. For example

```
void f(complex a, complex b)
{
    complex c = a + b;              // shorthand
    complex d = operator+(a,b); // explicit call
}
```

Given the preceding declaration of `complex`, the two initializers are synonymous.

7.2.1 Binary and Unary Operators

A binary operator can be defined by either a member function taking one argument or a global function taking two arguments. Thus, for any binary operator @, aa@bb can be interpreted as either `aa.operator@(bb)` or `operator@(aa,bb)`. If both are defined, argument matching (§r.13.2) determines which, if any, interpretation is used. A unary operator, whether prefix or postfix, can be defined by either a member function taking no arguments or a global function taking one argument. For any prefix unary operator @, @aa can be interpreted as either `aa.operator@()` or `operator@(aa)`. If both are defined, argument matching (§r.13.2) determines which, if any, interpretation is used. For any postfix unary operator @, aa@ can be interpreted as either `aa.operator@(int)` or `operator@(aa,int)`. This is explained further in §7.10. If both are defined, argument matching (§r.13.2) determines which, if any, interpretation is used. An operator can be specified only for the syntax defined for it in the C++ grammar. In particular, a user cannot define a unary %
or a ternary +. Consider these examples:

```
class X {
        // members (with implicit 'this' pointer):

        X* operator&();          // prefix unary & (address of)
        X operator&(X);          // binary & (and)
        X operator++(int);       // postfix increment
        X operator&(X,X);        // error: ternary
        X operator/();           // error: unary /
};

// global functions (often friends):

X operator-(X);               // prefix unary minus
X operator-(X,X);             // binary minus
X operator--(X&,int);         // postfix increment
X operator-();                // error: no operand
X operator-(X,X,X);           // error: ternary
X operator%(X);               // error: unary %
```

Operator [] is described in §7.7, operator () in §7.8, operator -> in §7.9, and operators ++ and -- in §7.10.

7.2.2 Predefined Meanings for Operators

Only a few assumptions are made about the meaning of a user-defined operator. In
particular, operator=, operator[], operator(), and operator-> must be
non-static member functions; this ensures that their first operands will be lvalues.

The meanings of some built-in operators are defined to be equivalent to some
combination of other operators on the same arguments. For example, if a is an int,
++a means a+=1, which in turn means a=a+1. Such relations do not hold for user-
defined operators unless the user happens to define them that way. For example, the
definition of operator+=() for a type complex cannot be deduced from the definitions of complex::operator+() and complex::operator=().

Because of historical accident, the operators = (assignment), & (address-of), and ,
(sequencing) have predefined meanings when applied to class objects. These predefined meanings can be made inaccessible to general users by making them private:

```
class X {
    // ...
private:
    void operator=(const X&);
    void operator&();
    void operator,(const X&);
    // ...
};

void f(X a, X b)
{
    a = b;    // error: operator= private
    &a;       // error: operator& private
    a,b;      // error: operator, private
}
```

Alternatively, they can be given new meanings by suitable definitions.

7.2.3 Operators and User-defined Types

An operator function must either be a member or take at least one class object argument (functions redefining the new and delete operators need not). This rule
ensures that a user cannot change the meaning of an expression unless it contains an
object of a user-defined type. In particular, it is not possible to define an operator
function that operates exclusively on pointers. This ensures that C++ is extensible but
not mutable (with the exception of operators =, &, and , for class objects).

An operator function intended to accept a basic type as its first operand cannot be
a member function. For example, consider adding a complex variable aa to the integer 2: aa+2 can, with a suitably declared member function, be interpreted as

`aa.operator+(2)`, but `2+aa` cannot because there is no class `int` for which to define `+` to mean `2.operator+(aa)`. Even if there were, two different member functions would be needed to cope with `2+aa` and `aa+2`. Because the compiler does not know the meaning of a user-defined `+`, it cannot assume that it is commutative and interpret `2+aa` as `aa+2`. This example is trivially handled using nonmember functions.

Every expression is checked for ambiguities. Where a user-defined operator provides a possible interpretation, the expression is checked according to the rules in §r.13.2.

7.3 User-defined Type Conversion

The implementation of complex numbers presented in the introduction is too restrictive to please anyone, so it must be extended. This is mostly a trivial repetition of the techniques previously presented. For example:

```
class complex {
    double   re, im;
public:
    complex(double r, double i) { re=r; im=i; }

    friend complex operator+(complex, complex);
    friend complex operator+(complex, double);
    friend complex operator+(double, complex);

    friend complex operator-(complex, complex);
    friend complex operator-(complex, double);
    friend complex operator-(double, complex);
    complex operator-();              // unary -

    friend complex operator*(complex, complex);
    friend complex operator*(complex, double);
    friend complex operator*(double, complex);

    // ...
};
```

With this declaration of `complex`, we can now write:

```
void f()
{
    complex a(1,1), b(2,2), c(3,3), d(4,4), e(5,5);
    a = -b-c;
    b = c*2.0*c;
    c = (d+e)*a;
}
```

However, writing a function for each combination of `complex` and `double`, as for `operator*()` above, is tedious. Furthermore, a realistic facility for complex arithmetic must provide at least a dozen such functions; see, for example, the type `complex` as declared in `<complex.h>`.

7.3.1 Constructors

An alternative to using several functions is to declare a constructor that, given a `double`, creates a `complex`. For example,

```
class complex {
    // ...
    complex(double r) { re=r; im=0; }
};
```

This specifies how to make a `complex` given a `double`. It specifies the traditional embedding of the real line in the complex plane.

A constructor requiring a single argument need not be called explicitly:

```
complex z1 = complex(23);
complex z2 = 23;
```

Both `z1` and `z2` will be initialized by calling `complex(23)`.

A constructor is a prescription for creating a value of a given type. When a value of a type is expected, and when such a value can be created by a constructor, given the value to be assigned, the constructor will be used. For example, class `complex` could be declared like this:

```
class complex {
    double re, im;
public:
    complex(double r, double i =0) { re=r; im=i; }

    friend complex operator+(complex, complex);
    friend complex operator*(complex, complex);

    complex operator+=(complex);
    complex operator*=(complex);

    // ...
};
```

and operations involving `complex` variables and integer constants would be legal. An integer constant will be interpreted as `complex` with the imaginary part zero. For example, `a=b*2` means

```
a = operator*( b, complex( double(2), double(0) ) )
```

Now extra versions of operators such as + need be defined only if experience shows that the improvement in efficiency achieved by avoiding the conversion is worth while. For example, if it was found that multiplying a complex variable by a `double` was a critical operation, we might add `operator*=(double)` to the set of operators:

```
class complex {
    double re, im;
public:
    complex(double r, double i =0) { re=r; im=i; }

    friend complex operator+(complex, complex);
    friend complex operator*(complex, complex);

    complex& operator+=(complex);
    complex& operator*=(complex);
    complex& operator*=(double);

    // ...
};
```

Assignment operators such as += and *= can be very useful for user-defined types because they tend to be simpler to write than their "simple" counterparts + and * and also because they help improve run-time efficiency by eliminating temporary variables. For example

```
inline complex& complex::operator+=(complex a)
{
    re += a.re;
    im += a.im;
    return *this;
}
```

does not require a temporary variable to hold the result and is simple for a compiler to inline "perfectly." A simple operation such as complex addition is also easy to write directly

```
inline complex operator+(complex a, complex b)
{
    return complex(a.re+b.re,a.im+b.im);
}
```

and the use of the constructor in the return statement provides compilers with a valuable clue to optimization. However, for more complicated types and operations, such as matrix operations, the result cannot be constructed in a single expression and implementing * and + in terms of *= and += becomes both simpler to write and easier for an optimizer to deal with:

```
matrix& matrix::operator*=(const matrix& a)
{
    // ...
    return *this;
}
```

```
matrix operator*(const matrix& a, const matrix& b)
{
    matrix prod = a;
    prod *= b;
    return prod;
}
```

Note that an operation defined this way requires no special access to the class it operates on; that is, it needs neither to be a friend nor a member.

A user-defined conversion is implicitly applied only if it is unique (§7.3.3).

An object constructed by explicit or implicit use of a constructor is automatic and will be destroyed at the first opportunity, typically immediately after the statement in which it was created.

7.3.2 Conversion Operators

Using a constructor to specify type conversion is convenient but has implications that can be undesirable:

[1]   There can be no implicit conversion from a user-defined type to a basic type (because the basic types are not classes);

[2]   it is not possible to specify a conversion from a new type to an old one without modifying the declaration for the old one; and

[3]   it is not possible to have a constructor with a single argument without also having a conversion.

The last does not appear to be a serious problem, and the first two problems can be coped with by defining a *conversion operator* for the source type. A member function X::operator T(), where T is a type name, defines a conversion from X to T. For example, one could define a type tiny that can take on values in the range 0..63 only but still can mix freely with integers in arithmetic operations:

```
class tiny {
    char v;
    void assign(int i)
    {   if (i>63) { error("range error"); v=i&~63; }
        v=i;
    }
public:
    tiny(int i) { assign(i); }
    tiny(const tiny& t) { v = t.v; }
    tiny& operator=(const tiny& t)
        { v = t.v; return *this; }
    tiny& operator=(int i) { assign(i); return *this; }
    operator int() { return v; }
};
```

The range is checked whenever a tiny is initialized by an int and whenever an int is assigned to one. One tiny can be assigned to another without a range check. To enable the usual integer operations on tiny variables the implicit conversion from `tiny` to `int`, `tiny::operator int()`, is defined. Whenever a `tiny` appears where an `int` is needed, the appropriate `int` is used. For example:

```
void main()
{
    tiny c1 = 2;
    tiny c2 = 62;
    tiny c3 = c2 - c1;    // c3 = 60
    tiny c4 = c3;         // no range check (not necessary)
    int i = c1 + c2;      // i = 64
    c1 = c2 + 2 * c1;     // range error: c1 = 0 (not 66)
    c2 = c1 - i;          // range error: c2 = 0
    c3 = c2;              // no range check (not necessary)
}
```

A type *vector of tiny* would appear to be more useful because it would also save space; the subscript operator `[]` can be used to make such a type convenient to use.

Another use of user-defined conversion operators is for types providing non-standard representations of numbers (base 100 arithmetic, fixed point arithmetic, Binary Coded Decimal representation, etc.); this will typically involve redefinition of operators such as `+` and `*`.

Conversion functions appear to be particularly useful for handling data structures when reading (implemented by a conversion operator) is trivial, while assignment and initialization are distinctly less trivial.

The `istream` and `ostream` types rely on a conversion function to make statements such as

```
while (cin>>x) cout<<x;
```

possible. The input operation `cin>>x` above returns an `istream&`. That value is implicitly converted to a value indicating the state of `cin`, and this value can then be tested by the `while` (see §10.3.2). However, it is typically *not* a good idea to define an implicit conversion from one type to another in such a way that information is lost in the conversion.

In general it is wise to be sparing in the introduction of conversion operators. When used in excess, they can lead to large numbers of ambiguities. Such ambiguities are caught by the compiler, but they can be a nuisance to resolve. Probably the best idea is initially to do conversions by named functions, such as `X::intof()` and only if such a function becomes used enough to make explicit use inelegant, to replace it with a conversion operator `X::operator int()`.

7.3.3 Ambiguities

An assignment to (or initialization of) an object of class X is legal if either the assigned value is an X or there is a unique conversion of the assigned value to type X.

In some cases, a value of the desired type can be constructed by repeated use of constructors or conversion operators. This must be handled by explicit use; only one level of user-defined implicit conversion is legal. In some cases, a value of the

desired type can be constructed in more than one way. Such cases are illegal. For
example:

```
class x { /* ... */ x(int); x(char*); };
class y { /* ... */ y(int); };
class z { /* ... */ z'(x); };

x f(x);
y f(y);

z g(z);

void k1()
{
    f(1);           // illegal: ambiguous f(x(1)) or f(y(1))
    f(x(1));
    f(y(1));
    g("asdf");      // illegal: g(z(x("asdf"))) not tried
    g(z("asdf"));
}
```

    User-defined conversions are considered only if a call cannot be resolved without
them. For example:

```
class x { /* ... */ x(int); };

void h(double);
void h(x);

void k2()
{
    h(1);
}
```

The call could be interpreted as either h(double(1)) or h(x(1)) and would
appear to be illegal according to the uniqueness rule. However, the first interpretation
uses only a standard conversion and will be chosen under the rules presented in §4.6.6
and §r.13.2.
    The rules for conversion are neither the simplest to implement, the simplest to
document, nor the most general that could be devised. Consider the requirement that
a conversion must be unique to be legal. A simpler approach would allow the compiler to use any conversion it could find; thus it would not be necessary to consider all
possible conversions before declaring an expression legal. Unfortunately, this would
imply that the meaning of a program depended on which conversion was found. In
effect, the meaning of a program would in some way depend on the order of the declaration of the conversions. Because these will often reside in different source files
(written by different programmers), the meaning of a program would depend on the
order in which its parts were merged. Alternatively, implicit conversions could be
disallowed. Nothing could be simpler, but this rule leads to either inelegant user

interfaces or an explosion of overloaded functions and operators, as seen in the class `complex` in the previous section.

The most general approach would take all available type information into account and consider all possible conversions. For example, using the preceding declarations, `aa=f(1)` could be handled because the type of `aa` determines a unique interpretation. If `aa` is an `x`, `f(x(1))` is the only one yielding the `x` needed in the assignment; if `aa` is a `y`, `f(y(1))` will be used instead. The most general approach would also cope with `g("asdf")` because `g(z(x("asdf")))` is a unique interpretation. The problem with this approach is that it requires extensive analysis of a complete expression to determine the interpretation of each operator and function call. This leads to slow compilation and also to surprising interpretations and error messages as the compiler considers conversions defined in libraries, etc. With this approach, the compiler takes more information into account than the programmer writing the code can be expected to know! With the chosen approach, checking is a strictly bottom up process where only one operator and its already type checked operands are considered at a time.

The insistence on strict bottom up analysis implies that the return type is not used in overloading resolution. For example:

```
class quad {
    // ...
public:
    quad(double);
    // ...
};


quad operator+(quad,quad);

void f(double a1, double a2)
{
    quad r1 = a1+a2;         // double-precision add
    quad r2 = quad(a1)+a2; // force quad arithmetic
}
```

The reason for this design choice is partly that strict bottom up analysis is more comprehensible, and partly that it is not considered the compiler's job to decide which precision the programmer might want for the addition.

However, note that once the types of both sides of an initialization or assignment have been determined, both types are used to resolve the initialization or assignment:

```
class real {
    // ...
public:
    operator double();
    operator int();
    // ...
};
```

```
void g(real a)
{
    double d = a;    // d = a.double();
    int i = a;       // i = a.int();

    d = a;           // d = a.double();
    i = a;           // i = a.int();
}
```

In these cases the type analysis is still bottom up, with only a single operator and its argument types considered at any one time.

7.4 Literals

It is not possible to define literals of a class type in the sense that 1.2 and 12e3 are literals of type double. However, literals of the basic types can often be used instead if class member functions are used to provide an interpretation for them. Constructors taking a single argument provide a general mechanism for this. When constructors are simple and inline substituted, it is quite reasonable to think of constructor invocations as literals. For example, given the declaration of class complex in <complex.h>, the expression zz1*3+zz2*complex(1,2) will cause two function calls and not five. The two * operations will cause real function calls, but the + operation and the constructor called to create complex(3) and complex(1,2) will be inline expanded.

7.5 Large Objects

For each use of a complex binary operator as previously declared, a copy of each operand is passed as an argument to the function implementing the operator. The overhead of copying two doubles is noticeable but probably acceptable. Unfortunately, not all classes have a conveniently small representation. To avoid excessive copying, one can declare functions to take reference arguments. For example:

```
class matrix {
    double m[4][4];
public:
    matrix();
    friend matrix operator+(const matrix&, const matrix&);
    friend matrix operator*(const matrix&, const matrix&);
};
```

References allow the use of expressions involving the usual arithmetic operators for large objects without excessive copying. Pointers can not be used because it is not possible to redefine the meaning of an operator when applied to a pointer. The plus operator could be defined like this:

```
matrix operator+(const matrix& arg1, const matrix& arg2)
{
    matrix sum;
    for (int i=0; i<4; i++)
        for (int j=0; j<4; j++)
            sum.m[i][j] = arg1.m[i][j] + arg2.m[i][j];
    return sum;
}
```

This `operator+()` accesses the operands of + through references, but returns an object value. Returning a reference would appear to be more efficient:

```
class matrix {
    // ...
    friend matrix& operator+(const matrix&, const matrix&);
    friend matrix& operator*(const matrix&, const matrix&);
};
```

This is legal, but causes a memory allocation problem. Because a reference to the result will be passed out of the function as a reference to the return value, the return value cannot be an automatic variable. Since an operator is often used more than once in an expression, the result cannot be a `static` local variable. The result would typically be allocated on the free store. Copying the return value is often cheaper (in execution time, code space, and data space) than allocating and (eventually) deallocating an object on free store. It is also much simpler to program.

7.6 Assignment and Initialization

Consider a simple class `string`:

```
struct string {
    char* p;
    int size;   // of vector pointed to by p

    string(int sz) { p = new char[size=sz]; }
    ~string() { delete p; }
};
```

A string is a data structure consisting of a pointer to a vector of characters and the size of that vector. The vector is created by the constructor and deleted by the destructor. However, as shown in §5.5.1, this can cause trouble. For example:

```
void f()
{
    string s1(10);
    string s2(20);
    s1 = s2;
}
```

will allocate two character vectors, but the assignment s1=s2 will destroy the pointer to one of them and duplicate the other. The destructor will be called for s1 and s2 on exit from f(), and it will then delete the same vector twice, with predictably disastrous results. The solution to this problem is to define assignment of string objects appropriately.

```
struct string {
    char* p;
    int size;   // of vector pointed to by p

    string(int sz) { p = new char[size=sz]; }
    ~string() { delete p; }
    string& operator=(const string&);
};
```

```
string& string::operator=(const string& a)
{
    if (this != &a) {   // beware of s=s;
        delete p;
        p = new char[size=a.size];
        strcpy(p,a.p);
    }
    return *this;
}
```

This definition of string will ensure that the preceding example will work as intended. However, a small modification to f() will cause the problem to reappear in a different guise:

```
void f()
{
    string s1(10);
    string s2 = s1;   // initialization, not assignment
}
```

Now only one string is constructed by string::string(int), but two strings are destroyed. The user-defined assignment operator is not applied to an uninitialized object. A quick look at string::operator=() shows why that would be unreasonable: the pointer p would contain an undefined and effectively random value. An assignment operator often relies on its arguments being initialized. For an initialization such as the preceding one this is by definition not so. Consequently, a similar, but separate, function must be defined to cope with initialization:

```
struct string {
    char* p;
    int size;   // of vector pointed to by p

    string(int sz) { p = new char[size=sz]; }
    ~string() { delete p; }
    string& operator=(const string&);
    string(const string&);
};

string::string(const string& a)
{
    p=new char[size=a.size];
    strcpy(p,a.p);
}
```

For a type X, the copy constructor X (const X&) takes care of initialization by an object of the same type X. It cannot be overemphasized that *assignment and initialization are different operations.* This is especially important when a destructor is declared. If a class X has a destructor that performs a nontrivial task, such as free store de-allocation, it is likely that it needs the full complement of functions for completely avoiding memberwise copying of objects:

```
class X {
    // ...
    X(something);          // constructor: create objects
    X(const X&);           // copy constructor
    operator=(const X&);   // assignment: cleanup and copy
    ~X();                  // destructor: cleanup
};
```

There are two more cases when an object is copied: as a function argument and as a function return value. When an argument is passed, a hitherto uninitialized variable – the formal argument – is initialized. The semantics are identical to those of other initializations. The same is the case for function return, though that is less obvious. In both cases, the copy constructor will be applied. For example,

```
string g(string arg)
{
    return arg;
}

main ()
{
    string s = "asdf";
    s = g(s);
}
```

Clearly, the value of s ought to be "asdf" after the call of g (). Getting a copy of the value of s into the argument `arg` is not difficult; a call of `string`'s copy constructor does that. Getting a copy of that value out of `g()` takes another call of `string(const string&)`; this time, the variable initialized is a temporary one, which is then assigned to s. Often one, but not both, of these copy operations can be optimized away. Such temporary variables are, of course, destroyed properly using `string::~string()`; see §r.12.2.

For a class X for which the assignment operator `X::operator=(const X&)` and the copy constructor `X::X(const X&)` are not explicitly declared by the programmer, the missing operation or operations will be generated by the compiler. The generated functions will do memberwise copy of the members of the class. Where the elements are simple values – as in the case of complex numbers – this is just right, and the generated operation degenerates into a simple and optimal bitwise copy. Where the members themselves have user-defined copy operations, these are called appropriately. For example:

```
class Record {
    String name, address, profession;
    // ..
};


void f(Record& r1)
{
    Record r2 = r1;
}
```

Here, `String::operator=(const string&)` must be called to copy each `String` member of r1. The original flawed version of class `String` above has a pointer member and a destructor. In this case the default memberwise copy is almost certainly wrong; a compiler can warn in such cases.

7.7 Subscripting

An `operator[]` function can be used to give subscripts a meaning for class objects. The second argument (the subscript) of an `operator[]` function may be of any type. This makes it possible to define associative arrays, etc. As an example, let us recode the example from §2.3.10 in which an associative array is used to write a small program for counting the number of occurrences of words in a file. There a function is used. Here a proper associative array type is defined:

```
class assoc {

    struct pair {
        char* name;
        int val;
    };
```

```
        pair* vec;
        int max;
        int free;

        assoc(const assoc&); // prevent copying
        assoc& operator=(const assoc&); // prevent copying
    public:
        assoc(int);
        int& operator[](const char*);
        void print_all();
    };
```

An assoc keeps a vector of pairs of size max. The index of the first unused vector element is kept in free.

The copy constructor and assignment operator are declared private to prevent copying of assocs. The constructor looks like this:

```
    assoc::assoc(int s)
    {
        max = (s<16) ? 16 : s;
        free = 0;
        vec = new pair[max];
    }
```

The implementation uses the same trivial and inefficient search method as in §2.3.10. However, an assoc grows in case of overflow:

```
    #include <string.h>

    int& assoc::operator[](const char* p)
    /*
        maintain a set of "pair"s:
        search for p,
        return a reference to the integer part of its "pair"
        make a new "pair" if "p" has not been seen
    */
    {
        register pair* pp;

        for (pp=&vec[free-1]; vec<=pp; pp-- )
            if (strcmp(p,pp->name)==0) return pp->val;
```

```
    if (free==max) {      // overflow: grow the vector
        pair* nvec = new pair[max*2];
        for (int i=0; i<max; i++) nvec[i] = vec[i];
        delete vec;
        vec. = nvec;
        max = 2*max;
    }

    pp = &vec[free++];
    pp->name = new char[strlen(p)+1];
    strcpy(pp->name,p);
    pp->val = 0;          // initial value: 0
    return pp->val;
}
```

Because the representation of an `assoc` is hidden, we need a way of printing it. The next section will show how a proper iterator can be defined. Here we will just use a simple print function:

```
void assoc::print_all()
{
    for (int i = 0; i<free; i++)
        cout << vec[i].name << ": " << vec[i].val << '\n';
}
```

Finally, we can write the trivial main program:

```
main()  // count the occurrences of each word on input
{
    const MAX = 256; // larger than the largest word
    char buf[MAX];
    assoc vec(512);
    while (cin>>buf) vec[buf]++;
    vec.print_all();
}
```

Experienced programmers will note that the second comment could easily be false; fixing this problem is left as an exercise (§7.14 [20]). A further development of the idea of an associative array can be found in §8.8.

An `operator[]()` must be a member function. This implies that the `x[y]==y[x]` equivalence does not necessarily hold where x is a class object. The "usual equivalences" between operators with operands of built-in types are not guaranteed for user-defined types (§7.2.2, see also §7.9).

7.8 Function Call

Function call, that is, the notation *expression(expression-list)*, can be interpreted as a binary operation with the *expression* as the left operand and the *expression-list* as the right operand. The call operator () can be overloaded in the same way as other operators. An argument list for an `operator()` function is evaluated and checked according to the usual argument-passing rules. Overloading function call seems to be useful primarily for defining types with only a single operation, and for types for which one operation is so predominant that others can be ignored in most contexts.

We did not define an iterator for the associative array type `assoc`. This could be done by defining a class `assoc_iterator` with the job of presenting elements from an `assoc` in some order. The iterator needs access to the data stored in an `assoc` and it is therefore made a `friend`:

```
class assoc {
friend class assoc_iterator;
    pair* vec;
    int max;
    int free;
public:
    assoc(int);
    int& operator[](const char*);
};
```

The iterator can be defined as:

```
class assoc_iterator {
    const assoc* cs;    // assoc array
    int i;              // current index
public:
    assoc_iterator(const assoc& s) { cs = &s; i = 0; }
    pair* operator()()
        { return (i<cs->free) ? &cs->vec[i++] : 0; }
};
```

An `assoc_iterator` must be initialized for an `assoc` array, and it will return a pointer to a (new) `pair` from that array each time it is activated using the () operator. When it reaches the end of the array, it returns 0:

```
main()   // count the occurrences of each word on input
{
    const MAX = 256; // larger than the largest word
    char buf[MAX];
    assoc vec(512);
    while (cin>>buf) vec[buf]++;
    assoc_iterator next(vec);
    pair* p;
    while ( p = next() )
        cout << p->name << ": " << p->val << '\n';
}
```

An iterator type like this has the advantage over a set of functions doing the same job: It has its own private data for keeping track of the iteration. It is typically also important that many iterators of such a type can be active simultaneously.

Naturally, this use of objects to represent iterators has nothing in particular to do

with operator overloading. Many people like iterators with operations such as
`first()`, `next()`, and `last()`; others like to overload `++` to provide an iterator
that can be used like a pointer (see §8.8). Other popular uses of `operator()` are as
a substring operator and as a subscripting operator for multi-dimensional arrays.

An `operator()()` must be a member function.

7.9 Dereferencing

The dereferencing operator `->` can be defined as a unary postfix operator. That is,
given a class

```
class Ptr {
    // ...
    X* operator->();
};
```

objects of class `Ptr` can be used to access members of class `X` in a very similar to the
way pointers are used. For example:

```
void f(Ptr p)
{
    p->m = 7;   // (p.operator->())->m = 7
}
```

The transformation of the object p into the pointer `p.operator->()` does not
depend on the member m pointed to. That is the sense in which `operator->()` is a
unary postfix operator. However, there is no new syntax introduced, so a member
name is still required after the `->`. For example:

```
void g(Ptr p)
{
    X* q1 = p->;     // syntax error
    X* q2 = p.operator->(); // ok
}
```

Overloading `->` is primarily useful for creating ''smart pointers,'' that is, objects
that act like pointers and in addition perform some action whenever an object is
accessed through them. For example, one could define a class `RecPtr` for accessing
objects of class `Rec` stored on disc. The constructor for `RecPtr` takes a name that
can be used to find the object on disc, `RecPtr::operator->()` brings the object
into main memory when accessed through its `RecPtr`, and `RecPtr`'s destructor
eventually writes the updated object back out to disc.

```
class RecPtr {
    Rec* in_core_address;
    const char* identifier;
    // ...
public:
```

```
        RecPtr(const char* p)
            : identifier(p) { in_core_address = 0; }
        ~RecPtr()
            { write_to_disc(in_core_address,identifier); }
        Rec* operator->();
    };

    Rec* RecPtr::operator->()
    {
        if (in_core_address == 0)
            in_core_address = read_from_disc(identifier);
        return in_core_address;
    }
```

This might be used like this:

```
    main(int argc, const char* argv)
    {
        for (int i = argc; i; i--) {
            RecPtr p(argv[i]);
            p->update();
        }
    }
```

Naturally, a real `RecPtr` would be a template (see §8) so that the `Record` type is a parameter. Also, a realistic program would contain error handling code and use a less naive way of interacting with the disc.

For ordinary pointers, use of `->` is synonymous with some uses of unary `*` and `[]`. For example, for

```
    Y* p;
```

it holds that

```
    p->m  ==  (*p).m  ==  p[0].m
```

As usual, no such guarantee is provided for user-defined operators. The equivalence can be provided where desired:

```
    class X {
        Y* p;
    public:
        Y* operator->() { return p; }
        Y& operator*() { return *p; }
        Y& operator[](int i) { return p[i]; }
    };
```

If you provide more than one of these operators it might be wise to provide the equivalence, just as it is wise to ensure that `++x` and `x+=1` have the same effect as `x=x+1` for a simple variable `x` of some class if `++`, `+=`, `=`, and `+` are provided.

The overloading of `->` is important to a class of interesting programs, just like overloading `[]`, and not just a minor curiosity. The reason is that *indirection* is a key

concept and that overloading -> provides a clean, direct, and efficient way of representing indirection in a program. Another way of looking at operator -> is to consider it a way of providing C++ with a limited, but useful, form of *delegation* (see
§12.2.8 and 13.9).

7.10 Increment and Decrement

Once people invent "smart pointers" they often decide to provide the increment operator ++ and the decrement operator -- to mirror these operators' use for built-in
types. This is especially obvious and necessary where the aim is to replace an ordinary pointer type with a "smart pointer" type that has the same semantics except for
doing a bit of run-time error checking. For example, given a troublesome traditional
program

```
void f1(T a)   // traditional use:
{
    T v[200];
    T* p = &v[0];
    p--;
    *p = a;   // Oops: 'p' out of range, uncaught
    ++p;
    *p = a;   // ok
}
```

one might want to replace the pointer p with an object of a class `CheckedPtrToT`
that can be dereferenced only provided it actually points to an object and incremented
and decremented only provided it points to an object within an array and the increment and decrement operations yield an object within the array:

```
class CheckedPtrToT {
    // ...
};

void f2(T a)   // checked:
{
    T v[200];
    CheckedPtrToT p(&v[0],v,200);
    p--;
    *p = a;   // run-time error: 'p' out of range
    ++p;
    *p = a;   // ok
}
```

The increment and decrement operators are unique among C++ operators in that they
can be used as both prefix and postfix operators. Consequently, we can define class
`CheckedPtrToT` only provided we can specify separate functions for prefix and
postfix increment and decrement. This can be done like this:

```
class CheckedPtrToT {
    T* p;
    T* array;
    int size;
public:
        // bind to array 'a' of size 's'
        // initial value 'p':
    CheckedPtrToT(T* p, T* a, int s);

        // bind to single object
        // initial value 'p':
    CheckedPtrToT(T* p);

    T* operator++();       // prefix
    T* operator++(int);    // postfix

    T* operator--();       // prefix
    T* operator--(int);    // postfix

    T& operator*();        // prefix
};
```

The `int` argument is used to indicate that the function is to be invoked for postfix
application of ++. This `int` is never used; the argument is simply a dummy used to
distinguish between prefix and postfix application. The way to remember which version of an `operator++` is prefix is to note that the version without the dummy argument is prefix exactly as all the other unary arithmetic and logical operators. The
dummy argument is used only for the "odd" postfix ++ and --.

Using `CheckedPtrToT`, the example is equivalent to:

```
void f3(T a)   // checked:
{
    T v[200];
    CheckedPtrToT p(&v[0],v,200);
    p.operator--(1);
    p.operator*() = a;   // run-time error: 'p' out of range
    p.operator++();
    p.operator*() = a;   // ok
}
```

Completing class `CheckedPtrToT` is left as an exercise (§7.14 [19]) and its elabo-
ration into a template using exceptions to report the run-time errors as another exercise (§9.10 [2]). An example of operators ++ and -- for iteration can be found in
§8.8.

7.11 A String Class

Here is a more realistic version of class `string`. It counts the references to a string
to minimize copying and uses standard C++ character strings as constants.

```cpp
#include <iostream.h>
#include <string.h>

class string {
    struct srep {
        char* s;            // pointer to data
        int   n;            // reference count
        srep() { n = 1; }
    };
    srep *p;

public:
    string(const char *);    // string x = "abc"
    string();                // string x;
    string(const string &);  // string x = string ...
    string& operator=(const char *);
    string& operator=(const string &);
    ~string();
    char& operator[](int i);

    friend ostream& operator<<(ostream&, const string&);
    friend istream& operator>>(istream&, string&);

    friend int operator==(const string &x, const char *s)
        { return strcmp(x.p->s, s) == 0; }

    friend int operator==(const string &x, const string &y)
        { return strcmp(x.p->s, y.p->s) == 0; }

    friend int operator!=(const string &x, const char *s)
        { return strcmp(x.p->s, s) != 0; }

    friend int operator!=(const string &x, const string &y)
        { return strcmp(x.p->s, y.p->s) != 0; }
};
```

The constructors and the destructor are trivial:

```cpp
string::string()
{
    p = new srep;
    p->s = 0;
}
```

```
string::string(const string& x)
{
    x.p->n++;
    p = x.p;
}

string::string(const char* s)
{
    p = new srep;
    p->s = new char[ strlen(s)+1 ];
    strcpy(p->s, s);
}

string::~string()
{
    if (--p->n == 0) {
        delete[] p->s;
        delete p;
    }
}
```

As usual, the assignment operators are similar to the constructors. They must handle cleanup of their first (left-hand) operand:

```
string& string::operator=(const char* s)
{
    if (p->n > 1) {          // disconnect self
        p->n--;
        p = new srep;
    }
    else                     // free old string
        delete[] p->s;

    p->s = new char[ strlen(s)+1 ];
    strcpy(p->s, s);
    return *this;
}

string& string::operator=(const string& x)
{
    x.p->n++; // protect against ``st = st''
    if (--p->n == 0) {
        delete[] p->s;
        delete p;
    }
    p = x.p;
    return *this;
}
```

The output operator is intended to demonstrate the use of reference counting. It echoes each input string (using the << operator, defined below):

```
ostream& operator<<(ostream& s, const string& x)
{
    return s << x.p->s << " [" << x.p->n << "]\n";
}
```

The input operation uses the standard character string input function (§10.3.1):

```
istream& operator>>(istream& s, string& x)
{
    char buf[256];
    s >> buf;  // unsafe, might overflow
               // see section 10.3.1 for alternative
    x = buf;
    cout << "echo: " << x << '\n';
    return s;
}
```

The subscript operator is provided for access to individual characters. The index is checked:

```
void error(const char* p)
{
    cerr << p << '\n';
    exit(1);
}
```

```
char& string::operator[](int i)
{
    if (i<0 || strlen(p->s)<i) error("index out of range");
    return p->s[i];
}
```

The main program simply exercises the string operators a bit. It reads words from input into strings and then prints the strings. It continues to do so until the string done is recognized, it runs out of strings to store words in, or it finds the end of file. Then it prints out all the strings in reverse order and terminates.

```
int main()
{
    string x[100];
    int n;

    cout << "here we go\n";
```

```
        for (n = 0; cin>>x[n]; n++) {
            if (n==100) {
                error("too many strings");
                return 99;
            }
            string y;
            cout << (y = x[n]);
            if (y=="done") break;
        }
        cout << "here we go back again\n";
        for (int i=n-1; 0<=i; i--) cout << x[i];
        return 0;
    }
```

7.12 Friends and Members

Finally, it is possible to discuss when to use members and when to use friends to access the private part of a user-defined type. Some operations must be members – for example constructors, destructors, and virtual functions (§r.12) – but typically there is a choice. Because members do not introduce new global names, members should be chosen in the absence of other reasons.

Consider a simple class X:

```
class X {
    // ...

    X(int);

    int m1();
    int m2() const;

    friend int f1(X&);
    friend int f2(const X&);
    friend int f3(X);
};
```

Note first that the members X::m1() and X::m2() can be invoked only for objects of class X. The conversion X(int) cannot be applied for the object for which X::m1() and X::m2() are invoked:

```
void g()
{
    1.m1();   // error: X(1).m1() not tried
    1.m2();   // error: X(1).m2() not tried
}
```

The global function f1() has a similar property (§4.6.3) because it takes a non-const reference; f2() and f3() behave differently:

```
void h()
{
    f1(1);   // error: f1(X(1)) not tried
    f2(1);   // ok: f2(X(1));
    f3(1);   // ok: f3(X(1));
}
```

An operation modifying the state of a class object should therefore be a member or a global function taking a non-const reference argument. Operators that require lvalue operands for the fundamental types (=, *=, ++, etc.) are most naturally defined as members for user-defined types.

Conversely, if implicit type conversion is desired for all operands of an operation, the function implementing it must be a global function taking a const reference argument or a non-reference argument, not a member. This is often the case for the functions implementing operators that do not require lvalue operands when applied to fundamental types (+, −, | |, etc.).

If no type conversions are defined, there appears to be no compelling reason to choose a member over a friend taking a reference argument or vice versa. In some cases the programmer may have a preference for one call syntax over another. For example, most people seem to prefer the notation inv(m) for inverting a matrix m to the alternative m.inv(). Naturally, if inv() really does invert m itself, rather than return a new matrix that is the inverse of m, it should be a member.

All other things considered equal, choose a member: It is not possible to know if someone some day will define a conversion operator. It is not always possible to predict if a future change may require changes to the state of the object involved. The member function call syntax makes it clear to the user that the object may be modified; a reference argument is far less obvious. Furthermore, expressions in the body of a member can be noticeably shorter than the equivalent expressions in a global function. The global function must use an explicit argument, whereas the member can use this implicitly. Also, because member names do not enter the global name space they tend to be shorter than the names of global functions.

7.13 Caveat

Like most programming language features, operator overloading can be both used and misused. In particular, the ability to define new meanings for old operators can be used to write programs that are well nigh incomprehensible. Imagine, for example, the problems facing a reader of a program in which the operator + has been made to denote subtraction. The mechanism presented here should protect the programmer/reader from the worst excesses of overloading by preventing a programmer from changing the meaning of operators for basic data types such as int, and by preserving the syntax of expressions and the precedence of operators.

It is probably wise to use operator overloading primarily to mimic conventional use of operators. The function call notation can be used when such conventional use of operators is not established or when the set of operators available for overloading in C++ is not adequate to mimic conventional usage.

7.14 Exercises

1. (*2) Define an iterator for class `string`. Define a concatenate operator + and an "add to the end" operator +=. What other operations would you like to be able to do on a `string`?
2. (*1.5) Provide a substring operator for a string class by overloading `()`.
3. (*3) Design class `string` so that the substring operator can be used on the left-hand side of an assignment. First write a version in which a string can be assigned to a substring of the same length, then a version in which the lengths may differ.
4. (*2) Design a class `string` so that it has value semantics for assignment, argument passing, etc.; that is, where the string representation, not just the controlling data structure in class `string`, is copied.
5. (*3) Modify the class `string` from the previous example to copy strings only when necessary. That is, keep a shared representation of two strings until one of the strings is modified. Do not try to have a substring operator that can be used on the left-hand side at the same time.
6. (*4) Design a class `string` with value semantics, delayed copy, and a substring operator that can be used on the left-hand side.
7. (*2) In the following program, which conversions are used in each expression?

```
struct X {
    int i;
    X(int);
    operator+(int);
};

struct Y {
    int i;
    Y(X);
    operator+(X);
    operator int();
};

extern X operator*(X, Y);
extern int f(X);

X x = 1;
Y y = x;
int i = 2;

int main()
{
    i + 10;          y + 10;          y + 10 * y;
```

```
x + y + i;       x * x + i;       f(7);
f(y);            y + y;           106 + y;
}
```

Define both X and Y to be integer types. Modify the program so that it will run and print the values of each legal expression.

8. (*2) Define a class INT that behaves exactly like an int. Hint: Define INT::operator int().

9. (*1) Define a class RINT that behaves like an int except that the only operations allowed are + (unary and binary), - (unary and binary), *, /, %. Hint: Do not define RINT::operator int().

10. (*3) Define a class LINT that behaves like a RINT except that it has at least 64 bits of precision.

11. (*4) Define a class implementing arbitrary precision arithmetic. Hint: You will need to manage storage in a way similar to what was done for class string.

12. (*2) Write a program that has been rendered unreadable through use of operator overloading and macros. An idea: Define + to mean − and vice versa for INTs; then use a macro to define int to mean INT. Redefining popular functions, using reference type arguments, and a few misleading comments can also create great confusion.

13. (*3) Swap the result of exercise [12] with a friend. Figure out what your friend's program does without running it. When you have completed this exercise you'll know what to avoid.

14. (*2) Re-write the complex example (§7.3), the tiny example (§7.3.2), and the string example (§7.11) without use of friend functions. Use only member functions. Test each of the new versions. Compare them with the versions using friend functions. Review Exercise 5.3.

15. (*2) Define a type vec4 as a vector of four floats. Define operator[] for vec4. Define operators +, −, *, /, =, +=, −=, *=, and /= for combinations of vectors and floating point numbers.

16. (*3) Define a class mat4 as a vector of four vec4s. Define operator[] returning a vec4 for mat4. Define the usual matrix operations for this type. Define a function doing Gaussian elimination for a mat4.

17. (*2) Define a class vector similar to vec4, but with the size given as an argument to the constructor vector::vector(int).

18. (*3) Define a class matrix similar to mat4, but with the dimensions given as arguments to the constructor matrix::matrix(int,int).

19. (*3) Complete class CheckedPtoT from §7.10 and test it. To be complete, CheckedPtoT must have at least the operators *, −>, =, ++, and −− defined. Do not cause a run-time error until a wild pointer is actually dereferenced.

20. (*1.5) Re-write the word-counting program from §7.7 so that it contain no arbitrary limit on the length of a word.

8

Templates

Your quote here.
– B.Stroustrup

This chapter introduces the template concept that allows container classes, such as lists and associative arrays, to be simply defined and implemented without loss of static type checking or run-time efficiency. Similarly, templates allow generic functions, such as `sort()`, to be defined once for a family of types. A family of list classes is defined as an example of templates and their interaction with other language features. Some variants of a `sort()` function template is presented to demonstrate techniques for using templates to compose code from semi-independent parts. Finally, a simple associative array template is defined and used in a couple of small example programs.

8.1 Introduction

One of the most useful kinds of classes is the container class, that is, a class that holds objects of some (other) type. Lists, arrays, associative arrays, and sets are container classes. Specifying a container of objects of a single known type can be done with the facilities described in Chapters 5 and 7. For example §5.3.2 defined a set of `int`s. However, container classes have the interesting property that the type of objects they contain is of little interest to the definer of a container class, but of crucial importance to the user of a particular container. Thus we want to have the type of the contained object be an argument to a container class: The definer specifies the container class in terms of that argument, and the users specify what the type of contained objects is to be for each particular container (each object of the container class). The `Vector` template in §1.4.3 was an example of this.

This chapter first presents the notion of a template class by examining a simple `stack` template. Then a more complete and realistic example of a couple of related list templates is presented. Function templates and the rules for what can be a function template argument are stated. Finally, an associative array template is presented.

8.2 A Simple Template

A class template specifies how individual classes can be constructed much as a class declaration specifies how individual objects can be constructed. We can define a `stack` of elements of an arbitrary type:

```
template<class T>
class stack {
    T* v;
    T* p;
    int sz;

public:
    stack(int s) { v = p = new T[sz=s]; }
    ˜stack() { delete[] v; }

    void push(T a) { *p++ = a; }
    T pop() { return *--p; }

    int size() const { return p-v; }
};
```

All run-time error checking has been left out for simplicity. Apart from that, the example is complete and realistic.

The `template <class T>` prefix specifies that a template is being declared and that an argument T of type *type* will be used in the declaration. After its introduction, T is used exactly like other type names. The scope of T extends to the end of the declaration that `template <class T>` prefixes. Note that `template<class T>` says that T is a *type* name; it need not actually be the name of a *class*. For sc below, T turns out to be `char`.

The name of a class template followed by a type bracketed by < > is the name of a class (as defined by the template) and can be used exactly like other class names. For example:

```
stack<char> sc(100);       // stack of characters
```

defines an object sc of a class `stack<char>`.

Except for the special syntax of its name, `stack<char>` works exactly as if it had been defined:

```
class stack_char {
    char* v;
    char* p;
    int sz;
public:
    stack_char(int s) { v = p = new char[sz=s]; }
    ~stack_char() { delete[] v; }

    void push(char a) { *p++ = a; }
    char pop() { return *--p; }

    int size() const { return p-v; }
};
```

One can think of a template as a clever kind of macro that obeys the scope, naming, and type rules of C++. That would be an oversimplification, but it is an oversimplification that might help avoid some gross misunderstandings. In particular, use of a template need not imply any run-time mechanisms beyond what is used for an equivalent ''hand-written'' class, nor does it necessarily imply any savings in the amount of code generated.

It is usually a good idea to debug a particular class, such as `stack_char`, before turning it into a template such as `stack<T>`. Similarly, when trying to understand a template it is often useful to imagine its behavior for a particular type such as `int` or `shape*` before trying to comprehend the template in its full generality.

Given the class template declaration, `stacks` can now be defined and used like this:

```
stack<shape*> ssp(200);   // stack of pointers to shapes
stack<Point> sp(400);     // stack of Points

void f(stack<complex>& sc)     // 'reference to stack
                               // of complex' argument
{
    sc.push(complex(1,2));
    complex z = 2.5*sc.pop();

    stack<int>*p = 0;          // pointer to stack of ints
    p = new stack<int>(800);   // stack of ints
                               // on the free store

    for (int i = 0; i<400; i++) {
        p->push(i);
        sp.push(Point(i,i+400));
    }

    // ...
}
```

Because the `stack` member functions were all inline, the only function calls generated for this example were the ones generated for free store allocation and deallocation.

Template functions need not be inline; stack could equally well have been defined:

```
template<class T> class stack {
    T* v;
    T* p;
    int sz;
public:
    stack(int);
    ~stack();

    void push(T);
    T pop();

    int size() const;
};
```

In that case, definitions of the stack member function must be provided somewhere exactly as for non-template class member functions. Such functions are themselves parameterized by the type argument to their template class; thus these functions are defined by function templates. When defined outside the template class, this must be explicit. For example:

```
template<class T> void stack<T>::push(T a)
{
    *p++ = a;
}

template<class T> stack<T>::stack(int s)
{
    v = p = new T[sz=s];
}
```

Note that within the scope of stack<T> qualification with <T> is redundant so that stack<T>::stack is the name for the constructor.

It is the implementation's job – *not* the programmer's – to ensure that versions of template functions are generated for each argument type to the template. Thus for the example above, the implementation would generate definitions for the constructors for stack<shape*>, stack<Point>, and stack<int>, the destructors for stack<shape*> and stack<Point>, the push() functions for stack<complex>, stack<int>, stack<Point>, and the pop() function for stack<complex>. The generated functions will be perfectly ordinary member functions. For example:

```
void stack<complex>::push(complex a) { *p++ = a; }
```

differs from ''ordinary member functions'' only in the syntax for the class name.

Just as there can be only one function defining a class member function in a program, there can be only one function template defining a class template member function in a program. When a function definition is needed for a class template member function for a particular type, it is the implementation's job to find the template for the member function and generate the appropriate version. An implementation may require the programmer to help find templates unless some convention is obeyed.

It is important to write templates so that they have as few dependencies on global information as possible. The reason is that a template will be used to generate functions and classes based on unknown types and in unknown contexts. Almost any subtle context dependency will surface as a debugging problem to a programmer who is unlikely to be the original author of the template. The rule of avoiding references to global names as far as possible should be taken extra seriously in template design.

8.3 List Templates

When writing a realistic collection class, one often needs to deal with relationships between the classes involved in the implementation, with memory management issues, and with the need to iterate over a collection. It is also common to design several related classes together (§12.2). As an example, we will present a family of singly linked list classes and templates.

8.3.1 An Intrusive List

First, we will build a simple list that relies on a link field in objects put onto the list. Later, we use that list as a building block for a more general list that does not require a link field in objects put onto it. The class declarations with only their public functions will be presented first; the implementation will be presented in the next section. The idea is to avoid obscuring the design points with implementation details.

First we define a type `slink`, that is, a link in a singly linked list:

```
struct slink {
    slink* next;
    slink() { next=0; }
    slink(slink* p) { next = p; }
};
```

We can now define a class that can contain objects of any class derived from `slink`:

```
class slist_base {
    // ...
public:
    int insert(slink*);    // add at head of list
    int append(slink*);    // add at tail of list
    slink* get();          // remove and return head of list
    // ...
};
```

This class is intrusive because it can be used only if the elements provide the `slink` as a handle for `slist_base` to use. The name `slist_base` indicates that the class will be used as a base for singly linked list classes. As ever, when one designs a family of related entities there is a problem selecting names for the various members of the family. Since class names cannot be overloaded the way function names can, we cannot use overloading to reduce the name proliferation.

An `slist_base` can be used like this:

```
void f()
{
    slist_base slb;
    slb.insert(new slink);
    // ...
    slink* p = slb.get();
    // ...
    delete p;
}
```

However, because `slink`s don't carry information (beyond their identity), this is not very interesting. To use a `slist_base`, one needs to derive a useful class from `slink`. In a compiler one might have a `name` node that needs to be on a list:

```
class name : public slink {
    // ...
};

void f(const char* s)
{
    slist_base slb;
    slb.insert(new name(s));
    // ...
    name* p = (name*)slb.get();
    // ...
    delete p;
}
```

This works, but because `slist_base` is defined in terms of `slink`s and not names, it is necessary to use an explicit cast to convert the `slink*` returned by `slist_base::get()` into a `name*`. This is inelegant. In a large program with many lists and many classes derived from `slink`, it is also error prone. What we would like is a type-safe version of `slist_base`:

```
template<class T>
class Islist : private slist_base {
public:
    void insert(T* a) { slist_base::insert(a); }
    T* get() { return (T*) slist_base::get(); }
    // ...
};
```

The cast inside `Islist::get()` is perfectly reasonable and safe because class
`Islist` ensures that every object on the list really is of type `T` or of a type derived
from `T`. Note that `slist_base` is a `private` base class of `Islist`. We do not
want users accidentally messing around with the unsafe implementation details.

The name `Islist` stands for ''intrusive singly linked list.'' This template can be
used like this:

```
void f(const char* s)
{
    Islist<name> ilst;
    ilst.insert(new name(s));
    // ...
    name* p = ilst.get();
    // ...
    delete p;
}
```

Attempted misuses are caught at compile time:

```
class expr : public slink {
    // ...
};

void g(expr* e)
{
    Islist<name> ilst;
    ilst.insert(e); // error: Islist<name>::insert()
                    // expects a name*
    // ...
}
```

There are several important things to note about the example so far. First, the scheme
is type safe (barring silly mistakes in the very limited context of the access functions
in `Islist`). Second, type safety is achieved without the expenditure of time or
space because the access functions in `Islist` are trivial inline functions. Third,
because all the real work is done by the – yet to be presented – implementation of
`slist_base`, there is no replication of code, and the source code of the implementation (the `slist_base` functions) need not be available to a user. This is considered commercially important by some. It also provides a separation between an interface and its implementation so that re-implementation without requiring recompilation of user code becomes possible. Finally, a simple intrusive list is close to
optimal in time and space. In other words, this strategy has near optimal properties of
time, space, data hiding, and type checking while providing great flexibility and econ-
omy of expression.

However, an object can be on an `Islist` only provided it is derived from
`slink`. This implies that we cannot have an `Islist` of `int`s, that we cannot have
a list of some previously defined type that is not based on `slink`, and that having an
object on two `Islist`s takes some work (§6.5.1).

8.3.2 A Non-intrusive List

After our "digression" into the building and use of intrusive lists, we can proceed to building a non-intrusive list, that is, a list that does not require its elements to provide facilities to help the implementation of the list class. Because we no longer can assume that an object on the list has link field, the list implementation will have to provide one:

```
template<class T>
struct Tlink : public slink {
    T info;
    Tlink(const T& a) : info(a) { }
};
```

A `Tlink<T>` holds a copy of an object of type `T` in addition to the link field provided by its base class `slink`. Note that the use of the initializer `info(a)`, rather than the assignment `info=a`, is essential for efficient operation for types with non-trivial copy constructors and assignment operators (§7.11). For such a type – say `String` – defining the constructor,

```
Tlink(const T& a) { info = a; }
```

would have caused a default `String` to be constructed and then assigned to.

Given this link class and the `Islist` class, the definition of the non-intrusive list is almost trivial:

```
template<class T>
class Slist : private slist_base {
public:
    void insert(const T& a)
        { slist_base::insert(new Tlink<T>(a)); }
    void append(const T& a)
        { slist_base::append(new Tlink<T>(a)); }
    T get();
    // ...
};


template<class T>
T Slist<T>::get()
{
    Tlink<T>* lnk = (Tlink<T>*) slist_base::get();
    T i = lnk->info;
    delete lnk;
    return i;
}
```

The use of `Slist` is as simple as the use of `Islist`. The difference is that it is possible to have an object on an `Slist` without first deriving its class from `slink` and to have an object on two lists:

```
void f(int i)
{
    Slist<int> lst1;
    Slist<int> lst2;

    lst1.insert(i);
    lst2.insert(i);
    // ...

    int i1 = lst1.get();
    int i2 = lst1.get();
    // ...
}
```

However, an intrusive list, such as `Islist`, does have a consistent advantage in run-time efficiency and most often in compactness: Each time we put an object on an `Slist`, the list needs to allocate a `Tlink` object; each time we take an object off an `Slist`, the list needs to deallocate a `Tlink` object; and in each case a `T` is copied. Where the overhead is a problem, two things can be done. First, `Tlink` is a prime candidate for a near-optimal special-purpose allocator as described in §5.5.6; this will reduce the run-time overhead to something that is most often acceptable. Second, it is often a good idea to keep objects on a "primary list" that is intrusive and to use non-intrusive lists only where membership of several lists is needed:

```
void f(name* p)
{
    Islist<name> lst1;
    Slist<name*> lst2;

    lst1.insert(p);    // link through object '*p'
    lst2.insert(p);    // use separate link object to hold 'p'
    // ...
}
```

Naturally, such tricks can typically be played only within a particular component of a program (to avoid confusion about the types of lists used in inter-component interfaces) but *that* is exactly where run-time efficiency and compactness games are worth playing.

Because of the copying of the argument to `insert()` in the `tlist` constructor, `Slist` is suitable only for small objects such as integers, `complex` numbers, and pointers. For objects where copying is expensive or unacceptable for semantic reasons, it is often a good idea to put pointers on the list rather than the objects themselves. This was done for `lst2` in `f()` above.

Note that because an argument to `Slist::insert()` is copied, passing an object of a derived class to an `insert()` function expecting an object of a base class will not work as (naively) expected:

```
class smiley : public circle { /* ... */ };

void g1(Slist<circle>& olist, const smiley& grin)
{
    olist.insert(grin);   // trap!
}
```

Only the `circle` part of the `smiley` will be stored. Note that this nasty problem is detected by the compiler in the case where it is most likely to occur. Had the base class in question been an abstract class, the compiler would have refused to ''slice'' the object of the derived class:

```
void g2(Slist<shape>& olist, const circle& c)
{
    olist.insert(c);   // error: attempt to create
                       // object of abstract class
}
```

Pointers must be used to avoid the problem of slicing:

```
void g3(Slist<shape*>& plist, const smiley& grin)
{
    plist.insert(&grin);   // fine
}
```

Don't use a reference as an argument to a class template. For example:

```
void g4(Slist<shape&>& rlist, const smiley& grin)
{
    rlist.insert(grin);   // error: generated code contains
                          // reference to reference (Shape&&)
}
```

References used like that most often cause type errors when the template is expanded. In this case the expansion of

```
Slist::insert(T&);
```

gives rise to the illegal declaration

```
Slist::insert(shape&&);
```

A reference is not an object, so it is not possible to have a reference to a reference.
    Since lists of pointers are so useful it is a good idea to name them specifically:

```
template<class T>
class Splist : private Slist<void*> {
public:
    void insert(T* p) { Slist<void*>::insert(p); }
    void append(T* p) { Slist<void*>::append(p); }
    T* get() { return (T*) Slist<void*>::get(); }
};
```

```
class Isplist : private slist_base {
public:
    void insert(T* p) { slist_base::insert(p); }
    void append(T* p) { slist_base::append(p); }
    T* get() { return (T*) slist_base::get(); }
};
```

This also improves type checking and further reduces code replication.

It is often useful for the element type of a template itself to be a template class. For example, a sparse matrix of dates could be defined like this:

```
typedef Slist< Slist<date> > dates;
```

Please note the use of spaces here. Leaving out the space between the first and the second > would cause a syntax error when >> in

```
typedef Slist<Slist<date>> dates;
```

was interpreted as a right shift operator. As ever, a name introduced by a `typedef` is a synonym for the type it names and not a new type. Typedefs can be useful for longer template class names just as they are for other longish type names.

Note that a template argument used in several ways in a template should be be mentioned once only in the list of template arguments. Thus, a template using a T object and a list of T's is defined like this

```
template<class T> class mytemplate {
    T obj;
    Slist<T> slst;
    // ...
};
```

and *not* like this

```
template<class T, class Slist<T> > class mytemplate {
    T obj;
    Slist<T> slst;
    // ...
};
```

The rules for what can be a template argument can be found in §8.6 and §r.14.2.

8.3.3 A List Implementation

Implementing the `slist_base` functions is straightforward. The only real problem is what to do in case of an error, for example, what to do in case a user tries to `get()` something off an empty list. This will be handled by providing an error function, `slist_handler()`. Further strategies relying on exceptions will be discussed in Chapter 9.

The complete declaration of class `slist_base` is:

```
class slist_base {
    slink* last;   // last->next is head of list
public:
    void insert(slink* a);  // add at head of list
    void append(slink* a);  // add at tail of list
    slink* get();           // return and remove head

    void clear() { last = 0; }

    slist_base() { last = 0; }
    slist_base(slink* a) { last = a->next = a; }

    friend class slist_base_iter;
};
```

Storing a pointer to the last element of the circular list enables simple implementation
of both an append() and an insert() operation:

```
void slist_base::insert(slink* a)   // add to head of list
{
    if (last)
        a->next = last->next;
    else
        last = a;
    last->next = a;
}
```

Note that last->next is the first element on the list.

```
void slist_base::append(slink* a)   //  add to tail of list
{
    if (last) {
        a->next = last->next;
        last = last->next = a;
    }
    else
        last = a->next = a;
}
```

```
slist* slist_base::get()   // return and remove head of list
{
    if (last == 0) slist_handler("get from empty slist");
    slink* f = last->next;
    if (f == last)
        last = 0;
    else
        last->next = f->next;
    return f;
}
```

For flexibility, it is a good idea to have slist_handler be a pointer to function rather than a function. The call

```
slist_handler("get from empty list");
```

will then be equivalent to

```
(*slist_handler)("get from empty list");
```

As in the case of the new_handler() (§3.2.6) it is useful to provide a function

```
typedef void (*PFV)(const char*);

PFV set_slist_handler(PFV a)
{
    PFV old = slist_handler;
    slist_handler = a;
    return old;
}

PFV slist_handler = &default_slist_handler;
```

to help users manage their handlers. Exceptions, as described in Chapter 9, provide both an alternative way of handling errors and a way of implementing an slist_handler.

8.3.4 Iteration

Class slist_base provides no facilities for looking into a list, only the means for inserting and deleting members. It does, however, declare a class slist_base_iter to be a friend, so we can declare a suitable iterator. Here is one in the style presented in §7.8:

```
class slist_base_iter {
    slink* ce;        // curent element
    slist_base* cs;   // current list
public:
    inline slist_base_iter(slist_base& s);
    inline slink* operator()();
};


slist_base_iter::slist_base_iter(slist_base& s)
{
    cs = &s;
    ce = cs->last;
}
```

```
slink* slist_base_iter::operator()()
    // return 0 to indicate end of iteration
{
    slink* ret = ce ? (ce=ce->next) : 0;
    if (ce == cs->last) ce = 0;
    return ret;
}
```

From this, iterators for `Slist` and `Islist` are easily constructed. First we must declare the iterators `friends` of their respective collection classes:

```
template<class T> class Islist_iter;

template<class T> class Islist {
    friend class Islist_iter<T>;
    // ...
};


template<class T> class Slist_iter;

template<class T> class Slist {
    friend class Slist_iter<T>;
    // ...
};
```

Note the way the names of the iterators are introduced without defining their template classes. This is the way one handles mutual dependencies between templates.

Next we can define the iterators:

```
template<class T>
class Islist_iter : private slist_base_iter {
public:
    Islist_iter(Islist<T>& s) : slist_base_iter(s) { }

    T* operator()()
        { return (T*) slist_base_iter::operator()(); }
};


template<class T>
class Slist_iter : private slist_base_iter {
public:
    Slist_iter(Slist<T>& s) : slist_base_iter(s) { }
    inline T* operator()();
};


T* Slist_iter::operator()()
{
    return ((Tlink<T>*) slist_base_iter::operator()())->info;
}
```

Note that we again used the trick of deriving a family of classes (that is, a class template) from a unique base class. This uses inheritance to express commonality and to prevent unnecessary code replication. The importance of avoiding code replication in the implementation of simple, frequently used classes such as lists and iterators cannot be overstated. Such iterators can be used like this:

```
void f(name* p)
{
    Islist<name> lst1;
    Slist<name> lst2;

    lst1.insert(p);
    lst2.insert(p);
    // ...

    Islist_iter<name> iter1(lst1);
    const name* p;
    while (p=iter1()) {
        list_iter<name> iter2(lst1);
        const name* q;
        while (q=iter2()) {
            if (p == q) cout << "found " << *p << '\n';
        }
    }
}
```

There are several techniques for providing iteration for container classes. A designer of a program or a library will have to choose one style and stick to it. The style presented above is sometimes deemed "too cute." A less cute variant can be had by simply renaming `operator()()` as `next()`. Both variants have the property that cooperation between the iterator class and its container class is assumed so that it is possible to handle the case where elements are added to or removed from the container while an iterator is active. This and several other techniques would not be feasible if iteration depended on user code holding pointers to elements in the container. Typically, a container or its iterator supports a notion of resetting an iteration to "the beginning" and the notion of a "current element."

If the notion of a current element is provided by the container itself rather than by the iterator, the iteration becomes intrusive to the container in the same way links stored in element were to the contained objects. That is, it becomes hard to have two simultaneous iterations for a container, but the time and space properties of iteration approach optimum. For example:

```
class slist_base {
    // ...
    slink* last;  // last->next is head of list
    slink* current; // current element
public:
```

```
        // ...
        slink* head() { return last?last->next:0; }
        slink* current() { return current; }
        void   set_current(slink* p) { current = p; }
        slink* first() { set_current(head()); return current; }
        slink* next();
        slink* prev();
    };
```

In the same way as both intrusive and non-intrusive lists could be used for the same
object for space and time efficiency, both intrusive and non-intrusive iteration can be
used for the same container:

```
    void f(Islist<name>& ilst)
    // dumb search for duplicates:
    {
        list_iter<name> slow(ilst); // use iterator
        name* p;
        while (p = slow()) {
            ilst.set_current(p); // rely on current element
            name* q;
            while (q = ilist.next())
                if (strcmp(p->string,q->string) == 0)
                    cout << "duplicate " << p << '\n';
        }
    }
```

For yet another style of iterator see §8.8.

8.4 Function Templates

The use of template classes implies template member functions. In addition, global
function templates, that is function templates that are not members of a class, can be
defined. A function template defines a family of functions in the same way a class
template defines a family of classes. This idea will be explored through a series of
examples of how one might provide a sort() function. Each variant of sort() in
the subsections below illustrates a general technique.

    As ever, the focus of the discussion is program organization rather than algorithm
design so a trivial algorithm is used. These variants of the sort() template are presented to demonstrate language features and useful techniques. The variants are not
ordered according to "how good" they are, and there is also a lot to be said for the
traditional non-template version (passing a pointer to a comparison function) in many
contexts.

8.4.1 A Simple Global Function Template

Consider first the simplest `sort ()` template:

```
template<class T> void sort(Vector<T>&);

void f(Vector<int>& vi,
       Vector<String>& vc,
       Vector<int>& vi2,
       Vector<char*>& vs)
{
    sort(vi);     // sort(Vector<int>& v);
    sort(vc);     // sort(Vector<String>& v);
    sort(vi2);    // sort(Vector<int>& v);
    sort(vs);     // sort(Vector<char*>& v);
}
```

For each call, the argument type determines the sort function to be used. The programmer must provide a definition for the function template, and the language implementation must ensure that the proper variants of the template are created and called. For example, a simple bubble sort template might look like this:

```
template<class T> void sort(Vector<T>& v)
/*
    Sort the elements into increasing order

    Algorithm: bubble sort
*/
{
    unsigned n = v.size();

    for (int i=0; i<n-1; i++)
        for (int j=n-1; i<j; j--)
            if (v[j] < v[j-1]) { // swap v[j] and v[j-1]
                T temp = v[j];
                v[j] = v[j-1];
                v[j-1] = temp;
            }
}
```

Please compare this to the bubble sort function from §4.6.9. The significant difference is that in the version here all the information needed is passed in the single argument v. Because the type of the elements is known (from the argument type), the comparison operator can be used directly rather than being passed as a pointer to function, and there is no need to mess around with the `sizeof` operator. This seems more elegant and is also more efficient than the traditional version. There is a problem, though. Some types do not have a < operator, and others, such as `char*`, have a < that does not do what is intended by the template function definition above. In the former case, an attempt to generate a version of `sort ()` for such a type will fail (as one would hope it would); in the latter, surprising code will be generated.

To sort a Vector of char*s, we can simply specify a suitable implementation
of sort (Vector<char*>&):

```
void sort(Vector<char*>& v)
{
    unsigned n = v.size();

    for (int i=0; i<n-1; i++)
        for (int j=n-1; i<j; j--)
            if (strcmp(v[j],v[j-1])<0) {
                // swap v[j] and v[j-1]
                char* temp = v[j];
                v[j] = v[j-1];
                v[j-1] = temp;
            }
}
```

Because a user-specified "special" definition of sort () is provided for vectors of
character pointers, that special definition will be used, and no version sort () needs
to be generated from the template for arguments of type Vector<char*>&. The
ability for the programmer to provide separate definitions of template functions for
specially important or "odd" types provides a valuable degree of flexibility and can
be an important tool for performance tuning.

8.4.2 Adding Operations by Derivation

In the example above, the comparison function was "hard-wired" into the sort ()
function. An alternative would be to require the Vector class template to provide it.
However, that requirement makes sense only for element types that have meaningful
concepts of comparison. An traditional solution to that dilemma is to define sort ()
only for vectors that do have < defined:

```
template<class T> void sort(SortableVector<T>& v)
{
    unsigned n = v.size();

    for (int i=0; i<n-1; i++)
        for (int j=n-1; i<j; j--)
            if (v.lessthan(v[j],v[j-1])) {
                // swap v[j] and v[j-1]
                T temp = v[j];
                v[j] = v[j-1];
                v[j-1] = temp;
            }
}
```

Class SortableVector might be defined like this:

```
template<class T> class SortableVector
    : public Vector<T>, public Comparator<T> {
public:
    SortableVector(int s) : Vector<T>(s) { }
};
```

To make this work we need to define a general `Comparator` class template:

```
template<class T> class Comparator {
public:
    inline static lessthan(T& a, T& b)
        { return a<b; }
    // ...
};
```

To handle the problem that < has the wrong semantics (for our purpose) for type
`char*`, we define a special version of the class:

```
class Comparator<char*> {
public:
    inline static lessthan(const char* a, const char* b)
        { return strcmp(a,b)<0; }
    // ...
};
```

This declaration of a special version of a class template for `char*` closely mirrors the
use of a special version of a function template for `char*` above. To have effect such
a specialized version of a template class must be seen before its use. Otherwise, the
class generated from the template will be used. Since a class must have exactly one
definition in a program, attempting to use both a specialized version of a template
class and the version generated from the template is an error.

Since we already have a special version of `Comparator` for `char*` we don't
need a special version of `SortableVector` for `char*`, so we can finally write:

```
void f(SortableVector<int>& vi,
       SortableVector<String>& vc,
       SortableVector<int>& vi2,
       SortableVector<char*>& vs)
{
    sort(vi);
    sort(vc);
    sort(vi2);
    sort(vs);
}
```

Having two kinds of `Vectors` can be a bit of a nuisance, but at least
`SortableVector` is derived from `Vector` so that a function that does not care
about sorting need not worry about `SortableVectors`; the implicit conversion of
a reference to a derived class to a reference to its public base takes care of that. The
reason `SortableVector` was derived from both `Vector` and `Comparator`

(rather than adding functions to a class derived from `Vector` only) was simply that we had `Comparator` lying around from a previous example. This illustrates a style of composition found in larger libraries. A class like `Comparator` is a likely candidate for a library class, where it could be used to express the requirements for comparisons in many contexts.

8.4.3 Passing Operations as Function Arguments

An alternative to passing the comparison function as part of the `Vector` type is to pass it as a second argument to the `sort()` function. This second argument is an object of a class that specifies how comparison is to be done:

```
template<class T> void sort(Vector<T>& v, Comparator<T>& cmp)
{
    unsigned n = v.size();

    for (int i=0; i<n-1; i++)
        for (int j=n-1; i<j; j--)
            if (cmp.lessthan(v[j],v[j-1])) {
                // swap v[j] and v[j-1]
                T temp = v[j];
                v[j] = v[j-1];
                v[j-1] = temp;
            }
}
```

This variant is a generalization of the traditional technique of passing the comparison operator as a pointer to function. We can now rewrite the user code:

```
void f(Vector<int>& vi,
       Vector<String>& vc,
       Vector<int>& vi2,
       Vector<char*>& vs)
{
    Comparator<int> ci;
    Comparator<char*> cs;
    Comparator<String> cc;

    sort(vi,ci);      // sort(Vector<int>&);
    sort(vc,cc);      // sort(Vector<String>&);
    sort(vi2,ci);     // sort(Vector<int>&);
    sort(vs,cs);      // sort(Vector<char*>&);
}
```

Note that including the `Comparator` as a template argument ensures that inlining can be used for the `lessthan` operator. This technique is particularly useful if the function template requires several functions rather than a single comparison function and especially if the behavior of these functions are controlled by some data in the object they are part of.

8.4.4 Passing Operations Implicitly

In the previous section, the Comparator objects are not really used in the computation; they are simply "dummy arguments" used to drive the type system. Such a "dummy argument" is a useful and general – if not completely elegant – technique. However, where – as in the example above – an object used to pass in operations *only*, that is, where the object's value and address is not used at all in the called function, the operations can be passed implicitly instead. For example:

```
template<class T> void sort(Vector<T>& v)
{
    unsigned n = v.size();

    for (int i=0; i<n-1; i++)
        for (int j=n-1; i<j; j--)
            if (Comparator<T>::lessthan(v[j],v[j-1])) {
                // swap v[j] and v[j-1]
                T temp = v[j];
                v[j] = v[j-1];
                v[j-1] = temp;
            }
}
```

This allows our example to revert to its original version:

```
void f(Vector<int>& vi,
       Vector<String>& vc,
       Vector<int>& vi2,
       Vector<char*>& vs)
{
    sort(vi);    // sort(Vector<int>&);
    sort(vc);    // sort(Vector<String>&);
    sort(vi2);   // sort(Vector<int>&);
    sort(vs);    // sort(Vector<char*>&);
}
```

The key advantage of this version and the previous (two versions) compared to the original simple sort() template is that the code for the sorting algorithm is separated from the code doing element-type-specific operations such as lessthan. This separation of concerns increases in importance as programs grow and is of particular interest in the context of library design where the library designer cannot know the template argument types and the users cannot know (or do not want to know) the details of the algorithms. In particular, had the sort() routine been a more complicated, optimized, "industrial strength" algorithm from a library, a user would have been reluctant to write the special version for type char* as was done in §8.4.1. Providing the special char* version of the Comparator class is trivial, though, and will have a variety of uses.

8.4.5 Adding Operations as Class Template Arguments

In some cases, having the connection between the `sort()` function template and the `Comparator` class template implicit can be a problem. The implicit connection can easily be overlooked and can also be hard to understand. Also, since it is "wired into" the `sort()` function it is not possible to use that `sort()` function to sort `Vectors` of a single type using different comparison criteria (see exercise 3 in §8.9). By wrapping the `sort()` function in a class we can allow the `Comparator` to be specified directly:

```
template<class T, class Comp> class Sort {
public:
    static void sort(Vector<T>&);
};
```

The repetition of the element type is tedious, and we can avoid it by placing a `typedef` in the `Comparator` template:

```
template<class T> class Comparator {
public:
    typedef T T; // define Comparator<T>::T
    static int lessthan (T& a, T& b) {
        return a < b;
    }
    // ...
};
```

and in its special version for character strings:

```
class Comparator<char*> {
public:
    typedef char* T;
    static int lessthan (T a, T b) {
        return strcmp(a,b) < 0;
    }
    // ...
};
```

With that change, we can eliminate the element type argument from class `Sort` like this

```
template<class T, class Comp> class Sort {
public:
    static void sort(Vector<T>&);
};
```

Now that we can write:

```
void f(Vector<int>& vi,
       Vector<String>& vc,
       Vector<int>& vi2,
       Vector<char*>& vs)
{
    Sort< int,Comparator<int> >::sort(vi);
    Sort< String,Comparator<String> >::sort(vc);
    Sort< int,Comparator<int> >::sort(vi2);
    Sort< char*,Comparator<char*> >::sort(vs);
}
```

and define sort () like this:

```
template<class T, class Comp>
void Sort<T,Comp>::sort(Vector<T>& v)
{
    for (int i=0; i<n-1; i++)
        for (int j=n-1; i<j; j--)
            if (Comp::lessthan(v[j],v[j-1])) {
                T temp = v[j];
                v[j] = v[j-1];
                v[j-1] = temp;
            }
}
```

This last variant is a powerful model for composition of code from separate parts. The example can even be further simplified by using the comparator type as the only template argument. In that case, the element type is referred to as Comp::T in the definition of Sort and Sort::sort().

8.5 Template Function Overloading Resolution

No conversions are applied to arguments on template functions. Instead, new versions are generated whereever possible. For example:

```
template<class T> T sqrt(T);

void f(int i, double d, complex z)
{
    complex z1 = sqrt(i);   // sqrt(int)
    complex z2 = sqrt(d);   // sqrt(double)
    complex z3 = sqrt(z);   // sqrt(complex)
    // ...
}
```

This will generate a sqrt function from the template for each of the three argument types. If the user wants something different – say a call of sqrt(double) given an int argument – explicit type conversion must be used:

```
template<class T> T sqrt(T);

void f(int i, double d, complex z)
{
    complex z1 = sqrt(double(i));   // sqrt(double)
    complex z2 = sqrt(d);   // sqrt(double)
    complex z3 = sqrt(z);   // sqrt(complex)
    // ...
}
```

Here, only sqrt(double) and sqrt(complex) definitions will be generated
from the template.

A template function may be overloaded either by other functions of its name or by
other template functions of that same name. Overloading resolution for template
functions and other functions of the same name is done in three steps†:

[1] Look for an exact match (§r.13.2) on functions; if found, call it.

[2] Look for a function template from which a function that can be called with an
exact match can be generated; if found, call it.

[3] Try ordinary overloading resolution (§r.13.2) for the functions; if a function is
found, call it. If no match is found the call is an error.

In each case, if there is more than one alternative in the first step that finds a match,
the call is ambiguous and is an error. For example:

```
template<class T>
    T max(T a, T b) { return a>b?a:b; };

void f(int a, int b, char c, char d)
{
    int m1 = max(a,b);   // max(int,int)
    char m2 = max(c,d);  // max(char,char)
    int m3 = max(a,c);   // error: cannot generate
                         // max(int,char)
}
```

Because no conversions are applied before selecting a template function to generate
and call (rule 2 above), the last call cannot be resolved to max(a, int(c)). The
programmer can resolve this by explicitly declaring max(int,int). This would
bring rule 3 into action:

```
template<class T>
    T max(T a, T b) { return a>b?a:b; };

int max(int,int);
```

---

† These rules are very strict and likely to be relaxed to allow pointer and reference conversions and possibly
also other standard conversions. In that case, ambiguity control would be applied as always.

```
void f(int a, int b, char c, char d)
{
    int m1 = max(a,b);   // max(int,int)
    char m2 = max(c,d);  // max(char,char)
    int m3 = max(a,c);   // max(int,int)
}
```

There is no need to provide a definition for max(int,int); it will be generated from the template by default.

The max() template could have been written to accept the example as originally written:

```
template<class T1, class T2>
    T1 max(T1 a, T2 b) { return a>b?a:b; };

void f(int a, int b, char c, char d)
{
    int m1 = max(a,b);   // int max(int,int)
    char m2 = max(c,d);  // char max(char,char)
    int m3 = max(a,c);   // int max(int,char)
}
```

However, the C and C++ type rules for built-in types and operators are such that definition and use of such two-argument templates often get tricky. For example, the choice of T1 as the result type would be wrong, or at least surprising, for a call

```
max(c,i);    // char max(char,int)
```

The use of two (or more) template arguments for functions taking a variety of arithmetic types can also lead to the generation of a surprising number of different functions and thus to a surprising amount of generated code. Forcing type conversion by explicit function declarations is most often a more manageable alternative.

8.6 Template Arguments

A template argument need not be a type name; see §r.14.2. In addition to type arguments, character strings, function names, and constant expressions can be used. In particular, integers can be useful as template arguments:

```
template<class T, int sz> class buffer {
    T v[sz];
    // ...
};
```

```
void f()
{
    buffer<char,128> buf1;
    buffer<complex,20> buf2;
    // ...
}
```

Making `sz` an argument of the template `buffer` itself rather than of its objects implies that the size of a `buffer` is known at compile time so that a `buffer` can be allocated without use of free store. This makes a template such as `buffer` useful for implementing container classes, where the use of free store can be the prime factor determining their run-time efficiency. For example, implementing a `string` class so that short strings are allocated on the stack is often a win because in many applications almost all strings are very short. The `buffer` template is useful in the implementation of such types.

Each template argument of a function template must affect the type of the function by affecting at least one argument type of functions generated from the template. This ensures that functions can be selected and generated based on their arguments. For example:

```
template<class T> void f1(T);         // fine
template<class T> void f2(T*);        // fine
template<class T> T f3(int);          // error
template<int i> void f4(int[][i]);    // error
template<int i> void f5(int = i);     // error
template<class T, class C> void f6(T);  // error
template<class T> void f7(const T&, complex);   // fine
template<class T> void f8(Vector< List<T> >);   // fine
```

In each case, the error is caused by a type argument not being used in a way that affects the argument types of the function.

There are no such constraints on arguments to class templates. The reason is that the arguments to a class template must be specified whenever an object of a template class is specified. On the other hand, for class templates we must answer the question, "When are two types the same?" Two template class names refer to the same class if their template names are identical and their arguments have identical values (modulo typedefs, constant expression evaluation, etc.). For example, consider the `buffer` template again:

```
template<class T, int sz>
class buffer {
    T v[sz];
    // ...
};
```

```
void f()
{
    buffer<char,20> buf1;
    buffer<complex,20> buf2;
    buffer<char,20> buf3;
    buffer<char,100> buf4;

    buf1 = buf2;   // error: type mismatch
    buf1 = buf3;   // fine
    buf1 = buf4;   // error: type mismatch

    // ...
}
```

Where non-type arguments are used for class templates, it is possible to construct some ambiguous looking constructs. For example:

```
template<int i>
class X { /* ... */ };

void f(int a, int b)
{
    X < a > b >; // X<a> b followed by a syntax error
                 // or X< (a>b) >; ?
}
```

This example is a syntax error because the first matching > terminates the template argument. In the unlikely case that you would want to specify a class template argument by a greater than expression, use parentheses: X< (a>b) >.

8.7 Derivation and Templates

As demonstrated above, the combination of derivation (inheritance) with templates can be a powerful tool. A template expresses a commonality across the types used as template arguments, and a base class expresses commonality of representation and calling interface. A few simple mistakes should be avoided.

Two types generated from a common template are different, and have no inheritance relationship, unless their template arguments are identical. For example:

```
template<class T>
class Vector { /* ... */ };

Vector<int> v1;
Vector<short> v2;
Vector<int> v3;
```

Here v1 and v3 are of the same type and v2 is of a completely different type. The fact that there is an implicit conversion from short to int does not imply that there is an implicit conversions from Vector<short> to Vector<int>:

```
v2 = v3;   // error: type mismatch
```

This is, I suspect, what one would expect since no built-in conversions exists between int[] and short[].

Similarly:

```
class circle : public shape { /* ... */ };

Vector<circle*> v4;
Vector<shape*> v5;
Vector<circle*> v6;
```

Here v4 and v6 are of the same type and v5 is of a completely different type. The fact that there are implicit conversions from circle to shape and from circle* to shape* does not imply that there are implicit conversions from Vector<circle*> to Vector<shape*> or from Vector<circle*>* to Vector<shape*>*:

```
v5 = v6;   // error: type mismatch
```

The reason is that, in general, the structure (representation) of one class generated from a class template is such that an inheritance relationship cannot be assumed. For example, the generated class may contain an object of the argument type rather than just a pointer. Furthermore, had such conversions been allowed, we would have been vulnerable to a hole in the type system. For example:

```
void f(Vector<circle>* pc)
{
    Vector<shape>* ps = pc;   // error: type mismatch
    (*ps)[2] = new square;    // put a square peg
                              // into a round hole
}
```

As shown with Islist, Tlink, Slist, Splist, Islist_iter, Slist_iter, and SortableVector, templates provide a useful way of deriving families of classes. Without templates the derivation of similar classes can become tedious and thus error prone. Conversely, without derivation, use of templates would imply massive replication of class template member function code, massive replication of declarative information in class templates, and massive replication of functions using the templates.

8.7.1 Specifying Implementation through Template Arguments

Container classes often have to allocate storage. Occasionally, it is necessary – or simply convenient – to give users the opportunity to chose between different allocation strategies and to supply their own. This can be done in several ways. One way is to use a template to compose a new class out of the interface to the desired container and an allocator class using the placement technique described in §6.7.2:

```
template<class T, class A> class Controlled_container
    : public Container<T>, private A {

    // ...
    void some_function()
    {
        // ...
        T* p = new(A::operator new(sizeof(T))) T;
        // ...
    }
    // ...
};
```

Here it is necessary to use a template because we are designing a container class; derivation from `Container<T>` is needed to allow a `Controlled_container` to be used as a container; and the use of the template argument A is necessary to allow a variety of allocators to be used. For example:

```
class Shared : public Arena { /* ... */ };
class Fast_allocator { /* ...*/ };
class Persistent : public Arena { /* ... */ };


Controlled_container<Process_descriptor,Shared> ptbl;

Controlled_container<Node,Fast_allocator> tree;

Controlled_container<Personnel_record,Persistent> payroll;
```

This is a general strategy for providing non-trivial implementation information for a derived class. It has the advantage of being systematic and allowing inlining to be used. It does tend to lead to extraordinarily long names, though. As usual, `typedef` can be used to introduce synonyms for type names of undesirable length. For example:

```
typedef
Controlled_container<Personnel_record,Persistent> pp_record;

pp_record payroll;
```

Typically, one would use a template to define a class such as `pp_record` only if the "implementation information" added is significant enough to make hand coding it into a derived class unattractive. Examples are a general (and possibly standard in some library) `Comparator` class template (§8.4.2) and non-trivial (and possibly standard in some library) `Allocator` classes. Note that the derivation in such examples has a distinct "main line" (here the `Container`) that provides the user interface and "side lines" that provide implementation details.

8.8 An Associative Array

An associative array is probably the most useful general non-built-in type. An associative array, often called a *map* and sometimes a *dictionary*, keeps pairs of values. Given the one value, called the *key*, one can access the other, called the *value*. An associative array can be thought of as an array where the index need not be an integer:

```
template<class K, class V> class Map {
    // ...
public:
    V& operator[](const K&);  // find the V
                              // corresponding to K
                              // and return
                              // a reference to it
    // ...
};
```

Thus a key of type K names a value of type V. We assume that keys can be compared using equality, ==, and the less-than operator, <, so that we can keep the array sorted. Note that a Map differs from the assoc type presented in §7.8 in that it requires a less-than operator rather than a hash function.

Here is a simple word count program written using a Map template and a String type:

```
#include <String.h>
#include <iostream.h>
#include "Map.h"

int main()
{
    Map<String,int> count;
    String word;

    while (cin >> word) count[word]++;

    for (Mapiter<String,int> p = count.first(); p; p++)
        cout << p.value() << '\t' << p.key() << '\n';

    return 0;
}
```

The String was used to avoid having to worry about memory management and overflows the way one would have to with a char*. An iterator, MapIter, was used to visit (and write) each value in order; MapIter provides iteration by imitating pointers. Given

```
It was new. It was singular. It was simple. It must succeed.
```

as input this program produced:

```
4        It
1        must
1        new.
1        simple.
1        singular.
3        was
```

There are, of course, many ways of designing an associative array, and given a definition of Map and its associated iterator class, there are many ways of implementing
them. Here, a trivial implementation is chosen. It uses a linear search that makes it
unsuitable for large arrays. An "industrial strength" implementation would be
designed with criteria, such as speed of lookup and compactness of representation, in
mind; see Exercise 4 in §8.9.

The implementation is based on a doubly linked list of Links:

```
template<class K, class V> class Map;
template<class K, class V> class Mapiter;

template<class K, class V> class Link {
    friend class Map<K,V>;
    friend class Mapiter<K,V>;
private:
    const K key;
    V value;

    Link* pre;
    Link* suc;

    Link(const K& k, const V& v) : key(k), value(v) { }
    ~Link() { delete suc; } // delete all links recursively
};
```

Each Link holds a (key,value) pair. Friendship is used to ensure that Links
can be created, manipulated, and destroyed only by the appropriate Map and iterator
classes. Note the forward declarations of the Map and Mapiter class templates.

The Map template itself looks like this:

```
template<class K, class V> class Map {
    friend class Mapiter<K,V>;
    Link<K,V>* head;
    Link<K,V>* current;
    V def_val;
    K def_key;
    int sz;

    void find(const K&);
    void init() { sz = 0; head = 0; current = 0; }
```

```
public:

     Map() { init(); }
     Map(const K& k,const V& d)
          : def_key(k), def_val(d) { init(); }
     ~Map() { delete head; } // delete all links recursively

     Map(const Map&);
     Map& operator= (const Map&);

     V& operator[] (const K&);

     int size() const { return sz; }
     void clear() { delete head; init(); }
     void remove(const K& k);

          // iteration functions:

     Mapiter<K,V> element(const K& k)
     {
          (void) operator[](k);   // move current to k
          return Mapiter<K,V>(this,current);
     }
     Mapiter<K,V> first() { return Mapiter<K,V>(this,head); }
     Mapiter<K,V> last();
};
```

The elements are stored in a sorted doubly linked list. For simplicity, no attempt is made to minimize lookup time (see Exercise 4 in §8.9). The critical operation is `operator[]()`:

```
template<class K, class V>
V& Map<K,V>::operator[](const K& k)
{
     if (head == 0) {
          current = head = new Link<K,V>(k,def_val);
          current->pre = current->suc = 0;
          return current->value;
     }

     Link<K,V>* p = head;
     for (;;) {
          if (p->key == k) {   // found
               current = p;
               return current->value;
          }
```

```
        if (k < p->key) {    // insert before p
            current = new Link<K,V>(k,def_val);
            current->pre = p->pre;
            current->suc = p;
            if (p == head)   // becomes new head
                head = current;
            else
                p->pre->suc = current;
            p->pre = current;
            return current->value;
        }

        Link<K,V>* s = p->suc;
        if (s == 0) {           // insert after p (at end)
            current = new Link<K,V>(k,def_val);
            current->pre = p;
            current->suc = 0;
            p->suc = current;
            return current->value;
        }
        p = s;
    }
}
```

The subscript operator returns a reference to the value corresponding to the key given as an argument. If no corresponding value is found, a new element with a default value is returned. This allows the subscript operator to be used on the left hand side of assignments. The default values for keys and values is set by the Map constructors. The subscript operator also sets the value current used by the iterators.

The implementation of the remaining member functions is left as an exercise for the reader:

```
template<class K, class V>
void Map<K,V>::remove(const K& k)
{
    // see exercise section 8.10 [2]
}



template<class K, class V>
Map<K,V>::Map(const Map<K,V>& m)
{
    // copy the map and all its elements
}
```

```
template<class K, class V>
Map& Map<K,V>::operator=(const Map<K,V>& m)
{
    // copy the map and all its elements
}
```

Now all we need is a notion of iteration. A Map has member functions first(),
last(), and element(const K&) that return an iterator positioned at the first
element, the last element, and the element with key indicated by an argument, respectively. This makes sense because we keep the elements ordered by their keys.

A Map iterator Mapiter looks like this:

```
template <class K, class V> class Mapiter {
    friend class Map<K,V>;

    Map<K,V>* m;
    Link<K,V>* p;

    Mapiter(Map<K,V>* mm, Link<K,V>* pp)
        { m = mm; p = pp; }
public:
    Mapiter() { m = 0; p = 0; }
    Mapiter(Map<K,V>& mm);

    operator void*() { return p; }

    const K& key();
    V& value();

    Mapiter& operator--();     // prefix
    void operator--(int);      // postfix
    Mapiter& operator++();     // prefix
    void operator++(int);      // postfix
};
```

Once positioned, Mapiter's key() and value() functions refer to the key and
value of the element referred to by the iterator, respectively.

```
template<class K, class V> const K& Mapiter<K,V>::key()
{
    if (p) return p->key; else return m->def_key;
}
```

```
template<class K, class V> V& Mapiter<K,V>::value()
{
    if (p) return p->value; else return m->def_val;
}
```

In analogy to pointers, operators ++ and -- are provided for moving forward and
backward in the Map:

```
Mapiter<K,V>& Mapiter<K,V>::operator--() // prefix decrement
{
    if (p) p = p->pre;
    return *this;
}

void Mapiter<K,V>::operator--(int)   // postfix decrement
{
    if (p) p = p->pre;
}

Mapiter<K,V>& Mapiter<K,V>::operator++() // prefix increment
{
    if (p) p = p->suc;
    return *this;
}

void Mapiter<K,V>::operator++(int)   // postfix increment
{
    if (p) p = p->suc;
}
```

The postfix operations were made to return no value because the cost of creating and returning a new `Mapiter` on each iteration could be significant and because the usefulness of doing that would be slight.

A `Mapiter` can be initialized to refer to the head of a Map:

```
template<class K, class V> Mapiter<K,V>::Mapiter(Map<K,V>& mm)
{
    m = &mm; p = m->head;
}
```

The conversion operator `operator void*()` returns zero if the iterator does not refer to an element, and non-zero otherwise. This means that one can test an iterator `iter` like this:

```
void f(Mapiter<const char*,Shape*>& iter)
{
    // ...

    if (iter) {
        // refers to element of map
    }
    else {
        // doesn't refer to element of map
    }

    // ...
}
```

The same technique is used to control stream I/O operations §10.3.2.

If an iterator doesn't refer to an element of a map, its key() and value() functions return references to the default objects.

In case you have now forgotten the purpose of all this, here is another little program using a Map. We will assume that the input is a list of pairs of values such as:

```
hammer   2
nail     100
saw      3
saw      4
hammer   7
nail     1000
nail     250
```

We would like to sort this, to have values of matching items added, and to print them together with the sum of the values:

```
hammer   9
nail     1350
saw      7
----------------
total    1366
```

First we will write a function that reads lines and enters the items found into a table keyed on the first item on the line:

```cpp
template<class K, class V>
    void readlines (Map<K,V>& key)
    {
        K word;
        while (cin >> word) {
            V val = 0;
            if (cin >> val)
                key[word] += val;
            else
                return;
        }
    }
```

Next we provide a simple main() program to call the readlines() function and print the resulting table:

```
main()
{
    Map<String,int> tbl("nil",0);
    readlines(tbl);

    int total = 0;
    for (Mapiter<String,int> p(tbl); p; ++p) {
        int val = p.value();
        total += val;
        cout << p.key() << '\t' << val << '\n';
    }

    cout << "----------------\n";
    cout << "total\t" << total << '\n';
}
```

8.9 Exercises

1. (*2) Write a set of doubly linked lists to complement the family of singly linked lists defined in §8.3.
2. (*3) Define a `String` template that takes the character type as a template argument and show how it could be used for both ''ordinary characters'' and a hypothetical `lchar` class (supposed to represent characters in a non-English or extended character set). Make sure that people who use this template does not suffer significantly in time, space, or convenience compared to an ordinary string class.
3. (*1.5) Define a class `Record` with two data members `count` and `price`. Sort a `Vector` or `Records` on each field. Do not modify the sort function or the `Vector` template.
4. (*2) Complete the `Map` class template by defining the missing member functions.
5. (*2) Re-implement `Map` from §8.8 using a doubly linked list class.
6. (*2.5) Re-implement `Map` from §8.8 using a balanced tree as described in Knuth vol. 3, §6.2.3.
7. (*2) Compare the performance of a `Map` where `Link` is implemented with and without a class specific allocator.
8. (*3) Compare the performance of the word count program from §8.8 against a program not using a `Map`. Use the same style of I/O in both cases. Do the comparison against several versions of the `Map` class including the one from your library (if yours provides a `Map`).
9. (*2.5) Use `Map` to implement a topological sort function. Topological sort is described in Knuth vol. 1 (second edition), pp 262.
10. (*2) Make the sum program from §8.8 work correctly for long names and names containing spaces such as ''thumb tack.''
11. (*2) Make `readline` templates for different kinds of lines. For example

(item,count,price).

12. (*2) Write a shell sort variant of the `Sort` class from §8.4.5 and show how to choose the sorting algorithm used through the template argument. Shell sort is described in Knuth vol. 3, §5.2.1.

13. (*1) Change `Map` and `Mapiter` so that postfix `++` and `--` returns a `Mapiter`.

14. (*1.5) Use the templates-as-modules technique from §8.4.5 to write a sort function that will work on both `Vector<T>` and `T[]` inputs.

9

Exception Handling

Don't interrupt me
while I'm interrupting.
– Winston S. Churchill

This chapter presents the exception handling mechanism and some of the error-handling techniques it supports. The mechanism is based on an expression that throws an exception to be caught by a handler. The rules for catching exceptions are described, as are the rules for dealing with uncaught and unexpected exceptions. Groups of exceptions can be defined as derived classes. A technique for using destructors and exception handling to ensure reliable, implicit resource management is presented.

9.1 Error Handling

The author of a library can detect run-time errors but does not in general have any idea what to do about them. The user of a library may know how to cope with such errors but cannot detect them – or else they would have been handled in the user's code and not left for the library to find. The notion of an *exception* is provided to help deal with such problems†. The fundamental idea is that a function that finds a problem that it cannot cope with *throws* an exception, hoping that its (direct or indirect) caller can handle the problem. A function that wants to handle that kind of problem can indicate that it is willing to *catch* that exception.

For example, consider how to represent and handle a range error from a `Vector`

---

† Exceptions have only recently been accepted by the ANSI C++ standards committee, and implementations are at the time of writing not widely available.

class:

```
class Vector {
    int* p;
    int sz;
public:
    class Range { };   // exception class

    int& operator[](int i);

    // ...
};
```

Objects of class Range are intended to be used as exceptions and thrown like this:

```
int& Vector::operator[](int i)
{
    if (0<=i && i<sz) return p[i];
    throw Range();
}
```

A function that needs to detect the use of an out-of-range index states its interest by enclosing the code in which it wants to catch range errors in a t r y statement with an exception handler. For example:

```
void f(Vector& v)
{
    // ...

    try {
        do_something(v);
    }
    catch (Vector::Range) {
        // handler for Vector::Range exception:

        // do_something() failed, do something else

        // we get here if and only if
        // the call do_something() results
        // in a call of Vector::operator[]()
        // with a bad index
    }

    // ...
}
```

The construct

```
catch ( /* ... */ ) {
    // ...
}
```

is called an *exception handler*. It can be used only immediately after a block prefixed with the keyword `try` or immediately after another exception handler; `catch` is also a keyword. The parentheses contain a declaration that is used in a way similar to the way a function argument declaration is used: It specifies the type of the objects with which the handler can be entered and optionally names the argument; see §9.3. If `do_something()` or any function called by `do_something()` causes a range error (on any `Vector`) the exception will be caught by the handler and the exception-handling code executed. For example, the following definitions would cause the handler in `f()` to be entered:

```
void do_something(Vector& v)
{
    // ...
    crash(v);
    // ...
}


void crash(Vector& v)
{
    v[v.size()+10]; // trigger range error!
}
```

The process of throwing and catching an exception involves searching the call chain for a handler from the throw point up through its callers. In this process, the call stack is unwound to the stack frame of the catching function, and destructors for local objects on such stack frames are invoked along the way; see §9.4.1 for details.

If a function throws an exception for which there is no matching exception handler on the call chain leading to the function throwing the exception, the program will be terminated; see §9.7 for details.

Once a handler has caught an exception, that exception has been dealt with and other handlers that might exist for it become irrelevant. In other words, only the active handler most recently encountered by the thread of control will be invoked. For example, because the function `f()` catches `Vector::Range` a caller of `f()` will never get a `Vector::Range` exception:

```
int ff(Vector& v)
{
    try {
        f(v);                       // f() catches Vector::Range
    }
    catch (Vector::Range) {   // so we will not get here
        // ...
    }
}
```

9.1.1 Exceptions and Traditional Error Handling

This style of error handling compares favorably with more traditional techniques in many ways. Consider the alternatives for `Vector::operator[]()`. Upon detecting an out-of-range index the subscript operator could:

[1] terminate the program,
[2] return a value representing ''error,''
[3] return a legal value and leave the program in an illegal state, or
[4] call a function supplied to be called in case of ''error.''

Case [1] ''terminate the program,'' is what by default happens when an exception isn't caught. For most errors we can and must do better.

Case [2] ''return an error value,'' isn't always feasible because there is often no acceptable ''error value.'' For example, *every* `int` is a legal return value for our subscript operator. Where the approach is feasible, it is often inconvenient because every call must be checked for the error value. This can easily double the size of a program. Consequently, the approach is rarely used systematically enough to detect all errors.

Case [3] ''leave the program in an illegal state,'' has the problem that the calling function may not notice that the program has been put in an illegal state. For example, many standard C library functions set the global variable `errno` to indicate an error. However, programs typically fail to test `errno` consistently enough to avoid consequential errors caused by bad values returned from failed calls. Furthermore, the use of a single global variable for several error conditions is a disaster in the presence of concurrency.

Exception handling is not meant to handle problems for which case [4], ''call an error-handler function,'' is relevant. However, note that – in the absence of exceptions – an error-handler function has exactly the three other cases as alternatives for how *it* handles the error. See §9.4.3 for a further discussion of error-handling functions and exceptions.

The exception-handling mechanism provides an alternative to the traditional techniques in the cases where the traditional techniques are insufficient, inelegant, and error-prone. It provides a way of explicitly separating error handling code from ''ordinary'' code, thus making the program more readable and more amenable to tools. The exception handling mechanism provides a more regular style of error handling, thus simplifying cooperation between separately written program fragments.

One aspect of the exception-handling scheme that will appear novel to C programmers is that the default response to an error (especially to an error in a library) is to terminate the program. The traditional response has been to muddle through and hope for the best. Thus exception handling makes programs more ''brittle'' in the sense that more care and effort must be taken to get a program to run acceptably. This seems preferable, though, to getting wrong results later in the development process (or after the development process was considered complete and the program handed over to innocent users). Where termination is unacceptable, the traditional approach can be simulated by catching *all* exceptions or by catching all exceptions belonging to a specific class (§9.3.2).

The exception-handling mechanism can be seen as a run-time analog to the compile-time type checking and ambiguity control mechanisms. It makes the design process more important and the work involved in getting a program running harder than for C. However, the result is code that has a much better chance to run as expected, to run as an acceptable part of a larger program, to be comprehensible to other programmers, and to be amenable to manipulation by tools. Similarly, exception handling provides specific language features to support "good style" in the same way other C++ features support "good style" that can only be practiced informally and incompletely in languages such as C.

It should be recognized that error handling will remain a difficult task and that the exception handling mechanism – although more formalized than the techniques it replaces – is still relatively unstructured compared with language features involving only local control flow.

9.1.2 Alternative Views on Exceptions

"Exception" is one of those words that mean different things to different people. The C++ exception handling mechanism is designed to support error handling. In particular, it is intended to support error handling in programs composed of independently developed components.

The mechanism is designed to handle only synchronous exceptions, such as array range checks. Asynchronous exceptions, such as keyboard interrupts, are not handled directly by this mechanism. Other mechanisms, such as signals, exist on various systems; because they tend to be system dependent, they are not described here.

The exception handling mechanism is a non-local control structure that can be seen as an alternative return mechanism. There are therefore legitimate uses of exceptions that have nothing to do with errors (§9.5). However, the primary aim of the exception mechanism and the focus of this chapter is error handling and the support of fault tolerance.

9.2   Discrimination of Exceptions

Naturally, a program will have several different possible run-time errors. Such errors can be mapped into exceptions with distinct names. For example, a Vector class will typically have to detect and report two kinds of errors: range errors and errors caused by an unsuitable constructor argument:

```
class Vector {
    int* p;
    int sz;
public:
    enum { max = 32000 };
    class Range { };  // range exception
    class Size { };   // bad size exception
```

```
        Vector(int sz);
        int& operator[](int i);

    // ...
};
```

As before, the subscript operator will throw a `Range` exception if presented with an out-of-range index. Similarly, the constructor will throw a `Size` error if presented with an unacceptable size:

```
Vector::Vector(int sz)
{
    if (sz<0 || max<sz) throw Size();
    // ...
}
```

A user of class `Vector` can discriminate between the two exceptions by adding handlers for both to a `try` block:

```
void f()
{
    try {
        use_vectors();
    }
    catch (Vector::Range) {
        // ...
    }
    catch (Vector::Size) {
        // ...
    }
}
```

Where needed, the appropriate handler will be entered. If we ''fall through the bottom'' of a handler the execution continues at the end of the list of handlers. For example:

```
void f()
{
    try {
        use_vectors();
    }
    catch (Vector::Range) {
        // adjust the use of vectors
        // try again:
        f();
    }
    catch (Vector::Size) {
        cerr << "Vector::Size error" ;
        exit(99);
    }
```

```
    // we get here if there was no Vector exception
    // or if a Range exception was handled
}
```

A list of handlers may look a bit like a `switch` statement but there is no need for `break` statements. The syntax of a list of handlers differ from the syntax of a list of cases partly for that reason and partly to indicate that each handler is a scope (see §9.8).

A function need not catch all possible exceptions. For example:

```
void f1()
{
    try {
        f2(v);
    }
    catch (Vector::Size) {
    // ...
    }
}
```

```
void f2(Vector& v)
{
    try {
        use_vectors();
    }
    catch (Vector::Range) {
    // ...
    }
}
```

Here, `f2()` will catch `Range` errors from `use_vectors()` and pass `Size` errors on to `f1()`.

From the language's point of view, an exception is considered handled immediately upon entry into its handler so that any exceptions thrown while executing a handler must be dealt with by the callers of the try block. For example, assuming that `input_overflow` is a global name of a class:

```
try {
    // ...
}
catch (input_overflow) {
    // ...
    throw input_overflow();
}
```

does not cause an infinite loop.

Exception handlers can be nested. For example:

```
try {
    // ...
}
catch (xxii) {
    try {
        // something complicated
    }
    catch (xxii) {
        // complicated handler code failed
    }
}
```

However, such nesting is rarely useful in human-written code and is more often than not an indication of poor style.

9.3 Naming of Exceptions

An exception is caught by specifying its type. However, what is thrown is not a type but an object. If we need to transmit extra information from the throw point to the handler we can do so by putting data into that object. For example, we might like to know the index that caused a range error:

```
class Vector {
    // ...
public:
    class Range {
    public:
        int index;
        Range(int i) : index(i) { }
    };
    // ...
    int& operator[](int i)
    // ...
};
```

```
int& Vector::operator[](int i)
{
    if (0<=i && i<sz) return p[i];
    throw Range(i);
}
```

To examine the bad index, the handler must give a name to the exception object:

```
void f(Vector& v)
{
    // ...

    try {
        do_something(v);
    }
    catch (Vector::Range r) {
        cerr << "bad index" << r.index << '\n';
        // ...
    }

    // ...
}
```

The construct in the parentheses after catch is in fact a declaration and is similar to
a formal argument declaration for a function. It specifies what argument (exception)
type is acceptable and optionally names the actual exception.

Note that for templates we have a choice when naming an exception. Each class
generated can have its own exception class:

```
template<class T> class Allocator {
    // ...
    class Exhausted { };
    // ...
    T* get();
};

void f(Allocator<int>& ai, Allocator<double>& ad)
{
    try {
        // ...
    }
    catch (Allocator<int>::Exhausted) {
        // ...
    }
    catch (Allocator<double>::Exhausted) {
        // ...
    }
}
```

Alternatively, an exception can be common to all classes generated from the template:

```
class Allocator_Exhausted { };

template<class T> class Allocator {
    // ...
    T* get();
};
```

```
void f(Allocator<int>& ai, Allocator<double>& ad)
{
    try {
        // ...
    }
    catch (Allocator_Exhausted) {
        // ...
    }
}
```

I know of no general rule for choosing the one style over the other; the choice depends on the meaning of the template in question.

9.3.1 Grouping of Exceptions

Exceptions often fall naturally into families. For example, one could imagine a Matherr exception that includes Overflow, Underflow, and other possible exceptions. The Matherr exceptions could be the set of exceptions potentially thrown by a standard library of mathematical functions.

One way of doing this might be to define Matherr as a type whose possible values include Overflow and the others:

```
enum Matherr { Overflow, Underflow, Zerodivide, /* ... */ };

try {
    // ...
}
catch (Matherr m) {
    switch (m) {
    case Overflow:
        // ...
    case Underflow:
        // ...
    // ...
    }
    // ...
}
```

In other contexts, C++ uses inheritance and virtual functions to avoid this kind of switch on a type field. Similarly, it is possible to use inheritance to describe collections of exceptions. For example:

```
class Matherr { };
class Overflow: public Matherr { };
class Underflow: public Matherr { };
class Zerodivide: public Matherr { };
// ...
```

There are many occasions where one would like to handle any Matherr without caring precisely which kind it was. Using inheritance makes it possible to say

```
try {
    // ...
}
catch (Overflow) {
    // handle Overflow or anything derived from Overflow
}
catch (Matherr) {
    // handle any Matherr that is not Overflow
}
```

Here an `Overflow` is handled specifically, and all other `Matherr` exceptions will be handled by the general case. Of course, a program that says `catch(Matherr)` will not know what kind of `Matherr` it has caught; whatever it was, its copy will be a `Matherr` by the time the handler is entered. This is often exactly what is desired. Where it is not, the exception can be caught by reference; see §9.3.2.

Organizing exceptions into hierarchies can be important for robustness of code. For example, consider handling all exceptions from a standard library of mathematical functions without such a grouping mechanism. This would have to be done by exhaustively listing the exceptions:

```
try {
    // ...
}
catch (Overflow) { /* ... */ }
catch (Underflow) { /* ... */ }
catch (Zerodivide) { /* ... */ }
// ...
```

This is not only tedious, but one can accidentally leave out exceptions from the list. Further, listing all exceptions for a library in a try block almost guarantees that errors will creep into a program when an exception is added to the set of library exceptions. For example, if an exception is added to the math library, every piece of code that tries to catch all math exceptions must be recompiled. In general, such universal recompilation is not feasible. Often, there is no way of finding every piece of code that needs recompilation, and even if there were we cannot in general assume that the source code is available for every piece of code in the system or that we would be willing to make changes to every piece of code in the system if it were available. For example, we are not supposed to have to worry about the internals of libraries. These recompilation and maintenance problems would lead to a policy that no new exceptions can be added to a library after its first release, and *that* would be unacceptable for almost all libraries.

This reasoning leads exceptions to be defined as class hierarchies (see also §9.6.1). This in turn leads to exceptions that are members of more than one group. For example:

```
class network_file_err
    : public network_err, public file_system_err {
    // ...
};
```

Such a `network_file_err` can be caught by functions dealing with network exceptions:

```
void f()
{
    try {
        // something
    }
    catch(network_err) {
        // ...
    }
}
```

and functions dealing with file system exceptions:

```
void g()
{
    try {
        // something else
    }
    catch(file_system_err) {
        // ...
    }
}
```

This is important because services, such as networking, can be transparent so that the writer of g() might not even be aware that a network is involved.

Note that there currently isn't a set of standard exceptions defined for standard math and I/O libraries. The job of deciding if such exceptions should be defined and what exactly their names and classes would be will probably fall to the ANSI and ISO C++ standards committees.

It is possible to catch *all* exceptions (see §9.3.2) so there is no absolute need to create a common base class for all exceptions for that purpose. However, deriving all exceptions from an empty class `Exception` would allow a more uniform treatment of exceptions in interfaces (see §9.6). If you use a common base class `Exception` make sure that it is empty except for a virtual destructor so that it does not clash with a potential standard.

9.3.2 Derived Exceptions

The use of class hierarchies for exception handling naturally leads to handlers that are interested only in a subset of the information carried by exceptions. In other words, an exception is typically caught by a handler for its base class rather than a handler for its exact class. The semantics for a handler catching and naming an exception are identical to that of a function accepting an argument. That is, the formal argument is initialized with the argument value. This implies that the exception thrown is ''cut down'' to the exception caught. For example:

```
class Matherr {
    // ...
    virtual void debug_print();
};

class Int_overflow: public Matherr {
public:
    char* op;
    int opr1, opr2;
    Int_overflow(const char* p, int a, int b)
        { op = p; opr1 = a; opr2 = b; }
    virtual void debug_print()
        { cerr << op << '(' << opr1 << ',' << opr2 << ')'; }
};


void f()
{
    try {
        g();
    }
    catch (Matherr m) {
        // ...
    }
}
```

When the `Matherr` handler is entered, m is a `Matherr` object, even if the call to g() threw `Int_overflow`. This implies that the extra information found in an `Int_overflow` is inaccessible.

As ever, pointers or references can be used to avoid losing information permanently. For example, we might write:

```
int add(int x, int y)
{
    if (x > 0 && y > 0 && x > MAXINT - y
    || x < 0 && y < 0 && x < MININT + y)
        throw Int_overflow("+", x, y);

    // If we get here, either overflow has
    // been checked and will not occur, or
    // overflow is impossible because
    // x and y have opposite sign

    return x + y;
}
```

```
void f()
{
    try {
        add(1,2);
        add(MAXINT,-2);
        add(MAXINT,2);        // here we go!
    }
    catch (Matherr& m) {
        // ...
        m.debug_print();
    }
}
```

Here, the last call of add() will trigger an exception that will cause
Int_overflow's debug_print() to be invoked. Had the exception been
caught by value rather than by reference, Matherr's debug_print() would have
been invoked instead.

Having caught an exception, it is not uncommon for a handler to decide that it
really can do nothing about the error. In that case, the typical thing to do is to throw
the exception again, hoping some other handler can do better. For example:

```
void h()
{
    try {
        // something
    }
    catch (Matherr) {
        if (can_handle_it) {
            // handle
        }
        else {
            throw; // re-throw the exception caught
        }
    }
}
```

A re-throw is indicated by a throw without an argument. The exception re-thrown is
the original exception caught and not just the part of it that was accessible as a
Matherr. In other words, had an Int_overflow been thrown, a caller of h()
could still catch an Int_overflow that h() had caught as a Matherr and
decided to re-throw:

```
void k()
{
    try {
        h();
        // ...
    }
```

```
        catch (Int_overflow) {
            // ...
        }
    }
```

A degenerate version of this can be useful. As for functions, the ellipsis . . . indicates "any argument," so that `catch(...)` means catch any exception. For example:

```
    void m()
    {
        try {
            // something
        }
        catch (...) {
            // cleanup
            throw;
        }
    }
```

That is, if any exception occurs as the result of executing the main part of `m()` the cleanup action in the handler is invoked; and once the cleanup is done, the exception that caused the cleanup is re-thrown.

Because a derived exception can be caught by handlers for more than one exception type the order in which the handlers are written in a `try` statement is significant. The handlers are tried in order. For example:

```
    try {
        // ...
    }
    catch (ibuf) {
        // handle input buffer overflow
    }
    catch (io) {
        // handle any io error
    }
    catch (stdlib) {
        // handle any library exception
    }
    catch (...) {
        // handle any other exception
    }
```

The type in a handler matches if it directly refers to the exception thrown, if it is of an accessible base class of that exception, or if the exception thrown is a pointer and the exception caught is a pointer to an accessible base class (§r.4.6) of that exception.

Because the compiler knows the class hierarchy, it can catch sillinesses such as a (...) handler that is not the last handler or a handler for a base class preceding a handler for a class derived from it (§r.15.4). In both cases, the later handler(s) could never be invoked because they were masked.

9.4 Resource Acquisition

When a function acquires a resource – that is, opens a file, allocates some memory from the free store, sets an access control lock, etc., – it is often most important for the future running of the system that the resource is properly released. Often that ''proper release'' is achieved by the function that acquired it releasing it again before returning to its caller. For example:

```
void use_file(const char* fn)
{
    FILE* f = fopen(fn,"w");

    // use f

    fclose(f);
}
```

This looks plausible until you realize that, if something goes wrong after the call of `fopen()` and before the call of `fclose()`, an exception may cause `use_file()` to be exited without calling `fclose()`†. If we want to write a fault-tolerant system we must solve this problem. A primitive solution looks like this:

```
void use_file(const char* fn)
{
    FILE* f = fopen(fn,"r");
    try {
        // use f
    }
    catch (...) {
        fclose(f);
        throw;
    }
    fclose(f);
}
```

All the code using the file is enclosed in a `try` block that catches every exception, closes the file, and re-throws the exception.

The problem with this solution is that it is verbose, tedious, and potentially expensive. Furthermore, any verbose and tedious solution is error-prone because programmers get bored. Fortunately, there is a more elegant solution. The general form of the problem looks like this:

---

† Please note that exactly the same problem can occur in languages that do not support exception handling. For example, a call of the standard C library function `longjmp()` would have the same bad effects.

```
void acquire()
{
    // acquire resource 1
    // ...
    // acquire resource n

    // use resources

    // release resource n
    // ...
    // release resource 1
}
```

It is typically important that resources are released in the reverse order of their acquisition. This strongly resembles the behavior of local objects created by constructors and destroyed by destructors. Thus we can handle such resource acquisition and release problems by a suitable use of objects of classes with constructors and destructors. For example, we can define a class `FilePtr` that acts like a `FILE*`:

```
class FilePtr {
    FILE* p;
Public:
    FilePtr(const char* n, const char* a)
        { p = fopen(n,a); }
    FilePtr(FILE* pp) { p = pp; }
    ~FilePtr() { fclose(p); }

    operator FILE*() { return p; }
}
```

We can construct a `FilePtr` given either a `FILE*` or the arguments required for `fopen()`. In either case a `FilePtr` will be destroyed at the end of its scope and its destructor closes the file. Our program now shrinks to to this minimum

```
void use_file(const char* fn)
{
    FilePtr f(fn,"r");
    // use f
}
```

and the destructor will be called independently of whether the function is exited normally or because an exception is thrown.

9.4.1 Constructors and Destructors

This technique for managing resources is usually referred to as ''resource acquisition is initialization.'' It is a general technique that relies on the properties of constructors and destructors and their interaction with exception handling.

An object is not considered constructed until its constructor has completed. Then and only then will stack unwinding call the destructor for the object. An object composed of sub-objects is constructed to the extent that its sub-objects have been constructed.

A well written constructor should ensure that its object is completely and correctly constructed. Failing that, the constructor should – as far as possible – restore the state of the system to what it was before creation. It would be ideal for naively written constructors always to achieve one of these alternatives and not leave their objects in some "half-constructed" state. This can be achieved by applying the "resource acquisition is initialization" technique to the members.

Consider a class X for which a constructor needs to acquire two resources, a file x and a lock y. This acquisition might fail and throw an exception. Without imposing a burden of complexity on the programmer, the class X constructor must never return having acquired the file but not the lock. We use objects of two classes, FilePtr and LockPtr, to represent the acquired resources (naturally, a single class would be sufficient if the resources x and y are of the same kind). The acquisition of a resource is represented by the initialization of the local object that represents the resource:

```
class X {
    FilePtr aa;
    LockPtr bb;
    // ...
    X(const char* x, const char* y)
            : aa(x),      // acquire 'x'
            bb(y)         // acquire 'y'
    {}
    // ...
};
```

Now, as in the local object case, the implementation can take care of all the bookkeeping. The user doesn't have to keep track at all. For example, if an exception occurs after aa has been constructed but before bb has been, then the destructor for aa but not for bb will be invoked.

This implies that where this simple model for acquisition of resources is adhered to, all is well and – importantly – the author of the constructor need not write explicit exception-handling code.

The most common resource acquired in an ad hoc manner is free store. You have seen examples like this several times in this book:

```
class X {
    int* p;
    // ...
public:
    X(int s) { p = new int[s]; init(); }
    ˜X() { delete[] p; }
    // ...
};
```

This practice is common and can lead to "memory leaks" when used together with exceptions. In particular, if an exception is thrown by init() then the store acquired will not be freed; the destructor will not be called because the object wasn't completely constructed. A safe variant is:

```
template<class T> class MemPtr {
public:
    T* p;
    MemPtr(size_t s) { p = new T[s]; }
    ~MemPtr() { delete[] p; }
    operator T*() { return p; }
};

class X {
    MemPtr<int> cp;
    // ...
public:
    X(int s) :cp(s) { init(); }
    // ...
};
```

The destruction of the array pointed to by p is now implicit in the MemPtr. If init() now throws an exception the memory acquired will be freed when the completely constructed sub-object cp is (implicitly) invoked.

Note also that the C++ default memory-allocation strategy guarantees that the code for a constructor will never be called if operator new() fails to provide memory for an object. That means that a user need not worry that constructor (or destructor) code might be executed for a non-existent object.

Theoretically, the overhead incurred by exception handling can be reduced to zero in the case where no exception is called. However, this minimum is unlikely to be reached in early implementations, so at least for a while it will be wise to avoid the use of local variables of classes with destructors in critical inner loops.

9.4.2 Caveat

Not all programs need to be resilient against all forms of failure, and not all resources are critical enough to warrant the effort to protect them through the "resource acquisition is initialization" strategy presented here. For example, for many programs that simply read an input and run to completion, the most suitable response to a serious run-time error is to abort the process (after producing a suitable diagnostic) and leave it to the system to release all acquired resources and to the user to re-run the program with a more suitable input. The strategy discussed here is intended for applications where such a simplistic response to a run-time error is unacceptable. In particular, a library designer cannot usually make assumptions about the fault tolerance requirements of a program using the library and is thus forced to avoid all unconditional run-time failures and to release all resources before a library function returns to the calling program. The "resource acquisition is initialization" strategy, together with the use of exceptions to signal failure, is suitable for many such libraries.

9.4.3 Resource Exhaustion

One of the recurring problems of programming is what to do when an attempt to acquire a resource fails. For example, above we blithely opened files (using `fopen()`) and requested memory from the free store (using operator new) without worrying about what happened if the file wasn't there or if we had run out of free store. When confronted with such problems programmers come up with two styles of solutions:

Resumption:Ask the caller to fix the problem and carry on.

Termination:Ask for more resources, and if none are found throw an exception.

In the former case a caller must be prepared to help out with the resource acquisition problem; in the latter a caller must be prepared to cope with failure of the attempt to acquire the resource. The latter is in most cases far simpler and allows a system to maintain a better separation of levels of abstraction.

In C++, the former model is supported by the function-call mechanism, the latter by the exception-handling mechanism. Both can be illustrated by the implementation and use of the new operator:

```
#include <stdlib.h>

extern void* _last_allocation;

extern void* operator new(size_t size)
{
    void* p;

    while ( (p=malloc(size))==0 ) {
        if (_new_handler)
            (*_new_handler)();   // ask for help
        else
            return 0;
    }
    return _last_allocation=p;
}
```

If `operator new()` cannot find memory it calls `_new_handler()`. If `_new_handler()` can supply enough memory for `malloc()`, all is fine. If it can't, the handler cannot return to `operator new()` without causing an infinite loop. The new-handler might then choose to throw an exception, thus leaving the mess for some caller to handle:

```
void my_new_handler()
{
    try_to_find_some_memory();
    if (found_some()) return;
    throw Memory_exhausted();   // give up
}
```

Somewhere, there ought to be a try block with a suitable handler:

```
try {
    // ...
}
catch (Memory_exhausted) {
    // ...
}
```

The `_new_handler` used in the implementation of `operator new()` is a pointer to function maintained by the standard function `set_new_handler()`. If I want my new handler used I can say:

```
set_new_handler(&my_new_handler);
```

If I also want to catch `Memory_exhausted` I might say:

```
void(*oldnh)() = set_new_handler(&my_new_handler);

try {
    // ...
}
catch (Memory_exhausted) {
    // ...
}
catch (...) {
    set_new_handler(oldnh); // re-set handler
    throw;   // re-throw
}

set_new_handler(oldnh); // re-set handler
```

Or even better, apply the ''resource acquisition is initialization'' technique described in §9.4 to the new handler and avoid the `catch(...)` handler.

With the new handler, no extra information is passed along from where the error is detected to the helper function. If it is necessary to pass more information, the user-supplied helper function can be part of a class and the function needing help can place the information needed in an object of that class. The function objects used to implement manipulators in §10.4.2 are an example of this. A pointer to a function or function object used by a server to call ''back'' to code that requested the service is often called a _callback._

It should be realized that the more information is passed between the code detecting a run-time error and a function helping correct that error, the more the two pieces of code become dependent on each other. It is generally a good idea to minimize such dependencies, because changes to the one piece of code require understanding of and maybe even changes to the other. In general, we would like to keep separate pieces of software separate. The exception handling mechanism supports such separation better than function calls to helper routines provided by a caller.

In general, it is wise to organize resource allocation in layers (levels of abstraction) and avoid one layer depending on help from the layer that called it. Experience with larger systems shows that over years successful systems evolve in this direction.

9.4.4 Exceptions and Constructors

Exceptions provide a solution to the problem of how to report errors from a constructor. Because a constructor does not return a separate value that a caller can test, the traditional (that is, non-exception-handling) alternatives are:

[1] Return an object in a bad state – and trust the user to test the state.

[2] Set a non-local variable indicating that the creation failed.

Exception handling allows the information that a construction failed to be transmitted out of the constructor. For example:

```
Vector::Vector(int size)
{
    if (sz<0 || max<sz) throw Size();
    // ...
}
```

Code creating Vectors can now catch Size errors and hopefully do something sensible with them:

```
Vector* f(int i)
{
    Vector* p;
    try {
        p = new Vector v(i);
    }
    catch(Vector::Size) {
        // deal with the bad size error
    }
    // ...
    return p;
}
```

The handler can then deal with the error in a suitable way. As ever, the error handler itself can use the standard set of fundamental techniques for error reporting and recovery. Each time an exception is passed along to a caller, the view of what went wrong changes. If suitable information is passed along in the exception, the amount of information available to deal with the problem increases. In other words, the fundamental aim of the error-handling techniques is to reliably and conveniently pass information about an error from the original point of detection to a point where there is sufficient information available to recover from the problem.

The ''resource acquisition is initialization'' technique is the safest and most elegant way of handling constructors that acquire more than one resource. In essence, the technique reduces the problem of handling many resources to repeated application of the (simple) technique for handling one resource.

9.5   Exceptions that are not Errors

If an exception is expected and caught so that it has no bad effects on the behavior of
the program, then how can it be an error? Only because the programmer thinks of it
as an error and of the exception handling mechanisms as a tool for handling errors.
Alternatively, one might think of the exception handling mechanisms as simply
another control structure. For example,

```
class message { /* ... */ };

class queue {
    // ...
    message* get(); // return 0 if queue empty
    // ...
};

void f1(queue& q)
{
    message* m = q.get();
    if (m == 0) {  // queue empty
        // ...
    }
    // use m
}
```

could be written as

```
class Empty { }; // exception type

class queue {
    // ...
    message* get(); // throw Empty if queue empty
    // ...
};

void f2(queue& q)
{
    try {
        message* m = q.get();
        // use m
    }
    catch (Empty) {  // queue empty
        // ...
    }
}
```

The exception handling version actually has some charm, so this is a good example of
a case where it is not entirely clear what should be considered an error and what
should not. If the queue is not supposed to be empty – if it is actually empty very
rarely ("only one time in a thousand") – and the action taken is some kind of

recovery action, then f2 () comes close to following the "exception handling is error handling" view that has been presented in this chapter so far. If the queue is often empty and the action taken upon finding the queue empty is simply an alternative in the course of normal processing, one has departed from the "exception handling is error handling" view and the code should be rewritten. For example:

```
class queue {
    // ...
    message* get();   // throw Empty if queue empty
    int empty();
    // ...
};

void f3(queue& q)
{
    if (q.empty()) {  // queue empty
        // ...
    }
    else {
        message* m = q.get();
        // use m
    }
}
```

However, separating the test from the get operation will work only if concurrency is not an issue for the queue.

One should not depart lightly from the "exception handling is error handling" view. As long as one sticks to it, code is clearly separated into two categories: ordinary code and error-handling code. This makes code more comprehensible. Unfortunately, the real world isn't so clear cut, and program organization will (and should) reflect that. For example, if a queue is empty exactly once – as is the case where the get() operation is used in a loop and where "queue empty" indicates end of loop – then there clearly isn't anything unusual or erroneous about the queue being empty, so using an exception to indicate "end of queue" is stretching the "exception handling is error handling" view quite a bit. On the other hand, the action taken when such a queue is empty is clearly different from what goes on in "the usual case" of the loop.

Exception handling is a less structured mechanism than the more localized control structures, such as if and for, and often far less efficient in the case where an exception is actually thrown. Therefore exceptions should be used only where the more traditional control structures are inelegant or impossible to use. For example, in the queue example there is a perfectly good "queue empty" value available in the form of the zero pointer, so using exceptions is unnecessary. However, had the queue returned an int instead of a pointer to a message, then there might not have been a value available to represent "queue empty." In that sense the queue get() would be equivalent to the subscript operator from §9.1, and an exception would become attractive as a way of representing "queue empty." This argument indicates that a perfectly general queue template will need to use exceptions to indicate "queue empty,'' leading to code like this:

```
void f(Queue<X>& q)
{
    try {
        for (;;) {  // ``infinite loop''
                    // broken by an exception
            X m = q.get();
            // ...
        }
    }
    catch (Queue<X>::Empty) {
        return;
    }
}
```

If a loop like the one above usually iterates thousands of times, it will probably be more efficient than an ordinary loop with a test of a condition. If the loop typically iterates only a few times it will almost certainly be less efficient.

In the general queue, the exception is used as an alternate return path from the get() function. Using exceptions as alternate returns can be an elegant technique for terminating search functions – especially highly recursive search functions such as a lookup in a tree structure. However, such use of exceptions could easily be overused and lead to obscure code. Wherever reasonable, one should stick to the ''exception handling is error handling'' view. Error handling is inherently difficult, and anything that helps preserve a clear model of what is an error and how it is handled should be treasured.

9.6 Interface Specifications

Throwing or catching an exception affects the way a function relates to other functions. It can therefore be worthwhile to specify the set of exceptions that might be thrown as part of the function declaration. For example:

```
void f(int a) throw (x2, x3, x4);
```

This specifies that f() may throw exceptions x2, x3, and x4, and exceptions derived from these types, but no others. When a function says something about its exceptions, it is effectively making a guarantee to its caller; if during execution that function does something that tries to abrogate the guarantee, the attempt will be transformed into a call of unexpected(). The default meaning of unexpected() is terminate(), which in turn normally calls abort(); see §9.7 for details.

In effect, writing:

```
void f() throw (x2, x3, x4)
{
    // stuff
}
```

is equivalent to writing this:

```
void f()
{
    try {
        // stuff
    }
    catch (x2) {
        throw;      // re-throw
    }
    catch (x3) {
        throw;      // re-throw
    }
    catch (x4) {
        throw;      // re-throw
    }
    catch (...) {
        unexpected();
    }
}
```

The advantage of the explicit declaration of exceptions that a function can throw compared to the equivalent checking in the code is not just that it saves keystrokes. The most important advantage is that the function *declaration* belongs to an interface that is visible to its callers. Function *definitions*, on the other hand, are not universally available; and even if we do have access to the source code of all our libraries, we strongly prefer not to have to look at it very often.

A function declared without an exception specification is assumed to throw every exception.

```
int f();               // can throw any exception
```

A function that will throw no exceptions can be declared with an explicitly empty list:

```
int g() throw ();   // no exception thrown
```

One might think that the default should be that a function throws no exceptions; but that would require exception specifications for essentially every function, would be a significant cause for recompilation, and would inhibit cooperation with software written in other languages. This would encourage programmers to subvert the exception-handling mechanisms and to write spurious code to suppress exceptions. It would provide a false sense of security to people who failed to notice the subversion.

9.6.1 Unexpected Exceptions

Carelessly used exception specifications can lead to calls to unexpected(), which are typically undesirable except during testing. Such calls can be avoided through careful organization of exceptions and specification of interfaces. Alternatively, calls to unexpected() can be intercepted and rendered harmless.

A well defined sub-system Y would have all its exceptions derived from a class Yerr. For example, given

```
class someYerr : public Yerr { /* ... */ };
```

a function declared

```
void f() throw (Xerr, Yerr, IOerr);
```

will pass any Yerr on to its caller. In particular, f() would handle a someYerr by passing it on to its caller.

Occasionally, the policy of terminating a program upon encountering an unexpected exception is too Draconian. For example, consider calling a function g() written for a non-networked environment in a distributed system. Naturally, g() will not know about network exceptions and will call unexpected() when it encounters one. To use g() in a distributed environment we must provide code that handles network exceptions – or rewrite g(). Assuming a re-write is infeasible or undesirable, we can handle the problem by redefining the meaning of unexpected(). The function set_unexpected() can be used to achieve that. First we define a class to allow us to use the ''resource acquisition is initialization'' technique for unexpected() functions:

```
typedef void(*PFV)();
PFV set_unexpected(PFV);

class STC {     // store and reset class
    PFV old;
public:
    STC(PFV f) { old = set_unexpected(f); }
    ~STC() { set_unexpected(old); }
};
```

Then we define a function with the meaning we want for unexpected in this case:

```
void rethrow() { throw; }
```

and finally we provide a version of g() to be used in the networked environment:

```
void networked_g()
{
    STC xx(&rethrow); // now unexpected() calls rethrow()
    g();
}
```

As shown above, unexpected() is conceptually called from a catch(...)

handler. There is therefore definitely an exception to re-throw. A re-throw done when no exception is thrown causes a call of `terminate()`. Similarly, because the `catch(...)` handler is outside the scope where the original exception was thrown there is no possibility for infinite loops.

A somewhat dangerous approach would be to suppress an unexpected exception and muddle on:

```
void muddle_on() { cerr << "muddling on\n"; }
// ...
STC xx(&muddle_on); // now unexpected()
                    // just prints the message
```

This will cause a normal return from a function detecting an unexpected exception. Despite its obvious dangers this approach has uses. It does, for example, allow a part of a system to "muddle on" so that other parts can be tested. This can be important in development/debug situations and where a system is being converted from a non-exception-handling style of code. More often, though, it is preferable for errors to manifest themselves as soon as possible.

An alternative would be to turn a call of `unexpected()` into a `throw` of an exception `Fail`:

```
void fail() { throw Fail; }
// ...
STC yy(&fail);
```

That would save calling functions from knowing about the details of the called function: It will either succeed and return normally or `Fail`. The obvious drawback of this approach is that it suppresses potentially useful information about the cause of the exception. If necessary, this problem could be alleviated by storing information in `Fail` exceptions.

9.7 Uncaught Exceptions

If an exception is thrown but not caught the function `terminate()` will be called; `terminate()` will also be called when the exception handling mechanism finds the stack corrupted, and when a destructor called during stack unwinding caused by an exception tries to exit using an exception.

The `terminate()` function executes the most recent function given as an argument to the function `set_terminate()`:

```
typedef void(*PFV)();
PFV set_terminate(PFV);
```

The return value is the previous function given to `set_terminate()`.

The reason for `terminate()` is that exception handling must occasionally be abandoned for less subtle error handling techniques. For example, `terminate()` could be used to abort a process or maybe to re-initialize a system. The intent is for `terminate()` to be a drastic measure to be applied when the error-recovery strategy implemented by the exception handling mechanism has failed and it is time to go to another level of a fault tolerance strategy.

The `unexpected()` function is used to handle the related but slightly less serious issue of a function throwing an exception that wasn't declared in its exception specification. The `unexpected()` function executes the last function given as an argument to the function `set_unexpected()`.

By default `unexpected()` will call `terminate()` and `terminate()` will call `abort()`. These defaults are expected to be the correct choice for most users.

A call of `terminate()` is assumed not to return to its caller.

Note that `abort()` indicates abnormal exit from the program. The function `exit()` can be used to exit a program with a return value that indicates to the surrounding system whether the exit is normal or abnormal.

9.8 Error-Handling Alternatives

The purpose of the exception handling mechanism is to provide a means for one part of a program to inform another part of a program that an "exceptional circumstance" has been detected. The assumption is that the two parts of the program are written independently and that the part of the program that handles the exception often can do something sensible about the error.

What kind of code could one reasonably expect to find in an exception handler? Here are some examples:

```
int f(int arg)
{
    try {
        g(arg);
    }
    catch (x1) {
        // fix something and retry:
        g(arg);
    }
    catch (x2) {
        // calculate and return a result:
        return 2;
    }
    catch (x3) {
        // pass the bug
        throw;
    }
    catch (x4) {
        // turn x4 into some other exception
        throw xxii;
    }
```

```
catch (x5) {
    // fix up and carry on with next statement
}
catch (...) {
    // give up:
    terminate();
}
// ...
}
```

Note that a handler can access variables in the scope surrounding its `try` block but not, of course, variables declared in other handlers or in the `try` block:

```
void f()
{
    int i1;
    // ...
    try {
        int i2;
        // ...
    }
    catch (x1) {
        int i3;
        // ...
    }
    catch (x4) {
        i1 = 1;   // ok
        i2 = 2;   // error: i2 not in scope
        i3 = 3;   // error: i3 not in scope
    }
}
```

To use handlers effectively in a program, an overall strategy is needed; that is, the various parts of the program must agree on how exceptions are used and where errors are dealt with. The exception handling mechanisms are inherently non-local so that adherence to an overall strategy is essential. This implies that the error-handling strategy must be considered even in the earliest phases of a design. It also implies that the strategy must be simple (relative to the complexity of the total program) and explicit; something complicated would simply never be consistently adhered to in an area as inherently tricky as error recovery.

First of all, the idea that a single mechanism or technique can handle all errors must be dispelled; that would lead to complexity. Instead, successful fault-tolerant systems are multi-level. Each level copes with as many errors as it can without getting too contorted and leaves the rest of the problems to higher levels. The notion of `terminate()` is intended to support this view by providing an escape when the exception-handling mechanism itself is corrupted or if it has been incompletely used, leaving exceptions uncaught. Similarly, the notion of `unexpected()` is intended to provide an escape when the strategy using exception specifications to provide firewalls fails.

Note that not every function should be a firewall. Trying to have every function do sufficient checking to ensure that it either completes successfully or fails in a well defined way will fail. The reasons for this failure will vary from program to program and from programmer to programmer, but for larger programs

[1] the amount of work needed to ensure this notion of ''reliability'' is too great to be done consistently;

[2] the overheads in time and space are too great for the system to run acceptably (there will be a tendency to check for the same errors, e.g., valid arguments, over and over again);

[3] functions written in other languages won't obey the rules; and

[4] this purely local notion of ''reliability'' leads to complexities that actually become a burden to overall system reliability.

Separating the program into distinct subsystems that either complete successfully or fail in a well-defined way is, however, essential, feasible, and economical. Thus, a major library, sub-system, or key function should be designed in this way. Exception specifications are intended for interfaces to such libraries and sub-systems.

Occasionally, it is necessary to convert from one style of error reporting to another – for example, checking `errno` and possibly throwing an exception after a call to a C library or, conversely, catching an exception and setting `errno` before returning to a C program from a C++ library:

```
void callC()
{
    errno = 0;
    cfunction();
    if (errno) throw some_exception(errno);
}

void fromC()
{
    try {
        c_pl_pl_function();
    }
    catch (...) {
        errno = E_CPLPLFCTBLEWIT;
    }
}
```

In such cases it is important to be systematic enough to ensure that the conversion of error reporting styles is complete.

Error handling should be – as far as possible – strictly hierarchical. If a function detects a run-time error it should not ask its caller for help with recovery or resource acquisition; such requests set up cycles in the system dependencies, and that makes the program hard to understand and introduces the possibility of infinite loops in the error-handling and recovery code.

Simplifying techniques such as ''resource acquisition is initialization'' and simplifying assumptions such a ''exceptions represent errors'' should be used to make the error handling code more regular.

9.9 Exercises

1. (*2) Genralize the STC class to a template that can store and reset functions of a variety of types.
2. (*3) Complete the CheckedPtrToT class from §7.10 as a template using exceptions to signal run-time errors.
3. (*3) Write a function that searches a binary tree of nodes based on a char* field for a match. If a node containing hello is found , find("hello") will return a pointer to that node. Use an exception to indicate ''not found.''
4. (*1) Define a class Int that acts exactly like the built-in type int except that it throws exceptions rather than overflow or underflow. Hint: §9.3.2.
5. (*2) Take the basic operations for opening, closing, reading, and writing from the C interface to your operating system and provide equivalent C++ functions that call the C functions but throw exceptions in case of errors.
6. (*1) Write a complete Vector template with Range and Size exceptions. Hint: 9.3.
7. (*1) Write a loop that computes the sum of a Vector as defined in exercise 6 without examining the size of the Vector. Why is this a bad idea?
8. (*2.5) Consider using a class Exception as the base of all classes used as exceptions. What should it look like? How should it be used? What good might it do? What disadvantages might a requirement to use such a class cause?
9. (*2) Write a class or template suitable for implementing callbacks.
10. (*2) Write a Lock class for some system supporting concurrency.
11. (*1) Given a

```
int main() { /* ... */ }
```

change it to catch all exceptions, turn them into error messages, and abort(). Hint: fromC() in §9.8 doesn't quite handle all cases.

10

Streams

What you see is all you get.
– Brian Kernighan

The C++ language does not provide facilities for input or output. It does
not need to; such facilities can be simply and elegantly created using the
language itself. The standard stream input/output library described here
provides a type-secure, flexible, and efficient method for handling character input and output of integers, floating-point numbers, and character
strings, and a model for extending it to handle user-defined types. Its user
interfaces can be found in `<iostream.h>`. This chapter presents the
stream library itself, some ways of using it, and some of the techniques
used to implement it.

10.1 Introduction

Designing and implementing a standard input/output facility for a programming language is notoriously difficult. Traditionally, I/O facilities have been designed exclusively to handle a few built-in data types. However, a nontrivial C++ program uses
many user-defined types, and input and output of values of those types must be handled. An I/O facility should clearly be easy, convenient, and safe to use, efficient and
flexible, and above all complete. Nobody has come up with a solution that pleases
everyone; it should therefore be possible for a user to provide alternative I/O facilities
and to extend the standard I/O facilities to cope with special applications.

C++ was designed to enable a user to define new types that are as efficient and
convenient to use as built-in types. It is therefore a reasonable requirement that an
input/output facility for C++ should be provided in C++ using only facilities available
to every programmer. The stream I/O facilities presented here are the result of an

effort to meet this challenge.

The stream I/O facilities are exclusively concerned with the process of converting typed objects into sequences of characters, and vice versa. There are other models for I/O, but this one is fundamental; and many forms of binary I/O can be handled by considering a character as simply a bit pattern and ignoring its conventional correspondence with the alphabet. The key problem for the programmer is, then, to specify a correspondence between a typed object and an essentially untyped string.

The sections below describe the major parts of the C++ streams library:

§10.2   *Output*: What the application programmer thinks of as output is really the conversion of objects of types such as `int`, `char*`, `complex`, and `Employee_record` into a sequence of characters. The facilities for writing built-in and user-defined types to output are described.

§10.3   *Input*: The functions for requesting input of characters, strings, and values of other built-in and user-defined types are presented.

§10.4   *Formatting*: There are often specific requirements for the layout of the output; for example, `int`s may have to be printed in decimal and pointers in hexadecimal, or floating-point numbers must appear with exactly specified precision within a fixed-size space. The formatting functions and the programming techniques used to define them – in particular *manipulators*– are discussed.

§10.5   *Files and Streams*: By default, every C++ program can use three streams, standard output (`cout`), standard input (`cin`), and error output (`cerr`). To use other devices or files, streams must be created and attached to those files or devices. The mechanisms for opening and closing files and for attaching files to streams are described.

§10.6   *C Input/Output*: The `printf()` function from the C `<stdio.h>` library and the C library's relation to the C++ `<iostream.h>` library are discussed.

Note that there are many independent implementations of the stream I/O library and that the set of facilities described here is only a subset of those found in your library. It is said that inside every large program there is a small program struggling to get out. This chapter is an attempt to describe that small stream I/O library and thus give an appreciation of the fundamentals of stream I/O and a guide to its most useful facilities. Many programs can be written using only the facilities described here; if necessary, consult the manual for your C++ library for further details. The header file `<iostream.h>` defines the interface to the stream library. Older versions of the stream library use the header `<stream.h>`. Where both exist, `<iostream.h>` defines the full set of facilities and `<stream.h>` defines a subset that is compatible with older, less comprehensive, stream libraries.

Naturally, knowledge of the techniques used to implement the stream library is not needed to use it, and the techniques used for different implementations will differ. However, implementing I/O is a challenging task, and therefore an implementation will contain examples of techniques that can be applied to many other tasks and is thus worthy of study.

10.2 Output

Type-secure and uniform treatment of both built-in and user-defined types can be achieved by using a single overloaded function name for a set of output functions. For example:

```
put(cerr,"x = "); // cerr is the error output stream
put(cerr,x);
put(cerr,'\n');
```

The type of the argument determines which `put` function will be invoked for each argument. This solution has been used in several languages. However, it is verbose. Overloading the operator << to mean ''put to'' gives a better notation and lets the programmer put out a sequence of objects in a single statement, for example,

```
cerr << "x = " << x << '\n';
```

where `cerr` is the standard error output stream. So, if x is an `int` with the value 123, this statement would print

```
x = 123
```

and a newline onto the standard error output stream. Similarly, if x is of the user-defined type `complex` with the value (1,2.4), the statement above will print

```
x = (1,2.4)
```

on `cerr`. This style can be used as long as x is of a type for which operator << is defined, and a user can trivially define operator << for a new type.

An output operator is needed to avoid the verbosity that would have resulted from using an output function. But why <<? It is not possible to invent a new lexical token (see §7.2). The assignment operator was a candidate for both input and output, but most people seemed to prefer the input operator to be different from the output operator. Furthermore, = binds the wrong way; that is, cout=a=b means cout=(a=b). The operators < and > were tried, but the meanings ''less than'' and ''greater than'' were so firmly implanted in people's minds that the new I/O statements were for all practical purposes unreadable.

The operators << and >> do not appear to cause that kind of problem. They are asymmetric in a way that can be used to suggest ''to'' and ''from,'' they are not among the most commonly used operations on built-in types, and the precedence of << is low enough to allow arithmetic expressions as operands without using parentheses. For example:

```
cout << "a*b+c=" << a*b+c << '\n';
```

Parentheses must be used to write expressions containing operators of lower precedence. For example:

```
cout << "a^b|c=" << (a^b|c) << '\n';
```

The left shift operator can be used in an output statement, but of course it too must appear within parentheses:

```
cout << "a<<b=" << (a<<b) << '\n';
```

10.2.1 Output of Built-in Types

The class ostream is defined with the operator << (''put to'') to handle output of
the built-in types:

```
class ostream : public virtual ios {
    // ...
public:
    ostream& operator<<(const char*);   // strings
    ostream& operator<<(char);
    ostream& operator<<(short i)
        { return *this << int(i); }
    ostream& operator<<(int);
    ostream& operator<<(long);
    ostream& operator<<(double);
    ostream& operator<<(const void*);   // pointers
    // ...
};
```

Naturally, ostream also has a set of operator<<() functions dealing with
unsigned types.

An operator<< function returns a reference to the ostream it was called for,
so that another operator<< can be applied to it. For example,

```
cerr << "x = " << x;
```

where x is an int, will be interpreted as:

```
(cerr.operator<<("x = ")).operator<<(x);
```

In particular, this implies that when several items are printed by a single output statement, they will be printed in the expected order: left to right.

The function ostream::operator<<(int) prints integer values and
ostream::operator<<(char) prints characters. For example:

```
void val(char c)
{
    cout << "int('" << c << "') = " << int(c) << '\n';
}
```

prints integer values of characters:

```
main()
{
    val('A');
    val('Z');
}
```

printed

```
int ('A') = 65
int ('Z') = 90
```

My machine uses ASCII; yours may give a different result. Note that a character literal has type char so that cout<<'Z' will print the letter Z and not the integer value 90.

The function ostream::operator<<(const void*) prints a pointer value in a form appropriate to the architecture of the machine used. For example:

```
main ()
{
    int i = 0;
    int* p = new int (1);
    cout << "local " << &i
         << ", free store " << p << '\n';
}
```

printed

```
local 0x7fffead0, free store 0x500c
```

on my machine. Other systems have different conventions for printing pointer values.

The base class ios will be discussed in §10.4.1.

10.2.2 Output of User-defined Types

Consider a user-defined type:

```
class complex {
    double re, im;
public:
    complex (double r = 0, double i = 0) { re=r; im=i; }

    friend double real (complex& a) { return a.re; }
    friend double imag (complex& a) { return a.im; }

    friend complex operator+ (complex, complex);
    friend complex operator- (complex, complex);
    friend complex operator* (complex, complex);
    friend complex operator/ (complex, complex);
    // ...
};
```

Operator << can be defined for the new type complex like this:

```
ostream& operator<< (ostream&s, complex z)
{
    return s << '(' << real (z) << ',' << imag (z) << ')';
};
```

and used exactly like operator<< for a built-in type. For example:

```
main()
{
    complex x(1,2);
    cout << "x = " << x << '\n';
}
```

produced

```
x = (1,2)
```

Defining an output operation for a user-defined type does not require modification of the declaration of class ostream nor access to the (hidden) data structure maintained by it. The former is fortunate because the declaration of class ostream resides among the standard header files to which most users do not have write access and that they wouldn't want to modify even if they did have access. The latter is also important because it provides protection against accidental corruption of that data structure. It also makes it possible to change the implementation of an ostream without affecting user programs.

10.3 Input

Input is similar to output. There is a class istream providing an input operator >> (''get from'') for a small set of standard types. A function operator>> can then be defined for a user-defined type.

10.3.1 Input of Built-in Types

Class istream is defined like this:

```
class istream : public virtual ios {
    // ...
public:
    istream& operator>>(char*);        // string
    istream& operator>>(char&);        // character
    istream& operator>>(short&);
    istream& operator>>(int&);
    istream& operator>>(long&);
    istream& operator>>(float&);
    istream& operator>>(double&);
    // ...
};
```

The operator>> input functions are defined in this style:

```
istream& istream::operator>>(T& tvar)
{
    // skip whitespace
    // somehow read a T into 'tvar'

    return *this;
}
```

Thus one can read a sequence of whitespace-separated integers into a `Vector` like this:

```
int readints(Vector<int>& v)
// return number of ints read
{
    for (int i = 0; i<v.size(); i++)
    {
        if (cin>>v[i]) continue;
        return i;
    }
    // too many ints for the size of the vector
    // do appropriate error handling
}
```

A non-`int` on the input will cause the input operation to fail and thus terminate the input loop. For example, the input:

```
1 2 3 4 5. 6 7 8.
```

would have `readints()` read in the five integers

```
1 2 3 4 5
```

leaving the dot as the next character to be read from input. Whitespace is defined as the standard C whitespace (blank, tab, newline, formfeed, and carriage return) by a call to `isspace()` as defined in `<ctype.h>`.

Alternatively one might use the `get()` functions:

```
class istream : public virtual ios {
    // ...
    istream& get(char& c);                      // char
    istream& get(char* p, int n, char ='\n');  // string
};
```

They treat whitespace characters like other characters. They are intended for input operations where one doesn't make assumptions about the meaning of the characters read.

The function `istream::get(char&)` reads a single character into its argument. For example, a character by character copy program can be written like this:

```
main()
{
    char c;
    while(cin.get(c)) cout<<c;
}
```

This looks a bit asymmetric, so the << operator for chars has an equivalent counter-part called put() so that we could write:

```
main()
{
    char c;
    while(cin.get(c)) cout.put(c);
}
```

The three argument istream::get() reads at most n characters into a character vector starting at p. A call of get() will always place a 0 at the end of the characters (if any) it placed in the buffer, so that at most n−1 characters are read given n as the second argument. The third argument specifies a terminator. A typical use of the three argument get() is to read a "line" into a fixed size buffer for further analysis. For example:

```
void f()
{
    char buf[100];

    cin >> buf;                // suspect
    cin.get(buf,100,'\n');     // safe
    // ...
}
```

The cin>>buf is suspect because a string of more than 99 characters will cause the buffer to overflow. If the terminator is found, it is left as the first unread character on the stream. This allows a check for buffer overflow:

```
void f()
{
    char buf[100];

    cin.get(buf,100,'\n');     // safe

    char c;
    if (cin.get(c) && c!='\n') {
        // input string longer than expected
    }
    // ...
}
```

Naturally, there are also versions of get() for unsigned chars.

The standard header <ctype.h> defines several functions that can be useful when processing input:

```
int isalpha(char)      // 'a'..'z' 'A'..'Z'
int isupper(char)      // 'A'..'Z'
int islower(char)      // 'a'..'z'
int isdigit(char)      // '0'..'9'
int isxdigit(char)     // '0'..'9' 'a'..'f' 'A'..'F'
int isspace(char)      // ' ' '\t' return newline formfeed
int iscntrl(char)      // control character
                       // (ASCII 0..31 and 127)
int ispunct(char)      // punctuation: none of the above
int isalnum(char)      // isalpha() | isdigit()
int isprint(char)      // printable: ascii ' '..'~'
int isgraph(char)      // isalpha() | isdigit() | ispunct()
int isascii(char c) { return 0<=c && c<=127; }
```

All but `isascii()` are implemented by a simple lookup, using the character as an index into a table of character attributes. Expressions such as

```
(('a'<=c && c<='z') || ('A'<=c && c<='Z')) // alphabetic
```

are therefore not only tedious to write and error-prone (on a machine with the EBCDIC character set, this will accept nonalphabetic characters), they are also less efficient than using a standard function:

```
isalpha(c)
```

For example, an `eatwhite()` function that reads whitespace characters from a stream could be defined like this:

```
istream& eatwhite(istream& is)
{
    char c;
    while (is.get(c)) {
        if (isspace(c)==0) {
            is.putback(c);
            break;
        }
    }
    return is;
}
```

using the `putback()` function that puts a character back to be the next character read from a stream.

10.3.2 Stream States

Every stream (`istream` or `ostream`) has a *state* associated with it. Errors and non-standard conditions are handled by setting and testing this state appropriately.

The stream state can be examined by operations on class `ios`:

```
class ios {   // ios is a base of ostream and istream
    // ...
public:
    int eof() const;   // end of file seen
    int fail() const;  // next operation will fail
    int bad() const;   // stream corrupted
    int good() const;  // next operation might succeed
    // ...
};
```

If the state is good() or eof(), the previous input operation succeeded. If the state
is good(), the next input operation might succeed; otherwise, it will fail. Applying
an input operation to a stream that is not in the good() state is a null operation. If
one tries to read into a variable v and the operation fails, the value of v should be
unchanged (it is unchanged if v is of one of the types handled by istream or
ostream member functions). The difference between the states fail() and
bad() is subtle and only really interesting to implementers of input operations. In
the state fail(), it is assumed that the stream is uncorrupted and that no characters
have been lost. In the state bad(), all bets are off.

The values used to represent those states are also defined in class ios:

```
class ios {
    // ...
public:
    enum io_state {
        goodbit=0,
        eofbit=1,
        failbit=2,
        badbit=4,
    };
    // ...
};
```

The values of the bits are implementation dependent and are presented here only to
avoid presenting syntactically incorrect code.

One can examine the state of a stream like this:

```
switch (cin.rdstate()) {
case ios::goodbit:
    // the last operation on cin succeeded
    break;
case ios::eofbit:
    // at end of file
    break;
case ios::failbit:
    // some kind of formatting error
    // probably not too bad
    break;
```

```
case ios::badbit:
    // cin characters possibly lost
    break;
}
```

Older implementations used global names for the state values. This caused undesirable name space pollution, so new names were defined within the scope of ios. If you need to use the old names with a new library you can use these definitions:

```
const int _good = ios::goodbit;
const int _bad = ios::badbit;
const int _fail = ios::failbit;
const int _eof = ios::eofbit;

typedef ios::io_state state_value ;
```

Library designers should be careful to avoid adding names to the global name space. If enumerators must be part of the public interface of a library, they should almost always be nested within a class the way ios::goodbit and ios::io_state are.

For any variable z of a type for which the operators >> and << have been defined, a copy loop can be written like this:

```
while (cin>>z) cout << z << '\n';
```

When a stream is used as a condition, the state of the stream is tested and the test *succeeds* (that is, the value of the condition is nonzero) only if the state is good(). In particular, the state of the istream returned by the cin>>z in the preceding loop is tested. To find out why a loop or test failed, one can examine the state. This test of a stream is implemented by a conversion operator (§7.3.2).

For example, if z is a character vector, this loop will take standard input and put it one word (that is, a sequence of non-whitespace characters) per line onto standard output. If z is of type complex this loop will copy complex numbers using the I/O operations described in §10.2.2 and §10.3.3. A template function for copying streams of values of arbitrary type might be written like this:

```
template<class T> void iocopy(T z, istream& is, ostream& os)
{
    while (is>>z) os << z << '\n';
}
```

The variable of type T is passed as an argument to tell the template what type of objects to copy. Its value is not used. For example:

```
complex z;
iocopy(z,cin,cout);   // copy complex numbers

double d;
iocopy(d,cin,cout);   // copy doubles
```

```
char c;
iocopy(c,cin,cout);    // copy chars
```

It is not convenient to test for errors after each input or output operation, so a common cause of error is a programmer failing to do so in a place where it matters. For example, output operations are typically unchecked, but they can occasionally fail. The stream I/O paradigm is designed so that when exceptions become widely available it will be easy to apply them to simplify stream I/O error handling.

10.3.3 Input of User-defined Types

An input operation can be defined for a user-defined type exactly as an output operation was, but for an input operation it is essential that the second argument is of reference type. For example:

```
istream& operator>>(istream& s, complex& a)
/*
    input formats for a complex; "f" indicates a float:
        f
        ( f )
        ( f , f )
*/
{
    double re = 0, im = 0;
    char   c = 0;

    s >> c;
    if (c == '(') {
        s >> re >> c;
        if (c == ',') s >> im >> c;
        if (c != ')') s.clear(ios::badbit);    // set state
    }
    else {
        s.putback(c);
        s >> re;
    }

    if (s) a = complex(re,im);
    return s;
}
```

Despite the scarcity of error-handling code, this will actually handle most kinds of errors. The local variable c is initialized to avoid having its value accidentally ' (' after a failed operation. The final check of the stream state ensures that the value of the argument a is changed only if everything went well.

The operation for setting a stream state is called clear() because its most common use is to reset the state of a stream to good(); ios::goodbit is the default argument value for ios::clear().

10.4 Formatting

The examples in §10.2 were all of unformatted output; that is, an object was turned into a sequence of characters according to default rules and of the length needed to hold it under these rules. Often the programmer needs more detailed control. For example, we need to be able to control the amount of space used for an output operation and the format used for output of numbers. Similarly, some aspects of input can be explicitly controlled.

10.4.1 Class `ios`

Many aspects of the control of input and output reside in class `ios`, which is a base class of `ostream` and `istream`. Basically, an `ios` controls the connection between an `istream` or an `ostream` and the buffer used for the input or output operations. Therefore an `ios` controls exactly how characters are inserted into the buffer or extracted from the buffer. For example, class `ios` has members that hold the information about the base (octal, decimal, or hexadecimal) to be used when integers are written or read, the precision of floating-point numbers written or read, etc., and functions to set and examine these per-stream control variables.

```
class ios {
    // ...
public:
    ostream* tie(ostream* s);  // tie input to output
    ostream* tie();            // return ''tie''


    int width(int w);    // set field width
    int width() const;

    char fill(char);     // set fill character
    char fill() const;   // return fill character


    long flags(long f);
    long flags() const;

    long setf(long setbits, long field);
    long setf(long);
    long unsetf(long);


    int precision(int);  // set floating point precision
    int precision() const;
```

```
    int rdstate(); const; // stream states, see §10.3.2
    int eof() const;
    int fail() const;
    int bad() const;
    int good() const;
    void clear(int i =0);

    // ...
};
```

The functions relating to stream states were described in §10.3.2; the others are described below.

10.4.1.1 Tying of Streams

The tie() function is used to set up and break connections between an istream and an ostream. Consider:

```
main()
{
    String s;
    cout << "Password: ";
    cin >> s;
    // ...
}
```

How can we be sure that Password: appears on the screen before the read operation is executed? The output on cout is buffered, so had cin and cout been independent Password: would not have appeared on the screen until the output buffer was terminated at the end of the program.

The answer is that cout is tied to cin by the operation cin.tie(cout).

When an ostream is tied to an istream the ostream is flushed whenever an input operation is attempted on the istream. Thus,

```
    cout << "Password: ";
    cin >> s;
```

is equivalent to:

```
    cout << "Password: ";
    cout.flush();
    cin >> s;
```

A call is.tie(0) unties the stream is from the stream it was tied to, if any. Like most other stream functions that set a value, tie(s) returns the previous value, that is, returns the previously tied stream or 0. A call without an argument, tie(), returns the current value.

10.4.1.2 Output Fields

The `width()` function specifies the the minimum number of characters to be used for the next numeric or string output operation. For example:

```
cout.width(4)
cout << '(' << 12 << ')';
```

will print `12` in a field of 4 characters giving the output

```
(  12)
```

The ''padding'' or ''filler'' character can be specified by the `fill()` function. For example:

```
cout.width(4)
cout.fill('#');
cout << '(' << "ab" << ')';
```

gives this output:

```
(##ab)
```

The default fill character is space and the default field size is 0, meaning ''as many characters as needed.'' The field size can be reset to its default value like this:

```
cout.width(0);  // ''as many characters as needed''
```

The `width()` function sets the minimum number of characters. If more characters are provided they will all be printed. For example

```
cout.width(4);
cout << '(' << 121212 << ")\n";
```

produced

```
(121212)
```

The reason for letting the fields overflow rather than truncating the output to fit the field is to avoid quiet errors. It is better to get the right output looking ugly than to get the wrong output looking just fine.

A call of `width()` affects only the immediate following output operation, so

```
cout.width(4);
cout.fill('#');
cout << '(' << 12 << "),(" << '(' << 12 << ")\n";
```

produced

```
(##12),(12)
```

and not

```
(##12),(##12)
```

as one might have expected. However, note that had all the numeric and string output operations been affected this – even more surprising – would have been the result:

```
(##12#),(##12##
)
```

The standard manipulator presented in §10.4.2.1 provides a more elegant way of specifying the width of an output field.

10.4.1.3 Format State

An `ios` has a format state that is controlled by the `flags()` and `setf()` functions. Basically, these functions are used to set and unset these flags:

```
class ios {
public:
        // flags for controlling format:
    enum {
        skipws=01,              // skip whitespace on input
                                // field adjustment:
        left=02,                // padding after value
        right=04,               // padding before value
        internal=010,           // padding between sign and value
                                // integer base:
        dec=020,                // octal
        oct=040,                // decimal
        hex=0100,               // hexadecimal
        showbase=0200,          // show integer base
        showpoint=0400,         // print trailing zeros
        uppercase=01000,        // 'E', 'X' rather than 'e', 'x'
        showpos=02000,          // explicit '+' for positive ints
                                // floating point notation:
        scientific=04000,       // .dddddd Edd
        fixed=010000,           // dddd.dd
                                // flush output:
        unitbuf=020000,         // after each output operation
        stdio=040000            // after each character
    };
    // ...
};
```

The meaning of the flags will be explained in the subsections below. The values of the flags are implementation dependent and are presented here only to avoid presenting syntactically incorrect code.

Defining an interface as a set of flags and operations for setting and clearing them is a time honored if somewhat old-fashioned technique. Its main virtue is that a user can compose a set of options. For example:

```
const int my_io_options =
    ios::left|ios::oct|ios::showpoint|ios::fixed;
```

Such a set of options can be installed by a single operation

```
cout.flags(my_io_options);
```

and also trivially passed around in a program:

```
void your_function(int ios_options);

void my_function()
{
    // ...
    your_function(my_io_options);
    // ...
};
```

A set of options can be installed using the function `flags()`. For example:

```
void your_function(int ios_options)
{
    int old_options = cout.flags(ios_options);
    // ...
    cout.flags(old_options);   // reset options
}
```

The `flags()` function returns the old option set. This allows re-setting of all options as shown above and also the setting of an individual flag. For example:

```
myostream.flags(myostream.flags()|ios::showpos);
```

makes `mystream` display an explicit + in front of positive numbers without affecting other options. The old options are read and `showpos` is set by or-ing it into the set. `setf()` does exactly that, so the example could equivalently have been written:

```
myostream.setf(ios::showpos);
```

Once set, a flag retains its meaning until unset.

Controlling I/O options by explicitly setting and clearing flags is crude and error-prone. It is better avoided (in favor of the manipulators described in §10.4.2.1) except after careful examination of your implementation manual and in the simple cases found in the following subsections. This technique of dealing with stream state is a better study in implementation techniques than in interface design technique.

10.4.1.4 Integer Output

The technique of or-ing in a new option with `flags()` or `setf()` works only where a single bit controls a feature. This is not the case for options such as the base used for printing integers and the style of floating-point output. Here, the value that specifies a style cannot be represented by a single bit or as a set of independent single bits.

The solution adopted in `<iostream.h>` is to provide a version of `setf()` that takes a second "pseudo argument" indicating which kind of option we want to set in addition to the new value. For example:

```
cout.setf(ios::oct,ios::basefield); // octal
cout.setf(ios::dec,ios::basefield); // decimal
cout.setf(ios::hex,ios::basefield); // hexadecimal
```

sets the base of integers without side effects on other parts of the stream state. Once set, a base is used until reset. For example:

```
cout << 1234 << ' '; //default: decimal
cout << 1234 << ' ';

cout.setf(ios::oct,ios::basefield); // octal
cout << 1234 << ' ';
cout << 1234 << ' ';

cout.setf(ios::hex,ios::basefield); // hexadecimal
cout << 1234 << ' ';
cout << 1234 << ' ';
```

produced

```
1234 1234 2322 2322 4d2 4d2
```

If one needs to be able to tell which base was used for each number one can set showbase. Thus, adding

```
cout.setf(ios::showbase);
```

before the operations above we get:

```
1234 1234 02322 02322 0x4d2 0x4d2
```

The standard manipulators presented in §10.4.2.1 provide a more elegant way of specifying the base of integer output.

10.4.1.5 Field Adjustment

The adjustment of characters within a field can be controlled by setf() calls:

```
cout.setf(ios::left,ios::adjustfield);     // left
cout.setf(ios::right,ios::adjustfield);    // right
cout.setf(ios::internal,ios::adjustfield); // internal
```

sets the adjustment of output within an output field defined by ios::width() without side effects on other parts of the stream state.

Adjustment can be specified like this:

```
cout.width(4);
cout << '(' << -12 << ")\n";

cout.width(4);
cout.setf(ios::left,ios::adjustfield);
cout << '(' << -12 << ")\n";

cout.width(4);
cout.setf(ios::internal,ios::adjustfield);
cout << '(' << -12 << ")\n";
```

This produced:

```
( -12)
(-12 )
(- 12)
```

Internal adjustment places fill characters between the sign and the value. As shown, right adjustment is the default.

10.4.1.6 Floating-Point Output

The state manipulation functions also control the output of floating-point values. In particular:

```
cout.setf(ios::scientific,ios::floatfield);
cout.setf(ios::fixed,ios::floatfield);
cout.setf(0,ios::floatfield); // reset to default
```

sets the notation used for printing floating-point values without side effects on other parts of the stream state.

For example:

```
cout << 1234.56789 << '\n';

cout.setf(ios::scientific,ios::floatfield);
cout << 1234.56789 << '\n';

cout.setf(ios::fixed,ios::floatfield);
cout << 1234.56789 << '\n';
```

produced

```
1234.57
1.234568e+03
1234.567890
```

The default is n digits as specified by a call of

```
cout.precision(n)
```

The default is n==6. A call of precision affects all floating-point I/O operations up until the next call of precision:

```
cout.precision(8);
cout << 1234.56789 << '\n';
cout << 1234.56789 << '\n';

cout.precision(4);
cout << 1234.56789 << '\n';
cout << 1234.56789 << '\n';
```

produced

```
1234.5679
1234.5679
1235
1235
```

Note that values are rounded rather than just truncated.

The standard manipulators presented in §10.4.2.1 provide a more elegant way of specifying output format for floating-point output.

10.4.2 Manipulators

There is a wide variety of operations one might like to perform just before or just after an input or output operation. For example:

```
cout << x;
cout.flush();
cout << y;

cin.eatwhite();
cin >> x;
```

When written as separate statements as above, the logical connections between the operations are not obvious; and once the logical connection is lost, the code gets harder to understand.

The notion of manipulators allows operations such as flush() and eatwhite() to be inserted directly in the list of input or output operations. Consider the flush() operation. We can define a class with an operator<<() that calls flush:

```
class Flushtype { };

ostream& operator<<(ostream& os, Flushtype)
{
    return flush(os);
}
```

define an object

```
Flushtype FLUSH;
```

and get flushing done by inserting FLUSH into the list of objects to be output:

```
cout << x << FLUSH << y << FLUSH ;
```

We now have the explicit connection between the flush operation and the output operations. However, having to define a class and an object for each operation we want to apply to an output stream soon gets tedious. Fortunately, we can do better. Consider this function:

```
typedef ostream& (*Omanip)(ostream&);

ostream& operator<<(ostream& os, Omanip f)
{
    return f(os);
}
```

This output operator takes arguments of type "pointer to function taking an ostream& argument and returning an ostream&." Noting that flush() is a function of type "function taking an ostream& argument and returning an ostream&" we can write

```
cout << x << flush << y << flush;
```

and have the function flush() called. In fact, flush() is declared

```
ostream& flush(ostream&);
```

in <iostream.h>, and class ostream does have an operator<< that takes pointer to function as described above:

```
class ostream : public virtual ios {
    // ...
public:
    ostream& operator<<(ostream&, ostream& (*)(ostream&));
    // ...
};
```

Thus, this does flush cout twice at the appropriate times:

```
cout << x << flush << y << flush;
```

Similar declarations are found for class istream:

```
istream& ws(istream& is ) { return is.eatwhite(); }

class istream : public virtual ios {
    // ...
public:
    istream& operator>>(istream&, istream& (*)(istream&));
    // ...
};
```

so

```
cin >> ws >> x;
```

does indeed ensure that whitespace has been removed before the attempt to read into
x. However, because eating whitespace is the default for >> this particular use of ws
is redundant.

Naturally, manipulators that take arguments can also be useful. For example, one
might want to write:

```
cout << setprecision(4) << angle;
```

to print the value of the floating point variable angle with four digits after the point.

To do this we need to be able to invoke a function that sets the variable in the
ostream that controls the precision. We can achieve that by having
setprecision(4) build an object that can be "output" by applying an
operator<<():

```
class Omanip_int {
    int i;
    ostream& (*f)(ostream&,int);
public:
    Omanip_int(ostream& (*ff)(ostream&,int), int ii)
        : f(ff), i(ii) { }

    friend ostream& operator<<(ostream& os, Omanip& m)
        { return m.f(os,m.i); }
};
```

The Omanip_int constructor stores its arguments in i and f, and operator<<
calls f() with the argument i. Objects of such classes are often called *function
objects*. To make the example

```
cout << setprecision(4) << angle ;
```

work as described we need to make setprecision(4) to create an (unnamed)
object of class Omanip_int containing 4 and a pointer to the function that sets the
variable in the ostream that controls the precision:

```
ostream& _set_precision(ostream&,int);

Omanip_int setprecision(int i)
{
    return Omanip_int(&_set_precision,i);
}
```

Given these definitions operator<<() will cause a call of precision(i).

Defining a class like Omanip_int for each argument type is tedious, so we
define a template instead:

```
template<class T> class OMANIP {
    T i;
    ostream& (*f)(ostream&,T);
public:
    OMANIP(ostream& (*ff)(ostream&,T), T ii)
        : f(ff), i(ii) { }

    friend ostream& operator<<(ostream& os, OMANIP& m)
        { return m.f(os,m.i); }
};
```

Using OMANIP, the setprecision() example can be abbreviated to:

```
ostream& precision(ostream& os, int i)
{
    os.precision(i);
    return os;
}


OMANIP<int> setprecision(int i)
{
    return OMANIP<int>(&precision,i);
}
```

The OMANIP template, its IMANIP counterpart for istreams, and its SMANIP counterpart for ioss can be found in <iomanip.h>.

Some of the standard manipulators supplied by the stream library are described in the subsections below. Note that a programmer can define new manipulators as needed without touching the definitions of istream, ostream, OMANIP, IMANIP, or SMANIP.

The idea of manipulators was pioneered by Andrew Koenig. He was inspired by the layout procedures in Algol68's I/O system. The technique has many interesting applications beyond the confines of input and output. Essentially, an object is made that can be passed anywhere and used like a function. Passing the object is much more flexible in that the details of the execution can be determined partially by the creator of the object and partially by the caller.

10.4.2.1 Standard I/O Manipulators

The standard I/O manipulators are

```
// Simple manipulators:

ios& oct(ios&); // used octal notation
ios& dec(ios&); // used decimal notation
ios& hex(ios&); // used hexadecimal notation
```

```
ostream& endl(ostream&);     // add '\n' and flush
ostream& ends(ostream&);     // add '\0' and flush
ostream& flush(ostream&);    // flush stream

istream& ws(istream&);       // eat whitespace



// Manipulators taking arguments:

SMANIP<int>   setbase(int b);
SMANIP<int>   setfill(int f);
SMANIP<int>   setprecision(int p);
SMANIP<int>   setw(int w);
SMANIP<long>  resetiosflags(long b);
SMANIP<long>  setiosflags(long b);
```

For example,

```
cout << 1234 << ' '
     << hex << 1234 << ' '
     << oct << 1234 << endl;
```

produced

```
1234 4d2 2322
```

and

```
cout << setw(4) << setfill('#') << '(' << 12 << ")\n";
cout << '(' << 12 << ")\n";
```

produced

```
(##12)
(12)
```

Remember to include `<iomanip.h>` when trying to use manipulators that take arguments.

10.4.3 Members of `ostream`

Class `ostream` provides only a few functions for controlling output; most such functions are provided by the base class `ios`.

```
class ostream : public virtual ios {
     // ...
public:
     ostream&   flush();

     ostream&   seekp(streampos);
     ostream&   seekp(streamoff, seek_dir);
     streampos tellp();
     // ...
};
```

As we have seen, `flush()` empties the buffer onto the output. The other functions are used to position an `ostream` for writing. The p suffix indicates that it is the position used for *putting* characters into the stream that is manipulated. Naturally, these functions have no effect unless the stream is attached to something for which positioning is meaningful, such as a file. The `streampos` type represents a character position in a file, and the `streamoff` type represents an offset from a point indicated by `seek_dir`. All are defined in class `ios`:

```
class ios {
     // ...
     enum seek_dir {
          beg=0,  // seek from beginning of file
          cur=1,  // seek from current position in file
          end=2   // seek from end of file
     };
     // ...
};
```

Stream positions start at 0, so if we think of a file as an array of n characters,

```
char file[n-1];
```

then if `fout` is attached to `file`

```
fout.seekp(10);
fout<<'#';
```

will place a # into `file[10]`.

10.4.4 Members of `istream`

As in the case of `ostream`, most formatting and control functions for an `istream` are found in the base class `ios`.

```
class istream : public virtual ios {
    // ...
public:
    int        peek()
    istream&   putback(char c);

    istream&   seekg(streampos);
    istream&   seekg(streamoff, seek_dir);
    streampos  tellg();
    // ...
};
```

The positioning functions work like their counterparts in ostream. The g suffix indicates that it is the position used for *getting* characters from the stream that is manipulated. The p and g suffixes are needed because we can create iostreams derived from both istream and ostream and such a stream needs to keep track of both a get position and a put position.

The peek() function allows a program to determine the next character to be read without affecting the result of the next read operation. The putback() function allows a program to put an unwanted character back to be read some other time, as shown in §10.3.3.

10.5 Files and Streams

Here is a complete program that copies one file to another. The file names are taken as command line arguments:

```
#include <fstream.h>
#include <libc.h>

void error(char* s, char* s2 = "")
{
    cerr << s << ' ' << s2 << '\n';
    exit(1);
}

int main(int argc, char* argv[])
{
    if (argc != 3) error("wrong number of arguments");

    ifstream from(argv[1]);
    if (!from) error("cannot open input file",argv[1]);

    ofstream to(argv[2]);
    if (!to) error("cannot open output file",argv[2]);
```

```
        char ch;
        while (from.get(ch)) to.put(ch);

        if (!from.eof() || to.bad())
            error("something strange happened");

        return 0;
    }
```

A file is opened for output by creating an object of class ofstream, output file stream, given its name as the argument. Similarly, a file is opened for output by creating an object of class ifstream, input file stream, given its name as the argument. In both cases one can test the state of the created object to see if the file was successfully opened; if not, operations on it will fail quietly.

An ofstream is by default opened for writing, and ifstream is by default opened for reading. Both ifstream and ofstream optionally take a second argument specifying alternative modes of opening:

```
    class ios {
    public:
        // ...
        enum open_mode {
                in=1,              // open for reading
                out=2,             // open for output
                ate=4,             // open and seek to end of file
                app=010,           // append
                trunc=020,         // truncate file to 0-length
                nocreate=040,      // fail if file does not exist
                noreplace=0100     // fail if file exists
        };
        // ...
    };
```

The actual values of these open_modes and their meaning are likely to be implementation specific. Please consult your library manual for details, or experiment. The comments should give some idea of their intended meaning. For example, one can open a file with the proviso that the open operation must fail if the file doesn't already exist:

```
    void f()
    {
        ofstream mystream(name,ios::out|ios::nocreate);

        if (ofstream.bad()) {
            // ...
        }
        // ...
    }
```

It is also possible to open a file for both input and output. For example:

```
fstream dictionary("concordance",ios::in|ios::out);
```

All the operations on istreams and ostreams can be applied to an fstream. In fact, fstream is derived from class iostream, which is derived from both istream and ostream. The reason that the buffering and formatting information of an istream and an ostream reside in a *virtual* base class ios is to make this series of derivations work. This is also the reason that the positioning operations in ostream and istream have different names, seekp() versus seekg(). An iostream has separate positions for reading and writing.

10.5.1 Closing of Streams

A file can be explicitly closed by calling close() on its stream:

```
mystream.close();
```

However, this is implicitly done by the stream's destructor, so an explicit call of close() is needed only if the file must be closed before reaching the end of the scope in which the stream was declared.

This raises the question of how an implementation can ensure that the predefined streams cout, cin, and cerr are created before their first use and closed (only) after the last use. Naturally, different implementations of the <iostream.h> stream library can used different techniques to achieve this. After all, exactly how it is done is an implementation detail that ought not be visible to the user. Here, I will present just one technique that is used in one implementation and that is general enough to be used to ensure proper order of construction and destruction of global objects of a variety of types.

The fundamental idea is to define a helper class that basically is a counter that keeps track of how many times <iostream.h> has been included in a separately compiled source file:

```
class Io_init {
    static int count;
    // ...
public:
    Io_init();
    ˜Io_init();
};
```

```
static Io_init io_init ;
```

Each such file declares its own object called io_init. The constructor for the io_init objects uses Io_init::count as a first-time switch to ensure that actual initialization of the global objects of the stream I/O library is done exactly once:

```
Io_init::Io_init()
{
    if (count++ == 0) {
        // initialize cout
        // initialize cerr
        // initialize cin
        // etc.
    }
}
```

Conversely, the destructor for the io_init objects uses Io_init::count as a last-time switch to ensure that the streams are closed:

```
Io_init::~Io_init()
{
    if (--count == 0) {
        // clean up cout (flush, etc.)
        // clean up cerr (flush, etc.)
        // clean up cin
        // etc.
    }
}
```

This is a general technique for dealing with libraries that require initialization and cleanup of global objects. It was pioneered in C++ by Jerry Schwarz. In a system where all code resides in main memory during execution, the technique is almost free; where that is not the case, the overhead of bringing each object file into main memory to execute its initialization function can be noticeable. As ever, it is better to avoid having global objects wherever possible. For a class where each operation performs significant work, it can be reasonable to test a first-time switch (like Io_init::count, above) in each operation to ensure initialization. However, for streams that approach would have been prohibitively expensive.

10.5.2 String Streams

As shown, a stream can be bound to a file, that is, to an array of characters stored on some secondary storage device, such as a disc. Similarly, a stream can be attached to an array of characters in main memory. For example, an output string stream ostrstream can be used to format messages that should not be printed immediately:

```
char* p = new char[message_size];
ostrstream ost(p,message_size);
do_something(arguments,ost);
display(p);
```

An operation such as do_something can write to the stream ost, pass ost on to its suboperations, etc., using the standard output operations. There is no need to check for overflow because ost knows its size and will go into fail() state when it is full. Finally, `display` can write the message to a "real" output stream. This technique can be most useful to cope with cases in which the final display operation involves writing to something more complicated than a traditional line-oriented output device. For example, the text from `ost` could be placed in a fixed-sized area somewhere on a screen.

Similarly, class `istrstream` is an input string stream reading from a zero terminated string of characters:

```
void word_per_line(char v[], int sz)
/*
    print "v" of size "sz" one word per line
*/
{
    istrstream ist(v,sz);  // make an istream for v
    char b2[MAX];          // larger than largest word
    while (ist>>b2) cout << b2 << "\n";
}
```

The terminating zero character is interpreted as end-of-file.

The `strstreams` are declared in `<strstream.h>`.

10.5.3 Buffering

The I/O operations are specified without any mention of file types, but not all devices can be treated identically with respect to buffering strategies. For example, an `ostream` bound to a character string needs a different kind of buffer that does an `ostream` bound to a file. These problems are handled by providing different buffer types for different streams at the time of initialization. There is only one set of operations on these buffer types, so the `ostream` functions do not contain code distinguishing them. However, the functions handling overflow and underflow are `virtual`. This is sufficient to cope with the buffering strategies needed to date, and it is a good example of the use of virtual functions to allow uniform treatment of logically equivalent facilities with different implementations. The declaration of a stream buffer in `<iostream.h>` might look like this:

```
class streambuf {     // manage a stream buffer
protected:
    char* base;       // start of buffer
    char* pptr;       // next free char
    char* gptr;       // next filled char
    char* eptr;       // one off the end of buffer
    char  alloc;      // buffer allocated by "new"
    // ...
```

```
        // Empty a buffer:
        // Return EOF on error, 0 on success
    virtual int overflow(int c =EOF);

        // Fill a buffer:
        // Return EOF on error or end of input,
        // next char otherwise
    virtual int underflow();
    // ...
public:
    streambuf();
    streambuf(char* p, int l);
    virtual ~streambuf();

    int snextc()           // get the next char
    {
        return (++gptr==pptr) ? underflow() : *gptr&0377;
    }

    int allocate();        // allocate some buffer space
    // ...
};
```

The details of class `streambuf` are presented here for exposition only. I don't believe any generally available implementation of iostreams uses these particular names. Note that the pointers needed to maintain the buffer are specified here so that the common per-character operations can be defined (once only) as maximally efficient inline functions. Only the `overflow()` and `underflow()` functions need to be implemented for each particular buffering strategy. For example:

```
    class filebuf : public streambuf {
    protected:
        int  fd;               // file descriptor
        char opened;           // file opened
    public:
        filebuf() { opened = 0; }
        filebuf(int nfd, char* p, int l)
            : streambuf(p,l) { /* ... */ }
        ~filebuf() { close(); }

        int overflow(int c =EOF);
        int underflow();

        filebuf* open(char *name, ios::open_mode om);
        int close() { /* ... */ }
        // ...
    };
```

```
int filebuf::underflow()          // fill buffer from "fd"
{
    if (!opened || allocate()==EOF) return EOF;

    int count = read(fd, base, eptr-base);
    if (count < 1) return EOF;

    gptr = base;
    pptr = base + count;
    return *gptr & 0377;   // &0377 prevents sign extension
}
```

See your implementation manual for more details of class `streambuf`.

10.6 C Input/Output

Because C++ and C code are often intermixed, C++ stream I/O must sometimes be mixed with the C `printf()` family of input and output functions. Also, because C functions can be called from C++, some programmers may prefer to use the more familiar C I/O functions.

Consequently, the basics of the C I/O functions will be explained here. Typically, C and C++ input and output can be mixed on a per-line basis. Mixing at a per-character basis is possible on some implementations but cannot be relied on for portable code. Some implementations of the C++ stream library require a call of the static member function `ios::sync_with_stdio()` when mixing with C I/O.

The general advantage of the stream output functions over the C standard library function `printf()` is that the stream functions are type safe and have a common style for specifying output of objects of built-in and user-defined types.

The general C output function

```
int printf(const char* format, ...)
```

produces formatted output of an arbitrary sequence of arguments under control of the format string `format`. The format string contains two types of objects: plain characters, which are simply copied to the output stream, and conversion specifications, each of which causes conversion and printing of the next argument. Each conversion specification is introduced by the character %. For example

```
printf("there were %d members present.",no_of_members);
```

Here %d specifies that `no_of_members` is to be treated as an `int` and printed as the appropriate sequence of decimal digits. With `no_of_members==127`, the output is

```
there were 127 members present.
```

The set of conversion specifications is quite large and provides a great degree of flexibility. Following the %, there may be:

- an optional minus sign that specifies left-adjustment of the converted value in the indicated field;

d an optional digit string specifying a field width; if the converted value has fewer characters than the field width, it will be blank-padded on the left (or right, if the left-adjustment indicator has been given) to make up the field width; if the field width begins with a zero, zero-padding will be done instead of blank-padding;

. an optional period that serves to separate the field width from the next digit string;

d an optional digit string specifying a precision that specifies the number of digits to appear after the decimal point, for e- and f-conversion, or the maximum number of characters to be printed from a string;

* a field width or precision may be * instead of a digit string. In this case an integer argument supplies the field width or precision;

h an optional character h, specifying that a following d, o, x, or u corresponds to a short integer argument;

l an optional character l, specifying that a following d, o, x, or u corresponds to a long integer argument;

% indicating that the character % is to be printed; no argument is used;

c a character that indicates the type of conversion to be applied. The conversion characters and their meanings are:

    d   The integer argument is converted to decimal notation;

    o   The integer argument is converted to octal notation;

    x   The integer argument is converted to hexadecimal notation;

    f   The `float` or `double` argument is converted to decimal notation in the style *[-]ddd.ddd*, where the number of d's after the decimal point is equal to the precision specification for the argument. If the precision is missing, six digits are given; if the precision is explicitly 0, no digits and no decimal point are printed;

    e   The `float` or `double` argument is converted to decimal notation in the style *[-]d.ddde+dd*, where there is one digit before the decimal point and the number of digits after the decimal point is equal to the precision specification for the argument; when the precision is missing, six digits are produced;

    g   The `float` or `double` argument is printed in style d, in style f, or in style e, whichever gives full precision in minimum space;

    c   The character argument is printed. Null characters are ignored;

    s   The argument is taken to be a string (character pointer), and characters from the string are printed until a null character or until the number of characters indicated by the precision specification is reached; however, if the precision is 0 or missing, all characters up to a null are printed.

    p   The argument is taken to be a pointer. The representation printed is implementation dependent.

    u   The unsigned integer argument is converted to decimal notation;

In no case does a nonexistent or small field width cause truncation of a field; padding takes place only if the specified field width exceeds the actual width.
Here is a more elaborate example:

```
char* src_file_name;
int line;
char* line_format = "\n#line %d \"%s\"\n";
main()
{
    line = 13;
    src_file_name = "C++/main.c";

    printf("int a;\n");
    printf(line_format,line,src_file_name);
    printf("int b;\n");
}
```

which produces:

```
int a;

#line 13 "C++/main.c"
int b;
```

Using `printf()` is unsafe in the sense that type checking is not done. For
example, here is a well-known way of getting unpredictable output, a core dump, or
worse:

```
char x;
// ...
printf("bad input char: %s",x);
```

It does, however, provide great flexibility in a form that is familiar to C programmers.
Similarly `getchar()` provides a familiar way of reading characters from input:

```
int i;
while ((i=getchar())!=EOF) {   // C character input
    // use i
}
```

Note that to be able to test for end of file against the `int` value `EOF`, the value of
`getchar()` must be put into an `int` rather than into a `char`.
For further details of C input/output operations see your C manual or Kernighan
and Ritchie: *The C Programming Language.*

10.7 Exercises

1. (*1.5) Read a file of floating point numbers, make complex numbers out of pairs
   of numbers read, and write out the complex numbers.
2. (*1.5) Define a type name_and_address. Define << and >> for it. Copy a

stream of `name_and_address` objects.

3. (*2) Design some functions for requesting and reading information of various types. Ideas: integer, floating-point number, file name, mail address, date, personal information, etc. Try to make them foolproof.

4. (*1.5) Write a program that prints (1) all lowercase letters, (2) all letters, (3) all letters and digits, (4) all characters that may appear in a C++ identifier on your system, (5) all punctuation characters, (6) the integer value of all control characters, (7) all whitespace characters, (8) the integer value of all whitespace characters, and finally (9) all printing characters.

5. (*4) Implement the C standard I/O library (`<stdio.h>`) using the C++ standard I/O library (`<iostream.h>`).

6. (*4) Implement the C++ standard I/O library (`<iostream.h>`) using the C standard I/O library (`<stdio.h>`).

7. (*4) Implement the C and C++ libraries so that they can be used simultaneously.

8. (*2) Implement a class for which `[]` is overloaded to implement random reading of characters from a file.

9. (*3) Repeat Exercise 8, but make `[]` useful for both reading and writing. Hint: Make `[]` return an object of a ''descriptor type'' for which assignment means assign through descriptor to file, and implicit conversion to `char` means read from file through descriptor.

10. (*2) Repeat Exercise 9, but let `[]` index objects of arbitrary types, not just characters.

11. (*3.5) Design and implement a pattern-matching input operation. Use `printf`-style format strings to specify a pattern. It should be possible to try out several patterns against some input to find the actual format. One might derive a pattern-matching input class from `istream`.

12. (*4) Invent (and implement) a much better kind of pattern.

13. (**2) Define an output manipulator `based` that takes two arguments, a base and an `int` value, and outputs the integer in the representation specified by the base. For example, `based(2,9)` should print `1001`.

14. (**2) Write a ''minuature'' stream I/O system that provides classes `istream`, `ostream`, `ifstream`, `ofstream` providing functions such as `operator<<()` and `operator>>()` for integers and operations such as `open()` and `close()` for files. Use exceptions, rather than, state variables to communicate error conditions.

15. (**2) Write manipulators that turns character echoing on and off.

11

Design and Development

There is no silver bullet.
– F. Brooks

This chapter discusses approaches to software construction. The discussion covers both technical and sociological aspects of software development. A program is seen as a model of reality, with each class representing a concept. The key task of design is to specify the public and protected interfaces of the classes that define the different parts of a program. Defining these interfaces is an iterative process that typically requires experimentation. The importance of design and of attention to organizational factors in the development of software is emphasized.

11.1 Introduction

Constructing any non-trivial piece of software is a complex and often daunting task. Even for an individual programmer, the actual writing of program statements is only one part of the process. Typically, issues of problem analysis, overall program design, documentation, testing, maintenance, and the management of all of this dwarfs the task of writing and debugging individual pieces of code. Naturally, one might simply label the totality of these activities ''programming'' and thereafter make a logically coherent claim that ''I don't design, I just program;'' but whatever one calls the activity it is important sometimes to focus on individual parts of it – just as it is important occasionally to consider the complete process. Neither the details nor the big picture must be permanently lost in the rush to get a system shipped – although often enough that is exactly what happens.

This chapter will focus on the parts of program development that do not involve writing and debugging individual pieces of code. The discussion is less precise and detailed than the discussions of individual language features and specific programming techniques presented elsewhere in this book. This is necessary because there can be no cookbook method for creating good software. Detailed ''how to'' descriptions can exist for specific well-understood kinds of applications, but not for more general application areas. There is no substitute for intelligence, experience, and taste in programming. In consequence, this chapter offers only general advice, alternative approaches, and cautionary observations.

The discussion is hampered by the abstract nature of software and the fact that techniques that work for smaller projects (say, for one or two people writing 10,000 lines of code) do not necessarily scale to medium and large projects. For this reason, some discussions are formulated in terms of analogies from less abstract engineering disciplines rather than in terms of code examples. Please remember that ''proof by analogy'' is fraud so that analogy is used here for exposition only. Discussions of design issues phrased in C++ specific terms and with examples can be found in Chapters 12 and 13. The ideas expressed in this chapter are reflected in both the C++ language itself and in the presentation of the individual examples throughout this book.

Please also remember that because of the extraordinary diversity of application areas, people, and program-development environments, you cannot expect every observation made here to apply directly to your current problem. The observations made here apply to a wide variety of situations, but they cannot be considered universal laws. Look at these observations with a healthy degree of skepticism.

C++ can be used simply as a better C. However, doing so leaves the most powerful techniques and language features unused so that only a small fraction of the potential benefits of using C++ will be gained. This chapter focuses on approaches to design that enable the data abstraction and object-oriented programming facilities of C++ to be used well; such techniques are often called object-oriented design. Chapter 12 contains a discussion of the main styles of C++ usage together with a warning against the curious ideas that there is ''one right way'' to use C++ and that every C++ feature must be employed in every program to gain maximum benefits from the language (§12.1).

A few major themes run through this chapter:
- The most important single aspect of software development is to be clear about what you are trying to build.
- Successful software development is a long term activity.
- The systems we construct tend to be at the limit of the complexity that we and our tools can handle.
- There are no ''cookbook'' methods that can replace intelligence, experience, and good taste in design and programming.
- Experimentation is essential for all non-trivial software development.
- Design and programming are iterative activities.
- The different phases of a software project, such as design, programming, and testing, cannot be strictly separated.
- Programming and design cannot be considered without also considering the management of these activities.

It is easy – and typically expensive – to underestimate any of these points. It is also hard to transform the abstract ideas they embody into practice. The need for experience should be noted. Like boat building, bicycling, and programming, design is not a skill that can be mastered through theoretical study alone.

Maybe even these highly condensed points could be united into one:

> *Design and programming are human activities;*
> *forget that and all is lost.*

All too often we forget and consider the software development process as simply "a series of well-defined steps, each performing specific actions on inputs according to predefined rules to produce the desired outputs." The very language used in the previous statement conceals the human involvement!

This chapter is concerned with the design of systems that are ambitious relative to the experience and resources of the people building the system. It seems to be the nature of individuals and organizations to attempt projects that are at the limits of their ability. Projects that don't offer such challenges don't need a discussion of design. Such projects already have established frameworks that need not be upset. Only when something ambitious is attempted is there a need to adopt new and better tools and procedures. There is also a tendency to assign projects that "we know how to do" to relative novices who don't.

There is no "one right way" to design and build all systems. I would consider belief in "the one right way" a childhood disease if experienced programmers and designers didn't succumb to it so often. Please remember that, just because a technique worked for you last year and for one project, it does not follow that it will work unmodified for someone else or for a different project. It is most important to keep an open mind.

The conviction that there is no one right way permeates the design of C++ and was the major reason there was no section on "design" in the first edition of this book: I didn't want it to turn into a "manifesto" for my personal preferences. For the same reason the discussions in this chapter and in Chapters 12 and 13 do not present a single sharply delimited view of software development; rather, they provide a discussion of a set of issues that often have to be faced and some approaches that have proved useful in addressing them in some contexts.

After this introduction and a brief discussion of the aims and means of software development in §11.2, this chapter has two major parts:

–   §11.3 presents a view of the software development process.
–   §11.4 presents some practical observations about the organization of software development.

The relationship between design and programming language is discussed in Chapter 12 and issues specifically related to the design of C++ libraries in Chapter 13.

Clearly, much of the discussion here relates to larger scale software development. Readers who are not involved in such development can sit back and enjoy a look at the horrors they have escaped. Alternatively, they can look for the subset of the discussion that relates to individual work. There is no lower limit to the size of programs for which it is sensible to design before starting to code. There is, however, a lower limit for which any particular approach to design and documentation is appropriate. See §11.4.2 for a discussion of issues of scale.

The most fundamental problem in software development is complexity. There is only one basic way of dealing with complexity: Divide and conquer. A problem that can be separated into two sub-problems that can be handled separately is more than half solved by that separation. This simple principle can be applied in an amazing variety of ways. In particular, the use of a module or a class in the design of systems separates the program into two parts – the implementation and its users – connected only by an (ideally) well defined interface; this is the fundamental approach to handling the inherent complexity of a program. Similarly, the process of designing a program can be broken into distinct activities with (ideally) well defined interactions between the people involved; this is the basic approach to handling the inherent complexity of the development process and the people involved in it.

In both cases, the selection of the parts and the specification of the interfaces between the parts is where the most experience and taste is required. Such selection is not a simple mechanical process but typically requires insights that can be achieved only through a thorough understanding of a system at suitable levels of abstraction (see §11.3.3, §12.2.1, and §13.3). A myopic view of a program or of a software development process often leads to seriously flawed systems. Note also that for both people and programs *separation* is easy. The hard part is to ensure effective *communication* between parties on different sides of a barrier without destroying the barrier or stifling the communication necessary to achieve cooperation.

This chapter presents an approach to design, not a complete formal design method. A complete formal design method is beyond the scope of this book; the approach presented here can be used with different degrees of formalization and as the basis for different formalizations. Similarly, this chapter is not a literature survey and does not attempt to touch every topic relevant to software development or to present every viewpoint. Again, that is beyond the scope of this book. A literature survey can be found in reference [2]. Note that terms are used here in fairly general and conventional ways. Most ''interesting'' terms, such as design, prototype, and programmer, have several different and often conflicting definitions in the literature. Please be careful not to read something unintended into what is said here based on specialized or locally precise definitions of the terms.

11.2 Aims and Means

The purpose of programming is to deliver a product that satisfies its users. The primary means of doing so is to produce software with a clean internal structure and to grow a group of designers and programmers skilled enough and motivated enough to respond quickly and effectively to change and opportunities.

Why? The internal structure of the program and the process by which it was created are ideally of no concern to the end user. Stronger: If the end user has to worry about how the program was written then there is something wrong with that program. Given that, what is the importance of the structure of a program and of the people who create the program? After all, neither should be seen by the end user.

A program needs a clean internal structure to ease:

- testing,
- porting,
- maintenance,
- extension,
- re-organization, and
- understanding.

The main point is that every successful major piece of software has an extended life in which it is worked on by a succession of programmers and designers, ported to new hardware, adapted to unanticipated uses, and re-organized several times. Throughout its life, versions have to be produced with acceptable error rates and on time. Not planning for this is planning to fail.

Note that even though end users ideally don't have to know the internal structure of a system, they might actually want to. For example, a user might want to know the design of a system in detail to be able to assess its likely reliability and potential for revision and extension. If the software in question is not a complete system, but a set of libraries for building other software, then the users will want to know more ''details'' to be able to use the libraries better and also as a source of ideas.

A balance has to be struck between the lack of an overall design for a piece of software and overemphasis on structure. The former leads to endless cutting of corners (''we'll just ship this one and fix the problem in the next release''). The latter leads to overelaborate designs where essentials are lost in formalism, where implementation gets delayed by program reorganizations (''but this new structure is *much* better that the old one, people will want to wait for it''), and often results in systems so demanding of resources that they are unaffordable to most potential users. Such balancing acts are the most difficult aspects of design and the area where talent and experience show themselves. The choices are hard for the individual designer or programmer and harder for the larger projects where more people with differing skills are involved.

A program needs to be produced and maintained by an organization that can do this despite changes of personnel, direction, and management structure. A popular approach to coping with this problem has been to try to reduce system development into a few relatively low-level tasks slotted into a rigid framework; that is, create a class of easy-to-train (cheap) and interchangeable low-level programmers (''coders''), and a class of somewhat less cheap but equally interchangeable (and therefore equally dispensable) designers. The coders are not supposed to make design decisions, and the designers are not supposed to concern themselves with the grubby details of coding. This approach often fails, and where it does work it produces overly large systems with poor performance.

The problems with this approach are
- insufficient communication between implementers and designers leads to missed opportunities, delays, inefficiencies, and repeated problems due to failure to learn from experience;
- insufficient scope for initiative among implementers leads to lack of professional growth, lack of initiative, sloppiness, and high turnover.

Basically, such a system is wasteful of scarce human talent. Creating a framework within which people can utilize diverse talents, develop new skills, and contribute ideas is not just the only decent thing to do but also makes practical and economic sense.

On the other hand, a system cannot be built, documented, and maintained indefinitely without some form of formal structure. Simply finding the best people and letting them attack the problem as they think best is often a good start for a project requiring innovation; but as the project progresses, more scheduling, specialization, and formalized communication between the people involved in the project become necessary. By ''formal'' I don't mean a mathematical or mechanically verifiable notation (though that is nice, where available and applicable), but rather a set of guidelines for notation, naming, documentation, testing, etc. Again, a balance and a sense of appropriateness is necessary. A too rigid system can prevent growth and stifle innovation. In this case it is the manager's talent and experience that is tested. For the individual the equivalent dilemma is to choose where to try to be clever and where to simply ''do it by the book.''

The recommendation is to plan not just for the next release of the current project, but for the longer term. Looking only to the next release is planning to fail. We must develop organizations and software development strategies aimed at producing and maintaining many releases of many projects; that is, we must plan for a series of successes.

The purpose of ''design'' is to create a clean and relatively simple internal structure, sometimes also called an architecture, for a program – in other words, to create a framework into which the individual pieces of code can fit and thereby guide the writing of these individual pieces of code.

A design is the end product of the design process (as far as there is an *end* product of an iterative process). It is the focus of the communication between the designer and the programmer and between programmers. It is important to have a sense of proportion here. If I – as an individual programmer – design a small program that I'm going to implement tomorrow, the appropriate level of precision and detail may be some scribbles on the back of an envelope. At the other extreme, the development of a system involving hundreds of designers and programmers may require books of specifications carefully written using formal or semi-formal notations. Determining a suitable level of detail, precision, and formality for a design is in itself a challenging technical and managerial task.

Below, I will assume that the design of a system is expressed as a set of class declarations (typically with their private declarations omitted as spurious detail) and their relationships. This is a simplification: Issues of concurrency, management of the global name space, uses of global function and data, organization of code to minimize re-compilation, persistence, use of multiple computers, etc., may all enter into a specific design. However, simplification is necessary for a discussion at this level of detail, and classes are the proper focus of design in the context of C++. Some of these other issues are mentioned in passing below, and some that directly affect the design of C++ libraries are discussed in Chapter 13. For more detailed discussion and examples of a specific object-oriented design method, see reference [2].

I'm leaving the distinction between analysis and design vague because a discussion of this issue is beyond the scope of this book and is sensitive to variations in specific design methods. The important thing is to pick an analysis method to match the design method and to pick a design method to match the programming style and language used.

11.3 The Development Process

Software development is an iterative and incremental process. Each stage of the process is revisited repeatedly through the development, and each visit refines the end products of that stage. In general, the process has no beginning and no end. When designing and implementing a system, you start from a base of other people's designs, libraries, and application software. When you finish, you leave a body of design and code for others to refine, revise, extend, and port. Naturally, a specific project can have a definite beginning and end, and it is important (though often surprisingly hard) to delimit the project cleanly and precisely in time and scope. However, pretending that you are starting from a clean slate can cause serious problems, and pretending that the world ends at the ''final delivery'' can cause equally serious problems for your successors (often yourself in a different role).

One implication of this is that the following sections could be read in any order because the aspects of design and implementation can be almost arbitrarily interleaved in a real project. That is, ''design'' is almost always re-design based on a previous design, some implementation experience, and constrained by schedules, the skills of the people involved, compatibility issues, etc. A major challenge to a designer/manager/programmer is to create order in this process without stifling innovation and destroying the feedback loops that are necessary for successful development.

The development process has three stages:
- Analysis: Defining the scope of the problem to be solved.
- Design: Creating an overall structure for a system.
- Implementation: Writing and testing the code.

Please remember the iterative nature of this process (it is significant that these stages are not numbered) and note that some major aspects of program development don't appear as separate stages because they ought to permeate the process:
- Experimentation.
- Testing.

 –   Analysis of the design and the implementation.
 –   Documentation.
 –   Management.

Software "maintenance" is seen as simply more iterations through this development process (see also §11.3.6).

It is most important that analysis, design, and implementation don't become too detached from each other, and that the people involved share a culture so that they can communicate effectively. In larger projects this is all too often not the case. Ideally, individuals move from one stage to another during a project: The best way to transfer subtle information is in a person's head. Unfortunately, organizations often establish barriers against such transfers, for example, by giving designers higher status and/or higher pay than "mere programmers." If it is not practical for people to move around to learn and teach, they should at least be encouraged to talk regularly with individuals involved in "the other" stages of the development.

For small to medium projects there often is no distinction made between analysis and design: These two phases have been merged into one. Similarly, in small projects there often is no distinction made between design and programming. Naturally, this solves the communication problems. It is important to apply an appropriate degree of formality for a given project and to maintain an appropriate degree of separation between these phases (§11.4.2). There is no one right way to do this.

The model of software development described here differs radically from the traditional "waterfall model." In a waterfall model, the development progresses in an orderly and linear fashion through the development stages from analysis to testing. The waterfall model suffers from the fundamental problem that information tends to flow only one way. As problems are found "downstream" there is often strong methodological and organizational pressure to provide a local fix; that is, there is pressure to solve the problem without affecting the previous stages of the process. This lack of feedback leads to deficient designs, and the local fixes lead to contorted implementations. In the inevitable cases where information does flow back toward the source and cause changes to the design, the result is a slow and cumbersome ripple effect through a system that is geared to prevent the need for change and therefore unwilling and slow to respond to change. The argument for "no change" or for a "local fix" thus becomes that one sub-organization cannot impose large amounts of work on other sub-organizations "for its own convenience." In particular, by the time a major flaw is found there has often been so much paperwork generated relating to the flawed decision that the effort involved in modifying the documentation dwarfs the effort needed to fix the code. Thus paperwork can become the major problem of software development. Naturally, such problems can – and do – occur however one organizes the development of large systems. After all, *some* paperwork is essential. However, the pretense of a linear model of development (a waterfall) greatly increases the likelihood that this problem will get out of hand.

The problem with the waterfall model is insufficient feedback and inability to respond to change; the danger of the iterative approach outlined here is a temptation to substitute a series of non-converging changes for real thought and progress. Both problems are easier to diagnose than to solve, and however one organizes a task it is easy and tempting to mistake activity for progress.

Remember that no amount of attention to detail, no application of proper management technique, no amount of advanced technology can help you if you don't have a clear idea of what you are trying to achieve. More projects fail for lack of well-defined and realistic goals than for any other reason. Whatever you do and however you go about it, be clear about your aims, define tangible goals and milestones, and don't look for technological solutions to sociological problems. On the other hand, do use whatever *appropriate* technology is available – even if it involves an investment; people do work better with appropriate tools and in reasonable surroundings. Don't get fooled into believing that following this advice is easy.

11.3.1 The Development Cycle

Developing a system should be an iterative activity. The main loop consists of repeated trips through this sequence:
　[1] Create overall design.
　[2] Find standard components.
　　[a] Customize the components for this design.
　[3] Create new standard components.
　　[a] Customize the components for this design.
　[4] Assemble design.
As an analogy, consider a car factory. For a project to start, there needs to be an overall design for a new type of car. This first cut will be based on some kind of analysis and specifies the car in general terms related mostly to its intended use rather than to details of how to achieve these desirable properties. Deciding which properties are desirable – or even better, providing a relatively simple guide to deciding which properties are desirable – is often the hardest part of a project. When done well, this is typically the work of a single insightful individual and is often called a vision. It is quite common for projects to lack such clear goals – and for projects to falter or fail for that reason.

Say we want to build a medium sized car with four doors and a fairly powerful engine. The first stage in the design is most definitely not to start designing the car (and all of its sub-components) from scratch. A software designer or programmer in a similar circumstance might unwisely do exactly that.

The first stage will be to consider which components are available from the factory's own inventory and from reliable suppliers. The components thus found need not be exactly right for the new car. There will be ways of customizing the components. It might even be possible to affect the specification of the "next release" of such components to make them more suitable for our project. For example, there may be an engine available with the right properties except a slight deficiency in delivered power. Either we or the engine supplier might be able to add a turbocharger to compensate without affecting the basic design. Note that making such a change "without affecting the basic design" is unlikely unless the original design anticipated at least some form of customization. Such customization will typically require cooperation between you and your engine supplier. A software designer or programmer has similar options. In particular, derived classes can often be used effectively for customization. However, don't expect to be able to effect arbitrary extensions without foresight by or cooperation with the provider of such a class.

Having run out of suitable standard components, the car designer doesn't rush to design optimal new components for the new car. That would simply be too expensive. Assume that there were no suitable air conditioning unit available and that there was a suitable L-shaped space available in the engine compartment. One solution would be to design an L-shaped air conditioning unit. However, the probability that this oddity could be used in other car types – even after extensive customization – is low. This implies that our car designer will not be able to share the cost of producing such units with the designers of other car types and that the useful life of the unit will be short. It will thus be worthwhile to design a unit that has a wider appeal, that is, design a unit that has a cleaner design and is more suited for customization than our hypothetical L-shaped oddity. This will probably involve more work than the L-shaped unit and might even involve a modification of the overall design of our car to accommodate the more general purpose unit. Because the new unit was designed to be more widely useful than our L-shaped wonder, it will presumably need a bit of customization to fit our revised needs perfectly. Again, the software designer or programmer has a similar option: Rather than writing project-specific code, he designer can design a new component of a generality that makes it a good candidate to become a standard in some universe.

Finally, when we have run out of potential standard components we assemble the "final" design. We use as few specially designed widgets as possible, because next year we will have to go through a variant of this exercise again for the next new model and the specially designed widgets will be the ones we most likely would have to redo or throw away. Sadly, the experience with traditionally designed software is that few parts of a system can even be recognized as discrete components, and few of those are of use outside their original project.

I'm not saying that all car designers are as rational as I have outlined in this analogy or that all software designers make the mistakes mentioned. On the contrary, this model can be made to work with software. In particular, this chapter and the next present techniques for making it work with C++. I do claim, however, that the intangible nature of software makes those mistakes harder to avoid (§12.2.1 and §12.2.5), and in §11.4.3 I argue that corporate culture often discourages people from using the model outlined here.

Note that this model of development really works well only when you consider the longer term. If your horizon extends only to the next release, the creation and maintenance of standard components makes no sense. It will simply be seen as spurious overhead. This model is suggested for an organization with a life that spans several projects and of a size that makes the necessary extra investment in tools (for design, programming, and project management) and education (of designers, programmers, and managers) worth while. It is a sketch of a kind of software factory. Curiously enough, it differs only in scale from the practices of the best individual programmers, who over the years build up a stock of techniques, designs, tools, and libraries to enhance their personal effectiveness. It seems, in fact, that most organizations have failed to take advantage of the best personal practices due to both a lack of vision and an inability to manage such practices on more than a very small scale.

Note that it is unreasonable to expect ''standard components'' to be universally standard. There will exist a few international standard libraries. However, most components will be standard (only) within a country, an industry, a company, a product line, a department, an application area, etc. The world is simply too large for universal standards to be a realistic or indeed a desirable aim for all components and tools.

11.3.2 Design Aims

What are the overall aims of a design? Simplicity is one, of course, but simplicity according to what criteria? Because we assume that a design will have to evolve – that is, the system will have to be extended, ported, tuned, and generally changed in a number of ways that cannot all be foreseen – we must aim for a design and an implemented system that is simple under the constraint that it will be changed in many ways. In fact, it is realistic to assume that the requirements for the system will change several times between the time of the initial design and the first release of the system.

The implication is that the system must be designed to *remain* as simple as possible under a sequence of changes. We must design for change; that is, we must aim for

  – flexibility,
  – extensibility, and
  – portability.

This is best done by trying to encapsulate the areas of a system that are likely to change and by providing non-intrusive ways for a later designer/programmer to modify the behavior of the code. This is done by identifying the key concepts of an application and giving each class the responsibility for the maintenance of all information relating to a single concept (only). In that case, a change can be effected by a modification of that class only. Ideally, that change can be done by deriving a new class or by passing a different argument to objects of that class. Naturally, this ideal is much easier to state than to follow.

Consider an example: In a simulation involving meteorological phenomena we want to display a rain cloud. How do we do that? We cannot have a general routine display the cloud because what a cloud looks like depends on the internal state of the cloud, and that state should be the sole responsibility of the cloud.

A first solution to this problem is to let the cloud display itself. This style of solution is acceptable in many limited contexts. However, it is not general because there are many ways to view a cloud: as a detailed picture, as a rough outline, as an icon on a map, etc. In other words, what a cloud looks like depends on both the cloud and its environment.

A second solution to the problem is to make the cloud aware of its environment and then let the cloud display itself. This solution is acceptable in even more contexts. However, it is still not a general solution. Having the cloud know about such details of its environment violates the dictum that a class is responsible for one thing only and that every "thing" is the responsibility of some class. It may not be possible to come up with a coherent notion of "the cloud's environment" because in general what a cloud looks like depends on both the cloud and the viewer. What the cloud looks like to me depends rather strongly on how I look at it: with my naked eyes, through a polarizing filter, with a weather radar, etc. In addition to the viewer and the cloud, some "general background" such as the relative position of the sun might have to be taken into account. Adding other objects, such as other clouds and airplanes, further complicates the matter. To make life really hard for the designer, add the possibility of having several simultaneous viewers.

A third solution is to have the cloud – and other objects such as airplanes and the sun – describe themselves to a viewer. This solution has sufficient generality to serve most purposes†. It may, however, impose a significant cost in both complexity and run-time overhead. For example, how do we arrange that a viewer understands the descriptions produced by clouds and other objects?

Rain clouds are not particularly common in programs, but objects that need to be involved in a variety of input and output operations are. This makes the cloud example relevant to programs in general and to the design of libraries in particular. C++ code for a logically similar example can be found in the manipulators used for formatted output in the stream I/O system (§10.4.2). Note that the third solution is not "the right solution;" it is simply the most general solution. A designer must balance the various needs of a system to choose the level of generality and abstraction that is appropriate for a given problem in a given system. As a rule of thumb, the right level of abstraction for a long-lived program is the most general you can comprehend and afford, *not* the absolutely most general. Generalization beyond the scope of a given project and beyond the experience of the people involved can be harmful (that is, can cause delays, unacceptable inefficiencies, unmanageable designs, and plain failure).

To make such techniques manageable and economical, we must also design and manage for re-use as described in §11.4.1 and not completely forget about efficiency (see §11.3.7).

11.3.3 Design Steps

Consider designing a single class. Typically, this is *not* a good idea. Concepts do *not* exist in isolation; rather, a concept is defined in the context of other concepts. Similarly, a class does not exist in isolation but is defined together with logically related classes. Typically, one works on a set of related classes. Such a set is often called a *class library* or a *component*. Sometimes all classes in a component constitute a single class hierarchy, sometimes they do not (see §12.3).

The set of classes in a component is united by some logical criteria, often by a

---

† Even this model is unlikely to be sufficient for extreme cases like high-quality graphics based on ray tracing. I suspect achieving such detail requires the designer to move to a different level of abstraction.

common style, and often by a reliance on common services. A component is thus the unit of design, documentation, ownership, and often re-use. This does not mean that if you use one class from a component you must understand and use all the classes from the component or maybe get the code for every class in the component loaded into your program. On the contrary, one typically strives to ensure that a class can be used with only minimal overhead in machine resources and human effort. However, to use any part of a component, one needs to understand the logical criteria that define the component (hopefully made abundantly clear in the documentation), the conventions and style embodied in the design of the component and its documentation, and the common services (if any).

So consider how one might approach the design of a component. Because this is often a challenging task, it is worthwhile breaking it into steps to help focus on the various sub-tasks in a logical and complete way. As usual, there is no one right way of doing this. However, here is a series of steps that has worked for some people:

[1] Find the concepts/classes and their most fundamental relationships.

[2] Refine the classes by specifying the sets of operations on them.

    [a] Classify these operations. In particular, consider the needs for construction, copying, and destruction.

    [b] Consider minimalism, completeness, and convenience.

[3] Refine the classes by specifying their dependencies on other classes:

    [a] Inheritance.

    [b] Use dependencies.

[4] Specify the interfaces for the classes.

    [a] Separate functions into public and protected operations.

    [b] Specify the exact type of the operations on the classes.

Note that these are steps in an iterative process. Typically, several loops through this sequence are needed to produce a design one can comfortably use for an initial implementation or a re-implementation. One advantage of well-done analysis and data abstraction as described here is that it becomes relatively easy to reshuffle class relationships even after code has been written. This is never a trivial task, though.

After that, we implement the classes and go back and review the design based on what was learned from implementing them. Consider these steps one by one:

11.3.3.1 Step 1: Find Classes

Find the concepts/classes and their most fundamental relationships. The key to a good design is to model some aspect of "reality" directly – that is, capture the concepts of an application as classes, represent the relationships between classes in well-defined ways such as inheritance, and do this repeatedly at different levels of abstraction. But how do we go about finding those concepts? What is a practical approach to deciding which classes we need?

The best place to start looking is in the application itself – as opposed to looking in the computer scientist's bag of abstractions and concepts. Listen to someone who will become an expert user of the system once it has been built and to someone who is a somewhat dissatisfied user of the system being replaced. Note the vocabulary used.

It is often said that the nouns will correspond to the classes and objects needed in the program; often that is indeed the case. However, that is by no means the end of the story: Verbs may denote operations on objects, traditional (global) functions that produce new values based on the value of their arguments, or even classes. As an example of the latter, note the function objects described in §10.4.2. Verbs such as "iterate" or "commit" can be represented by an iterator object and an object representing a database commit operation, respectively. Even adjectives can often usefully be represented by classes. Consider, the adjectives "storable," "concurrent," "registered," "bounded." These may be classes intended to allow a designer or programmer to pick and choose among desirable attributes for later designed classes by specifying virtual base classes.

The best tool for finding these initial key concepts/classes is a blackboard. The best method for their initial refinement is discussions with experts in the application domain and a couple of friends. Discussion is necessary to develop a viable initial vocabulary and conceptual framework. Few people can do that alone. See reference [11] for a way of structuring such refinement.

Not all classes correspond to application level concepts. For example, others represent system resources and implementation level abstractions; see §12.2.1.

The relationships mentioned here are the ones that come naturally from our understanding of the application area or (in the case of later iterations through the design steps) arise from further work on the class structure. They represent our fundamental understanding of the application. Often, they are classifications of the fundamental concepts. For example, a hook-and-ladder is a fire engine is a truck is a vehicle. Sections §11.3.3.2 and §11.3.3.5 explain a few ways of looking at classes and class hierarchies with the view of making improvements.

11.3.3.2 Step 2: Specify Operations

Refine the classes by specifying the sets of operations on them. Naturally, it is not possible to separate finding the classes from figuring out what operations are needed on them. However, there is a practical difference in that finding the classes focuses on the key concepts and deliberately de-emphasizes the computational aspects of the classes, whereas specifying the operations focuses on finding a complete and usable set of operations. It is most often too hard to consider both at the same time, especially considering that related classes should be designed together.

In considering what functions are to be provided, several philosophies are possible. I suggest the following strategy:

[1] Consider how an object of the class is to be constructed, copied (if at all), and destroyed.

[2] Define the *minimal* set of operations required by the concept the class is representing.

[3] Consider which operations could be added for notational convenience – and include only a few really important ones.

[4] Consider which operations are to be virtual, that is, operations for which the class can act as an interface for an implementation supplied by a derived class.

[5] Consider what commonality of naming and functionality can be achieved across all the classes of the component.

This is clearly a statement of minimalism. It is far easier to add any function that could conceivably be useful and to make all operations virtual. However, the more functions, the more likely they are to remain unused and the more likely they are to constrain the implementation and the further evolution of the system. In particular, functions that directly read or write part of the state of an object of a class often constrain the class to a single implementation strategy and severely limit the potential for redesign. Such functions lower the level of abstraction from a concept to one implementation of it. Adding functions also causes more work for the implementer – and for the designer in the next redesign. It is *much* easier to add a function to an interface once the need for it has been clearly established than to remove it once it has become a liability.

The reason for requiring the decision to make a function virtual to be explicit rather than a default or an implementation detail is that making a function virtual critically affects the use of its class and the relationships between that class and other classes. Objects of a class with even a single virtual function have a non-trivial layout compared to objects in languages such as C and Fortran. A class with even a single virtual function potentially acts as the interface to yet-to-be-defined classes, and a virtual function implies a dependency on yet-to-be-defined classes (see §12.2.3).

Note that minimalism requires more work from the designer rather than less.

When choosing operations, it is important to focus on what is to be done rather than how it is to be done.

It is sometimes useful to classify operations on a class in terms of their use of the internal state of objects:

   – Foundation operators: constructors, destructors and copy operators.
   – Selectors: operations that do not modify the state of an object.
   – Modifiers: operations that do modify the state of an object.
   – Conversion operators: operations that produce an object of another type based on the value (state) of the object to which they are applied.
   – Iterators: operations that somehow allow access to or use of a sequence of contained objects.

These categories are not orthogonal. For example, an iterator can be designed to be either a selector or a modifier. These categories are simply a classification that has helped people approach design of class interfaces. Naturally, other classifications are possible. Such classifications are especially useful for maintaining consistency across a set of classes within a component.

C++ provides support for the notion of selectors and modifiers in the form of `const` and non-`const` member functions. Similarly, the notions of constructors, destructors, and conversion functions are directly supported. The notion of copy operations is supported through assignment operators and copy constructors.

11.3.3.3 Step 3: Specify Dependencies

Refine the classes by specifying their dependencies on other classes. The various dependencies are discussed in §12.2. The key ones to consider in the context of design are *inheritance* and *use* relationships. Both involve consideration of what it means for a class to be responsible for a single property of a system. To be responsible certainly doesn't mean that the class has to hold all the data itself or that its member functions have to perform all the necessary operations directly. On the contrary, each class having a single area of responsibility ensures that much of the work of a class is done by directing requests "elsewhere" for handling by some other class that has that particular sub-task as its responsibility. However, be warned that overuse of this technique can lead to inefficient and incomprehensible designs by proliferating classes and objects to the point where no work is done except by a cascade of forwarded requests for service. What *can* be done here and now, should be.

The need to consider inheritance and use relationships at the design stage (and not just during implementation) follows directly from the use of classes to represent concepts. This also implies that the component (that is, a set of related classes), and not the individual class, is the unit of design.

11.3.3.4 Step 4: Specify Interfaces

Specify the interfaces for the classes. Private functions don't usually need to be considered at the design stage. What implementation issues must be considered in the design stage are best dealt with as part of the consideration of dependencies in step 2. Stronger: I use as a rule of thumb that unless at least two significantly different implementations of a class are possible, then there is probably something wrong with the class: It is simply an implementation in disguise and not a representation of a proper concept. In many cases, considering if a lazy evaluation scheme is feasible for a class is a good way of approaching the question, "Is the interface to this class sufficiently implementation independent?"

Note that public bases and friends are part of the public interface of a class; see also §5.4.1 and §12.4. Providing separate interfaces for inheriting and general clients by defining separate protected and public interfaces can be a rewarding exercise.

This is the step where the exact types of arguments are considered and specified. The ideal is to have as many interfaces as possible statically typed with application level types; see §12.1.3 and §12.4.

When specifying the interfaces, one should look out for classes where the operations seem to support more than one level of abstraction. For example, some member functions of a class `file` may take arguments of type `file_descriptor` and others character string arguments to be interpreted as file names. The `file_descriptor` operations operates on a different (lower) level of abstraction than the file name operations, so one must wonder whether they belong in the same class. Maybe it would be better to have two file classes, one supporting the notion of a file descriptor and another supporting the notion of a file name. Typically, all operations on a class should support the same level of abstraction. Where they don't, a reorganization of the class and related classes should be considered.

11.3.3.5 Reorganization of Class Hierarchies

In step 1 and again in step 3 we have to examine the classes and class hierarchies to see if they adequately serve our needs. Typically they don't, and we have to reorganize to improve that structure or a design and/or an implementation.

The most common reorganizations of a class hierarchy are factoring the common part of two classes into a new class and splitting a class into two new ones. In both cases the result is three classes: a base class and two derived classes. When should such reorganizations be done? What are common indicators that such a reorganization might be useful?

Unfortunately, there are no simple, general answers to such questions. This is not really surprising because what we are talking about is not simply minor implementation details, but changes to the basic concepts of a system. The fundamental – and non-trivial – operation is to look for commonality between classes and factor out the common part. The exact criteria for commonality are undefined but should reflect commonality in the concepts of the system, not just implementation conveniences. Clues that two or more classes have commonality that might be factored out into a common base class are common patterns of use, similarity of sets of operations, similarity of implementations, and simply that these classes often turn up together in design discussions. Conversely, if subsets of the operations of a class have distinct usage patterns, if such subsets access separate subsets of the representation, and if the class turns up in apparently unrelated design discussions, then that class might be a good candidate for splitting into two.

Because of the close relationship between classes and concepts, problems with the organization of a class hierarchy often surface as problems with the naming of classes and the use of class names in design discussions. If design discussion using class names and the classification implied by the class hierarchies sounds awkward, then there is probably an opportunity to improve the hierarchies. Note that I'm implying that two people are much better at analyzing a class hierarchy than one. Should you happen to be without someone with whom to discuss a design, then trying to write a tutorial description of the design using the class names can be a useful alternative.

11.3.3.6 Use of Models

When I write an article I try to find a suitable model to follow. That is, rather than immediately starting to type, I look for papers on a similar topic, to see if I can find one to be an initial pattern for my paper. If the model I choose is a paper I wrote myself on a related topic, I might even be able to leave parts of the text in place, modify other parts as needed, and add new information only where the logic of the information I'm trying to convey requires it. This book is written that way based on its first edition. An extreme form of this writing technique is the form letter. In that case, I simply fill in a name and maybe add a few lines to "personalize" the letter. In essence I'm writing such letters by specifying the differences from a standard.

Such use of existing systems as models for new designs is the norm rather than the exception in all forms of creative endeavors. Wherever possible, design and programming should be based on previous work. This limits the degrees of freedom that the designer has to deal with and allows attention to be focussed on a few issues at a time. Starting a major project ''completely from scratch'' can be exhilarating, but often a more accurate description is ''intoxicating'' and results in a drunkard's walk through the design alternatives. Having a model is not constraining and does not require that the model should be slavishly followed; it simply frees the designer to consider one aspect of a design at a time.

Note that the use of models is inevitable because any design will be synthesized from the experiences of its designers. Having an explicit model makes the choice of a model a conscious decision, makes assumptions explicit, defines a common vocabulary, provides an initial framework for the design, and increases the likelihood that the designers have a common approach.

Naturally, the choice of an initial model is in itself an important design decision and often can be made only after a search for potential models and careful evaluation of alternatives. Furthermore, in many cases a model is suitable only with the understanding that major modification is necessary to adapt the ideas to a particular new application. Software design is hard, and we need all the help we can get. We should not reject the use of models out of misplaced disdain for ''imitation.'' Imitation is the sincerest form of flattery, and the use of models and previous work as inspiration is – within the bounds of propriety and copyright law – acceptable technique for innovative work in all fields: What was good enough for Shakespeare is good enough for us. Some people refer to such use of models in design as ''design re-use.''

11.3.4 Experimentation and Analysis

At the start of an ambitious development project, we do not know the best way to structure the system. Often we don't even know precisely what the system should do because particulars will become clear only through the effort of building, testing, and using the system. How – short of building the complete system – do we get the information necessary to understand what design decisions are significant and to estimate their ramifications?

We conduct experiments. Also, we analyze the design and implementation as soon as we have something to analyze. Most frequently and importantly we discuss the design and implementation alternatives. In all but the rarest cases, design is a social activity where designs are developed through presentations and discussions. Often, the most important design tool is a blackboard; without it the embryonic concepts of a design cannot be developed and shared among designers and programmers.

The most popular form of experiment seems to be to build a prototype, that is, a scaled down version of the system. A prototype doesn't have stringent performance criteria, machine and programming environment resources are typically ample, and the designers and programmers tend to be uncommonly well educated, experienced, and motivated. The idea is to get a version running as fast as possible to enable exploration of design and implementation choices.

This approach can be very successful when done well. It can also be an excuse for sloppiness. The problem is that the emphasis of a prototype can easily shift from ''exploring design alternatives'' to ''getting some sort of system running as soon as possible.'' This can easily lead to a disinterest in the internal structure of the prototype (''after all, it is only a prototype'') and a neglect of the design effort in favor of playing around with the prototype implementation. The snag is that such an implementation can easily degenerate into the worst kind of resource hog and maintenance nightmare while giving the illusion of an ''almost complete'' system. In that state, the ''prototype'' soaks up time and energy that could been better spent on the product. The temptation for both developers and managers is to make the prototype into a product and postpone ''performance engineering'' until the next release. Misused this way, prototyping is the negation of all that design stands for.

A related problem is that the prototype developers can fall in love with their prototyping tools and forget that the expense of their (necessary) convenience cannot always be afforded by a production system and that the freedom from constraints and formalities offered by their small research group cannot easily be maintained for a larger group working toward a set of interlocking deadlines.

On the other hand, prototypes can be invaluable. Consider designing a user interface. In this case the internal structure of the part of the system that doesn't interact directly with the user often *is* irrelevant and there are no other feasible ways of getting experience with users' reaction to the look and feel of a system. Another example is a prototype designed strictly for studying the internal workings of a system. Here, the user interface can be rudimentary – possibly with simulated users instead of real ones.

Prototyping is a way of experimenting. The desired result from building a prototype is the insights building it brings and not the prototype itself. Maybe the most important criteria for a prototype is that it has to be so incomplete that it is obviously an experimental vehicle and cannot be turned into a product without a major redesign and reimplementation. Having a prototype ''incomplete'' helps keep the focus on the experiment and minimizes the danger of having the prototype become a product. It also minimizes the temptation to try to base the design of the product too closely on the design of the prototype – thus forgetting or ignoring the inherent limitations of the prototype. After use, a prototype should be thrown away.

It should be remembered that there are experimental techniques that can be used as alternatives to prototyping in many cases, and where they can be used they are often preferable because of their greater rigor and lower demands on designer time and system resources. Examples are mathematical models and various forms of simulators. In fact, one can see a continuum from mathematical models, through more and more detailed simulations, through prototypes, through partial implementations, to a complete system.

This leads to the idea of growing a system from an initial design and implementation through repeated redesign and reimplementation. This is the ideal strategy, but it can be very demanding on design and implementation tools, and the approach suffers from the risk of getting burdened with so much code reflecting initial design decisions that a better design cannot be implemented. At least for now, this strategy seems limited to small-to-medium-scale projects, where major changes to the overall design are unlikely, and for redesigns and reimplementations after the initial release of the system, where such a strategy is inevitable.

In addition to experiments designed to provide insights into design choices, analysis of a design and/or an implementation itself can be an important source of further insights. For example, studies of the various dependencies between classes (see §12.2) can be most helpful, and traditional implementer's tools such as call graphs, performance measurements, etc., must not be ignored.

Note that specifications (the output of the analysis phase) and designs are as prone to errors as is the implementation – more so, maybe, because they are even less concrete, are often specified less precisely, are not executable, and typically are not supported by tools of a sophistication comparable to what is available for checking and analyzing the implementation. Increasing the formality of the language/notation used to express a design can go some way toward enabling the application of tools to help the designer. As mentioned in §12.1.1, this must not be done at the cost of impoverishing the programming language used for implementation. Also, a formal notation can itself be a source of complexity and problems. This happens when the formalism is ill suited to the practical problem to which it is applied, when the rigor of the formalism exceeds the mathematical background and maturity of the designers and programmers involved, and when the formal description of a system gets out of touch with the system it is supposedly describing.

The observation that experience is necessary and that design is inherently error-prone and hard to support with tools is the major reason for the emphasis on the iterative model of design and implementation. The alternative – considering the software-development process a linear process starting with analysis and ending with testing – is fundamentally flawed because it does not allow for sufficient feedback from experience gained during the various stages of development.

11.3.5 Testing

A program that has not been tested does not work. The ideal of designing and/or verifying a program so that it works the first time is unattainable for all but the most trivial programs. We should strive toward that ideal, but we should not be fooled into thinking that testing is easy.

"How to test?" is a question that cannot be answered in general. "When to test?" however, does have a general answer: As early and as often as possible. Test strategies should be generated as part of the design and implementation efforts or at least should be developed in parallel with them. As soon as there is a running system, testing should begin. Postponing serious testing until "after the implementation is complete" is a prescription for slipped schedules and/or flawed releases.

Whereever possible, a system should be designed specifically so that it is relatively easy to test. In particular, mechanisms for testing can often be designed right into the system. Sometimes this is not done out of fear of causing expensive run-time testing or because of fear that the redundancy necessary for consistency checks will unduly enlarge data structures. Such fear is usually misplaced because most actual testing code and redundancy can, if necessary, be stripped out of the code before the system is shipped. Assertions (§12.2.7) are sometimes useful here.

More important than specific tests is the idea that the structure of the system should be such that we have a reasonable chance of convincing ourselves and our users/customers that we can eliminate errors by a combination of static checking, static analysis, and testing. Where a strategy for fault tolerance is developed (§9.8) a testing strategy can usually be designed as a complementary and closely related aspect of the total design.

If testing issues are completely discounted in the design phase, testing, delivery date, and maintenance problems will result. The class interfaces and the class dependencies (as described in §12.2 and §12.4) are usually a good place to start work on a testing strategy.

Determining how much testing is enough is usually hard. However, it is clear that too little testing is a more common problem than too much. Exactly how many resources should be allocated to testing compared to design and implementation naturally depends on the nature of the system and the methods used to construct it. However, as a rule of thumb I can suggest that more resources in time, effort, and talent should be spent testing a system than on constructing the initial implementation.

11.3.6 Software Maintenance

''Software maintenance'' is a misnomer. The word ''maintenance'' suggest a misleading analogy to hardware. Software doesn't need oiling, doesn't have moving parts that wear down so that they must be replaced, and doesn't have crevices where water collects to cause rust. Software can be replicated *exactly* and transported over long distances at minute costs. Software is not hardware.

The activities that go under the name of software maintenance are really redesign and reimplementation and thus belong under the usual program development cycle. When flexibility, extensibility, and portability are emphasized in the design, the traditional sources of maintenance problems are addressed directly.

Just like testing, maintenance must not be an afterthought or an activity segregated from the mainstream of development.

11.3.7 Efficiency

Donald Knuth observed that ''premature optimization is the root of all evil.'' Some people have learned that lesson all too well and consider all concern for efficiency evil. On the contrary, efficiency must be kept in mind throughout the design and implementation effort. However, that does not mean the the designer should be concerned with micro-efficiencies, but that first order efficiency issues must be considered.

The best strategy for efficiency is to produce a clean and simple design. Only such a design can remain relatively stable over the lifetime of the project and serve as a base for performance tuning. Avoiding the gargantuism that plagues large projects is essential. Far too often people add features ''just in case'' (see §11.3.3.2 and §11.4.3) and end up doubling and quadrupling the size and run-time of systems to support frills. Worse, such overelaborate systems are often unnecessarily hard to analyze so that it becomes difficult to distinguish the avoidable overheads from the unavoidable, thus discouraging even basic analysis and optimization. Optimization should be the result of analysis and performance measurement, not random fiddling with the code; especially in larger systems, a designer's or programmer's ''intuition'' is an unreliable guide in matters of efficiency.

It is important to avoid inherently inefficient constructs and constructs that will take much time and cleverness to optimize to an acceptable performance level. Similarly, it is important to minimize the use of inherently non-portable constructs and tools because using such tools and constructs condemns the project to run on older (less powerful and/or more expensive) computers.

11.4 Management

Provided it makes some minimum of sense, most people do what they are encouraged to do. In particular, if in the context of a programming project you reward certain ways of operating and penalize others, only exceptional programmers and designers will risk their careers to do what they consider right in the face of management opposition, indifference, and red tape†. It follows that an organization should have a reward structure that matches its stated aims of design and programming. However, all too often this is not the case: A major change of programming style can be achieved only through a matching change of design style, and both typically require changes in management style to be effective. Mental and organizational inertia all too easily lead to a local change that is not supported by global changes required to ensure its success. Fairly typical examples are a change to a language supporting object-oriented programming, such as C++, without a matching change in the design strategies to take advantage of its facilities (see also §12.1) and a change to ''object-oriented design'' without the introduction of a programming language to support it.

11.4.1 Re-use

Increased re-use of code and design is often cited as a major reason for adopting a new programming language or design strategy. However, most organizations reward individuals and groups that choose to re-invent the wheel. For example, a programmer may have his productivity measured in lines of code; will he produce small programs relying on standard libraries at the cost of income and, possibly, status? A manager may be paid somewhat proportionally to the number of people in her group;

---

† An organization that treats its programmers as morons will soon have programmers that are willing and able to act like morons only.

is she going to use software produced in another group when she can hire another couple of programmers for her own group? A company can be awarded a government contract where the profit is a fixed percentage of the development cost; is that company going to minimize its profits by using the most effective development tools? Rewarding re-use is hard, but unless management finds ways to encourage and reward it, re-use will not happen.

Re-use is primarily a social phenomenon. I can use someone else's software provided that

[1] it works: to be re-usable, software must first be usable;

[2] it is comprehensible: program structure, comments, documentation, and tutorial material are important;

[3] it can co-exist with software not specifically written to coexist with it;

[4] it is supported (or I'm willing to support it myself; typically, I'm not);

[5] it is economical (I can share the development and maintenance costs with other users?); and

[6] I can find it.

To this, we may add that a component is not re-usable until someone has "re-used" it. The task of fitting a component into an environment typically leads to refinements in its operation, generalizations of its behavior, and improvements in its ability to co-exist with other software. Until this exercise has been done at least once, even components that have been designed and implemented with the greatest care tend to have unintended and unexpected rough corners.

My experience is that the conditions necessary for re-use will exist only if someone makes it their business to make such sharing work. In a small group, this typically means that an individual, by design or by accident, becomes the keeper of common libraries and documentation. In a larger organization, this means that a group or department is chartered to gather, build, document, popularize, and maintain software for use by many groups.

The importance of such a "standard components" group cannot be underestimated. Note that as a first approximation, a system reflects the organization that produced it. If an organization has no mechanism for promoting and rewarding cooperation and sharing, cooperation and sharing will be rare. A standard components group must actively promote its components. This implies that good traditional documentation is essential, but insufficient. In addition, the components group must provide tutorials and other information that allows a potential user to find a component and understand why it might be of help. This implies that activities that traditionally are associated with marketing and education must be undertaken by the components group.

Wherever possible, the members of such a components group should work in close cooperation with applications builders. Only then can they be sufficiently aware of the needs of users and alert to the opportunities for sharing of components between different applications. This argues for a consultancy role for such an organization and for the use of internships to transfer information into and out of the components group.

Note that not all code needs to be re-usable and that re-usability is not a universal property. Saying that a component is "re-usable" means that its re-use within a certain framework requires little or no work. In most cases, moving to a different framework will require significant work. In this respect, re-use strongly resembles portability. It is important to note that re-use is the result of design aimed at re-use, refinement of components based on experience, and deliberate effort to search out existing components to (re)use. Re-use does not magically arise from mindless use of specific language features or coding techniques. C++ features such as classes, virtual functions, and templates allow designs to be expressed so that re-use is made easier (and thus more likely), but in themselves such features do not ensure re-usability.

11.4.2 Scale

It is easy for an individual or an organization to get excited about "doing things right." In an institutional setting, this often translates into "developing and strictly following proper procedures." In both cases, common sense can be the first victim of a genuine and often ardent desire to improve the way things are done. Unfortunately, once common sense is missing there is no limit to the damage that can unwittingly be done.

Consider the stages of the development process listed in §11.3 and the stages of the design steps listed in §11.3.3. It is relatively easy to elaborate these stages into a proper design method where each stage is more precisely defined, and has well defined inputs and output and a semi-formal notation for expressing these inputs and outputs. Checklists can be developed to ensure that the design method is adhered to, and tools can be developed to enforce a large number of the procedural and notational conventions. Further, looking at the classification of dependencies presented in §12.2 one could decree that certain dependencies were good and others bad and provide analysis tools to ensure that these value judgements were applied uniformly across a project. To complete this "firming up" of the software-production process, one would define standards for documentation (including rules for spelling and grammar, and typesetting conventions) and for the general look of the code (including specifications of which language features can and cannot be used, specifications of what kinds of libraries can and cannot be used, conventions for indentation and the naming of functions, variables, and types, etc.).

Much of this can be helpful for the success of a project. At least, it would be a folly to set out to design a system that will eventually contain ten million lines of code that will be developed by hundreds of people and maintained and supported by thousands more over a decade or more without a fairly well defined and somewhat rigid framework along the lines described above.

Fortunately, most systems do not fall into this category. However, once the idea is accepted that such a design method or adherence to such a set of coding and documentation standards is "the right way," pressure builds to apply it universally. This can lead to ludicrous constraints and overheads on small projects. In particular, it can lead to paper shuffling and forms filling replacing productive work as the measure of progress and success. If that happens, real designers and programmers will leave the project and be replaced with bureaucrats.

Once such a ridiculous misapplication of a (hopefully perfectly reasonable) design method has occurred in a community, its failure becomes the excuse for avoiding almost all formality in the development process. This in turn naturally leads to the kind of messes and failures that the design method was designed to prevent in the first place.

The real problem is to find an appropriate degree of formality for the development of a particular project. Don't expect to find an easy answer to this problem. Essentially every approach works for a small project. Worse; it seems that essentially every approach – however ill conceived and however cruel to the individuals involved – also works for a large project, provided you are willing to throw indecent amounts of time and money at the problem.

A key problem in every software project is to maintain the integrity of the design. This problem increases more than linearly with scale. Only an individual or a small group of people can grasp and keep sight of the overall aims of a major project. Most people must spend so much of their time on sub-projects, technical details, or day-to-day administration that the overall design aims are easily forgotten or subordinated to more local and immediate goals. It is a recipe for failure not to have an individual or group with the explicit task of maintaining the integrity of the design. It is a recipe for failure not to enable such an individual or group to have an effect on the project as a whole.

Lack of a consistent long-term aim is much more damaging to a project and an organization than the lack of any individual feature. It should be the job of some small number of individuals to formulate such an overall aim, to keep that aim in mind, to write the key overall design documents, to write the introductions to the key concepts, and generally to help others to keep the overall aim in mind.

11.4.3 Individuals

Use of design as described here places a premium on skillful designers and programmers; thus it makes the choice of designers and programmers critical to the success of an organization.

Managers often forget that organizations consist of individuals. A popular notion is that programmers are equal and interchangeable. This is a fallacy that can destroy an organization by driving out many of the most effective individuals and condemning the people remaining to work at levels well below their potential. Individuals are interchangeable only if they are not allowed to take advantage of skills that raise them above the absolute minimum required for the task in question. Thus the fiction of interchangeability is inhumane and inherently wasteful.

Most programming performance measures encourage wasteful practices and fail to take critical individual contributions into account. The most obvious example is the relatively widespread practice of measuring progress in number of lines of code produced, number of pages of documentation produced, number of tests passed, etc.

Such figures look good on management charts but bear only the most tenuous relation to reality. For example, if productivity is measured in number of lines of code produced a successful application of re-use will appear to cause negative performance of programmers. A successful application of the best principles in the re-design of a major piece of software typically has the same effect.

Quality is far harder to measure than quantity of output, yet individuals and groups must be rewarded based on the quality of their output rather than by crude quantity measures. Unfortunately, the design of practical quality measures has – to the best of my knowledge – hardly begun. In addition, measures that incompletely describe the state of a project tend to warp development. People adapt to meet local deadlines and to optimize individual and group performance as defined by the measures. As a direct result, overall system integrity and performance suffers. For example, if a deadline is defined in terms of bugs removed or bugs remaining, we may see that deadline met at the expense of run-time performance or hardware resources needed to run the system. Conversely, if only run-time performance is measured, the error rate will surely rise if the developers are under time pressure. The lack of good and comprehensive quality measures places great demands on the technical expertise of managers, but the alternative is a systematic tendency to reward random activity rather than progress. Don't forget that managers are also individuals. Managers need as least as much education on new techniques as do the people they manage.

As in all other areas of software development, it is necessary to consider the longer term. It is essentially impossible to judge the performance of an individual on the basis of a single year's work. Most individuals do, however, have consistent long term track records that can be reliable predictors of technical judgement and a useful help in evaluating immediate past performance. Disregard of such records – as is done where individuals are considered merely as interchangeable cogs in the wheels of an organization – leaves managers at the mercy of misleading quantity measurements.

One consequence of taking a long term view and avoiding the ''interchangeable morons school of management'' is that individuals (both developers and managers) need longer to grow into the more demanding and interesting jobs. This discourages job hopping as well as job rotation for ''career development.'' A low turnover of both key technical people and key managers must be a goal. No manager can succeed without a rapport with key designers and programmers and some recent and relevant technical knowledge. Conversely, no group of designers and developers can succeed in the long run without support from competent managers and a minimum of understanding of the larger non-technical context in which they work.

Where innovation is needed, senior technical people, analysts, designers, programmers, etc., have a critical and difficult role to play in the introduction of new techniques. These are the people who must learn new techniques and in many cases unlearn old habits. This is not easy. These individuals have made great personal investments in the old ways of doing things and rely on successes achieved using these ways of operating for their technical reputation. So do many technical managers.

Naturally, there is often a fear of change among such individuals. This can lead to an overestimate of the problems involved in a change and a reluctance to acknowledge problems with the old ways of doing things. Equally naturally, people arguing for change tend to overestimate the beneficial effects of new ways of doing things and to underestimate the problems involved in a change. These two groups of individuals *must* communicate, they *must* learn to talk the same language, they *must* help each other hammer out a model for transition. The alternative is organizational paralysis and the departure of the most capable individuals from both groups. Both groups should remember that the most successful ''old timers'' are often the ''young turks'' of yesteryear, and given a chance to learn without humiliation some can become the most successful and insightful proponents of change. Their healthy skepticism, knowledge of users, and acquaintance with the organizational hurdles can be invaluable. Proponents of immediate and radical change must realize that a transition, often involving a gradual adoption of new techniques, is more often than not necessary. Conversely, individuals that have no desire to change should search out areas where no change is needed rather than fighting vicious rearguard battles in areas where new demands have already significantly altered the conditions for success.

11.5 Rules of Thumb

This chapter has touched upon many subjects and generally refrained from making strong specific recommendations about how to do things. This reflects my view that there is no ''one right way.'' Techniques and principles have to be applied in ways appropriate to a specific tasks. This requires taste, experience and intelligence. It is possible, however, to outline a few rules of thumb that a designer might use as a guide while gaining sufficient experience to develop better ones. This section presents such a set of rules.

These rules can be used as a starting point for developing design guidelines for specific projects or organizations or as a checklist. I emphasize that these are not absolute rules and cannot act as a substitute for thought.

- Know what you are trying to achieve.
- Have specific and tangible aims.
- Don't try technological fixes for sociological problems.
- Consider the longer term
    - in design, and
    - in the treatment of people.
- Use existing systems as models, as inspiration, and as starting points.
- Design for change:
    - flexibility,
    - extensibility,
    - portability, and
    - re-use.
- Document, market, and support re-usable components.

- Reward and encourage re-use of
    - designs,
    - libraries, and
    - classes.
- Focus on component design.
    - Use classes to represent concepts.
    - Define interfaces to reveal the minimal amount of information needed.
    - Keep interfaces strongly typed wherever possible.
    - Use application level types in interfaces wherever possible.
- Repeatedly review and refine both the design and the implementation.
- Use the best tools available for testing and for analysing
    - the design, and
    - the implementation.
- Experiment, analyze, and test as early as possible and as often as possible.
- Keep it simple; as simple as possible, but no simpler.
- Keep it small; don't add features "just in case."
- Don't forget about efficiency.
- Keep the level of formality appropriate to the scale of the project.
- Don't forget that designers, programmers, and even managers are human.

More rules of thumb can be found in §12.5.

11.6 Annotated Bibliography

This chapter only scratches the surface of the issues of design and of the management of programming projects. For that reason, a short annotated bibliography is provided. A much more extensive annotated bibliography can be found in reference [2].

[1]   Bruce Anderson and Sanjiv Gossain: *An Iterative Design Model for Reusable Object-Oriented Software*. Proc. OOPSLA'90. Ottawa, Canada. pp. 12-27. A description of an iterative design and re-design model with a specific example and a discussion of experience.

[2]   Grady Booch: *Object Oriented Design*. Benjamin Cummings. 1991. This book contains a detailed description of design, a specific design method with a graphical notation, and several large examples of designs expressed in different languages. It is an excellent book to which this chapter owes much. It provides a more in-depth treatment of many of the issues in this chapter.

[3]   Fred Brooks: *The Mythical Man Month*. Addison Wesley. 1982. Everyone should read it every couple of years. A warning against hubris. It is a bit dated on technical matters, but it is not at all dated in matters related to individuals, organizations, and scale.

[4]   Fred Brooks: *No Silver Bullet*. IEEE Computer, Vol.20 No.4. April 1987. A summary of approaches to large-scale software development with a much needed warning against belief in miracle cures ("silver bullets").

[5]   DeMarco and Lister: *Peopleware*. Dorset House Publishing Co. 1987. One
        of the few books that focuses on the role of people in the production of soft-
        ware. A must for every manager. Smooth enough for bedside reading. An
        antidote for much silliness.

[6]   Ron Kerr: *A Materialistic View of the Software "Engineering" Analogy*. in
        SIGPLAN Notices, March 1987. pp. 123-125. The use of analogy in this
        chapter and the next owes much to the observations in this paper and to the
        presentations by and discussions with Ron that preceded it.

[7]   Barbara Liskov: *Data Abstraction and Hierarchy*. Proc. OOPSLA'87
        (Addendum). Orlando, Florida. pp. 17-34. A discussion of how the use of
        inheritance can compromise data abstraction. Please note that C++ has spe-
        cific language support to help avoid most of the problems mentioned
        (§12.2.5).

[8]   C. N. Parkinson: *Parkinson's Law and other Studies in Administration*.
        Houghton-Mifflin. Boston. 1957. One of the funniest and most cutting
        descriptions of disasters caused by administrative processes.

[9]   Bertrand Meyer: *Object Oriented Software Construction*. Prentice Hall.
        1988. Pages 1-64 and 323-334 give a good introduction to one view of
        object-oriented programming and design with many sound pieces of practi-
        cal advice. The rest of the book describes the Eiffel language.

[10]   Alan Snyder: *Encapsulation and Inheritance in Object-Oriented Program-
        ming Languages*. Proc. OOPSLA'86. Portland, Oregon. pp. 38-45. Proba-
        bly the first good description of the interaction between encapsulation and
        inheritance. This article also provides a nice discussion of some notions of
        multiple inheritance.

[11]   Rebecca Wirfs-Brock, Brian Wilkerson, and Lauren Wiener: *Designing
        Object-Oriented Software*. Prentice Hall. 1990. Describes an anthropomor-
        phic design method based on role playing using CRC (Classes, Responsibil-
        ities, and Collaboration) cards. The text, if not the method itself, is biased
        toward Smalltalk.

12

Design and C++

Keep it simple:
as simple as possible,
but no simpler.
– A.Einstein

This chapter discusses the relation between design and the C++ programming language. It examines the use of classes in design and presents the kinds of dependencies that must be considered within and between C++ classes. The role of static type checking is examined. The uses of inheritance and inheritance's relationship to containment are explored. The notion of a *component* is discussed, and some ideals for interfaces are presented.

12.1 Design and Programming Language

If I were to build a bridge, I would seriously consider what material to build it out of, and the design of the bridge would be heavily influenced by the choice of material and vice versa: Reasonable designs for stone bridges differ from reasonable designs for steel bridges, from reasonable designs for wooden bridges, etc. I would not expect to be able even to select the proper material for a bridge without knowing a bit about the various materials and their uses. Naturally, you don't have to be an expert carpenter to design a wooden bridge, but you do have to know the fundamentals of wooden constructions to choose between wood and iron as the material for a bridge. Furthermore, even though you don't personally have to be an expert carpenter to design a wooden bridge, you do need quite a detailed knowledge of the properties of wood and the mores of carpenters.

The analogy is that to choose a language for some software requires knowledge of several languages, and to design a piece of software successfully you need a fairly detailed knowledge of the chosen implementation language – even if you never personally write a single line of that software. The good bridge designer respects the properties of his materials and uses them to enhance the design. Similarly, the good software designer builds on the strengths of her implementation language and – as far as possible – avoids using it in ways that cause problems for implementers.

One might think that this came naturally when only a single designer/programmer was involved, but even in such cases the programmer can be seduced into misusing the language due to inadequate experience or undue respect for styles of programming established for radically different languages. Where the designer is different from the programmer – and especially where they do not share a common culture – the likelihood of introducing error, inelegance, and inefficiencies into the resulting system approaches certainty.

So what can a programming language do for a designer? A programming language can provide features that allow the fundamental notions of the design to be represented directly in the programming language. This eases the implementation, makes it easier to maintain the correspondence between the design and the implementation, enables better communication between designers and implementers, and allows better tools to be built to support both designers and implementers.

For example, most design methods are concerned about dependencies between different parts of a program (usually to minimize them and to ensure that they are well defined and understood). A language supporting explicit interfaces between parts of a program can support such design notions. It can guarantee that only the expected dependencies actually exist. Because many dependencies are explicit in code written in such a language, tools that read a program to produce charts of dependencies can be provided. This eases the job of designers and others that need to understand the structure of a program. A programming language such as C++ can be used to decrease the gap between design and program and consequently reduce the scope for confusion and misunderstandings.

The key notion of C++ is that of a class. A C++ class is a type. The class is also the primary mechanism for information hiding. Programs can be specified in terms of user-defined types and hierarchies of such user-defined types. Both built-in and user-defined types obey statically checked type rules. Virtual functions provide a mechanism for run-time binding without breaking the static type rules. Templates support the design of parameterized types. Exceptions provide a way of making error handling more regular. These C++ features can be used without incurring overhead compared to C programs. These are the first-order properties of C++ that must be understood and considered by a designer. In addition, generally available major libraries – such as matrix libraries, database interfaces, graphical user interface libraries, concurrency support libraries, etc. – can strongly affect design choices.

Fear of novelty; misapplication of lessons from other languages, systems, and application areas; and poor design tools sometimes lead to sub-optimal use of C++. Three ways designers fail to take advantage of language features and fail to respect limitations are worth mentioning:

[1] Ignore classes and express the design in a way that constrains implementers to use the C subset only.

[2] Ignore derived classes and virtual functions and use only the data abstraction subset.

[3] Ignore the static type checking and express the design in such a way that implementers are constrained to simulate dynamic type checking.

These three variants are typical for designers with

[1] a C, traditional CASE, or structured design background,

[2] an Ada or data abstraction background,

[3] a Smalltalk or Lisp background,

respectively. In each case one must wonder if either the implementation language was ill chosen (assuming that the design method was well chosen) or if the designer had failed to adapt to and appreciate the tool in hand (assuming that the implementation language was well chosen).

It should be noted that there is nothing unusual or shameful in such a mismatch. It is simply a mismatch that delivers sub-optimal designs and imposes unnecessary burdens on programmers and – in the case where the conceptual framework of the design method is noticeably poorer than C++'s conceptual framework – on the designers.

Note also that not all programs need to be structured around classes and/or class hierarchies and that not every part of a program needs to use every feature that C++ has to offer. On the contrary, it is essential for the success of a project that people do not indulge in massive use of features that they are only just learning. The point of the discussion below is not to encourage dogmatic use of classes, hierarchies, and strongly typed interfaces but to suggest an open mind about their use wherever appropriate given the nature of an application, the limitations of C++, and the experience of the individuals involved. Section §12.1.4 will discuss approaches to the use of more than one style of C++ usage in a project under the heading of "Hybrid Design."

12.1.1 Ignoring Classes

Consider case 1 – the design that ignores classes. Here, the resulting C++ program will be roughly equivalent to the C program that would have resulted from the same design process – and this program would again be roughly equivalent to the Ada or COBOL program that would have resulted from the same design process. In essence, the design has been made "programming language independent" at the cost of forcing the programmer to code in the common subset of C, Ada, and COBOL. This has advantages. For example, the strict separation of data and code that results makes it easy to use traditional databases that are designed for such programs. Because a minimal programming language is used, it would appear that less skill – or at least different skills – would be required from programmers. For many applications – say, a traditional sequential database update program – this way of thinking is quite reasonable, and the traditional techniques developed over decades are adequate for the job.

However, where the application differs sufficiently from traditional sequential processing of records (or characters) or the complexity involved is higher – say, in an interactive CASE system – the lack of language support for data abstraction implied by the decision (or default) to ignore classes will hurt. The complexity is still there and because the system now is implemented in an impoverished language, the code does not reflect the design directly. It consists of too many lines of code, lacks type checking, and is in general not amenable to tools. This is the prescription for a maintenance nightmare.

A common band-aid for this problem is to build specific tools to support the notions of the design method. These tools then provide higher level constructs and checking to compensate for deficiencies of the (deliberately impoverished) implementation language. Thus the design method becomes a special purpose and typically corporately owned programming language. Such programming languages are in most contexts poor substitutes for a widely available general purpose programming language supported by suitable design tools. Using C++ with a design method and tools enforcing such restrictive conventions is a waste. It may not be a total waste, though. The mismatch between programming language and tools may simply be part of a transition process and thus temporary.

The most common reason for ignoring classes in design is simple inertia. Traditional programming languages simply don't support the notion of a class, and traditional design techniques reflect this deficiency. The most common focus of design has been the decomposition of the problems into a set of procedures performing required actions. This notion, called procedural programming in Chapter 1, is in the context of design often called functional decomposition. A common question is, "Can we use C++ together with a design method based on functional decomposition?" You can, but you will most likely end up using C++ as simply a better C and will suffer the problems mentioned above. This may be acceptable in a transition period, for already completed designs, and for sub-systems where classes do not appear to offer significant benefits (given the experience of the individuals involved at this time); but for the longer term and in general the policy against large-scale use of classes implied by functional decomposition is not compatible with effective use of C++.

The procedure-oriented and object-oriented views of programming are fundamentally different and typically lead to radically different solutions to the same problem. This observation is as true for the design phase as it is for the implementation phase: You can focus the design on the actions taken or on the entities represented, but not simultaneously on both.

So why prefer "object-oriented design" over the traditional design methods based on functional decomposition? A first-order answer is that functional decomposition leads to insufficient data abstraction. From this, it follows that the resulting design is
  – less resilient to change,
  – less amenable to tools,
  – less suited for parallel development, and
  – less suited for concurrent execution.
The problem is that functional decomposition causes interesting data to become global because when a system is structured as a tree of functions, any data accessed by

two functions must be global to both. This ensures that "interesting" data bubble up toward the top of the tree as more and more functions require access to it†. Focussing on the specification of classes and the encapsulation of data addresses this problem by making the dependencies between different parts of a program explicit and tractable. More importantly, though, it reduces the number of dependencies in a system by improving locality of reference to data.

However, some problems are best solved by writing a set of procedures. The point of an "object oriented" approach to design is not that there should never be any global procedures in a program or that no part of a system may be procedure oriented. Rather, the key point is that classes and not global procedures are the primary focus on the design effort. The use of a procedural style should be a conscious decision and not a simple default. Both classes and procedures should be used appropriately relative to the application and not simply as artifacts of an inflexible design method.

12.1.2 Avoiding Inheritance

Consider case 2 – the design that avoids inheritance. Here the resulting programs simply fail to take advantage of a key C++ feature while still reaping many benefits of C++ compared to C, Pascal, Fortran, COBOL, etc. Common reasons for doing that – apart from inertia – are claims that "inheritance is an implementation detail" and "inheritance violates information hiding," and "inheritance makes cooperation with other software harder."

Considering inheritance merely an implementation detail ignores the way that class hierarchies can directly model key relationships between concepts in the application domain. Such relationships should be explicit in the design to allow designers to reason about them.

A strong case can be made for excluding inheritance from the parts of a C++ program that must interface directly with code written in other languages. This is, however, *not* a sufficient reason for avoiding the use of inheritance throughout a system; it is simply a reason for carefully specifying and encapsulating a program's interface to "the outer world." Similarly, worries about compromising information hiding through the use of inheritance (see §12.2.3) is a reason to be careful with the use of virtual functions and protected members, not a reason for general avoidance.

There are many cases where there is no real advantage of using inheritance, but in a large project a policy of "no inheritance" will result in a less comprehensible and flexible system where inheritance is "faked" using more traditional language and design constructs. Further, I suspect that despite such a policy inheritance will eventually be used anyway because C++ programmers will find convincing arguments for inheritance-based designs in various parts of the system. Therefore a "no inheritance" policy will ensure only that a coherent overall architecture will be missing and will restrict the use of class hierarchies to specific sub-systems.

---

† Exactly the same process can be seen in single rooted class hierarchies where "interesting" data and functions tend to bubble up toward a root class. See also §12.3.

In other words, keep an open mind. Class hierarchies are not an essential part of every good program, but there are many cases where they can help in both the understanding of the application and the expression of a solution. The fact that inheritance can be misused and overused is a reason for caution; it is a not reason for prohibition.

12.1.3 Ignoring Static Type Checking

Consider case 3 – the design that ignores static type checking. Commonly stated reasons to ignore static type checking in the design phase are that ''types are an artifact of the programming language,'' that ''it is more natural to think about objects without bothering about types,'' and that ''static type checking forces us to think about implementation issues too early.'' This attitude is fine as far as it goes and harmless up to a point. It is certainly reasonable to ignore details of type checking in the design stage, and it is often safe to ignore type issues almost completely in the analysis stage and early design stages. However, classes and class hierarchies are very useful in the design; in particular, they allow us to be specific about concepts, allow us to be precise about their relationships, and help us reason about the concepts. As the design progresses, this precision takes the form of increasingly precise statements about classes and their interfaces.

It is important to realize that precisely specified and strongly typed interfaces are a fundamental design tool. C++ was designed with this in mind. A strongly typed interface ensures (up to a point) that only compatible pieces of software can be compiled and linked together and thus allows these pieces of software to make relatively strong assumptions about each other. These assumptions are guaranteed by the type system. The effect of this is to minimize the use of run-time tests, thus promoting efficiency and causing significant reductions in the integration phase of multi-person projects. In fact, strong positive experience with integrating systems with strongly typed interfaces is the reason integration isn't a major topic of this chapter.

Consider an analogy: In the physical world we plug gadgets together all the time, and a seemingly infinite number of standards for plugs exists. The most obvious thing about these plugs is that they are specifically designed to make it impossible to plug two gadgets together unless they were designed to be plugged together and then only in the right way. You cannot plug a shaver into a high-power socket. Had you been able to you would have ended up with a fried shaver or a fried shavee. Much ingenuity is expended on ensuring that incompatible pieces of hardware cannot be plugged together. The alternative to using many incompatible plugs is gadgets that protect themselves against undesirable behavior from gadgets plugged into their sockets. A surge protector is a good example of this. Because perfect compatibility cannot be guaranteed at the ''plug compatibility level,'' we occasionally need the more expensive protection of circuitry that dynamically adapts to and/or protects from a range of inputs.

The analogy is almost exact: Static type checking is equivalent to plug compatibility, and dynamic checking corresponds to protection/adaption circuitry. If both checks fail – in either the physical world or the software world – serious damage can result. In large systems both forms of checking are used. In the early stages of a design it may be reasonable simply to say, "These two gadgets should be plugged together," but soon it becomes relevant exactly how they should be plugged together: What guarantees does the plug provide about behavior? What error conditions are possible? What are the first order cost estimates?

The use of "static typing" is not limited to the physical world. The use of units (for example, meters, kilograms, and seconds) to prevent the mixing of incompatible entities is pervasive in physics and engineering.

In the description of the design steps in §11.3.3, type information enters the picture in step 2 (presumably after having been superficially considered in step 1) and becomes a major issue in step 4.

Statically checked interfaces are the prime vehicle for ensuring cooperation between C++ software developed by different groups, and the documentation of these interfaces (including the exact types involved) is the primary means of communication between separate groups of programmers. These interfaces are one of the prime outputs of the design process and a prime means of communication between designers and programmers.

Ignoring this leads to designs that obscure the structure of the program, that postpone error detection until run time, and that might be difficult to implement well in C++.

Consider an interface specified in terms of self-identifying "objects." For example, "Function `f()` takes an argument that *must be* a `plane`" (checked by the called function at run time), rather than, "Function `f()` takes an argument that *is* a `plane`" (guaranteed by the compiler). The former is a severe underspecification of the interface that forces dynamic rather than static checking. A similar point was made by the airplane example in §1.5.2. There, a more precise specification – a template plus virtual functions rather than unconstrained dynamic type checking – was used to move error detection from run-time to compile-time. The difference in run-time between dynamic and static checking can be significant, usually a factor in the range of 3 to 10.

One should not go to the other extreme, though. It is not possible to catch all errors by static checking. For example, even the most thoroughly statically checked program is vulnerable to hardware failures. However, the ideal is to have the vast majority of interfaces be statically typed with application-level types; see §12.4.

Another problem is that a design can be perfectly reasonable in the abstract but cause serious trouble because it fails to take limitations of a basic tool, in this case C++, into account. For example, reliance on names rather than types for the structuring of a system can cause unnecessary problems for C++'s type system and thus can become a cause of run-time errors and overheads. Consider three classes:

```
class X {   // pseudo code, not C++
    f()
    g()
}
```

```
class Y {
    g()
    h()
}

class Z {
    h()
    f()
}
```

used by some function in an untyped design:

```
k(a, b, c)   // pseudo code, not C++
{
    a.f()
    b.g()
    c.h()
}
```

Here the calls

```
X x
Y y
Z z

k(x,y,z)      // ok
k(z,x,y)      // ok
```

will succeed because k() simply requires that its first argument must have an operation f(), its second argument an operation g(), and its third argument an operation h(). On the other hand,

```
k(y,x,z)      // fail
k(x,z,y)      // fail
```

will fail. This example has perfectly reasonable implementations in a completely run time checked language (say Smalltalk or CLOS), but because C++ requires commonality between types to be represented as a base class relationship it has no direct representation in C++. Often, examples such as this *can* be mapped into C++ by expressing the assumptions about commonality explicitly in the class declarations, but it requires an undesirable amount of mechanism and cleverness. For example:

```
class F {
    virtual void f();
};

class G {
    virtual void g();
};
```

```
class H {
    virtual void h();
};

class X : public virtual F, public virtual G {
    void f();
    void g();
};

class Y : public virtual G, public virtual H {
    void g();
    void h();
};

class Z : public virtual H, public virtual F {
    void h();
    void f();
};

k(const F& a, const G& b, const H& c)
{
    a.f();
    b.g();
    c.h();
}

main()
{
    X x;
    Y y;
    Z z;

    k(x,y,z);     // ok
    k(z,x,y);     // ok

    k(y,x,z);     // error F required for first argument
    k(x,z,y);     // error G required for second argument
}
```

Note that making k()'s assumptions about its argument explicit moved the error detection from run time to compile time. Elaborate examples like the one above result from trying to implement designs on the basis of experience with a different type model in C++. It is usually possible, but it does lead to "unnatural" looking and typically inefficient code. Such a mismatch between the design technique and the programming language used could be compared with the result of word-for-word translation between natural languages. For example, English with German grammar is as awkward as German with English grammar, and both can be close to incomprehensible to someone fluent in only one of those languages.

This example reflects the observation that the classes in a program are the concrete representation of the concepts of the design, so that obscuring the relationships between the classes obscures the fundamental concepts of the design.

12.1.4 Hybrid Design

Introducing new ways of doing things into an organization can be painful. The disruption to the organization and the individuals in the organization can be significant. In particular, an abrupt change that overnight turns productive and proficient members of ''the old school'' into ineffective novices in ''the new school'' is typically unacceptable. However, it is rare to achieve major gains without changes, and significant changes typically involve risks.

C++ was designed to minimize such risks by allowing a gradual adoption of techniques. Although it is clear that the largest benefits from using C++ are achieved through data abstraction, object-oriented programming, and object-oriented design, it is not clear that the fastest way to achieve these gains is a radical break with the past. Occasionally such a clean break is feasible; more often the desire for improvement is – or ought to be – tempered by concerns about how to manage the transition. Consider:

- Designers and programmers need time to acquire new skills.
- New code needs to cooperate with old code.
- Old code needs to be maintained (often indefinitely).
- Work on existing designs and programs needs to be completed (on time).
- Tools supporting the new techniques need to be introduced into the local environment.

This section is concerned with situations where these concerns are relevant. It is easy to underestimate the first two points.

By supporting several programming paradigms C++ supports the notion of a gradual introduction into an organization in several ways:

- Programmers can remain productive while learning C++.
- C++ can yield significant benefits in a tool-poor environment.
- C++ program fragments can cooperate well with code written·in C and other traditional languages.
- C++ has a large C-compatible subset.

The idea is that programmers can make the move to C++ from a traditional language by first adopting C++ while retaining a traditional (procedural) style of programming, then using the data abstraction techniques, and finally – when the language and its associated tools have been mastered – object-oriented programming. Note that a well designed library is much easier to use than it was to design and implement, so a novice can benefit from the more advanced uses of C++ even during the early stages of this progress.

The idea of climbing the C++ learning curve in stages and the ability to mix C++ code with code written in languages that do not support C++'s notions of data abstraction and object-oriented programming naturally leads to a hybrid style of design.

Many interfaces can simply be left procedural because there will be no immediate benefits in doing anything more complicated. For example, the C standard math library is interfaced to C++ like this:

```
extern "C" {
    #include <math.h>
}
```

and the C math functions can then be used exactly as in C. For many key libraries this will already have been done by the library provider so that the C++ programmer can stay ignorant of the actual implementation language. Using libraries written in languages such as C is the first, and initially most important, form of re-use in C++.

The next stage – to be used only where a more elaborate technique is actually needed – is to present facilities written in languages such as C and Fortran as classes by encapsulating the data structures and functions in C++ interface classes. A simple example of lifting the semantics from the procedure plus data structure level to the data abstraction level is the string class from §7.6. There, encapsulation of the C character string representation and the standard C string functions are used to produce a string type that is much simpler to use.

A similar technique can be used to fit a built-in or stand-alone type into a class hierarchy. For example, int can be fitted into a class hierarchy:

```
class Int : public My_object {
    int i;
public:
    // definition of operations
    // see exercises [8]-[11] in section 7.14 for ideas
};
```

Again, this should be done only where there actually is a need to fit such types into a hierarchy.

Conversely, C++ classes can be presented to C and Fortran code fragments as functions and data structures. For example:

```
class myclass {
    // representation
public:
    void f();
    T1 g(T2);
    // ...
};


extern "C" {      // map myclass into C callable functions:

    void myclass_f(myclass* p) { p->f(); }
    T1 myclass_g(myclass* p, T2 a) { return p->g(a); }
    // ...
}
```

The C program would declare these functions in a header file like this:

```
// in C header file:

extern void myclass_f(struct myclass*);
extern T1 myclass_g(struct myclass*, T2);
```

This allows designs for C++ to evolve to use data abstraction and class hierarchies in the presence of code written in languages in which these concepts are missing and even under the constraint that the resulting code must be callable from procedural languages.

12.2 Classes

The most fundamental notion of object-oriented design and programming is that the program is a model of some aspects of reality. The classes in the program represent the fundamental concepts of the application and, in particular, the fundamental concepts of the "reality" being modeled. Real-world objects and artifacts of the implementation are represented by objects of these classes.

In this section we examine the structure of a program as seen by the relationships between the classes:
- inheritance relationships,
- containment relationships,
- use relationships, and
- programmed-in relationships.

Implicit in the discussion of these relationships is the assumption that the analysis of such relationships is central to the design of a system. In §12.4 we examine the properties that make a class and its interfaces useful for representing concepts. Basically, the ideal class has a minimal and well-defined dependence on the rest of the world and presents an interface exposing the minimal amount of information necessary to the rest of the world.

Note that a C++ class is a type, so that classes and the relationships between classes receive significant support from compilers and are generally amenable to static analysis.

12.2.1 What Do Classes Represent?

There are essentially two kinds of classes in a system:
- [1] the classes that directly reflect the concepts in the application domain, that is, concepts that are used by end-users to describe their problems and solutions; and
- [2] the classes that are artifacts of the implementation, that is, concepts that are used by the designers and programmers to describe their implementation techniques.

Some of the classes that are artifacts of the implementation may also represent real-world entities. For example, the hardware and software resources of a system provide good candidates for classes in an application. This reflects the fact that a system can be viewed from several viewpoints, so that one person's implementation detail is another person's application. A well designed system will contain classes supporting logically separate views of the system. For example:

[1] classes representing user-level concepts (e.g., cars and trucks),

[2] classes representing generalizations of the user-level concepts (vehicles),

[3] classes representing hardware resources (e.g., a memory management class),

[4] classes representing system resources (e.g., output streams),

[5] classes used to implement other classes (e.g., lists, queues, locks), and

[6] built-in data types and control structures.

In larger systems, keeping logically separate types of classes separate and maintaining separation between several levels of abstraction becomes a challenge. The simple example above could be considered to have three levels of abstraction:

[1+2] provides an application level view of the system,

[3+4] represents the machine on which the model runs, and

[5+6] represents a low-level (programming language) view of the implementation.

The larger the system, the more levels of abstraction are typically needed for the description of the system and the more difficult it becomes to define and maintain such levels of abstraction. Note that such levels of abstraction have direct counterparts in nature and in other types of human constructions. For example, a house can be considered as consisting of

[1] atoms;

[2] molecules;

[3] lumber and bricks;

[4] floors, walls, and ceilings; and

[5] rooms

As long as these levels of abstraction are kept separate, you can maintain a coherent view of the house. However, if you mix them, absurdities arise. For example, the statement, "My house consists of several thousand pounds of carbon, some complex polymers, about 5000 bricks, two bathrooms, and 13 ceilings," is silly. Given the abstract nature of software, the equivalent statement about a complex system is not always recognized for what it is.

The translation of a concept in the application area into a class in a design is not a simple mechanical operation. It is often a task that requires significant insights. Note that the concepts in an application area are themselves abstractions. For example, "taxpayers," "monks," and "employees" don't really exist in nature; such concepts are themselves labels put on the poor individuals to classify them relative to some system. The real or even the imagined world (literature, especially science fiction) is sometimes simply a source of ideas for concepts that mutate radically in the transition into classes: The screen of my Mac doesn't really resemble my desktop despite being designed to support the desktop metaphor†, and the windows on my terminal bear

---

† I wouldn't be able to tolerate such mess on my screen anyway.

only the slightest relation to the contraptions that let drafts into my office. The point about modeling reality is not to slavishly follow what we see but to use it as a starting point for design, a source of inspiration, and an anchor to hold on to when the intangible nature of software threatens to overcome our ability to understand our programs.

A word of caution may be in place: Beginners often find it hard to "find the classes," but that problem is usually soon overcome without long-term ill effects. Next, however, often follows a phase where classes – and their inheritance relationships – seem to multiply uncontrollably. This can cause long-term problems with the complexity, comprehensibility, and efficiency of the resulting program. Not every minute detail needs to be represented by a distinct class, and not every relationship between classes needs to be represented as an inheritance relationship. Try to remember that the aim of a design is to model a system at an *appropriate* level of detail and at *appropriate* levels of abstraction. Finding a balance between simplicity and generality for a significant system is not an easy task.

12.2.2 Class Hierarchies

Consider simulating the traffic flow of a city to determine the likely times needed for emergency vehicles to reach their destinations. Clearly we need to represent cars, trucks, ambulances, fire engines of various sorts, police cars, busses, etc. Inheritance comes into play because a real-world concept does not exist in isolation; it exists with numerous relationships to other concepts. Without understanding these concepts and appreciating their relationships we cannot understand any of them. Consequently, a model that does not represent such relationships does not adequately represent our concepts. That is, in our programs we need classes to represent concepts, but that is not enough. We also need ways of representing relationships between classes. Inheritance is one powerful way of representing hierarchical relationships directly. In our example, we would probably consider emergency vehicles special and probably want also to distinguish between car-like and truck-like vehicles. This would yield a class hierarchy along these lines:

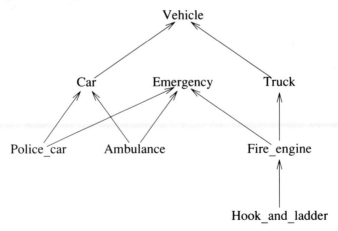

Here, `Emergency` represents the aspects of an emergency vehicle that are relevant to the simulation: It can violate some traffic rules and has priority in intersections when on an emergency call, it is under control of a dispatcher, etc.

Here is the C++ version:

```
class Vehicle { /* ... */ };
class Emergency { /* ... */ };
class Car : public Vehicle { /* ... */ };
class Truck : public Vehicle { /* ... */ };
class Police_car : public Car , public Emergency {
    // ...
};
class Ambulance : public Car , public Emergency {
    // ...
};
class Fire_engine : public Truck , public Emergency {
    // ...
};
class Hook_and_ladder : public Fire_engine {
    // ...
};
```

Inheritance is the highest level relationship that can be represented directly in C++ and the one that figures largest in the early stages of a design. Often there is a choice between using inheritance to represent a relationship and using membership. Consider an alternative notion of being an emergency vehicle: A vehicle is an emergency vehicle if it displays a flashing light. This would allow a simplification of the class hierarchy by replacing the `Emergency` class by a member in class `Vehicle`:

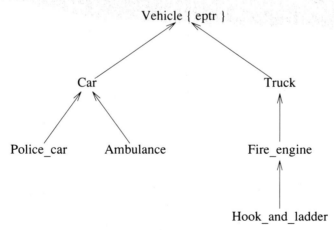

Class `Emergency` is now simply used as a member in classes that might need to act as emergency vehicles:

```
class Emergency { /* ... */ };
class Vehicle { public: Emergency* eptr;   /* ... */ };
class Car : public Vehicle { /* ... */ };
class Truck : public Vehicle { /* ... */ };
class Police_car : public Car { /* ... */ };
class Ambulance : public Car { /* ... */ };
class Fire_engine : public Truck { /* ... */ };
class Hook_and_ladder : public Fire_engine { /* ... */ };
```

Here, a vehicle is an emergency vehicle if `Vehicle::eptr` is non-zero. The
"plain" cars and trucks are initialized with `Vehicle::eptr` zero, the others with
`Vehicle::eptr` non-zero. For example:

```
Car::Car()      // Car constructor
{
     eptr = 0;
}


Police_car::Police_car()     // Police_car constructor
{
     eptr = new Emergency;
}
```

Defining things this way enables a simple conversion of an emergency vehicle to an
ordinary vehicle and vice versa:

```
void f(Vehicle* p)
{
     delete p->eptr;
     p->eptr = 0;   // no longer an emergency vehicle

     // ...

     p->eptr = new Emergency;   // an emergency vehicle again
}
```

So, which variant of the class hierarchy is best? The general answer is, "The program that most directly models the real world is the best." That is, in choosing
between models we should aim for greater realism under the inevitable constraints of
efficiency and simplicity. In this case, the easy conversion between ordinary vehicles
and emergency vehicles seems unrealistic to me. Fire engines and ambulances are
purpose-built vehicles manned by trained personnel and operated using dispatch procedures requiring specialized communication equipment. This view indicates that
being an emergency vehicle should be a fundamental concept and represented directly
in the program to improve type checking and other uses of tools. Had we been modeling a place where the roles of vehicles were less firmly defined – say, an area where
private vehicles were routinely used to carry emergency personnel to accident sites
and where communication was primarily based on portable radios – the other way of

modeling the system might have been more appropriate.

For people who consider traffic simulations esoteric, it might be worth pointing out that such tradeoffs between inheritance and membership almost invariably occur in a design. The scrollbar example in §12.2.5 is an equivalent example.

12.2.3 Dependencies within a Class Hierarchy

Naturally, a derived class depends on its base classes. It is less often appreciated that the opposite can also be true†. If a class has a virtual function, it depends on derived classes to implement part of its functionality whenever a derived class overrides that function. If a member of a base class itself calls one of the class's virtual functions, then the base class depends on its derived classes for its own implementation. Similarly, if a class uses a protected member, then it is again dependent on its derived classes for its own implementation. Consider:

```
class B {
    // ...
protected:
    int a;
public:
    virtual int f();
    int g() { int x = f(); return x-a; }
};
```

What does g() do? The answer critically depends on the definition on f() in some derived class. Here is a version that will ensure that g() returns 1:

```
class D1 : public B {
    int f() { return a+1; }
};
```

and a version that makes g() write ``Hello, World'' and return 0:

```
class D1 : public B {
    int f() { cout<<"Hello, World\n"; return a; }
};
```

This example illustrates one of the most important points about virtual functions. Why is it silly? Why wouldn't a programmer ever write something like that? The answer is that a virtual function is part of an interface to a base class, and that class can supposedly be used without knowledge of the classes derived from it. Consequently, it must be possible to describe the expected behavior of an object of the base class in such a way that programs can be written without knowledge of the derived classes. Every class that overrides the virtual function must implement a variant of that behavior. For example, the virtual function rotate() of a Shape class rotates a shape; the rotate() functions for derived classes such as Circle and

---

† This observation has been summarized as: ``Insanity is hereditary, you get it from your children.''

Triangle must rotate objects of their respective type – otherwise a fundamental assumption about class Shape is violated. No such assumption about behavior is made for class B or its derived classes D1 and D2; thus the example appears nonsensical. The specification of the expected behavior of virtual functions is a *major* focus of class design.

Is a dependency on unknown (possibly yet unwritten) derived classes good or bad? Naturally, that depends on the intent of the programmer. If the intent is to isolate a class from all external influences so that it can be proven to behave in a specific way, then protected members and virtual functions are best avoided. If, however, the intent is to provide a framework into which a later programmer (such as the same programmer a few weeks later) can add code, then virtual functions are often an elegant mechanism for achieving this; and protected members have proven convenient for supporting such use.

For example, consider a simple buffer template:

```
template<class T> class buffer {
    // ...
    void put(T);
    T get();
};
```

If the policy of what to do in case of overflow and underflow is hard-wired into the class, its usefulness is somewhat limited. If, however, the put() and get() functions call virtual functions overflow() and underflow(), respectively, then a user can tailor different buffer types to suit a variety of needs:

```
template<class T> class buffer {
    // ...
    virtual int overflow(T);
    virtual int underflow();
    void put(T);   // call overflow(T) if buffer is full
    T get(); // call underflow(T) if buffer is empty
};


template<class T> class circular_buffer : public buffer<T> {
    // ...
    int overflow(T); // wrap around if full
    int underflow();
};


template<class T> class expanding_buffer : public buffer<T> {
    // ...
    int overflow(T); // increase buffer size if full
    int underflow();
};
```

This technique is used in the stream input/output library (§10.5.3).

12.2.4 Containment Relationships

Where containment is used there are two major alternatives for representing an object of a class X:

    [1] Declare a member of type X.

    [2] Declare a member of type X* or type X&.

If the value of the pointer is never changed these alternatives are equivalent except for efficiency issues:

```
class X {
    // ...
public:
    X(int);
    // ...
};


class C {
    X a;
    X* p;
public:
    C(int i, int j) : a(i), p(new X(j)) { }
    ~C() { delete p; }
};
```

In such cases membership of the object itself, as in the case of X::a above, is usually preferable because it is the most efficient in time, space, and keystrokes. However, see also §12.4 and §13.9.

    The pointer solution should be used where there is a need to change the pointer to the ''contained'' object during the life of the ''containing'' object. For example:

```
class C2 {
    X* p;
public:
    C(int i) : p(new X(i)) { }
    ~C() { delete p; }

    X* change(X* q)
    {
        X* t = p;
        p = q;
        return t;
    }
};
```

Another reason for using a pointer member is to allow the ''contained'' member to be passed in as an argument:

```
class C3 {
    X* p;
public:
    C(X* q) : p(q) { }
    // ...
};
```

By having objects contain pointers to other objects, one creates what is often called "object hierarchies." This is an alternative and complementary technique to using class hierarchies. As shown in the emergency vehicle example in §12.2.2, it is often a tricky design issue to choose between representing a property of a class as a base class or as a member. A need to override is an indication that the former is the best choice. Conversely, a need to be able to allow the property to be represented by a variety of types is an indication that the latter is the best choice. For example:

```
class XX : public X { /* ... */ };

class XXX : public X { /* ... */ };

void f()
{
    C3* p1 = new C3(new X);      // C3 ``contains'' an X
    C3* p2 = new C3(new XX);     // C3 ``contains'' an XX
    C3* p3 = new C3(new XXX);    // C3 ``contains'' an XXX
    // ...
}
```

This could not be modeled by a derivation of C3 from X or by C3 having a member of type X because the exact type of a member need to be used. This is important for classes with virtual functions, such as a shape class (§1.1.2.5) or an abstract set class (§13.3).

Note that references can be used to simplify classes based on pointer membership when only one object is referred to during the life of the containing object. For example:

```
class C4 {
    X& r;
public:
    C(X& q) : r(q) { }
    // ...
};
```

12.2.5 Containment and Inheritance

Given the importance of inheritance relationships, it is not surprising that they are frequently overused and misunderstood. When a class D is publicly derived from another class B it is often said that a D *is a* B:

```
class B { /* ... */ };
class D : public B { /* ... */ };   // D is a kind of B
```

Alternatively, this is expressed by saying that inheritance is an *isa* relationship or –
somewhat more precisely – that a D is a kind of B. In contrast, a class D that has a
member of another class B is often said to *have a* B:

```
class D {      // D contains a B
    // ...
public:
    B b;
    // ...
};
```

Alternatively, this is expressed by saying that membership is a *hasa* relationship or
that D contains a B.

For given classes B and D, how do we choose between inheritance and membership? Consider an `airplane` and an `engine`: Novices often wonder if it might be
a good idea to derive class `airplane` from `engine`. This is a bad idea, though,
because an `airplane` *is* not an `engine`; it *has* an `engine`. One way of seeing
that is to consider if an `airplane` might have two or more engines. Because that
seems feasible (even if we are considering a program where all our `airplanes` will
be single-engine ones) we should use membership rather than inheritance. The "can
it have two?" question is useful in the surprisingly many cases where there is doubt.
As usual, it is the intangible nature of software that makes this discussion relevant.
Had all classes been as easy to visualize as `airplane` and `engine`, trivial mistakes
like deriving an `airplane` from an `engine` would be easily avoided. They are,
however, quite frequent – particularly among people who consider derivation as simply another mechanism for combining programming language level constructs.
Despite the conveniences and shorthand notation derivation provides, it should be
used almost exclusively to express relationships that are well defined in a design.
Consider:

```
class B {
public:
    virtual void f();
    void g();
};
```

```
class D1 {      // D1 contains a B
public:
    B b;
    void f();   // does not override b.f()
};
```

```
void h1(D1* pd)
{
    B* pb = pd; // error: no D1* to B* conversion
    pb = &pd->b;
    pb->g();      // calls B::g
    pd->g();      // error: D1 doesn't have a member g()
    pd->b.g();
    pb->f();      // calls B::f (not overridden by D1::f)
    pd->f();      // calls D1::f
}
```

Note that there is no implicit conversion from a class to one of its members and that a class containing a member of another class does not override the virtual functions of that member. This contrasts with the derivation case:

```
class D2 : public B {       // D2 is a B
public:
    void f();                 // overrides B::f()
};
```

```
void h2(D2* pd)
{
    B* pb = pd; // ok: implicit D2* to B* conversion
    pb->g();      // calls B::g
    pd->g();      // calls B::g
    pb->f();      // virtual call: invokes D2::f
    pd->f();      // invokes D2::f
}
```

The notational convenience provided by the D2 example compared to the D1 example is a factor that can lead to overuse. It should be remembered, though, that there is a cost of increased dependency between B and D2 to be paid for that notational convenience (see §12.2.3). In particular, it is easy to forget the implicit conversion from D2 to B. Unless such conversions are an acceptable part of the semantics of your classes, *public* derivation is to be avoided. When a class is used to represent a concept and derivation is used to represent an *isa* relationship, such conversions are most often exactly what is desired.

There are cases, though, where you would like inheritance but cannot afford to have the conversion happen. Consider writing a class cfield (controlled field) that – in addition to whatever else it does – provides run-time access control for another class field. At first glance, defining cfield by deriving it from field seems just right:

```
class cfield : public field {
    // ...
};
```

This expresses the notion that a cfield really is a kind of field, allows notational convenience when writing a cfield function that uses a member of the field part of the `cfield`, and – most importantly – allows a `cfield` to override `field` virtual functions. The snag is that the `cfield*` to `field*` conversion implied in the declaration of `cfield` defeats all attempts to control access to the `field`:

```
void g(cfield* p)
{
    *p = "asdf";   // access to field controlled by
                   // cfield's assignment operator:
                   // p->cfield::operator=("asdf")

    field* q = p;  // implicit cfield* to field* conversion
    *q = "asdf";   // OOPS! no control
}
```

A solution would be to define `cfield` to have a `field` as a member, but that precludes `cfield` from overriding `field` virtual functions. A better solution would be to use *private* derivation:

```
    class cfield : private field { /* ... */ };
```

From a design perspective, private derivation is equivalent to containment except for the (occasionally important) issue of overriding. An important use of this is the technique of deriving a class publicly from an abstract base class defining an interface and privately from a concrete class providing an implementation (§13.3). Because the inheritance implied in *private* derivation is an implementation detail that is not reflected in the type of the derived class, it is sometimes called ''implementation inheritance'' and contrasted to *public* derivation, where the interface of the base class is inherited and the implicit conversion to the base type is allowed. The latter is sometimes referred to as sub-typing or ''interface inheritance.''

To further examine the design choices involving containment and inheritance, consider how to represent a scrollbar in an interactive graphics system and how to attach a scrollbar to a window. We need two kinds of scrollbars, horizontal and vertical. We can represent this by two types, `horizontal_scrollbar` and `vertical_scrollbar` or by a single `scrollbar` type that takes an argument that says whether its layout is horizontal or vertical. The former choice implies the need for a third type, the plain `scrollbar`, as the base class of the two specific scollbar types. The latter choice implies an extra argument to the scrollbar type and the need to choose values to represent the two kinds of scrollbars. For example:

```
    enum orientation { horizontal, vertical };
```

Once a choice is made, it determines the kind of change needed to extend the system. In the scrollbar example, we might want to introduce a third type of scrollbar. We may originally have thought that there could be only two kinds of scrollbars (''after all a window has only two dimensions'') but in this case – as in most others – there are possible extensions that surface as re-design issues. For example, one might like to use a ''navigation button'' instead of two scrollbars. Such a button would cause scrolling in different directions dependent on where a user pressed it: pressing at the middle of the top would cause ''scrolling up,'' pressing at the middle left would cause ''scrolling left,'' pressing at the top left corner would cause ''scrolling up and left.'' Such buttons are not uncommon and can be seen as a refinement of the notion of a scrollbar that is particularly suited to applications where the information scrolled over isn't plain text but more general sorts of pictures.

Adding a navigation button to a program with a three-scrollbar class hierarchy involves adding a new class, but it requires no changes to the old scrollbar code:

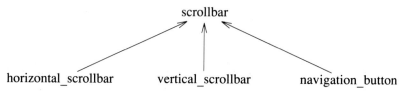

scrollbar

horizontal_scrollbar   vertical_scrollbar   navigation_button

This is the nice aspect of the ''hierarchical'' solution.

Passing the orientation of the scrollbar as an argument implies the presence of type fields in the scrollbar objects and the use of switch statements in the code of the scrollbar member functions. That is, we are facing a tradeoff between expressing this aspect of the structure of the system in terms of declarations or in terms of code. The former increases the degree of static checking and the amount of information that tools have to work on. The latter postpones decisions to run time and allows changes to be made by modifying individual functions without affecting the overall structure of the system as seen by the type checker and other tools. In most situations, I recommend the former approach.

The nice aspect of the single scrollbar type solution is that it is easy to pass information about what kind of scrollbar I want to another function to use:

```
void helper(orientation oo)
{
    // ...
    p = new scrollbar(oo);
    // ...
}

void me()
{
    helper(horizontal);
}
```

This representation would also make it easy to re-orient a scrollbar at run-time. This is unlikely to be of major importance in the case of scrollbars, but it can be important for equivalent examples. The point here is that there are always tradeoffs, and the tradeoffs are often non-trivial.

Now consider how to attach a scrollbar to a window. If we consider a `window_with_scrollbar` as something that is both a `window` and a `scrollbar`, we get something like:

```
class window_with_scrollbar
: public window, public scrollbar {
    // ...
};
```

This allows any `window_with_scrollbar` to act like a `scrollbar` and like a `window` but constrains us to using the single scrollbar type solution.

If, on the other hand, we consider a `window_with_scrollbar` as a `window` that has a `scrollbar`, we get something like:

```
class window_with_scrollbar : public window {
    // ...
    scrollbar* sb;
public:
    window_with_scrollbar(scrollbar* p, /* ... */)
        :window(/* ...*/), sb(p)
        {
            // ...
        }
    // ...
};
```

This allows us to use the three scrollbar types solution. Passing the scrollbar as an argument allows the window to be oblivious to the exact type of its scrollbar. If we want a `window_with_scrollbar` to act as a scrollbar, we can add a conversion operator:

```
window_with_scrollbar::operator scrollbar&()
{
    return *sb;
}
```

My preference would be to have a window contain a scrollbar. I find it easier to think of a window *having* a scrollbar than of a window *being* a scrollbar. In fact, my favorite design strategy involves a scrollbar being a special kind of window. That strategy would force the decision in favor of the containment solution. An alternative argument for the containment solution comes from the "can it have two?" rule of thumb mentioned above. Because there is no logical reason why a window shouldn't have two scrollbars (in fact, many windows do have both a horizontal and a vertical scrollbar) a `window_with_scrollbar` ought not be derived from `scrollbar`.

Note that it is not possible to derive from an unknown class. The exact type of a base class must be known at compile time. In particular, if an attribute of a class needs to be passed as an argument to its constructor, then somewhere in the class there must be a member that represents it.

12.2.6 Use Relationships

Knowledge of what other classes a class uses and in which ways is often critical to express and understand a design. Such dependencies are supported only implicitly by C++. A class can use only names that have been declared (somewhere), but there is no place in the C++ source containing the full list of names used. Tools (or in the absence of suitable tools, careful reading) are necessary for extracting such information. The ways a class X can use another class Y can be classified in several ways. Here is one way:

- X uses the name Y
- X uses Y
  - X calls a Y member function
  - X reads a member of Y
  - X writes a member of Y
- X creates a Y
  - X allocates an `auto` or `static` variable of Y
  - X creates a Y using `new`
  - X takes the size of a Y

The reason that taking the size of an object is classified as creation is that it requires knowledge of the complete class declaration. Conversely, the reason naming Y is classified as a separate dependency is that just doing that – for example, in declaring a Y* or mentioning Y in the declaration of an external function – doesn't require access to the declaration of Y at all:

```
class Y;      // Y is the name of a class
Y* p;
extern Y f(const Y&);
```

The reason creation using `new` is mentioned separately from variable declaration is that it is possible to implement C++ so that creation of a Y using `new` does not require knowledge of the size of Y. This can be important to limit dependencies in a design and to minimize recompilation after a change.

C++ doesn't require the implementer of a class to specify in detail what other classes are used and how. One reason for this is that most significant.classes depend on so many other classes that an abbreviation of the list of those classes, such as an `#include` directive, would be necessary for readability. Another is that the classification of such dependencies, and in particular the granularity of such dependencies, doesn't appear to be a programming language issue. Rather, exactly how *uses* dependencies are viewed depends on the purpose of the designer, programmer, or tool. Finally, what dependencies are interesting may also depend on details of the language implementation.

12.2.7 Relationships within a Class

Up until now I have talked primarily of classes; operations have been mentioned, but except for particular stages of the development process (e.g., §11.3.3.2) they have been considered strictly secondary; objects have hardly been mentioned at all. The reason for that is simple: In C++, the class, and not the function or the object, is the primary unit of system organization.

A class can conceal just about any implementation detail and just about any amount of dirt – and sometimes it has to. However, the objects of most classes do themselves have a regular structure and are manipulated in ways that are fairly easy to describe. An object of a class is a collection of other sub-objects (often called members), and many of these are pointers and references to other objects. Thus an object can be seen as the root of a tree of objects, and the objects involved can be seen as constituting an "object hierarchy" that is complementary to the class hierarchy as described in §12.2.4. For example, consider the string class from §7.6:

```
class String {
    int sz;
    char* p;
public:
    String(const char* q);
    ~String();
    // ...
};
```

A `String` object can be drawn as:

12.2.7.1 Invariants

The value of the members and the objects referred to by members is called the state of the object (or simply its value). A major concern of a class design is to get an object into a well defined state (initialization), to maintain a well defined state as operations are performed, and finally to destroy the object gracefully. The property that makes the state of an object well defined is called an invariant.

Thus the purpose of initialization is to establish the invariant for an object. Each operation on a class can assume it will find the invariant true on entry and must leave the invariant true on exit. The destructor finally invalidates the invariant by destroying the object. For example, the constructor `String::String(const char*)` ensures that `p` points to an array of at least `sz` elements where `sz` has a reasonable value and where `v[sz-1]==0`. Every string operation must leave that assertion true.

Much of the skill in class design involves making the implementation of a class simple enough to make it possible to have a useful invariant that can be expressed simply. It is easy enough to state that every class needs an invariant; the hard part is to come up with a useful invariant that is easy to comprehend and doesn't impose unacceptable constraints on the implementer or on the efficiency of the operations. Note ''invariant'' here is used to denote a piece of code that can be run to check the state of an object. A stricter and more mathematical notion is clearly possible and, in some contexts, more appropriate. An invariant, as discussed here, is a practical – and therefore typically economical and logically incomplete – check on an object's state.

The notion of invariants has its origins in the work of Floyd, Naur, and Hoare on pre- and post-conditions and is present in essentially all work on abstract data types and program verification done over the last 20 years or so. It is also a staple of C debugging.

Typically, the invariant is not maintained during the execution of a member function. Functions that may be called while the invariant is invalid should not be part of the public interface. Private and protected functions can serve that purpose.

How can we express the notion of an invariant in a C++ program? A simple way is to define an invariant-checking function and insert calls to it in the public operations. For example:

```
class String {
    int sz;
    int* p;
public:
    class Range {};
    class Invariant {};

    void check();

    String(const char* q);
    ~String();
    char& operator[](int i);
    int size() { return sz; }
    // ...
};

void String::check()
{
    if (p==0 || sz<0 || TOO_LARGE<=sz || p[sz-1])
        throw Invariant;
}

char& String::operator[](int i)
{
    check();                              // check on entry
    if (i<0 || i<sz) throw Range;         // do work
    check();                              // check on exit
    return v[i];
}
```

This will work nicely and is hardly any work for the programmer. However, for a simple class like `String` the invariant checking will dominate the run-time and maybe even the code size. Therefore programmers often execute the invariant checks only during debugging:

```
inline void String::check()
{
    if (!NDEBUG)
        if (p==0 || sz<0 || TOO_LARGE<=sz || p[sz])
            throw Invariant;
}
```

The name NDEBUG was chosen because it is a macro used in a similar way in the standard C `assert()` macro. NDEBUG is conventionally set to indicate that debugging is not being done. Making `check()` inline ensures that no code is generated unless the constant NDEBUG is set to indicate no ''debugging code'' is to be executed.

An `Assert()` template can be used to express less regular assertions:

```
template<class T, class X> inline void Assert(T expr,X x)
{
    if (!NDEBUG)
        if (!expr) throw x;
}
```

will throw exception x if `expr` is false and we have not turned off checking by setting NDEBUG. For example:

```
class Bad_f_arg { };

void f(String& s, int i)
{
    Assert(0<=i && i<s.size(),Bad_f_arg());
    // ...
}
```

This `Assert()` template mimics the C `assert()` macro. The `Bad_f_arg` exception will be thrown unless `i` is in the expected range.

Checking this style of assertions and invariants is an all or nothing affair based on a single constant or, alternatively, based on a per-class constant. If, instead, one wants to check invariants on a per-object basis one can derive a class with checked operations from a class without checking; see exercise 8 in §13.11.

For classes with more elaborate operations, the overhead of invariant checking can be insignificant and the checking can be left in permanently to catch various forms of hard-to-detect errors. It is usually a good idea to leave at least some checks active in even the best checked program. In all cases, the simple act of defining invariants and using them during debugging is an invaluable help in getting the code right and – more importantly – in getting the concepts represented by the classes well defined and regular. The point is that, when you are designing invariants, a class will be considered from an alternative viewpoint and the code will contain redundancy. Both increase the likelihood of spotting mistakes, inconsistencies, and oversights.

In §11.3.3.5 it was mentioned that the two most common forms of class hierarchy reorganizations were splitting a class into two and factoring the common part of two classes out into a base class. In both cases, well-designed invariants can give a clue to the potential for reorganization. Comparing the invariant with the code of operations will show most of the invariant checking to be redundant in a class that is ripe for splitting. In such cases, subsets of the operations will access only subsets of the object state. Conversely, classes that are ripe for merging will have similar invariants even if their detailed implementations differ.

12.2.7.2 Encapsulation

Note that in C++ the class – and not the individual object – is the unit of encapsulation. For example:

```
class list {
    list* next;
public:
    int on(list*);
};

int list::on(list* p)
{
    list* q = this;
    for(;;) {
        if (p == q) return 1;
        if (q == 0) return 0;
        q = q->next;
    }
}
```

The chasing of the private `list::next` pointer is accepted because `list::on()` has access to every object of class `list` it can somehow reference. Where that is inconvenient, matters can be simplified by not taking advantage of the ability to access the representation of other objects from a member function. For example:

```
int list::on(list* p)
{
    if (p == this) return 1;
    if (p == 0) return 0;
    return next->on(p);
}
```

However, this turns iteration into recursion, and that can cause a major performance hit where a compiler isn't able to optimize the recursion back into an iteration.

12.2.8 Programmed-in Relationships

A given programming language cannot directly support every concept from every design method. Where a programming language cannot represent a concept from the

design directly, a conventional mapping between the design construct and the programming language constructs should be used. For example, a design method may
have a notion of delegation. That is, the design can specify that every operation not
defined for a class A should be serviced by an object of a class B pointed to by a
pointer p. C++ cannot express this directly. However, the expression of that idea in
C++ is so stylized that one could easily imagine a program generating the code. Consider:

```
class A {
    B* p;
    // ...
    void f();
    void ff();
};

class B {
    // ...
    void f();
    void g();
    void h();
};
```

A specification that A delegated to B through A::p would result in code like this:

```
class A {
    B* p;        // delegation through p
    // ...
    void f();
    void ff();
    void g() { p->g(); }     // delegate g()
    void h() { p->h(); }     // delegate h()
};
```

It is fairly obvious to a programmer what is going on here, but it is clearly inferior to a
one-to-one correspondence. Such "programmed-in" relationships are not as well
"understood" by the programming language and are therefore less amenable to
manipulation by tools. For example, standard tools would not recognize the "delegation" from A to B through A::p as different from any other use of a B*.

A one-to-one mapping between the design concepts and the programming language concepts should be used where ever possible. A one-to-one mapping ensures
simplicity and guarantees that the design really is reflected in the program so that programmers and tools can take advantage of it.

Conversion operators provide a language mechanism for expressing a class of
programmed-in relationships; that is, a conversion operator X::operator Y()
specifies that wherever a Y is acceptable an X can be used. A constructor Y::Y(X)
expresses the same relationship. Note that a conversion operator (and a constructor)
produces a new object rather than changing the type of an existing object. Declaring a
conversion function to Y is simply a way of requesting *implicit* application of a

function returning a Y. Because the implicit application of conversions defined by constructors and conversion operators can be treacherous, it is sometimes useful to analyze them separately in a design.

It is important to ensure that the conversion graphs for a program do not contain cycles. If they do, the resulting ambiguity errors will render the types involved in the cycles unusable in combination. For example

```
class Big_int {
    // ...
    friend Big_int operator+(Big_int,Big_int);
    // ...
    operator Rational();
    // ...
};


class Rational {
    // ...
    friend Rational operator+(Rational,Rational);
    // ...
    operator Big_int();
};
```

The Rational and Big_int types will not interact as smoothly as one might have hoped:

```
void f(Rational r, Big_int i)
{
    // ...
    g(r+i);  // error, ambiguous:
             //          operator+(r,Rational(i)) or
             //          operator+(Big_int(r),i)
    g(r,Rational(i)); // one explicit resolution
    g(Big_int(r),i);  // another explicit resolution
}
```

One can avoid such "mutual" conversions by making at least some of them explicit. For example, the Big_int to Rational conversion might have been defined as make_Rational() instead of as a conversion operator, and the addition above would have been resolved to g(Big_int(r),i). Where "mutual" conversion operators cannot be avoided one must either resolve the resulting clashes by explicit conversions as shown above or by defining many separate versions of binary operators such as +.

12.3 Components

C++ does not provide constructs that allow us to map the notion of a component, that is a set of related classes, directly into a program. The primary reason for that is a set of classes (maybe with associated global functions, etc.) can be considered a component for a variety of reasons. The absence of direct support of the concept leads to difficulties in expressing the difference between information (names) shared within a component and information (names) exported by the component to users.

Ideally, a component is described by the set of interfaces it uses for its implementation plus the set of interfaces it provides for its users; everything else is "implementation detail" and hidden from the rest of the system. This may indeed be the designer's description of a component. The programmer will have to cope with the fact that C++ doesn't provide a general notion of a component name space so that this has to be "simulated" through the notions of classes and translation units, which are the facilities C++ does provide for limiting the scope of non-local names.

Consider two classes that need to share a function f() and a variable v. The simplest solution is to declare f and v as global names. However, all experienced programmers know that this "name space pollution" will eventually lead to trouble when someone else innocently use the names f and v for something unrelated or – not so innocently – accesses f and v directly, thus bypassing the explicit component interfaces, and uses these "implementation details" directly. Three solutions exist:

[1] Give "unusual names" to the objects and functions that are not meant for users.

[2] Declare the objects and functions that are not meant for users static in some source file.

[3] Place the objects and functions that are not meant for users in a class and don't make the declaration of that class available to users.

The first technique is crude and somewhat inconvenient to the implementer – but it is effective:

```
// compX implementation details.
// Don't use unless you are a compX implementer:

extern void compX_f(T2*, const char*);
extern T3 compX_v;
// ...
```

Names such as compX_f and compX_v are unlikely to clash with anything and the fact that a user can cheat and use them directly is mitigated by the fact that users can always cheat anyway: Language-level protection mechanisms are protection against accident, not against fraud. This technique has the benefit of being perfectly general and well known. However, it is unsafe, inelegant, and a nuisance to poor typists.

The second technique is safer but less general:

```
// compX implementation details:

static void compX_f(T2* a1, const char* a2) { /* ...*/ }
static T3 compX_v;
// ...
```

It is not easy to ensure that information shared by the classes in a component is accessible only within a single translation unit because the operations used to access this

information must be generally accessible. This technique can also lead to giant translation units, and some C++ debuggers lack access to the names of static functions and
variables. However, the technique is safe and often ideal for smaller components.

The third technique can be seen as a formalization and generalization of the first
two techniques:

```
class compX_details {    // compX implementation details
public:
    static void f(T2*, const char*);
    static T3 v;
    // ...
}
```

Only the implementer will use the `compX_details` declaration; others need not
include it in their programs.

A component can of course have many classes that are not intended for general
use. If their names are intended for local use only, then they too could be "hidden"
within implementation classes:

```
class compX_details {    // compX implementation details.
public:
    // ...

    class widget {
        // ...
    };

    // ...
};
```

Note, however, that the nesting is a barrier to the use of `widgets` in other parts of the
program. Often classes that represent coherent concepts are better considered candidates for re-use and thus part of the interface of the component rather than implementation details. In other words, even though the sub-objects used to implement an
object of a class are best treated as hidden implementation details to maintain proper
levels of abstraction, the classes defining such sub-objects need not be hidden if they
are of sufficient generality. For example:

```
class Car {
    class Wheel {
        // ...
    };

    Wheel flw, frw, rlw, rrw;
    // ...
};
```

seems to be excess hiding. In most contexts, we need to have the actual wheels hidden to maintain the abstraction of a car (when you use a car you cannot operate on the
wheels independently). However, the `Wheel` class itself seems a good candidate for

wider use so that moving it outside class `Car` might be better:

```
class Wheel {
    // ...
};

class Car {
    Wheel flw, frw, rlw, rrw;
    // ...
};
```

The decision to nest or not depends on the aims of the design and the generality of the concepts involved. Both nesting and ''non-nesting'' are widely applicable techniques for expressing a design. Because nesting avoids name-space pollution, a rule of thumb would be to nest unless there is a reason not to.

Note that header files provide a powerful mechanism for supplying different views of a component to different users and for excluding classes that are considered part of the implementation from the user's view.

Another way of organizing a component and presenting it to its users is as a hierarchy. In this case, a base class acts as the repository for common data and functions. This avoids the problem of having global data and functions to implement common services for the classes in the component. On the other hand, it ties the component classes tightly together and forces a user to depend directly on all the base classes of the classes actually used. There also is a tendency for ''interesting'' functions and data members to ''bubble up'' to an ultimate base class so that if a hierarchy gets too large the problems associated with global data and global functions reappear within the hierarchy. This is most likely to happen in a single rooted hierarchy; virtual base classes (§6.5.4) can be used to combat this phenomenon. Sometimes a hierarchy is the best choice for representing a component; sometimes it is not. As ever, it is up to the designer to evaluate the tradeoffs.

12.4 Interfaces and Implementations

The ideal interface
- presents a complete and coherent set of concepts to a user,
- is consistent over all parts of a component,
- does not reveal implementation details to a user,
- can be implemented in several ways,
- is statically typed,
- is expressed using application level types, and
- depends in limited and well-defined ways on other interfaces.

Having noted the need for consistency across the classes that present the component's interface to the rest of the world, we can simplify the discussion by looking at only a single class. Consider:

```
class X {      // example of poor interface style
     Y a;
     Z b;
public:
     void f(const char * ...);
     void g(int[],int);
     void set_a(Y&);
     Y& get_a();
};
```

This interface has several potential problems:
  - The interface uses the types Y and Z in a way that requires the declarations of Y and Z to be known to compile it.
  - The function X::f takes an arbitrary number of arguments of unknown types (probably somehow controlled by a ''format string'' supplied as the first argument).
  - The function X::g takes an int[] argument. This may be OK, but typically it is a sign that the level of abstraction is too low. An array of integers is not self-describing, so it is not obvious how many elements it is supposed to have.
  - The set_a() and get_a() most likely expose the representation of objects of class X by allowing direct access to X::a.

These member functions provide an interface at a very low level of abstraction. Basically, classes with interfaces at this level belong among the implementation details of a larger component – if they belong anywhere at all. Ideally, an argument of an interface function carries enough information to make it self-describing. A rule of thumb is that it should be possible to transmit the request for service over a thin wire for service at a remote server.

C++ exposes the representation of a class as part of the interface. This representation may be hidden (using private or protected), but it is available to the compiler to allow allocation of automatic variables, to allow inline substitution of functions, etc. The negative effect of this is that use of class types in the representation of a class may introduce undesirable dependencies. Whether the use of members of type Y and Z is a problem depends on what kind of types Y and Z actually are. If they are simple types, such as complex or String, their use is quite appropriate in most cases. Such types can be considered stable, and the need to include their class declarations is an acceptable burden on the compiler. However, had Y and Z themselves been interface classes of significant components, such as a graphics system or a bank account management system, it may be wise not to depend too directly on them. In such cases, using a pointer or a reference member is often a better choice:

```
class X {
     Y* a;
     Z& b;
     // ...
};
```

This decouples the declaration of X from the declarations of Y and Z; that is, the declaration of X depends on the names Y and Z only. The implementation of X will of course still depend on the declarations of Y and Z, but this will not adversely affect the users of X.

This illustrates an important point: An interface that hides significant amounts of information – as a useful interface ought to – will have far fewer dependencies than the implementation it hides. For example, the declaration of class X can be compiled without access to the declarations of Y and Z. The definitions of X's member functions that manipulates the Y and Z objects referred to, however, will need access to the definitions of Y and Z. When dependencies are analyzed, the dependencies of the interface and the implementation must be considered separately. In both cases, the ideal is for the dependency graphs of a system to be a directed acyclic graph to ease understanding and testing of the system. However, this idea is far more critical and far more often achievable for implementations than for interfaces.

Note that a class defines three interfaces:

```
class X {
private:
        // accessible to members and friends only
protected:
        // accessible to members and friends and
        // to members and friends of derived classes only
public:
        // accessible to the general public
};
```

A member should be part of the most restrictive interface possible. That is, a member should be `private` unless there is a reason for it to be more accessible; and if so it should be `protected` unless there is a reason for it to be `public`. It is almost always a bad idea to make data members `public`. The functions and classes that constitute the public interface should be designed to present a view of the class that fits with its role as representing a concept. Remember that friends are part of the public interface.

Note that abstract classes can be used to provide a further level of representation hiding (§1.4.6, §6.3, §13.3).

12.5 Rules of Thumb

This chapter has touched upon many subjects and generally refrained from making strong specific recommendations about how to do things. This reflects my view that there is no "one right way." Techniques and principles have to be applied in ways appropriate to a specific tasks. This requires taste, experience, and intelligence. It is possible, however, to outline a few rules of thumb that a designer might use as a guide while gaining sufficient experience to develop better ones. This section presents such a set of rules.

These rules can be used as a starting point for developing design guidelines for specific projects or organizations or as a checklist. I emphasize that these are not absolute rules and cannot act as a substitute for thought.

- Evolve use towards data abstraction and object-oriented programming.
    - Adopt new techniques gradually; don't rush.
    - Use C++ features and techniques as needed (only).
    - Match design and programming styles.
- Focus on component design.
- Use classes to represent concepts.
    - Use public inheritance to represent *isa* relationships.
    - Use membership to represent *hasa* relationships.
    - Make sure that the *uses* dependencies are understood, non-cyclic wherever possible, and minimal.
    - Actively search for commonality in the concepts of the application and implementation, and represent the resulting more general concepts as base classes.
- Define interfaces to reveal the minimal amount of information needed:
    - Use `private` data and member functions wherever possible.
    - Use the `public/protected` distinction to distinguish between the needs of designers of derived classes and general users.
- Minimize an interface's dependencies on other interfaces.
- Keep interfaces strongly typed.
- Express interfaces in terms of application-level types.

More rules of thumb can be found in §11.5.

13

Design of Libraries

Library design is language design,
– Bell Labs proverb

and vice versa.
– A.R.Koenig

This chapter presents a variety of techniques that have proven useful in designing C++ libraries. In particular, concrete types, abstract types, node classes, handle classes, and interface classes are presented. In addition, fat interfaces, application frameworks, the use of run-time type information, and memory management techniques are discussed. The discussion focuses on desirable properties of library classes, rather than on details of the language features used to implement such classes or on particular services that a library might provide.

13.1 Introduction

Designing a general library is much harder than designing an ordinary program. A program is a solution to a particular problem in a particular context, but a library must be the solution to a set of problems encountered in a number of projects. An ordinary program can make strong assumptions about its environment, but a good library has to operate successfully in the contexts provided by a number of programs. The more general and useful a library is, the more environments it will be tried in and the stronger are the requirements of correctness, flexibility, efficiency, extensibility, portability, consistency, simplicity, completeness, ease of use, etc. Also, a library cannot be everything to all people so tradeoffs will have to be made. A library is the most interesting special case of what has been called a component in the preceding chapters. Every recommendation for the design and maintenance of components is extra-critical for libraries. Conversely, most ideas for organizing libraries have uses in the design of other components.

It would be presumptuous to try to describe how libraries *should* be constructed: Several dissimilar strategies have worked for people in the past, and the whole topic is the subject of active debate and experimentation. Instead, this chapter examines a few key problem areas and presents a few key techniques that have proven useful in the context of libraries. It should also be remembered that libraries are used to support many different areas of programming, and there is no reason to believe that a single strategy will be the most appropriate for all libraries. For example, I see no fundamental reason why techniques that are successful for supplying concurrency features for a multi-processor operating system kernel should also be the most successful for writing a library to support scientific programming or a graphical user interface library.

The C++ class concept can be used in a variety of ways, and the diversity of possible styles can be a source of confusion. A good library presents a consistent style or at most few consistent styles to its users to minimize such confusion. This makes a library more predictable and thus relatively easy to learn and to use well. Five "archetypical" kinds of classes are described and their inherent strengths and weaknesses discussed: Concrete types (§13.2), abstract types (§13.3), node classes (§13.4), interface classes (§13.8), and handle classes (§13.9). These kinds of classes are design notions and not language constructs. Each notion is implemented through a use of the class concept. The unattained, and probably unattainable, ideal is to have a minimal set of simple and orthogonal kinds of classes from which all well-behaved and useful classes could be constructed. It is important to note that each of these kinds of classes has a place in library design and none is inherently better than the others for all uses.

The concept of a "fat" interface (§13.6) is introduced to describe a common variant of several of these kinds of classes and to introduce the notion of an application framework (§13.7).

The description emphasizes the pure forms of these kinds of classes. Naturally, hybrid forms can also be used. However, a hybrid ought to appear as the result of a design decision based on an evaluation of the engineering tradeoffs, and not a result of some misguided attempt to avoid making decisions ("delaying decisions" is too often a euphemism for "avoiding thinking"). Novice library designers will usually do best by staying away from hybrids and also by following the style of an existing library with properties that resemble the desired properties for the new library. Only experienced programmers should even dream about writing a general-purpose library, and every library designer should be "condemned" to use, document, and support his or her creation for some years. Also note §11.4.1.

C++ relies on static type information. However, it is occasionally necessary to write code that relies on dynamic type information in excess of what is directly supported by virtual functions; a way of handling this is described in §13.5. Finally, every non-trivial library must deal with memory management; §13.10 discusses techniques for this. Naturally, this chapter cannot describe all techniques that can be useful in the context of library design. In particular, note §9.8 on error handling and fault tolerance, §10.4.2 and §9.4.3 on the use of functional objects and callbacks, and §8.4 on the use of templates for composing classes.

Many discussions in this chapter center on container classes, such as arrays and lists. Naturally, such container classes should be templates (as shown in §1.4.3 and §8). However, to simplify the presentation here, the examples are expressed in terms of classes containing pointers to objects of a type T. To generalize for real code, use templates as shown in Chapter 8.

13.2 Concrete Types

Classes such as vector (§1.4), Slist (§8.3), date (§5.2.2), and complex (§7.3) are *concrete* in the sense that each is the representation of a relatively simple concept with all the operations essential for the support of that concept, has a one-to-one correspondence between its interface and an implementation, and each is not (primarily) intended as a base for derivation. Typically, concrete types are not fitted into a general system of related classes. Each concrete type can be understood in isolation without reference to other classes. If a concrete type is implemented well, programs using it are comparable in size and speed to programs a user would write using a hand-crafted and specialized version of the concept. Similarly, if the implementation changes significantly, the interface is usually modified to reflect the change. The exact nature of the interface determines what implementation changes are significant in this context; more abstract interfaces leave more scope for implementation changes but can compromise run-time efficiency. Furthermore, a good implementation does not depend on more other classes than necessary so that it is possible to use the class without compile-time or run-time overheads caused by the accommodation of other ''similar'' classes in a program.

To sum up, a class providing a concrete type aims to:
[1] be a close match to a particular concept and implementation strategy;
[2] provide run-time and space efficiency comparable to ''hand-crafted'' code through the use of inlining and of operations taking full advantage of the properties of the concept and its implementation;
[3] have only minimal dependency on other classes;
[4] be comprehensible and usable in isolation.
The result is a tight binding between user and implementation code. If the implementation changes in any way, user code will have to be recompiled, because user code almost always contains calls of inline functions and local variables of a concrete type.

Concrete types often provide fundamental types for some application domain not provided directly by C++, such as complex numbers, vectors, lists, matrices, dates, associative arrays, character strings, and characters of a non-English alphabet. Note that in a world made up of concrete types, there really isn't such a thing as a list. Instead, there are many list classes, each specialized to match a variant of that concept. There could be a dozen list classes, including a singly-linked list, a doubly-linked list, a singly-linked list not requiring a link field in an object, a doubly-linked list not requiring a link field in an object, a singly-linked list where it is easy and efficient to determine if an object is on a list, a doubly linked list where it is easy and efficient to determine if an object is on a list, etc.

The name ''concrete type'' (''concrete data type'' or CDT) was chosen in contrast to the common term ''abstract type'' (''abstract data type'' or ADT). The relationship between CDTs and ADTs will be discussed in §13.3.

In essence, concrete types cannot explicitly express commonality. For example, an slist and a vector can be used as alternative implementations of the concept of a set, but that is not expressed directly. A programmer who wants to express the concept of a set must – if using concrete types and not having a set class available – choose between an slist and a vector. The program is then written in terms of the chosen class – say, slist – and if it is later decided to use the other alternative, the code must be changed.

This potential nuisance is compensated for by having all the ''natural'' operations for the chosen class, such as indexing for an array and element removal for a list, available in their optimal form without having ''unnatural'' operations, such as indexing for a list or element removal for an array, around to confuse issues. For example:

```
void my(slist& sl)
{
    for (T* p = sl.first(); p; p = sl.next())
    {
        // my stuff
    }
    // ...
}

void your(vector& v)
{
    for (int i = 0; i<v.size(); i++)
    {
        // your stuff
    }
    // ...
}
```

The availability of operations that are ''natural'' relative to a chosen implementation strategy is often crucial for efficiency and important for ease of writing the code. In addition, inlining is usually feasible for the simplest operations, such as array indexing and getting the next element from a list. The effect on run-time efficiency can be significant. One snag is that the code for fundamentally similar operations, such as the two loops above, can look dissimilar, and code that uses different concrete types for similar operations cannot be used interchangeably. It is usually not possible to factor out the similar code.

A user of a function must use the exact type expected by that function. For example:

```
void user()
{
    slist sl;
    vector v(100);

    my(sl);
    your(v);

    my(v);        // error: type mismatch
    your(sl);     // error: type mismatch
}
```

To compensate, the provider of a service can supply several versions of a function to give users a choice:

```
void my(slist&);
void my(vector&);

void your(slist&);
void your(vector&);

void user()
{
    slist sl;
    vector v(100);

    my(sl);
    your(v);

    my(v);        // now ok: call my(vector&)
    your(sl);     // now ok: call your(slist&)
}
```

Because the code of a function depends critically on its argument type, each version of my() and your() needs to be written separately. That can be a nuisance.

In all the aspects mentioned, a concrete type resembles the built-in types. The net effect is a tight coupling between users of a type and its implementer and also between users that create objects and users that provide functions operating on such objects. To use a concrete type well, the user must understand its particular details. There are (typically) no general properties that hold for all concrete types in a library that can be relied on to save the user the bother of knowing the individual classes. This is the price of run-time compactness and efficiency. Sometimes that is a price well worth paying; sometimes it is not. It can also be the case that an individual concrete class is easier to understand and use than a more general (abstract) class. This is often the case for classes that represent well-known data types such as arrays and lists.

Note, however, that the ideal is still to hide as much of the implementation as is feasible without seriously hurting performance. Inline functions can be a great win in this context, and exposing member variables by making them public or by providing set and get functions that allow the user to manipulate them directly is almost never a good idea. Concrete types should still be types and not just bags of bits with a few functions added for convenience.

13.3 Abstract Types

The simplest way of loosening the coupling between users of a class and its implementers and also between code that creates objects and code that uses such objects is to introduce an abstract base class that represents the interface to a set of implementations of a common concept. Consider a set of objects of some type T:

```
class set {
public:
    virtual void insert(T*) = 0;
    virtual void remove(T*) = 0;

    virtual int is_member(T*) = 0;

    virtual T* first() = 0;
    virtual T* next() = 0;

    virtual ~set() { }
};
```

defines an interface to a set with a built-in notion of iteration over its elements. The absence of a constructor and the presence of a virtual destructor is typical; see also §6.7. Several implementations are possible. For example:

```
class slist_set : public set, private slist {
    slink* current_elem;
public:
    void insert(T*);
    void remove(T*);

    int is_member(T*);

    virtual T* first();
    virtual T* next();

    slist_set() : slist(), current_elem(0) { }
};
```

```
class vector_set : public set, private vector {
    int current_index;
public:
    void insert(T*);
    void remove(T*);

    int is_member(T*);

    T* first() { current_index = 0; return next(); }
    T* next();

    vector_set(int initial_size)
        : array(initial_size), current_index(0) { }
};
```

The concrete implementation type is used as a private base class instead of as a member for notational convenience and also because some concrete types may have protected interfaces exactly to allow more direct access to their representations from derived classes. Furthermore, some classes used this way in an implementation are not concrete types and have virtual functions; only through derivation can the new class elegantly override virtual functions from an implementation class. The abstract class provides the interface.

A user can now write the examples from §13.2 like this:

```
void my(set& s)
{
    for (T* p = s.first(); p; p = s.next())
    {
        // my stuff
    }
    // ...
}
```

```
void your(set& s)
{
    for (T* p = s.first(); p; p = s.next())
    {
        // your stuff
    }
    // ...
}
```

The similarity between these functions is now obvious, and only a single version of each of my() and your() is now needed, because they use the set interface to both slist_sets and vector_sets:

```
void user()
{
    slist_set sl;
    vector_set v(100);

    my(sl);
    your(v);

    my(v);
    your(sl);
}
```

Furthermore, the implementers of my() and your() need not know the declarations of slist_set and vector_set, so my() and your() do not depend on these declarations in any way and need not be recompiled or in any way changed if slist_set or vector_set changes or even if a new implementation of set – say tree_set – is introduced. All dependencies are contained in functions that explicitly use – say, vector_set. In particular, assuming the conventional use of header files, the programmer writing my() or your() need only include set.h and not slist_set.h or vector_set.h.

Typically, an abstract type has its operations specified as pure virtual functions and has no data members (except an implicit pointer to a table of virtual functions). The reason is simply that, in most cases, adding a non-virtual function or a data member would require assumptions that would constrain the possible implementations. The notion of an abstract type as presented here is closely akin to the traditional notion of providing a clean separation between an interface and its implementations. An abstract type is an interface, and concrete types are used to provide implementations.

This separation of the interface from the implementations implies the absence of access to operations that are ''natural'' to a particular implementation but not general enough to be part of the interface. For example, because a set doesn't have a notion of ordering, we cannot support a subscripting operator in the set interface even if we happen to be implementing a particular set using an array. This implies a run-time cost due to missed hand optimizations. Furthermore, inlining typically becomes infeasible (except in a local context where the compiler knows the real type), and all interesting operations on the interface become virtual function calls. As with concrete types, sometimes the cost of an abstract type is worth it; sometimes it is not.

To sum up, an abstract type aims to:

[1] define a single concept in a way that allows several implementations of it to coexist in a program;

[2] provide reasonable run-time and space efficiency through the use of virtual functions;

[3] let each implementation have only minimal dependency on other classes; and

[4] be comprehensible in isolation.

Note that abstract types are not better than concrete types, just different. There is a difficult and important tradeoff for the user to make. The library provider can dodge the issue by providing both, thus leaving the choice to the user. The important thing is to be clear about which world a class belongs to. Limiting the generality of an abstract type to attempt to compete in speed with a concrete type usually fails. It compromises the ability to use interchangeable implementations without significant re-compilation after change. Similarly, attempting to provide "generality" in concrete types to compete with the abstract type notion also usually fails. It compromises the efficiency and appropriateness of a simple class. The two notions can coexist – indeed, they *must* coexist because concrete classes provide the implementations for the abstract types – but they must not be muddled together.

Note that neither concrete types nor abstract types are primarily intended to be bases for further derivation. In the case of abstract types, derivation is used to supply implementation rather than to evolve the concept or interface. Each concrete or abstract type aims at providing a clean and efficient representation of a single concept. A class that does that well is rarely a good candidate for the creation of different but related classes through derivation. For example, attempts to derive "more advanced" classes from concrete or abstract types, such as strings, complex numbers, lists, or associative arrays typically lead to awkwardness. Such classes are more often useful as members or private base classes, where they can be used effectively without having their interfaces and implementations mixed up with and compromised by those of the new classes.

When a concrete or abstract type is designed care must be taken to provide a simple interface supporting a single well defined concept. Attempts to broaden the appeal of a class by loading its declaration with all kinds of "useful features" lead to confusion and inefficiency. So do misguided attempts to make a class re-usable by adding `virtual` to each member function without thought of why or how someone would override such functions.

Why didn't we derive `slist` and `vector` from `set` in the first place to save the introduction of `slist_set` and `vector_set` classes? In other words, what are the reasons for having concrete types when we can have abstract types? I can see three reasons:

[1] *Efficiency*: We want to have types like as `vector` and `slist` without the overheads implied by decoupling the implementations from the interfaces (as implied by the abstract type style).

[2] *Multiple interfaces*: Often different concepts are best implemented as derived from a single class.

[3] *Re-use*: We need a mechanism to fit types designed "elsewhere" into our own libraries.

Naturally, these points are related. As an example of 2 consider the notion of an iterator. We may want the notion of an iterator over any type that can yield a sequence of objects. Naturally, this includes `slists` as described above. However, we cannot simply build a general iterator on `slist` or even the set notion because we would also want to iterate over objects that are not sets, such as input streams and functions that compute the next value of a series when called. Thus we want both sets and

iterators, and we don't want to replicate the concrete types that are the obvious implementations of many kinds of sets and iterators. Graphically, we might represent our
desired organization like this:

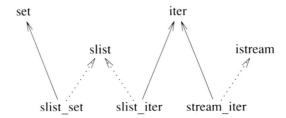

Here, set and iter provide the interfaces, and slist and istream are private
and provide the implementations. Clearly, we could not invert this hierarchy and
derive the concrete types from the abstract classes providing the general interfaces.
That would lead to a hierarchy where every useful operation on every useful abstraction would have to be supported by a common abstract base class. This issue is discussed further in §13.6.

Here is a simple abstract iterator type for containers of objects of type T:

```
class iter {
    virtual T* first() = 0;
    virtual T* next() = 0;
    virtual ~iter() { }
};


class slist_iter : public iter, private slist {
    slink* current_elem;
public:
    T* first();
    T* next();

    slist_iter() : current_elem(0) { }
};


class input_iter: public iter {
    istream& is;
public:
    T* first();
    T* next();

    input_iter(istream& r) : is(r) { }
};
```

These types can be used like this:

```
void user(const iter& it)
{
    for (T* p = it.first(); p; p = it.next()) {
        // ...
    }
}


void caller()
{
    slist_iter sli;
    input_iter ii(cin);

    // fill sli

    user(sli);
    user(ii);
}
```

The use of a concrete type to implement an abstract type makes it possible to use the concrete type separately or directly for run-time efficiency; see also §13.5. It also makes it possible to use the concrete type as the implementation of several abstract types.

A more flexible iterator where the binding of the iterator to the implementation yielding the objects can be specified at the point of initialization and changed at run time is described in §13.9.

13.4 Node Classes

A class hierarchy is built with a view of derivation completely different from the interface/implementer view used for abstract types. Here a class is viewed as a foundation on which to build. Even if it is an abstract class, it usually has some representation and provides some services for its derived classes. Examples of node classes are rectangle (§6.4.2) and satellite (§6.5.1). Typically, a class in a hierarchy represents a general concept of which its derived classes can be seen as specializations. The typical class designed as an integral part of a hierarchy, a *node class*, relies on services from base classes, provides some services itself, and provides virtual functions and/or a protected interface to allow further refinement of its operations by its derived classes.

A typical node class provides not just an implementation of the interface specified by its base class (the way an implementation class does for an abstract type), but it adds new functions itself, thus providing a wider interface. For example, a dialog_box is a kind of window that displays a query to the user and receives an answer in the form of a mouse click on some button:

```
class dialog_box : public window {
    // ...
public:
    dialog_box(const char* ...); // zero terminated list
                                 // of button labels
    // ...
    virtual int ask();
};
```

The important functions are the constructor through which the programmer specifies the buttons and their associated labels and the function `ask()` that displays the `dialog_box` and reports back the number of the button that was clicked in response. One could imagine a use like this:

```
void user()
{
    for(;;) {
        // do something

        dialog_box cont("continue",
                        "try again",
                        "abort",
                        (char*)0);

        switch (cont.ask()) {
        case 0:    return;
        case 1:    break;
        case 2:    abort();
        }
    }
}
```

Note the importance of the constructor. A node class usually needs constructors and often needs a nontrivial constructor; in this, node classes differ from abstract types that rarely have constructors.

The user of a `dialog_box` (and not just the implementer of class `dialog_box`) relies on services from its base classes. In particular, the example above relies on some form of default placement on the screen of a new window, and if the user wanted explicit control of the placement, the `window` base class of `dialog_box` would provide it. For example:

```
dialog_box cont("continue","try again","abort",(char*)0);
cont.move(some_point);
```

The `move()` operation would again rely on services provided by base classes.

A `dialog_box` is itself a good candidate for derivation. For example, it is not uncommon to have a dialog box that accepts a character string (say, a file name) in addition to a click on a button. Such a `dbox_w_str` could be derived from a ''plain'' `dialog_box`:

```
class dbox_w_str : public dialog_box {
    // ...
public:
    dbox_w_str (
        const char* sl,    // string request label
        const char* ...    // list of button labels
    );

    int ask();
    virtual char* get_string();
    // ...
};
```

The get_string() operation is the operation by which the programmer gains
access to the string supplied by the user. The ask() operation supplied by
dbox_w_str will ensure that such a string is entered correctly and that a suitable
value (such as 0) is available to the program if the user declined to supply a string.

```
void user2()
{
    // ...

    dbox_w_str file_name("please enter file name",
                         "done",
                         (char*)0);

    file_name.ask();
    char* p = file_name.get_string();
    if (p) {
        // use file name
    }
    else {
        // no file name given
    }
    // ...
}
```

To sum up, a node class
    [1] relies on its base classes both for its implementation and for supplying services
        to its users;
    [2] provides a wider interface (that is, an interface with more public member func-
        tions) to its users than do its base classes;
    [3] relies primarily (though not necessarily exclusively) on virtual functions in its
        public interface;
    [4] depends on all of its (direct and indirect) base classes;
    [5] can be understood only in the context of its base classes;
    [6] can be used as a base for further derivation;
    [7] can be instantiated.

Not every node class will conform to all of points 1, 2, 6, and 7, but most do. A class that does not conform to point 6 resembles a concrete type and could be called a concrete node class. A class that does not conform to point 7 resembles an abstract type and could be called an abstract node class. Many node classes have at least some `protected` members to provide a less restricted interface for derived classes.

Note an implication of point 4: To compile, a user of a node class must include the declarations of all of its direct and indirect base classes and all of the declarations that they, in turn, depend on. In this, a node class again provides a contrast to an abstract type. A user of an abstract type does not depend on the classes used to implement it and need not include them to compile.

13.5 Run-time Type Information

Sometimes it is useful to find the actual type of an object without entering it to perform an operation. For example, consider the function my (`set&`) from §13.3.

```
void my(set& s)
{
    for (T* p = s.first(); p; p = s.next()) {

        // my stuff
    }

    // ...
}
```

It is nice and general, but what if I knew that many of the `set`s passed were implemented by `slist`s, if I knew an algorithm for the loop that was significantly more efficient for lists than for general sets, and if I knew (from measurement) that this loop was a bottleneck for my system? It would then be worth my while to expand my code to handle `slist`s separately. Assuming that it was possible to determine the actual type of the `set` argument, I could write:

```
void my(set& s)
{
    if (ref_type_info(s) == static_type_info(slist_set)) {
        // compare run-time type representations

        // s is an slist

        slist& sl = (slist&)s;
        for (T* p = sl.first(); p; p = sl.next()) {

            // souped up list algorithm
        }
    }
}
```

```
        else {

            for (T* p = s.first(); p; p = s.next()) {

                // ordinary set algorithm
            }
        }

        // ...
    }
```

Note that once the concrete type `slist` is used, not only are the special list operations available but inlining can also be used for key operations.

This version works well because `slist` is a concrete class, and we really do want the special code only when the argument is exactly an `slist_set`. However, consider a case where we want to provide special code for a class and all classes derived from it. Say we have a `dialog_box` as defined in §13.4 and want to know if it is a `dbox_w_str`. Just checking if it is exactly a `dbox_w_str` would not be a good idea because in a real system there will most likely be quite a few classes derived from `dbox_w_str`. Such derived classes would provide a variety of ways of asking the user for a string. For example, one class derived from `dbox_w_str` may offer the user a set of alternatives to chose from, another may allow the user to search a dictionary for candidates, etc. Consequently, we need to test for a `dbox_w_str` and any class derived from it. This is typical for node classes in the same way as the test for an exact type is typical for abstract classes implemented by concrete classes.

```
    void f(dialog_box& db)
    {
        dbox_w_str* dbws = ptr_cast(dbox_w_str,&db);

        if (dbws) {   // dbox_w_str

            // here we can use dbox_w_str::get_string()
        }
        else {

            // ``plain'' dialog box
        }

        // ...
    }
```

The `ptr_cast()` "operator" casts its second operand (a pointer) to a pointer to its first (a type) provided the object pointed to really is of the type specified (or a class derived from that). A pointer was used to manipulate the `dialog_box` so that we could test for zero after the pointer cast.

As an alternative to manipulating a `dbox_w_str` argument through a pointer, we could manipulate it through a reference:

```
void g(dialog_box& db)
{
    try {
        dbox_w_str& dbws = ref_cast(dialog_box,db);

        // here we can use dbox_w_str::get_string()

    }
    catch(Bad_cast) {

        // ''plain'' dialog box

    }

    // ...
}
```

An exception is used to indicate a bad cast because there is no acceptable null reference to test and because it is sometimes preferable to avoid an explicit test on the
result of a cast.

The difference between `ref_cast()` and `ptr_cast()` is a good illustration of
the difference between pointers and references: A reference refers to an object,
whereas a pointer *might* refer to an object and thus can and often must be checked
before use.

13.5.1 Type Information

C++ does not provide a standard way of doing run-time type inquiries† – only virtual
function calls. However, it is relatively easy to simulate such a facility, and most
major libraries do provide some way of doing run-time type inquiries. The system
described here has the interesting property that the information available for a type is
arbitrarily extendible, can be implemented using virtual function calls, and could be
supported by an enhanced C++ implementation.

The "operators"

```
typeid static_type_info(type)     // get typeid for type name
typeid ptr_type_info(pointer)     // get typeid for pointer
typeid ref_type_info(reference)   // get typeid for reference
pointer ptr_cast(type,pointer)    // convert pointer
reference ref_cast(type,reference) // convert reference
```

provide a reasonably convenient interface to any type inquiry mechanism. A class
user can use these operators exclusively; a class implementer may have to provide
some "scaffolding" in class declarations to conform to a library's implementation
conventions.

---

† Several proposals for extending C++ in this direction have been made, though.

Most users who need to use run-time type identification at all can use the conditional cast operators `ptr_cast()` and `ref_cast()` exclusively. That insulates the user completely from the further complexities of run-time type identification. It is by far the least error-prone way of using run-time type identification.

For applications, such as object I/O, where the exact type must be known – rather than just the knowledge that a cast is safe – the run-time type inquiry operators `static_type_info()`, `ptr_type_info()`, and `ref_type_info()` can be used. They return an object of class `typeid`. Objects of class `typeid` can be compared as was shown in the `set` and `slist_set` example above. Many applications need to know no more about `typeid`s. However, class `typeid` does provide a function `get_type_info()` for applications that need even more information about a type:

```
class typeid {
    friend class Type_info;
private:
    const Type_info* id;
public:
    typeid(const Type_info* p) :id(p) { }
    const Type_info* get_type_info() const { return id; }
    int operator==(typeid i) const ;
};
```

The `get_type_info()` function returns a pointer to a constant object of class `Type_info` from the `typeid`. The "constant" is important to ensure that the run-time type information corresponds to the static type information in the source text. Having type information mutate at run-time is generally not a good idea.

By extracting a pointer to a `Type_info` object describing a type from a `typeid`, a user becomes dependent on details of the run-time type inquiry system and the mechanism for run-time description of types that has not been standardized and cannot easily be covered by a few well-chosen macros.

13.5.2 Class **Type_info**

A `Type_info` holds the minimal information to implement the `ptr_cast()` operator. Class `Type_info` might be defined like this:

```
class Type_info {
    const char* n;          // name
    const Type_info** b;    // list of bases
public:
    Type_info(const char* name, const Type_info* bases[]);

    const char* name() const;
    Base_iterator bases(int direct=0) const;
```

```
int same(const Type_info* p) const;
int has_base(const Type_info*, int direct=0) const;
int can_cast(const Type_info* p) const;

static const Type_info info_obj;
virtual typeid get_info() const;
static typeid info();
};
```

The last two functions must be defined for every class derived from Type_info.

The representation of a Type_info object should be of no concern to a user. It is presented here for completeness, though. The name string is there to allow lookup in tables, such as debugger tables, based on the name of a class and to enable better messages to be composed based on the information found in Type_info objects. The name also serves as a unique key for Type_info objects should there be a reason to replicate such objects for a single type.

```
const char* Type_info::name() const
{
    return n;
}

int Type_info::same(const Type_info* p) const
{
    return this==p || strcmp(n,p->n)==0;
}

int Type_info::can_cast(const Type_info* p) const
{
    return same(p) || p->has_base(this);
}
```

The functions bases() and has_base() provide an interface to the base class information; bases() returns an iterator that can be used to get the pointers to the bases's Type_info objects, and has_base() can be used to ask if the class has a particular base class. The optional direct arguments to has_base() and bases() are used to determine if all base classes (direct==0) or only direct base classes (direct==1) are to be considered. Finally, get_info() and info() can be used to apply these facilities to Type_info itself, as described below.

I am deliberately using only trivial classes in the implementation of this type inquiry mechanism. This avoids dependence on any particular library. An implementation in the context of a particular library might choose to do things differently. Naturally, users will be wise to avoid unnecessary dependence on implementation details.

The list of base classes allows has_base() to do a search for all base classes. There is no need to store information about whether a base is private or virtual because any errors caused by access restrictions and ambiguities will be caught at compile time.

```
class base_iterator {
    short i;
    short alloc;
    const Type_info* b;
public:
    const Type_info* operator()();
    void reset() { i = 0; }

    base_iterator(const Type_info* bb, int direct=0);
    ~base_iterator() { if (alloc) delete[] (Type_info*)b; }
};
```

The optional argument is used to determine if all base classes (`direct==0`) or only direct base classes (`direct==1`) are to be considered.

```
base_iterator::base_iterator(const Type_info* bb, int direct)
{
    i = 0;

    if (direct) { // use list of direct bases
        b = bb;
        alloc = 0;
        return;
    }

    // create list of all bases:

    // int n = number of bases
    b = new const Type_info*[n+1];
    // put bases into b

    alloc = 1;
    return;
}


const Type_info* base_iterator::operator()()
{
    const Type_info * p = &b[i];
    if (p) i++;
    return p;
}
```

We can now define the type inquiry operators as macros:

```
#define static_type_info(T)  T::info()


#define ptr_type_info(p)  ((p)->get_info())
#define ref_type_info(r)  ((r).get_info())
```

```
#define ptr_cast(T,p) \
    (T::info()->can_cast((p)->get_info())  ?  (T*)(p)  :  0)
#define ref_cast(T,r) \
    (T::info()->can_cast((r).get_info()) \
        ? 0 : throw Bad_cast(T::info()->name()),  (T&)(r))
```

The exception type Bad_cast is assumed to be declared

```
class Bad_cast {
    const char* tn;
    // ...
public:
    Bad_cast(const char* p) : tn(p) { }
    const char* cast_to() { return tn; }
    // ...
};
```

As noted in §4.7 the use of macros is an indication of a problem. In this case, the problem is that only the compiler can deal directly with literal types. Macros were used to hide implementation details. In essence, the virtual function table is made to hold the information needed to do run-time type inquiry. An implementation directly supporting the run-time type identification operators can implement these operators slightly more directly, efficiently, and elegantly. In particular, it would be trivial to support a ptr_cast() from a virtual base class to its derived class.

13.5.3 Scaffolding for Run-time Type Inquiries

This section demonstrates how run-time type inquiry can be done explicitly by the programmer where no compiler support is provided. Providing such scaffolding without compiler support can be quite tedious so you might consider skipping this section; it contains only implementation details.

Consider how the set and slist_set classes from §13.3 could be modified to make the type inquiry operators work. First the base class set must be given the member functions used by the type inquiry operators:

```
class set {
public:
    static const Type_info info_obj;
    virtual typeid get_info() const;
    static typeid info();

    // ...
};
```

The set::info_obj object is the (unique) run-time representation of the type set. It must be defined:

```
const Type_info set::info_obj("set",0);
```

Given that, the definition of the functions are trivial:

```
typeid set::get_info() const { return &info_obj; }
typeid set::info() { return &info_obj; }
typeid slist_set::get_info() const { return &info_obj; }
typeid slist_set::info() { return &info_obj; }
```

The virtual function get_info() will support the ref_type_info() and
ptr_type_info() operators, and the static function info() will support the
static_type_info() operator.

The greatest practical problem in building this form of scaffolding for type
inquiries is to ensure that the Type_info object and the two functions returning
pointers to it are defined exactly once for each class.

Class slist_set can now be similarly modified:

```
class slist_set : public set, private slist {
    // ...
public:
    static const Type_info info_obj;
    virtual typeid get_info() const;
    static typeid info();

    // ...
};


static const Type_info* slist_set_b[]
    = { &set::info_obj, &slist::info_obj, 0 };
const Type_info slist_set::info_obj("slist_set",slist_set_b);


typeid slist_set::get_info() const { return &info_obj; }
typeid slist_set::info() { return &info_obj; }
```

13.5.4 Extending the Amount of Run-time Type Information

Class Type_info contains only the minimal information needed to do type identification and safe casting. However, because class Type_info has itself been supplied
with the info() and get_info() member functions, it is possible to derive
classes from it and at run-time to determine which kind of Type_info object was
returned. This ensures that people can extend the amount of information available by
the object returned by dynamic_type() and static_type() without modifying class Type_info. For example, many uses of dynamic type information require
a map of the object:

```
struct Member_info {
    char* name;
    Type_info* tp;
    int offset;
};
```

```
class Map_info : public Type_info {
    Member_info** mi;
public:
    static const Type_info info_obj;
    virtual typeid get_info() const;
    static typeid info();

    // access functions
};
```

Class `Type_info` is a good candidate for a standard library. It provides the minimal
base from which classes providing further information can be derived. Such derived
classes can be provided by users writing code, by stand-alone tools reading C++
source code, or by compilers.

13.5.5 Uses and Misuses of Run-time Type Inquiry

Run-time type information has many uses including support for object I/O, persistent
objects, object-oriented databases, and debugging. However, it also has an enormous
potential for misuse. Simula provided such a facility, and it was widely misused.
Consequently, no such facility was included in C++. It is *very* seductive to use a run-
time type inquiry where a virtual function call would be a better choice. For example,
consider the shape example from §1.2.5. It could have been written like this:

```
void rotate(const Shape& s)
    // misuse of run-time type inquiry
{
    if (ref_type_info(s)==static_type_info(Circle)) {
        // do nothing
    }
    else if (ref_type_info(s)==static_type_info(Triangle)) {
        // rotate triangle
    }
    else if (ref_type_info(s)==static_type_info(Square)) {
        // rotate square
    }
    // ...
}
```

Using run-time type inquiries to implement a switch statement on a type field destroys
all modularity in a program and negates the aims of object-oriented programming. It
is also error-prone; the example above will fail when given an object of a class
derived from `circle` as argument. Experience shows that programmers brought up
with languages such as Pascal or C find this trap is very hard to resist. One reason is
that this style requires less forethought in the design of libraries. In this context, such
lack of forethought is often simple sloppiness.

One might wonder why the conditional cast `ptr_cast()` was chosen as the
interface to the type inquiry mechanism and not an `is_base()` operator (built

directly on the has_base() operation of class Type_info). Consider this example:

```
void f(dialog_box& db)
{
    if (is_base(&db,dbox_w_str)) { // is db's class
                                   // a base of dbox_w_str?

        dbox_w_str* dbws = (dbox_w_str*)&db;

        // ...
    }

    // ...
}
```

This is more verbose than the "equivalent" example using ptr_cast (§13.5) and the explicit and unconditional type conversion is separated from the test, thus introducing the possibility of mistake, inefficiency, and even wrong results. The wrong results occur in the rare case when the run-time inquiry mechanism knows one type is derived from another but the compiler does not. For example:

```
class D;
class B;

void g(B* pb)
{
    if (is_base(pb,D)) {

        D* pb = (D*)pb;

        // ...
    }

    // ...
}
```

but unbeknownst to the compiler the declaration of D is

```
class D : public A, public B {
    // ...
};
```

so that a correct conversion of pb to a D* involves a change in pointer value. The ptr_cast() technique does not suffer from this problem because ptr_cast() can only be used if the declarations for both its arguments have been seen. Casting between undeclared classes as demonstrated above is inherently unsafe but cannot be prohibited without introducing a major incompatibility with C.

13.6 Fat Interfaces

In the sections on abstract types (§13.3) and node classes (§13.4), it was emphasized that all functions of a base class were implemented by either the base or the derived class. However, there is a different way of defining classes. Consider lists, arrays, associative arrays, trees, etc. It is tempting to provide a generalization of all of these types, usually called a container, that can be used as the interface to every one of those. That (apparently) relieves the user of dealing with the details of all of these containers. However, defining the interface of a general container class is non-trivial. Assume that we want to define `container` as an abstract type. What operations do we want `container` to provide? We could provide only the operations that every container can support, the intersection of the sets of operations, but that is a ridiculously narrow interface. In fact, in many interesting cases that intersection is empty. Alternatively, we could provide the union of all the sets of operations and give a run-time error if a ''non-existent'' operation is applied to an object through this interface. An interface that is such a union of interfaces to a set of concepts is called a *fat interface*. Consider a ''general container'' of objects of type `T`:

```
class container {
public:
    struct Bad_operation {      // exception class
        const char* p;
        Bad_operation(const char* pp) :  p(pp) { }
    };


    virtual void put(const T*)
        { throw Bad_operation("container::put"); }
    virtual T* get()
        { throw Bad_operation("container::get"); }


    virtual T*& operator[](int)
        { throw Bad_operation("container::[](int)"); }
    virtual T*& operator[](const char*)
        { throw Bad_operation("container::[](char*)"); }
    // ...
};
```

Few implementations can support both the subscripting and the list-style operations well and it is probably not a good idea to do that anyway.

Note that where a true abstract type uses pure virtual functions to ensure compile-time checking, a fat interface uses functions that throw exceptions to ensure run-time error detection.

A `container` implemented by a singly linked list could then be declared like this:

```
class slist_container : public container, private slist {
public:
    void put(const T*);
    T* get();

    T*& operator[](int)
        { throw Bad_operation("slist::[](int)"); }
    T*& operator[](const char*)
        { throw Bad_operation("slist::[](char*)"); }
    // ...
};
```

The subscripting operators are defined to improve the run-time error handling.
Instead, one might simply rely on the less detailed information provided by the exceptions thrown by the container class and leave unimplemented functions unmen-
tioned:

```
class vector_container : public container, private vector {
public:
    T*& operator[](int);
    T*& operator[](const char*);
    // ...
};
```

As long as one is careful, all is well:

```
void f()
{
    slist_container sc;
    vector_container vc;
    // ...
    user(sc,vc);
}
```

```
void user(container& c1, container& c2)
{
    T* p1 = c1.get();
    T* p2 = c2[3];
    // don't use c2.get() or c1[3]
    // ...
}
```

However, run-time type-inquiry (§13.5) or exception handling (§9) is often needed to
avoid run-time errors. For example:

```
void user2(container& c1, container& c2)
/*
    detection is easy, but recovery can be hard
*/
{
    try {
        T* p1 = c1.get();
        T* p2 = c2[3];
        // ...
    }
    catch(container::Bad_operation& bad) {
        // Oops!
        // Now what?
    }
}
```

or

```
void user3(container& c1, container& c2)
/*
    detection is tedious
    and recovery can still be hard
*/
{
    slist* sl = ptr_cast(slist_container,&c1);
    vector* v = ptr_cast(vector_container,&c2);

    if (sl && v) {
        T* p1 = c1.get();
        T* p2 = c2[3];
        // ...
    }
    else {
        // Oops!
        // Now what?
    }
}
```

In both cases, run-time performance can suffer and the generated code can be surprisingly large. As a result, people are tempted to ignore the potential errors and hope that they don't actually occur when the program is in the hands of users. The problem with this approach is that exhaustive testing is also hard and expensive.

Consequently, fat interfaces are best avoided where run-time performance is at a premium, where strong guarantees about the correctness of code are required, and in general whereever there is a good alternative. Also, the use of fat interfaces weakens the correspondence between concepts and classes and thus opens the floodgates for the use of derivation as a mere implementation convenience.

13.7 Application Frameworks

Libraries built out of the kinds of classes described above support design and re-use of code by supplying building blocks and ways of combining them; the application builder designs a framework into which these common building blocks are fitted. An alternative, and sometimes more ambitious, approach to the support of design and re-use is to provide code that establishes a common framework into which the application builder fits application-specific code as building blocks. Such an approach is often called an application framework. The classes establishing such a framework often have such fat interfaces that they are hardly types in the traditional sense. They approximate the ideal of being complete applications, except that they don't do anything. The specific actions are supplied by the application programmer.

As an example, consider a filter, that is, a program that reads an input stream, (maybe) performs some actions based on that input, (maybe) produces an output stream, and (maybe) produces a final result. A naive framework for such programs would provide a set of operations that an applications programmer might supply:

```
class filter {
public:
    class Retry {
    public:
        virtual const char* message() { return 0; }
    };

    virtual void start() { }
    virtual int retry() { return 2; }
    virtual int read() = 0;
    virtual void write() { }
    virtual void compute() { }
    virtual int result() = 0;
};
```

Functions that are required of a derived class are declared pure virtual; others are simply defined to do nothing. The framework also provides a main loop and a rudimentary error handling mechanism:

```
int main_loop(filter* p)
{
    for(;;) {
        try {
            p->start();
            while (p->read()) {
                p->compute();
                p->write();
            }
            return p->result();
        }
```

```
            catch (filter::Retry& m) {
                cout << m.message() << '\n';
                int i = p->retry();
                if (i) return i;
            }
            catch (...) {
                cout << "Fatal filter error\n";
                return 1;
            }
        }
    }
```

Finally, I could write my program like this:

```
    class myfilter : public filter {
        istream& is;
        ostream& os;
        char c;
        int nchar;


    public:
        int read() { is.get(c); return is.good(); }
        void compute() { nchar++; };
        int result()
            { os << nchar
                << " characters read\n";
              return 0;
            }


        myfilter(istream& ii, ostream& oo)
            : is(ii), os(oo), nchar(0) { }
    };
```

and activate it like this:

```
    int main()
    {
        myfilter f(cin,cout);
        return main_loop(&f);
    }
```

Naturally, to be of significant use a real framework must provide more structure and
many more services than this simple example. In particular, a framework is typically
a hierarchy of node classes. Having the application programmer supply leaf classes in
a deeply nested hierarchy allows commonality between applications and reuse of services provided by such a hierarchy. A framework will also be supported by a library
providing classes, such as scroll_bar (§12.2.5) and dialog_box (§13.4), that
are useful for the application programmer when specifying the action classes.

13.8 Interface Classes

One of the most important kinds of classes is the humble and mostly overlooked interface class. An interface class doesn't do much – if it did it wouldn't be an interface class. It simply adjusts the appearance of some service to local needs. Because it is in principle impossible to serve all needs equally well all the time, interface classes are essential to allow sharing yet not force all use into a common straightjacket.

The purest form of an interface doesn't even cause any code to be generated. Consider the `Splist` template from §8.3.2:

```
template<class T>
class Splist : private Slist<void*> {
public:
    void insert(T* p) { Slist<void*>::insert(p); }
    void append(T* p) { Slist<void*>::append(p); }
    T* get() { return (T*) Slist<void*>::get(); }
};
```

Here, `Splist` turns the unsafe, but generic, list of `void*` pointers into a much more useful family of type-safe list classes. Inline functions are often essential for making interface classes affordable. In cases such as this, where an inline forwarding functions does only type adjustment, there is no added overhead in time or space.

Naturally, an abstract base class representing an abstract type implemented by concrete types (§13.3) is a form of interface class, as are the handles from section §13.9. However, here we will focus on classes that have no more specific function than adjusting an interface.

Consider the problem of merging two hierarchies using multiple inheritance. What can be done if there is a name clash, that is, where two classes have used the same name for virtual functions performing completely different operations? For example, consider a wild-west videogame where user interactions are handled by a general window class:

```
class Window {
    // ...
    virtual void draw();
};

class Cowboy {
    // ...
    virtual void draw();
};

class CowboyWindow : public Cowboy, public Window {
    // ...
};
```

A CowboyWindow represents the animation of a cowboy in the game and handles the user/player's interactions with the cowboy character. We would prefer to use multiple inheritance, rather than declaring either the `Window` or the `Cowboy` as members, because there will be many service functions defined for both `Windows` and `Cowboys`. We would like to pass a `CowboyWindow` to such functions without special actions required by the programmer. However, this leads to a problem defining `CowboyWindow` versions of `Cowboy::draw()` and `Window::draw()`.

There can be only one function defined in `CowboyWindow` called `draw()`; yet because service functions manipulate `Windows` and `Cowboys` without knowledge of `CowboyWindows`, `CowboyWindow` must override both `Cowboy`'s `draw()` and `Window`'s `draw()`. Overriding both functions by a single `draw()` function would be wrong because, despite the common name, the `draw()` functions are unrelated and cannot be redefined by a common function.

Finally, we would also like `CowboyWindow` to have distinct, unambiguous names for the inherited functions `Cowboy::draw()` and `Window::draw()`.

To solve this problem, we need to introduce an extra class for `Cowboy` and an extra class for `Window`. These classes introduce the two new names for the `draw()` functions and ensure that a call of the `draw()` functions in `Cowboy` and `Window` calls the functions with the new names:

```
class CCowboy : public Cowboy {
    virtual int cow_draw(int) = 0;
    void draw() { cow_draw(i); } // overrides Cowboy::draw

};

class WWindow : public Window {
    virtual int win_draw() = 0;
    void draw() { win_draw(); } // overrides Window::draw

};
```

We can now compose a `CowboyWindow` from the interface classes `CCowboy` and `WWindow` and override `cow_draw()` and `win_draw()` with the desired effect:

```
class CowboyWindow : public CCowboy, public WWindow {
    // ...
    void cow_draw();
    void win_draw();
};
```

Note that only because the two `draw()` functions had the same argument type was this problem serious. Had the two `draw()` functions had different argument types, the usual overloading resolution rules would have ensured that no problem manifested itself despite the unrelated functions having the same name.

For each use of an interface class one could imagine a special purpose language extension that could perform the desired adjustment a little bit more efficiently or a little more elegantly. However, each use of an interface class is infrequent and supporting them all with specialized language constructs would impose a prohibitive burden of complexity. In particular, name clashes arising from the merging of class hierarchies are not common (compared with the frequency that a programmer will write a class) and tend to arise from the merging of hierarchies generated from dissimilar cultures – such as games and operating systems, in this example. Merging such dissimilar hierarchies is not easy, and the resolution of name clashes will more often than not be the least of the programmer's problems. Other problems include dissimilar error handling, dissimilar initialization, and dissimilar memory management strategies. The resolution of name clashes was discussed here because the technique of introducing a interface class with a forwarding function has many other applications; it can be used not only to change names, but also to change argument and return types, to introduce run-time checking, etc.

Because the forwarding functions `CCowboy::draw()` and `WWindow::draw()` are virtual functions they cannot be optimized away by simple inlining. It is, however, possible for a compiler to recognize them as simple forwarding functions and then optimize them out of the call chains that go through them.

A major use of interface functions is to adjust an interface to match user's expectations better, thus moving code that would have been scattered through a user's code into an interface. Consider class `vector` from §1.4. Such `vector`s, like arrays, are zero-based. Users who want ranges other than 0 to `size-1` must adjust their usage. For example

```
void f()
{
    vector v(10);      // range [0:9]

    // pretend v is in the range [1::10]:

    for (int i = 1; i<=10; i++) {
        v[i-1] = ...  // remember to adjust index


    }
    // ...
}
```

A better way is to provide a `vector` with arbitrary bounds:

```
class vec : public vector {
    int lb;
public:
    vec(int low, int high)
        : vector(high-low+1) { lb=low; }

    int& operator[](int i)
        { return vector::operator[](i-lb); }

    int low() { return lb; }
    int high() { return lb+size()-1; }
};
```

A `vec` can be used like this:

```
void g()
{
    vec v(1,10);        // range [1:10]

    for (int i = 1; i<=10; i++) {
        v[i] = ...

    }
    // ...
}
```

without overhead compared to the example above. Clearly, the vec version is easier to read and write and less error prone.

Another important use is to provide C++ interfaces to non-C++ code, as described in §12.1.4, or to C++ libraries following "strange" conventions.

13.9 Handle Classes

An abstract type provides an effective separation between an interface and its implementations. However, as used above, the connection between an interface provided by an abstract type and its implementation provided by a concrete type is permanent. For example, it is not possible to rebind an abstract iterator from one source – say, a set – to another – say, a stream – once the original source becomes exhausted.

Furthermore, unless one manipulates abstract type objects through pointers or references, the benefits of virtual functions are lost. The user code becomes dependent on details of the implementation classes because even an abstract type cannot be allocated on the stack (including being accepted as a by-value argument) or statically without its size being known. However, using pointers and references implies that the burden of memory management falls on the user (§13.10).

Another limitation of the abstract class approach is that a class object is of fixed size, but classes are used to represent concepts that require varying amounts of storage to implement them.

A popular technique for dealing with these issues is to separate what is used as a single object into two parts: A handle providing the user interface and a representation holding all or most of the object's state. The connection between the handle and the representation is typically a pointer in the handle. Often, handles have a bit more data than the simple representation pointer, but not much more. This implies that the layout of a handle is typically stable even when the representation changes and also that handles are small enough to move around relatively freely so that pointers and references need not be used by the user.

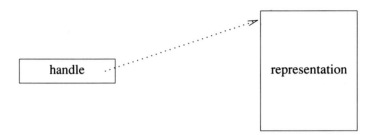

The `string` class from §7.6 is a simple example of a handle. The handle provides an interface to, access control for, and memory management for the representation. In this case, both the handle and the representation are concrete types, but the representation class is often an abstract class.

Consider the abstract type `set` from §13.3. How could one provide a handle for it, and what benefits and cost would that involve? Given a set class, one might simply define a handle by overloading the `->` operator:

```
class set_handle {
    set* rep;
public:
    set* operator->() { return rep; }

    set_handle(set* pp) : rep(pp) { }
};
```

This doesn't significantly affect the way `sets` are used; one simply passes `set_handles` around instead of `set&s` or `set*s`. For example:

```
void my(set_handle s)
{
    for (T* p = s->first(); p; p = s->next())
    {
        // ...
    }
    // ...
}
```

```
void your(set_handle s)
{
    for (T* p = s->first(); p; p = s->next())
    {
        // ...
    }
    // ...
}
```

```
void user()
{
    set_handle sl(new slist_set);
    set_handle v(new vector_set v(100));

    my(sl);
    your(v);

    my(v);
    your(sl);
}
```

If the set class and the set_handle class are designed together it is easy to do reference counting:

```
class set {
friend class set_handle;
protected:
    int handle_count;
public:
    virtual void insert(T*) = 0;
    virtual void remove(T*) = 0;

    virtual int is_member(T*) = 0;

    virtual T* first() = 0;
    virtual T* next() = 0;

    set() : handle_count(0) { }
};
```

The handle_count is incremented and decremented by the handles to reflect the number of set_handles active for the given set:

```
class set_handle {
    set* rep;
public:
    set* operator->() { return rep; }



    set_handle(set* pp)
        : rep(pp) { pp->handle_count++; }
    set_handle(const set_handle& r)
        : rep(r.rep) { rep->handle_count++; }
```

```
        set_handle& operator=(const set_handle& r)
        {
            rep->handle_count++;
            if (--rep->handle_count == 0) delete rep;
            rep = r.rep;
            return *this;
        }

        ~set_handle()
            { if (--rep->handle_count == 0) delete rep; }
    };
```

Provided that all references to a set go through set_handles, the user can forget about memory management for that set.

Realistically, though, it will sometimes be useful to extract the representation pointer from a handle and use it directly. An example would be to pass it to a function that does not know about handles. This works nicely provided the called function does not destroy the object passed to it or store a pointer to it for use after returning to its caller. An operation for rebinding a handle to a new representation can also be useful:

```
    class set_handle {
        set* rep;
    public:
        // ...

        set* get_rep()   { return rep; }

        void bind(set* pp)
        {
            pp->handle_count++;
            if (--rep->handle_count == 0) delete rep;
            rep = pp;
        }
    };
```

Note that derivation of new classes from set_handle isn't particularly useful. It is a concrete type without virtual functions. The idea is to have one handle class for a family of classes defined by a base class. Derivation from this base class can be a powerful technique. It applies to node classes as well as to abstract types.

A handle class is an obvious candidate for a template:

```
    template <class T> class handle {
        T* rep;
    public:
        T* operator->() { return rep; }
        // ...
    };
```

A problem with this technique is that it requires cooperation between the handle class and the "handled" class. When designing the handle and the handled class together for a library this may be reasonable, though, and alternatives do exist (§13.10).

Overloading –> enables a handle to gain control and do some work on each access to an object. For example, one could collect statistics about the number of uses of the object accessed through a handle:

```
template <class T>
    class Xhandle {
        T* rep;
        int count;
    public:
        T* operator->() { count++; return rep; }

        // ...
    };
```

Handles for which work needs to be done both before *and* after access require much more elaborate programming. For example, one might want a set with locking while an insertion or a removal is being done. Essentially, the representation class's interface needs to be replicated in the handle class:

```
class set_controller {
    set* rep;
    // ...
public:

    lock();
    unlock();

    virtual void insert(T* p)
        { lock(); rep->insert(p); unlock(); }
    virtual void remove(T* p)
        { lock(); rep->remove(p); unlock(); }

    virtual int is_member(T* p)
        { return rep->is_member(p); }

    virtual T* first() { return rep->first(); }
    virtual T* next() { return rep->insert(); }

    // ...
};
```

Providing these forwarding functions is tedious (and therefore somewhat error-prone), though neither difficult nor costly in run-time.

Note that only some of the set functions required locking. In my experience, it is typical that a class needing pre- and post-actions requires them only for some and not all member functions. In the case of locking, locking on all operations – as is done for monitors in some systems – leads to excess locking and sometimes causes a noticeable decrease in concurrency.

An advantage of the elaborate definition of all operations on the handle over the overloading of `->` style of handles is that it is possible to derive from class `set_controller`. Unfortunately, some of the benefits of being a handle are compromised if data members are added in the derived class. In particular, the amount of code shared (in the handled class) decreases compared to the amount of code written in each handle.

13.10 Memory Management

One of the most critical issues of the design of libraries and long running programs is memory management. A library writer doesn't in general know if a library will be part of an application where memory is scarce, where a memory leak would be a serious problem, or where memory-management overhead could be a serious liability.

The fundamental question about memory management can be stated in this way: If `f()` passes or returns a pointer to an object to `g()`, who is responsible for the object's destruction? A secondary question must also be answered: When can it be destroyed? In particular, these questions are critical to designers and users of container classes, such as lists, arrays, and associative arrays. From the point of view of a library provider, the ideal answers are ''the system'' and ''whenever nobody is using the object any longer.'' A system doing this is usually said to be garbage collecting, and the part of the system that determines that nobody uses a given object and destroys it is called the garbage collector.

Unfortunately, garbage collection implies overheads in runtime and space, service interruptions, special supportive hardware, trouble with linking to program fragments written in other languages, or system complexity. This, many users cannot afford†. Consequently, although garbage collecting implementations of C++ exist, most C++ programs cannot rely on garbage collection and must devise strategies for managing objects on the free store without help from the system.

Consider the simplest possible memory management scheme in a C++ program. Replace `operator new()` with the simplest allocator and `operator delete()` with the null operation:

---

† It is said that Lisp programmers know that memory management is so important that it cannot be left to the users and C programmers know that memory management is so important that it cannot be left to the system.

```
inline size_t align(size_t s)
/*
    Even a simple allocator needs to align memory
    so that it can be pointed to
    by a pointer of arbitrary type
*/
{
    union Word { void* p; long double d; long l; };

    int x = s + sizeof(Word) - 1;
    x -= x%sizeof(Word);
    return x;
}


static void* freep; // initialize to the start of free memory

void* operator new(size_t s) // simple linear allocation
{
    void* p = freep;
    s = align(s);
    freep += s;
    return p;
}


void operator delete(void*) { }  // no-op
```

Given an infinite memory, this equals garbage collection without the overheads and complexities. This strategy is unsuitable for a library where the pattern of memory use cannot be known in advance and where programs using the library may be required to run for long periods of time. For programs where memory use is limited or proportional to the size of some input, it can be the ideal memory-management technique, though.

13.10.1 Garbage Collection

Garbage collection can be seen as a way of simulating an infinite memory in a limited memory. With this in mind, we can answer a common question: Should a garbage collector call the destructor for an object it recycles? The answer is no, because an object placed on free store and never deleted is never destroyed. Seen in this light, using delete is simply a way of requesting the destructor to be called (together with a notification to the system that the object's memory may be recycled). But what if we actually do want an action performed for an object allocated on the free store but never deleted? Note that this problem does not arise for static and automatic objects; their destructors are always called implicitly. Note also that actions performed "at garbage-collection time" are unpredictable because they may happen at essentially any time between the last use of the object and "the end of the program." This implies that the state of the program at the time of their execution is unknown. This again makes such actions hard to program correctly and less useful than is sometimes imagined.

Where such actions are needed, the problem of performing an action at some unspecified ''destruction time'' can be solved by providing a registration server. An object that needs a service performed ''at the end of the program'' places its address and a pointer to a ''cleanup'' function in a global associative array. If the object is explicitly deleted this registration is removed. When the registration server is destroyed (''at the end of the program'') all remaining registered objects have their cleanup functions called. This solution applies to the garbage collection case also (because garbage collection is seen as a simulation of infinite memory). In the garbage collection case, a choice must be made between deleting an object when its last reference is the one in the registration server and the (default) approach of having the registration of an object cause the object to live until the end of the program (because it now has a reference in the registration server).

The registration server might be implemented as an associative array (§8.8):

```
class Register {
    Map<void*,void (*)(void*)> m;
public:
    insert(void* po, void (*pf)()) { m[po]=pf; }
    remove(void* po) { m.remove(po); }
};

Register cleanup_register;
```

A class using it systematically could look like this:

```
class X {
    // ...
    static void cleanup(void*);
public:


    X()
    {
        cleanup_register.insert(this,&cleanup);
        // ...
    }


    ˜X() { cleanup(this); }

    // ...
};
```

```
void X::cleanup(void* pv)
{
    X* px = (X*)pv;
    cleanup_register.remove(pv);
    // clean up
}
```

The reason for using a static member function and a `void*` pointer is to avoid having the cleanup register deal with type information.

13.10.2 Containers and Deletion

Assuming that we do not have infinite memory or garbage collection, what options for memory management does the designer of a container class such as `Vector` have? For some types of elements, such as `int`s, the right choice is clearly to copy the integers into the container. For other types, such as the abstract class `Shape`, it is equally clear that a pointer must be stored. Consequently, a library designer must typically provide both alternatives. Consider the obvious skeleton implementation:

```
template<class T> Vector {
    T* p;
    int sz;
public:
    Vector(int s) { p = new T[sz=s]; }
    // ...
};
```

This serves both alternatives provided the user inserts pointers to `Shapes` and not `Shape` objects themselves.

```
Vector<Shape*> vsp(200);    // fine
Vector<Shape> vs(200);      // compile time error
```

Fortunately, the compiler catches attempts to create an array of objects of the abstract base class `Shape`.

However, using pointers implies that the library and the user must agree on who is responsible for the deletion of the objects stored in the container. For example:

```
void f()
    // confused use of memory management facilities
{
    Vector<Shape*> v(10);
    Circle* cp = new Circle;
    v[0] = cp;
    v[1] = new Triangle;
    Square s;
    v[2] = &s;
    delete cp; // does not delete objects pointed to
               // by contained pointers
}
```

Given the implementation of Vector from §1.4.3, the Triangle now remains unreferenced (forever, assuming that we are not employing a garbage collector). In memory management, consistency is everything. For example:

```
void g()
    // consistent use of memory management facilities
{
    Vector<Shape*> v(10);
    Circle* cp = new Circle;
    v[0] = cp;
    v[1] = new Triangle;
    Square s;
    v[2] = &s;
    delete cp;
    delete v[1];
}
```

Consider a vector class that assumes responsibility for pointers passed to it:

```
template<class T> MVector {
    T* p;
    int sz;
public:
    MVector(int s);
    ~MVector();
    // ...
};


template<class T> MVector<T>::MVector(int s)
{
    // check s
    p = new T[sz=s];
    for (int i=0; i<s; i++) p[i] = 0;
}
```

```
template<class T> MVector<T>::~MVector()
{
    for (int i=0; i<s; i++) delete p[i];
    delete p;
}
```

The user can rely on the `MVector` to delete its contained pointer. The implication is that the user may not hold on to a pointer to an object given to the `MVector` after the `MVector` is deleted, and no pointers to static or automatic objects may be in the `MVector` at the point of its destruction. For example:

```
void h()
        // consistent use of memory management facilities
{
    MVector<Shape*> v(10);
    Circle* cp = new circle();
    v[0] = cp;
    v[1] = new Triangle;
    Square s;
    v[2] = &s;
    v[2] = 0;  // prevent deletion of s

    // all remaining pointers automatically
    // deleted at exit from f()
}
```

Naturally, this technique is applicable only to containers that do not contain duplicates such as `Map` (§8.8). The simple `MVector` destructor above contains the error that it will delete a pointer entered twice two times.

Note that the construction and destruction of containers that take responsibility for their contents is relatively expensive and that copying of such containers must be prohibited (which copy would be responsible?) or at least severely restricted:

```
template<class T> MVector {
    // ...
private:
    MVector(const MVector&);                //prevent copying
    MVector& operator=(const MVector&);  //prevent copying
    // ...
};
```

This implies that such containers must be passed by reference or by pointers (if passed at all), thus creating a problem of memory management at a different level.

However, it is often useful to reduce the number of pointers that a user has to manage: It is much easier to manage 100 first-level objects that themselves are responsible for the management of 1000 objects than it is to manage 1100 objects directly. One way of viewing the techniques in this section and some of the techniques relying on constructors and destructors for memory management is that they allow the programmer to reduce the memory-management problem from the well nigh unmanageable – say, 100,000 objects – to the easily handled – say, 100 objects – by automating and stylizing the memory management of almost all objects.

Can a container class be written so that it offers the creator of an individual container the choice of management strategy yet presents users with only a single container type? If so, would that be a good idea? To answer the second question first: It would be a good idea because most functions in a system do not have to be concerned with memory management and having two (or more) distinct types for each container class would place an unnecessary burden on users. A library must either provide only one kind of container class (`Vector` or `MVector`) or provide both as variants of the same type. For example:

```
template<class T> PVector {
    T** p;
    int sz;
    int managed;
public:
    PVector(int s, int managed = 0);
    ~PVector();
    // ...
};
```

```
template<class T> PVector<T>::PVector(int s, int m)
{
    // check s
    p = new T*[sz=s];
    if (managed = m)
        for (int i=0; i<s; i++) p[i] = 0;
}
```

```
template<class T> PVector<T>::~PVector()
{
    if (managed) {
        for (int i=0; i<s; i++) delete p[i];
    }
    delete p;
}
```

The handle class from §13.9 is an example of a class that a library might provide to help users manage memory. The use counting in the handles ensures that one can pass handles freely without worrying about who deletes the object referred to by the handle – the handle does. This approach is intrusive; it requires a use count field in the objects managed through the handles. Naturally, this can be avoided through the use of an additional object:

```
template<class T>
class Handle {
    T* rep;
    int* pcount;
public:
    T* operator->() { return rep; }

    Handle(const T* pp)
        : rep(pp), pcount(new int) { (*pcount) = 0; }
    Handle(const Handle& r)
        : rep(r.rep), pcount(r.count) { (*pcount)++; }

    void bind(const Handle& r)
    {
        if (rep == r.rep) return;
        if (--(*pcount) == 0) { delete rep; delete pcount; }
        rep = r.rep;
        pcount = r.pcount;
        (*pcount)++;
    }

    Handle& operator=(const Handle& r)
    {
        bind(r);
        return *this;
    }

    ~Handle()
    {
        if (--(*pcount) == 0) { delete rep; delete pcount; }
    }
};
```

13.10.3 Allocators and Deallocators

The examples above all treat memory as something given. However, ordinary general-purpose free store managers are surprisingly inefficient compared with special-purpose allocators. The most extreme example was the ''infinite memory'' allocator with a null deallocator described above. Less extreme special purpose allocators can be provided by a library and can often be used to double the speed of a program. Please profile your program and determine the memory management overhead *before* trying to optimize it away, though.

Sections §5.5.6 and §6.7 showed how to attach a memory allocator to a class X by defining X::operator new() and X::operator delete(). A problem with that approach is that the allocators we would like for two classes X and Y are so similar that we would like them to be identical. In other words, we want a library class that does allocation and deallocation suitable for class-specific allocators. Given that,

writing class-specific allocators becomes a simple matter of attaching an allocator to
the class:

```
class X {
    static Pool my_pool;
    // ...
public:
    // ...
    void* operator new(size_t) { return my_pool.alloc(); }
    void operator delete(void* p) { my_pool.free(p); }
};

Pool X::my_pool(sizeof(X));
```

A `Pool` provides a set of memory blocks all of the same size. For example,
`my_pool` in the example allocates chunks of memory of size `sizeof(X)`.

The declaration of class `X` and the use of the `Pool` is optimized for speed and
compactness of representation. Note that the size of the blocks of memory allocated
is "wired in" so that the size argument to `X::operator new()` isn't used and the
version of `X::operator delete()` without a size argument is used. If you
derive a class `Y` from `X` so that `sizeof(Y)>sizeof(X)`, then class `Y` must provide
its own allocation and deallocation; inheriting class `X`'s would be a disaster. Fortunately, providing an allocator for `Y` is trivial.

A `Pool` maintains a linked list of elements of the right size. It gets the elements
from fixed-sized blocks of memory and allocates new such blocks as needed. The
reason for having elements in blocks is for the `Pool` to minimize the number of times
it has to ask the general-purpose allocator for more memory. A `Pool` never hands
memory back to the general-purpose allocator until the `Pool` itself is destroyed.

The declaration of class `Pool` is:

```
class Pool {

    struct Link { Link* next; };

    const unsigned esize;
    Link* head;

    Pool(Pool&);                // copy protection
    void operator= (Pool&);     // copy protection
    void grow();
public:
    Pool(unsigned n);
    ~Pool();

    void* alloc();
    void free(void* b);
};
```

```
inline void* Pool::alloc()
{
    if (head==0) grow();
    Link* p = head;
    head = p->next;
    return p;
}

inline void Pool::free(void* b)
{
    Link* p = (Link*) b;
    p->next = head;
    head = p;
}
```

The declarations above would be in a `Pool.h` header. The definitions below would reside elsewhere and complete the definition. The constructor must initialize the `Pool`:

```
Pool::Pool(unsigned sz)
    : esize(sz)
{
    head = 0;
}
```

and `Pool::grow()` must link all elements in a new block onto the list of free elements, `head`. The definition of the rest of the member functions is left as exercises 5 and 6 in §13.11.

```
void Pool::grow()
{
    const int overhead = 12;
    const int chunk_size = 8*1024-overhead;
    const int nelem = (chunk_size-esize)/esize;

    char* start = new char[chunk_size];
    char* last = &start[(nelem-1)*esize];

    for (char* p = start; p<last; p+=esize)
        ((Link*)p)->next = ((Link*)p)+1;
    ((Link*)last)->next = 0;
    head = (Link*)start;
}
```

13.11 Exercises

1. (*3) Complete the definitions of the member functions of class `Type_info`.
2. (*3) Draw an object layout that would make `Type_info::get_info()`

redundant and rewrite the `Type_info` member functions to take advantage of it.

3. (*2.5) How convenient can you make the notation for the `Dialog_box` examples without using any macros (and no language extensions)? How convenient can you make the notation for the `Dialog_box` if language extensions were allowed?

4. (*4) Study two widely used libraries. Classify the library classes in terms of concrete types, abstract types, node classes, handle classes, and interface classes. Are abstract node classes and concrete node classes used? Is there a more appropriate classification for the classes in these libraries? Are fat interfaces used? What facilities – if any – are provided for run-time type information? What is the memory management strategy?

5. (*3) Define a template version of the `Pool` class from (§13.10.3). Make the size of the elements allocated a template argument rather than a constructor argument.

6. (*2.5) Refine the `Pool` template from the previous exercise by having it preallocate some elements at the time of construction. Also, find the portability problem that can manifest itself if `Pool` is used with `char` as the element type and fix it.

7. (*3) If your C++ implementation doesn't directly support run-time type inquiry, have a look at your favorite library. Does it implement a mechanism run-time type inquiry? If so, implement the operators from §13.5 on top of that mechanism.

8. (*2.5) Write a string class that performs no error checking at all plus another string class from it that performs only checking and calls to to its unchecked base. Discuss the pros and cons of this approach to selective checking of a class and the ''invariant approach'' described in §12.2.7.1. To which extent can the two techniques be used in combination?

9. (*4) Define a class `Storable` as an abstract base class with virtual functions `writeout()` and `readin()`. For simplicity, assume that a character string is sufficient to specify a permanent storage location. Use class `Storable` to provide a facility for writing objects of to and from disc. Test it with a couple of classes of your own choice.

10. (*4) Define a base class `Persistent` with operations `save()` and `nosave()` that control whether an object is written to permanent storage by a destructor. In addition to `save()` and `nosave()`, what operations could `Persistent` usefully provide? Test class `Persistent` it with a couple of classes of your own choice. Is `Persistent` a node class, a concrete type, or an abstract type? Why?

11. (*3) Write the class declaration (only) for a class `stack` that implements the notion of stacks by providing operations `create()` (create a stack), `delete()`, `push()`, and `pop()`. Use static members only. Provide a class `id` for identifying and referencing stacks. Ensure that users can copy `stack::ids` but cannot manipulate them in other ways. Compare this stack to the stack class found in §8.2.

12. (*3) Write the class declaration for a class `stack` that is an abstract type (§13.3). Provide two different implementations for this interface. Write a small program to exercise these classes. Compare this stack to the stack classes found in the

previous exercise and in §8.2.

13. (*3) Write the class declaration for a class `stack` for which it is possible to change implementation at run time. Hint: "Every problem is solved by yet another indirection."

14. (*3.5) Define a class `Oper` holding an identifier (of some suitable type), and an operation (some form of pointer to function). Define a class `cat_object` that holds a list of `Opers` and a `void*`. Provide `cat_object` with operations `add_oper()` that adds an `Oper` to the list, `remove_oper(id)` that removes an `Oper` identified by `id` from the list, and an `operator()(id,arg)` that invokes the `Oper` identified by `id`. Implement a stack of cats by a `cat_object`. Write a small program to exercise these classes.

15. (*3) Define a template `Object` base of class `cat_object`. Use `Object` to implement a stack of `Strings`. Write a small program to exercise this template.

16. (*3) Define a variant of class `Object` called `Class` that ensures that objects with identical operations share a list of operations. Write a small program to exercise this template.

17. (*3) Define a `Stack` template that provides a conventional and type-safe interface to a stack implemented by the `Object` template. Compare this stack to the stack classes found in the previous exercises. Write a small program to exercise this template.

R

Reference Manual

r.1 Introduction

This manual describes the C++ programming language as of May 1991. C++ is a general purpose programming language based on the C programming language*. In addition to the facilities provided by C, C++ provides classes, inline functions, operator overloading, function name overloading, constant types, references, free store management operators, and function argument checking and type conversion. These extensions to C are summarized in §r.18.1. The differences between C++ and ANSI C† are summarized in §r.18.2. The extensions to C++ since the 1985 edition of this manual are summarized in §r.18.1.2. The sections related to templates (§r.14) and exception handling (§r.15) are placeholders for planned language extensions.

r.1.1 Overview

This manual is organized like this:

1. Introduction	10. Derived Classes
2. Lexical Conventions	11. Member Access Control
3. Basic Concepts	12. Special Member Functions
4. Standard Conversions	13. Overloading
5. Expressions	14. Templates
6. Statements	15. Exception Handling
7. Declarations	16. Preprocessing
8. Declarators	Appendix A: Grammar Summary
9. Classes	Appendix B: Compatibility

---

* ''The C Programming Language'' by Brian W. Kernighan and Dennis M. Ritchie, Prentice Hall, 1978 and 1988.
† American National Standard X3.159-1989.

r.1.2 Syntax Notation

In the syntax notation used in this manual, syntactic categories are indicated by *italic* type, and literal words and characters in `constant width` type. Alternatives are listed on separate lines except in a few cases where a long set of alternatives is presented on one line, marked by the phrase "one of." An optional terminal or nonterminal symbol is indicated by the subscript "*opt*," so

> { *expression*$_{opt}$ }

indicates an optional expression enclosed in braces.

r.2   Lexical Conventions

A C++ program consists of one or more *files* (§r.3.3). A file is conceptually translated in several phases. The first phase is preprocessing (§r.16), which performs file inclusion and macro substitution. Preprocessing is controlled by directives introduced by lines having # as the first character other than white space (§r.2.1). The result of preprocessing is a sequence of tokens. Such a sequence a tokens, that is, a file after preprocessing is called a *translation unit*.

r.2.1 Tokens

There are five kinds of tokens: identifiers, keywords, literals, operators, and other separators. Blanks, horizontal and vertical tabs, newlines, formfeeds, and comments (collectively, "white space"), as described below, are ignored except as they serve to separate tokens. Some white space is required to separate otherwise adjacent identifiers, keywords, and constants.

   If the input stream has been parsed into tokens up to a given character, the next token is taken to be the longest string of characters that could possibly constitute a token.

r.2.2 Comments

The characters `/*` start a comment, which terminates with the characters `*/`. These comments do not nest. The characters `//` start a comment, which terminates at the end of the line on which they occur. The comment characters `//`, `/*`, and `*/` have no special meaning within a `//` comment and are treated just like other characters. Similarly, the comment characters `//` and `/*` have no special meaning within a `/*` comment.

r.2.3 Identifiers

An identifier is an arbitrarily long sequence of letters and digits. The first character must be a letter; the underscore _ counts as a letter. Upper- and lower-case letters are different. All characters are significant.

r.2.4 Keywords

The following identifiers are reserved for use as keywords, and may not be used otherwise:

```
asm       continue   float    new         signed     try
auto      default    for      operator    sizeof     typedef
break     delete     friend   private     static     union
case      do         goto     protected   struct     unsigned
catch     double     if       public      switch     virtual
char      else       inline   register    template   void
class     enum       int      return      this       volatile
const     extern     long     short       throw      while
```

In addition, identifiers containing a double underscore (_ _) are reserved for use by C++ implementations and standard libraries and should be avoided by users.

The ASCII representation of C++ programs uses the following characters as operators or for punctuation:

```
!    %    ^    &    *    (    )    -    +    =    {    }    |    ~
[    ]    \    ;    '    :    "    <    >    ?    ,    .    /
```

and the following character combinations are used as operators:

```
->    ++    --    .*    ->*    <<    >>     <=    >=    ==    !=    &&
||    *=    /=    %=    +=     -=    <<=    >>=   &=    ^=    |=    ::
```

Each is a single token.

In addition, the following tokens are used by the preprocessor:

```
#    ##
```

Certain implementation-dependent properties, such as the type of a `sizeof` (§r.5.3.2) and the ranges of fundamental types (§r.3.6.1), are defined in the standard header files (§r.16.4)

```
<float.h>    <limits.h>    <stddef.h>
```

These headers are part of the ANSI C standard. In addition the headers

```
<new.h>    <stdarg.h>    <stdlib.h>
```

define the types of the most basic library functions. The last two headers are part of the ANSI C standard; `<new.h>` is C++ specific.

r.2.5 Literals

There are several kinds of literals (often referred to as "constants").

> *literal:*
>> *integer-constant*
>> *character-constant*
>> *floating-constant*
>> *string-literal*

r.2.5.1 Integer Constants

An integer constant consisting of a sequence of digits is taken to be decimal (base ten) unless it begins with 0 (digit zero). A sequence of digits starting with 0 is taken to be an octal integer (base eight). The digits 8 and 9 are not octal digits. A sequence of digits preceded by 0x or 0X is taken to be a hexadecimal integer (base sixteen). The hexadecimal digits include a or A through f or F with decimal values ten through fifteen. For example, the number twelve can be written 12, 014, or 0XC.

The type of an integer constant depends on its form, value, and suffix. If it is decimal and has no suffix, it has the first of these types in which its value can be represented: int, long int, unsigned long int. If it is octal or hexadecimal and has no suffix, it has the first of these types in which its value can be represented: int, unsigned int, long int, unsigned long int. If it is suffixed by u or U, its type is the first of these types in which its value can be represented: unsigned int, unsigned long int. If it is suffixed by l or L, its type is the first of these types in which its value can be represented: long int, unsigned long int. If it is suffixed by ul, lu, uL, Lu, Ul, lU, UL, or LU, its type is unsigned long int.

r.2.5.2 Character Constants

A character constant is one or more characters enclosed in single quotes, as in 'x'. Single character constants have type char. The value of a single character constant is the numerical value of the character in the machine's character set. Multicharacter constants have type int. The value of a multicharacter constant is implementation dependent.

Certain nongraphic characters, the single quote ', the double quote ", the question mark ?, and the backslash \, may be represented according to the following table of escape sequences:

new-line	NL (LF)	\n
horizontal tab	HT	\t
vertical tab	VT	\v
backspace	BS	\b
carriage return	CR	\r
form feed	FF	\f

alert	BEL	\a
backslash	\	\\
question mark	?	\?
single quote	'	\'
double quote	"	\"
octal number	*ooo*	*ooo*
hex number	*hhh*	\x*hhh*

If the character following a backslash is not one of those specified, the behavior is undefined. An escape sequence specifies a single character.

The escape *ooo* consists of the backslash followed by one, two, or three octal digits that are taken to specify the value of the desired character. The escape \x*hhh* consists of the backslash followed by x followed by a sequence of hexadecimal digits that are taken to specify the value of the desired character. There is no limit to the number of hexadecimal digits in the sequence. A sequence of octal or hexadecimal digits is terminated by the first character that is not an octal digit or a hexadecimal digit, respectively. The value of a character constant is implementation dependent if it exceeds that of the largest char.

A character constant immediately preceded by the letter L, for example, L'ab', is a wide-character constant. A wide-character constant is of type wchar_t, an integral type (§r.3.6.1) defined in the standard header <stddef.h>. Wide-characters are intended for character sets where a character does not fit into a single byte.

r.2.5.3 Floating Constants

A floating constant consists of an integer part, a decimal point, a fraction part, an e or E, an optionally signed integer exponent, and an optional type suffix. The integer and fraction parts both consist of a sequence of decimal (base ten) digits. Either the integer part or the fraction part (not both) may be missing; either the decimal point or the letter e (or E) and the exponent (not both) may be missing. The type of a floating constant is double unless explicitly specified by a suffix. The suffixes f and F specify float, the suffixes l and L specify long double.

r.2.5.4 String Literals

A string literal is a sequence of characters (as defined in §r.2.5.2) surrounded by double quotes, as in "...". A string has type "array of char" and storage class *static* (§r.3.5), and is initialized with the given characters. Whether all string literals are distinct (that is, are stored in nonoverlapping objects) is implementation dependent. The effect of attempting to modify a string literal is undefined.

Adjacent string literals are concatenated. Characters in concatenated strings are kept distinct. For example,

        "\xA" "B"

contains the two characters '\xA' and 'B' after concatenation (and not the single hexadecimal character `'\xAB'`).

After any necessary concatenation `'\0'` is appended so that programs that scan a string can find its end. The size of a string is the number of its characters including this terminator. Within a string, the double quote character `"` must be preceded by a `\`.

A string literal immediately preceded by the letter `L`, for example, `L"asdf"`, is a wide-character string. A wide-character string is of type "array of `wchar_t`," where `wchar_t` is an integral type defined in the standard header `<stddef.h>`. Concatenation of ordinary and wide-character string literals is undefined.

r.3 Basic Concepts

A name denotes an object, a function, a set of functions, an enumerator, a type, a class member, a template, a value, or a label. A name is introduced into a program by a declaration. A name can be used only within a region of program text called its *scope*. A name has a type, which determines its use. A name used in more than one translation unit may (or may not) refer to the same object, function, type, template, or value in these translation units depending on the linkage (§r.3.3) specified in the translation units.

An object is a region of storage (§r.3.7). A named object has a storage class (§r.3.5) that determines its lifetime. The meaning of the values found in an object is determined by the type of the expression used to access it.

r.3.1 Declarations and Definitions

A declaration (§r.7) introduces one or more names into a program. A declaration is a definition unless it declares a function without specifying the body (§r.8.3), it contains the `extern` specifier (§r.7.1.1) and no initializer or function body, it is the declaration of a static data member in a class declaration (§r.9.4), it is a class name declaration (§r.9.1), or it is a typedef declaration (§r.7.1.3). The following, for example, are definitions:

```
int a;
extern const c = 1;
int f(int x) { return x+a; }
struct S { int a; int b; };
enum { up, down };
```

whereas these are just declarations:

```
extern int a;
extern const c;
int f(int);
struct S;
typedef int Int;
```

There must be exactly one definition of each object, function, class, and enumerator used in a program (§r.3.3). If a function is never called and its address is never taken, it need not be defined. Similarly, if the name of a class is used only in a way that does not require its definition to be known, it need not be defined.

r.3.2 Scopes

There are four kinds of scope: local, function, file, and class.

Local: A name declared in a block (§r.6.3) is local to that block and can be used only in it and in blocks enclosed by it after the point of declaration. Names of formal arguments for a function are treated as if they were declared in the outermost block of that function.

Function: Labels (§r.6.1) can be used anywhere in the function in which they are declared. Only labels have function scope.

File: A name declared outside all blocks (§r.6.3) and classes (§r.9) has file scope and can be used in the translation unit in which it is declared after the point of declaration. Names declared with *file* scope are said to be *global*.

Class: The name of a class member is local to its class and can be used only in a member function of that class (§r.9.3), after the . operator applied to an object of its class (§r.5.2.4) or a class derived from (§r.10) its class, after the −> operator applied to a pointer to an object of its class (§r.5.2.4) or a class derived from its class, or after the : : scope resolution operator (§r.5.1) applied to the name of its class or a class derived from its class. A name first declared by a `friend` declaration (§r.11.4) belongs to the same scope as the class containing the `friend` declaration. A class first declared in a return or argument type belongs to the global scope.

Special rules apply to names declared in function argument declarations (§r.8.2.5), and friend declarations (§r.11.4).

A name may be hidden by an explicit declaration of that same name in an enclosed block or in a class. A hidden class member name can still be used when it is qualified by its class name using the : : operator (§r.5.1, §r.9.4, §r.10). A hidden name of an object, function, type, or enumerator with file scope can still be used when it is qualified by the unary : : operator (§r.5.1). In addition, a class name (§r.9.1) may be hidden by the name of an object, function, or enumerator declared in the same scope. If a class and an object, function, or enumerator are declared in the same scope (in any order) with the same name the class name is hidden. A class name hidden by a name of an object, function, or enumerator in local or class scope can still be used when appropriately (§r.7.1.6) prefixed with `class`, `struct`, or `union`. Similarly, a hidden enumeration name can be used when appropriately (§r.7.1.6) prefixed with `enum`. The scope rules are summarized in §r.10.4.

The *point of declaration* for a name is immediately after its complete declarator (§r.8) and before its initializer (if any). For example,

```
int x = 12;
{ int x = x; }
```

Here the second x is initialized with its own (unspecified) value.

The point of declaration for an enumerator is immediately after the identifier that names it. For example,

```
enum { x = x };
```

Here, again, the enumerator x is initialized to its own (uninitialized) value.

r.3.3 Program and Linkage

A program consists of one or more files (§r.2) linked together. A file consists of a sequence of declarations.

A name of file scope that is explicitly declared static is local to its translation unit and can be used as a name for other objects, functions, and so on, in other translation units. Such names are said to have internal linkage. A name of file scope that is explicitly declared inline is local to its translation unit. A name of file scope that is explicitly declared const and not explicitly declared extern is local to its translation unit. So is the name of a class that has not been used in the declaration of an object, function, or class that is not local to its translation unit and has no static members (§r.9.4) and no noninline member functions (§r.9.3.2). Every declaration of a particular name of file scope that is not declared to have internal linkage in one of these ways in a multifile program refers to the same object (§r.3.7), function (§r.8.2.5), or class (§r.9). Such names are said to be external or to have external linkage. In particular, since it is not possible to declare a class name static, every use of a particular file scope class name that has been used in the declaration of an object or function with external linkage or has a static member or a noninline member function refers to the same class.

Typedef names (§r.7.1.3), enumerators (§r.7.2), and template names (§r.14) do not have external linkage.

Static class members (§r.9.4) have external linkage.

Noninline class member functions have external linkage. Inline class member functions must have exactly one definition in a program.

Local names (§r.3.2) explicitly declared extern have external linkage unless already declared static (§r.7.1.1).

The types specified in all declarations of a particular external name must be identical except for the use of typedef names (§r.7.1.3) and unspecified array bounds (§r.8.2.4). There must be exactly one definition for each function, object, class and enumerator used in a program. If, however, a function is never called and its address is never taken, it need not be defined. Similarly, if the name of a class is used only in a way that does not require its definition to be known, it need not be defined.

A function may be defined only in file or class scope.

Linkage to non-C++ declarations can be achieved using a *linkage-specification* (§r.7.4).

r.3.4 Start and Termination

A program must contain a function called `main()`. This function is the designated start of the program. This function is not predefined by the compiler, it cannot be overloaded, and its type is implementation dependent. It is recommended that the two examples below be allowed on any implementation and that any further arguments required be added after `argv`. The function `main()` may be defined as

```
int main() { /* ... */ }
```

or

```
int main(int argc, char* argv[]) { /* ... */ }
```

In the latter form `argc` shall be the number of parameters passed to the program from an environment in which the program is run. If `argc` is nonzero these parameters shall be supplied as zero-terminated strings in `argv[0]` through `argv[argc-1]` and `argv[0]` shall be the name used to invoke the program or `""`. It is guaranteed that `argv[argc]==0`.

The function `main()` may not be called from within a program. The linkage (§r.3.3) of `main()` is implementation dependent. The address of `main()` cannot be taken and `main()` may not be declared `inline` or `static`.

Calling the function

```
void exit(int);
```

declared in `<stdlib.h>` terminates the program. The argument value is returned to the program's environment as the value of the program.

A return statement in `main()` has the effect of calling `exit()` with the return value as the argument.

The initialization of nonlocal static objects (§r.3.5) in a translation unit is done before the first use of any function or object defined in that translation unit. Such initializations (§r.8.4, §r.9.4, §r.12.1, §r.12.6.1) may be done before the first statement of `main()` or deferred to any point in time before the first use of a function or object defined in that translation unit. The default initialization of all static objects to zero (§r.8.4) is performed before any dynamic (that is, run-time) initialization. No further order is imposed on the initialization of objects from different translation units. The initialization of local static objects is described in §r.8.4.

Destructors (§r.12.4) for initialized static objects are called when returning from `main()` and when calling `exit()`. Destruction is done in reverse order of initialization. The function `atexit()` from `<stdlib.h>` can be used to specify that a function must be called at exit. If `atexit()` is to be called, objects initialized before an `atexit()` call may not be destroyed until after the function specified in the `atexit()` call has been called. Where a C++ implementation coexists with a C implementation, any actions specified by the C implementation to take place after the `atexit()` functions have been called take place after all destructors have been called.

Calling the function

```
void abort();
```

declared in `<stdlib.h>` terminates the program without executing destructors for static objects and without calling the functions passed to `atexit()`.

r.3.5 Storage Classes

There are two declarable storage classes: automatic and static.

> *Automatic* objects are local to each invocation of a block.

> *Static* objects exist and retain their values throughout the execution of the entire program.

Automatic objects are initialized (§r.12.1) each time the control flow reaches their definition and destroyed (§r.12.4) on exit from their block (§r.6.7).

A named automatic object may not be destroyed before the end of its block nor may an automatic named object of a class with a constructor or a destructor with side effects be eliminated even if it appears to be unused.

Similarly, a global object of a class with a constructor or a destructor with side effects may not be eliminated even if it appears to be unused.

Static objects are initialized and destroyed as described in §r.3.4 and §r.6.7. Some objects are not associated with names; see §r.5.3.3 and §r.12.2. All global objects have storage class *static*. Local objects and class members can be given static storage class by explicit use of the `static` storage class specifier (§r.7.1.1).

r.3.6 Types

There are two kinds of types: fundamental types and derived types.

r.3.6.1 Fundamental Types

There are several fundamental types. The standard header `<limits.h>` specifies the largest and smallest values of each for an implementation.

Objects declared as characters (`char`) are large enough to store any member of the implementation's basic character set. If a character from this set is stored in a character variable, its value is equivalent to the integer code of that character. Characters may be explicitly declared `unsigned` or `signed`. Plain `char`, `signed char`, and `unsigned char` are three distinct types. A `char`, a `signed char`, and an `unsigned char` consume the same amount of space.

Up to three sizes of integer, declared `short int`, `int`, and `long int`, are available. Longer integers provide no less storage than shorter ones, but the implementation may make either short integers or long integers, or both, equivalent to plain integers. Plain integers have the natural size suggested by the machine architecture; the other sizes are provided to meet special needs.

For each of the types signed char, short, int, and long, there exists a corresponding unsigned type, which occupies the same amount of storage and has the same alignment requirements. An *alignment requirement* is an implementation-dependent restriction on the value of a pointer to an object of a given type (§r.5.4).

Unsigned integers, declared unsigned, obey the laws of arithmetic modulo 2^n where n is the number of bits in the representation. This implies that unsigned arithmetic does not overflow.

There are three *floating* types: float, double, and long double. The type double provides no less precision than float, and the type long double provides no less precision than double. An implementation will define the characteristics of the fundamental floating point types in the standard header <float.h>.

Types char, int of all sizes, and enumerations (§r.7.2) are collectively called *integral* types. *Integral* and *floating* types are collectively called *arithmetic* types.

The void type specifies an empty set of values. It is used as the return type for functions that do not return a value. No object of type void may be declared. Any expression may be explicitly converted to type void (§r.5.4); the resulting expression may be used only as an expression statement (§r.6.2), as the left operand of a comma expression (§r.5.18), or as a second or third operand of ? : (§r.5.16).

r.3.6.2 Derived Types

There is a conceptually infinite number of derived types constructed from the fundamental types in the following ways:

arrays of objects of a given type, §r.8.2.4;

functions, which take arguments of given types and return objects of a given type, §r.8.2.5;

pointers to objects or functions of a given type, §r.8.2.1;

references to objects or functions of a given type, §r.8.2.2;

constants, which are values of a given type, §r.7.1.6;

classes containing a sequence of objects of various types (§r.9), a set of functions for manipulating these objects (§r.9.3), and a set of restrictions on the access to these objects and functions, §r.11;

structures, which are classes without default access restrictions, §r.11;

unions, which are structures capable of containing objects of different types at different times, §r.9.5;

pointers to class members, which identify members of a given type within objects of a given class, §r.8.2.3.

In general, these methods of constructing objects can be applied recursively; restrictions are mentioned in §r.8.2.1, §r.8.2.4, §r.8.2.5, and §r.8.2.2.

A pointer to objects of a type T is referred to as a "pointer to T." For example, a pointer to an object of type int is referred to as "pointer to int" and a pointer to an object of class X is called a "pointer to X."

Objects of type void* (pointer to void), const void*, and volatile void* can be used to point to objects of unknown type. A void* must have enough bits to hold any object pointer.

Except for pointers to static members, text referring to "pointers" does not apply to pointers to members.

r.3.6.3 Type Names

Fundamental and derived types can be given names by the typedef mechanism (§r.7.1.3), and families of types and functions can be specified and named by the template mechanism (§r.14).

r.3.7 Lvalues

An *object* is a region of storage; an *lvalue* is an expression referring to an object or function. An obvious example of an lvalue expression is the name of an object. Some operators yield lvalues. For example, if E is an expression of pointer type, then *E is an lvalue expression referring to the object to which E points. The name "lvalue" comes from the assignment expression E1 = E2 in which the left operand E1 must be an lvalue expression. The discussion of each operator in §r.5 indicates whether it expects lvalue operands and whether it yields an lvalue. An lvalue is *modifiable* if it is not a function name, an array name, or const.

r.4   Standard Conversions

Some operators may, depending on their operands, cause conversion of the value of an operand from one type to another. This section summarizes the conversions demanded by most ordinary operators and explains the result to be expected from such conversions; it will be supplemented as required by the discussion of each operator. These conversions are also used in initialization (§r.8.4, §r.8.4.3, §r.12.8, §r.12.1). §r.12.3 and §r.13.2 describe user-defined conversions and their interaction with standard conversions. The result of a conversion is an lvalue only if the result is a reference (§r.8.2.2).

r.4.1 Integral Promotions

A char, a short int, enumerator, object of enumeration type (§r.7.2), or an int bit-field (§r.9.6) (in both their signed and unsigned varieties) may be used wherever an integer may be used. If an int can represent all the values of the original type, the value is converted to int; otherwise it is converted to unsigned int. This process is called *integral promotion*.

r.4.2 Integral Conversions

When an integer is converted to an *unsigned* type, the value is the least unsigned integer congruent to the signed integer (modulo 2^n where n is the number of bits used to represent the unsigned type). In a two's complement representation, this conversion is conceptual and there is no change in the bit pattern.

When an integer is converted to a signed type, the value is unchanged if it can be represented in the new type; otherwise the value is implementation dependent.

r.4.3 Float and Double

Single-precision floating point arithmetic may be used for float expressions. When a less precise floating value is converted to an equally or more precise floating type, the value is unchanged. When a more precise floating value is converted to a less precise floating type and the value is within representable range, the result may be either the next higher or the next lower representable value. If the result is out of range, the behavior is undefined.

r.4.4 Floating and Integral

Conversion of a floating value to an integral type truncates; that is, the fractional part is discarded. Such conversions are machine dependent; for example, the direction of truncation of negative numbers varies from machine to machine. The result is undefined if the value cannot be represented in the integral type.

Conversions of integral values to floating type are as mathematically correct as the hardware allows. Loss of precision occurs if an integral value cannot be represented exactly as a value of the floating type.

r.4.5 Arithmetic Conversions

Many operators cause conversions and yield result types in a similar way. This pattern will be called the "usual arithmetic conversions."

> If either operand is of type long double, the other is converted to long double.

> Otherwise, if either operand is double, the other is converted to double.

Otherwise, if either operand is `float`, the other is converted to `float`.

Otherwise, the integral promotions (§r.4.1) are performed on both operands.

Then, if either operand is `unsigned long` the other is converted to `unsigned long`.

Otherwise, if one operand is a `long int` and the other `unsigned int`, then if a `long int` can represent all the values of an `unsigned int`, the `unsigned int` is converted to a `long int`; otherwise both operands are converted to `unsigned long int`.

Otherwise, if either operand is `long`, the other is converted to `long`.

Otherwise, if either operand is `unsigned`, the other is converted to `unsigned`.

Otherwise, both operands are `int`.

r.4.6 Pointer Conversions

The following conversions may be performed wherever pointers (§r.8.2.1) are assigned, initialized, compared, or otherwise used:

A constant expression (§r.5.19) that evaluates to zero is converted to a pointer, commonly called the null pointer. It is guaranteed that this value will produce a pointer distinguishable from a pointer to any object or function.

A pointer to any non-`const` and non-`volatile` object type may be converted to a `void*`.

A pointer to function may be converted to a `void*` provided a `void*` has sufficient bits to hold it.

A pointer to a class may be converted to a pointer to an accessible base class of that class (§r.10) provided the conversion is unambiguous (§r.10.1); a base class is accessible if its public members are accessible (§r.11.1). The result of the conversion is a pointer to the base class sub-object of the derived class object. The null pointer (0) is converted into itself.

An expression with type "array of T" may be converted to a pointer to the initial element of the array.

An expression with type "function returning `T`" is converted to "pointer to function returning `T`" except when used as the operand of the address-of operator `&` or the function call operator `()`.

r.4.7 Reference Conversions

The following conversion may be performed wherever references (§r.8.2.2) are initialized (including argument passing (§r.5.2.2) and function value return (§r.6.6.3)) or otherwise used:

A reference to a class may be converted to a reference to an accessible base class (§r.10, §r.11.1) of that class (§r.8.4.3) provided this conversion can be done unambiguously (§r.10.1.1). The result of the conversion is a reference to the base class sub-object of the derived class object.

r.4.8 Pointers to Members

The following conversion may be performed wherever pointers to members (§r.8.2.3) are initialized, assigned, compared, or otherwise used:

A constant expression (§r.5.19) that evaluates to zero is converted to a pointer to member. It is guaranteed that this value will produce a pointer to member distinguishable from any other pointer to member.

A pointer to a member of a class may be converted to a pointer to member of a class derived from that class provided the (inverse) conversion from the derived class to the base class pointer is accessible (§r.11.1) and provided this conversion can be done unambiguously (§r.10.1.1).

The rule for conversion of pointers to members (from pointer to member of base to pointer to member of derived) appears inverted compared to the rule for pointers to objects (from pointer to derived to pointer to base) (§r.4.6, §r.10). This inversion is necessary to ensure type safety.

Note that a pointer to member is not a pointer to object or a pointer to function and the rules for conversions of such pointers do not apply to pointers to members. In particular, a pointer to member cannot be converted to a `void*`.

r.5 Expressions

This section defines the syntax, order of evaluation, and meaning of expressions. An expression is a sequence of operators and operands that specifies a computation. An expression may result in a value and may cause side effects.

Operators can be overloaded, that is, given meaning when applied to expressions of class type (§r.9). Uses of overloaded operators are transformed into function calls as described in §r.13.4. Overloaded operators obey the rules for syntax specified in this section, but the requirements of operand type, lvalue, and evaluation order are replaced by the rules for function call. Relations between operators, such as ++a meaning a+=1, are not guaranteed for overloaded operators (§r.13.4).

This section defines the operators when applied to types for which they have not been overloaded. Operator overloading cannot modify the rules for operators applied to types for which they are defined by the language itself.

The order of evaluation of subexpressions is determined by the precedence and grouping of the operators. The usual mathematical rules for associativity and commutativity of operators may be applied only where the operators really are associative and commutative. Except where noted, the order of evaluation of operands of individual operators is undefined. In particular, if a value is modified twice in an expression, the result of the expression is undefined except where an ordering is guaranteed by the operators involved. For example,

```
i = v[i++];      // the value of 'i' is undefined
i=7,i++,i++;     // 'i' becomes 9
```

The handling of overflow and divide check in expression evaluation is implementation dependent. Most existing implementations of C++ ignore integer overflows. Treatment of division by zero and all floating point exceptions vary among machines, and is usually adjustable by a library function.

Except where noted, operands of types const T, volatile T, T&, const T&, and volatile T& can be used as if they were of the plain type T. Similarly, except where noted, operands of type T*const and T*volatile can be used as if they were of the plain type T*. Similarly, a plain T can be used where a volatile T or a const T is required. These rules apply in combination so that, except where noted, a const T*volatile can be used where a T* is required. Such uses do not count as standard conversions when considering overloading resolution (§r.13.2).

If an expression has the type "reference to T" (§r.8.2.2, §r.8.4.3), the value of the expression is the object of type "T" denoted by the reference. The expression is an lvalue. A reference can be thought of as a name of an object.

User-defined conversions of class objects to and from fundamental types, pointers, and so on, can be defined (§r.12.3). If unambiguous (§r.13.2), such conversions may be applied by the compiler wherever a class object appears as an operand of an operator, as an initializer (§r.8.4), as the controlling expression in a selection (§r.6.4) or iteration (§r.6.5) statement, as a function return value (§r.6.6.3), or as a function argument (§r.5.2.2).

r.5.1 Primary Expressions

Primary expressions are literals, names, and names qualified by the scope resolution operator : :.

> *primary-expression:*
> > *literal*
> > `this`
> > : : *identifier*
> > : : *operator-function-name*
> > : : *qualified-name*
> > (*expression*)
> > *name*

A *literal* is a primary expression. Its type depends on its form (§r.2.5).

In the body of a nonstatic member function (§r.9.3), the keyword `this` names a pointer to the object for which the function was invoked. The keyword `this` cannot be used outside a class member function body.

The operator : : followed by an *identifier*, a *qualified-name*, or an *operator-function-name* is a primary expression. Its type is specified by the declaration of the identifier, name, or *operator-function-name*. The result is the identifier, name, or *operator-function-name*. The result is an lvalue if the identifier is. The identifier or *operator-function-name* must be of file scope. Use of : : allows a type, an object, a function, or an enumerator to be referred to even if its identifier has been hidden (§r.3.2).

A parenthesized expression is a primary expression whose type and value are identical to those of the unadorned expression. The presence of parentheses does not affect whether the expression is an lvalue.

A *name* is a restricted form of a *primary-expression* that can appear after . and -> (§r.5.2.4):

> *name:*
> > *identifier*
> > *operator-function-name*
> > *conversion-function-name*
> > ˜ *class-name*
> > *qualified-name*

An *identifier* is a *name* provided it has been suitably declared (§r.7). For *operator-function-name*s, see §r.13.4. For *conversion-function-name*s, see §r.12.3.2. A *class-name* prefixed by ˜ denotes a destructor; see §r.12.4.

> *qualified-name:*
> > *qualified-class-name* : : *name*

A *qualified-class-name* (§r.7.1.6) followed by : : and the name of a member of that class (§r.9.2), or a member of a base of that class (§r.10), is a *qualified-name*; its type is the type of the member. The result is the member. The result is an lvalue if the member is. The *class-name* may be hidden by a nontype name, in which case the *class-name* is still found and used. Where *class-name* : : *class-name* or *class-name* : : ˜ *class-name* is used, the two *class-name*s must refer to the same class; this notation names constructors (§r.12.1) and destructors (§r.12.4), respectively. Multiply qualified names, such as N1::N2::N3::n, can be used to refer to nested types (§r.9.7).

r.5.2 Postfix Expressions

Postfix expressions group left-to-right.

> *postfix-expression:*
>> *primary-expression*
>> *postfix-expression* [*expression*]
>> *postfix-expression* (*expression-list$_{opt}$*)
>> *simple-type-name* (*expression-list$_{opt}$*)
>> *postfix-expression* . *name*
>> *postfix-expression* −> *name*
>> *postfix-expression* ++
>> *postfix-expression* −−
>
> *expression-list:*
>> *assignment-expression*
>> *expression-list* , *assignment-expression*

r.5.2.1 Subscripting

A postfix expression followed by an expression in square brackets is a postfix expression. The intuitive meaning is that of a subscript. One of the expressions must have the type "pointer to T" and the other must be of integral type. The type of the result is "T." The expression E1[E2] is identical (by definition) to *((E1)+(E2)). See §r.5.3 and §r.5.7 for details of * and + and §r.8.2.4 for details of arrays.

r.5.2.2 Function Call

A function call is a postfix expression followed by parentheses containing a possibly empty, comma-separated list of expressions which constitute the actual arguments to the function. The postfix expression must be of type "function returning T," "pointer to function returning T," or "reference to function returning T," and the result of the function call is of type "T."

When a function is called, each formal argument is initialized (§r.8.4.3, §r.12.8, §r.12.1) with its actual argument. Standard (§r.4) and user-defined (§r.12.3) conversions are performed. A function may change the values of its nonconstant formal arguments, but these changes cannot affect the values of the actual arguments except where a formal argument is of a non-const reference type (§r.8.2.2). Where a formal argument is of reference type a temporary variable is introduced if needed (§r.7.1.6, §r.2.5, §r.2.5.4, §r.8.2.4, §r.12.2). In addition, it is possible to modify the values of nonconstant objects through pointer arguments.

A function may be declared to accept fewer arguments (by declaring default arguments §r.8.2.6) or more arguments (by using the ellipsis, . . . §r.8.2.5) than are specified in the function definition (§r.8.3).

A function can be called only if a declaration of it is accessible from the scope of the call. This implies that, except where the ellipsis (. . .) is used, a formal argument is available for each actual argument.

Any actual argument of type `float` for which there is no formal argument is converted to `double` before the call; any of `char`, `short`, enumeration, or a bit-field type for which there is no formal argument are converted to `int` or `unsigned` by integral promotion (§r.4.1). An object of a class for which no formal argument is declared is passed as a data structure.

An object of a class for which a formal argument is declared is passed by initializing the formal argument with the actual argument by a constructor call before the function is entered (§r.12.2, §r.12.8).

The order of evaluation of arguments is undefined; take note that compilers differ. All side effects of argument expressions take effect before the function is entered. The order of evaluation of the postfix expression and the argument expression list is undefined.

Recursive calls are permitted.

A function call is an lvalue only if the result type is a reference.

r.5.2.3 Explicit Type Conversion

A *simple-type-name* (§r.7.1.6) followed by a parenthesized *expression-list* constructs a value of the specified type given the expression list. If the expression list specifies more than a single value, the type must be a class with a suitably declared constructor (§r.8.4, §r.12.1).

A *simple-type-name* (§r.7.1.6) followed by a (empty) pair of parentheses constructs a value of the specified type. If the type is a class with a suitably declared constructor that constructor will be called; otherwise the result is an undefined value of the specified type. See also (§r.5.4).

r.5.2.4 Class Member Access

A postfix expression followed by a dot (`.`) followed by a *name* is a postfix expression. The first expression must be a class object, and the *name* must name a member of that class. The result is the named member of the object, and it is an lvalue if the member is an lvalue.

A postfix expression followed by an arrow (`->`) followed by a *name* is a postfix expression. The first expression must be a pointer to a class object and the *name* must name a member of that class. The result is the named member of the object to which the pointer points and it is an lvalue if the member is an lvalue. Thus the expression `E1->MOS` is the same as `(*E1).MOS`.

Note that "class objects" can be structures (§r.9.2) and unions (§r.9.5). Classes are discussed in §r.9.

r.5.2.5 Increment and Decrement

The value obtained by applying a postfix ++ is the value of the operand. The operand must be a modifiable lvalue. The type of the operand must be an arithmetic type or a pointer type. After the result is noted, the object is incremented by 1. The type of the result is the same as the type of the operand, but it is not an lvalue. See also §r.5.7 and §r.5.17.

The operand of postfix −− is decremented analogously to the postfix ++ operator.

r.5.3 Unary Operators

Expressions with unary operators group right-to-left.

> *unary-expression:*
>> *postfix-expression*
>> ++ *unary-expression*
>> −− *unary-expression*
>> *unary-operator cast-expression*
>> sizeof *unary-expression*
>> sizeof (*type-name*)
>> *allocation-expression*
>> *deallocation-expression*

> *unary-operator:* one of
>> *   &   +   −   !   ˜

The unary * operator means *indirection*: the expression must be a pointer, and the result is an lvalue referring to the object to which the expression points. If the type of the expression is "pointer to T," the type of the result is "T."

The result of the unary & operator is a pointer to its operand. The operand must be a function, an lvalue, or a *qualified-name*. In the first two cases, if the type of the expression is "T," the type of the result is "pointer to T." In particular, the address of an object of type const T has type const T*; volatile is handled similarly. For a *qualified-name*, if the member is not static and of type "T" in class "C," the type of the result is "pointer to member of C of type T." For a static member of type T, the type is plain "pointer to T." The address of an overloaded function (§r.13) can be taken only in an initialization or an assignment where the left side uniquely determines which version of the overloaded function is referred to (§r.13.3).

The operand of the unary + operator must have arithmetic or pointer type and the result is the value of the argument. Integral promotion is performed on integral operands. The type of the result is the type of the promoted operand.

The operand of the unary − operator must have arithmetic type and the result is the negation of its operand. Integral promotion is performed on integral operands. The negative of an unsigned quantity is computed by subtracting its value from 2^n, where n is the number of bits in the promoted operand. The type of the result is the type of the promoted operand.

The operand of the logical negation operator ! must have arithmetic type or be a pointer; its value is 1 if the value of its operand is 0 and 0 if the value of its operand is nonzero. The type of the result is int.

The operand of ~ must have integral type; the result is the one's complement of its operand. Integral promotions are performed. The type of the result is the type of the promoted operand.

r.5.3.1 Increment and Decrement

The operand of prefix ++ is incremented by 1. The operand must be a modifiable lvalue. The type of the operand must be an arithmetic type or a pointer type. The value is the new value of the operand; it is an lvalue. The expression ++x is equivalent to x+=1. See the discussions of addition (§r.5.7) and assignment operators (§r.5.17) for information on conversions.

The operand of prefix -- is decremented analogously to the prefix ++ operator.

r.5.3.2 Sizeof

The sizeof operator yields the size, in bytes, of its operand. The operand is either an expression, which is not evaluated, or a parenthesized type name. The sizeof operator may not be applied to a function, a bit-field, an undefined class, the type void, or an array with an unspecified dimension. A *byte* is undefined by the language except in terms of the value of sizeof; sizeof(char) is 1.

When applied to a reference, the result is the size of the referenced object. When applied to a class, the result is the number of bytes in an object of that class including any padding required for placing such objects in an array. The size of any class or class object is larger than zero. When applied to an array, the result is the total number of bytes in the array. This implies that the size of an array of *n* elements is *n* times the size of an element.

The sizeof operator may be applied to a pointer to a function, but not to a function.

The result is a constant of type size_t, an implementation-dependent unsigned integral type defined in the standard header <stddef.h>.

r.5.3.3 New

The new operator attempts to create an object of the *type-name* (§r.8.1) to which it is applied. This type must be an object type; functions cannot be allocated this way, though pointers to functions can.

> *allocation-expression:*
> $::_{opt}$ new *placement*$_{opt}$ *new-type-name new-initializer*$_{opt}$
> $::_{opt}$ new *placement*$_{opt}$ (*type-name*) *new-initializer*$_{opt}$

> *placement:*
> (*expression-list*)

new-type-name:
> *type-specifier-list new-declarator_{opt}*

new-declarator:
> * *cv-qualifier-list_{opt} new-declarator_{opt}*
> *class-name* :: * *cv-qualifier-list_{opt} new-declarator_{opt}*
> *new-declarator_{opt}* [*expression*]

new-initializer:
> (*initializer-list_{opt}*)

The lifetime of an object created by `new` is not restricted to the scope in which it is created. The `new` operator returns a pointer to the object created. When that object is an array, a pointer to its initial element is returned. For example, both `new int` and `new int[10]` return an `int*` and the type of `new int[i][10]` is `int (*)[10]`. Where an array type (§r.8.2.4) is specified all array dimensions but the first must be constant expressions (§r.5.19) with positive values. The first array dimension can be a general *expression* even when the *type-name* is used (despite the general restriction of array dimensions in *type-name*s to *constant-expression*s (§r.5.19)).

This implies that an `operator new()` can be called with the argument zero. In this case, a pointer to an object is returned. Repeated such calls return pointers to distinct objects.

The *type-specifier-list* may not contain `const`, `volatile`, class declarations, or enumeration declarations.

The `new` operator will call the function `operator new()` to obtain storage (§r.12.5). A first argument of `sizeof(T)` is supplied when allocating an object of type `T`. The *placement* syntax can be used to supply additional arguments. For example, `new T` results in a call of `operator new(sizeof(T))` and `new(2,f) T` results in a call `operator new(sizeof(T),2,f)`.

The *placement* syntax can be used only provided an `operator new()` with suitable argument types (§r.13.2) has been declared.

When an object of a nonclass type (including arrays of class objects) is created with operator new, the global `::operator new()` is used. When an object of a class `T` is created with operator new, `T::operator new()` is used if it exists (using the usual lookup rules for finding members of a class and its base classes; §r.10.1.1); otherwise the global `::operator new()` is used. Using `::new` ensures that the global `::operator new()` is used even if `T::operator new()` exists.

A *new-initializer* may be supplied in an *allocation-expression*. For objects of classes with a constructor (§r.12.1) this argument list will be used in a constructor call; otherwise the initializer must be of the form (*expression*) or (). If present, the expression will be used to initialize the object; if not, the object will start out with an undefined value.

If a class has a constructor an object of that class can be created by `new` only if suitable arguments are provided or if the class has a default constructor (§r.12.1). Whether `operator new` allocates the memory itself or leaves that up to the constructor when creating an object of a class with a constructor is implementation dependent. Access and ambiguity control are done for both `operator new()` and the constructor; see §r.12.

No initializers can be specified for arrays. Arrays of objects of a class with constructors can be created by operator `new` only if the class has a default constructor (§r.12.1). In that case, the default constructor will be called for each element of the array.

Initialization is done only if the value returned by `operator new()` is nonzero. If the value returned by the `operator new()` is 0 (the null pointer) the value of the expression is 0.

The order of evaluation of the call to an `operator new()` to get memory and the evaluation of arguments to constructors is undefined. It is also undefined if the arguments to a constructor are evaluated if `operator new()` returns 0.

In a *new-type-name* used as the operand for new, parentheses may not be used. This implies that

```
new int(*[10])();        // error
```

is an error because the binding is

```
(new int) (*[10])();     // error
```

Objects of general type can be expressed using the explicitly parenthesized version of the new operator. For example,

```
new (int (*[10])());
```

allocates an array of 10 pointers to functions (taking no argument and returning `int`).

The *new-type-name* in an *allocation-expression* is the longest possible sequence of *new-declarator*s. This prevents ambiguities between declarator operators &, *, [], and their expression counterparts. For example,

```
new int*i;       // syntax error: parsed as '(new int*) i'
                 //               not as '(new int)*i'
```

The * is the pointer declarator and not the multiplication operator.

r.5.3.4 Delete

The `delete` operator destroys an object created by the new operator.

> *deallocation-expression:*
> ::ₒₚₜ `delete` *cast-expression*
> ::ₒₚₜ `delete` [ ] *cast-expression*

The result has type `void`. The operand of `delete` must be a pointer returned by new. The effect of applying `delete` to a pointer not obtained from the new operator without a placement specification is undefined and usually harmful. Deleting a pointer with the value zero, however, is guaranteed to be harmless.

The effect of accessing a deleted object is undefined and the deletion of an object may change its value. Furthermore, if the expression denoting the object in a `delete` expression is a modifiable lvalue, its value is undefined after the deletion.

A pointer to constant cannot be deleted.

The `delete` operator will invoke the destructor (if any, §r.12.4) for the object pointed to.

To free the storage pointed to, the `delete` operator will call the function `operator delete()`; see §r.12.5. For objects of a nonclass type (including arrays of class objects), the global `::operator delete()` is used. For an object of a class T, `T::operator delete()` is used if it exists (using the usual lookup rules for finding members of a class and its base classes; §r.10.1.1); otherwise the global `::operator delete()` is used. Using `::delete` ensures that the global `::operator delete()` is used even if `T::operator delete()` exists.

The form

> `delete [ ]` *cast-expression*

is used to delete arrays. The expression points to an array. The destructors (if any) for the objects pointed to will be invoked.

The effect of deleting an array with the plain `delete` syntax is undefined, as is deleting an individual object with the `delete[]` syntax.

r.5.4 Explicit Type Conversion

An explicit type conversion can be expressed using either functional notation (§r.5.2.3) or the *cast* notation.

> *cast-expression:*
> > *unary-expression*
> > (*type-name*) *cast-expression*

The *cast* notation is needed to express conversion to a type that does not have a *simple-type-name*.

Types may not be defined in casts.

Any type conversion not mentioned below and not explicitly defined by the user (§r.12.3) is an error.

Any type that can be converted to another by a standard conversion (§r.4) can also be converted by explicit conversion and the meaning is the same.

A pointer may be explicitly converted to any integral type large enough to hold it. The mapping function is implementation dependent, but is intended to be unsurprising to those who know the addressing structure of the underlying machine.

A value of integral type may be explicitly converted to a pointer. A pointer converted to an integer of sufficient size (if any such exists on the implementation) and back to the same pointer type will have its original value; mappings between pointers and integers are otherwise implementation dependent.

A pointer to one object type may be explicitly converted to a pointer to another object type (subject to the restrictions mentioned in this section). The resulting pointer may cause addressing exceptions on use if the subject pointer does not refer to an object suitably aligned in storage. It is guaranteed that a pointer to an object of a given size may be converted to a pointer to an object of the same or smaller size and back again without change. Different machines may differ in the number of bits in pointers and in alignment requirements for objects. Aggregates are aligned on the strictest boundary required by any of their constituents. A void* is considered a pointer to object type.

A pointer to a class B may be explicitly converted to a pointer to a class D that has B as a direct or indirect base class if an unambiguous conversion from D to B exists (§r.4.6, §r.10.1.1) and if B is not a virtual base class (§r.10.1). Such a cast from a base to a derived class assumes that the object of the base class is a sub-object of an object of the derived class; the resulting pointer points to the enclosing object of the derived class. If the object of the base class is not a sub-object of an object of the derived class, the cast may cause an exception.

The null pointer (0) is converted into itself.

A yet undefined class may be used in a pointer cast, in which case no assumptions will be made about class lattices (§r.10.1).

An object may be explicitly converted to a reference type X& if a pointer to that object may be explicitly converted to an X*. Constructors or conversion functions are not called as the result of a cast to a reference. Conversion of a reference to a base class to a reference to a derived class is handled similarly to the conversion of a pointer to a base class to a pointer to a derived class with respect to ambiguity, virtual classes, and so on.

The result of a cast to a reference type is an lvalue; the results of other casts are not. Operations performed on the result of a pointer or reference cast refer to the same object as the original (uncast) expression.

A pointer to function may be explicitly converted to a pointer to an object type provided the object pointer type has enough bits to hold the function pointer. A pointer to an object type may be explicitly converted to a pointer to function provided the function pointer type has enough bits to hold the object pointer. In both cases, use of the resulting pointer may cause addressing exceptions, or worse, if the subject pointer does not refer to suitable storage.

A pointer to a function may be explicitly converted to a pointer to a function of a different type. The effect of calling a function through a pointer to a function type that differs from the type used in the definition of the function is undefined. See also §r.4.6.

An object or a value may be converted to a class object (only) if an appropriate constructor or conversion operator has been declared (§r.12.3).

A pointer to member may be explicitly converted into a different pointer to member type when the two types are both pointers to members of the same class or when the two types are pointers to member functions of classes one of which is unambiguously derived from the other (§r.4.8).

A pointer to an object of a const type can be cast into a pointer to a non-const type. The resulting pointer will refer to the original object. An object of a `const` type or a reference to an object of a `const` type can be cast into a reference to a non-`const` type. The resulting reference will refer to the original object. The result of attempting to modify that object through such a pointer or reference will either cause an addressing exception or be the same as if the original pointer or reference had referred a non-`const` object. It is implementation dependent whether the addressing exception occurs.

A pointer to an object of a `volatile` type can be cast into a pointer to a non-`volatile` type. The resulting pointer will refer to the original object. An object of a `volatile` type or a reference to an object of a `volatile` type can be cast into a reference to a non-`volatile` type.

r.5.5 Pointer-to-Member Operators

The pointer-to-member operators `->*` and `.*` group left-to-right.

> *pm-expression:*
>> *cast-expression*
>> *pm-expression* `.*` *cast-expression*
>> *pm-expression* `->*` *cast-expression*

The binary operator `.*` binds its second operand, which must be of type "pointer to member of class `T`" to its first operand, which must be of class `T` or of a class of which `T` is an unambiguous and accessible base class. The result is an object or a function of the type specified by the second operand.

The binary operator `->*` binds its second operand, which must be of type "pointer to member of `T`" to its first operand, which must be of type "pointer to `T`" or "pointer to a class of which `T` is an unambiguous and accessible base class." The result is an object or a function of the type specified by the second operand.

If the result of `.*` or `->*` is a function, then that result can be used only as the operand for the function call operator `()`. For example,

```
(ptr_to_obj->*ptr_to_mfct)(10);
```

calls the member function denoted by `ptr_to_mfct` for the object pointed to by `ptr_to_obj`. The result of an `.*` expression or a `->*` expression is an lvalue if its second operand is an lvalue.

r.5.6 Multiplicative Operators

The multiplicative operators `*`, `/`, and `%` group left-to-right.

> *multiplicative-expression:*
>> *pm-expression*
>> *multiplicative-expression* `*` *pm-expression*
>> *multiplicative-expression* `/` *pm-expression*
>> *multiplicative-expression* `%` *pm-expression*

The operands of `*` and `/` must have arithmetic type; the operands of `%` must have integral type. The usual arithmetic conversions (§r.4.5) are performed on the operands and determine the type of the result.

The binary * operator indicates multiplication.

The binary / operator yields the quotient, and the binary % operator yields the remainder from the division of the first expression by the second. If the second operand of / or % is 0 the result is undefined; otherwise (a/b)*b + a%b is equal to a. If both operands are nonnegative then the remainder is nonnegative; if not, the sign of the remainder is implementation dependent.

r.5.7 Additive Operators

The additive operators + and − group left-to-right. The usual arithmetic conversions (§r.4.5) are performed for operands of arithmetic type.

>   *additive-expression:*
>   *multiplicative-expression*
>   *additive-expression* + *multiplicative-expression*
>   *additive-expression* − *multiplicative-expression*

The operands must be of arithmetic or pointer type. The result of the + operator is the sum of the operands. A pointer to an object in an array and a value of any integral type may be added. The result is a pointer of the same type as the original pointer, which points to another object in the same array, appropriately offset from the original object. Thus if P is a pointer to an object in an array, the expression P+1 is a pointer to the next object in the array. If the resulting pointer points outside the bounds of the array, except at the first location beyond the high end of the array, the result is undefined.

The result of the − operator is the difference of the operands. A value of any integral type may be subtracted from a pointer, and then the same conversions apply as for addition.

No further type combinations are allowed for pointers.

If two pointers to objects of the same type are subtracted, the result is a signed integral value representing the number of objects separating the pointed-to objects. Pointers to successive elements of an array differ by 1. The type of the result is implementation dependent, but is defined as ptrdiff_t in the standard header <stddef.h>. The value is undefined unless the pointers point to elements of the same array; however, if P points to the last element of an array then (P+1)−1 is P.

r.5.8 Shift Operators

The shift operators << and >> group left-to-right.

>   *shift-expression:*
>   *additive-expression*
>   *shift-expression* << *additive-expression*
>   *shift-expression* >> *additive-expression*

The operands must be of integral type and integral promotions are performed. The type of the result is that of the promoted left operand. The result is undefined if the right operand is negative, or greater than or equal to the length in bits of the promoted left operand. The value of E1<<E2 is E1 (interpreted as a bit pattern) left-shifted E2 bits; vacated bits are 0-filled. The value of E1>>E2 is E1 right-shifted E2 bit positions. The right shift is guaranteed to be logical (0-fill) if E1 has an unsigned type or if it has a nonnegative value; otherwise the result is implementation dependent.

r.5.9 Relational Operators

The relational operators group left-to-right, but this fact is not very useful; a<b<c means (a<b)<c and *not* (a<b)&&(b<c).

> *relational-expression:*
>> *shift-expression*
>> *relational-expression* < *shift-expression*
>> *relational-expression* > *shift-expression*
>> *relational-expression* <= *shift-expression*
>> *relational-expression* >= *shift-expression*

The operands must have arithmetic or pointer type. The operators < (less than), > (greater than), <= (less than or equal to), and >= (greater than or equal to) all yield 0 if the specified relation is false and 1 if it is true. The type of the result is int.

The usual arithmetic conversions are performed on arithmetic operands. Pointer conversions are performed on pointer operands. This implies that any pointer may be compared to a constant expression evaluating to 0 and any pointer can be compared to a pointer of type void* (in the latter case the pointer is first converted to void*). Pointers to objects or functions of the same type (after pointer conversions) may be compared; the result depends on the relative positions of the pointed-to objects or functions in the address space.

Two pointers to the same object compare equal. If two pointers point to nonstatic members of the same object, the pointer to the later declared member compares higher provided the two members not separated by an *access-specifier* label (§r.11.1) and provided their class is not a union. If two pointers point to nonstatic members of the same object separated by an *access-specifier* label (§r.11.1) the result is undefined. If two pointers point to data members of the same union, they compare equal. If two pointers point to elements of the same array or one beyond the end of the array, the pointer to the object with the higher subscript compares higher. Other pointer comparisons are implementation dependent.

r.5.10 Equality Operators

> *equality-expression:*
>> *relational-expression*
>> *equality-expression* == *relational-expression*
>> *equality-expression* != *relational-expression*

The == (equal to) and the != (not equal to) operators are exactly analogous to the relational operators except for their lower precedence. (Thus a<b == c<d is 1 whenever a<b and c<d have the same truth-value.)

In addition, pointers to members of the same type may be compared. Pointer to member conversions (§r.4.8) are performed. A pointer to member may be compared to a constant expression that evaluates to 0.

r.5.11 Bitwise AND Operator

> *and-expression:*
> > *equality-expression*
> > *and-expression* & *equality-expression*

The usual arithmetic conversions are performed; the result is the bitwise AND function of the operands. The operator applies only to integral operands.

r.5.12 Bitwise Exclusive OR Operator

> *exclusive-or-expression:*
> > *and-expression*
> > *exclusive-or-expression* ^ *and-expression*

The usual arithmetic conversions are performed; the result is the bitwise exclusive OR function of the operands. The operator applies only to integral operands.

r.5.13 Bitwise Inclusive OR Operator

> *inclusive-or-expression:*
> > *exclusive-or-expression*
> > *inclusive-or-expression* | *exclusive-or-expression*

The usual arithmetic conversions are performed; the result is the bitwise inclusive OR function of its operands. The operator applies only to integral operands.

r.5.14 Logical AND Operator

> *logical-and-expression:*
> > *inclusive-or-expression*
> > *logical-and-expression* && *inclusive-or-expression*

The && operator groups left-to-right. It returns 1 if both its operands are nonzero, 0 otherwise. Unlike &, && guarantees left-to-right evaluation; moreover the second operand is not evaluated if the first operand evaluates to 0.

The operands need not have the same type, but each must have arithmetic type or be a pointer. The result is an int. All side effects of the first expression happen before the second expression is evaluated.

r.5.15 Logical OR Operator

> *logical-or-expression:*
> > *logical-and-expression*
> > *logical-or-expression* | | *logical-and-expression*

The | | operator groups left-to-right. It returns 1 if either of its operands is nonzero, and 0 otherwise. Unlike |, | | guarantees left-to-right evaluation; moreover, the second operand is not evaluated if the first operand evaluates to nonzero.

The operands need not have the same type, but each must have arithmetic type or be a pointer. The result is an int. All side effects of the first expression happen before the second expression is evaluated.

r.5.16 Conditional Operator

> *conditional-expression:*
> > *logical-or-expression*
> > *logical-or-expression* ? *expression* : *conditional-expression*

Conditional expressions group right-to-left. The first expression must have arithmetic type or be a pointer type. It is evaluated and if it is nonzero, the result of the conditional expression is the value of the second expression, otherwise that of the third expression. All side effects of the first expression happen before the second or third expression is evaluated.

If both the second and the third expressions are of arithmetic type, then if they are of the same type the result is of that type; otherwise the usual arithmetic conversions are performed to bring them to a common type. Otherwise, if both the second and the third expressions are either a pointer or a constant expression that evaluates to 0, pointer conversions are performed to bring them to a common type. Otherwise, if both the second and the third expressions are references, reference conversions are performed to bring them to a common type. Otherwise, if both the second and the third expressions are void, the common type is void. Otherwise, if both the second and the third expressions are of the same class T, the common type is T. Otherwise the expression is illegal. The result has the common type; only one of the second and third expressions is evaluated. The result is an lvalue if the second and the third operands are of the same type and both are lvalues.

r.5.17 Assignment Operators

There are several assignment operators, all of which group right-to-left. All require a modifiable lvalue as their left operand, and the type of an assignment expression is that of its left operand. The result of the assignment operation is the value stored in the left operand after the assignment has taken place; the result is an lvalue.

assignment-expression:
    conditional-expression
    unary-expression assignment-operator assignment-expression

assignment-operator: one of
    `=`   `*=`   `/=`   `%=`   `+=`   `-=`   `>>=`   `<<=`   `&=`   `^=`   `|=`

In simple assignment (=), the value of the expression replaces that of the object referred to by the left operand. If both operands have arithmetic type, the right operand is converted to the type of the left preparatory to the assignment. There is no implicit conversion to an enumeration (§r.7.2), so if the left operand is of an enumeration type the right operand must be of the same type. If the left operand is of pointer type, the right operand must be of pointer type or a constant expression that evaluates to 0; the right operand is converted to the type of the left before the assignment.

A pointer of type `T*const` can be assigned to a pointer of type `T*`, but the reverse assignment is illegal (§r.7.1.6). Objects of types `const T` and `volatile T` can be assigned to plain `T` lvalues and to lvalues of type `volatile T`; see also (§r.8.4).

If the left operand is of pointer to member type, the right operand must be of pointer to member type or a constant expression that evaluates to 0; the right operand is converted to the type of the left before the assignment.

Assignment to objects of a class (§r.9) `X` is defined by the function `X::operator=()` (§r.13.4.3). Unless the user defines an `X::operator=()`, the default version is used for assignment (§r.12.8). This implies that an object of a class derived from `X` (directly or indirectly) by unambiguous public derivation (§r.4.6) can be assigned to an `X`.

A pointer to a member of class B may be assigned to a pointer to a member of class D of the same type provided D is derived from B (directly or indirectly) by unambiguous public derivation (§r.10.1.1).

Assignment to an object of type "reference to `T`" assigns to the object of type `T` denoted by the reference.

The behavior of an expression of the form E1 *op*= E2 is equivalent to E1 = E1 *op* (E2); except that E1 is evaluated only once. In += and -=, the left operand may be a pointer, in which case the (integral) right operand is converted as explained in §r.5.7; all right operands and all nonpointer left operands must have arithmetic type.

For class objects, assignment is not in general the same as initialization (§r.8.4, §r.12.1, §r.12.6, §r.12.8).

r.5.18 Comma Operator

The comma operator groups left-to-right.

expression:
>   *assignment-expression*
>   *expression* , *assignment-expression*

A pair of expressions separated by a comma is evaluated left-to-right and the value of the left expression is discarded. All side effects of the left expression are performed before the evaluation of the right expression. The type and value of the result are the type and value of the right operand; the result is an lvalue if its right operand is.

In contexts where comma is given a special meaning, for example, in lists of actual arguments to functions (§r.5.2.2) and lists of initializers (§r.8.4), the comma operator as described in this section can appear only in parentheses; for example,

```
f(a, (t=3, t+2), c);
```

has three arguments, the second of which has the value 5.

r.5.19 Constant Expressions

In several places, C++ requires expressions that evaluate to an integral constant: as array bounds (§r.8.2.4), as `case` expressions (§r.6.4.2), as bit-field lengths (§r.9.6), and as enumerator initializers (§r.7.2).

constant-expression:
>   *conditional-expression*

A *constant-expression* can involve only literals (§r.2.5), enumerators, `const` values of integral types initialized with constant expressions (§r.8.4), and `sizeof` expressions. Floating constants (§r.2.5.3) must be cast to integral types. Only type conversions to integral types may be used. In particular, except in `sizeof` expressions, functions, class objects, pointers, and references cannot be used. The comma operator and *assignment-operator*s may not be used in a constant expression.

r.6 Statements

Except as indicated, statements are executed in sequence.

statement:
>   *labeled-statement*
>   *expression-statement*
>   *compound-statement*
>   *selection-statement*
>   *iteration-statement*
>   *jump-statement*
>   *declaration-statement*

r.6.1 Labeled Statement

A statement may be labeled.

> *labeled-statement:*
> > *identifier* : *statement*
> > `case` *constant-expression* : *statement*
> > `default` : *statement*

An identifier label declares the identifier. The only use of an identifier label is as the target of a `goto`. The scope of a label is the function in which it appears. Labels cannot be redeclared within a function. A label can be used in a `goto` statement before its definition. Labels have their own name space and do not interfere with other identifiers.

Case labels and default labels may occur only in switch statements.

r.6.2 Expression Statement

Most statements are expression statements, which have the form

> *expression-statement:*
> > *expression*$_{opt}$;

Usually expression statements are assignments or function calls. All side effects from an expression statement are completed before the next statement is executed. An expression statement with the expression missing is called a null statement; it is useful to carry a label just before the } of a compound statement and to supply a null body to an iteration statement such as `while` (§r.6.5.1).

r.6.3 Compound Statement, or Block

So that several statements can be used where one is expected, the compound statement (also, and equivalently, called "block") is provided.

> *compound-statement:*
> > { *statement-list*$_{opt}$ }

> *statement-list:*
> > *statement*
> > *statement-list statement*

Note that a declaration is a *statement* (§r.6.7).

r.6.4 Selection Statements

Selection statements choose one of several flows of control.

selection-statement:
> if (*expression*) *statement*
> if (*expression*) *statement* else *statement*
> switch (*expression*) *statement*

The *statement* in a *selection-statement* may not be a *declaration*.

r.6.4.1 The `if` Statement

The expression must be of arithmetic or pointer type or of a class type for which an unambiguous conversion to arithmetic or pointer type exists (§r.12.3).

 The expression is evaluated and if it is nonzero, the first substatement is executed. If else is used, the second substatement is executed if the expression is zero. The else ambiguity is resolved by connecting an else with the last encountered else-less if.

r.6.4.2 The `switch` Statement

The switch statement causes control to be transferred to one of several statements depending on the value of an expression.

 The expression must be of integral type or of a class type for which an unambiguous conversion to integral type exists (§r.12.3). Integral promotion is performed. Any statement within the statement may be labeled with one or more case labels as follows:

> case *constant-expression* :

where the *constant-expression* (§r.5.19) is converted to the promoted type of the switch expression. No two of the case constants in the same switch may have the same value.

 There may be at most one label of the form

> default :

within a switch statement.

 Switch statements may be nested; a case or default label is associated with the smallest switch enclosing it.

 When the switch statement is executed, its expression is evaluated and compared with each case constant. If one of the case constants is equal to the value of the expression, control is passed to the statement following the matched case label. If no case constant matches the expression, and if there is a default label, control passes to the statement labeled by the default label. If no case matches and if there is no default then none of the statements in the switch is executed.

 case and default labels in themselves do not alter the flow of control, which continues unimpeded across such labels. To exit from a switch, see break, §r.6.6.1.

 Usually, the statement that is the subject of a switch is compound. Declarations may appear in the *statement* of a switch-statement. It is illegal, however, to jump past a declaration with an explicit or implicit initializer unless the declaration is in an inner block that is not entered (that is, completely bypassed by the transfer of control; §r.6.7). This implies that declarations that contain explicit or implicit initializers must be contained in an inner block.

r.6.5 Iteration Statements

Iteration statements specify looping.

> *iteration-statement:*
>   `while` (*expression*) *statement*
>   `do` *statement* `while` (*expression*) `;`
>   `for` (*for-init-statement expression*$_{opt}$ `;` *expression*$_{opt}$) *statement*

> *for-init-statement:*
>   *expression-statement*
>   *declaration-statement*

Note that a *for-init-statement* ends with a semicolon.
The *statement* in an *iteration-statement* may not be a *declaration*.

r.6.5.1 The while Statement

In the `while` statement the substatement is executed repeatedly until the value of the expression becomes zero. The test takes place before each execution of the substatement.

The expression must be of arithmetic or pointer type or of a class type for which an unambiguous conversion to arithmetic or pointer type exists (§r.12.3).

r.6.5.2 Do statement

In the `do` statement the substatement is executed repeatedly until the value of the expression becomes zero. The test takes place after each execution of the substatement.

The expression must be of arithmetic or pointer type or of a class type for which an unambiguous conversion to arithmetic or pointer type exists (§r.12.3).

r.6.5.3 The for Statement

The `for` statement

> `for` (*for-init-statement expression-1*$_{opt}$ `;` *expression-2*$_{opt}$) *statement*

is equivalent to

```
        for-init-statement
        while ( expression-1 ) {
                statement
                expression-2 ;
        }
```

except that a `continue` in *statement* will execute *expression-2* before re-evaluating *expression-1*. Thus the first statement specifies initialization for the loop; the first expression specifies a test, made before each iteration, such that the loop is exited when the expression becomes zero; the second expression often specifies incrementing that is done after each iteration. The first expression must have arithmetic or pointer type or a class type for which an unambiguous conversion to arithmetic or pointer type exists (§r.12.3).

Either or both of the expressions may be dropped. A missing *expression-1* makes the implied `while` clause equivalent to `while (1)`.

If the *for-init-statement* is a declaration, the scope of the names declared extends to the end of the block enclosing the *for-statement*.

r.6.6 Jump Statements

Jump statements unconditionally transfer control.

> *jump-statement:*
>   `break` ;
>   `continue` ;
>   `return` *expression*_{opt} ;
>   `goto` *identifier* ;

On exit from a scope (however accomplished), destructors (§r.12.4) are called for all constructed class objects in that scope that have not yet been destroyed. This applies to both explicitly declared objects and temporaries (§r.12.2).

r.6.6.1 The `break` Statement

The `break` statement may occur only in an *iteration-statement* or a `switch` statement and causes termination of the smallest enclosing *iteration-statement* or `switch` statement; control passes to the statement following the terminated statement, if any.

r.6.6.2 The `continue` Statement

The `continue` statement may occur only in an *iteration-statement* and causes control to pass to the loop-continuation portion of the smallest enclosing *iteration-statement*, that is, to the end of the loop. More precisely, in each of the statements

```
while (foo) {          do {                  for (;;) {
    // ...                 // ...                // ...
    contin: ;             contin: ;             contin: ;
}                      } while (foo);         }
```

a continue not contained in an enclosed iteration statement is equivalent to goto contin.

r.6.6.3 The return Statement

A function returns to its caller by the return statement.

A return statement without an expression can be used only in functions that do not return a value, that is, a function with the return value type void, a constructor (§r.12.1), or a destructor (§r.12.4). A return statement with an expression can be used only in functions returning a value; the value of the expression is returned to the caller of the function. If required, the expression is converted, as in an initialization, to the return type of the function in which it appears. This may involve the construction and copy of a temporary object (§r.12.2). Flowing off the end of a function is equivalent to a return with no value; this is illegal in a value-returning function.

r.6.6.4 The goto Statement

The goto statement unconditionally transfers control to the statement labeled by the identifier. The identifier must be a label (§r.6.1) located in the current function.

r.6.7 Declaration Statement

A declaration statement introduces a new identifier into a block; it has the form

> *declaration-statement:*
>   *declaration*

If an identifier introduced by a declaration was previously declared in an outer block, the outer declaration is hidden for the remainder of the block, after which it resumes its force.

Any initializations of auto or register variables are done each time their *declaration-statement* is executed. Destruction of local variables declared in the block is done on exit from the block (§r.6.6). Destruction of auto variables defined in a loop is done once per iteration. For example, here the Index j is created and destroyed once each time round the i loop:

```
for (int i = 0; i<100; i++)
    for (Index j = 0; j<100; j++) {
        // ...
    }
```

Transfer out of a loop, out of a block, or back past an initialized auto variable involves the destruction of auto variables declared at the point transferred from but not at the point transferred to.

It is possible to transfer into a block, but not in a way that causes initializations not to be done. It is illegal to jump past a declaration with an explicit or implicit initializer unless the declaration is in an inner block that is not entered (that is, completely bypassed by the transfer of control) or unless the jump is from a point where the variable has already been initialized. For example,

```
void f()
{
    // ...
    goto lx;        // error: jump past initializer
    // ...
ly:
    X a = 1;
    // ...
lx:
    goto ly;        // ok, jump implies destructor
                    // call for 'a'
}
```

An `auto` variable constructed under a condition is destroyed under that condition and cannot be accessed outside that condition. For example,

```
if (i)
    for (int j = 0; j<100; j++) {
        // ...
    }
if (j!=100)      // error: access outside condition
    // ...
;
```

Initialization of a local object with storage class `static` (§r.7.1.1) is done the first time control passes through its declaration (only). Where a `static` variable is initialized with an expression that is not a *constant-expression*, default initialization to 0 of the appropriate type (§r.8.4) happens before its block is first entered.

The destructor for a local `static` object will be executed if and only if the variable was constructed. The destructor must be called either immediately before or as part of the calls of the `atexit()` functions (§r.3.4). Exactly when is undefined.

r.6.8 Ambiguity Resolution

There is an ambiguity in the grammar involving *expression-statement*s and *declaration*s: An *expression-statement* with a function-style explicit type conversion (§r.5.2.3) as its leftmost subexpression can be indistinguishable from a *declaration* where the first *declarator* starts with a (. In those cases the *statement* is a *declaration*.

To disambiguate, the whole *statement* may have to be examined to determine if it is an *expression-statement* or a *declaration*. This disambiguates many examples. For example, assuming T is a *simple-type-name* (§r.7.1.6),

```
T(a)->m = 7;        // expression-statement
T(a)++;             // expression-statement
T(a,5)<<c;          // expression-statement

T(*e)(int);         // declaration
T(f)[];             // declaration
T(g) = { 1, 2 };    // declaration
T(*d)(double(3));   // declaration
```

The remaining cases are *declaration*s. For example,

```
T(a);               // declaration
T(*b)();            // declaration
T(c)=7;             // declaration
T(d),e,f=3;         // declaration
T(g)(h,2);          // declaration
```

The disambiguation is purely syntactic; that is, the meaning of the names, beyond whether they are *type-name*s or not, is not used in the disambiguation.

A slightly different ambiguity between *expression-statement*s and *declaration*s is resolved by requiring a *type-name* for function declarations within a block (§r.6.3). For example,

```
void g()
{
    int f();        // declaration
    int a;          // declaration
    f();            // expression-statement
    a;              // expression-statement
}
```

r.7 Declarations

Declarations specify the interpretation given to each identifier; they do not necessarily reserve storage associated with the identifier (§r.3.1). Declarations have the form

> *declaration:*
> > *decl-specifiers*$_{opt}$ *declarator-list*$_{opt}$;
> > *asm-declaration*
> > *function-definition*
> > *linkage-specification*

The declarators in the *declarator-list* (§r.8) contain the identifiers being declared. Only in function definitions (§r.8.3) and function declarations may the *decl-specifiers* be omitted. Only when declaring a class (§r.9) or enumeration (§r.7.2), that is, when the *decl-specifier* is a *class-specifier* or *enum-specifier*, may the *declarator-list* be empty. *asm-declaration*s are described in §r.7.3, and *linkage-specification*s in §r.7.4. A declaration occurs in a scope (§r.3.2); the scope rules are summarized in §r.10.4.

r.7.1 Specifiers

The specifiers that can be used in a declaration are

> *decl-specifier:*
>> *storage-class-specifier*
>> *type-specifier*
>> *fct-specifier*
>> *template-specifier*
>> `friend`
>> `typedef`

> *decl-specifiers:*
>> *decl-specifiers*_{opt} *decl-specifier*

The longest sequence of *decl-specifiers* that could possibly be a type name is taken as the *decl-specifiers* of a *declaration*. The sequence must be self-consistent as described below. For example,

```
typedef char* Pc;
static Pc;                  // error: name missing
```

Here, the declaration `static Pc` is illegal because no name was specified for the static variable of type `Pc`. To get a variable of type `int` called `Pc`, the *type-specifier* `int` must be present to indicate that the *typedef-name* `Pc` is the name being (re)declared, rather than being part of the *decl-specifier* sequence. For example,

```
void f(const Pc);        // void f(char*const)
void g(const int Pc);    // void g(const int)
```

Note that since `signed`, `unsigned`, `long`, and `short` by default imply `int`, a *typedef-name* appearing after one of those specifiers must be the name being (re)declared. For example,

```
void h(unsigned Pc);        // void h(unsigned int)
void k(unsigned int Pc);    // void k(unsigned int)
```

r.7.1.1 Storage Class Specifiers

The storage class specifiers are

> *storage-class-specifier:*
>> `auto`
>> `register`
>> `static`
>> `extern`

The `auto` or `register` specifiers can be applied only to names of objects declared in a block (§r.6.3) and for formal arguments (§r.8.3). The `auto` declarator is almost always redundant and not often used; one use of `auto` is to distinguish a *declaration-statement* from an *expression-statement* (§r.6.2) explicitly.

A `register` declaration is an `auto` declaration, together with a hint to the compiler that the variables declared will be heavily used. The hint may be ignored and in most implementations it will be ignored if the address of the variable is taken.

An object declaration is a definition unless it contains the `extern` specifier and has no initializer (§r.3.1).

A definition causes the appropriate amount of storage to be reserved and any appropriate initialization (§r.8.4) to be done.

The `static` and `extern` specifiers can be applied only to names of objects and functions and to anonymous unions. There can be no `static` function declarations within a block, nor any `static` or `extern` formal arguments. Static class members are described in (§r.9.4); `extern` cannot be used for class members.

A name specified `static` has internal linkage. Objects declared `const` have internal linkage unless they have previously been given external linkage. A name specified `extern` has external linkage unless it has previously been given internal linkage. A file scope name without a *storage-class-specifier* has external linkage unless it has previously been given internal linkage and provided it is not declared `const`. For a nonmember function an `inline` specifier is equivalent to a `static` specifier for linkage purposes (§r.3.3). All linkage specifications for a name must agree. For example,

```
static char* f(); // f() has internal linkage
char* f()         // f() still has internal linkage
    { /* ... */ }


char* g();        // g() has external linkage
static char* g()  // error: inconsistent linkage
    { /* ... */ }


static int a;     // 'a' has internal linkage
int a;            // error: two definitions


static int b;     // 'b' has internal linkage
extern int b;     // 'b' still has internal linkage


int c;            // 'c' has external linkage
static int c;     // error: inconsistent linkage


extern int d;     // 'd' has external linkage
static int d;     // error: inconsistent linkage
```

The name of an undefined class can be used in an `extern` declaration. Such a declaration, however, cannot be used before the class has been defined. For example,

```
struct S;
extern S a;
extern S f();
extern void g(S);

void h()
{
    g(a);           // error: S undefined
    f();            // error: S undefined
}
```

r.7.1.2 Function Specifiers

Some specifiers can be used only in function declarations.

> *fct-specifier:*
> > inline
> > virtual

The inline specifier is a hint to the compiler that inline substitution of the function body is to be preferred to the usual function call implementation. The hint may be ignored. For a nonmember function inline specifier also gives the function default internal linkage (§r.3.3). A function (§r.5.2.2, §r.8.2.5) defined within the declaration of a class is inline by default.

An inline member function must have exactly the same definition in every compilation in which it appears.

A class member function need not be explicitly declared inline in the class declaration to be inline. When no inline specifier is used, linkage will be external unless an inline definition appears before the first call.

```
class X {
public:
    int f();
    inline int g();   // X::g() has internal linkage
    int h();
};
```

```
void k(X* p)
{
    int i = p->f();   // now X::f() has external linkage
    int j = p->g();
    // ...
}
```

```
inline int X::f()      // error: called before defined
                       // as inline
{
    // ...
}


inline int X::g()
{
    // ...
}


inline int X::h()      // now X::h() has internal linkage
{
    // ...
}
```

The `virtual` specifier may be used only in declarations of nonstatic class member functions within a class declaration; see §r.10.2.

r.7.1.3 The `typedef` Specifier

Declarations containing the *decl-specifier* `typedef` declare identifiers that can be used later for naming fundamental or derived types. The `typedef` specifier may not be used in a *function-definition* (§r.8.3).

> *typedef-name:*
> > *identifier*

Within the scope (§r.3.2) of a `typedef` declaration, each identifier appearing as part of any declarator therein becomes syntactically equivalent to a keyword and names the type associated with the identifier in the way described in §r.8. A *typedef-name* is thus a synonym for another type. A *typedef-name* does not introduce a new type the way a class declaration (§r.9.1) does. For example, after

```
typedef int MILES, *KLICKSP;
```

the constructions

```
MILES distance;
extern KLICKSP metricp;
```

are all legal declarations; the type of `distance` is `int`; that of `metricp` is "pointer to `int`."

A `typedef` may be used to redefine a name to refer to the type to which it already refers – even in the scope where the type was originally declared. For example,

```
typedef struct s { /* ... */ } s;
typedef int I;
typedef int I;
typedef I I;
```

An unnamed class defined in a typedef gets its typedef name as its name. For example,

```
typedef struct { /* ... */ } S; // the struct is named S
```

A `typedef` may not redefine a name of a type declared in the same scope to refer to a different type. For example,

```
class complex { /* ... */ };
typedef int complex;    // error: redefinition
```

Similarly, a class may not be declared with the name of a type declared in the same scope to refer to a different type. For example,

```
typedef int complex;
class complex { /* ... */ };   // error: redefinition
```

A *typedef-name* that names a class is a *class-name* (§r.9.1). The synonym may not be used after a `class`, `struct`, or `union` prefix and not in the names for constructors and destructors within the class declaration itself. For example,

```
struct S {
    S();
    ˜S();
};

typedef struct S T;

S a = T();      // ok
struct T * p;   // error
```

r.7.1.4 The `template` Specifier

The `template` specifier is used to specify families of types or functions; see §r.14.

r.7.1.5 The `friend` Specifier

The `friend` specifier is used to specify access to class members; see §r.11.4.

r.7.1.6 Type Specifiers

The type-specifiers are

type-specifier:
> *simple-type-name*
> *class-specifier*
> *enum-specifier*
> *elaborated-type-specifier*
> `: :`   *class-name*
> `const`
> `volatile`

The words `const` and `volatile` may be added to any legal *type-specifier* in the declaration of an object. Otherwise, at most one *type-specifier* may be given in a declaration. A `const` object may be initialized, but its value may not be changed thereafter. Unless explicitly declared `extern`, a `const` object does not have external linkage and must be initialized (§r.8.4; §r.12.1). An integer `const` initialized by a constant expression may be used in constant expressions (§r.5.19). Each element of a `const` array is `const` and each nonfunction, nonstatic member of a `const` class object is `const` (§r.9.3.1). A `const` object of a type that does not have a constructor or a destructor may be placed in readonly memory. The effect of a write operation on any part of such an object is either an addressing exception or the same as if the object had been non-`const`.

There are no implementation-independent semantics for `volatile` objects; `volatile` is a hint to the compiler to avoid aggressive optimization involving the object because the value of the object may be changed by means undetectable by a compiler. Each element of a `volatile` array is `volatile` and each nonfunction, nonstatic member of a `volatile` class object is `volatile` (§r.9.3.1).

If the *type-specifier* is missing from a declaration, it is taken to be `int`.

simple-type-name:
> *complete-class-name*
> *qualified-type-name*
> `char`
> `short`
> `int`
> `long`
> `signed`
> `unsigned`
> `float`
> `double`
> `void`

At most one of the words `long` or `short` may be specified together with `int`. Either may appear alone, in which case `int` is understood. The word `long` may appear together with `double`. At most one of the words `signed` and `unsigned` may be specified together with `char`, `short`, `int`, or `long`. Either may appear alone, in which case `int` is understood. The `signed` specifier forces `char` objects and bit-fields to be signed; it is redundant with other integral types.

class-specifiers and *enum-specifiers* are discussed in §r.9 and §r.7.2, respectively.

> *elaborated-type-specifier:*
>> *class-key class-name*
>> *class-key identifier*
>> `enum` *enum-name*

> *class-key:*
>> `class`
>> `struct`
>> `union`

If an *identifier* is specified, the *elaborated-type-specifier* declares it to be a *class-name*; see §r.9.1.

If defined, a name declared using the `union` specifier must be defined as a union. If defined, a name declared using the `class` specifier must be defined using the `class` or `struct` specifier. If defined, a name declared using the `struct` specifier must be defined using the `class` or `struct` specifier. Names of nested types (§r.9.7) can be qualified by the name of their enclosing class:

> *qualified-type-name:*
>> *typedef-name*
>> *class-name* `::` *qualified-type-name.*

> *complete-class-name:*
>> *qualified-class-name*
>> `::` *qualified-class-name*

> *qualified-class-name:*
>> *class-name*
>> *class-name* `::` *qualified-class-name*

A name qualified by a *class-name* must be a type defined in that class or in a base class of that class. As usual, a name declared in a derived class hides members of that name declared in base classes; see §r.3.2.

r.7.2 Enumeration Declarations

An enumeration is a distinct integral type (§r.3.6.1) with named constants. Its name becomes an *enum-name*, that is, a reserved word within its scope.

> *enum-name:*
>> *identifier*

> *enum-specifier:*
>> `enum` *identifier*$_{opt}$ `{` *enum-list*$_{opt}$ `}`

> *enum-list:*
>> *enumerator*
>> *enum-list* `,` *enumerator*

enumerator:
> *identifier*
> *identifier* = *constant-expression*

The identifiers in an *enum-list* are declared as constants, and may appear wherever constants are required. If no enumerators with = appear, then the values of the corresponding constants begin at zero and increase by one as the declaration is read from left to right. An enumerator with = gives the associated identifier the value indicated; subsequent identifiers without initializers continue the progression from the assigned value. The value of an enumerator must be an int or a value that can be promoted to int by integral promotion (§r.4.1).

The names of enumerators must be distinct from those of ordinary variables and other enumerators in the same scope. The values of the enumerators need not be distinct. An enumerator is considered defined immediately after it and its initializer, if any, has been seen. For example,

```
enum { a, b, c=0 };
enum { d, e, f=e+2 };
```

defines a, c, and d to be 0, b and e to be 1, and f to be 3.

Each enumeration defines an integral type that is different from all other integral types. The type of an enumerator is its enumeration. The value of an enumerator or an object of an enumeration type is converted to an integer by integral promotion (§r.4.1). For example,

```
enum color { red, yellow, green=20, blue };
color col = red;
color* cp = &col;
if (*cp == blue) // ...
```

makes color an integral type describing various colors, and then declares col as an object of that type, and cp as a pointer to an object of that type. The possible values of an object of type color are red, yellow, green, blue; these values can be converted to the int values 0, 1, 20, and 21. Since enumerations are distinct types, objects of type color may be assigned only values of type color. For example,

```
color c = 1;      // error: type mismatch,
                  // no conversion from int to color

int i = yellow;   // ok: yellow converted to int value 1
                  // integral promotion
```

See also §r.18.3.

Enumerators defined in a class (§r.9) are in the scope of that class and can be referred to outside member functions of that class only by explicit qualification with the class name (§r.5.1). The name of the enumeration itself is also local to the class (§r.9.7). For example,

```
class X {
public:
    enum direction { left='l', right='r' };
    int f(int i)
        { return i==left ? 0 : i==right ? 1 : 2; }
};

void g(X* p)
{
    direction d;           // error: 'direction' not in scope
    int i;
    i = p->f(left);        // error: 'left' not in scope
    i = p->f(X::right);    // ok
    // ...
}
```

r.7.3 Asm Declarations

An asm declaration has the form

> *asm-declaration:*
>> asm (*string-literal*) ;

The meaning of an asm declaration is implementation dependent. Typically it is used to pass information through the compiler to an assembler.

r.7.4 Linkage Specifications

Linkage (§r.3.3) between C++ and non-C++ code fragments can be achieved using a *linkage-specification*:

> *linkage-specification:*
>> extern *string-literal* { *declaration-list*$_{opt}$ }
>> extern *string-literal* *declaration*
>
> *declaration-list:*
>> *declaration*
>> *declaration-list declaration*

The *string-literal* indicates the required linkage. The meaning of the *string-literal* is implementation dependent. Linkage to a function written in the C programming language, "C", and linkage to a C++ function, "C++", must be provided by every implementation. Default linkage is "C++". For example,

```
complex sqrt(complex);    // C++ linkage by default
extern "C" {
    double sqrt(double);  // C linkage
}
```

Linkage specifications nest. A linkage specification does not establish a scope. A *linkage-specification* may occur only in *file* scope (§r.3.2). A *linkage-specification* for a class applies to nonmember functions and objects declared within it. A *linkage-specification* for a function also applies to functions and objects declared within it. A linkage declaration with a string that is unknown to the implementation is an error.

If a function has more than one *linkage-specification*, they must agree; that is, they must specify the same *string-literal*. A function declaration without a linkage specification may not precede the first linkage specification for that function. A function may be declared without a linkage specification after an explicit linkage specification has been seen; the linkage explicitly specified in the earlier declaration is not affected by such a function declaration.

At most one of a set of overloaded functions (§r.13) with a particular name can have C linkage. See §r.7.4.

Linkage can be specified for objects. For example,

```
extern "C" {
    // ...
    _iobuf _iob[_NFILE];
    // ...
    int _flsbuf(unsigned,_iobuf*);
    // ...
}
```

Functions and objects may be declared static within the { } of a linkage specification. The linkage directive is ignored for such a function or object. Otherwise, a function declared in a linkage specification behaves as if it was explicitly declared extern. For example,

```
extern "C" double f();
static double f();        // error
```

is an error (§r.7.1.1). An object defined within an

```
extern "C" { /* ... */ }
```

construct is still defined (and not just declared).

Linkage from C++ to objects defined in other languages and to objects defined in C++ from other languages is implementation and language dependent. Only where the object layout strategies of two language implementations are similar enough can such linkage be achieved.

When the name of a programming language is used to name a style of linkage in the *string-literal* in a *linkage-specification*, it is recommended that the spelling be taken from the document defining that language, for example, Ada (not ADA) and FORTRAN (not Fortran).

r.8   Declarators

The *declarator-list* appearing in a declaration is a comma-separated sequence of declarators, each of which may have an initializer.

> *declarator-list:*
> > *init-declarator*
> > *declarator-list* ,   *init-declarator*

> *init-declarator:*
> > *declarator   initializer*$_{opt}$

The two components of a *declaration* are the specifiers (*decl-specifiers*; §r.7.1) and the declarators (*declarator-list*). The specifiers indicate the fundamental type, storage class, or other properties of the objects and functions being declared. The declarators specify the names of these objects and functions and (optionally) modify the type with operators such as * (pointer to) and () (function returning). Initial values can also be specified in a declarator; initializers are discussed in §r.8.4 and §r.12.6.

Declarators have the syntax

> *declarator:*
> > *dname*
> > *ptr-operator declarator*
> > *declarator* (*argument-declaration-list*)   *cv-qualifier-list*$_{opt}$
> > *declarator* [*constant-expression*$_{opt}$]
> > (*declarator*)

> *ptr-operator:*
> > *   *cv-qualifier-list*$_{opt}$
> > &   *cv-qualifier-list*$_{opt}$
> > *complete-class-name* : :   *   *cv-qualifier-list*$_{opt}$

> *cv-qualifier-list:*
> > *cv-qualifier   cv-qualifier-list*$_{opt}$

> *cv-qualifier:*
> > const
> > volatile

> *dname:*
> > *name*
> > *class-name*
> > ˜ *class-name*
> > *typedef-name*
> > *qualified-type-name*

A *class-name* has special meaning in a declaration of the class of that name and when qualified by that name using the scope resolution operator : : (§r.12.1, §r.12.4).

r.8.1 Type Names

To specify type conversions explicitly, and as an argument of `sizeof` or `new`, the name of a type must be specified. This is done with a *type-name*, which is syntactically a declaration for an object or function of that type that omits the name of the object or function.

> *type-name:*
> > *type-specifier-list abstract-declarator*$_{opt}$
>
> *type-specifier-list:*
> > *type-specifier type-specifier-list*$_{opt}$
>
> *abstract-declarator:*
> > *ptr-operator abstract-declarator*$_{opt}$
> > *abstract-declarator*$_{opt}$ (*argument-declaration-list*) *cv-qualifier-list*$_{opt}$
> > *abstract-declarator*$_{opt}$ [*constant-expression*$_{opt}$]
> > (*abstract-declarator*)

It is possible to identify uniquely the location in the *abstract-declarator* where the identifier would appear if the construction were a declarator in a declaration. The named type is then the same as the type of the hypothetical identifier. For example,

```
int                    // int i
int *                  // int *pi
int *[3]               // int *p[3]
int (*)[3]             // int (*p3i)[3]
int *()                // int *f()
int (*)(double)        // int (*pf)(double)
```

name respectively the types "integer," "pointer to integer," "array of 3 pointers to integers," "pointer to array of 3 integers," "function taking no arguments and returning pointer to integer," and "pointer to function taking a `double` argument and returning an integer."

r.8.1.1 Ambiguity Resolution

The ambiguity arising from the similarity between a function-style cast and a declaration mentioned in §r.6.8 can also occur in the context of a declaration. In that context, it surfaces as a choice between a function declaration with a redundant set of parentheses around an argument name and an object declaration with a function-style cast as the initializer. Just as for statements, the resolution is to consider any construct that could possibly be a declaration a declaration. A declaration can be explicitly disambiguated by a nonfunction-style cast or a = to indicate initialization. For example,

```
struct S {
    S(int);
};
```

```
void foo(double a)
{
    S x(int(a));          // function declaration
    S y((int)a);          // object declaration
    S z = int(a);         // object declaration
}
```

r.8.2 Meaning of Declarators

A list of declarators appears after a (possibly empty) list of *decl-specifiers* (§r.7.1).
Each declarator contains exactly one *dname*; it specifies the identifier that is declared.
Except for the declarations of some special functions (§r.12.3, §r.13.4) a *dname* will
be a simple *identifier*. An auto, static, extern, register, friend,
inline, virtual, or typedef specifier applies directly to each *dname* in a
declarator-list; the type of each *dname* depends on both the *decl-specifiers* (§r.7.1)
and its *declarator*.

Thus, a declaration of a particular identifier has the form

    T D

where T is a type and D is a declarator. In a declaration where D is an unadorned
identifier the type of this identifier is T.

In a declaration where D has the form

    (D1)

the type of D1 is the same as that of D. Parentheses do not alter the type of the
embedded *dname*, but they may alter the binding of complex declarators.

r.8.2.1 Pointers

In a declaration T D where D has the form

    * *cv-qualifier-list*$_{opt}$ D1

the type of the contained identifier is "... *cv-qualifier-list* pointer to T." The *cv-
qualifiers* apply to the pointer and not to the object pointed to.

For example, the declarations

```
const ci = 10, *pc = &ci, *const cpc = pc;
int i, *p, *const cp = &i;
```

declare ci, a constant integer; pc, a pointer to a constant integer; cpc, a constant
pointer to a constant integer; i, an integer; p, a pointer to integer; and cp, a constant
pointer to integer. The value of ci, cpc, and cp cannot be changed after initialization. The value of pc can be changed, and so can the object pointed to by cp.
Examples of legal operations are

```
i = ci;
*cp = ci;
pc++;
pc = cpc;
pc = p;
```

Examples of illegal operations are

```
ci = 1;       // error
ci++;         // error
*pc = 2;      // error
cp = &ci;     // error
cpc++;        // error
p = pc;       // error
```

Each is illegal because it would either change the value of an object declared `const` or allow it to be changed through an unqualified pointer later.

`volatile` specifiers are handled similarly.

See also §r.5.17 and §r.8.4.

There can be no pointers to references (§r.8.2.2) or pointers to bit-fields (§r.9.6).

r.8.2.2 References

In a declaration T D where D has the form

> & *cv-qualifier-list*$_{opt}$ D1

the type of the contained identifier is ''... *cv-qualifier-list* reference to T.'' The type `void&` is not permitted.

For example,

```
void f(double& a) { a += 3.14; }
// ...
    double d = 0;
    f(d);
```

declares a to be a reference argument of `f` so the call `f(d)` will add `3.14` to d.

```
int v[20];
// ...
int& g(int i) { return v[i]; }
// ...
g(3) = 7;
```

declares the function `g()` to return a reference to an integer so `g(3)=7` will assign 7 to the fourth element of the array v.

```
struct link {
    link* next;
};

link* first;

void h(link*& p)  // 'p' is a reference to pointer
{
    p->next = first;
    first = p;
    p = 0;
}

void k()
{
        link* q = new link;
        h(q);
}
```

declares p to be a reference to a pointer to link so h(q) will leave q with the value
0. See also §r.8.4.3.

There can be no references to references, no references to bit-fields (§r.9.6), no
arrays of references, and no pointers to references. The declaration of a reference
must contain an *initializer* (§r.8.4.3) except when the declaration contains an explicit
extern specifier (§r.7.1.1), is a class member (§r.9.2) declaration within a class declaration, or is the declaration of an argument or a return type (§r.8.2.5); see §r.3.1.

r.8.2.3 Pointers to Members

In a declaration T D where D has the form

> *complete-class-name* :: * *cv-qualifier-list$_{opt}$* D1

the type of the contained identifier is "... *cv-qualifier-list* pointer to member of class
complete-class-name of type T."

For example,

```
class X {
public:
    void f(int);
    int a;
};

int X::* pmi = &X::a;
void (X::* pmf)(int) = &X::f;
```

declares pmi and pmf to be a pointer to a member of X of type int and a pointer to a
member of X of type void(int), respectively. They can be used like this:

```
X obj;
//...
obj.*pmi = 7;      // assign 7 to an integer
                   // member of obj
(obj.*pmf)(7);     // call a function member of obj
                   // with the argument 7
```

Note that a pointer to member cannot point to a static member of a class (§r.9.4). See also §r.5.5 and §r.5.3.

r.8.2.4 Arrays

In a declaration T D where D has the form

> D1 [*constant-expression*_{opt}]

then the contained identifier has type "... array of T." If the *constant-expression* (§r.5.19) is present, it must be of integral type and have a value greater than 0. The constant expression specifies the number of elements in the array. If the constant expression is N, the array has N elements numbered 0 to N−1.

An array may be constructed from one of the fundamental types (except void), from a pointer, from a pointer to member, from a class, from an enumeration, or from another array.

When several "array of" specifications are adjacent, a multidimensional array is created; the constant expressions that specify the bounds of the arrays may be omitted only for the first member of the sequence. This elision is useful for function arguments of array types, and when the array is external and the definition, which allocates storage, is given elsewhere. The first *constant-expression* may also be omitted when the declarator is followed by an *initializer-list* (§r.8.4). In this case the size is calculated from the number of initial elements supplied (§r.8.4.1).

The declaration

```
float fa[17], *afp[17];
```

declares an array of float numbers and an array of pointers to float numbers. The declaration

```
static int x3d[3][5][7];
```

declares a static three-dimensional array of integers, with rank 3×5×7. In complete detail, x3d is an array of three items; each item is an array of five arrays; each of the latter arrays is an array of seven integers. Any of the expressions x3d, x3d[i], x3d[i][j], x3d[i][j][k] may reasonably appear in an expression.

When an identifier of array type appears in an expression, except as the operand of sizeof or & or used to initialize a reference (§r.8.4.3), it is converted into a pointer to the first member of the array. Because of this conversion, arrays are not modifiable lvalues. Except where it has been declared for a class (§r.13.4.5), the subscript operator [] is interpreted in such a way that E1[E2] is identical to *((E1)+(E2)).

Because of the conversion rules that apply to +, if E1 is an array and E2 an integer, then E1[E2] refers to the E2-th member of E1. Therefore, despite its asymmetric appearance, subscripting is a commutative operation.

A consistent rule is followed for multidimensional arrays. If E is an n-dimensional array of rank $i \times j \times \cdots \times k$, then E appearing in an expression is converted to a pointer to an $(n-1)$-dimensional array with rank $j \times \cdots \times k$. If the * operator, either explicitly or implicitly as a result of subscripting, is applied to this pointer, the result is the pointed-to $(n-1)$-dimensional array, which itself is immediately converted into a pointer.

For example, consider

```
int x[3][5];
```

Here x is a 3×5 array of integers. When x appears in an expression, it is converted to a pointer to (the first of three) five-membered arrays of integers. In the expression x[i], which is equivalent to *(x+i), x is first converted to a pointer as described; then x+i is converted to the type of x, which involves multiplying i by the length of the object to which the pointer points, namely five integer objects. The results are added and indirection applied to yield an array (of five integers), which in turn is converted to a pointer to the first of the integers. If there is another subscript the same argument applies again; this time the result is an integer.

It follows from all this that arrays in C++ are stored row-wise (last subscript varies fastest) and that the first subscript in the declaration helps determine the amount of storage consumed by an array but plays no other part in subscript calculations.

r.8.2.5 Functions

In a declaration T D where D has the form

> D1 (*argument-declaration-list*) *cv-qualifier-list*$_{opt}$

the contained identifier has the type "... *cv-qualifier-list*$_{opt}$ function taking arguments of type *argument-declaration-list* and returning T."

> *argument-declaration-list:*
> > *arg-declaration-list*$_{opt}$ $\cdots$$_{opt}$
> > *arg-declaration-list* , $\ldots$

> *arg-declaration-list:*
> > *argument-declaration*
> > *arg-declaration-list* , *argument-declaration*

> *argument-declaration:*
> > *decl-specifiers declarator*
> > *decl-specifiers declarator* = *expression*
> > *decl-specifiers abstract-declarator*$_{opt}$
> > *decl-specifiers abstract-declarator*$_{opt}$ = *expression*

If the *argument-declaration-list* terminates with an ellipsis, the number of arguments is known only to be equal to or greater than the number of argument types specified; if it is empty, the function takes no arguments. The argument list (void) is equivalent to the empty argument list. Except for this special case void may not be an argument type (though types derived from void, such as void*, may). Where legal, '', ...'' is synonymous with ''...''. The standard header <stdarg.h> contains a mechanism for accessing arguments passed using the ellipsis. See §r.12.1 for the treatment of array arguments.

A single name may be used for several different functions in a single scope; this is function overloading (§r.13). All declarations for a function taking a given set of arguments must agree exactly both in the type of the value returned and in the number and type of arguments; the presence or absence of the ellipsis is considered part of the function type. Argument types that differ only in the use of typedef names or unspecified argument array bounds agree exactly. The return type and the argument types, but not the default arguments (§r.8.2.6), are part of the function type. A *cv-qualifier-list* can be part of a declaration or definition of a nonstatic member function, and of a pointer to a member function; see §r.9.3.1. It is part of the function type.

Functions cannot return arrays or functions, although they can return pointers and references to such things. There are no arrays of functions, although there may be arrays of pointers to functions.

Types may not be defined in return or argument types.

The *argument-declaration-list* is used to check and convert actual arguments in calls and to check pointer-to-function and reference-to-function assignments and initializations.

An identifier can optionally be provided as an argument name; if present in a function declaration, it cannot be used since it immediately goes out of scope; if present in a function definition (§r.8.3), it names a formal argument. In particular, argument names are also optional in function definitions and names used for an argument in different declarations and the definition of a function need not be the same.

The declaration

```
int i,
    *pi,
    f(),
    *fpi(int),
    (*pif)(const char*, const char*);
```

declares an integer i, a pointer pi to an integer, a function f taking no arguments and returning an integer, a function fpi taking an integer argument and returning a pointer to an integer, and a pointer pif to a function which takes two pointers to constant characters and returns an integer. It is especially useful to compare the last two. The binding of *fpi(int) is *(fpi(int)), so the declaration suggests, and the same construction in an expression requires, the calling of a function fpi, and then using indirection through the (pointer) result to yield an integer. In the declarator (*pif)(const char*, const char*), the extra parentheses are necessary to indicate that indirection through a pointer to a function yields a function,

which is then called.
  The declaration

```
fseek(FILE*, long, int);
```

declares a function taking three arguments of the specified types. Since no return value type is specified it is taken to be int (§r.7.1.6). The declaration

```
printf(const char* ...);
```

declares a function that can be called with varying number and types of arguments. For example,

```
printf("hello world");
printf("a=%d b=%d", a, b);
```

It must always have a value, however, that can be converted to a const char* as its first argument.

r.8.2.6 Default Arguments

If an expression is specified in an argument declaration this expression is used as a default argument. All subsequent arguments must have default arguments supplied in this or previous declarations of this function. Default arguments will be used in calls where trailing arguments are missing. A default argument cannot be redefined by a later declaration (not even to the same value). A declaration may add default arguments, however, not given in previous declarations.
  The declaration

```
point(int = 3, int = 4);
```

declares a function that can be called with zero, one, or two arguments of type int. It may be called in any of these ways:

```
point(1,2);   point(1);   point();
```

The last two calls are equivalent to point (1, 4) and point (3, 4), respectively.
  Default argument expressions have their names bound and their types checked at the point of declaration, and are evaluated at each point of call. In the following example, g will be called with the value f (2):

```
int a = 1;
int f(int);
int g(int x = f(a)); // default argument: f(::a)

void h() {
    a = 2;
    {
        int a = 3;
        g();            // g(f(::a))
    }
}
```

Local variables may not be used in default argument expressions. For example,

```
void f()
{
    int i;
    extern void g(int x = i);    // error
    // ...
}
```

Note that default arguments are evaluated before entry into a function and that the order of evaluation of function arguments is implementation dependent. Consequently, formal arguments of a function may not be used in default argument expressions. Formal arguments of a function declared before a default argument expression are in scope and may hide global and class member names. For example,

```
int a;
int f(int a, int b = a);      // error: argument 'a'
                              // used as default argument
typedef int I;
int g(int I, int b = I(2)); // error: 'int' called
```

Similarly, the declaration of X::mem1() in the following example is illegal because no object is supplied for the nonstatic member X::a used as an initializer.

```
class X {
    int a;
    static b;
    mem1(int i = a); // error: nonstatic member 'a'
                     // used as default argument
    mem2(int i = b); // ok
};
```

The declaration of X::mem2() is legal, however, since no object is needed to access the static member X::b. Classes, objects, and members are described in §r.9.

A default argument is not part of the type of a function.

```
int f(int = 0);

void h()
{
    int j = f(1);
    int k = f();              // fine, means f(0)
}

int (*p1)(int) = &f;
int (*p2)() = &f;         // error: type mismatch
```

An overloaded operator (§r.13.4) cannot have default arguments.

r.8.3 Function Definitions

Function definitions have the form

> *function-definition:*
> > *decl-specifiers*$_{opt}$ *declarator ctor-initializer*$_{opt}$ *fct-body*
>
> *fct-body:*
> > *compound-statement*

The *declarator* in a *function-definition* must contain a declarator with the form

> D1 (*argument-declaration-list*) *cv-qualifier-list*$_{opt}$

as described in §r.8.2.5.

The formal arguments are in the scope of the outermost block of the *fct-body*.

A simple example of a complete function definition is

```
int max(int a, int b, int c)
{
    int m = (a > b) ? a : b;
    return (m > c) ? m : c;
}
```

Here int is the *decl-specifiers*; max(int a, int b, int c) is the *declarator*; {
/* ... */ } is the *fct-body*.

A *ctor-initializer* is used only in a constructor; see §r.12.1 and §r.12.6.

A *cv-qualifier-list* can be part of a nonstatic member function declaration, non-static member function definition, or pointer to member function only; see §r.9.3.1. It is part of the function type.

Note that unused formal arguments need not be named. For example,

```
void print(int a, int)
{
    printf("a = %d\n",a);
}
```

r.8.4 Initializers

A declarator may specify an initial value for the identifier being declared.

> *initializer:*
> > = *assignment-expression*
> > = { *initializer-list* ₁ *opt* }
> > (*expression-list*)
>
> *initializer-list:*
> > *assignment-expression*
> > *initializer-list* , *assignment-expression*
> > { *initializer-list* ₁ *opt* }

Automatic, register, static, and external variables may be initialized by arbitrary expressions involving constants and previously declared variables and functions.

```
int f(int);
int a = 2;
int b = f(a);
int c(b);
```

A pointer of type const T*, that is, a pointer to constant T, can be initialized with a pointer of type T*, but the reverse initialization is illegal. Objects of type T can be initialized with objects of type T independently of const and volatile modifiers on both the initialized variable and on the initializer. For example,

```
int a;
const int b = a;
int c = b;

const int* p0 = &a;
const int* p1 = &b;
int* p2 = &b;          // error: makes a pointer to
                       // nonconst point to a const

int *const p3 = p2;
int *const p4 = p1;    // error: makes a pointer to
                       // nonconst point to a const
const int* p5 = p1;
```

The reason for the two errors is the same: had those initializations been allowed they would have allowed the value of something declared const to be changed through an unqualified pointer.

Default argument expressions are more restricted; see §r.8.2.6.

Initialization of objects of classes with constructors is described in §r.12.6.1. Copying of class objects is described in §r.12.8. The order of initialization of static objects is described in §r.3.4 and §r.6.7.

Variables with storage class static (§r.3.5) that are not initialized are guaranteed to start off as 0 converted to the appropriate type. So are members of static class objects. The initial values of automatic and register variables that are not initialized are undefined.

When an initializer applies to a pointer or an object of arithmetic type, it consists of a single expression, perhaps in braces. The initial value of the object is taken from the expression; the same conversions as for assignment are performed.

Note that since `()` is not an initializer,

```
X a();
```

is not the declaration of an object of class X, but the declaration of a function taking no argument and returning an X.

An initializer for a static member is in the scope of the member's class. For example,

```
int a;

struct X {
     static int a;
     static int b;
};

int X::a = 1;
int X::b = a;      // X::b = X::a
```

See §r.8.2.6 for initializers used as default arguments.

r.8.4.1 Aggregates

An *aggregate* is an array or an object of a class (§r.9) with no constructors (§r.12.1), no private or protected members (§r.11), no base classes (§r.10), and no virtual functions (§r.10.2). When an aggregate is initialized the *initializer* may be an *initializer-list* consisting of a brace-enclosed, comma-separated list of initializers for the members of the aggregate, written in increasing subscript or member order. If the aggregate contains subaggregates, this rule applies recursively to the members of the subaggregate. If there are fewer initializers in the list than there are members of the aggregate, then the aggregate is padded with zeros of the appropriate types.

For example,

```
struct S { int a; char* b; int c; };
S ss = { 1, "asdf" };
```

initializes `ss.a` with 1, `ss.b` with `"asdf"`, and `ss.c` with 0.

An aggregate that is a class may also be initialized with an object of its class or of a class publicly derived from it (§r.12.8).

Braces may be elided as follows. If the *initializer-list* begins with a left brace, then the succeeding comma-separated list of initializers initializes the members of the aggregate; it is erroneous for there to be more initializers than members. If, however, the *initializer-list* or a subaggregate does not begin with a left brace, then only enough elements from the list are taken to account for the members of the aggregate; any remaining members are left to initialize the next member of the aggregate of which the current aggregate is a part.

For example,

```
int x[] = { 1, 3, 5 };
```

declares and initializes x as a one-dimensional array that has three members, since no size was specified and there are three initializers.

```
float y[4][3] = {
        { 1, 3, 5 },
        { 2, 4, 6 },
        { 3, 5, 7 },
    };
```

is a completely-bracketed initialization: 1, 3, and 5 initialize the first row of the array y[0], namely y[0][0], y[0][1], and y[0][2]. Likewise the next two lines initialize y[1] and y[2]. The initializer ends early and therefore y[3] is initialized with zeros. Precisely the same effect could have been achieved by

```
float y[4][3] = {
        1, 3, 5, 2, 4, 6, 3, 5, 7
    };
```

The last (rightmost) index varies fastest (§r.8.2.4).

The initializer for y begins with a left brace, but the one for y[0] does not, therefore three elements from the list are used. Likewise the next three are taken successively for y[1] and y[2]. Also,

```
float y[4][3] = {
        { 1 }, { 2 }, { 3 }, { 4 }
    };
```

initializes the first column of y (regarded as a two-dimensional array) and leaves the rest 0.

Initialization of arrays of objects of a class with constructors is described in §r.12.6.1.

The initializer for a union with no constructor is either a single expression of the same type, or a brace-enclosed initializer for the first member of the union. For example,

```
union u { int a; char* b; };
```

```
u a = { 1 };
u b = a;
u c = 1;                    // error
u d = { 0, "asdf" };        // error
u e = { "asdf" };           // error
```

There may not be more initializers than there are members or elements to initialize. For example,

```
char cv[4] = { 'a', 's', 'd', 'f', 0 };   // error
```

is an error.

r.8.4.2 Character Arrays

A `char` array (whether signed or unsigned) may be initialized by a *string-literal*; successive characters of the string initialize the members of the array. For example,

```
char msg[] = "Syntax error on line %s\n";
```

shows a character array whose members are initialized with a string. Note that because `'\n'` is a single character and because a trailing `'\0'` is appended, `sizeof(msg)` is 25.

There may not be more initializers than there are array elements. For example,

```
char cv[4] = "asdf";   // error
```

is an error since there is no space for the implied trailing `'\0'`.

r.8.4.3 References

A variable declared to be a `T&`, that is "reference to type `T`" (§r.8.2.2), must be initialized by an object of type `T` or by an object that can be converted into a `T`. For example,

```
void f()
{
    int i;
    int& r = i;   // 'r' refers to 'i'
    r = 1;        // the value of 'i' becomes 1
    int* p = &r;  // 'p' points to 'i'
    int& rr = r;  // 'rr' refers to what 'r' refers to,
                  // that is, to 'i'
}
```

A reference cannot be changed to refer to another object after initialization. Note that initialization of a reference is treated very differently from assignment to it. Argument passing (§r.5.2.2) and function value return (§r.6.6.3) are initializations.

The initializer may be omitted for a reference only in an argument declaration (§r.8.2.5), in the declaration of a function return type, in the declaration of a class member within its class declaration (§r.9.2), and where the `extern` specifier is explicitly used. For example,

```
int& r1;          // error: initializer missing
extern int& r2;   // ok
```

If the initializer for a reference to type `T` is an lvalue of type `T` or of a type derived (§r.10) from `T` for which `T` is an accessible base (§r.4.6), the reference will refer to the initializer; otherwise, if and only if the reference is to a `const` an object of type `T` will be created and initialized with the initializer. The reference then becomes a name for that object. For example,

```
double d = 1.0;

double& rd = d;              // rd refers to 'd'
const double& rcd = d;       // rcd refers to 'd'

double& rd2 = 1;             // error: type mismatch
const double& rcd2 = 1;      // rcd2 refers to temporary
                             // with value '1'
```

A reference to a `volatile T` can be initialized with a `volatile T` or a plain `T` but not a `const T`. A reference to a `const T` can be initialized with a `const T` or a plain `T` or something that can be converted into a plain `T` but not a `volatile T`. A reference to a plain `T` can be initialized only with a plain `T`.

The lifetime of a temporary object created in this way is the scope in which it is created (§r.3.5). Note that a reference to a class B can be initialized by an object of a class D provided B is an accessible and unambiguous base class of D (in that case a D is a B); see §r.4.7.

r.9   Classes

A class is a type. Its name becomes a *class-name* (§r.9.1), that is, a reserved word within its scope.

> *class-name:*
> > *identifier*

*Class-specifier*s and *elaborated-type-specifier*s (§r.7.1.6) are used to make *class-name*s. An object of a class consists of a (possibly empty) sequence of members.

> *class-specifier:*
> > *class-head* { *member-list*$_{opt}$ }

> *class-head:*
> > *class-key identifier*$_{opt}$ *base-spec*$_{opt}$
> > *class-key class-name base-spec*$_{opt}$

> *class-key:*
> > `class`
> > `struct`
> > `union`

The name of a class can be used as a *class-name* even within the *member-list* of the class specifier itself. A *class-specifier* is commonly referred to as a class declaration. A class is considered defined when its *class-specifier* has been seen even though its member functions are in general not yet defined.

Objects of an empty class have a nonzero size.

Class objects may be assigned, passed as arguments to functions, and returned by functions (except objects of classes for which copying has been restricted; see §r.12.8). Other plausible operators, such as equality comparison, can be defined by the user; see §r.13.4.

A structure is a class declared with the *class-key* struct; its members and base classes (§r.10) are public by default (§r.11). A union is a class declared with the *class-key* union; its members are public by default and it holds only one member at a time (§r.9.5).

r.9.1 Class Names

A class declaration introduces a new type. For example,

```
struct X { int a; };
struct Y { int a; };
X a1;
Y a2;
int a3;
```

declares three variables of three different types. This implies that

```
a1 = a2;        // error: Y assigned to X
a1 = a3;        // error: int assigned to X
```

are type mismatches, and that

```
int f(X);
int f(Y);
```

declare an overloaded (§r.13) function f() and not simply a single function f() twice. For the same reason,

```
struct S { int a; };
struct S { int a; };  // error, double definition
```

is an error because it defines S twice.

A class declaration introduces the class name into the scope where it is declared and hides any class, object, function, or other declaration of that name in an enclosing scope (§r.3.2). If a class name is declared in a scope where an object, function, or enumerator of the same name is also declared the class can be referred to only using an *elaborated-type-specifier* (§r.7.1.6). For example,

```
struct stat {
    // ...
};

stat gstat;                // use plain 'stat' to
                           // define variable

int stat(struct stat*); // redefine 'stat' as function
```

```
void f()
{
    struct stat* ps;     // 'struct' prefix needed
                         // to name struct stat
    // ...
    stat(ps);            // call stat()
    // ...
}
```

An *elaborated-type-specifier* with a *class-key* used without declaring an object or function introduces a class name exactly like a class declaration but without defining a class. For example,

```
struct s { int a; };

void g()
{
    struct s;    // hide global struct 's'
    s* p;        // refer to local struct 's'
    struct s { char* p; };  // declare local struct 's'
}
```

Such declarations allow declaration of classes that refer to each other. For example,

```
class vector;

class matrix {
    // ...
    friend vector operator*(matrix&, vector&);
};


class vector {
    // ...
    friend vector operator*(matrix&, vector&);
};
```

Declaration of `friends` is described in §r.11.4, operator functions in §r.13.4. If a class mentioned as a `friend` has not been declared its name is entered in the same scope as the name of the class containing the friend declaration (§r.11.4).

An *elaborated-type-specifier* (§r.7.1.6) can also be used in the declarations of objects and functions. It differs from a class declaration in that if a class of the elaborated name is in scope the elaborated name will refer to it. For example,

```
struct s { int a; };

void g()
{
    struct s* p = new s;      // refer to global 's'
    p->a = 1;
}
```

A name declaration takes effect immediately after the *identifier* is seen. For example,

```
class A * A;
```

first specifies A to be the name of a class and then redefines it as the name of a pointer to an object of that class. This means that the elaborated form `class A` must be used to refer to the class. Such artistry with names can be confusing and is best avoided.

A *typedef-name* (§r.7.1.3) that names a class is a *class-name*; see also §r.7.1.3.

r.9.2 Class Members

> *member-list:*
>> *member-declaration member-list*$_{opt}$
>> *access-specifier : member-list*$_{opt}$
>
> *member-declaration:*
>> *decl-specifiers*$_{opt}$ *member-declarator-list*$_{opt}$;
>> *function-definition* ;$_{opt}$
>> *qualified-name* ;
>
> *member-declarator-list:*
>> *member-declarator*
>> *member-declarator-list , member-declarator*
>
> *member-declarator:*
>> *declarator pure-specifier*$_{opt}$
>> *identifier*$_{opt}$: *constant-expression*
>
> *pure-specifier:*
>> = 0

A *member-list* may declare data, functions, classes, enumerations (§r.7.2), bit-fields (§r.9.6), friends (§r.11.4), and type names (§r.7.1.3, §r.9.1). A *member-list* may also contain declarations adjusting the access to member names; see §r.11.3. A member may not be declared twice in the *member-list*. The *member-list* defines the full set of members of the class. No member can be added elsewhere.

Note that a single name can denote several function members provided their types are sufficiently different (§r.13). Note that a *member-declarator* cannot contain an *initializer* (§r.8.4). A member can be initialized using a constructor; see §r.12.1.

A member may not be `auto`, `extern`, or `register`.

The *decl-specifiers* can be omitted in function declarations only. The *member-declarator-list* can be omitted only after a *class-specifier*, an *enum-specifier*, or *decl-specifiers* of the form `friend` *elaborated-type-specifier*. A *pure-specifier* may be used only in the declaration of a virtual function (§r.10.2).

Members that are class objects must be objects of previously declared classes. In particular, a class `cl` may not contain an object of class `cl`, but it may contain a pointer or reference to an object of class `cl`. When an array is used as the type of a nonstatic member all dimensions must be specified.

A simple example of a class declaration is

```
struct tnode {
    char tword[20];
    int count;
    tnode *left;
    tnode *right;
};
```

which contains an array of twenty characters, an integer, and two pointers to similar structures. Once this declaration has been given, the declaration

```
tnode s, *sp;
```

declares s to be a `tnode` and sp to be a pointer to a `tnode`. With these declarations, `sp->count` refers to the `count` member of the structure to which sp points; `s.left` refers to the `left` subtree pointer of the structure s; and `s.right->tword[0]` refers to the initial character of the `tword` member of the `right` subtree of s.

Nonstatic data members of a class declared without an intervening *access-specifier* are allocated so that later members have higher addresses within a class object. The order of allocation of nonstatic data members separated by an *access-specifier* is implementation dependent (§r.11.1). Implementation alignment requirements may cause two adjacent members not to be allocated immediately after each other; so may requirements for space for managing virtual functions (§r.10.2) and virtual base classes (§r.10.1); see also §r.5.4.

A function member (§r.9.3) with the same name as its class is a constructor (§r.12.1). A static data member, enumerator, member of an anonymous union, or nested type may not have the same name as its class.

r.9.3 Member Functions

A function declared as a member (without the `friend` specifier; §r.11.4) is called a member function, and is called using the class member syntax (§r.5.2.4). For example,

```
struct tnode {
    char tword[20];
    int count;
    tnode *left;
    tnode *right;
    void set(char*, tnode* l, tnode* r);
};
```

Here set is a member function and can be called like this:

```
void f(tnode n1, tnode n2)
{
    n1.set("abc",&n2,0);
    n2.set("def",0,0);
}
```

The definition of a member function is considered to be within the scope of its class. This means that (provided it is nonstatic §r.9.4) it can use names of members of its class directly. A static member function can use only the names of static members, enumerators, and nested types directly. If the definition of a member function is lexically outside the class declaration, the member function name must be qualified by the class name using the : : operator. For example,

```
void tnode::set(char* w, tnode* l, tnode* r)
{
    count = strlen(w)+1;
    if (sizeof(tword)<=count)
        error("tnode string too long");
    strcpy(tword,w);
    left = l;
    right = r;
}
```

The notation tnode::set specifies that the function set is a member of and in the scope of class tnode. The member names tword, count, left, and right refer to members of the object for which the function was called. Thus, in the call n1.set("abc",&n2,0), tword refers to n1.tword, and in the call n2.set("def",0,0) it refers to n2.tword. The functions strlen, error, and strcpy must be declared elsewhere.

Members may be defined (§r.3.1) outside their class declaration if they have already been declared but not defined in the class declaration; they may not be redeclared. See also §r.3.3. Function members may be mentioned in friend declarations after their class has been defined. Each member function that is called must have exactly one definition in a program.

The effect of calling a nonstatic member function (§r.9.4) of a class X for something that is not an object of class X is undefined.

r.9.3.1 The this Pointer

In a nonstatic (§r.9.3) member function, the keyword `this` is a pointer to the object
for which the function is called. The type of `this` in a member function of a class X
is X `*const` unless the member function is declared `const` or `volatile`; in those
cases, the type of `this` is `const X *const` and `volatile X *const`, respectively. A function declared `const` and `volatile` has a `this` with the type
`const volatile X *const`. See also §r.18.3.3. For example,

```
struct s {
    int a;
    int f() const;
    int g() { return a++; }
    int h() const { return a++; } // error
};

int s::f() const { return a; }
```

The `a++` in the body of `s::h` is an error because it tries to modify (a part of) the
object for which `s::h()` is called. This is not allowed in a `const` member function
where `this` is a pointer to `const`, that is, `*this` is a `const`.

   A `const` member function (that is, a member function declared with the `const`
qualifier) may be called for `const` and non-const objects, whereas a non-const
member function may be called only for a non-const object. For example,

```
void k(s& x, const s& y)
{
    x.f();
    x.g();
    y.f();
    y.g();        // error
}
```

The call `y.g()` is an error because `y` is `const` and `s::g()` is a non-const member function that could (and does) modify the object for which it was called.

   Similarly, only `volatile` member functions (that is, a member function
declared with the `volatile` specifier) may be invoked for `volatile` objects. A
member function can be both `const` and `volatile`.

   Constructors (§r.12.1) and destructors (§r.12.4) may be invoked for a `const` or
`volatile` object. Constructors (§r.12.1) and destructors (§r.12.4) cannot be
declared `const` or `volatile`.

r.9.3.2 Inline Member Functions

A member function may be defined (§r.8.3) in the class declaration, in which case it is
`inline` (§r.7.1.2). Defining a function within a class declaration is equivalent to
declaring it `inline` and defining it immediately after the class declaration; this
rewriting is considered to be done after preprocessing but before syntax analysis and
type checking of the function definition. Thus

```
int b;
struct x {
    char* f() { return b; }
    char* b;
};
```

is equivalent to

```
int b;
struct x {
    char* f();
    char* b;
};

inline char* x::f() { return b; } // moved
```

Thus the b used in x::f() is X::b and not the global b.

Member functions can be defined even in local or nested class declarations where this rewriting would be syntactically illegal. See §r.9.8 for a discussion of local classes and §r.9.7 for a discussion of nested classes.

r.9.4 Static Members

A data or function member of a class may be declared static in the class declaration. There is only one copy of a static data member, shared by all objects of the class in a program. A static member is not part of objects of a class. Static members of a global class have external linkage (§r.3.3). The declaration of a static data member in its class declaration is *not* a definition. A definition is required elsewhere; see also §r.18.3.

A static member function does not have a this pointer so it can access nonstatic members of its class only by using . or ->. A static member function cannot be virtual. There cannot be a static and a nonstatic member function with the same name and the same argument types.

Static members of a local class (§r.9.8) have no linkage and cannot be defined outside the class declaration. It follows that a local class cannot have static data members.

A static member mem of class cl can be referred to as cl::mem (§r.5.1), that is, independently of any object. It can also be referred to using the . and -> member access operators (§r.5.2.4). When a static member is accessed through a member access operator, the expression on the left side of the . or -> is not evaluated. The static member mem exists even if no objects of class cl have been created. For example, in the following, run_chain, idle, and so on exist even if no process objects have been created:

```
class process {
    static int no_of_processes;
    static process* run_chain;
    static process* running;
    static process* idle;
    // ...
public:
    // ...
    int state();
    static void reschedule();
    // ...
};
```

and `reschedule` can be used without reference to a `process` object, as follows:

```
void f()
{
    process::reschedule();
}
```

Static members of a global class are initialized exactly like global objects and only in file scope. For example,

```
void process::reschedule() { /* ... */ };
int process::no_of_processes = 1;
process* process::running = get_main();
process* process::run_chain = process::running;
```

Static members obey the usual class member access rules (§r.11) except that they can be initialized (in file scope).

The type of a static member does not involve its class name; thus the type of `pro-cess :: no_of_processes` is `int` and the type of `&process :: reschedule` is `void(*)()`.

r.9.5 Unions

A union may be thought of as a structure whose member objects all begin at offset zero and whose size is sufficient to contain any of its member objects. At most one of the member objects can be stored in a union at any time. A union may have member functions (including constructors and destructors), but not virtual (§r.10.2) functions. A union may not have base classes. A union may not be used as a base class. An object of a class with a constructor or a destructor or a user-defined assignment operator (§r.13.4.3) cannot be a member of a union. A union can have no `static` data members.

A union of the form

```
union { member-list } ;
```

is called an anonymous union; it defines an unnamed object (and not a type). The names of the members of an anonymous union must be distinct from other names in the scope in which the union is declared; they are used directly in that scope without the usual member access syntax (§r.5.2.4). For example,

```
void f()
{
    union { int a; char* p; };
    a = 1;
    // ...
    p = "Jennifer";
    // ...
}
```

Here a and p are used like ordinary (nonmember) variables, but since they are union members they have the same address.

A global anonymous union must be declared static. An anonymous union may not have private or protected members (§r.11). An anonymous union may not have function members.

A union for which objects or pointers are declared is not an anonymous union. For example,

```
union { int aa; char* p; } obj, *ptr = &obj;
aa = 1;          // error
ptr->aa = 1;    // ok
```

The assignment to plain aa is illegal since the member name is not associated with any particular object.

Initialization of unions that do not have constructors is described in §r.8.4.1.

r.9.6 Bit-Fields

A *member-declarator* of the form

> *identifier*$_{opt}$: *constant-expression*

specifies a bit-field; its length is set off from the bit-field name by a colon. Allocation of bit-fields within a class object is implementation dependent. Fields are packed into some addressable allocation unit. Fields straddle allocation units on some machines and not on others. Alignment of bit-fields is implementation dependent. Fields are assigned right-to-left on some machines, left-to-right on others.

An unnamed bit-field is useful for padding to conform to externally-imposed layouts. As a special case, an unnamed bit-field with a width of zero specifies alignment of the next bit-field at an allocation unit boundary.

An unnamed field is not a member and cannot be initialized.

A bit-field must have integral type (§r.3.6.1). It is implementation dependent whether a plain (neither explicitly signed nor unsigned) int field is signed or unsigned. The address-of operator & may not be applied to a bit-field, so there are no pointers to bit-fields. Nor are there references to bit-fields.

r.9.7 Nested Class Declarations

A class may be declared within another class. A class declared within another is called a *nested* class. The name of a nested class is local to its enclosing class. The nested class is in the scope of its enclosing class. Except by using explicit pointers, references, and object names, declarations in a nested class can use only type names, static members, and enumerators from the enclosing class.

```
int x;
int y;

class enclose {
public:
      int x;
      static int s;


      class inner {


          void f(int i)
          {
              x = i;    // error: assign to enclose::x
              s = i;    // ok: assign to enclose::s
              ::x = i; // ok: assign to global x
              y = i;        // ok: assign to global y
          }


          void g(enclose* p, int i)
          {
              p->x = i;    // ok: assign to enclose::x
          }


      };
};

inner* p = 0;    // error 'inner' not in scope
```

Member functions of a nested class have no special access to members of an enclosing class; they obey the usual access rules (§r.11). Member functions of an enclosing class have no special access to members of a nested class; they obey the usual access rules. For example,

```
class E {
      int x;
```

```
class I {
    int y;
    void f(E* p, int i)
    {
        p->x = i;    // error: E::x is private
    }
};

    int g(I* p)
    {
        return p->y;    // error: I::y is private
    }
};
```

Member functions and static data members of a nested class can be defined in the global scope. For example,

```
class enclose {
    class inner {
        static int x;
        void f(int i);
    };
};

typedef enclose::inner ei;
int ei::x = 1;

void enclose::inner::f(int i) { /* ... */ }
```

Like a member function, a friend function defined within a class is in the lexical scope of that class; it obeys the same rules for name binding as the member functions (described above and in §r.10.4) and like them has no special access rights to members of an enclosing class or local variables of an enclosing function (§r.11).

r.9.8 Local Class Declarations

A class can be declared within a function definition; such a class is called a *local* class. The name of a local class is local to its enclosing scope. The local class is in the scope of the enclosing scope. Declarations in a local class can use only type names, static variables, `extern` variables and functions, and enumerators from the enclosing scope. For example,

```
int x;
void f()
{
    static int s ;
    int x;
    extern int g();
```

```
struct local {
        int h() { return x; }    // error: 'x' is auto
        int j() { return s; }    // ok
        int k() { return ::x; }  // ok
        int l() { return g(); }  // ok
};
// ...
}

local* p = 0;    // error: 'local' not in scope
```

An enclosing function has no special access to members of the local class; it obeys the usual access rules (§r.11). Member functions of a local class must be defined within their class definition. A local class may not have static data members.

r.9.9 Local Type Names

Type names obey exactly the same scope rules as other names. In particular, type names defined within a class declaration cannot be used outside their class without qualification. For example,

```
class X {
public:
    typedef int I;
    class Y { /* ... */ };
    I a;
};

I b;      // error
Y c;      // error
X::Y d;   // ok
```

The following rule limits the context sensitivity of the rewrite rules for inline functions and for class member declarations in general. A *class-name* or a *typedef-name* or the name of a constant used in a type name may not be redefined in a class declaration after being used in the class declaration, nor may a name that is not a *class-name* or a *typedef-name* be redefined to a *class-name* or a *typedef-name* in a class declaration after being used in the class declaration. For example,

```
typedef int c;
enum { i = 1 };
```

```
class X {
    char v[i];
    int f() { return sizeof(c); }
    char c;                 // error: typedef name
                            // redefined after use
    enum { i = 2 };         // error: 'i' redefined after
                            // use in type name 'char[i]'
};

typedef char* T;

struct Y {
        T a;
        typedef long T; // error: T already used
        T b;
};
```

r.10   Derived Classes

A list of base classes may be specified in a class declaration using the notation:

> *base-spec:*
>> : *base-list*

> *base-list:*
>> *base-specifier*
>> *base-list* , *base-specifier*

> *base-specifier:*
>> *complete-class-name*
>> virtual *access-specifier*$_{opt}$ *complete-class-name*
>> *access-specifier* virtual$_{opt}$ *complete-class-name*

> *access-specifier:*
>> private
>> protected
>> public

The *class-name* in a *base-specifier* must denote a previously declared class (§r.9), which is called a base class for the class being declared. A class is said to be derived from its base classes. For the meaning of *access-specifier* see §r.11. Unless redefined in the derived class, members of a base class can be referred to as if they were members of the derived class. The base class members are said to be *inherited* by the derived class. The scope resolution operator :: (§r.5.1) may be used to refer to a base member explicitly. This allows access to a name that has been redefined in the derived class. A derived class can itself serve as a base class subject to access control; see §r.11.2. A pointer to a derived class may be implicitly converted to a pointer to an accessible unambiguous base class (§r.4.6). A reference to a derived class may be implicitly converted to a reference to an accessible unambiguous base class (§r.4.7).

For example,

```
class base {
public:
     int a, b;
};

class derived : public base {
public:
     int b, c;
};

void f()
{
     derived d;
     d.a = 1;
     d.base::b = 2;
     d.b = 3;
     d.c = 4;
     base* bp = &d;   // standard conversion:
                      // derived* to base*
}
```

assigns to the four members of d and makes bp point to d.

A class is called a *direct base* if it is mentioned in the *base-list* and an *indirect base* if it is not a direct base but is a base class of one of the classes mentioned in the *base-list*.

Note that in the *class-name* : : *name* notation, *name* may be a name of a member of an indirect base class; the notation simply specifies a class in which to start looking for *name*. For example,

```
class A { public: void f(); };
class B : public A { };
class C : public B { public: void f(); };

void C::f()
{
     f();     // Call C's f()
     A::f(); // call A's f()
     B::f(); // call A's f()
}
```

Here, A: : f () is called twice since it is the only f () in B.

Initialization of objects representing base classes can be specified in constructors; see §r.12.6.2.

r.10.1 Multiple Base Classes

A class may be derived from any number of base classes. For example,

```
class A { /* ... */ };
class B { /* ... */ };
class C { /* ... */ };
class D : public A, public B, public C { /* ... */ };
```

The use of more than one direct base class is often called multiple inheritance.

The order of derivation is not significant except possibly for default initialization by constructor (§r.12.1), for cleanup (§r.12.4), and for storage layout (§r.5.4, §r.9.2, §r.11.1). The order in which storage is allocated for base classes is implementation dependent.

A class may not be specified as a direct base class of a derived class more than once but it may be an indirect base class more than once.

```
class B { /* ... */ };
class D : public B, public B { /* ... */ };   // illegal

class L { /* ... */ };
class A : public L { /* ... */ };
class B : public L { /* ... */ };
class C : public A, public B { /* ... */ };    // legal
```

Here, an object of class C will have two sub-objects of class L.

The keyword `virtual` may be added to a base class specifier. A single sub-object of the virtual base class is shared by every base class that specified the base class to be virtual. For example,

```
class V { /* ... */ };
class A : virtual public V { /* ... */ };
class B : virtual public V { /* ... */ };
class C : public A, public B { /* ... */ };
```

Here class C has only one sub-object of class V.

A class may have both virtual and nonvirtual base classes of a given type.

```
class B { /* ... */ };
class X : virtual public B { /* ... */ };
class Y : virtual public B { /* ... */ };
class Z : public B { /* ... */ };
class AA : public X, public Y, public Z { /* ... */ };
```

Here class AA has two sub-objects of class B: Z's B and the virtual B shared by X and Y.

r.10.1.1 Ambiguities

Access to base class members must be unambiguous. Access to a base class member is ambiguous if the expression used refers to more than one function, object, type, or enumerator. The check for ambiguity takes place before access control (§r.11). For example,

```
class A {
public:
    int a;
    int (*b)();
    int f();
    int f(int);
    int g();
};

class B {
    int a;
    int b();
public:
    int f();
    int g;
    int h();
    int h(int);
};

class C : public A, public B {};

void g(C* pc)
{
    pc->a = 1;   // error: ambiguous: A::a or B::a
    pc->b();     // error: ambiguous: A::b or B::b
    pc->f();     // error: ambiguous: A::f or B::f
    pc->f(1);    // error: ambiguous: A::f or B::f
    pc->g();     // error: ambiguous: A::g or B::g
    pc->g = 1;   // error: ambiguous: A::g or B::g
    pc->h();     // ok
    pc->h(1);    // ok
}
```

If the name of an overloaded function is unambiguously found overloading resolution also takes place before access control. Ambiguities can be resolved by qualifying a name with its class name. For example,

```
class A {
public:
    int f();
};

class B {
public:
    int f();
};
```

```
class C : public A, public B {
    int f() { return A::f() + B::f(); }
};
```

When virtual base classes are used, a single function, object, type, or enumerator may be reached through more than one path through the directed acyclic graph of base classes. This is not an ambiguity. The identical use with nonvirtual base classes is an ambiguity; in that case more than one sub-object is involved. For example,

```
class V { public: int v; };
class A { public: int a; };
class B : public A, public virtual V {};
class C : public A, public virtual V {};


class D : public B, public C { public: void f(); };

void D::f()
{
    v++;        // ok: only one 'v' in 'D'
    a++;        // error, ambiguous: two 'a's in 'D'
}
```

When virtual base classes are used, more than one function, object, or enumerator may be reached through paths through the directed acyclic graph of base classes. This is an ambiguity unless one of the names found *dominates* the others. The identical use with nonvirtual base classes is an ambiguity; in that case more than one sub-object is involved.

A name B::f *dominates* a name A::f if its class B has A as a base. If a name dominates another no ambiguity exists between the two; the dominant name is used when there is a choice. For example,

```
class V { public: int f(); int x; };
class B : public virtual V { public: int f(); int x; };
class C : public virtual V { };


class D : public B, public C { void g(); };

void D::g()
{
    x++;        // ok: B::x dominates V::x
    f();        // ok: B::f() dominates V::f()
}
```

An explicit or implicit conversion from a pointer or reference to a derived class to a pointer or reference to one of its base classes must unambiguously refer to the same object representing the base class. For example,

```
class V { };
class A { };
class B : public A, public virtual V { };
class C : public A, public virtual V { };
class D : public B, public C { };


void g()
{
    D d;
    B* pb = &d;
    A* pa = &d;   // error, ambiguous: C's A or B's A ?
    V* pv = &d;   // fine: only one V sub-object
}
```

r.10.2 Virtual Functions

If a class base contains a virtual (§r.7.1.2) function vf, and a class derived
derived from it also contains a function vf of the same type, then a call of vf for an
object of class derived invokes derived::vf (even if the access is through a
pointer or reference to base). The derived class function is said to *override* the base
class function. If the function types (§r.8.2.5) are different, however, the functions are
considered different and the virtual mechanism is not invoked (see also §r.13.1).
It is an error for a derived class function to differ from a base class' virtual function in
the return type only. For example,

```
struct base {
    virtual void vf1();
    virtual void vf2();
    virtual void vf3();
    void f();
};


class derived : public base {
public:
    void vf1();
    void vf2(int);       // hides base::vf2()
    char vf3();   // error: differs in return type only
    void f();
};
```

```
void g()
{
    derived d;
    base* bp = &d;   // standard conversion:
                     // derived* to base*
    bp->vf1();       // calls derived::vf1
    bp->vf2();       // calls base::vf2
    bp->f();         // calls base::f
}
```

The calls invoke derived::vf1, base::vf2, and base::f, respectively, for the class derived object named d. That is, the interpretation of the call of a virtual function depends on the type of the object for which it is called, whereas the interpretation of a call of a nonvirtual member function depends only on the type of the pointer or reference denoting that object. For example, bp->vf1() calls derived::vf1() because bp points to an object of class derived in which derived::vf1() has overridden the virtual function base::vf1().

The virtual specifier implies membership, so a virtual function cannot be a global (nonmember) (§r.7.1.2) function. Nor can a virtual function be a static member, since a virtual function call relies on a specific object for determining which function to invoke. A virtual function can be declared a friend in another class. An overriding function is itself considered virtual. The virtual specifier may be used for an overriding function in the derived class, but such use is redundant. A virtual function in a base class must be defined or declared pure (§r.10.3). A virtual function that has been defined in a base class need not be defined in a derived class. If it is not, the function defined for the base class is used in all calls.

Explicit qualification with the scope operator (§r.5.1) suppresses the virtual call mechanism. For example,

```
class B { public: virtual void f(); };
class D : public B { public: void f(); };

void D::f() { /* ... */ B::f(); }
```

Here, the call of f in D really does call B::f and not D::f.

r.10.3 Abstract Classes

The abstract class mechanism supports the notion of a general concept, such as a shape, of which only more concrete variants, such as circle and square, can actually be used. An abstract class can also be used to define an interface for which derived classes provide a variety of implementations.

An *abstract class* is a class that can be used only as a base class of some other class; no objects of an abstract class may be created except as objects representing a base class of a class derived from it. A class is abstract if it has at least one *pure virtual function*. A virtual function is specified *pure* by using a *pure-specifier* (§r.9.2) in the function declaration in the class declaration. A pure virtual function need be defined only if explicitly called with the *qualified-name* syntax (§r.5.1). For example,

```
class point { /* ... */ };
class shape {              // abstract class
    point center;
    // ...
public:
    point where() { return center; }
    void move(point p) { center=p; draw(); }
    virtual void rotate(int) = 0;   // pure virtual
    virtual void draw() = 0;        // pure virtual
    // ...
};
```

An abstract class may not be used as an argument type, as a function return type, or as the type of an explicit conversion. Pointers and references to an abstract class may be declared. For example,

```
shape x;            // error: object of abstract class
shape* p;           // ok
shape f();          // error
void g(shape);      // error
shape& h(shape&);   // ok
```

Pure virtual functions are inherited as pure virtual functions. For example,

```
class ab_circle : public shape {
    int radius;
public:
    void rotate(int) {}
    // ab_circle::draw() is a pure virtual
};
```

Since shape::draw() is a pure virtual function ab_circle::draw() is a pure virtual by default. The alternative declaration,

```
class circle : public shape {
    int radius;
public:
    void rotate(int) {}
    void draw(); // must be defined somewhere
};
```

would make class circle nonabstract and a definition of circle::draw() must be provided somewhere.

    Member functions can be called from a constructor of an abstract class; the effect of calling a pure virtual function directly or indirectly for the object being created from such a constructor is undefined.

r.10.4 Summary of Scope Rules

The scope rules for C++ programs can now be summarized. These rules apply uniformly for all names (including *typedef-names* (§r.7.1.3) and *class-names* (§r.9.1))
wherever the grammar allows such names in the context discussed by a particular
rule. This section discusses lexical scope only; see §r.3.3 for an explanation of linkage issues. The notion of point of declaration is discussed in (§r.3.2).

Any use of a name must be unambiguous (up to overloading) in its scope
(§r.10.1.1). Only if the name is found to be unambiguous in its scope are access rules
considered (§r.11). Only if no access control errors are found is the type of the object,
function, or enumerator named considered.

A name used outside any function and class or prefixed by the unary scope operator : : (and *not* qualified by the binary : : operator or the -> or . operators) must be
the name of a global object, function, enumerator, or type.

A name specified after X: :, after obj., where obj is an X or a reference to X, or
after ptr->, where ptr is a pointer to X must be the name of a member of class X or
be a member of a base class of X. In addition, ptr in ptr-> may be an object of a
class Y that has operator->() declared so ptr->operator->() eventually
resolves to a pointer to X (§r.13.4.6).

A name that is not qualified in any of the ways described above and that is used in
a function that is not a class member must be declared in the block in which it occurs
or in an enclosing block or be a global name. The declaration of a local name hides
declarations of the same name in enclosing blocks and global names. In particular, no
overloading occurs of names in different scopes (§r.13.4).

A name that is not qualified in any of the ways described above and that is used in
a function that is a nonstatic member of class X must be declared in the block in
which it occurs or in an enclosing block, be a member of class X or a base class of
class X, or be a global name. The declaration of a local name hides declarations of the
same name in enclosing blocks, members of the function's class, and global names.
The declaration of a member name hides declarations of the same name in base
classes and global names.

A name that is not qualified in one of the ways described above and is used in a
static member function of a class X must be declared in the block in which it occurs,
in an enclosing block, be a static member of class X, or a base class of class X, or be a
global name.

A function argument name in a function definition (§r.8.3) is in the scope of the
outermost block of the function (in particular, it is a local name). A function argument name in a function declaration (§r.8.2.5) that is not a function definition is in a
local scope that disappears immediately after the function declaration. A default argument is in the scope determined by the point of declaration (§r.3.2) of its formal argument, but may not access local variables or nonstatic class members; it is evaluated at
each point of call (§r.8.2.6).

A *ctor-initializer* (§r.12.6.2) is evaluated in the scope of the outermost block of
the constructor it is specified for. In particular, it can refer to the constructor's

argument names.

r.11 Member Access Control

A member of a class can be

> `private`; that is, its name can be used only by member functions and friends of the class in which it is declared.

> `protected`; that is, its name can be used only by member functions and friends of the class in which it is declared and by member functions and friends of classes derived from this class (see §r.11.5).

> `public`; that is, its name can be used by any function.

Members of a class declared with the keyword `class` are `private` by default. Members of a class declared with the keywords `struct` or `union` are `public` by default. For example,

```
class X {
    int a;  // X::a is private by default
};
```

```
struct S {
    int a;  // S::a is public by default
};
```

r.11.1 Access Specifiers

Member declarations may be labeled by an *access-specifier* (§r.10):

> *access-specifier* : *member-list*_{opt}

An *access-specifier* specifies the access rules for members following it until the end of the class or until another *access-specifier* is encountered. For example,

```
class X {
    int a;  // X::a is private by default: 'class' used
public:
    int b;  // X::b is public
    int c;  // X::c is public
};
```

Any number of access specifiers is allowed and no particular order is required. For example,

```
struct S {
    int a;    // S::a is public by default: 'struct' used
protected:
    int b;    // S::b is protected
private:
    int c;    // S::c is private
public:
    int d;    // S::d is public
};
```

The order of allocation of data members with separate *access-specifier* labels is implementation dependent (§r.9.2).

r.11.2 Access Specifiers for Base Classes

If a class is declared to be a base class (§r.10) for another class using the `public` access specifier, the `public` members of the base class are `public` members of the derived class and `protected` members of the base class are `protected` members of the derived class. If a class is declared to be a base class for another class using the `private` access specifier, the `public` and `protected` members of the base class are `private` members of the derived class. Private members of a base class remain inaccessible even to derived classes unless `friend` declarations within the base class declaration are used to grant access explicitly.

In the absence of an *access-specifier* for a base class, `public` is assumed when the derived class is declared `struct` and `private` is assumed when the class is declared `class`. For example,

```
class B { /* ... */ };
class D1 : private B { /* ... */ };
class D2 : public B { /* ... */ };
class D3 : B { /* ... */ };        // 'B' private by default
struct D4 : public B { /* ... */ };
struct D5 : private B { /* ... */ };
struct D6 : B { /* ... */ };       // 'B' public by default
```

Here B is a public base of D2, D4, and D6, and a private base of D1, D3, and D5.

Specifying a base class *private* does not affect access to static members of the base class. If, however, an object or a pointer requiring conversion is used to select the static member the usual rules for pointer conversions apply.

Members and friends of a class X can implicitly convert an X* to a pointer to a private immediate base class of X.

r.11.3 Access Declarations

The access to a member of a base class in a derived class can be adjusted by mentioning its *qualified-name* in the `public` or `protected` part of a derived class declaration. Such mention is called an *access declaration*.

For example,

```
class B {
    int a;
public:
    int b, c;
    int bf();
};


class D : private B {
    int d;
public:
    B::c;   // adjust access to 'B::c'
    int e;
    int df();
};

int ef(D&);
```

The external function ef can use only the names c, e, and df. Being a member of D, the function df can use the names b, c, bf, d, e, and df, but not a. Being a member of B, the function bf can use the members a, b, c, and bf.

An access declaration may not be used to restrict access to a member that is accessible in the base class, nor may it be used to enable access to a member that is not accessible in the base class. For example,

```
class B {
public:
    int a;
private:
    int b;
protected:
    int c;
};


class D : private B {
public:
    B::a;   // make 'a' a public member of D
    B::b;   // error: attempt to grant access
            // can't make 'b' a public member of D
protected:
    B::c;   // make 'c' a protected member of D
    B::a;   // error: attempt to reduce access
            // can't make 'a' a protected member of D
};
```

An access declaration for the name of an overloaded function adjusts the access to all functions of that name in the base class. For example,

```
class X {
public:
    f();
    f(int);
};

class Y : private X {
public:
    X::f;   // makes X::f() and X::f(int) public in Y
};
```

   The access to a base class member cannot be adjusted in a derived class that also defines a member of that name. For example,

```
class X {
public:
    void f();
};

class Y : private X {
public:
    void f(int);
    X::f;   // error: two declarations of f
};
```

r.11.4 Friends

A friend of a class is a function that is not a member of the class but is permitted to use the private and protected member names from the class. The name of a friend is not in the scope of the class, and the friend is not called with the member access operators (§r.5.2.4) unless it is a member of another class. The following example illustrates the differences between members and friends:

```
class X {
    int a;
    friend void friend_set(X*, int);
public:
    void member_set(int);
};


void friend_set(X* p, int i) { p->a = i; }
void X::member_set(int i) { a = i; }
```

```
void f()
{
    X obj;
    friend_set(&obj,10);
    obj.member_set(10);
}
```

When a `friend` declaration refers to an overloaded name or operator, only the function specified by the argument types becomes a friend. A member function of a class X can be a friend of a class Y. For example,

```
class Y {
    friend char* X::foo(int);
    // ...
};
```

All the functions of a class X can be made friends of a class Y by a single declaration using an *elaborated-type-specifier* (§r.9.1):

```
class Y {
    friend class X;
    // ...
};
```

Declaring a class to be a friend also implies that private and protected names from the class granting friendship can be used in the class receiving it. For example,

```
class X {
    enum { a=100 };
    friend class Y;
};

class Y {
    int v[X::a];   // ok, Y is a friend of X
};

class Z {
    int v[X::a];   // error: X::a is private
};
```

If a class or a function mentioned as a friend has not been declared its name is entered in the same scope as the name of the class containing the friend declaration (§r.9.1).

A function first declared in a friend declaration is equivalent to an `extern` declaration (§r.3.3, §r.7.1.1).

A `friend` function defined in a class declaration is `inline` and the rewriting rule specified for member functions (§r.9.3.2) is applied. A `friend` function defined in a class is in the (lexical) scope of the class in which it is defined. A friend function defined outside the class is not.

Friend declarations are not affected by *access-specifiers* (§r.9.2).

Friendship is neither inherited nor transitive. For example,

```
class A {
    friend class B;
    int a;
};


class B {
    friend class C;
};


class C   {
    void f(A* p)
    {
        p->a++;   // error: C is not a friend of A
                  // despite being a friend of a friend
    }
};


class D : public B  {
    void f(A* p)
    {
        p->a++;   // error: D is not a friend of A
                  // despite being derived from a friend
    }
};
```

r.11.5 Protected Member Access

A friend or a member function of a derived class can access a protected static member
of a base class. A friend or a member function of a derived class can access a protected nonstatic member of one of its base classes only through a pointer to, reference
to, or object of the derived class (or any class derived from that class). For example,

```
class B {
protected:
    int i;
};


class D1 : public B {
};


class D2 : public B {
    friend void fr(B*,D1*,D2*);
    void mem(B*,D1*);
};
```

```
void fr(B* pb, D1* p1, D2* p2)
{
    pb->i = 1;   // illegal
    p1->i = 2;   // illegal
    p2->i = 3;   // ok (access through a D2)
}

void D2::mem(B* pb, D1* p1)
{
    pb->i = 1;   // illegal
    p1->i = 2;   // illegal
    i = 3;       // ok (access through 'this')
}

void g(B* pb, D1* p1, D2* p2)
{
    pb->i = 1;   // illegal
    p1->i = 2;   // illegal
    p2->i = 3;   // illegal
}
```

r.11.6 Access to Virtual Functions

The access rules (§r.11) for a virtual function are determined by its declaration and are not affected by the rules for a function that later overrides it. For example,

```
class B {
public:
    virtual f();
};

class D : public B {
private:
    f();
};

void f()
{
    D d;
    B* pb = &d;
    D* pd = &d;

    pb->f();   // ok: B::f() is public,
               // D::f() is invoked
    pd->f();   // error: D::f() is private
}
```

Access is checked at the call point using the type of the expression used to denote the object for which the member function is called (B* in the example above). The access of the member function in the class in which it was defined (D in the example above) is in general not known.

r.11.7 Multiple Access

If a name can be reached by several paths through a multiple inheritance graph, the access is that of the path that gives most access. For example,

```
class W { public: void f(); };
class A : private virtual W { };
class B : public virtual W { };
class C : public A, public B {
    void f() { W::f(); }   // ok
};
```

Since W::f() is available to C::f() along the public path through B, access is legal.

r.12   Special Member Functions

Some member functions are special in that they affect the way objects of a class are created, copied, and destroyed, and how values may be converted to values of other types. Often such special functions are called implicitly.

These member functions obey the usual access rules (§r.11). For example, declaring a constructor protected ensures that only derived classes and friends can create objects using it.

r.12.1 Constructors

A member function with the same name as its class is called a constructor; it is used to construct values of its class type. If a class has a constructor, each object of that class will be initialized before any use is made of the object; see §r.12.6.

A constructor can be invoked for a const or volatile object. A constructor may not be declared const or volatile (§r.9.3.1). A constructor may not be virtual. A constructor may not be static.

Constructors are not inherited. Default constructors and copy constructors, however, are generated (by the compiler) where needed (§r.12.8). Generated constructors are public.

A *default constructor* for a class X is a constructor of class X that can be called without an argument. A default constructor will be generated for a class X only if no constructor has been declared for class X.

A *copy constructor* for a class X is a constructor that can be called to copy an object of class X; that is, one that can be called with a single argument of type X. For example, X::X(const X&) and X::X(X&,int=0) are copy constructors. A copy constructor is generated only if no copy constructor is declared.

A copy constructor for a class X may not take an argument of type X. For example, `X::X(X)` is illegal.

Constructors for array elements are called in order of increasing addresses (§r.8.2.4).

If a class has base classes or member objects with constructors, their constructors are called before the constructor for the derived class. The constructors for base classes are called first. See §r.12.6.2 for an explanation of how arguments can be specified for such constructors and how the order of constructor calls is determined.

An object of a class with a constructor cannot be a member of a union.

No return type (not even `void`) can be specified for a constructor. A `return` statement in the body of a constructor may not specify a return value. It is not possible to take the address of a constructor.

A constructor can be used explicitly to create new objects of its type, using the syntax

> *class-name* (*expression-list$_{opt}$*)

For example,

```
complex zz = complex(1,2.3);
cprint( complex(7.8,1.2) );
```

An object created in this way is unnamed (unless the constructor was used as an initializer for a named variable as for `zz` above), with its lifetime limited to the expression in which it is created; see §r.12.2.

Member functions may be called from within a constructor; see §r.12.7.

r.12.2 Temporary Objects

In some circumstances it may be necessary or convenient for the compiler to generate a temporary object. Such introduction of temporaries is implementation dependent. When a compiler introduces a temporary object of a class that has a constructor it must ensure that a constructor is called for the temporary object. Similarly, the destructor must be called for a temporary object of a class where a destructor is declared. For example,

```
class X {
    // ...
public:
    // ...
    X(int);
    X(X&);
    ~X();
};

X f(X);
```

```
void g()
{
    X a(1);
    X b = f(X(2));
    a = f(a);
}
```

Here, one might use a temporary in which to construct X(2) before passing it to f()
by X(X&); alternatively, X(2) might be constructed in the space used to hold the
argument for the first call of f(). Also, a temporary might be used to hold the result
of f(X(2)) before copying it to b by X(X&); alternatively, f()'s result might be
constructed in b. On the other hand, for many functions f(), the expression
a=f(a) requires a temporary for either the argument a or the result of f(a) to
avoid undesired aliasing of a.

The compiler must ensure that a temporary object is destroyed. The exact point of
destruction is implementation dependent. There are only two things that can be done
with a temporary: fetch its value (implicitly copying it) to use in some other expression, or bind a reference to it. If the value of a temporary is fetched, that temporary is
then dead and can be destroyed immediately. If a reference is bound to a temporary,
the temporary must not be destroyed until the reference is. This destruction must take
place before exit from the scope in which the temporary is created.

Another form of temporaries is discussed in §r.8.4.3.

r.12.3 Conversions

Type conversions of class objects can be specified by constructors and by conversion
functions.

Such conversions, often called *user-defined conversions*, are used implicitly in
addition to standard conversions (§r.4). For example, a function expecting an argument of type X can be called not only with an argument of type X but also with an
argument of type T where a conversion from T to X exists. User-defined conversions
are used similarly for conversion of initializers (§r.8.4), function arguments (§r.5.2.2,
§r.8.2.5), function return values (§r.6.6.3, §r.8.2.5), expression operands (§r.5),
expressions controlling iteration and selection statements (§r.6.4, §r.6.5), and explicit
type conversions (§r.5.2.3, §r.5.4).

User-defined conversions are applied only where they are unambiguous (§r.10.1.1,
§r.12.3.2). Conversions obey the access control rules (§r.11). As ever access control
is applied after ambiguity resolution (§r.10.4).

See §r.13.2 for a discussion of the use of conversions in function calls as well as
examples below.

r.12.3.1 Conversion by Constructor

A constructor accepting a single argument specifies a conversion from its argument
type to the type of its class. For example,

```
class X {
    // ...
public:
    X(int);
    X(const char*, int = 0);
};


void f(X arg) {
    X a = 1;            // a = X(1)
    X b = "Jessie";     // b = X("Jessie",0)
    a = 2;              // a = X(2)
    f(3);               // f(X(3))
}
```

When no constructor for class X accepts the given type, no attempt is made to find other constructors or conversion functions to convert the assigned value into a type acceptable to a constructor for class X. For example,

```
class X { /* ... */ X(int); };
class Y { /* ... */ Y(X); };
Y a = 1;                          // illegal: Y(X(1)) not tried
```

r.12.3.2 Conversion Functions

A member function of a class X with a name of the form

> *conversion-function-name:*
> > operator *conversion-type-name*

> *conversion-type-name:*
> > *type-specifier-list ptr-operator*_{opt}

specifies a conversion from X to the type specified by the *conversion-type-name*. Such member functions are called conversion functions. Classes, enumerations, and *typedef-name*s may not be declared in the *type-specifier-list*. Neither argument types nor return type may be specified.

Here is an example:

```
class X {
    // ...
public:
    operator int();
};
```

```
void f(X a)
{
    int i = int(a);
    i = (int)a;
    i = a;
}
```

In all three cases the value assigned will be converted by X::operator int().
User-defined conversions are not restricted to use in assignments and initializations.
For example,

```
void g(X a, X b)
{
    int i = (a) ? 1+a : 0;
    int j = (a&&b) ? a+b : i;
    if (a) { // ...
    }
}
```

Conversion operators are inherited.

Conversion functions can be virtual.

At most one user-defined conversion (constructor or conversion function) is
implicitly applied to a single value. For example,

```
class X {
    // ...
public:
    operator int();
};


class Y {
    // ...
public:
    operator X();
};


Y a;
int b = a;    // illegal:
              // a.operator X().operator int() not tried
int c = X(a); // ok: a.operator X().operator int()
```

User-defined conversions are used implicitly only if they are unambiguous. A
conversion function in a derived class does not hide a conversion function in a base
class unless the two functions convert to the same type. For example,

```
class X {
public:
    // ...
    operator int ();
};

class Y : public X {
public:
    // ...
    operator void* ();
};

void f (Y& a)
{
    if (a) {     // error: ambiguous
        // ...
    }
}
```

r.12.4 Destructors

A member function of class `cl` named `~cl` is called a destructor; it is used to destroy values of type `cl` immediately before the object containing them is destroyed. A destructor takes no arguments, and no return type can be specified for it (not even `void`). It is not possible to take the address of a destructor. A destructor can be invoked for a `const` or `volatile` object. A destructor may not be declared `const` or `volatile` (§r.9.3.1). A destructor may not be `static`.

Destructors are not inherited. If a base or a member has a destructor and no destructor is declared for its derived class a default destructor is generated. This generated destructor calls the destructors for bases and members of the derived class. Generated destructors are `public`.

The body of a destructor is executed before the destructors for member objects. Destructors for nonstatic member objects are executed before the destructors for base classes. Destructors for nonvirtual base classes are executed before destructors for virtual base classes. Destructors for nonvirtual base classes are executed in reverse order of their declaration in the derived class. Destructors for virtual base classes are executed in the reverse order of their appearance in a depth-first left-to-right traversal of the directed acyclic graph of base classes; ''left-to-right'' is the order of appearance of the base class names in the declaration of the derived class.

Destructors for elements of an array are called in reverse order of their construction.

A destructor may be `virtual`.

Member functions may be called from within a destructor; see §r.12.7.

An object of a class with a destructor cannot be a member of a union.

Destructors are invoked implicitly (1) when an `auto` (§r.3.5) or temporary

(§r.12.2, §r.8.4.3) object goes out of scope, (2) for constructed static (§r.3.5) objects at program termination (§r.3.4), (3) through use of the delete operator (§r.5.3.4) for objects allocated by the new operator (§r.5.3.3), and (4) explicitly called. When invoked by the delete operator, memory is freed by the destructor for the most derived class (§r.12.6.2) of the object using an operator delete() (§r.5.3.4). For example,

```
class X {
    // ...
public:
    X(int);
    ˜X();
};

void g(X*);

void f()            // common use:
{
    X* p = new X(111);   // allocate and initialize
    g(p);
    delete p;            // cleanup and deallocate
}
```

Explicit calls of destructors are rarely needed. One use of such calls is for objects placed at specific addresses using a new operator. Such use of explicit placement and destruction of objects can be necessary to cope with dedicated hardware resources and for writing memory management facilities. For example,

```
void* operator new(size_t, void* p) { return p; }

void f(X* p);

static char buf[sizeof(X)];

void g()            // rare, specialized use:
{
    X* p = new(buf) X(222);   // use buf[]
                              // and initialize
    f(p);
    p->X::˜X();               // cleanup
}
```

The notation for explicit call of a destructor may be used for any simple type name. For example,

```
int* p;
// ...
p->int::˜int();
```

Using the notation for a type that does not have a destructor has no effect. Allowing this enables people to write code without having to know if a destructor exists for a given type.

r.12.5 Free Store

When an object is created with the `new` operator, an `operator new()` function is (implicitly) used to obtain the store needed (§r.5.3.3).

If `operator new()` cannot allocate storage it will return 0.

An `X::operator new()` for a class X is a static member (even if not explicitly declared `static`). Its first argument must be of type `size_t`, an implementation-dependent integral type defined in the standard header `<stddef.h>`; it must return `void*`. For example,

```
class X {
    // ...
    void* operator new(size_t);
    void* operator new(size_t, Arena*);
};
```

See §r.5.3.3 for the rules for selecting an `operator new()`.

An `X::operator delete()` for a class X is a static member (even if not explicitly declared `static`) and must have its first argument of type `void*`; a second argument of type `size_t` may be added. It cannot return a value; its return type must be `void`. For example,

```
class X {
    // ...
    void operator delete(void*);
};

class Y {
    // ...
    void operator delete(void*, size_t);
};
```

Only one `operator delete()` may be declared for a single class; thus `operator delete()` cannot be overloaded. The global `operator delete()` takes a single argument of type `void*`.

If the two argument style is used, `operator delete()` will be called with a second argument indicating the size of the object being deleted. The size passed is determined by the destructor (if any) or by the (static) type of the pointer being deleted; that is, it will be correct either if the type of the pointer argument to the `delete` operator is the exact type of the object (and not, for example, just the type of base class) or if the type is that of a base class with a virtual destructor.

The global `operator new()` and `operator delete()` are used for arrays of class objects (§r.5.3.3, §r.5.3.4).

Since `X::operator new()` and `X::operator delete()` are static they cannot be `virtual`. A destructor finds the `operator delete()` to use for freeing store using the usual scope rules. For example,

```
struct B {
    virtual ~B();
    void* operator new(size_t);
    void operator delete(void*);
};



struct D : B {
    ~D();
    void* operator new(size_t);
    void operator delete(void*);
};



void f()
{
    B* p = new D;
    delete p;
}
```

Here, storage for the object of class D is allocated by `D::operator new()` and, thanks to the virtual destructor, deallocated by `D::operator delete()`.

r.12.6 Initialization

An object of a class with no constructors, no private or protected members, no virtual functions, and no base classes can be initialized using an initializer list; see §r.8.4.1. An object of a class with a constructor must either be initialized or have a default constructor (§r.12.1). The default constructor is used for objects that are not explicitly initialized.

r.12.6.1 Explicit Initialization

Objects of classes with constructors (§r.12.1) can be initialized with a parenthesized expression list. This list is taken as the argument list for a call of a constructor doing the initialization. Alternatively a single value is specified as the initializer using the = operator. This value is used as the argument to a copy constructor. Typically, that call of a copy constructor can be eliminated. For example,

```
class complex {
    // ...
public:
    complex();
    complex(double);
    complex(double,double);
    // ...
};

complex sqrt(complex,complex);

complex a(1);              // initialize by a call of
                           // complex(double)
complex b = a;             // initialize by a copy of 'a'
complex c = complex(1,2);  // construct complex(1,2)
                           // using complex(double,double)
                           // copy it into 'c'
complex d = sqrt(b,c);     // call sqrt(complex,complex)
                           // and copy the result into 'd'
complex e;                 // initialize by a call of
                           // complex()
complex f = 3;             // construct complex(3) using
                           // complex(double)
                           // copy it into 'f'
```

Overloading of the assignment operator = has no effect on initialization.

The initialization that occurs in argument passing and function return is equivalent to the form

```
T x = a;
```

The initialization that occurs in new expressions (§r.5.3.3) and in base and member initializers (§r.12.6.2) is equivalent to the form

```
T x(a);
```

Arrays of objects of a class with constructors use constructors in initialization (§r.12.1) just like individual objects. If there are fewer initializers in the list than elements in the array, the default constructor (§r.12.1) is used. If there is no default constructor the *initializer-list* must be complete. For example,

```
complex cc = { 1, 2 }; // error; use constructor
complex v[6] = { 1,complex(1,2),complex(),2 };
```

Here, v[0] and v[3] are initialized with complex::complex(double), v[1] is initialized with complex::complex(double,double), and v[2], v[4], and v[5] are initialized with complex::complex().

An object of class M can be a member of a class X only if (1) M does not have a constructor, or (2) M has a default constructor, or (3) X has a constructor and if every constructor of class X specifies a *ctor-initializer* (§r.12.6.2) for that member. In case

2 the default constructor is called when the aggregate is created. If a member of an aggregate has a destructor, then that destructor is called when the aggregate is destroyed.

Constructors for nonlocal static objects are called in the order they occur in a file; destructors are called in reverse order. See also §r.3.4, §r.6.7, §r.9.4.

r.12.6.2 Initializing Bases and Members

Initializers for immediate base classes and for members not inherited from a base class may be specified in the definition of a constructor. This is most useful for class objects, constants, and references where the semantics of initialization and assignment differ. A *ctor-initializer* has the form

> *ctor-initializer:*
>> :   *mem-initializer-list*

> *mem-initializer-list:*
>> *mem-initializer*
>> *mem-initializer* , *mem-initializer-list*

> *mem-initializer:*
>> *complete-class-name* (*expression-list$_{opt}$*)
>> *identifier* (*expression-list$_{opt}$*)

The argument list is used to initialize the named nonstatic member or base class object. This is the only way to initialize nonstatic `const` and reference members. For example,

```
struct B1 { B1(int); /* ... */ };
struct B2 { B2(int); /* ... */ };

struct D : B1, B2 {
    D(int);
    B1 b;
    const c;
};

D::D(int a) : B2(a+1), B1(a+2), c(a+3), b(a+4)
{ /* ... */ }

D d(10);
```

First, the base classes are initialized in declaration order (independent of the order of *mem-initializers*), then the members are initialized in declaration order (independent of the order of *mem-initializers*), then the body of `D::D()` is executed (§r.12.1). The declaration order is used to ensure that sub-objects and members are destroyed in the reverse order of initialization.

Virtual base classes constitute a special case. Virtual bases are constructed before any nonvirtual bases and in the order they appear on a depth-first left-to-right traversal of the directed acyclic graph of base classes; "left-to-right" is the order of appearance of the base class names in the declaration of the derived class.

A *complete object* is an object that is not a sub-object representing a base class. Its class is said to be the *most derived* class for the object. All sub-objects for virtual base classes are initialized by the constructor of the most derived class. If a constructor of the most derived class does not specify a *mem-initializer* for a virtual base class then that virtual base class must have a default constructor or no constructors. Any *mem-initializer*s for virtual classes specified in a constructor for a class that is not the class of the complete object are ignored. For example,

```
class V {
public:
    V();
    V(int);
    // ...
};

class A : public virtual V {
public:
    A();
    A(int);
    // ...
};

class B : public virtual V {
public:
    B();
    B(int);
    // ...
};

class C : public A, public B, private virtual V {
public:
    C();
    C(int);
    // ...
};

A::A(int i) : V(i) { /* ... */ }
B::B(int i) { /* ... */ }
C::C(int i) { /* ... */ }

V v(1); // use V(int)
A a(2); // use V(int)
B b(3); // use V()
C c(4); // use V()
```

A *mem-initializer* is evaluated in the scope of the constructor in which it appears. For example,

```
class X {
     int a;
public:
     const int& r;
     X(): r(a) {}
};
```

initializes X::r to refer to X::a for each object of class X.

r.12.7 Constructors and Destructors

Member functions may be called in constructors and destructors. This implies that virtual functions may be called (directly or indirectly). The function called will be the one defined in the constructor's (or destructor's) own class or its bases, but *not* any function overriding it in a derived class. This ensures that unconstructed objects will not be accessed during construction or destruction. For example,

```
class X {
public:
     virtual void f();
     X() { f(); }    // calls X::f()
     ˜X() { f(); }    // calls X::f()
};

class Y : public X {
     int& r;
public:
     void f()
     {
          r++;   // disaster if 'r' is uninitialized
     }
     Y(int& rr) :r(rr) {}
};
```

The effect of calling a pure virtual function directly or indirectly for the object being constructed from a constructor, except using explicit qualification, is undefined (§r.10.3).

r.12.8 Copying Class Objects

A class object can be copied in two ways, by assignment (§r.5.17) and by initialization (§r.12.1, §r.8.4) including function argument passing (§r.5.2.2) and function value return (§r.6.6.3). Conceptually, for a class X these two operations are implemented by an assignment operator and a copy constructor (§r.12.1). The programmer may define one or both of these. If not defined by the programmer, they will be defined as memberwise assignment and memberwise initialization of the members of X, respectively.

If all bases and members of a class X have copy constructors accepting const

arguments, the generated copy constructor for X will take a single argument of type
const X&, as follows:

```
X::X(const X&)
```

Otherwise it will take a single argument of type X&:

```
X::X(X&)
```

and initialization by copying of const X objects will not be possible.

Similarly, if all bases and members of a class X have assignment operators accepting const arguments, the generated assignment operator for X will take a single
argument of type const X&, asfollows:

```
X& X::operator=(const X&)
```

Otherwise it will take a single argument of type X&:

```
X& X::operator=(X&)
```

and assignment by copying of const X objects will not be possible. The default
assignment operator will return a reference to the object for which is invoked.

Objects representing virtual base classes will be initialized only once by a generated copy constructor. Objects representing virtual base classes will be assigned only
once by a generated assignment operator.

Memberwise assignment and memberwise initialization implies that if a class X
has a member of a class M, M's assignment operator and M's copy constructor are used
to implement assignment and initialization of the member, respectively. If a class has
a const member, a reference member, or a member or a base of a class with a private operator=(), the default assignment operation cannot be generated. Similarly, if a member or a base of a class M has a private copy constructor then the default
copy constructor cannot be generated.

The default assignment and copy constructor will be declared, but they will not be
defined (that is, a function body generated) unless needed. That is,
X::operator=() will be generated only if no assignment operation is explicitly
declared and an object of class X is assigned an object of class X or an object of a
class derived from X or if the address of X::operator= is taken. Initialization is
handled similarly.

If implicitly declared, the assignment and the copy constructor will be public
members and the assignment operator for a class X will be defined to return a reference of type X& referring to the object assigned to.

If a class X has any X::operator=() that takes an argument of class X, the
default assignment will not be generated. If a class has any copy constructor defined,
the default copy constructor will not be generated. For example,

```
class X {
    // ...
public:
    X(int);
    X(const X&, int = 1);
};

X a(1);              // calls X(int);
X b(a,0);            // calls X(const X&,int);
X c = b;             // calls X(const X&,int);
```

Assignment of class X objects is defined in terms of X::operator=(const X&). This implies (§r.12.3) that objects of a derived class can be assigned to objects of a public base class. For example,

```
class X {
public:
    int b;
};

class Y : public X {
public:
    int c;
};


void f()
{
    X x1;
    Y y1;

    x1 = y1;     // ok
    y1 = x1;     // error
}
```

Here y1.b is assigned to x1.b and y1.c is not copied.

Copying one object into another using the default copy constructor or the default assignment operator does not change the structure of either object. For example,

```
struct s {
    virtual f();
    // ...
};

struct ss : public s {
    f();
    // ...
};
```

```
void f()
{
      s a;
      ss b;
      a = b;      // really a.s::operator=(b)
      b = a;      // error
      a.f();      // calls s::f
      b.f();      // calls ss::f
      (s&)b = a;  // assign to b's s part
                  // really ((s&)b).s::operator=(a)
      b.f();      // still calls ss::f
}
```

The call `a.f()` will invoke `s::f()` (as is suitable for an object of class s (§r.10.2)) and the call `b.f()` will call `ss::f()` (as is suitable for an object of class ss).

r.13   Overloading

When several different function declarations are specified for a single name in the same scope, that name is said to be overloaded. When that name is used, the correct function is selected by comparing the types of the actual arguments with the types of the formal arguments. For example,

```
double abs(double);
int abs(int);

abs(1);        // call abs(int);
abs(1.0);      // call abs(double);
```

Since for any type T, a T and a T& accept the same set of initializer values, functions with argument types differing only in this respect may not have the same name. For example,

```
int f(int i)
{
      // ...
}

int f(int& r)   // error: function types
                // not sufficiently different
{
      // ...
}
```

Similarly, since for any type T, a T, a const T, and a volatile T accept the same set of initializer values, functions with argument types differing only in this respect may not have the same name. It is, however, possible to distinguish between const T&, volatile T&, and plain T& so functions that differ only in this respect may be defined. Similarly, it is possible to distinguish between const T*, volatile T*, and plain T* so functions that differ only in this respect may be defined.

Functions that differ only in the return type may not have the same name.

Member functions that differ only in that one is a static member and the other isn't may not have the same name (§r.9.4).

A typedef is not a separate type, but only a synonym for another type (§r.7.1.3). Therefore, functions that differ by typedef "types" only may not have the same name. For example,

```
typedef int Int;

void f(int i) { /* ... */ }
void f(Int i) { /* ... */ }  // error: redefinition of f
```

Enumerations, on the other hand, are distinct types and can be used to distinguish overloaded functions. For example,

```
enum E { a };

void f(int i) { /* ... */ }
void f(E i)   { /* ... */ }
```

Argument types that differ only in a pointer * versus an array [] are identical. Note that only the second and subsequent array dimensions are significant in argument types (§r.8.2.4).

```
f(char*);
f(char[]);       // same as f(char*);
f(char[7]);      // same as f(char*);
f(char[9]);      // same as f(char*);
```

```
g(char(*)[10]);
g(char[5][10]);  // same as g(char(*)[10]);
g(char[7][10]);  // same as g(char(*)[10]);
g(char(*)[20]);  // different from g(char(*)[10]);
```

r.13.1 Declaration Matching

Two function declarations of the same name refer to the same function if they are in the same scope and have identical argument types (§r.13). A function member of a derived class is *not* in the same scope as a function member of the same name in a base class. For example,

```
class B {
public:
    int f(int);
};

class D : public B {
public:
    int f(char*);
};
```

Here `D::f(char*)` hides `B::f(int)` rather than overloading it.

```
void h(D* pd)
{
    pd->f(1);         // error:
                      // D::f(char*) hides B::f(int)
    pd->B::f(1);      // ok
    pd->f("Ben");     // ok, calls D::f
}
```

A locally declared function is not in the same scope as a function in file scope.

```
int f(char*);
void g()
{
    extern f(int);
    f("asdf");   // error: f(int) hides f(char*)
                 // so there is no f(char*) in this scope
}
```

Different versions of an overloaded member function may be given different access rules. For example,

```
class buffer {
private:
    char* p;
    int size;

protected:
    buffer(int s, char* store) { size = s; p = store; }
    // ...

public:
    buffer(int s) { p = new char[size = s]; }
    // ...
};
```

r.13.2 Argument Matching

A call of a given function name chooses, from among all functions by that name that are in scope and for which a set of conversions exists so that the function could possibly be called, the function that best matches the actual arguments. The best-matching function is the intersection of sets of functions that best match on each argument. Unless this intersection has exactly one member, the call is illegal. The function thus selected must be a strictly better match for at least one argument than every other possible function (but not necessarily the same argument for each function). Otherwise, the call is illegal.

For purposes of argument matching, a function with n default arguments (§r.8.2.6) is considered to be $n+1$ functions with different numbers of arguments.

For purposes of argument matching, a nonstatic member function is considered to have an extra argument specifying the object for which it is called. This extra argument requires a match either by the object or pointer specified in the explicit member function call notation (§r.5.2.4) or by the first operand of an overloaded operator (§r.13.4). No temporaries will be introduced for this extra argument and no user-defined conversions will be applied to achieve a type match.

Where a member of a class X is explicitly called for a pointer using the -> operator, this extra argument is assumed to have type const X* for const members, volatile X* for volatile members, and X* for others. Where the member function is explicitly called for an object using the . operator or the function is invoked for the first operand of an overloaded operator (§r.13.4), this extra argument is assumed to have type const X& for const members, volatile X& for volatile members, and X& for others. The first operand of ->* and .* is treated in the same way as the first operand of -> and ., respectively.

An ellipsis in a formal argument list (§r.8.2.5) is a match for an actual argument of any type.

For a given actual argument, no sequence of conversions will be considered that contains more than one user-defined conversion or that can be shortened by deleting one or more conversions into another sequence that leads to the type of the corresponding formal argument of any function in consideration. Such a sequence is called a *best-matching* sequence.

For example, int→float→double is a sequence of conversions from int to double, but it is not a best-matching sequence because it contains the shorter sequence int→double.

Except as mentioned below, the following *trivial conversions* involving a type T do not affect which of two conversion sequences is better:

from:	to:
T	T&
T&	T
T[]	T*
T(args)	T(*)(args)

```
         T                          const  T
         T                          volatile  T
         T*                         const  T*
         T*                         volatile  T*
```

Sequences of trivial conversions that differ only in order are indistinguishable. Note that functions with arguments of type T, const T, volatile T, T&, const T&, and volatile T& accept exactly the same set of values. Where necessary, const and volatile are used as tie-breakers as described in rule [1] below.

A temporary variable is needed for a formal argument of type T& if the actual argument is not an lvalue, has a type different from T, or is a volatile and T isn't. This does not affect argument matching. It may, however, affect the legality of the resulting match since a temporary may not be used to initialize a non-const reference (§r.8.4.3).

Sequences of conversions are considered according to these rules:

[1] Exact match: Sequences of zero or more trivial conversions are better than all other sequences. Of these, those that do not convert T* to const T*, T* to volatile T*, T& to const T&, or T& to volatile T& are better than those that do.

[2] Match with promotions: Of sequences not mentioned in [1], those that contain only integral promotions (§r.4.1), conversions from float to double, and trivial conversions are better than all others.

[3] Match with standard conversions: Of sequences not mentioned in [2], those with only standard (§r.4.1, §r.4.2, §r.4.3, §r.4.4, §r.4.5, §r.4.6, §r.4.7, §r.4.8) and trivial conversions are better than all others. Of these, if B is publicly derived directly or indirectly from A, converting a B* to A* is better than converting to void* or const void*; further, if C is publicly derived directly or indirectly from B, converting a C* to B* is better than converting to A* and converting a C& to B& is better than converting to A&. The class hierarchy acts similarly as a selection mechanism for pointer to member conversions (§r.4.8).

[4] Match with user-defined conversions: Of sequences not mentioned in [3], those that involve only user-defined conversions (§r.12.3), standard (§r.4) and trivial conversions are better than all other sequences.

[5] Match with ellipsis: Sequences that involve matches with the ellipsis are worse than all others.

User-defined conversions are selected based on the type of variable being initialized or assigned to.

```
         class Y {
             // ...
         public:
             operator int();
             operator double();
         };
```

```
void f(Y y)
{
    int i = y;      // call Y::operator int()
    double d;
    d = y;          // call Y::operator double()
    float f = y;    // error: ambiguous
}
```

Standard conversions (§r.4) may be applied to the argument for a user-defined conversion, and to the result of a user-defined conversion.

```
struct S {  S(long); operator int(); };

void f(long), f(char*);
void g(S), g(char*);
void h(const S&), h(char*);

void k(S& a)
{
    f(a);       // f(long(a.operator int()))
    g(1);       // g(S(long(1)))
    h(1);       // h(S(long(1)))
}
```

If user-defined coercions are needed for an argument, no account is taken of any standard coercions that might also be involved. For example,

```
class x {
public:
    x(int);
};

class y {
public:
    y(long);
};

void f(x);
void f(y);

void g()
{
    f(1);           // ambiguous
}
```

The call f(1) is ambiguous despite f(y(long(1))) needing one more standard conversion than f(x(1)).

No preference is given to conversion by constructor (§r.12.1) over conversion by conversion function (§r.12.3.2) or vice versa.

```
struct X {
    operator int ();
};

struct Y {
    Y (X);
};

Y operator+ (Y, Y);

void f (X a,  X b)
{
    a+b;   // error, ambiguous:
           //      operator+ (Y (a),  Y (b))  or
           //      a.operator int ()  + b.operator int ()
}
```

r.13.3 Address of Overloaded Function

A use of a function name without arguments selects, among all functions of that name that are in scope, the (only) function that exactly matches the target. The target may be

an object being initialized (§r.8.4)

the left side of an assignment (§r.5.17)

a formal argument of a function (§r.5.2.2)

a formal argument of a user-defined operator (§r.13.4)

a function return type (§r.8.2.5)

Note that if f () and g () are both overloaded functions, the cross product of possibilities must be considered to resolve f (&g), or the equivalent expression f (g).
For example,

```
int  f (double);
int  f (int);
int  (*pfd) (double)  = &f;
int  (*pfi) (int)  = &f;
int  (*pfe) (...)  = &f; // error: type mismatch
```

The last initialization is an error because no f () with type int (...) has been defined, and not because of any ambiguity.
Note also that there are no standard conversions (§r.4) of one pointer to function type into another (§r.4.6). In particular, even if B is a public base of D we have

```
D* f();
B* (*p1)() = &f;          // error

void g(D*);
void (*p2)(B*) = &g;      // error
```

r.13.4 Overloaded Operators

Most operators can be overloaded.

> *operator-function-name:*
>   operator *operator*

> *operator:* one of
>   new   delete
>   +   -   *   /   %   ^   & | ~
>   !   =   <   >   +=   -=   *=   /=   %=
>   ^=   &= |=   <<   >>   >>=   <<=   ==   !=
>   <=   >=   && || ++   --   ,   ->*   ->
>   ()   []

The last two operators are function call (§r.5.2.2) and subscripting (§r.5.2.1).
Both the unary and binary forms of

>   +   -   *   &

can be overloaded.
The following operators cannot be overloaded:

>   .   .*   ::   ?:   sizeof

nor can the preprocessing symbols # and ## (§r.16).

Operator functions are usually not called directly; instead they are invoked to implement operators (§r.13.4.1, §r.13.4.2). They can be explicitly called, though. For example,

```
complex z = a.operator+(b);   // complex z = a+b;
void* p = operator new(sizeof(int)*n);
```

The operators new and delete are described in §r.5.3.3 and §r.5.3.4 and the rules described below in this section do not apply to them.

An operator function must either be a member function or take at least one argument of a class or a reference to a class. It is not possible to change the precedence, grouping, or number of operands of operators. The predefined meaning of the operators =, (unary) &, and , (comma) applied to class objects may be changed. Except for operator=(), operator functions are inherited; see §r.12.8 for the rules for operator=().

Identities among operators applied to basic types (for example, ++a ≡ a+=1) need not hold for operators applied to class types. Some operators, for example, +=, require an operand to be an lvalue when applied to basic types; this is not required when the operators are declared for class types.

An overloaded operator cannot have default arguments (§r.8.2.6).

Operators not mentioned explicitly below in §r.13.4.3 to §r.13.4.7 act as ordinary unary and binary operators obeying the rules of section §r.13.4.1 or §r.13.4.2.

r.13.4.1 Unary Operators

A prefix unary operator may be declared by a nonstatic member function (§r.9.3) taking no arguments or a nonmember function taking one argument. Thus, for any prefix unary operator @, @x can be interpreted as either x.operator@() or operator@(x). If both forms of the operator function have been declared, argument matching (§r.13.2) determines which, if any, interpretation is used. See §r.13.4.7 for an explanation of postfix unary operators, that is, ++ and --.

r.13.4.2 Binary Operators

A binary operator may be declared either by a nonstatic member function (§r.9.3) taking one argument or by a nonmember function taking two arguments. Thus, for any binary operator @, x@y can be interpreted as either x.operator@(y) or operator@(x,y). If both forms of the operator function have been declared, argument matching (§r.13.2) determines which, if any, interpretation is used.

r.13.4.3 Assignment

The assignment function operator=() must be a nonstatic member function; it is not inherited (§r.12.8). Instead, unless the user defines operator= for a class X, operator= is defined, by default, as memberwise assignment of the members of class X.

```
X& X::operator=(const X& from)
{
    // copy members of X
}
```

r.13.4.4 Function Call

Function call

      primary-expression (*expression-list*$_{opt}$)

is considered a binary operator with the *primary-expression* as the first operand and the possibly empty *expression-list* as the second. The name of the defining function is operator(). Thus, a call x(arg1,arg2,arg3) is interpreted as x.operator()(arg1,arg2,arg3) for a class object x. operator() must be a nonstatic member function.

r.13.4.5 Subscripting

Subscripting

> *primary-expression* [*expression*]

is considered a binary operator. A subscripting expression `x[y]` is interpreted as `x.operator[](y)` for a class object `x`. `operator[]` must be a nonstatic member function.

r.13.4.6 Class Member Access

Class member access using `->`

> *primary-expression* -> *primary-expression*

is considered a unary operator. An expression `x->m` is interpreted as `(x.operator->())->m` for a class object `x`. It follows that `operator->()` must return either a pointer to a class or an object of or a reference to a class for which `operator->()` is defined. `operator->` must be a nonstatic member function.

r.13.4.7 Increment and Decrement

A function called `operator++` taking one argument defines the prefix increment operator `++` for objects of some class. A function called `operator++` taking two arguments defines the postfix increment operator `++` for objects of some class. For postfix `operator++`, the second argument must be of type `int` and the `operator++()` will be called with the second argument `0` when invoked by a postfix increment expression. For example,

```
class X {
public:
    X operator++();       // prefix ++a
    X operator++(int);    // postfix a++
};


void f(X a)
{
    ++a;          // a.operator++();
    a++;          // a.operator++(0);


    a.operator++();     // explicit call: like ++a;
    a.operator++(0);    // explicit call: like a++;
}
```

The prefix and postfix decrement operators `--` are handled similarly.

r.14 Templates

r.14.1 Templates

A *template* defines a family of types or functions.

> *template-declaration:*
>   template < *template-argument-list* > *declaration*

> *template-argument-list:*
>   *template-argument*
>   *template-argument-list* , *template argument*

> *template-argument:*
>   *type-argument*
>   *argument-declaration*

> *type-argument:*
>   class *identifier*

The *declaration* in a *template-declaration* must declare or define a function or a class.

A *type-argument* defines its *identifier* to be a *type-name* in the scope of the template declaration.

Template names obey the usual scope and access control rules. A *template-declaration* is a *declaration*. A *template-declaration* may appear only as a global declaration.

r.14.2 Class Templates

A class template specifies how individual classes can be constructed much as a class declaration specifies how individual objects can be constructed. A vector class template might be declared like this:

```
template<class T> class vector {
    T* v;
    int sz;
public:
    vector(int);
    T& operator[](int);
    T& elem(int i) { return v[i]; }
    // ...
};
```

The prefix template <class T> specifies that a template is being declared and that a *type-name* T will be used in the declaration. In other words, vector is a parameterized type with T as its parameter.

A class can be specified by a *template-class-name*:

template-class-name:
        template-name < *template-arg-list* >

template-arg-list:
        template-arg
        template-arg-list , *template-arg*

template-arg:
        expression
        type-name

A *template-class-name* is a *class-name* (§r.9).

A class generated from a class template is called a template class, as is a class specifically defined with a *template-class-name* as its name; see §r.14.5.

A *template-class-name* where the *template-name* is not defined names an undefined class.

A class template name must be unique in a program and may not be declared to refer to any other template, class, function, object, value, or type in the same scope.

The types of the *template-args* specified in a *template-class-name* must match the types specified for the template in its *template-argument-list*.

Other *template-args* must be *constant-expressions*, addresses of objects or functions with external linkage, or of static class members. An exact match (§r.13.2) is required for nontype arguments.

For example, `vectors` can be used like this:

```
vector<int> v1(20);
vector<complex> v2(30);

typedef vector<complex> cvec;    // make cvec a synonym
                                 // for vector<complex>
cvec v3(40);   // v2 and v3 are of the same type

v1[3] = 7;
v2[3] = v3.elem(4) = complex(7,8);
```

Here, `vector<int>` and `vector<complex>` are template classes, and their definitions will by default be generated from the `vector` template.

Since a *template-class-name* is a *class-name*, it can be used wherever a *class-name* can be used. For example,

```
class vector<Shape*>;

vector<Window>* current_window;

class svector : public vector<Shape*> { /* ... */ };
```

Definition of class template member functions is described in §r.14.6.

r.14.3 Type Equivalence

Two *template-class-name*s refer to the same class if their *template* names are identical and their arguments have identical values. For example,

```
template<class E, int size> class buffer;

buffer<char,2*512> x;
buffer<char,1024> y;
buffer<char,512> z;
```

declares x and y to be of the same type and z of a different type, and

```
template<class T, void(*err_fct)()>
    class list { /* ... */ };

list<int,&error_handler1> x1;
list<int,&error_handler2> x2;
list<int,&error_handler2> x3;
list<char,&error_handler2> x4;
```

declares x2 and x3 to be of the same type. Their type differs from the types of x1 and x4.

r.14.4 Function Templates

A function template specifies how individual functions can be constructed. A family of sort functions, for example, might be declared like this:

```
template<class T> void sort(vector<T>);
```

A function template specifies an unbounded set of (overloaded) functions. A function generated from a function template is called a template function, as is a function defined with a type that matches a function template; see §r.14.5.

Template arguments are not explicitly specified when calling a function template; instead, overloading resolution is used. For example,

```
vector<complex> cv(100);
vector<int> ci(200);

void f(vector<complex>& cv, vector<int>& ci)
{
    sort(cv);    // invoke sort(vector<complex>)
    sort(ci);    // invoke sort(vector<int>)
}
```

A template function may be overloaded either by (other) functions of its name or by (other) template functions of that same name. Overloading resolution for template functions and other functions of the same name is done in three steps:

[1] Look for an exact match (§r.13.2) on functions; if found, call it.

[2] Look for a function template from which a function that can be called with an

exact match can be generated; if found, call it.
[3] Try ordinary overloading resolution (§r.13.2) for the functions; if a function is found, call it.

If no match is found the call is an error. In each case, if there is more than one alternative in the first step that finds a match, the call is ambiguous and is an error.

A match on a template (step [2]) implies that a specific template function with arguments that exactly matches the types of the arguments will be generated (§r.14.5). Not even trivial conversions (§r.13.2) will be applied in this case.

The same process is used for type matching for pointers to functions (§r.13.3).

Here is an example:

```
template<class T> T max(T a, T b) { return a>b?a:b; };

void f(int a, int b, char c, char d)
{
    int m1 = max(a,b);    // max(int a, int b)
    char m2 = max(c,d);   // max(char a, char b)
    int m3 = max(a,c);    // error: cannot generate
                          // max(int,char)
}
```

For example, adding

```
int max(int,int);
```

to the example above would resolve the third call, by providing a function that could be called for max(a, c) after using the standard conversion of char to int for c.

A function template definition is needed to generate specific versions of the template; only a function template declaration is needed to generate calls to specific versions.

Every *template-argument* specified in the *template-argument-list* must be used in the argument types of a function template.

```
template<class T> T* create();   // error

template<class T>
    void f() {   // error
        T a;
        // ...
    }
```

All *template-argument*s for a function template must be *type-argument*s.

r.14.5 Declarations and Definitions

There must be exactly one definition for each template of a given name in a program. There can be many declarations. The definition is used to generate specific template classes and template functions to match the uses of the template.

Using a *template-class-name* constitutes a declaration of a template class.

Calling a function template or taking its address constitutes a declaration of a template function. There is no special syntax for calling or taking the address of a template function; the name of a function template is used exactly as is a function name. Declaring a function with the same name as a function template with a matching type constitutes a declaration of a specific template function.

If the definition of a specific template function or specific template class is needed to perform some operation and if no explicit definition of that specific template function or class is found in the program, a definition is generated.

The definition of a (nontemplate) function with a type that exactly matches the type of a function template declaration is a definition of that specific template function. For example,

```
template<class T> void sort(vector<T>& v) { /* ... */ }

void sort(vector<char*>& v)   { /* ... */ }
```

Here, the function definition will be used as the sort function for arguments of type `vector<char*>`. For other `vector` types the appropriate function definition is generated from the template.

A class can be defined as the definition of a template class. For example,

```
template<class T> class stream { /* ... */ };

class stream<char> { /* ... */ };
```

Here, the class declaration will be used as the definition of streams of characters (`stream<char>`). Other streams will be handled by template functions generated from the function template.

No operation that requires a defined class can be performed on a template class until the class template has been seen. After that, a specific template class is considered defined immediately before the first global declaration that names it.

r.14.6 Member Function Templates

A member function of a template class is implicitly a template function with the template arguments of its class as its template arguments. For example,

```
template<class T> class vector {
    T* v;
    int sz;
public:
    vector(int);
    T& operator[](int);
    T& elem(int i) { return v[i]; }
    // ...
};
```

declares three function templates. The subscript function might be defined like this:

```
template<class T> T& vector<T>::operator[](int i)
{
    if (i<0 || sz<=i) error("vector: range error");
    return v[i];
}
```

The template argument for vector<T>::operator[]() will be determined by the vector to which the subscripting operation is applied.

```
vector<int> v1(20);
vector<complex> v2(30);

v1[3] = 7;                  // vector<int>::operator[]()
v2[3] = complex(7,8);       // vector<complex>::operator[]()
```

r.14.7 Friends

A friend function of a template is not implicitly a template function. For example,

```
template<class T> class task {
    // ...
    friend void next_time();
    friend task<T>* preempt(task<T>*);
    friend task* prmt(task*);              // error
    // ...
};
```

Here, next_time() becomes the friend of all task classes, and each task has an appropriately typed function called preempt() as a friend. The preempt functions might be defined as a template.

```
template<class T>
    task<T>* preempt(task<T>* t) { /* ... */ }
```

The declaration of prmt() is an error because there is no type task, only specific template types, task<int>, task<record>, and so on.

r.14.8 Static Members and Variables

Each template class or function generated from a template has its own copies of any static variables or members. For example,

```
template<class T> class X {
    static T s;
    // ...
};

X<int> aa;
X<char*> bb;
```

Here X<int> has a static member s of type int and X<char*> has a static

member s of type char*.
 Similarly,

```
template<class T> f(T* p)
{
    static T s;
    // ...
};

void g(int a, char* b)
{
    f(&a);
    f(&b);
}
```

Here f(int*) has a static member s of type int and f(char**) has a static
member s of type char**.

r.15 Exception Handling

r.15.1 Exception Handling

Exception handling provides a way of transferring control and information from a
point in the execution of a program to an *exception handler* associated with a point
previously passed by the execution. A handler will be invoked only by a *throw-
expression* invoked in code executed in the handler's *try-block* or in functions called
from the handler's *try-block*.

> *try-block:*
>   try *compound-statement handler-list*
>
> *handler-list:*
>   *handler handler-list*$_{opt}$
>
> *handler:*
>   catch (*exception-declaration*) *compound-statement*
>
> *exception-declaration:*
>   *type-specifier-list declarator*
>   *type-specifier-list abstract-declarator*
>   *type-specifier-list*
>   . . .
>
> *throw-expression:*
>   throw *expression*$_{opt}$

A *try-block* is a *statement* (§r.6). A *throw-expression* is a *unary-expression* (§r.5) of
type void. A *throw-expression* is sometimes referred to as a "*throw-point.*" Code

that executes a *throw-expression* is said to "throw an exception"; code that subsequently gets control is called a "*handler*."

r.15.2 Throwing an Exception

Throwing an exception transfers control to a handler. An object is passed and the type of that object determines which handlers can catch it. For example,

```
throw "Help!";
```

can be caught by a *handler* of some char* type:

```
try {
    // ...
}
catch(const char* p) {
    // handle character string exceptions here
}
```

and

```
class Overflow {
    // ...
public:
    Overflow(char,double,double);
};

void f(double x)
{
    // ...
    throw Overflow('+',x,3.45e107);
}
```

can be caught by a handler

```
try {
    // ...
    f(1.2);
    // ...
}
catch(Overflow& oo) {
    // handle exceptions of type Overflow here
}
```

When an exception is thrown, control is transferred to the nearest handler with an appropriate type; "nearest" means the handler whose *try-block* was most recently entered by the thread of control and not yet exited; "appropriate type" is defined in §r.15.4.

A *throw-expression* initializes a temporary object of the static type of the operand of throw and uses that temporary to initialize the appropriately-typed variable named in the handler. Except for the restrictions on type matching mentioned in

§r.15.4 and the use of a temporary variable, the operand of throw is treated exactly as a function argument in a call (§r.5.2.2) or the operand of a return statement.

If the use of the temporary object can be eliminated without changing the meaning of the program except for the execution of constructors and destructors associated with the use of the temporary object (§r.12.1c), then the exception in the handler may be initialized directly with the argument of the throw expression.

A *throw-expression* with no operand rethrows the exception being handled. A *throw-expression* with no operand may appear only in a handler or in a function directly or indirectly called from a handler. For example, code that must be executed because of an exception yet cannot completely handle the exception can be written like this:

```
try {
    // ...
}
catch (...) {   // catch all exceptions

    // respond (partially) to exception

    throw;      // pass the exception to some
                // other handler

}
```

r.15.3 Constructors and Destructors

As control passes from a throw-point to a handler, destructors are invoked for all automatic objects constructed since the *try-block* was entered.

An object that is partially constructed will have destructors executed only for its fully constructed sub-objects. Also, should a constructor for an element of an automatic array throw an exception, only the constructed elements of that array will be destroyed.

The process of calling destructors for automatic objects constructed on the path from a *try-block* to a *throw-expression* is called "*stack unwinding*".

r.15.4 Handling an Exception

A *handler* with type T, const T, T&, or const T& is a match for a *throw-expression* with an object of type E if

    [1] T and E are the same type, or
    [2] T is an accessible (§r.4.6) base class of E at the throw point, or
    [3] T is a pointer type and E is a pointer type that can be converted to T by a standard pointer conversion (§r.4.6) at the throw point.

For example,

```
class Matherr { /* ... */ virtual vf(); };
class Overflow: public Matherr { /* ... */ };
class Underflow: public Matherr { /* ... */ };
class Zerodivide: public Matherr { /* ... */ };


void f()
{
    try {
        g();
    }


    catch (Overflow oo) {
        // ...
    }
    catch (Matherr mm) {
        // ...
    }
}
```

Here, the `Overflow` handler will catch exceptions of type `Overflow` and the `Matherr` handler will catch exceptions of type `Matherr` and all types publicly derived from `Matherr` including `Underflow` and `Zerodivide`.

The handlers for a *try-block* are tried in order of appearance. It is an error to place a handler for a base class ahead of a handler for its derived class since that would ensure that the handler for the derived class would never be invoked.

A ... in a handler's *exception-declaration* functions similarly to ... in a function argument declaration; it specifies a match for any exception. If present, a ... handler must be the last handler for its *try-block*.

If no match is found among the handlers for a *try-block*, the search for a matching handler continues in a dynamically surrounding *try-block*. If no matching handler is found in a program, the function `terminate()` (§r.15.7) is called.

An exception is considered handled upon entry to a handler. The stack will have been unwound at that point.

r.15.5 Exception Specifications

Raising or catching an exception affects the way a function relates to other functions. It is possible to list the set of exceptions that a function may directly or indirectly throw as part of a function declaration. An *exception-specification* can be used as a suffix of a function declarator.

> *exception-specification:*
>   throw (*type-list*$_{opt}$)

type-list:
> *type-name*
> *type-list* , *type-name*

For example,

```
void f() throw (X,Y)
{
    // ...
}
```

An attempt by a function to throw an exception not in its exception list will cause a call of the function `unexpected()`; see §r.15.8.

An implementation may not reject an expression simply because it *may* throw an exception not specified in an *exception-specification* of the function containing the expression; the handling of violations of an *exception-specification* is done at run-time.

A function with no *exception-specification* may throw any exception.

A function with an empty *exception-specification*, `throw()`, may not throw any exception.

A function that may throw an exception of a class X may throw an exception of any class publicly derived from X.

An *exception-specification* is not considered part of a function's type.

r.15.6 Special Functions

The exception handling mechanism relies on two functions, `terminate()` and `unexpected()`, for coping with errors related to the exception handling mechanism itself.

r.15.6.1 The `terminate()` Function

Occasionally, exception handling must be abandoned for less subtle error handling techniques. For example,
- when the exception handling mechanism cannot find a handler for a thrown exception,
- when the exception handling mechanism finds the stack corrupted, or
- when a destructor called during stack unwinding caused by an exception tries to exit using an exception.

In such cases,

```
void terminate();
```

is called; `terminate()` calls the last function given as an argument to `set_terminate()`:

```
typedef void(*PFV)();
PFV set_terminate(PFV);
```

The previous function given to set_terminate() will be the return value; this enables users to implement a stack strategy for using terminate(). The default function called by terminate() is abort().

Selecting a terminate function that does not in fact terminate but tries to return to its caller is an error.

r.15.6.2 The **unexpected()** Function

If a function with an *exception-specification* throws an exception that is not listed in the *exception-specification*, the function

```
void unexpected();
```

is called; unexpected() calls the last function given as an argument to set_unexpected():

```
typedef void(*PFV)();
PFV set_unexpected(PFV);
```

The previous function given to set_unexpected() will be the return value; this enables users to implement a stack strategy for using unexpected(). The default function called by unexpected() is terminate(). Since the default function called by terminate() is abort(), this leads to immediate and precise detection of the error.

r.15.7 Exceptions and Access

The formal argument of a catch clause obeys the same access rules as an argument of the function in which the catch clause occurs.

An object may be thrown if it can be copied and destroyed in the context of the function in which the throw occurs.

r.16 Preprocessing

A C++ implementation contains a preprocessor capable of macro substitution, conditional compilation, and inclusion of named files.

Lines beginning with #, optionally preceded by space and horizontal tab characters, (also called "*directives*") communicate with this preprocessor. These lines have syntax independent of the rest of the language; they may appear anywhere and have effects that last (independent of the scoping rules of C++) until the end of the translation unit (§r.2).

A preprocessing directive (or any other line) may be continued on the next line in a source file by placing a backslash character, \, immediately before the new-line at the end of the line to be continued. The preprocessor effects the continuation by deleting the backslash and the new-line before the input sequence is divided into tokens. A backslash character may not be the last character in a source file.

A preprocessing token is a language token (§r.2.1), a file name as in a `#include` directive, or any single character, other than white space, that does not match another preprocessing token.

r.16.1 Phases of Preprocessing

Preprocessing is defined to occur in several phases. An implementation may collapse these phases, but the effect must be as though they had been executed.

If needed, new-line characters are introduced to replace system-dependent end-of-line indicators and any other necessary system-dependent character set translations are done. Trigraph sequences are replaced by their single character equivalents (§r.16.2).

Each pair of a backslash character \ immediately followed by a new-line is deleted, with the effect that the next source line is appended to the line that contained the sequence.

The source text is decomposed into preprocessing tokens and sequences of white space. A single white space replaces each comment. A source file may not end with a partial token or comment.

Preprocessing directives are executed and macros are expanded (§r.16.3, §r.16.4, §r.16.5, §r.16.6, §r.16.7, and §r.16.8).

Escape sequences in character constants and string literals are replaced by their equivalents (§r.2.5.2).

Adjacent string literals are concatenated.

The result of preprocessing is syntactically and semantically analyzed and translated, then linked together as necessary with other programs and libraries.

r.16.2 Trigraph Sequences

Before any other processing takes place, each occurrence of one of the following sequences of three characters (''*trigraph sequences*'') is replaced by the single character indicated in the table below.

??=	#	??(	[
??/	\	??)	]
??'	^	??!	|

For example,

```
??=define arraycheck(a,b)  a??(b??)  ??!??!  b??(a??)
```

becomes

```
#define arraycheck(a,b)  a[b]  ||  b[a]
```

r.16.3 Macro Definition and Expansion

A preprocessing directive of the form

#define *identifier token-string*

causes the preprocessor to replace subsequent instances of the identifier with the given sequence of tokens. White space surrounding the replacement token sequence is discarded. Given, for example,

```
#define SIDE 8
```

the declaration

```
char chessboard[SIDE][SIDE];
```

after macro expansion becomes

```
char chessboard[8][8];
```

An identifier defined in this form may be redefined only by another #define directive of this form provided the replacement list of the second definition is identical to that of the first. All white space separations are considered identical.

A line of the form

#define *identifier*(*identifier* , ... , *identifier*) *token-string*

where there is no space between the first identifier and the (is a macro definition with parameters, or a "*function-like*" macro definition. An identifier defined as a function-like macro may be redefined by another function-like macro definition provided the second definition has the same number and spelling of parameters and the two replacement lists are identical. White space separations are considered identical.

Subsequent appearances of an identifier defined as a function-like macro followed by a (, a sequence of tokens delimited by commas, and a) are replaced by the token string in the definition. White space surrounding the replacement token sequence is discarded. Each occurrence of an identifier mentioned in the parameter list of the definition is replaced by the tokens representing the corresponding actual argument in the call. The actual arguments are token strings separated by commas; commas in quoted strings, in character constants, or within nested parentheses do not separate arguments. The number of arguments in a macro invocation must be the same as the number of parameters in the macro definition.

Once the arguments to a function-like macro have been identified, argument substitution occurs. Unless it is preceded by a # token (§r.16.3.1) or is adjacent to a ##

token (§r.16.3.2), a parameter in the replacement list is replaced by the corresponding argument after any macros in the argument have been expanded (§r.16.3.3).

For example, given the macro definitions

```
#define index_mask        0XFF00
#define extract(word,mask)        word & mask
```

the call

```
index = extract(packed_data,index_mask);
```

expands to

```
index = packed_data & 0XFF00;
```

In both forms the replacement string is rescanned for more defined identifiers (§r.16.3.3).

r.16.3.1 The # Operator

If an occurrence of a parameter in a replacement token sequence is immediately preceded by a # token, the parameter and the # operator will be replaced in the expansion by a string literal containing the spelling of the corresponding argument. A \ character is inserted in the string literal before each occurrence of a \ or a " within or delimiting a character constant or string literal in the argument.

For example, given

```
#define path(logid,cmd)  "/usr/" #logid "/bin/" #cmd
#define joe              joseph
```

the call

```
char* mytool=path(joe,readmail);
```

yields

```
char* mytool="/usr/" "joe" "/bin/" "readmail";
```

which is later concatenated (§r.16.1) to become

```
char* mytool="/usr/joe/bin/readmail";
```

r.16.3.2 The ## Operator

If a ## operator appears in a replacement token sequence between two tokens, first if either of the adjacent tokens is a parameter it is replaced, then the ## operator and any white space surrounding it are deleted. The effect of the ## operator, therefore, is concatenation.

Given

```
#define inherit(basenum)  public Pubbase ## basenum, \
                          private Privbase ## basenum
```

the call

```
class D : inherit(1) { };
```

yields

```
class D : public Pubbase1, private Privbase1 { };
```

Any macros in the replaced tokens adjacent to the `##` are not available for further expansion, but the result of the concatenation is. Given

```
#define concat(a)      a ## ball
#define base           B
#define baseball        sport
```

the call

```
concat(base)
```

yields

```
sport
```

and *not*

```
Bball
```

r.16.3.3 Rescanning and Further Replacement

After all parameters in the replacement list have been replaced, the resulting list is rescanned for more macros to replace. If the name of the macro being replaced is found during this scan or during subsequent rescanning, it is not replaced.

A completely replaced macro expansion is not interpreted as a preprocessing directive, even if it appears to be one.

r.16.3.4 Scope of Macro Names and `#undef`

Once defined, a preprocessor identifier remains defined and in scope (independent of the scoping rules of C++) until the end of the translation unit or until it is undefined in a `#undef` directive.

A `#undef` directive has the form

```
#undef identifier
```

and causes the identifier's preprocessor definition to be forgotten. If the specified identifier is not currently defined as a macro name, the `#undef` is ignored.

r.16.4 File Inclusion

A control line of the form

```
#include <filename>
```

causes the replacement of that line by the entire contents of the file *filename*. The named file is searched for in an implementation-dependent sequence of places.

Similarly, a control line of the form

> `#include "`*filename*`"`

causes the replacement of that line by the contents of the file *filename*, which is searched for first in an implementation-dependent manner. If this search fails, the file is searched for as if the directive had been of the form

> `#include <`*filename*`>`

Neither the new-line character nor > may appear in *filename* delimited by < and >. If any of the characters `'`, `\`, or `"`, or either of the sequences `/*` or `//` appear in such a *filename* the behavior is undefined.

Neither the new-line character nor `"` may appear in a *filename* delimited by a `"` pair, although > may appear. If either of the characters `'` or `\` or either of the sequences `/*` or `//` appear in such a *filename* the behavior is undefined.

If a directive appears of the form

> `#include` *token-string*

not matching either of the forms given above, the preprocessing tokens within *token-string* will be processed as normal text. The resulting directive must match one of the forms defined above and will be treated as such.

A `#include` directive may appear within a file that is being processed as a result of another `#include` directive.

An implementation may impose a limit on the depth of nesting of `#include` directives within source files that have been read while processing a `#include` directive in another source file.

r.16.5 Conditional Compilation

The preprocessor allows conditional compilation of source code. The syntax for conditional compilation follows:

> *conditional:*
> > *if-part elif-parts$_{opt}$ else-part$_{opt}$ endif-line*

> *if-part:*
> > *if-line text*

> *if-line:*
> > `# if` *constant-expression*
> > `# ifdef` *identifier*
> > `# ifndef` *identifier*

elif-parts:
>
>> *elif-line text*
>> *elif-parts elif-line text*

elif-line:
>
>> `#  elif` *constant-expression*

else-part:
>
>> *else-line text*

else-line:
>
>> `#  else`

endif-line:
>
>> `#  endif`

The constant expression in the `#if` and `#elif`'s (if any) are evaluated in the order in which they appear until one of the expressions evaluates to a nonzero value. C++ statements following a line with a zero value are not compiled, nor do preprocessor directives following such a line have any effect. When a directive with a nonzero value is found, the succeeding `#elif`'s, and `#else`'s, together with their associated text (C++ statements and preprocessor directives) are ignored. The text associated with the successful directive (the first whose constant expression is nonzero) is preprocessed and compiled normally. If the expressions associated with the `#if` and all `#elif`'s evaluate to zero, then the text associated with the `#else` (if any) is treated normally.

Within the *constant-expression* in a `#if` or `#elif`, a unary operator `defined` can be used in either of the forms

>> `defined` *identifier*

or

>> `defined` (*identifier*)

When applied to an identifier, its value is 1 if that identifier has been defined with a `#define` directive and not later undefined using `#undef`; otherwise its value is 0. The identifier `defined` itself may not be undefined or redefined.

After any `defined` operators are evaluated, any remaining preprocessor macros appearing in the constant expression will be replaced as described in §r.16.3. The resulting expression must be an integral constant expression as defined in §r.5.19, except that types `int` and `unsigned  int` are treated as `long` and `unsigned long` respectively, and it may not contain a cast, a `sizeof` operator, or an enumeration constant.

A control line of the form

>> `#ifdef` *identifier*

is equivalent to

> #if defined *identifier*

A line of the form

> #ifndef *identifier*

is equivalent to

> #if !defined *identifier*

Conditional compilation constructs may be nested. An implementation may impose a limit on the depth of nesting of conditional compilation constructs.

r.16.6 Line Control

For the benefit of programs that generate C++ code, a line of the form

> #line *constant "filename "**opt*

sets the predefined macro _ _LINE_ _ (§r.16.10), for purposes of error diagnostics or symbolic debugging, such that the line number of the next source line is considered to be the given constant, which must be a decimal integer. If *"filename"* appears, _ _FILE_ _ (§r.16.10), is set to the file named. If *"filename"* is absent the remembered file name does not change.

Macros appearing on the line are replaced before the line is processed.

r.16.7 Error Directive

A line of the form

> #error *token-string*

causes the implementation to generate a diagnostic message that includes the given token sequence.

r.16.8 Pragmas

A line of the form

> #pragma *token-string*

causes an implementation-dependent behavior when the token sequence is of a form recognized by the implementation. An unrecognized pragma will be ignored.

r.16.9 Null Directive

The null preprocessor directive, which has the form

> #

has no effect.

r.16.10 Predefined Names

Certain information is available during compilation through predefined macros.

`__LINE__` A decimal constant containing the current line number in the C++ source file.

`__FILE__` A string literal containing the name of the source file being compiled.

`__DATE__` A string literal containing the date of the translation, in the form `"Mmm dd yyyy"`, or `"Mmm  d yyyy"` if the value of the date is less than `10`.

`__TIME__` A string literal containing the time of the translation, in the form `"hh:mm:ss"`.

In addition, the name `__cplusplus` is defined when compiling a C++ program. These names may not be undefined or redefined.

`__LINE__` and `__FILE__` can be set by the `#line` directive (§r.16.6).

Whether `__STDC__` is defined and, if so, what its value is are implementation dependent.

r.17   Appendix A: Grammar Summary

This appendix is not part of the C++ reference manual proper and does not define C++ language features.

This summary of C++ syntax is intended to be an aid to comprehension. It is not an exact statement of the language. In particular, the grammar described here accepts a superset of valid C++ constructs. Disambiguation rules (§r.6.8, §r.7.1, §r.10.1.1) must be applied to distinguish expressions from declarations. Further, access control, ambiguity, and type rules must be used to weed out syntactically valid but meaningless constructs.

r.17.1 Keywords

New context-dependent keywords are introduced into a program by `typedef` (§r.7.1.3), class (§r.9), enumeration (§r.7.2), and `template` (§r.14) declarations.

class-name:
> *identifier*

enum-name:
> *identifier*

typedef-name:
> *identifier*

Note that a *typedef-name* naming a class is also a *class-name* (§r.9.1).

r.17.2 Expressions

expression:
> *assignment-expression*
> *expression , assignment-expression*

assignment-expression:
> *conditional-expression*
> *unary-expression assignment-operator assignment-expression*

assignment-operator: one of
> =   *=   /=   %=   +=   -=   >>=   <<=   &=   ^= |=

conditional-expression:
> *logical-or-expression*
> *logical-or-expression ? expression : conditional-expression*

logical-or-expression:
> *logical-and-expression*
> *logical-or-expression | | logical-and-expression*

logical-and-expression:
> *inclusive-or-expression*
> *logical-and-expression && inclusive-or-expression*

inclusive-or-expression:
> *exclusive-or-expression*
> *inclusive-or-expression | exclusive-or-expression*

exclusive-or-expression:
> *and-expression*
> *exclusive-or-expression ^ and-expression*

and-expression:
> *equality-expression*
> *and-expression & equality-expression*

equality-expression:
> *relational-expression*
> *equality-expression == relational-expression*
> *equality-expression != relational-expression*

relational-expression:
> *shift-expression*
> *relational-expression* < *shift-expression*
> *relational-expression* > *shift-expression*
> *relational-expression* <= *shift-expression*
> *relational-expression* >= *shift-expression*

shift-expression:
> *additive-expression*
> *shift-expression* << *additive-expression*
> *shift-expression* >> *additive-expression*

additive-expression:
> *multiplicative-expression*
> *additive-expression* + *multiplicative-expression*
> *additive-expression* − *multiplicative-expression*

multiplicative-expression:
> *pm-expression*
> *multiplicative-expression* * *pm-expression*
> *multiplicative-expression* / *pm-expression*
> *multiplicative-expression* % *pm-expression*

pm-expression:
> *cast-expression*
> *pm-expression* .* *cast-expression*
> *pm-expression* −>* *cast-expression*

cast-expression:
> *unary-expression*
> (*type-name*) *cast-expression*

unary-expression:
> *postfix-expression*
> ++ *unary-expression*
> −− *unary-expression*
> *unary-operator* *cast-expression*
> `sizeof` *unary-expression*
> `sizeof` (*type-name*)
> *allocation-expression*
> *deallocation-expression*

unary-operator: one of
> *   &   +   −   !   ˜

allocation-expression:
> $::_{opt}$ new *placement$_{opt}$ new-type-name new-initializer$_{opt}$*
> $::_{opt}$ new *placement$_{opt}$* (*type-name*) *new-initializer$_{opt}$*

placement:
> (*expression-list*)

new-type-name:
> *type-specifier-list new-declarator$_{opt}$*

new-declarator:
> * *cv-qualifier-list$_{opt}$ new-declarator$_{opt}$*
> *complete-class-name* :: * *cv-qualifier-list$_{opt}$ new-declarator$_{opt}$*
> *new-declarator$_{opt}$* [*expression*]

new-initializer:
> (*initializer-list$_{opt}$*)

deallocation-expression:
> $::_{opt}$ delete *cast-expression*
> $::_{opt}$ delete [ ] *cast-expression*

postfix-expression:
> *primary-expression*
> *postfix-expression* [*expression*]
> *postfix-expression* (*expression-list$_{opt}$*)
> *simple-type-name* (*expression-list$_{opt}$*)
> *postfix-expression* . *name*
> *postfix-expression* -> *name*
> *postfix-expression* ++
> *postfix-expression* --

expression-list:
> *assignment-expression*
> *expression-list* , *assignment-expression*

primary-expression:
> *literal*
> this
> :: *identifier*
> :: *operator-function-name*
> :: *qualified-name*
> (*expression*)
> *name*

name:
>   *identifier*
>   *operator-function-name*
>   *conversion-function-name*
>   ~ *class-name*
>   *qualified-name*

qualified-name:
>   *qualified-class-name* : : *name*

literal:
>   *integer-constant*
>   *character-constant*
>   *floating-constant*
>   *string-literal*

r.17.3 Declarations

declaration:
>   *decl-specifiers$_{opt}$ declarator-list$_{opt}$* ;
>   *asm-declaration*
>   *function-definition*
>   *template-declaration*
>   *linkage-specification*

decl-specifier:
>   *storage-class-specifier*
>   *type-specifier*
>   *fct-specifier*
>   friend
>   typedef

decl-specifiers:
>   *decl-specifiers$_{opt}$ decl-specifier*

storage-class-specifier:
>   auto
>   register
>   static
>   extern

fct-specifier:
>   inline
>   virtual

type-specifier:
> *simple-type-name*
> *class-specifier*
> *enum-specifier*
> *elaborated-type-specifier*
> `const`
> `volatile`

simple-type-name:
> *complete-class-name*
> *qualified-type-name*
> `char`
> `short`
> `int`
> `long`
> `signed`
> `unsigned`
> `float`
> `double`
> `void`

elaborated-type-specifier:
> *class-key identifier*
> *class-key class-name*
> `enum` *enum-name*

class-key:
> `class`
> `struct`
> `union`

qualified-type-name:
> *typedef-name*
> *class-name* `::` *qualified-type-name*

complete-class-name:
> *qualified-class-name*
> `::` *qualified-class-name*

qualified-class-name:
> *class-name*
> *class-name* `::` *qualified-class-name*

enum-specifier:
> `enum` *identifier*$_{opt}$ `{` *enum-list*$_{opt}$ `}`

enum-list:
      enumerator
      enum-list , enumerator

enumerator:
      identifier
      identifier = constant-expression

constant-expression:
      conditional-expression

linkage-specification:
      `extern` *string-literal* { *declaration-list$_{opt}$* }
      `extern` *string-literal declaration*

declaration-list:
      declaration
      declaration-list declaration

asm-declaration:
      `asm` (*string-literal*) `;`

r.17.4 Declarators

declarator-list:
      init-declarator
      declarator-list , init-declarator

init-declarator:
      declarator initializer$_{opt}$

declarator:
      dname
      ptr-operator declarator
      declarator (*argument-declaration-list*) *cv-qualifier-list$_{opt}$*
      declarator [*constant-expression$_{opt}$*]
      (*declarator*)

ptr-operator:
      `*` *cv-qualifier-list$_{opt}$*
      `&` *cv-qualifier-list$_{opt}$*
      complete-class-name `::` `*` *cv-qualifier-list$_{opt}$*

cv-qualifier-list:
      cv-qualifier cv-qualifier-list$_{opt}$

cv-qualifier:
>   const
>   volatile

dname:
>   *name*
>   *class-name*
>   ˜ *class-name*
>   *typedef-name*
>   *qualified-type-name*

type-name:
>   *type-specifier-list abstract-declarator$_{opt}$*

type-specifier-list:
>   *type-specifier type-specifier-list$_{opt}$*

abstract-declarator:
>   *ptr-operator abstract-declarator$_{opt}$*
>   *abstract-declarator$_{opt}$* (*argument-declaration-list*) *cv-qualifier-list$_{opt}$*
>   *abstract-declarator$_{opt}$* [*constant-expression$_{opt}$*]
>   (*abstract-declarator*)

argument-declaration-list:
>   *arg-declaration-list$_{opt}$* $\cdots_{opt}$
>   *arg-declaration-list* , $\ldots$

arg-declaration-list:
>   *argument-declaration*
>   *arg-declaration-list* , *argument-declaration*

argument-declaration:
>   *decl-specifiers declarator*
>   *decl-specifiers declarator* = *expression*
>   *decl-specifiers abstract-declarator$_{opt}$*
>   *decl-specifiers abstract-declarator$_{opt}$* = *expression*

function-definition:
>   *decl-specifiers$_{opt}$ declarator ctor-initializer$_{opt}$ fct-body*

fct-body:
>   *compound-statement*

initializer:
>   = *assignment-expression*
>   = { *initializer-list* ,$_{opt}$ }
>   (*expression-list*)

initializer-list:
> *assignment-expression*
> *initializer-list , assignment-expression*
> { *initializer-list* $_{, opt}$ }

r.17.5 Class Declarations

class-specifier:
> *class-head* { *member-list$_{opt}$* }

class-head:
> *class-key identifier$_{opt}$ base-spec$_{opt}$*
> *class-key class-name base-spec$_{opt}$*

member-list:
> *member-declaration member-list$_{opt}$*
> *access-specifier : member-list$_{opt}$*

member-declaration:
> *decl-specifiers$_{opt}$ member-declarator-list$_{opt}$;*
> *function-definition ;$_{opt}$*
> *qualified-name ;*

member-declarator-list:
> *member-declarator*
> *member-declarator-list , member-declarator*

member-declarator:
> *declarator pure-specifier$_{opt}$*
> *identifier$_{opt}$: constant-expression*

pure-specifier:
> = 0

base-spec:
> : *base-list*

base-list:
> *base-specifier*
> *base-list , base-specifier*

base-specifier:
> *complete-class-name*
> `virtual` *access-specifier$_{opt}$ complete-class-name*
> *access-specifier* `virtual`$_{opt}$ *complete-class-name*

access-specifier:
>   private
>   protected
>   public

conversion-function-name:
>   operator *conversion-type-name*

conversion-type-name:
>   *type-specifier-list ptr-operator$_{opt}$*

ctor-initializer:
>   : *mem-initializer-list*

mem-initializer-list:
>   *mem-initializer*
>   *mem-initializer* , *mem-initializer-list*

mem-initializer:
>   *complete-class-name* (*expression-list$_{opt}$*)
>   *identifier* (*expression-list$_{opt}$*)

operator-function-name:
>   operator *operator*

operator: one of
>   new   delete
>   +   −   *   /   %   ^   & | ~
>   !   =   <   >   +=   −=   *=   /=   %=
>   ^=   &= |=   <<   >>   >>=   <<=   ==   !=
>   <=   >=   && || ++   −−   ,   −>*   −>
>   ()   []

r.17.6 Statements

statement:
>   *labeled-statement*
>   *expression-statement*
>   *compound-statement*
>   *selection-statement*
>   *iteration-statement*
>   *jump-statement*
>   *declaration-statement*

labeled-statement:
      identifier : *statement*
      case *constant-expression* : *statement*
      default : *statement*

expression-statement:
      expression$_{opt}$;

compound-statement:
      { *statement-list*$_{opt}$ }

statement-list:
      statement
      statement-list *statement*

selection-statement:
      if (*expression*) *statement*
      if (*expression*) *statement* else *statement*
      switch (*expression*) *statement*

iteration-statement:
      while (*expression*) *statement*
      do *statement* while (*expression*) ;
      for (*for-init-statement* *expression*$_{opt}$; *expression*$_{opt}$) *statement*

for-init-statement:
      expression-statement
      declaration-statement

jump-statement:
      break ;
      continue ;
      return *expression*$_{opt}$;
      goto *identifier* ;

declaration-statement:
      declaration

r.17.7 Preprocessor

```
#define identifier token-string
#define identifier( identifier , ... , identifier ) token-string

#include "filename"
#include <filename>
```

```
#line constant "filename"opt
#undef identifier
```

conditional:

  *if-part elif-parts*_{opt} *else-part*_{opt} *endif-line*

if-part:

  if-line text

if-line:

```
# if constant-expression
# ifdef identifier
# ifndef identifier
```

elif-parts:

  elif-line text
  elif-parts elif-line text

elif-line:

```
# elif constant-expression
```

else-part:

  else-line text

else-line:

```
# else
```

endif-line:

```
# endif
```

r.17.8 Templates

template-declaration:

  `template <` *template-argument-list* `>` *declaration*

template-argument-list:

  template-argument
  template-argument-list , *template argument*

template-argument:

  type-argument
  argument-declaration

type-argument:

  `class` *identifier*

> *template-class-name:*
>> *template-name* < *template-arg-list* >

> *template-arg-list:*
>> *template-arg*
>> *template-arg-list* , *template-arg*

> *template-arg:*
>> *expression*
>> *type-name*

r.17.9 Exception Handling

> *try-block:*
>> `try` *compound-statement handler-list*

> *handler-list:*
>> *handler handler-list$_{opt}$*

> *handler:*
>> `catch` (*exception-declaration*) *compound-statement*

> *exception-declaration:*
>> *type-specifier-list declarator*
>> *type-specifier-list abstract-declarator*
>> *type-specifier-list*
>> . . .

> *throw-expression:*
>> `throw` *expression$_{opt}$*

> *exception-specification:*
>> `throw` (*type-list$_{opt}$*)

> *type-list:*
>> *type-name*
>> *type-list* , *type-name*

r.18 Appendix B: Compatibility

This appendix is not part of the C++ reference manual proper and does not define C++ language features.

C++ is based on C (K&R78) and adopts most of the changes specified by the ANSI C standard. Converting programs among C++, K&R C, and ANSI C may be subject to vicissitudes of expression evaluation. All differences between C++ and

ANSI C can be diagnosed by a compiler. With the following three exceptions, programs that are both C++ and ANSI C have the same meaning in both languages:

In C, `sizeof('a')` equals `sizeof(int)`; in C++, it equals `sizeof(char)`.

In C, given

```
enum e { A };
```

`sizeof(A)` equals `sizeof(int)`; in C++, it equals `sizeof(e)`, which need not equal `sizeof(int)`.

A structure name declared in an inner scope can hide the name of an object, function, enumerator, or type in an outer scope. For example,

```
int x[99];
void f()
{
    struct x { int a; };
    sizeof(x);   /* size of the array in C */
                 /* size of the struct in C++ */
}
```

r.18.1 Extensions

This section summarizes the major extensions to C provided by C++.

r.18.1.1 C++ Features Available in 1985

This subsection summarizes the extensions to C provided by C++ in the 1985 version of this manual:

The types of function arguments can be specified (§r.8.2.5) and will be checked (§r.5.2.2). Type conversions will be performed (§r.5.2.2). This is also in ANSI C.

Single-precision floating point arithmetic may be used for `float` expressions; §r.3.6.1 and §r.4.3. This is also in ANSI C.

Function names can be overloaded; §r.13.

Operators can be overloaded; §r.13.4.

Functions can be inline substituted; §r.7.1.2.

Data objects can be `const`; §r.7.1.6. This is also in ANSI C.

Objects of reference type can be declared; §r.8.2.2 and §r.8.4.3.

A free store is provided by the `new` and `delete` operators; §r.5.3.3, §r.5.3.4.

Classes can provide data hiding (§r.11), guaranteed initialization (§r.12.1), user-defined conversions (§r.12.3), and dynamic typing through use of virtual functions (§r.10.2).

The name of a class or enumeration is a type name; §r.9.

A pointer to any non-`const` and non-`volatile` object type can be assigned to a `void*`; §r.4.6. This is also in ANSI C.

A pointer to function can be assigned to a `void*`; §r.4.6.

A declaration within a block is a statement; §r.6.7.

Anonymous unions can be declared; §r.9.5.

r.18.1.2 C++ Features Added Since 1985

This subsection summarizes the major extensions of C++ since the 1985 version of this manual:

A class can have more than one direct base class (multiple inheritance); §r.10.1.

Class members can be `protected`; §r.11 .

Pointers to class members can be declared and used; §r.8.2.3, §r.5.5.

Operators `new` and `delete` can be overloaded and declared for a class; §r.5.3.3, §r.5.3.4, §r.12.5. This allows the "assignment to `this`" technique for class specific storage management to be removed to the anachronism section; §r.18.3.3.

Objects can be explicitly destroyed; §r.12.4.

Assignment and initialization are defined as memberwise assignment and initialization; §r.12.8.

The `overload` keyword was made redundant and moved to the anachronism section; §r.18.3.

General expressions are allowed as initializers for static objects; §r.8.4.

Data objects can be `volatile`; §r.7.1.6. Also in ANSI C.

Initializers are allowed for `static` class members; §r.9.4.

Member functions can be `static`; §r.9.4.

Member functions can be `const` and `volatile`; §r.9.3.1.

Linkage to non-C++ program fragments can be explicitly declared; §r.7.4.

Operators `->`, `->*`, and `,` can be overloaded; §r.13.4.

Classes can be abstract; §r.10.3.

Prefix and postfix application of `++` and `--` on a user-defined type can be distinguished.

Templates; §r.14.

Exception handling; §r.15.

r.18.2 C++ and ANSI C

In general, C++ provides more language features and fewer restrictions than ANSI C so most constructs in ANSI C are legal in C++ with their meanings unchanged. The exceptions are:

ANSI C programs using any of the C++ keywords

`asm`	`catch`	`class`	`delete`	`friend`
`inline`	`new`	`operator`	`private`	`protected`
`public`	`template`	`try`	`this`	`virtual`
`throw`				

as identifiers are not C++ programs; §r.2.4.

Though deemed obsolescent in ANSI C, a C implementation may impose Draconian limits on the length of identifiers; a C++ implementation is not permitted to; §r.2.3.

In C++, a function must be declared before it can be called; §r.5.2.2.

The function declaration `f();` means that `f` takes no arguments (§r.8.2.5); in C it means that `f` can take any number of arguments of any type at all. Such use is deemed obsolescent in ANSI C.

In ANSI C a global data object may be declared several times without using the `extern` specifier; in C++ it must be defined exactly once; §r.3.3.

In C++, a class may not have the same name as a typedef declared to refer to a different type in the same scope; §r.9.1.

In ANSI C a `void*` may be used as the right-hand operand of an assignment to or initialization of a variable of any pointer type; in C++ it may not; §r.7.1.6.

C allows jumps to bypass an initialization; C++ does not.

In ANSI C, a global `const` by default has external linkage; in C++ it does not; §r.3.3.

"Old style" C function definitions and calls of undeclared functions are considered anachronisms in C++ and may not be supported by all implementations; §r.18.3.1. This is deemed obsolescent in ANSI C.

A `struct` is a scope in C++ (§r.3.2); in ANSI C a `struct`, an enumeration, or an enumerator declared in a `struct` is exported to scope enclosing the `struct`.

Assignment to an object of enumeration type with a value that is not of that enumeration type is considered an anachronism in C++ and may not be supported by all implementations; §r.7.2. ANSI C recommends a warning for such assignments.

Surplus characters are not allowed in strings used to initialize character arrays; §r.8.4.2.

The type of a character constant is `char` in C++ (§r.2.5.2) and `int` in C.

The type of an enumerator is the type of its enumeration in C++ (§r.7.2) and `int` in C.

In addition, the ANSI C standard allows conforming implementations to differ considerably; this may lead to further incompatibilities between C and C++ implementations. In particular, some C implementations may consider certain incompatible declarations legal. C++ requires consistency even across compilation boundaries; §r.3.3.

r.18.2.1 How to Cope

In general, a C++ program uses many features not provided by ANSI C. For such a program, the minor differences of §r.18.2 don't matter since they are dwarfed by the C++ extensions. Where ANSI C and C++ need to share header files, care must be taken so that such headers are written in the common subset of the two languages.

No advantage must be taken of C++ specific features such as classes, overloading, and so on.

A name should not be used both as a structure tag and as the name of a different type.

A function `f` taking no arguments should be declared `f(void)` and not simply `f()`.

Global `const`s must be declared explicitly `static` or `extern`.

Conditional compilation using the C++ predefined name `__cplusplus` may be used to distinguish information to be used by an ANSI C program from information to be used by a C++ program.

Functions that are to be callable from both languages must be explicitly declared to have C linkage.

r.18.3 Anachronisms

The extensions presented here may be provided by an implementation to ease the use of C programs as C++ programs or to provide continuity from earlier C++ implementations. Note that each of these features has undesirable aspects. An implementation providing them should also provide a way for the user to ensure that they do not occur in a source file. A C++ implementation is not obliged to provide these features.

The word `overload` may be used as a *decl-specifier* (§r.7) in a function declaration or a function definition. When used as a *decl-specifier*, `overload` is a reserved word and cannot also be used as an identifier.

The definition of a static data member of a class for which initialization by default to all zeros applies (§r.8.4, §r.9.4) may be omitted.

An old style (that is, pre-ANSI C) C preprocessor may be used.

An `int` may be assigned to an object of enumeration type.

The number of elements in an array may be specified when deleting an array of a type for which there is no destructor; §r.5.3.4.

A single function `operator++()` may be used to overload both prefix and postfix `++` and a single function `operator--()` may be used to overload both prefix and postfix `--`; §r.13.4.6.

r.18.3.1 Old Style Function Definitions

The C function definition syntax

> *old-function-definition:*
> > *decl-specifiers$_{opt}$ old-function-declarator declaration-list$_{opt}$ fct-body*

> *old-function-declarator:*
> > *declarator (parameter-list$_{opt}$)*

> *parameter-list:*
> > *identifier*
> > *parameter-list , identifier*

For example,

```
max(a,b) int b; { return (a<b) ? b : a; }
```

may be used. If a function defined like this has not been previously declared its argument type will be taken to be `(...)`, that is, unchecked. If it has been declared its type must agree with that of the declaration.

Class member functions may not be defined with this syntax.

r.18.3.2 Old Style Base Class Initializer

In a *mem-initializer*(§r.12.6.2), the *class-name* naming a base class may be left out provided there is exactly one immediate base class. For example,

```
class B {
    // ...
public:
    B (int);
};

class D : public B {
    // ...
    D(int i) : (i) { /* ... */ }
};
```

causes the B constructor to be called with the argument i.

r.18.3.3 Assignment to `this`

Memory management for objects of a specific class can be controlled by the user by suitable assignments to the this pointer. By assigning to the this pointer before any use of a member, a constructor can implement its own storage allocation. By assigning a zero value to this, a destructor can avoid the standard deallocation operation for objects of its class. Assigning a zero value to this in a destructor also suppressed the implicit calls of destructors for bases and members. For example,

```
class Z {
    int z[10];
    Z()  { this = my_allocator( sizeof(Z) ); }
    ~Z() { my_deallocator( this ); this = 0; }
};
```

On entry into a constructor, this is nonzero if allocation has already taken place (as it will have for auto, static, and member objects) and zero otherwise.

Calls to constructors for a base class and for member objects will take place (only) after an assignment to this. If a base class's constructor assigns to this, the new value will also be used by the derived class's constructor (if any).

Note that if this anachronism exists either the type of the this pointer cannot be a *const or the enforcement of the rules for assignment to a constant pointer must be subverted for the this pointer.

r.18.3.4 Cast of Bound Pointer

A pointer to member function for a particular object may be cast into a pointer to function, for example, (int (*) ())p->f. The result is a pointer to the function that would have been called using that member function for that particular object.

Any use of the resulting pointer is – as ever – undefined.

r.18.3.5 Nonnested Classes

Where a class is declared within another class and no other class of that name is declared in the program that class can be used as if it was declared outside its enclosing class (exactly as a C struct). For example,

```
struct S {
    struct T {
        int a;
    };
    int b;
};

struct T x;      // meaning 'S::T x;'
```

I

Index

A

call, explicit 576
call, implicit 575
call, undefined 514
constructor and 170, 173, 177
default 575
exception handling 603
extension to C 628
for derived class 186
for temporary 571
inheritance of 575
invocation 172
local object 486
order of execution 575
order of execution, base class 575
order of execution, member 575
program termination and 576
restriction 575
`static` object 485
`union` 549
virtual 575
˜ 152
destructors
exceptions and 309
garbage collection and 466
development
cycle 369
process 367
stages 367
`dialogbox` example 439
dictionary 284
difference
from ANSI C implementation dependency 629
from C expression evaluation 626
from C function declaration 629
from C initialization and `goto` 629
from C jump past initialization 629
from C linkage 629
from C name space 629
from C scope 627
from C `sizeof` 627
direct base class 555–556
directed acyclic graph 187
directive
error preprocessing 613
null preprocessing 613
pragma preprocessing 613
preprocessing 606
discriminating `union` 169
discrimination of exceptions 297
distinct string 481
divide and conquer, complexity 364
division
by zero, undefined 492, 503
implementation dependency 503
operator 502
dname 526

do statement 81, 511
documentation 382
dominance, virtual base class 558
Donald Knuth 381
dot operator – see class member access operator
double quote 66, 480
`double` 49
constant 481
type 487
type specifier 521
dynamic
binding – see virtual function
initialization 485
type checking 396
type checking, cost of 397

E

E suffix 481
EBCDIC character set 66
efficiency 6, 157, 177, 381
elaborated
class name 522, 543
`enum` name 522
type specifier – see elaborated class name
elaborated-type-specifier 522
`#elif` 612
elif-line 612
elif-parts 611
elimination of temporary 571
ellipsis
... 132
example 534
in function declaration 495, 532
overloading resolution and 588–589
`#else` 612
`else` 509
else-line 612
else-part 612
empty
argument list 533
class `sizeof` 541
queue 315
statement 509
encapsulation 41
complete 239
`#endif` 612
endif-line 612
`endl` 347
`ends` 347
`enum` 69
declaration { } 522
name, elaborated 522
overloading and 586
type of 522–523
type specifier 522

F

definition 484
definition anachronism, C 630
definition anachronism, old style 630
definition example 536
definition of `virtual` 190
definition, scope of 484
example of `virtual` 354
forwarding 457, 459
`friend` 161–162
`inline` 124
`inline` member 153
linkage specification 525
linkage specification overloaded 525
member 145
member – see member function
member declaration 545
name hiding 587
name, overloaded 27, 129, 585
object 346
`operator` 592
operator `::` and `virtual` 191
overloaded – see also overloading
pointer to 134
pointer to member 166
pointer to member 502
pure `virtual` 191
return – see `return`
return type – see return type
scope 483
specifier 518
template 270, 597
template declaration 598
template definition 598
type 487, 533
value `return` 126
`virtual` 189
virtual 9
virtual – see virtual function
functional decomposition 393
function-definition 536
function-like macro 608
functions
 exceptions and 317
 list of `operator` 226
fundamental
 type 23, 49, 486
 type conversion – see conversion, user-defined
   conversion
 type, destructor and 576

G

gap between design and language 392
garbage
 collection 465
 collection and destructors 466

collector 98–99
gargantuanism 381
generated
 constructor – see default constructor
 destructor – see default destructor
generic 32
global
 anonymous `union` 550
 data 10
 name 483
 `new` 498
 object storage class 486
 objects 353
 scope 45
 variable, constructor for 172
 variable, use of 79
`goto`
 difference from C initialization and 629
 initialization and 514
 non-logal 297
 statement 103, 509, 512–513
gradual adoption of C++ 400
grammar 614
graph, directed acyclic 187
greater
 than operator 504
 than or equal to operator 504
grouping of exceptions 302
growing systems 379

H

`.h` file 113
handle class 460
handler, exception 294, 603
handler 601
handler-list 601
hardware 50
header file 112–113
headers
 ANSI C 479
 ANSI C and shared 629
 library 479
 standard 479
hex number 481
`hex` 347
hexadecimal 65
 constant 480
hiding
 – see name hiding
 information 17
 name 45
hierarchies, exception 302
hierarchy
 class 9, 187
 object 410

J

K

L

M

N

P

Q

T

U

X

Z

W